Three Powers in Heaven

SYNKRISIS

Comparative Approaches to Early Christianity in Greco-Roman Culture

SERIES EDITORS

Dale B. Martin (Yale University) and L. L. Welborn (Fordham University)

Synkrisis is a project that invites scholars of early Christianity and the Greco-Roman world to collaborate toward the goal of rigorous comparison. Each volume in the series provides immersion in an aspect of Greco-Roman culture, so as to make possible a comparison of the controlling logics that emerge from the discourses of Greco-Roman and early Christian writers. In contrast to older "history of religions" approaches, which looked for similarities between religions in order to posit relations of influence and dependency, Synkrisis embraces a fuller conception of the complexities of culture, viewing Greco-Roman religions and early Christianity as members of a comparative class. The differential comparisons promoted by Synkrisis may serve to refine and correct the theoretical and historical models employed by scholars who seek to understand and interpret the Greco-Roman world. With its allusion to the rhetorical exercises of the Greco-Roman world, the series title recognizes that the comparative enterprise is a construction of the scholar's mind and serves the scholar's theoretical interests.

EDITORIAL BOARD

Loveday Alexander (Sheffield University)
John Bodel (Brown University)
Kimberly Bowes (University of Pennsylvania)
Daniel Boyarin (University of California, Berkeley)
Fritz Graf (Ohio State University)
Ronald F. Hock (University of Southern California)
Hans-Josef Klauck (University of Chicago)
Angela Standhartinger (Marburg University)
Stanley K. Stowers (Brown University)

Three Powers in Heaven

The Emergence of Theology and the Parting of the Ways

Emanuel Fiano

Yale UNIVERSITY PRESS NEW HAVEN AND LONDON

Published with assistance from the Louis Stern Memorial Fund.

Set in Scala type by Newgen.
Printed in the United States of America. Library of Congress Control Number: 2022948956
ISBN 978-0-300-26332-9 (hardcover: alk. paper)
A catalogue record for this book is available from the British Library.

This paper meets the requirements of ANSI/NISO Z39.48-1992 (Permanence of Paper).

10 9 8 7 6 5 4 3 2 1

First epigraph: Ancient Roman inscription, quoted in James Spencer Northcote, ed., *Epitaphs of the Catacombs, or Christian Inscriptions in Rome during the First Four Centuries* (London: Longmans, Green and Co., 1878), 102.

Second epigraph: משעול אגי, "הדרשה בלטרון", בתוך: 'ערה', הוצאת הקיבוץ המאוחד, 2013, עמ' 22–23.
Agi Mishol, "Hadrasha beLatrun," in *Era* (Hakibbutz Hameuchad Publishing House, 2013), 22–23.

Ai miei genitori

qui et filius diceris et pater inveniris
—Inscription found in Rome

הֲאִם לֹא שְׁמַעְתֶּם עַל אֱלוֹהִים
שֶׁאֵין לוֹ אֱלוֹהִים?
—Agi Mishol

Contents

Acknowledgments ix

Author's Note xi

Introduction 1

1. A Tale of Two Heretics 19

2. Credal Culture: The Trinitarian Debates, 318–362 51

3. Theological Labeling: Antioch and Alexandria in the 360s 79

4. Ortholalia: The Negotiation of Formulas in the 370s 122

5. The Ends of Dialogue 146

Conclusion 181

List of Abbreviations 185

Notes 187

List of Editions of Ancient Sources 287

Bibliography 305

Index of Subjects 395

Index of Ancient Sources 405

Index of Modern Authors 422

Acknowledgments

Among the many to whom I owe gratitude for acts of loving-kindness that have allowed this work to come to light, I wish to signal my debt to those who have offered advice about the manuscript of the book or provided help with some of its parts: Michael Ascoli, Lewis Ayres, Adam Becker, Phillip Blumberg, Daniel Boyarin, Hanns Christof Brennecke, Alberto Camplani, the late Elizabeth Clark, Emanuele Dattilo, Erez DeGolan, Benjamin Dunning, Samuel Fernández, Jacob Golan, Gabriela Goldin Marcovich, Francesca Gorgoni, Sarit Kattan Gribetz, Malachi Hacohen, Karina Hogan, Jaden Jarmel Schneider, Richard Kalmin, David Levene, Joseph Lienhard, Joel Marcus, Christoph Markschies, Xavier Morales, Ron Naiweld, Yakir Paz, Zlatko Pleše, Emanuela Prinzivalli, James Adam Redfield, Angelo Segneri, Columba Stewart, Susan Cook Summer, Richard Teverson, Lucas Van Rompay, Moulie Vidas, Erin Galgay Walsh, and Alex Weintraub. To all of them go my heartfelt thanks.

The Introduction reproduces in part, in English translation and with modifications, the contents of my article "El surgimiento de la teología cristiana y la separación de los caminos entre judaísmo y cristianismo," published in Spanish in two parts in *Teología: Revista de la Facultad de Teología de la Pontificia Universidad Católica Argentina* 68 (2020): 63–85, and 69 (2020): 37–52 (reprinted under Creative Commons License CC BY-NC-SA 4.0). Chapter 1 reproduces in part and with modifications the contents of my Introduction to select fragments of Paul of Samosata found in *The Cambridge Edition of Early Christian Writings*, Vol. 3, *Christ: Through the Nestorian Controversy*, ed. Mark DelCogliano (Cambridge: Cambridge University Press, 2022), 197–199 (© Cambridge University Press 2022, reprinted with permission). Chapter 3 reproduces in part and with modifications the contents of my articles "Splitting the Difference: Jerome and the Schism of Antioch in His *Letter 15*," published in *Sacris Erudiri: A Journal of Late Antique and Medieval Christianity* 59 (2020): 61–81 (reprinted with permission of the Editorial Board and of Brepols Publishers), and "The Council of the Thebaid, 362: Lucifer of Calaris, Eusebius of Vercellae, and the Readmission of the Clergy," published in *The Journal of Ecclesiastical History* 73 (2021): 1–19 (© Cambridge University Press 2021, reprinted with permission).

Author's Note

Save in some exceptional cases, passages from ancient works are set in the endnotes in their original language only when their text is examined at significant length. While these passages, and excerpts from them, are presented in the endnotes in the languages' original scripts, transliteration has been preferred for any words in non-Latin scripts in the main body of the text. The transliterations of words corresponding to common concepts expressed in these languages, as well as Latin expressions of the same kind, are italicized (with an English translation or explanation provided in parentheses) only on their first use, with ensuing occurrences in relative proximity to the first set in roman type. Common Hebrew proper names have been rendered according to their most common spelling rather than the transliteration system followed otherwise (e.g., Eliezer and not Eliʿezer, or Metatron in lieu of Meṭaṭron).

When either a particular locus in a source or the entirety of a short text (such as a letter or homily belonging to a larger collection) receives a citation in a note, a reference is given to the name of the scholar(s) responsible for the editions or translations consulted. Full bibliographic details for these, as well as occasionally for additional editions and translations not cited in the notes, may be found—under the name of the ancient work's author(s), or the work's title if the authorship is unknown—in the List of Editions of Ancient Sources at the end of the book. When words are also quoted from the passage, whether or not the original text is offered, a reference to page or column number in the edition or translation is provided in the notes. Spurious works are listed in the List of Editions of Ancient Sources under a separate entry for the author to whom they are attributed; dubious works are marked off as such next to their title, but are listed under the same author entry as genuine works. The list excludes for the most part fragments the history of whose editions is discussed in the endnotes.

References to translations included in Philip Schaff and Henry Wace's *A Select Library of the Nicene and Post-Nicene Fathers of the Christian Church* (Second Series) are omitted from the List of Editions of Ancient Sources and provided instead only in the notes, with the abbreviation *NPNF2* followed by a Roman numeral for the volume in the series. Citations from the Palestinian Talmud are given according to the Venice print, followed by a reference to the Vilna print. The works of *rishonim* and *aḥaronim* are excluded from the List of Editions of Ancient Sources as well as from the Bibliography at the end of the volume. The titles of all bibliographic items in languages that do not use the Latin script have been transliterated and any English title pages have been ignored. Transliterated titles are alphabetized in the Bibliography according to the order of the Latin alphabet and not to that of their original abjad. Occasional English renditions of passages from scholarly works in other languages are not marked as translations. Unless otherwise noted, all English translations of ancient and modern works are mine.

Three Powers in Heaven

Introduction

Nicaea's Jewish Question

In 314 CE, only one year after the practice of Christianity had been authorized in the Roman Empire, Emperor Constantine summoned a council to the city of Arles. Constantine tasked the bishops, drawn primarily from the Latin-speaking West, to repair a schism plaguing the Christian community of Carthage. However, before the bishops could begin their work, their attention shifted to another pressing issue. Perhaps directed by the emperor, who was acting as *pontifex maximus,* they examined a resurgent conflict that had afflicted Christianity in different forms since the second century: the timing of the Easter celebration.

Unlike their fellow Christians, members of the ancient Quartodeciman movement had the custom of cutting short their pre-paschal fast, ending it on the eve of the Jewish Passover instead of the following Sunday. This movement had subsided in the third century, but another aberrant practice still prevented the establishment of one common date for Easter observance across the Christian world. Followers of Protopaschism, who were mainly in the Asian churches, calculated the paschal full moon based on the Jewish lunar year, where it corresponded to the first day of the month of Nisan, instead of following the Julian solar calendar. In some years this caused the commemoration of Christ's resurrection to deviate up to one month relative to the western practice.[1] At Arles the bishops promoted the Julian computation, but their limited jurisdiction prevented their decision from carrying much weight. The problem continued to be perceived as important and was eventually put on the agenda for those gathered at the great Council of Nicaea in 325.[2]

What might appear as a minor calendric matter had, in fact, far greater cultural implications. Surely, the episcopal gathering of Nicaea attempted to solve the problem of determining the Easter calendar out of an interest in unifying imperial Christianity liturgically. However, the synod issued a letter, addressed to the "church of the Alexandrians," that reveals the anxiety evoked by these differences over dating. The document claims a definitive separation from the Jewish people as a central motivation for the council's deliberations, justifying in this way at considerable length the decision to distinguish Easter from celebrations of Passover.[3] The letter leaves little doubt that the council saw its gathering as an opportunity for reevaluating the role of the Jewish heritage in imperial Christendom.[4] Twelve years after Christianity had gained legal recognition through the Edict of Milan (313), the practices marking the life of the Church had to be severed from those that defined Jewish identity.

The Council of Nicaea is recorded in both ancient and modern accounts less for the bishops' intervention in the controversy surrounding Easter than as a first, failed attempt on the part of a Roman emperor to restore peace in the Church by resolving the theological strife among diverse forms of Christian confession. Significantly, at the same time they were debating the correct date when the resurrection of Jesus Christ ought to be celebrated, Christians were tussling over Christ's divine status and his role as a mediator between God and creation. Following the council, Christian thinkers remained embroiled for almost sixty years in acrimonious doctrinal dissension.

The resulting set of disputes about the Trinity has traditionally been termed "Arian," after the name of the Alexandrian presbyter of Libyan origin, Arius, whose preaching served as a catalyst for the eruption of the debates.[5] Around 318, Arius's interpretation of the begetting of the Son of God ignited a controversy in the Egyptian metropolis about the configuration of intra-divine relations. While his fellow Alexandrian theologians subordinated the Son to the Father only to a limited extent, Arius's teachings widened the ontological gap between these two members of the godhead in a manner unheard of within that theological tradition. Arius did not view Christ as merely one of God's creatures; instead, he took pains to label him as the most perfect among them. Despite these reassurances, his statements implying that Christ had been created punctiliarly and "out of nothing" were perceived as blasphemous by the Egyptian clergy. The controversy soon spread outside of Alexandria, eventually leading to the convocation of the Nicene council in 325.

Over the five and a half decades of heated Trinitarian debate that followed this synod, dissociation from Judaism was an integral aspect of Christian culture.[6] In skirmishes against those identified as heretics, allegations of association with Judaism or its perceived hybrids became a primary weapon in the rhetorical arsenal of many thinkers.[7] This rhetorical trick was by no means new. Second- and third-century apologists had already adopted it, and similar formulations would continue to appear in the polemics of self-styled orthodox authors of various stripes throughout late antiquity and into the early Middle Ages. Nevertheless, conflating Judaism with heresy became a distinctive feature of Trinitarian, and particularly pro-Nicene, rhetoric. Throughout the fourth-century debates surrounding the legacy of Nicaea, Christians were aware that their contemporary theological discussions had far-reaching consequences for their relations with Judaism. Under the force of the relentless undertow of anti-Jewish rhetoric, a sweeping historical process of separation was underway. Any attempt to determine just when and how Christianity recognizably broke away from its Jewish matrix, however, raises questions that find no univocal answers. The various theories set forth depend largely on the rubric under which the interrogation is pursued. The moment at which Jews and Christians ceased to behave or to think in similar ways within a particular domain, for example, may not coincide with the time when members of the two communities stopped seeing each other as belonging to the same collective.

In this book I pursue the subject of the parting of the ways under the rubric of intellectual culture, asking when Christianity and Judaism began to diverge qua intellectual traditions. I argue that the Trinitarian debates of the fourth century, which persisted within Christian-Jewish continuity from the viewpoint of beliefs about the divine, were uniquely crucial in the emergence of firmer demarcations between the two intellectual traditions. The Trinitarian controversies were the first war of words to unfold on a pan-Mediterranean stage. Thanks to their geographic scale, to the unprecedently thick web of literary exchanges in which they resulted, and above all to their novel embedment in the structures of the Roman Empire, these disputes had lasting effects on the religious landscape of late antiquity, and in particular on the shape of the Christian tradition. Ecclesiastical leaders' deployment of new methods for knowledge production, across doctrinal boundaries, gave rise to a method of inquiry that may be termed "theology." Through a selective sample of the writings they produced, I describe these shifts, which were central to Christianity's coming into its own as an intellectual tradition. Moreover, I frame them as relevant to the parting of the ways by delineating a contrast between aspects of late ancient Christian and Jewish discourse.

The Parting of the Ways

The title of this book adopts the metaphor of the "parting of the ways," common currency in studies of ancient Judaism and Christianity. This image requires us to imagine that prior to the moment it captures, the path on which the "twins in Rebecca's womb"—Jacob and Esau—were about to tread was one and the same, despite mutual grievances and pleas for separation.[8] Scholars of early Christianity have highlighted the struggles for authority that motivated the efforts of Christian writers to change this state of affairs by drawing and patrolling the borders of religious identity. In order to construct difference in a state of threatening similarity, these writers used their rhetorical weaponry to distance themselves from any form of kinship with the Jews. A comparably extensive anti-Christian polemic is absent from the late ancient rabbinic corpus, leading some to suppose a conspiratorial silence on the part of the rabbis. However, new insights about the belatedness with which the rabbinic world-view solidified and the bounded representativeness of the rabbinic movement have bolstered the idea that Christianity and Judaism continued to be, if not indistinguishable, then at least substantially interfused at least until the end of late antiquity.

As a result, in the quest to discover the origins of Christian-Jewish estrangement, attempts to locate a split in the first or second century have generally given way to an emphasis on the lack of historical evidence for such early severance. In recent decades, the image of "the ways that never parted" has been used to signal that an unbroken continuum between the two traditions persisted until a late date.[9] But even within this new paradigm positing a late, gradual, and geographically heterogeneous separation, disagreements continue regarding the nature of the relations between ancient Jesus-following Jews (and gentiles) and non-Jesus-following Jews. Students of ancient anti-Jewish literature have reached different conclusions about whether the sentiments of hostility expressed in early Christian treatises should be considered products of real-life interactions between the two communities or mere collections of rhetorical *topoi*.[10] Meanwhile, the category of "Jewish Christianity," traditionally used to describe phenomena that escaped an increasingly unsparing logic of dichotomous opposition between Christianity and Judaism, has been criticized for implicitly reinscribing "Jew" and "Christian" as stable identities through the construction of their hybrid as an exception.[11]

The general realization that Jews and Christians did not part ways in the second or even third century has led to the fourth century being considered in modern historiography "the first century of Judaism and Christianity."[12] Consensus has formed regarding the sway of Constantinian and post-Constantinian politics that converged to enforce one truth, while Jewry was becoming progressively estranged from a community with which it could previously have been identified. This historical description correctly grants the Jesus-following side of the Christian-Jewish continuum the priority of historical causality. Constantine's decision to summon a council at Nicaea ignited a steady integration of the Church and the imperial government, a turn whose momentousness can hardly be overstated.

At the same time, the image of an emperor willing into being Christianity and Judaism with a stroke of his stylus, by drawing between them the enforceable border of orthodoxy, seems simplistic. Friendly imperial policies proved instrumental to the independent constitution of a Christian intellectual tradition. The burgeoning working methods of Christian thinkers were incorporated into an institutional mechanism singularly privileged by political power. Those thinkers soon became skilled at manipulating the gears of that mechanism against an array of opponents, including the Jews.[13] Locating the parting of Christianity and Judaism in the context of the theological battles of the fourth century allows us to fill the political and institutional record with the practices of the Christian intellectual class.[14] The formation of a Christian discourse—and more specifically of theological codes as the primary mode of Christian intellectual pursuit—played a decisive role in giving historical effectiveness to the institutional sea changes of the fourth-century Church.

In any time of controversy, social and intellectual fields are torn by sectarianism and even violence. Controversies, however, can also function as unwitting rituals through which communities, eventually reconciled, set their broadest boundaries. The discursive field is thus constituted through a divisive intellectual exchange. In the Trinitarian debates, Christian believers who initially held each other as brethren suddenly discovered in one another foes and heretics. But it was not long after the final reckoning at the Council of Constantinople (381) that the cacophony of the Trinitarian battles subsided. Even in the regions of the Roman Empire where an anti-Constantinopolitan presence lingered, the struggle was over.[15] The war cries of homoousians, homoiousians, homoians, and heteroousians; the catchphrases of so-called Arians, Marcellans, Eustathians, Eusebians, Eunomians, Meletians, and Macedonians; the mutual reviling of westerners and easterners, the stirring missives of the ardent pro-Nicene advocates; the "meddlesome curiosity" of the lay anti-Nicene sympathizers[16]—all the voices that had loudly resonated for decades—faded away. At this time, the intellectual borders of imperial Christendom came to coincide to a substantial extent with those of the battlefield within which the Trinitarian conflict had taken place. Any actors who had preferred staying out of the disputes, seeing nothing at stake for them in the fight to establish in ontological terms Christ's identity, had sanctioned in effect their estrangement from the intellectual field of imperial Christendom.[17]

Such was the choice of non-Jesus-following Jews. This election was not dictated by lack of affinity for any one doctrinal outcome, whether potential or actual. "Binitarianism," a belief combining monotheism with the presence of a lower divine entity, was hardly unknown to the Jews.[18] As such, virtually all the options for the configuration of the relationship between the Father and the Son discussed during the controversies were compatible with positions about the divine realm held (though how widely is unknown) by Jews in the Second Temple period, and later even in circles at least adjacent to the rabbinic movement, especially in Babylonia. Different interpretations have been proposed to explain the persistence of a binitarian thread running through a millennium of Jewish literature, from the famous Son of Man passage of *Daniel* 7 (second century BCE) to the "Younger" or "Lesser Lord" starring in the *Third Book of Enoch* (seventh or eighth century CE). Opinions vary also about the role of the Jesus movement in the Jewish adoption or recuperation of these ideas after the composition of the New Testament.[19] However these scholarly disputes are settled, it is remarkable that centuries after the Trinitarian debates there existed Babylonian Jews with likely ties to the rabbinic world—and no discernible interest in the figure of Christ—who still remained unperturbed by the idea of a divine deuteragonist (they would likely have found Christian belief in the incarnation more unsettling).[20] Jewish extraneousness to the Trinitarian exchanges of the fourth century was not caused by apprehension about the integrity of a monotheistic ideal. It was the product, rather, of the development of new methods and practices for inquiry into the divine on the part of Jesus-followers.

It is common to see continued Jewish interest in exalted humans, personified attributes of the divinity, or chief angels employed as evidence to reverse the old-fashioned notion of an early Christian-Jewish separation.[21] Indeed, all too often in the search for moments of rupture between Christianity and Judaism—and for the continued presence of a Jewish-Christian group bridging the gap between the two communities—paramount importance is given to how key actors positioned themselves on questions central to a presumed ancient Jewish religion, issues such as the observance of the Mosaic precepts or the strict preservation of the divine monarchy. Though correct in dating the parting of the ways to the later part of late antiquity, this quest still assumes that religious constructs or religious praxis constitute the appropriate units by which to measure consistencies between the two traditions. A similar approach is only meaningful within a theoretical framework that presumes religious phenomena to constitute the ultimate lines of demarcation of identity. If this premise is held in abeyance—sidestepping a series of methodological problems that come with the category of religion—the parting of the ways can be modeled based on processes shared by literate societies at large.

To bracket off religion as a category pertinent to this examination, recasting the parting of the ways as a separation between two intellectual traditions, does not require denying that the problems Jews and Christians attempted to address through their distinct systems of reflection were of a kind that, from late modernity onward, would come to be defined as religious.[22] Rather, the continuum out of which the two traditions emerged stood on a foundation of intellectual engagement with a common conceptual structure inherited from Second Temple Judaism: Jewish monotheism.[23] Its fundamental problem could be expressed simply as follows: Once a deity is posited as a subject radically other from humanity and endowed with agency, how is humankind's relationship to this entity to be understood?[24]

Non-Jesus-following Jews shared with Jesus-following Jews (and with the gentiles who had joined their ranks) an interest in dealing with this theoretical tension. Indeed, it would be misleading to depict late ancient rabbinic Jews as indifferent to this quandary or uninterested in addressing it. A focus on the apprehension of the divine through words was hardly a prerogative of Christian thinkers.[25] Jewish sources exhibit a clear preoccupation with God and His activities, for example by famously going so far as to scrutinize His daily schedule.[26] Nevertheless, around the fourth century those with an interest in the figure of Jesus and the Jews who had no such interest began to engage differently with the monotheistic dilemma. Though addressing the same types of issues that busied rabbinic minds, believers in Jesus set about to do so in their own specialized ways and in manners that aimed at the establishment of correct speech about the divine. Eventually, their inquiries crystallized into a particular style of investigation, governed by a defined set of rules and sustained by a cohesive pattern of intellectual engagement.

The fourth century has long been seen as an era of intellectual decline in the Roman Empire.[27] The decreased literary production that marked this time puts in even greater relief the feverish scholarly activities of Christian intellectuals—the network of ecclesiastical leaders capable of mastering the methods of a new style of theological inquiry—in the period between the early 320s and 383.[28] Among the various forms of Christian literary activity were the release and circulation of myriad synodal documents, the exchange of epistles, and the publication of doctrinal treatises.[29] By virtue of the Trinitarian debates, the Christian theological production made up by far the most conspicuous literary corpus of the fourth century. Indifferent to sectarian divisions, the sheer density of literary transactions contributed to the constitution of a discrete tradition, distinct from that of the Jews.

The historical redescription tendered here may seem irreconcilable with a theory set forth by Daniel Boyarin over the course of several years, which has been gaining acceptance among scholars of Judaism. According to this view, it was late ancient Christians who rhetorically constituted the Jews, a group bound only by its "doings," into a (wrongheaded) religion called Judaism, after having established themselves as a religion called Christianity, in opposition to Romanness.[30] If this view is accepted, it might appear impossible to speak of a parting, as no Judaism would have existed for Christianity to splinter off from at the time of its emergence. However, the interrogation of the observable difference between the "doings" of the two communities can be distinguished from the inquiry into their rhetorical demarcations and production of difference. There is no denying that the two questions are related: proto-Christian (and proto-Jewish) activities aimed at extrojecting otherness could have been intensified as a result of increasing differentiation between the "doings" of the two groups; and conversely, the rhetorically effected separation may have led the two communities to intentionally take, in their "doings," routes not trodden by the other. But the two historical processes remain discrete and may have in principle followed different timelines. In other words, the field of observation for a redescription of the parting of the ways exceeds—though it certainly includes—the sum of rhetorical moves performed by actors in the processes of identity formation.

As explained above, this claim does not ask that we revert to identifying some core tenets of faith or praxis as key issues driving the separation. While it is true that Jews and Christians often built their separate identities around such matters, historical reality cannot be navigated by the same maps through which battling actors paradoxically agreed to represent their borders. A new survey of the territory is needed instead. My pursuit in this book can then also be qualified as an inquiry into the ways in which the Christian intellectual tradition came to diverge from that of the community whose "doings" were at some point called "Judaism." Furthermore, Boyarin's claim about the native meaninglessness of the category of religion to the cultural organization of ancient Jews, if accepted, bolsters the argument for the futility of privileging what we moderns most often consider quintessentially religious phenomena—the domains of the cultic and the doctrinal—in evaluating the separation between Christianity and Judaism.

My retelling of the parting of the ways undeniably assigns a prominent role to the activities and self-understanding of highly literate elites in determining the fate of the undifferentiated continuum between the Christian and Jewish traditions. This narrative takes note of the inescapably efficacious power of religious leaderships in setting the tone of Christian-Jewish relations in antiquity.[31] To be sure, though discretely formed, the discursive field of theology and the one constituted by rabbinic activities had spaces of interaction (a reality only conceivable, strictly speaking, within a state of distinction).[32] Theologians and rabbis, after all, by and large continued to inhabit a shared social reality. Complex phenomena of negotiation, convergence, intermixing, and boundary-crossing among Jews and Christians in the spheres of praxis and belief are also extensively documented in the non-elite social body well past the end of late antiquity. Nevertheless, these more flexible approaches to communal identity eventually did not carry the day. However late the parting is dated, few would question that the ties between the two groups were eventually severed.

Christianity as an Intellectual Tradition

My recasting of the parting of the ways as the separation of two intellectual traditions is inspired by an interweaving of the trajectories of three theoreticians: the discourse analyst Dominique Maingueneau, the sociologist Luc Boltanski, and the epistemologist and philosopher of science Larry Laudan. A certain articulation of these three perspectives makes it possible to address the rise of a new discursive field (Maingueneau) sustained by a social group, invested in a set of practices (Boltanski) that were related to a novel arc of inquiry (Laudan). The whole of these phenomena can be credited for the emergence of the Christian tradition.

The tradition under discussion does not have the traits of Alasdaire MacIntyre's "*living* tradition," defined as "an historically extended, socially embodied argument, and an argument precisely in part about the goods which constitute that tradition."[33] It is also unlike Talal Asad's more bio-politically inflected "*discursive* tradition," consisting "essentially of discourses that seek to instruct practitioners regarding the correct form and purpose of a given practice."[34] To be sure, more than the disembodied life of some episcopal minds is at stake in the establishment of Christianity as a self-standing tradition of inquiry, including such values as justice and social morality, central to MacIntyre's project. I also readily admit that a set of religious concerns gains hegemonic traction primarily through the means of social control borrowed by Asad from Foucault's inventory. However, my investigation pursues a different object: Christianity as an *intellectual* tradition, solidified around the discursive field constituted by theology.

Although they might not have always named it as such, Christians had arguably been pursuing theology in a broad sense since the first century.[35] After all, since early times, believers in Jesus had articulated a variety of views about God, the world, and Christ's identity. Had not the first-century author of the *Gospel of John,* who was referred to at least from the fourth century on as the theologian (*ho theologos*), inscribed at the beginning of his Prologue one of the most consequential lines in the history of Christian thought about God? Writings from the second and third century, such as *Ascension of Isaiah, Odes of Solomon,* Ignatius of Antioch's *Letters, Shepherd of Hermas,* and *Acts of Peter,* all testify to rich reflections on the question of Christ's identity.

Christoph Markschies, relying on a distinction between implicit and explicit theology—in which the former is construed as essential to any religious culture—remarks that the second and third centuries display "an increasing explication of 'implicit theology.'"[36] Indeed, the classical Christian argument emerged out of the identity-defining disputes of these two centuries in a more or less coherent shape, in which it was destined to perdure up to the end of late antiquity. This mode of expression and argumentation, prevalent in all Christian literary genres, entailed the integration of Greek *paideia*—in the form of grammatical, rhetorical, and philosophical learning—into the exegesis of Scripture.[37]

How, then, could the emergence of theological discourse be dated as late as the fourth century? The answer lies in an understanding of theology as other than the subjective endeavor of learned believers in Jesus to rationally comprehend their faith through tools borrowed from Hellenic education. Rather, the theology whose image I wish to capture here is a discipline of study resulting from the increasingly shared and regulated methods used by those who sought that understanding, a discipline practiced publicly and with close ties to civil society and institutional power. In the hands of fourth-century Greek-

and Latin-speaking Jesus-following intellectuals engaged in controversy about Christ's relation to God, this discipline assumed a new and distinctive shape.

The theology I am discussing is thus to be understood as a research tradition in the sense given to this term by Larry Laudan: "a set of general assumptions about the entities and processes in a domain of study, and about the appropriate methods to be used for investigating the problems and constructing the theories in that domain."[38] (Although Laudan set forth his research tradition as the fundamental unit of scientific development, he provided multiple examples of research traditions outside of the natural sciences.)[39] As the core of this book shows, actors engaged in Trinitarian debate developed a series of processual assumptions about the discussion of the divine, which may be captured under three headings: the importance placed on the creeds issued by councils, the recombination of geo-cultural traditions for the sake of their confrontation, and the production of a set of rules for the debate. Once bequeathed to the Christian intellectual tradition, these became as enduring a part of the Christian historical identity as the points of faith contained in the Niceno-Constantinopolitan Creed.

Fourth-century theology, however, was based not only on innovative and idiosyncratic methodological principles, but also on a novel set of practices. Three of these emerged as prominent. First, the recourse to synods—a supra-regional institution used since the beginning of the third century to clarify various aspects of Christian faith and life—for the purpose of settling doctrinal disagreements.[40] Second, the conversion of the synod into a judicial body put in charge not only of settling issues of doctrine, but also of trying individual clergy members.[41] Third, the establishment, through travel and epistolary exchange, of transregional episcopal ententes mediated by the granting, withdrawal, and withholding of sacramental communion. Through these and other patterns of activity, the research tradition that took shape during the Trinitarian controversies was embodied by an intellectual class whose uniform undertakings crossed doctrinal partisan lines. Although I do not pursue a historico-sociological account in this book, I find it important to heed sociologist Luc Boltanski's invitation "to treat [a] group not as a 'thing' but as the objectified product of a practice."[42] As the ancient Church became increasingly institutionalized, its structured doings—to borrow Boltanski's words—"made the group's existence seem more and more self-evident."[43]

Theology was crucially responsible for the production of a discursive field, which arose—as according to Dominique Maingueneau all discursive fields do—out of the competition between mutually delimiting positionings that vied for primacy of enunciative legitimacy.[44] In a general sense, the concept of a positioning refers to speakers locating themselves in a conflictual space; in a more restrictive sense, it designates "a strong enunciative identity [. . .], a well specified site of discursive production."[45] In the cases of philosophy or religion, positionings normally correspond to movements or schools.[46] During the Trinitarian disputes, the engenderment of multiple positionings on the question of divine relations led the proto-Christian positioning constituted by the sum of words exchanged by Jesus-followers—originally inscribed within a discursive field that underlay the undifferentiated Christian-Jewish continuum—to rise to the status of a discrete discursive field.[47] The importance of Christianity's embrace of theology for the constitution of the Christian intellectual tradition at large, and consequently for the parting of the ways, is best grasped through Maingueneau's notion of a constituting discourse (*discours constituant*), of which law or philosophy represent typical examples.[48] This is defined as a type of discourse based on no other discourse from which it could derive validation. "To found other discourses without being founded by them, [constituting discourses] must set themselves up as intimately bound with a legitimizing Source and show that they are in accordance with it, owing the way they emerge and develop to the operations by which they structure their texts and legitimate their own context."[49] At the same time, by founding and legitimizing themselves, constituting discourses can serve as guarantors for discourses of other kinds.[50] Christian theology as a constituting discourse, linked to divine revelation as the assumed transcendent source of its own authority, supported Christianity's inscription in the inter-discourse.[51] Thus, the Christian intellectual tradition as a whole—including literary domains ranging from exegesis to homiletics, from catechesis to apologetics, from liturgy to canon and historiography, and also involving features of lived religion—was established on the legitimizing basis of the theological field, built around theology as a research tradition.

To be clear, the public language about God studied in this book hardly exhausts the Christian literary production of the fourth or fifth centuries. Several crucial loci of what ancient writers called economy (*oikonomia*)—God's revelation to humanity through creation and redemption—fell outside of its purview. Even some argumentations that early Christians would have subsumed under the rubric of theology (*theologia*, the discussion of the mysteries of God's nature), and that were contained in Trinitarian and Christological works, escaped the tight grip of logical distillation, technical expression, and formulaic enunciation typical of conciliar and para-conciliar discussions.

There is no denying that in the fourth century the narrowing of the parameters for acceptable doctrinal opinions was still accompanied by the free exercise of thought about God. Indeed, the explosion of creativity demonstrated in the production by the Cappadocians—Basil of Caesarea, Gregory of Nazianzus, and Gregory of Nyssa—may even be evaluated as an expansion of speech about the divine in reaction to the more prescriptive modes of inquiry surveyed here.

Nevertheless, the privileged relationship between the civic and political sphere and the activities I am calling theological made the latter especially foundational for the identity of the Christian intellectual guild, facilitating its transformation into a constituting discourse. Maingueneau's concept of a constituting discourse helps explain how the emergence of a research tradition such as theology could have such lasting and percolating effects in various realms of the life of the Christian community, generating a dogmatic impulse that continued to support even less technical and specialized uses of language.[52]

The Legacy of Nicaea

Before discussing the relevance of the Trinitarian controversies for Christian-Jewish relations it is worth examining in some depth the history of these disputes' scholarly interpretations. Among the Christian theological debates of late antiquity, scholars have given the most attention to the fifth-century discussions about how divine and human elements coexisted in Jesus Christ. These so-called Christological controversies have provided historians with a multitude of occasions to study the state of Christendom in the post-Theodosian Empire.[53] By comparison, the fourth-century Trinitarian discussions have remained in the shadows, particularly in English-language scholarship focusing on late ancient cultural history.[54] Outside of theologically minded quarters, the phrase "Trinitarian controversies" points only to a time of barren contentiousness. There seems to be an unspoken consensus that little can be learned from these debates apart from the history of theological doctrines or the development of Christian dogma. As a result, they have been primarily mined in works either devoted to the meticulous reconstruction of facts and events (with a focus on chronology and prosopography) or inspired by theological concerns. An opportunity for different kinds of exploration is being missed.

For over sixteen centuries, the Council of Nicaea has been considered a milestone in the Trinitarian debates, and indeed in the history of Christian dogma. The Nicene fathers declared the Son "homoousios to the Father" (that is, sharing the same ousia as the Father), describing Christ as being "from" God's same ousia (*ek tēs ousias tou patros*).[55] In addition, the conciliar document included an anathema on those who affirmed that the Son "is from another hypostasis or ousia" (*ex heteras hypostaseōs ē ousias* [. . .] *einai*) than that of the Father.[56]

The phrasing of this anathematism, in which hypostasis and ousia appear to be treated as synonymous, provided the basis for a widespread scholarly narrative about the Trinitarian debates. Originating in the nineteenth century with Theodor Zahn and later disseminated by Adolf von Harnack and Friedrich Loofs, this now-obsolete account blamed the discord that followed the conclusion of the Nicene council on an inability to distinguish between ousia and hypostasis.[57] Only after this distinction was clarified did the term "homoousios" cease to convey the numeric—rather than generic—identity between the Father and His Son. According to Zahn, the Nicene concept of homoousios, allegedly preaching the numeric identity and the cohesiveness of the ousia of the godhead, was tantamount to the complete identification between the Father and the Son promoted by the Monarchians. While the partisans of Nicaea used the term "homoousios" to express the numeric identity of divine substance between God and Christ (unity of substance), the Cappadocian writers used the adjective to signify the generic identity between the two (equality of substance). Similar renditions often appear in early scholarship, with some versions finding their way into more recent work.[58] In essence, they posit a marked continuity between the contents of the creeds of the two councils, casting the Council of Constantinople of 381 (where agreement about the Trinitarian faith was reached among the vast majority of Church leaders) as a faithful interpreter of a logic that was outlined, though only imperfectly expressed, at Nicaea.[59]

Newer assessments have shown Zahn's narrative to be reliant on the ideological rendition of the debates that was produced in the fourth century by Athanasius, bishop of Alexandria and the foremost champion of Nicene orthodoxy. Athanasius and his allies were responsible for the definition of the specific meaning of homoousios as indicating unity of ousia. In reality, the issues addressed by the two councils were distinct: Nicaea dealt mainly with the consubstantiality between the Son and the Father, whereas Constantinople focused on the number of *hypostaseis* (plural of hypostasis) within the godhead. Any attempt to interpret the concerns of Constantinople as an explication of those of Nicaea is an instance of retrojection. As argued by George Leonard Prestige, the use of the term "homoousios" within Nicaea's pronouncements underscored Christ's absolute equality with God but could not possibly address the problem of God's unity, because that issue had not yet been raised in the fourth-century Trinitarian debate.[60] Additionally, Christopher Stead has demonstrated that no one in the immediate post-Nicene period considered the Nicene anathema on claims that the Son was "from another hypostasis" (*ex heteras hypostaseōs*) as equivalent to a condemnation of the view which held the Son's hypostasis as discrete. Rather, the phrase was understood as a denial of the Son having been created from nothing or from a substance coeternal with God himself.[61]

Building on Stead's thesis, André de Halleux criticized the anachronistic identification of early adherence to the Nicene Creed with the triadological question, that is, the issue concerning the number of hypostaseis. In his assessment, the Nicene fathers' only concern was defining God's generation of the Son (which they saw as eternal and natural, as opposed to willful) in terms on which Arius and his followers would no longer be able to quibble.[62] While past scholarship considered that the Council of Nicaea had condemned the entire Origenist theology of the Logos (and, with it, the doctrine of the three hypostaseis), de Halleux did not believe the council could proscribe a view so widespread in the East.[63] Thus, the only belief Nicaea had censured was the idea that the Son of God had a temporal, created, and mutable nature.[64]

Numerous aspects of the Trinitarian debates, which spanned the years 318–383, continued to be the object of critical reassessment throughout the second half of the twentieth century.[65] Scholars delved into the conceptual labor that took Christianity from the stalemate of Nicaea to the resolution at the Council of Constantinople. The settlement of 381 was shown to be not the inevitable outcome of the theological course inaugurated at Nicaea, but rather a product of the politicking and ingenuity of a group of post-Nicene theologians.

In his 2004 book *Nicaea and Its Legacy*, Lewis Ayres broke new historiographic ground by providing a synthetic account of those theological strands that would eventually come to be considered orthodox by Constantinopolitan standards. At the same time, Ayres aimed to displace a timeworn geographical paradigm of the development of Christian dogma, attributed to a three-volume study published at the end of the nineteenth century by Théodore de Régnon.[66] According to this paradigm, Trinitarian theology in the Greek-speaking East had as its point of departure plurality of principles within the godhead, and moved from there toward a recognition of divine unity. Conversely, de Régnon's model described western Christian thought as starting from the one and moving toward the triadic articulation of the divine.

Among the most significant innovations of *Nicaea and Its Legacy* is its identification of a non-geographically-bound "pro-Nicene culture."[67] Ayres's self-avowed theoretical reference for the concept of "culture" is Pierre Bourdieu. Countering the de Régnon model, Ayres formulates a four-part taxonomy of pre-Nicene Trinitarian postures, which he identifies—based on the unfolding of events over the subsequent years—as key avenues for the development of pro-Nicene culture.[68] Despite their differences in the "primary metaphors and analogies for speaking about the relationship between God and Word,"[69] all four parts shared a series of concerns. Of these, the most important were "a clear version of the person and nature distinction," "clear expression that the eternal generation of the Son occurs within the unitary and incomprehensible divine," and "clear expression of the doctrine that the persons work inseparably."[70]

The narrative of *Nicaea and Its Legacy* powerfully reimagines the fourth-century theological landscape, relegating the differences between those early-fourth-century traditions to the background and directing the reader's gaze to their ultimate convergence in Augustine's Trinitarian summa. The ghost of the Hegelian cunning of reason, or perhaps of salvation history, may be glimpsed behind the implicit rendition of those pre-Nicene theological trajectories as pre-oriented toward their eventual coherence in an orthodox pro-Nicene culture.[71] This line of interpretation, compelling for the historical theologian, might bear fewer rewards for readers with no stake in identifying in the debates around Nicaea a theoretical kernel capable of nurturing the faith of the Christian community. From the perspective of these readers, the problem of Trinitarian relations was not a timeless riddle urgently demanding a solution, finally identified by the Cappadocians. The very production of the questions that surfaced during the debates, along with the answers that were provided to those questions, was linked instead to subtle but decisive shifts in the working methods and intellectual practices of Christian thinkers.[72] These shifts are of great interest to the intellectual historian because of their effects on the constitution of the Christian tradition.

Additionally, while the concept of culture, on which the notion of a pro-Nicene culture is based, is central to historical accounts informed by social theory, its deployment as a descriptive category for the sole pro-Nicene perspective seems less fruitful. The culture of the pro-Nicene is defined in *Nicaea and Its Legacy* as an intellectual milieu "interweaving pro-Nicene Trinitarian theologies with discussions of cosmology, epistemology, anthropology and—importantly—with conceptions of how to read Scripture."[73] For Ayres, one can identify common themes reflecting an original Nicene theology: "Pro-Nicene theologies combined both doctrinal propositions and a complex of intellectual theological strategies. Together these doctrines and the strategies within which those doctrines were intended to be read constitute a theological culture."[74] This theorization of a pro-Nicene culture is declared to rest on the identification of material, social, and performative practices as constructing the Bordieusian habitus of pro-Nicene writers.[75]

Indeed, these practices are fundamental for the identification of any given culture based on the notion of habitus. However, the examination of multiple activities central to the advancement of the Trinitarian disputes—for example, epistolary practices, conciliar gatherings, literary circulation, the establishment and revocation of communion between different dioceses—reveals overwhelming commonalities between Nicaea's partisans and opponents alike. Thus, we can speak of a culture not exclusive to the victorious pro-Nicene, but common to all fourth-century Christian writers engaged in doctrinal controversy, irrespective of their doctrinal leanings.

The eventual convergence around a particular reinterpretation of the Nicene decree was not produced by the removal of hindrances to the natural unity of all pro-Nicene: it was the outcome of discursive conditions that prevailed in a field larger than the pro-Nicene field. In fact, the strategies that historical actors adopted regarding the issues highlighted by Ayres can be understood as articulating a culture only within an analytical framework that, standing in alignment with the pro-Nicene tradition, converts those theological problems into linchpins of a totalizing, normative historical anthropology. Once such a perspective is relinquished, we are left with too little ink to etch the contours of a Nicene culture. We ought to speak instead of a Christian culture.

Observed from a distance and with a dogmatic-historical interest, the Trinitarian controversies have looked to some like a clash between supporters and opponents of Arius, with a gradation of attachment to either cause. The earliest contemporary attempts to make sense of these disputes—the pioneering works of Adolf von Harnack, Eduard Schwartz, Theodor Zahn, Hans-Georg Opitz, and Friedrich Loofs—turned this mesh of exchanges into one cohesive crisis, unfolding systematically under the unfailing guidance of a transparent logic. These interpretations, however, failed to account for the ways in which theological trajectories pre-dating the Trinitarian controversies affected the emergence of the debate itself. This narrative also did not explain the volatile and continuous reconfigurations of ecclesiastical alliances throughout the crisis.[76] The histories published in the second half of the twentieth century—primarily by Manlio Simonetti and Richard Hanson[77]—have refined this picture by clearly demarcating distinct phases within the debate. As a result, it is now customary to criticize the earlier unitary interpretation, and to argue for the existence of multiple interlocking debates that, together, constituted the so-called Trinitarian dispute. Even these newer perspectives, however, eschew explicit discussion of how the controversies transformed Christian theological debate.

In order to seize elements of discontinuity in relation to the intellectual production that preceded their emergence, the Trinitarian controversies are to be apprehended again as a unitary whole. Upon entering the debates, participants did not share methods of inquiry into Trinitarian relations nor assumptions about how agreement could be reached. Actors holding disparate views on Christ's relation to the Father and to the cosmos expressed themselves in ways that resisted a synthesis. Their formulations could access a discussion only if the logics underpinning them could be made commensurable. Only a logical reconfiguration of the problem at hand into terms through which all battling positions could be expressed allowed those actors to gather in a shared polemical arena.

A reconstruction of key moments in the Trinitarian controversies shows them as a turning point not only in the formation of Christian dogma but also in the emergence of the rules governing theological exchange. The increasing cohesiveness and discreteness of this research tradition and of the discursive field underlying it led to the appearance of clearer partitions within the late ancient Christian-Jewish continuum. Each step toward defining clearer rules for thinking, speaking, and writing about God moved Christian culture closer to the dogmatic form in which it was to manifest itself at the turn of the fifth century. As it approached this form, the Christian intellectual tradition fell away from identification with Judaism. The Christian-Jewish continuum was eventually fractured as a result of transformations in the research methods and practices of Christian intellectuals.

1 • A Tale of Two Heretics

The Memory of Heresy

Christianity and Judaism, I have argued in the Introduction, separated as intellectual traditions only as a result of the crystallization of Jesus-believing thinkers' styles of inquiry. Before beginning to track the development of the Christian theological research tradition (in Chapters 2, 3, and 4), here I wish to clarify through a comparative reading the link between the Christian production of the theological discipline and the parting of the ways. Jews and Christians were interested in different avenues of religious investigation. The difference between the two groups emerged as one not of beliefs, but of methods. This reality led to an asymmetry in the distancing process. While Christians reproached Jews for their failure to believe in Christ, the rabbis' rejection of Christology was deployed on a different plane: irrespective of theological outcomes, Jewish thinkers saw as misguided the kind of speculations that their belief forced Christian intellectuals to embark on.

The larger discursive contexts and broader historical repercussions of this asymmetry are developed in Chapter 5. Here I would like simply to put its existence in relief through the juxtaposition of two sets of texts about heretics: the dossier related to the condemnation of the Antiochene bishop Paul of Samosata (200–275 CE) and the Talmudic story of the excommunication of the third-generation *tanna* (rabbinic sage) Elisha ben Abuyah (first to second century CE). Although these samples might appear disparate, we are dealing in both cases with the late ancient construction of an excommunication. The historical characters at the center of both episodes predated the Trinitarian controversies, but the narratives concerning them emerged and began to be transmitted in the fourth century. In both cases later writers projected the institutional workings and concerns of their own intellectual communities onto a previous era, which their historical accounts allowed them to construct as foundational. Christian and Jewish elites thus limned the image of the projects in which they saw themselves engaged by memorializing two figures who deviated from the ways of their communities. A parallel examination of these two episodes in Christian and Jewish heresiologies provides insights into the different ways in which elite thinkers on both sides reflected on the use of language about the divine, central to the practices of Christian theologians but not to the concerns of the rabbis.[1]

Our first and main object of interest is a *sugyah* (self-contained unit of discursive analysis), found in tractate *Ḥagigah* of the Babylonian Talmud, that describes the encounter between the first- to second-century CE tanna Elisha ben Abuyah and the angel Metatron. Elisha's vision of the heavenly being proved fateful as it led him to make a misguided statement, construable as binitarian, about the inner workings of the divine. While this sugyah has been interpreted as proscribing heterodox beliefs or upholding Torah praxis, I suggest reading it instead as containing a rabbinic reflection about the correct ways of producing religious knowledge. The core of Elisha's transgression is thus presented in this passage neither as heterodox belief in two powers in heaven nor as a sin of orthopraxy, but as the pursuit of certain modes of religious inquiry about the divine realm that are misaligned with the broader rabbinic worldview.

In a supplementary bit of analysis, I propose that the conclusion of the sugyah, which describes Elisha's transgression of Sabbath regulations in the aftermath of his vision, should be understood in light of a crucial nuance in those laws. A discussion found only a few folios earlier, in the same Talmudic treatise, points to the fact that Elisha's flagrant Sabbath violation is in reality only rabbinic in nature. This circumstance mitigates the wrong he has committed: a rabbinic leniency saves him from being punished with complete excision from the Jewish people through the divine punishment of *karet*. The rabbinic legal system is thus exalted for its saving power.

Elisha's tale is told by the rabbis not to safeguard monotheism, as it has nearly always been claimed, but to discourage anyone from abandoning the practices of the rabbinic academy, chief among them the jurisprudential articulation of orthopraxy, and from embracing instead an inquiry into the inner dynamics of heaven. Any quest for an exact grasp of the divine realm is disallowed, as the rabbis find it irreconcilable with the way of life their research community upholds. This episode in Talmudic heresiology, then, points to the rabbis' dismissal of theology as foreign to their intellectual concerns.

For purposes of comparison, we then consider the historiographic arc of the Christian arch-heretic Paul of Samosata. It is an established fact that around 260, as the recently elected bishop of Antioch, Paul faced an offensive from fellow Syrian Church leaders, ostensibly on account of his theological persuasions. After several councils, he was eventually defeated in a public debate and deposed by a synod convened in 268/9. The later memorialization of Paul's affair in Christian sources is often inaccurate, and assigns to the bishop a conglomerate of deviant forms of difference. Fourth- and fifth-century Christian authors who reported his story levied against Paul charges of Judaizing, heterodoxy, suspicious association with women, and collusion with an enemy of the Roman Empire. The supra-diocesan level at which the discussion unfolded led those writers to read back into this third-century series of events the first appearance of the working methods and institutional circumstances that had become typical of the theological field in the post-Constantinian and post-Theodosian period. As a result, the process that paved the way to Paul's condemnation was presented in late ancient Christian sources as heralding the emergence of theology in an orthodox Christendom ruled by a cohesive clerical class, released from its ties to contemporary Jewry, and constituted into the religion of the Roman Empire.

A parallel reading of the historical files on Paul of Samosata and Elisha ben Abuyah ultimately evidences an instructive asymmetry between the Christian and the Jewish relationship to the intellectual tradition of the other group, whose foreignness had by then solidified. Christian historiography inscribed the bishop's story as foundational to theologians' way of doing their thinking publicly in an empire where Christianity had garnered the support of political power. In this process of memorialization, the heterodox theological views of the heretic Paul were explicitly and repeatedly linked to Jewish otherness. In contrast, in the story in *Ḥagigah* the rabbis made no clear allusions to Christianity and passed over in silence the similarity between Elisha's interests and their Christian counterparts' theological activities.

Elisha's Misprision

The Babylonian Talmud recounts the encounter between the tanna Elisha ben Abuyah and the angel Metatron (*b.* Ḥagigah 15a).[2] This sugyah refers to a famous tale contained in the Tosefta (a collection of teachings that is largely a supplement to the Mishnah, itself a compilation of oral laws; the tale also appears with variants in the Mishnah at *b.* Ḥagigah 14b):

> Four entered the *pardes* (orchard): Ben Azzai, Ben Zoma, Acher, and Rabbi ʿAkiva. One gazed and perished, one gazed and was smitten, one gazed and cut the shoots, and one went up whole and came down whole. Ben Azzai gazed and perished. Concerning him scripture says, "The death of his faithful ones is grievous in the Lord's sight" (Ps 116:15). Ben Zoma gazed and was smitten. Concerning him scripture says, "If you find honey, eat only what you need, lest, surfeiting yourself, you throw it up" (Prov 25:16). Elisha gazed and cut the shoots. Concerning him scripture says, "Let not your mouth lead you into sin" (Qoh 5:5).[3]

The *gemara* (the commentary on the Mishnah, which along with it constitutes the Talmud) inquires into the pithy descriptions of the earthly lots of the protagonists and into the meaning of the biblical quotes used as "hazy hints at the[ir] fate[s],"[4] interpreting the various phrases used by the Tosefta and the scriptural citations "as referents of the events of a story."[5] The events of the story concerning Elisha ben Abuyah run as follows:

> [a] Acher cut the shoots. Of him Scripture says, "Do not let your mouth lead you into sin" (Qoh 5:5). [b] What is this [in reference to]? He saw Metatron, that authority had been given to him to sit down to write the merits of Israel. [c] He said: "It is taught [as a tradition] that above there is no sitting, and no competition, and no turning of the back, and no proliferation. Perhaps there are—God forbid—two authorities!" [d] They led Metatron out and punished him with sixty fiery lashes. [e] They told him: "Why is it that, when you saw him, you did not rise before him?" [f] Authority was given to him to strike out the merits of Acher. [g] A heavenly voice came out and said: "'Return, ye backsliding children (Jer 3:22)'—except Acher." [h] He said: "Since I have been driven out from that world, let me go enjoy this world."[6] [i] Acher went into evil ways. He went and found a prostitute and propositioned her. [j] She said to him: "And are you not Elisha ben Abuyah?" He uprooted a radish from [its] bed on a Sabbath and gave it to her. She said: "He is Acher" [or: "He is *aḥer* (i.e., another/other)"].[7]

The story of the fateful meeting between the sage and the heavenly creature, of which I offer a detailed reading below, is transmitted in different forms by several texts, including, among other *Hekhalot*-literature texts, one known as *3*

Enoch.[8] The various attestations narrate Elisha's ascent to a mystical realm, his vision of Metatron, and a statement he made that contained the phrase "two sovereignties" (*shetei reshuyot*).[9] This expression is known in the Talmud and in rabbinic literature as a catchword for different theological postures alien to the rabbinic movement, and most notably for dualistic or binitarian beliefs.[10] As a result, the account of *b.* Ḥagigah 15a has been traditionally interpreted as a proscription of such heterodox beliefs.

More recently a new line of interpretation has developed that sees the sugyah as preoccupied with upholding not rabbinic monotheism, but Torah praxis. However, both the theological and the orthopractical interpretations, while seizing important aspects of the narrative, fail to account for other parts of the story. In order to elucidate the broader ideological dynamic at play in this passage, I suggest reading the latter as a rabbinic expression of concern with both correct belief and observance of the precepts, in which a sharp contrast is also drawn between legitimate and illegitimate ways of producing religious knowledge. Using the pretext of Elisha's incorrect binitarian conclusion, forms of speech claiming exact knowledge about the divine realm are condemned by the editors of this sugyah inasmuch as they cannot be reconciled with the model of piety the rabbis advocate. This proposal, I argue, finds additional support by reading the story of Elisha's transgression in the context of a neighboring sugyah that discusses Sabbath law (*b.* Ḥagigah 10b).[11]

In my reading, the Acher sugyah in *b.* Ḥagigah 15a interprets the connection between mouth and flesh, established in the verse of Qohelet ("Do not suffer your mouth to cause your flesh to sin") cited by the *mishnah*, as binding together speech and praxis. Although the problematic outcome of Elisha's mistaking one kind of *reshuta* (permission, delegated authority) for another (a sovereignty) is undeniably related to his expression of an incorrect belief, the structure of the narrative highlights the process by which the ill-conceived conclusion is reached.

It is likely that the line "He saw Metatron, that authority had been given to him to sit down in order to write down the merits of Israel" (*b*) implies that, when seeing the heavenly figure, Elisha is not privy to the fact that the angel has been granted permission to sit down to perform this task, presumably delegated to him by God.[12] Metatron's sitting prompts Elisha's citation of a traditional teaching that he has previously learned (*c*): "It is taught [as a tradition] that above there is no sitting, and no competition, and no turning of the back, and no proliferation." From this teaching, describing activities and states of being precluded to the creatures that crowd the heavenly court, the tanna draws the obvious conclusion that the being he saw seated could not be one of those creatures. His status, then, has to be divine.

Elisha's reasoning is based on an implicit syllogism. The major premise, consisting in information conveyed by the traditional teaching, states that no creature may sit in God's presence. The minor premise, reposing on information gleaned through a vision, is that Metatron is sitting in God's presence. From the conclusion that Metatron is not a creature, the sage makes a final and for him fatal inference, namely that the angel Metatron must represent an independent celestial *reshuta* (sovereignty). The binitarian formulation is produced as the result of a collision between two distinct domains of knowledge, to which the major and minor premises of the implicit syllogism respectively pertain: the authoritative tradition of the rabbis and a form of knowledge about God obtained through direct revelation, which we may call theosophy.

The epistemic basis of Elisha's misprision is evidenced by the logic underlying his exclamation: since an authoritative tradition teaches that no sitting is allowed in heaven, and since he did see an entity sitting, the latter must belong to a category to which the authoritative tradition would not apply, namely a sovereignty. Elisha incorrectly draws conclusions from a teaching introduced by the expression *gemire/gemiri* (it is taught [as a tradition], literally, they have learned) in a domain to which teachings of that kind were never meant to be applied.[13] This application of a traditional teaching to a theosophical vision leads him dangerously close to a quest for exact knowledge about intra-divine dynamics.

The sugyah therefore proscribes the inappropriate intersection of two vectors of inquiry that, if taken separately, constitute legitimate avenues of attaining knowledge. The disapproval the text expresses about the failure to observe the epistemic boundaries within which the objects of visionary experience are to be maintained should not be mistaken for a delegitimization of that experience tout court. The Babylonian Talmud as a whole, insofar as such a generalization is permissible, does not appear to hold principled objections to Hekhalot-like visionary experiences. The whole second chapter of tractate *Ḥagigah*, containing the narrative of Elisha, after taking as its point of departure the Mishnah's proscription of esoteric teaching, surprisingly proceeds to describe wild speculations of that very kind. The sugyah on the work of creation (*ma ʿaśeh bereshit*) contained in the preceding pages of the second chapter of *Ḥagigah* has been recognized to incorporate major aspects of ascent apocalypse and Merkabah mysticism, while restricting the value of those revelations.[14] Similarly, the sugyah in *b.* Ḥagigah 15a marginalizes theosophical speculations by limiting their epistemic purview.

As mentioned above, scholarship has traditionally claimed that this sugyah should be understood as an expression of the rabbinic struggle with competing Jewish theological postures that celebrated an exalted binitarian figure.[15] But this reading fails to account for the citation of the traditional teaching introduced by the word *gemire/gemiri*, for the text's detailing of the logical process by which Elisha arrived at his mistaken conclusion, and for its insistence on the writing and erasure of merits. If the editor of this sugyah had simply meant to censure binitarian statements, a more parsimonious way to do so could certainly have been found. A deviant Elisha could have been represented, for example, as misled by his vision of Metatron into confessing a second God, without any reference to the teaching about sitting and to his interpretation thereof.

The existence of a dense cluster of cognate versions for the text of this sugyah has led to speculations about a deep textual prehistory.[16] Even if correct, these hypotheses do not preclude the possibility that some original or adventitious elements of the story may have been retained and re-signified in the hands of the editors.[17] The materials the editor of the sugyah received did not bind him to any specific organization. Indeed, the more dramatic the narrative variance is—both in relation to the configuration of the story in *y.* Ḥagigah 2:1 (77b) (this story's parallel in the Palestinian Talmud) and to other presumed or extant versions of *b.* Ḥagigah 15a—the more transparently we can perceive the editor's ideological agenda.

The expression *gemire/gemiri* is found over a hundred times in the Babylonian Talmud.[18] It is used to express a variety of concepts, including an ancient and reliable tradition, a tradition rooted in a reading of the Torah and not based on rabbinic innovation, and a tradition that can be formally categorized as *halakhah le-Mosheh mi-Sinai* (a law given to Moses at Sinai). What appears certain is that a traditional aura is attached to the teachings this formula introduces.[19] The phrase is often employed in the Babylonian Talmud to establish a contrast between traditional teaching and a product of experience, observation, or analysis. The tradition introduced by *gemire/gemiri* retains its validity; at the same time, by being marked as opposed to—at least in this case—incontrovertible observation, its authoritative value is irremediably fractured and thus distanced from the truly authoritative voice of the *stam* (the anonymous voice prominent in the gemara), even when a compromise is eventually formulated.

The teaching reported by Elisha ben Abuyah appears to be treated in a similar manner to cases in which *gemire/gemiri* conveys some form of lore. An example may be found in *b.* Berakhot 59a:

> [The mishnah taught that the blessing "Blessed be He whose strength and power fill the world" is recited] over winds. What are winds? Abaye said: "A hurricane." And Abaye [further] said: "It is taught as a tradition [*gemiri*] that a hurricane cannot happen at night, but lo, we see that it does!" It is one that began during the day. And Abaye said: "It is taught as a tradition [*gemiri*] that a hurricane does not last two hours, to fulfill that which was said (Nah 1:9): 'Disgrace will not rise twice,' but lo, we see that it does!" It [was one that] stop[ped] in the middle.[20]

Like in *b.* Ḥagigah 15a, here the contents of the authoritative traditional teaching do not comport with empirical reality. A third statement must be adduced in order to reconcile the two seemingly conflicting affirmations through an exception not accounted for by the original teaching. In the case of *b.* Ḥagigah 15a, the solution according to which "there are two sovereignties" is the only one capable of accounting logically for both the vision and the teaching. However, while the quest for logical reconciliation between a traditional teaching and an empirical observation is harmless when dealing with meteorological phenomena, when the most intimate realm of the divine is at issue the consequences can be dreadful.

There is, to the modern ear, an irresistibly tragicomic overtone to the series of mechanical reactions precipitated by Elisha's exclamation about "two sovereignties in heaven." The narrative shows an irreversible domino effect of infelicitous consequences, without providing a credible set of well-integrated interactions, out of which a coherent understanding may be drawn. Metatron and his angelic tormentors go through the motions of a punishment staged exclusively for Elisha's edification in order to reinforce the notion that the demoted angel is no God.[21]

When Elisha's merits are subsequently effaced, the fact that Metatron requires permission or authority (*reshuta*) to erase them should not mislead us. The sentence "Authority was given to him to strike out the merits of Acher" (*ityehiva leih reshuta le-mimḥaḳ zakhṿata de-ʾAḥer*) is meant to parallel "That authority had been given to him to sit down to write the merits of Israel" (*de-ʾityahava leih reshuta lemeitav lemikhtav zakhṿata de-Iśraʾel*). The parallelism conveys the notion that the angel's previous recording of merits is fully undone for this one deviant member of the people of Israel. The expression is also needed to inculcate again the idea that Metatron is not allowed to perform the function of soteriological scribe except by the granting of special permission. It could even be speculated that the words "authority was given to him" (*ityehiva/ ityahava leih reshuta*), repeated twice with a slight orthographical variation, are used again so that in the comparison between the two sentences the absence of any mention of sitting after the punishment may—as it were—stand out.

The removal of Elisha's *mitsvot* (precepts or, in this context, an equivalent of *zakhvata*, merits) is no petty initiative of Metatron's. No rage or request for revenge on his part is recorded. The erasure is, rather, an act of divinely sanctioned annihilation of the capital of mitsvot Elisha has accrued through a system mediated by rabbinic authority. After Elisha's recognition of a second sovereignty leads him to mistake an angel for a soteriological figure, he is forced to pay for his error by experiencing an alternate regimen of deliverance, wherein his fate is indeed entrusted to an angel, and to bear witness to the inefficacy and arbitrariness of such a system. The creature whom God had appointed to preside over the accounting of Israel's mitsvot, and whom Elisha has mistaken for an independent guarantor of his own righteousness, becomes responsible, in a dramatic turn of events, for the tanna's perdition.

Following the erasure of Elisha's mitsvot, a heavenly voice calls out, declaring that there will be no possibility of repentance. On the one hand, this voice might be understood as proclaiming Elisha's sin to be of the kind that the quadripartite expiatory taxonomy (*ḥillukei kaparah*) attributed to Rabbi Yishmael terms "profanation of the heavenly name" (*ḥillul shem shamayim*). Such transgressions can neither have their punishment suspended by repentance (*teshuvah*) nor be cleansed by tribulations (*yissurim*), nor atoned for by Yom Kippur: they are extinguished only by death.[22] On the other hand, the heavenly voice embodies a form of direct relationship with the divine about which the Talmud repeatedly records the rabbis' sentiment of at best ambiguity and at worst competitiveness.[23] Elisha's establishment of an unmediated soteriological link with God indicates that, as a result of his direct scrutiny of the divine realm, he is now put under a different aegis than that of the rabbis.[24] His inability to repent stems from his sudden placement outside of a legal system in which the possibility of repentance is tightly linked to the acceptance of rabbinic authority.

Having learned of his fate from the heavenly utterance, the outcast Elisha ben Abuyah, left with no way to remedy his statement or relieve its consequences, resolves to enjoy his earthly existence without regard to religious prohibitions. He propositions a prostitute, who upon recognizing him cannot believe her eyes (maybe an ironic reduplication, as Elisha, too, had balked before his own vision). Witnessing Elisha's theatrical uprooting of a radish, in saying "He is Acher" she does not so much recognize him as other (*aḥer*) from the pious Rabbi Elisha ben Abuyah she had previously known or heard about, as bestow that title upon him. In Mira Balberg's words, "the naming establishes her [. . .] as a privileged cultural agent of rabbinic society."[25] From this moment on, through the prostitute's proclamation, Elisha will be an outcast to the rabbinic community.

Cutting the Shoots

From a formal standpoint, the entire sugyah is structured as a response to the inquiry, contained in *b*, into the real-life referent of the statement found in *a* and quoted from the mishnah: "Acher cut the shoots. Of him Scripture says, 'Do not let your mouth lead you into sin' (Qoh 5:5)." The text pursues a full exegesis of Qoh 5:5:

> [a] Do not let your mouth lead you into sin
> [b] and do not say to the messenger: "It was a mistake."
> [c] Why should God be angry at your voice and destroy the work of your hands?[26]

An instance of straying speech (an incorrect use of his "mouth") leads Elisha's self (his "flesh," *baśar*, in the language of the Hebrew Bible) to commit a sin (Qoh 5:5a).[27] Just like a vow (see Qoh 5:4), blasphemous speech cannot be recanted or repented for (Qoh 5:5b); here the ambiguity of the term *mal'akh* ("angel"/"envoy") and a certain referential vagueness for the word *shegagah* ("mistake") allow the gemara to craftily read a statement that in the Hebrew Bible meant: "Do not tell the [Temple] messenger that [your vow] was a mistake" (see Qoh 5:5b) as meaning instead: "Do not [put yourself into the position of having to] tell the angel that [your vision] was a mistake."[28] Elisha's exclamation (his "voice," *ḳol*, in the word used by Qoh 5:5c) is what angers God, leading to a destruction of his merits ("the work of [his] hands").

The answer to the question concerning the referent of the cutting of the shoots comes at the end of the sugyah. There, after a diegetic progression, we learn that the mention of Acher's cutting the shoots in the garden (*a*) is a literal reference to his uprooting a radish on the Sabbath while visiting a prostitute (*j*). It is only through this action that Acher commits a trespass.[29]

This interpretation secures an inclusio between Acher's final action and the incipit of the discussion[30] and forcibly reduces the enigmatic and possibly esoteric meaning implied by the mishnah's citation of Qohelet to a celebration of halakhic observance. However, cutting the shoots of a plant and removing its root are different actions with dissimilar (literal and metaphorical) outcomes. As the Hebrew Bible teaches, cutting a plant's shoots endangers it, while uprooting it definitively ends its life.[31] Through his decision to violate rabbinic orthopraxis, Elisha definitively destroys (removes the root of) something he has previously only put at risk (cut the shoots of), namely his link to the rabbinic community and his resulting ability to be saved.

Until the uprooting of the radish Elisha was no transgressor; he had simply placed himself in jeopardy, predisposing himself to transgression. The "two sovereignties in heaven" statement is not Elisha's trespass. In this regard, I register my partial agreement with David Grossberg's comparative study of *b.* Ḥagigah 15a and *3 Enoch*.[32] According to Grossberg, the two narratives display a primary emphasis on orthopraxy and orthodoxy, respectively, an emphasis that reflects the concerns of those responsible for editing the narratives. For Grossberg the focus of the passage in *b.* Ḥagigah 15a lies not on Elisha's statement about the existence of two heavenly sovereignties, but on the fact that the events which that statement occasioned caused him to sin by violating rabbinic orthopraxis.[33] But reading the sugyah as "a cautionary tale warning the reader not to abandon the praxis of Torah even if it seems to you that a heavenly voice implies that you should"[34] prevents us from accounting for the presence of the vision of Metatron busily writing down the merits of Israel as well as of Elisha's ensuing declaration. If the editors of the sugyah were simply trying to convey the importance of orthopraxy, why involve the vision of an angel? It would also seem unreasonable, on the other hand, to consider half of the contents of this artfully crafted sugyah merely vestigial.

Grossberg argues that the sugyah's representation of Elisha's sin as a belief in two sovereignties reveals editorial awareness of a potential similarity of such a belief to Christian doctrine.[35] In his judgment, *3 Enoch*'s version may reflect a need to deal with questions of heresy and orthodoxy that were not pressing to the editors of *b.* Ḥagigah 15a. I see instead the issue of correct belief as not only present in the mind of the editor of the sugyah, but consciously thematized as such. However, such thematization leads him to a resolute rejection not of heterodox belief, but of styles of religious inquiry that aim at exact knowledge about the divine realm.

Grossberg's reading was partly anticipated by Alon Goshen-Gottstein. Countering a tendency to consider the expression "perhaps, God forbid" (*shemma ḥas ve-shalom*) in *c* as the product of a gradual softening of Elisha's blasphemous language on the part of the literary or even scribal tradition,[36] Goshen-Gottstein argued that here the phrase has the same function it generally plays in the Talmud, namely that of indicating a momentary and regrettable wavering on the part of a rabbi, who immediately corrects himself by uttering a correct judgment. Building on Goshen-Gottstein's insight, Grossberg claimed that the attribution of the words "perhaps, God forbid" to the rabbi himself existed in the original teaching and was not the product of a later interpolation.[37] According to Grossberg, in the Babylonian Talmud this phrase generally "functions simultaneously as an exclamation of worry and fear that something might be true and an implicit acknowledgement that it is not true."[38] The implication of its usage in *b.* Ḥagigah 15a would then be that Elisha is piously expressing concern that someone might draw from Metatron's sitting position the mistaken conclusion that there are two sovereignties in heaven.[39]

Daniel Boyarin, turning Goshen-Gottstein's intuition against his own intention, proposed that the dubitative value of the standard Talmudic expression "perhaps, God forbid" served here the purpose of enhancing the portrayal of the binitarian belief as dangerous. If Elisha is punished for a momentary faltering, the belief in two sovereignties in heaven must be a truly grave sin indeed.[40] While adopting the standard view, held also by Schäfer, that "Metatron clearly assumes here a very high position in heaven, in fact so high that Acher mistakes him for a second God,"[41] Boyarin connected the reference to sitting contained in both *b.* Ḥagigah 15a and *3 Enoch* to the famous enthronement scene in *Daniel* 7:13, and the mention of a "sovereignty" in the sugyah to the authority (*shilton*, or *exousia* in the LXX) that the "One like a Son of Man" is granted in the following verse.[42] Differing also from Boyarin's reading, I see the text as expressing a concern with both precepts and the question of expressed belief. It is specifically detailed speech about the divine that is declared illegitimate and irreconcilable with the model of piety administered by the rabbis.

Mountains Hanging by a Strand

Although the interpretation proposed above stands or falls on its own merits, further support for it may be found by reading Elisha's Sabbath transgression, described toward the end of the story, in light of another passage in the treatise within which the sugyah is folded. The rabbis, seeking a way to make actionable the scriptural commandment to abstain from work on the Sabbath (Lev 23:3), asserted that the Torah prohibited any *melakhah* (plural *melakhot*, loosely, work) whose performance was necessary for the construction of the Tabernacle.[43] The tanna'im famously identified thirty-nine categories of such work proscribed on the Sabbath (*avot melakhah*, fathers of work—e.g., *qotser*, reaping), and extended the ban to activities that expressed the same ultimate goal as those actions (*toldot melakhah*, offspring of work—e.g., honey-harvesting as derived from reaping). At the same time, the rabbis limited the Torah's ban on work to the kinds of work that are described by the expression "thoughtful work" (*melekhet maḥashevet*).[44] The above-mentioned thirty-nine melakhot were only forbidden if they constituted such thoughtful work, as identified through some criteria. To be sure, the rabbis multiplied prohibitions on the kinds of work that did not meet the criteria for thoughtful work, but they recognized that these bans were the product of their own legislation and distinct from the mandates they read in (or into) the Torah.

The distinction between prohibitions declared by the Torah (*mi-de'oraita*) and by the rabbis (*mi-derabanan*) was juridically consequential. The conscious transgressor (*mezid*) of the Torah prohibition of thoughtful work was considered punishable by excision (*karet*) (whatever this fate meant) or, if the trespass was committed in the presence of two warning witnesses, by stoning (*seḳilah*), while an involuntary transgressor (*shogeg*) needed to bring a sin offering (*ḳorban ḥaṭat*). On the other hand, when it came to rabbinic prohibitions, a voluntary transgressor was only punished with a beating for rebelliousness (*makat mardut*), while an involuntary violator was not liable at all.[45] Additionally, the rabbis envisioned cases in which leniency could be used toward the transgressor of Sabbath norms of their own derivation, while they applied stringency to rules understood as being spelled out by the Torah.

The Babylonian Talmud builds a complex casuistry for Sabbath transgressions using a multiplicity of partly interrelated legal categories, including but not limited to such notions as *ke-darkah* (expressing the need that an action prohibited mi-de'oraita be accomplished "according to its [usual] manner"),[46] *mitḳayyem* (indicating that the outcome of the action needs to be foreseen to be "persistent" for a reasonable amount of time in order for it to incur sanction), and *davar she-'eino mitkayyein* (exempting an "unintentional action" from the Torah's prohibition).[47] Talmudic commentators discuss the relationships of interdependence between these as well as other categories, and debate in particular their connection to the central notion of thoughtful work. This complex conceptual mesh cannot be charted in this chapter.[48] What is relevant to the argument pursued here is that for the definition of thoughtful work to be fulfilled, two criteria must be met: that the action be *metaḳḳen* ("constructive") and that it be a *melakhah ha-tserikhah le-gufah* ("a work necessary for its own sake").[49]

The criterion of constructiveness prescribes that, in order to be prohibited by the Torah as thoughtful work, any activity—including a physically destructive one—needs to be performed with a constructive intent. An act performed without such intent is allowed by the Torah on the Sabbath, as it is considered destructive (*meḳalḳel*).[50] For example, tearing down a wall on the Sabbath in order to clear an area so that one may later build on it would be prohibited by the Torah, whereas tearing it down with the sole aim of getting rid of it would be allowed mi-de᾽oraita, and only prohibited mi-derabanan.

Another criterion for qualification as thoughtful work, summarized by the formula "a work necessary for its own sake," stipulates that a prohibited action needs to be performed for the same purpose for which it was performed during the construction of the Tabernacle. When an action constitutes a "work not necessary for its own sake" (*melakhah she-᾽einah tserikhah le-gufah*), the Torah allows it. For example, putting out a fire on the Sabbath for the purpose of creating embers would be prohibited by the Torah, while extinguishing it to save oil would be permitted. As in the case of a destructive action, actions falling under the category of work not necessary for its own sake were still prohibited by the rabbis.

It does not seem coincidental that one of the main Talmudic sources for the rabbinic development of the notion of work necessary for its own sake is preserved only in five folios before the Metatron sugyah, in *b.* Hagigah 10b. The gemara takes up here a curious statement by the Mishnah, which articulates with rare bluntness and a surprising degree of self-awareness the relationship between the halakhic tradition originating from the rabbis and the commandments of the Torah:

> The dissolution of vows floats in the air and has nothing to lean on. The laws of the Sabbath, festal-offerings, and acts of sancta violation are as mountains hanging by a strand, [since they are] little scripture and [many] laws. Civil cases, temple services, purities and impurities, and forbidden relations have what to lean upon, and it is they that are the bodies of the Torah.[51]

As David Weiss Halivni explained, by the "bodies of the Torah" (*gufei ha-Torah*)—its essence—the Mishnah means that corpus of halakhic traditions that stand on firmest textual ground.[52] At the same time, as Martin Jaffee remarks, the Torah is treated in this passage "as a synthetic category that encompasses in its purview both halakhic judgments of Sages and scripturally grounded textual interpretations."[53]

Per its custom, the gemara takes up the Mishnah's syntagms one by one. When it begins discussing the rules of the Sabbath, we read:

> [The Mishnah taught that] "the rules of the Sabbath" [are like mountains hanging by a strand]. [But how is it possible if] they are indeed written [in the Torah]! No, it was necessary [for the mishnah to include them in the list of rules that are like mountains hanging by a strand], in agreement with Rabbi Aba. For Rabbi Aba said: "He who digs a hole on the Sabbath and only needs the earth [as opposed to the hole itself][54] is not liable for it." Who[se view is this one] like? Like [that of] Rabbi Shimon, who said: "As for 'a work not necessary for its own sake,' one is not liable for it." You [could even] say [that it is like the view] of Rabbi Judah [according to whom a work not necessary for its own sake is prohibited].[55] [For] there he [scil. the corpse-carrier] was constructive, [whereas] here he [scil. the hole-digger] is destructive [which is permitted by the Torah]. What [does] "like mountains hanging by a strand" [refer to]? [To the fact that] the Torah prohibited [only] thoughtful work, but "thoughtful work" is not written [explicitly in the Torah].[56]

The gemara's initial rebuttal to the mishnah is forcefully defensive: the rules concerning the Sabbath, we are told, are indeed found in the Torah. At the end of the brief discussion, we learn that the characterization of those rules as mountains hanging by a strand is justified insofar as the narrowing down of prohibited work to thoughtful work, on which Rabbi Aba's lenient opinion is based, is not made explicit anywhere in the Torah. Rabbi Aba believes that the hole-digger is not liable from the viewpoint of the Torah. His teaching is first found to be compatible with Rabbi Shimon's principled view that accomplishing a work not necessary for its own sake on the Sabbath does not carry mi-de'oraita liability. Rabbi Aba's exemption of the hole-digger is then also found to be compatible with the line of thinking of Rabbi Judah, identified as the original tanna who in the mishnah cited in *b.* Shabat 93b prohibited carrying out a dead person—or even a minimal part thereof—into the public domain on the Sabbath, despite the fact that it would be a work not necessary for its own sake.[57] Rabbi Judah's prohibition, it is explained, was not based on any putative disagreement about lack of liability for work not necessary for its own sake (a question on which he agreed with Rabbi Shimon), but on an application of the prohibition of constructive work. Since there is nothing constructive about digging a hole for the sake of gathering dirt, Rabbi Judah, just like Rabbi Aba, would not see the Torah as objecting to the hole-digger's Sabbath activities.

Thus, the gemara concludes that thoughtful work is what the mishnah must have meant to refer to in applying to Sabbath rules the hermeneutically terrifying image of mountains hanging by a strand.[58] The reluctant admission that one tidbit of rabbinic teaching concerning Sabbath regulations has but a loose textual foothold allows the gemara to perform damage control, effectively limiting to that sole case the reach of the mishnah's devastating statement. The rabbis' legislative authority is protected from charges of widespread abuse by sacrificing the soundly scriptural foundation of the sole category of thoughtful work. At the same time, the validity of the latter, endowed with exculpating potential, is unapologetically restated. In expressing anxiety about the relationship between the production of rules based on *midrash halakhah* (legal interpretation) and its scriptural anchorage, and in then reinscribing the rabbinic right to elaborate new legal categories, this passage displays a rhetorical dynamic akin to what Christine Hayes has described as the "amoraic discomfort with and reduced exercise of some aspects of rabbinic authority, coupled with hyperbolic and rhetorical assertions of that very authority."[59]

The same coupling of rabbinic discomfort and authority emerges in the story of Acher. As seen above, after hearing the heavenly voice barring him from repentance Elisha sets out to enjoy his life. As a way of addressing the disbelief of the prostitute he propositions, he purposefully proceeds to transgress a commandment of the Torah. Nevertheless, thanks to the intervention of rabbinic legislation, this act is insufficient to place him in violation of a Torah prohibition. This crucial halakhic detail about Acher's act would not have been lost on ancient readers of the Talmud, who would have been well conditioned to interrogate the nature of his trespass. The very intention behind plucking the radish, which is purely demonstrative, causes the act to fail to meet the criterion of thoughtful work, discussed in *b.* Ḥagigah 10a. The performative intent behind the gesture makes it fall short of constructiveness while also making it fail to meet the criterion of "a work necessary for its own sake" (although dissatisfaction of either criterion would have sufficed).

Acher's otherwise cryptic gesture in handing the radish to the prostitute clarifies the juridical status of the plucking. Getting rid of the vegetable immediately after plucking it guarantees its technical disqualification as thoughtful work under both rubrics and ensures Acher's lack of mi-deʾoraita liability.

The likelihood that the editors of *b.* Ḥagigah 15a had *b.* Ḥagigah 10b in mind when describing Acher's act is increased by the fact that the radish (*pugla*) is no stranger to discussions of Sabbath regulations in the Babylonian Talmud, making two appearances as a paradigmatic example in a debate concerning the moving of objects on the Sabbath.[60] By choosing a vegetable discussed elsewhere in relation to rules of the Sabbath, the text secures the reader's attention to the halakhic minutiae of the scene.

The prostitute, presumably unschooled in the subtleties of Sabbath legislation, is persuaded of the trespassing nature of Elisha's act and feels the need to ask no further questions. In any event, she would have been justified in seeing him as other (*aḥer*) from the sage she knew even based on a mi-derabanan transgression. A functional equivalent to the heavenly voice, the prostitute confers on him this title on behalf of the rabbis. What she is unwittingly sanctioning, however, is Elisha's extraneity not to the Torah, but to the rabbinic community. The rabbis' category of thoughtful work, whose validity was anxiously reaffirmed after careful scrutiny in *b.* Ḥagigah 10b, saves Elisha from the grave punishment of excision to which the violation of a Torah prohibition would have condemned him.

At the same time, however, Elisha becomes alienated from the community of the rabbis by transgressing the standing rabbinic prohibition of non-thoughtful work, a violation punishable with a beating for rebelliousness.[61] It is significant, in this regard, that the version of the story attested by two of the manuscripts has the heavenly voice explicitly denote Elisha's sin as an act of rebelliousness.[62] Elisha's act results in his being ostracized by the rabbis at the same time as he is reinscribed within their hegemonic sphere. The heavenly voice revealed that a juridical subject's direct relationship with the divine, unbrokered by the rabbis, would be inevitably damning. The prostitute announces the good news that such a relationship is in fact impossible: the rabbis' claim of Metatron's mediating position for themselves is in a sense inescapable.

A passage from *Genesis Rabbah*, focusing on the sin of the protoplasts, offers external support for this reading. The exegesis this midrash pursues centers on Adam's addition, in his report to Eve, of the prohibition of touching the tree to the ban uttered by God, which contained no such warning:[63]

> "But as for the fruit of the tree in the middle of the garden [. . .] nor touch it" (Gen 3:3): This is what is written: "Do not add to His words, lest He rebuke you and you be shown to be a liar" (Prov 30:6). Rabbi Hiyya taught: "Do not make the fence greater than the root [or: main object], lest he fall and cut the shoots."[64]

Although the subject of the falling and cutting of shoots has been understood by commentators to be the fence (*gader*) itself (which would require the translation "lest *it* fall"),[65] given the topic with which the statement is preoccupied—the transgression of commandments—it seems more reasonable to read here a hypothetical male human subject. The extended metaphor could be taken as a generic warning against the unreasonable proliferation of self-avowedly rabbinic decrees, which risk leading one to trip up and trespass against the legal core they are meant to protect. However, the fact that the passage transposes into the rabbinic jurisprudential realm the scriptural theme of an unwarranted addition to the direct report of God's words opens up the possibility that the cautionary dictum has a more specific target: prohibitions unduly alleged to be mi-de'oraita.[66]

The rabbis' development of the category of thoughtful work and their determination to exclude non-thoughtful work from Torah-sanctioned prohibitions of Sabbath work fufilled Rabbi Hiyya's request to refrain from the intemperately stringent adjudication of debates about the mi-de'oraita nature of a prohibition. By removing non-thoughtful work from the types of Sabbath activity sanctioned by the Torah, the rabbis pruned an overgrowth of the fence (an undue mi-de'oraita burden). In so doing, they prevented the body of rabbinic legislation (the fence) from collapsing onto the actual mi-de'oraita prohibitions (the *'iḳḳar*, root or main thing) it was meant to protect, a circumstance that would lead one to jeopardize his or her connection to the rabbinic community (i.e., to cutting the shoots). In the case of Elisha, the rabbis' relieving effort proved providential in preventing his definitive downfall: though severed from the rabbinic community as a result of his rebelliousness, he was not smitten by excision. In using cutting-of-the-shoots imagery to discuss the relationship between Torah commandments and rabbinic legislation, and in establishing the same shoots/root link on which the Acher sugyah is premised,[67] this midrash independently strengthens the argument for a connection between *b.* Ḥagigah 10a and 15a.[68]

A Rabbinic Reflection on Religious Knowledge

My reading of the story of Acher finds in *b.* Ḥagigah 15a a programmatic passage, in which the rabbis approximate an explicit articulation of the avenues of intellectual inquiry they consider legitimate and aligned with their value system. This sugyah does not primarily dismiss this or that belief about the nature of God. Rather, it proscribes—and resolutely so—a style of inquiry that aims at exact knowledge about the divine realm. It is undeniable that Elisha's curiosity led him to place excessive (quasi-binitarian or binitarian) trust in the independent soteriological function of the angel Metatron, at least for the brief time of his unfortunate ejaculation. Binitarian tenets, however, as unfavorably as they might be portrayed, are not made the object of overt proscription. The narrative structure of the sugyah is such that the focus of its condemnation lies not on binitarianism per se, but on the straight line that leads from dabbling in the kind of speech with which Elisha experimented to the wholesale rejection of rabbinic authority.

The "two sovereignties in heaven" utterance is used as a plot device for unleashing a chain of dramatic consequences that should suffice to dissuade anybody from an idle search for knowledge about the essential composition of the divine. Late ancient rabbis show no interest in this undertaking throughout the literary corpus they have left behind, as it diverts one from virtuous adherence to the system of Torah precepts mediated by their academy. The execrated type of religious knowledge practiced by Elisha and resulting in his incorrect form of speech is linked to a soteriology based on direct relationship with the divine, and as such incompatible with the rabbis' normative claims. As a result of his participation in an alien type of religious speech, Elisha is hurled into a system of deliverance alternative to that of halakhic observance. Forced to experience in his own flesh the ineffectual redemptive power of that regimen, he is eventually rescued from excision by the rabbis' all-encompassing legal discourse.

Reading *b.* Ḥagigah 15a as a programmatic text allows us to recognize that in rabbinic ideology the nexus between licit styles of religious inquiry and adherence to the normative regimen was at least as significant a preoccupation as (if not, as I propose, more significant a preoccupation than) the holding of correct beliefs about the structure of the divine.

The Excommunication of Paul of Samosata

The rabbis' attitude of relative indifference toward theological constructs, displayed in this sugyah, lies at the antipodes of the all-consuming attention that the Christian clergy paid, beginning in the fourth century, to collective agreement on the correct belief, a preoccupation anticipated, at least in the renditions of later Christian historians, in the third-century condemnation of the arch-heretic Paul of Samosata. The phantasmatic role that, as I demonstrate shortly, Judaism played in the memorialization of the events surrounding Paul's deposition is not without interest for an understanding of the enduring and unreciprocated Christian investment in Jewry's fate. For this reason, a contrastive reading of the two sets of materials imposes itself as appropriate.

Granted, the story narrated in *b.* Ḥagigah 15a is of a different order altogether from Christian reports about Paul. While the historical factuality of the bishop's ousting is not in question according to any scholar, from the viewpoint of positivist history the angelic vision from which the Elisha narrative unfurls is simply unverifiable. In any event, Haggadic passages in the Talmud are far from claiming historical truthfulness in the sense in which ecclesiastical histories do (although also the latter do so always within a providential frame of reference).[69] It should also be acknowledged that my study of the memorialization of Acher focuses on one relatively self-contained passage from the Babylonian Talmud culled out of a more extensive cycle, whereas the lore about Paul's deposition is preserved in a large corpus of Christian works, in which a heresiological approach to this episode prevails. Despite these caveats, the similar ideological dynamic structuring both narratives—the projection of the institutional and discursive workings of a present intellectual community onto an old story about a heretic—justifies a comparison.

The facts about the deposition of the Antiochene bishop Paul of Samosata are well known. In the 260s, Paul came under the attack of his Syrian colleagues. Although the accusations brought against him were theological in nature, he was also subjected to the supplementary charges of autocratic conduct and of committing acts unbecoming to his rank.[70] It seems likely that his opponents' conspiracy was part of the resistance to an onrush of monocratic forms of episcopal governance among the churches of Syria.[71]

In his *Ecclesiastical History* Eusebius of Caesarea reports that as soon as it became clear that Paul equated Christ with a common human being,[72] a first synod was summoned (around 264), to which clergymen hastened from across the empire. Shortly after this synod, and probably after a few others, Bishop Hymenaeus of Jerusalem and five colleagues composed a letter full of ad hominem attacks against Paul. The six bishops wrote that they had already discussed their faith with Paul, but that for the sake of clarity they wanted to expound their teaching again. They appended a long creed, emphasizing the eternity of the Son, and asked Paul to indicate whether he agreed with this expression of faith. At a synod that gathered in the year 268 or 269 Paul was finally cornered in a theological debate with Malchion, an Antiochene priest of much-praised rhetorical skill. Deposed, Paul was replaced by Domnus, the son of the bishop Demetrianus, who had either died or been kidnapped during the Persian invasion of the city.

The doctrine Paul professed is difficult to retrieve. One of the four excerpts from the synodal letter cited by Eusebius accuses Paul of claiming that the Son of God came "from below" (*katōthen*).[73] This report is exposed as incomplete by some historical documents, including Greek, Syriac, Armenian, and Latin fragments from the synodal letter of the council that deposed Paul in 268/269 and from the report of his discussion with Malchion, which was included in the synodal acts.[74]

To be sure, the evidence contained in the fragments confirms that Paul was a Monarchian. His doctrine was at the antipodes of the Logos Christology professed by his Origenist accusers. On the other hand, Paul deviated from the typical Monarchian views that reduced Christ to a creature adopted by God (adoptionism) in whom the divine *dynamis* (power)—Wisdom or Word of God—is present, or to a mere human being (psilanthropism). He posited the preexistence of God's Word, which he equated with his Wisdom (on occasion, Wisdom acquired in his writings the features of the Holy Spirit). This Word, though not endowed with hypostatic subsistence, had all the markers of a divine or semi-divine entity, including incorporeality and the inability to be mixed with other substances. Consequently, Paul did not see the incarnation as a substantial union between the Word and Jesus's body. He insisted instead on the inhabitation of the full humanity of Jesus on the part of the preexistent Word of God. Although this inhabitation did not result in an ontological union, it was in his view still of a more full and permanent kind than the presence the Holy Spirit enjoyed in other human beings, such as the prophets of the Old Testament.

Paul's Affair in Its Geo-ecclesiological Context

Whatever the nature of Paul's theology, the Syrian argument surrounding it quickly became a pan-Mediterranean dispute. Responding to the call for a synod, Church leaders from all over the Roman Empire came to Antioch. Of these, Eusebius says, the most eminent were Firmilian (bishop of Caesarea of Cappadocia), Gregory the Wonder-Worker and Athenodorus (pastors of the churches in Pontus), Helenus of Tarsus, Nicomas of Iconium, Hymenaeus of Jerusalem, Theotecnus of Caesarea of Palestine, and Maximus of Bosra. Dionysius of Alexandria, unable to attend, sent a letter to the Antiochene community.

In summoning churchmen from Asia Minor, Palestine, Arabia, and Egypt, the Syrian clergy was working to promote Antioch's integration into the developing ecclesiastical global network. Through the regional and transregional connections that were woven at this time, Antioch made the headlines, so to speak, of fourth- and fifth-century Church histories. The men convened were of no mean fame.[75] Helenus, one of the signatories of the synodal letter, had written to Dionysius of Alexandria at the time of the Novatian schism to summon him to a council assembled in Antioch. At that gathering, Helenus had agreed with Church leaders from Cilicia, Cappadocia, and Galatia on the need to rebaptize the heretics, and had as a result been excommunicated by Stephanus of Rome.

The most noteworthy figures connected to Paul's condemnation, Firmilian of Caesarea of Cappadocia and Dionysius of Alexandria, fully embodied the novel global outlook of the mid-third-century Church. Firmilian was a champion of long-distance networking. During his forty-year episcopal career, he induced Origen to visit him in Cappadocia, corresponded with Cyprian about the rebaptizing of those who had been baptized by heretics, and partook in numerous synods. Dionysius corresponded with Fabius of Antioch, Novatian, and the Roman bishops Cornelius, Sixtus II, and Dionysius. Writing in 254, after the end of the Novatian schism, he described the situation of the Church in idyllic terms to Stephen of Rome. The broad project of ecumenical integration, he reassured Stephen, was being implemented: the Church was serrying its ranks, strengthening its network of communications, and globalizing its operations.[76] Only seven years before the beginning of turmoil in Antioch, Church histories record Dionysius of Alexandria's name in relation to a feud about Trinitarian matters in which he opposed his namesake and fellow bishop in Rome.[77] By seeking the support of both Dionysii, Paul's Syrian opponents secured the involvement of the two most theologically active and geo-ecclesiologically prominent bishoprics in the Roman Empire.

The measures the Syrian clergy took to coordinate with other important episcopal sees throughout the Mediterranean were consistent with the unfolding ecclesiastical climate. Antioch was on the rise on the horizon of the triarchy, the inter-patriarchal structure including Rome and Alexandria and destined to morph into a tetrarchy, and then a pentarchy, over the next two centuries (through the inclusion of Jerusalem and Constantinople).[78] Through its inter-diocesan scheming to condemn Paul, the Syrian episcopate was also working toward the promotion of global ecclesial integration under its own aegis. The Church of Syria was claiming part of the limelight on the expanding ecclesiastical stage in the Roman Empire.[79]

After being condemned by the Antiochene synod of 268/269, Paul was not willing to go without a fight. Eusebius writes:

> As Paul had fallen off, along with the orthodoxy of faith, also from the episcopacy, Domnus, as has been said, received the office of the Church in Antioch. But, since Paul was in no way willing to give up the building of the church, the Emperor Aurelian, petitioned, settled the matter most equitably, ordering that the building be given to those to whom the bishops of Italy and of the city of Rome should issue judgment [for it to be given]. Thus the above-mentioned man was indeed driven out of the Church with the uttermost shame by the worldly power.[80]

It is likely that the bishops' decision to petition Emperor Aurelian (270–275) after Paul's refusal to leave the church house[81] appealed to an ordinance by Gallienus (253–268) recommending that bishops be allowed to access their houses of worship.[82] The Syrian clergy may even have meant to involve the secular power of Rome and the Italian clergy as part of their initiative of integration into global Christendom and of promotion of Syrian leadership within the Church.

Some scholars have found in the emperor's decision to drive Paul away from his church a record of the earliest intervention of the secular Roman power in ecclesiastical matters.[83] In reality it is more probable that Aurelian simply accepted the bishops' request just as he would have done with any other plea, according to the imperial practice of the rescript.[84] By the same token, Aurelian's reliance on the determination of the Roman and Italian clergy—his decision "that the building be given to those to whom the bishops of Italy and of the city of Rome should issue judgment [for it to be given]"—was hardly a precocious recognition of papal privilege. His statement was either merely a customary form of echoing verbiage contained in the (now lost) petition or a typical consequence of the centralizing and Italo-centric religious policy the emperor had adopted regarding all cults.[85] As such, his involvement in the matter cannot be described in any meaningful way as proto-Constantinian.

Nevertheless, Eusebius and his epigones did read Aurelian's decision to support the majority of Syrian bishops in their clash with Paul as anticipating the increasing backing that the Roman Empire from Constantine on—with the exclusion of the brief parenthesis of Julian's reign—would provide orthodox subjects.[86] Eusebius's feelings about the events are entrusted to the following words:

> Such was Aurelian's treatment of us at that time; but as his reign went on, having changed his mind in regard to us, he was moved by certain advisers to raise up a persecution against us, and there was great talk about this among all.[87]

Eusebius's historical sensitivity allowed him to recognize Aurelian was no Constantine, not even in the earlier stages of his imperial tenure. However, Aurelian's rescript undeniably had the effect of undermining the activities of a heretic through civic power. Nothing was more familiar to late ancient Christian intellectuals, used to routine imperial interventions in support of this or that position in Christian theological debates. For Eusebius's epigones who wrote about Paul, the emperor's act was fully understandable in light of the support that the Roman power of their own times lent to the institutions that regulated theological exchange.[88]

Similarly, the epistolary transregional scheming in the ecclesiastical and civic sphere that facilitated Paul's prosecution and the condemnation of his theological views must have appeared to those authors as a precursor to the global system of capillary Church organization, sponsored by the State, that they saw effectively at work in contemporary theological controversies. As a result, the deposition of Paul of Samosata was inscribed in Christian memory as a formational moment in the development of the discursive field of theology—a field profoundly interwoven, from the fourth century on, with ecclesiastical and secular institutions.

Paul the Jew

A reading of the ancient sources has suggested to some historians that Paul, a native of Samosata, was the champion of the Syriac-speaking element in the Antiochene Church. The opposition that coalesced against him, according to this theory, was representative of the Hellenic party within the Christianity of Syria. Some scholars have also added a national dimension to this ethnic schematism: Aurelian's approval of Paul's opponents' petition would be a sign of their affiliation with the Roman Empire. Additionally, some have lent credence to the notion, transmitted by some sources, that Paul established a relationship of tutelage with Queen Zenobia of Palmyra, who around those same years briefly took over Antioch, until Aurelian reconquered it in 272.[89] Within this interpretive frame, it has been speculated that the claim made by the synodal letter that Paul preferred to be called *procurator ducenarius* indicates not only that he held this civil office, but that he did so on behalf of Zenobia during the Palmyrene occupation of Antioch.[90]

Multiple late ancient authors reported about Paul's relationship to the Palmyrene queen Zenobia, finding in their political liaison an intriguing subplot to the story.[91] Given the nature of some of the attacks hurled at Paul, it is remarkable that the link between the two was never explicitly portrayed as other than one of patronage and ideological consonance. Their relationship is blamed, instead, on their allegedly shared Judaic leanings. In a passage in which he condemned Emperor Constantius's conduct by unfavorably comparing it to Zenobia's, Athanasius of Alexandria counted the queen among the members of the Jewish people and depicted her as a supporter of Paul:

> When was such an iniquity heard of? When was such an evil deed ever perpetrated, even in a persecution? The heathens were those who persecuted first; but they did not bring images into the churches. Zenobia was a Jewess, and a protector of Paul of Samosata; but she did not give up the churches to the Jews as synagogues.[92]

This report seems to suggest that Paul was not just a theologian with a mistaken notion of Christ's nature: he was a Jew out-and-out, protected by the Jewish queen of Palmyra.

According to Athanasius's contemporary and fellow pro-Nicene Philastrius of Brescia,

> [Paul] preached that Christ was a just man, not the true God; rather, he Judaized, teaching even circumcision; as a result, he also taught a certain Zenobia, a queen in the east at that time, to Judaize.[93]

While Athanasius's Paul may have had a connection with the synagogue, Philastrius's was a Judaizer not only in his Christology, but also in terms of religious practices. By encouraging Christian males to be circumcised, Paul removed what had been the bedrock of mainstream Christian soteriology since his namesake of Tarsus had written his letters.[94] The Judaizing tendencies of Zenobia, we learn on the other hand from Philastrius, were a product of her following Paul's doctrine, rather than, as Athanasius appeared to suggest, the other way around.

The tie John Chrysostom established between the heresiarch and the queen is more similar to the relationship envisioned by Athanasius:

> Indeed [Paul] did not err out of ignorance but being quite aware, the matter with him being the same as with the Jews. For just as those,

> looking towards human beings, gave up the soundness of the faith, knowing that [Christ] is God's only-begotten Son yet not confessing [it] out of [fear of the] powerful [and] lest they become synagogue outcasts, so do they say that [Paul], too, relinquished his salvation to gratify a certain woman.[95]

Though Zenobia remained unnamed, her figure was obviously evoked. The parallel Chrysostom drew in this passage between the Jews' and Paul's unbelief was merely formal: they had both knowingly renounced the true faith in fear of retaliation from the powerful. At the same time, the comparison itself was justified by the implicit notion that Paul's very doctrines were Judaizing. Paul propounded his heretical Christology only to obtain the favor of the Jewish Zenobia. A similar idea was also expressed by Theodoret:

> Paul of Samosata was Bishop of Antioch, and while Zenobia was at that time toparch (for the Persians, having defeated the Romans, had given her the government of Syria and Phoenicia) he drifted into the heresy of Artemon, thinking that through it he would flatter her, who held the opinions of the Jews.[96]

In Theodoret's account, Paul's fall into heresy coincided chronologically with Zenobia's toparchy and was a consequence, rather than a cause, of her own beliefs.

Several more late ancient testimonies mention the unlikely pair. A fragment attributed to Athanasius informs us that "the Jewess Zenobia protected [Paul]; but her protection did not benefit him."[97] Two fragments allegedly drawn from a writing "of the impious Paul of Samosata, from the (words) he wrote to Zenobia" are contained in Pamphilus the Theologian's *Explanation of Various Articles or Doubts* (sixth to seventh century CE).[98] As their contents reveal, these excerpts are not the work of Paul.[99] It is likely that there never existed a work *To Zenobia*; if there ever was one, either it was falsely attributed to Paul of Samosata, or the two excerpts were never part of it. Someone intrigued by the relationship between the heresiarch and the queen must have produced those passages and assigned them to a composition attributed to Paul and addressed to the queen (or written such a treatise, from which those passages were excerpted).

The connection between Zenobia and Judaism continued to capture the imagination of Christian historians in the Middle Ages. References to her Judaizing are found in the *Library* of the ninth-century Patriarch of Constantinople Photius:

> [Longinus] lived under Claudius and he often assisted Zenobia, Queen of Osrohene, who took power after her husband Odenathus died, and whom an old tradition reports to have converted to Jewish customs from the Hellenic superstition.[100]

Photius's passage makes no reference to Paul of Samosata. Paul is again mentioned with Zenobia in the works of the twelfth-century Syriac Orthodox patriarch Michael the Great:

> <And the reason> he lapsed <was a Jewish woman by the name of> Zenobia, whom the Persians <had appointed> over the regions of Syria when they had defeated the Romans. Since she was pleased with [the doctrines] of the Jews, the wretched Paul wanted to please her and lapsed into the heresy of Artemon. And attached to Paul were some women, who sang to him in his name. And it was said that he was also a fornicator. When he was anathematized by the bishops, he placed his trust in that woman who had been appointed ruler over all of Syria by the Persians. The bishops, then, told the emperor of the Romans, Aurelian, about the matter concerning him and, though being a heathen, he ordered that Paul be expelled from the Church.[101]

Michael agreed with Theodoret in portraying Paul's lapse into heretical doctrines (here specified as being those of Artemon) as a consequence of his desire to ingratiate Zenobia, who took pleasure in Jewish ideas. Also the thirteenth-century Syriac Orthodox bishop and polymath Grigorios Bar ʿEbroyo, who often drew on Michael the Syrian, wrote about Paul and Zenobia (both in the Syriac *Chronicon* and in the Arabic *Epitome of the History of the Dynasties*):

> Then he took shelter with a certain Jewish woman whose name was Zenobia, whom the Persians had appointed over the regions of Syria against the Romans, and to whom Paul's words were very pleasing. The bishops, then, told Aurelian, the emperor of the Romans, and, though being very much of a heathen, he sent to expel Paul.[102]

> And Eusebius the historian mentioned about this Paul that he used the assistance of a Jewish woman whom Gallus Caesar had made ruler over Syria and who appreciated his teaching and words. And she handed to him the patriarchy of Antioch.[103]

The cause-and-effect relationship between Paul's theology and his affiliation with the queen is not clarified in these bits. In the latter passage, Eusebius is identified as the source of the story about the link between the two, which is curious, given that neither Eusebius's account in *Church History* nor the synodal letter of which he cites portions includes any reference to Zenobia.[104]

Finally, Bar ʿEbroyo's near contemporary Nikephoros Kallistos Xanthopoulos mentioned the liaison in his *Church History*, largely plagiarizing Theodoret:

> At that time, when Demetrianus, Bishop of Antioch, died, Paul of Samosata replace[d] [him] to the see. Indeed, while Zenobia was at that time toparch (for the Persians, having defeated the Romans, had given her the government of Syria and Phoenicia), this Paul, desiring to perform religious matters for her, who held the opinions of the Jews, and trying to flatter as much as possible, drifted into the heresy of Artemon.[105]

From a historical standpoint, Zenobia was not Jewish in any possible sense of the adjective. A story in the Jerusalem Talmud has sometimes been interpreted as indicating that she might have been sympathetic to the Jewish people:

> Zeir bar Ḥinena was arrested in Saphsupha [or: during a riot]. Rabbi Ammi and Rabbi Shemuel went to beseech [him (?)] on his behalf. Zenobia the queen said to them: "He teaches that your creator performs wonders for you" [or: "Your creator is accustomed to performing wonders for you"]. [While] they were oppressing him [scil. Zeir bar Ḥinena], a Saracen entered with a sword. He said to them: "With this sword Bar Nitsor [scil. Odenathus] killed his brother," and Zeir bar Ḥinena was rescued.[106]

The meaning of the passage is fairly obscure.[107] Nowhere does the story suggest, however, that Zenobia was perceived by the rabbis as either Jewish or Judaizing: her speaking is defiant, and she refers to the Jewish God as "your creator."

It is true that the Palmyrene queen might be the Zenobia who is recorded to have financed the construction of a synagogue in Egypt;[108] she might also have restored the right of asylum of another synagogue, possibly in the Delta.[109] In addition, a Jewish Zenobius is recorded in a Palmyrene inscription,[110] and henotheistic or monolatristic elements in Palmyran religion might testify to the penetration of Jewish cultic ideas.[111] None of this, however, indicates that Zenobia was either a Jewess or a Judaizer. Had she been, it is still unlikely that this alone would have disposed her toward patronizing a Christian bishop by sheer virtue of his idiosyncratic views about Christ (far in any event from being able to be legitimately qualified as Judaizing). The idea that Zenobia's putative Judaism or Judaizing influenced Paul's doctrine is also incompatible with chronology: her accession to power only began after her husband's death in 267/268, while the first synod against Paul dates to 264 and any notion of a Palmyrene influence over Antioch prior to 270 is purely speculative.[112] All in all, the allegation of a Jewish connection uniting Paul and Zenobia, echoing from one author to another across the centuries, does not withstand the test of historical documentation.

The Asymmetric Parting of the Ways

Paul's deposition assumed the status of a foundational moment in late ancient Christian memory. It heralded a new era in Christian theological debates by precociously exhibiting some of the characteristics of the intellectual exchanges of the times of Constantine and his successors: among others, the use of synods to adjudicate theological as well as disciplinary matters, the hierarchization and centralization of ecclesiastical structures, the establishment of transregional episcopal alliances, and the proximity of such alliances to political power. Paul's condemnation was momentous, as it manifested for the first time a series of institutional dynamics that had just begun to coalesce. Later Christian intellectuals recognized those dynamics to be fully congruous with the working methods they had taken for granted since the second quarter of the fourth century.

What is more, by weaving together, in different combinations, Paul's alleged xenophilia, Judeophilia, heresy, and appreciation for a powerful woman, authors such as Athanasius, Philastrius, Chrysostom, Theodoret, and those responsible for the composition of the *Fragment of the Great Athanasius* and for the invention of a work *To Zenobia* (or for attributing spurious excerpts of Paul's to a lost work with this title) labored at painting the reversed image of the Christian intellectual tradition they knew and cherished: one fully identified with the Roman Empire, ruled by a male emperor; separated from the scholarly practices of Jewish literate elites; and entrenched behind the wordy barricades of orthodoxy. In particular, late ancient Christian writers' keen insistence on Paul's association with the Palmyrene queen, grounded in the penchant for Judaism the two allegedly shared, clearly shows an ideological investment outweighing—or more accurately being built into—historiographic concerns.

The heresiological memorialization of Paul of Samosata is infused through and through with polemical references to Judaism, from the fourth to the thirteenth century. Contrastingly, the narrative of *b.* Ḥagigah 15a contains no polemics against or even explicit reference to Christianity, despite its dismissal of a model of piety based on something other than the mitsvot. It is not impossible to detect subtle polemical hints at the Christian tradition in the Talmudic narrative. The representation of the bureaucratic ease with which Elisha's record of mitsvot is turned into tabula rasa, suggesting that its inscription had been a similarly perfunctory act, may evoke through a biting parody the workings of Paul's doctrine of justification. Elisha's association with a prostitute and plucking of a plant on the Sabbath might lead to reading his affiliation with a lesser deity as resembling that of Jesus's disciples.[113] The ousting and lashing of a soteriological figure could be a satire of the incarnation and passion of Jesus Christ. Finally, a few lines before the Acher sugyah (*b.* Ḥagigah 14b) the gemara asks whether a high priest is allowed to marry a maiden who has become pregnant. This questioning of the virginity of a woman who conceived without intercourse might contain a polemical reference to the figure of Mary.[114]

The validity of these links partly rests on views more broadly held regarding the presence of references to Jesus and Christianity in the Talmud.[115] Generally speaking, however, caution is needed in establishing a rhetorical connection between Elisha's story and Christianity. Prostitutes are ubiquitous in the Babylonian Talmud. The uprooting of the radish from its bed has a verbatim parallel in a thematically unrelated Talmudic context where it simply represents destruction (perhaps brought about in a piecemeal manner).[116] The symbolism of Metatron's flogging is also of disputed origin; the angel Gabriel is lashed elsewhere in the Talmud.[117] Moreover, the representation of Metatron in *b.* Ḥagigah 15a was influenced by Zoroastrian and Manichaean reports about the Iranian hero Yima.[118]

Whatever one might think of the possibility that the sugyah contains vague intimations of the rabbis' awareness of Christian beliefs and practice, however, it is undeniable that the text does not openly discuss Christianity as such. Unsurprisingly for anybody familiar with the silence the Babylonian Talmud by and large reserves for Jesus-followers, Acher's attempt at discerning intra-divine dynamics, an easy target for potential charges of Christian-like behavior, is never explicitly characterized as Christian, whether in its binitarian contents or in its methodology. In composing a narrative reflection about appropriate ways of producing religious knowledge, the editor of the sugyah repudiated Acher's style of investigation without invoking the intellectual practices or the beliefs of the rival religious tradition.

To be sure, this sugyah represents but one voice not only in the diverse landscape of late ancient Judaism, but even within the multifaceted rabbinic movement. It is, however, a voice representative of an attitude of rhetorical disengagement from Christianity that is pervasive in the Talmud. Acher's deviant choice, despite its proximity, arguably both in methods and in content, to the speculations of Christian theologians, made him foreign to the rabbinic academy without visibly turning him into a Christian. Christian heresiographers, on the other hand, exerted themselves to assign their heretical opponents' intellectual activities to a fictional Jewess like Zenobia, alleging her predilection for a particular kind of Christology. In other words, our rabbinic source condemns the kind of inquiry that Acher was conducting rather than polemically associating its content with the Christian tradition, as it could have, whereas the Christian tradition condemns Paul of Samosata as a heretic because of the content of his doctrine, which it speciously connects to Judaism.

When noticing that the editor of the sugyah passed over in silence the reality of his Christian counterparts' intellectual interests, we ought to wonder whether the rabbinic rejection of a style of inquiry akin to Christian theology was articulated in dissimulating reaction to the Christian constitution of theology as a research tradition or in autonomy from that historical process. While the question cannot be adjudged, the interlocking receptions of Acher and Paul of Samosata point, as anticipated at the beginning of this chapter, to asymmetric relations beween Christianity and Judaism, two intellectual traditions whose mutual extraneousness was by then becoming starker. The juxtaposition of these two chapters in late ancient religious memory reveals that on the Jewish side interactions with Christian elite intellectuals were marked less by polemic, engagement, and confrontation than by an acknowledgment of the progressive divergence of institutionally embedded styles of inquiry.

As I attempt to demonstrate in the next three chapters, in the case of Christianity a theological practice was founded. Within rabbinic Judaism, that same practice was rejected in favor of other approaches to investigation, first and foremost *midrash halakhah*, that is, scriptural exegesis in the service of juridical elaboration. In labeling Paul of Samosata's Christology as Judaizing, Christian heresiographers continued for centuries to bark up the wrong tree. The rabbis, uninterested in the very epistemic premises of the intellectual activities in which Christians were engaged, had silently left the arena of theological debate, retreating into the schoolhouse.

While Paul of Samosata rose in the Christian tradition to the status of an archetypal anti-hero, being quoted in much later generations as the progenitor of long-lasting heretical genealogies, the rejection of Elisha ben Abuyah was much more casual. Acher never assumed in the rabbinic tradition the status of a true antitype of the sage, thereby making effectively unviable, besides the practice of theological debate, even a theoretical discussion of theological debate as an option for intellectual inquiry. A cultural system devoid of a theological inquiry capable of producing dogma had no use for a paradigmatic heretic akin to Paul. The heresiology developed by Christian authors could only be promoted by a content-based intolerance, whose contours are described in the last chapter of this book. That intolerance derived, in turn, from the constitution of the theological field, selectively examined in the next three chapters.

2 • Credal Culture

The Trinitarian Debates, 318–362

> Everything that is, is either unbegotten or begotten or made. There is therefore something that is neither born nor made. And there is something that is born and not made. And there is something that is neither born nor made. And there is something that is made and not born. And there is something that is made and born and reborn. And there is something that is made and born and not reborn. Now, remembering the(se) intentions, we will assign a substance to the individual things. Therefore, that which is neither born nor made is the Father, for He is not from something. On the other hand, that which is born and is not made is the Son, who was begotten by the Father. And again, that which is neither born nor made is the Holy Spirit, who proceeds from the Father.[1]

We are informed of this set of simple truths, concerning the three members of the Christian Trinity, at the outset of an obscure late-fourth-century treatise of Spanish provenance, titled *Rules of Interpretation Issued against the Heretics*. In this work the formulaic exposition of Trinitarian doctrine reaches a uniquely virtuosic peak. The tendency to condense theological truths in formulas, however, was a common feature of theological treatises written at the end of the fourth century.

Christians, even those whose reflection about the divine was most thoroughly imbued with Greek philosophical thinking, had not always written and spoken in this manner. But by the time the bishops gathered at Constantinople in 381 had reaffirmed (and reinterpreted) the *Nicaenum*, and Emperor Theodosius had issued his edict requiring all churches to conform to that faith, Christian authors of various stripes shared the idea that truth could be encapsulated in a formula, with the occasional addition of qualifications or anathematisms.[2] But how had this unspoken consensus been reached? In this chapter and the next two I attempt to provide an answer to this question. After introducing the Trinitarian controversies, their origins, and their unfolding up to 340, the present chapter examines, without any claim to exhaustiveness, creeds and related documents produced between 340 and 362.

Credal declaration during this period developed a polemical ethos previously unknown to the genre. Creeds had been traditionally produced in response to local needs, and recited during baptisms, catechesis, worship, and exorcisms, or in opposition to pagans or heretics perceived to be definitively outside the Christian camp.[3] During the Trinitarian controversies, these documents were made to interact polemically with one another on a wide Mediterranean scale. The two main alliances involved in this battle—easterners and westerners—accused each other of doctrinal inadequacy. Though fairly uniformly distributed from the geographic point of view, these alliances were mainly identified through their respective antagonisms toward "Arianism" and Monarchianism.

Credal declarations required actors to position themselves on the doctrinal battleground. In these documents, Church leaders began to deploy a novel polemical style, which led to two important developments: a greater emphasis on credal formulas as the key to solving theoretical problems and their rise to quasi-scriptural status. As seen in the Introduction, scholarship on the Trinitarian controversies has largely focused on the winding path leading from the deliberations of Nicaea to the settlement achieved in Constantinople. But in order for the Constantinopolitan consensus to be reached, it was necessary that the actors involved in the dispute develop a shared manner of discussing the divine. Through the counterpoint of eastern and western conciliar texts, the problem of the status of the Son, framed at Nicaea as concerning the manner of his begetting, was logically reconfigured into an interrogation of his personal subsistence. This controversy, its actors began to see, was going to be solved only by agreeing about how to name plurality in the deity.[4] This realization led to the construction of shared technical terminologies as tools for the negotiation of theological constructs. Once these terminologies gained wider acceptance, the phrases that utilized them crystallized into formulas.

This chapter also highlights the epistemic shifts that enabled the ratification of the Nicene Creed as the touchstone of orthodoxy, not only among the traditionally pro-Nicene milieus but also, beginning with the Council of Antioch of 363, among theologians of various provenances. Athanasius of Alexandria is commonly credited with single-handedly carrying out this revolution in the mid-350s. In reality, however, the debates of the early 340s surrounding the production of other formulas than the *Nicaenum* had paved the way for the elevation of conciliar creeds to quasi-scriptural status. As a case study in the scripturalization of creeds, here I track the immediate background and reception of the western Council of Sardica of 343. The processes of formularization and scripturalization bequeathed a dogmatic legacy to the Christian practice of discussing the divine.[5]

The Origins of the Trinitarian Controversies

The fourth-century Trinitarian controversies were set in motion around 318 by the teaching of the Alexandrian priest Arius.[6] The most contentious feature of his doctrine was the idea that the Son of God had been created. Arius, to be more precise, characterized the generation of Christ through the verbs "to beget" (*gennaō*), "to place into existence" (*hyphistēmi*), and "to create" (*ktizō*). The concept that Christ had been the object of begetting was accepted without reservations by Arius's opponents in Alexandria, and the notion that the Son of God might have been placed into existence was still found acceptable due to its ambiguity. But, with his idea that the Son had been the object of an act of creation, Arius could not but run afoul of other Alexandrian theologians.[7] Although his preaching met with some approval among the laypeople of his church, soon enough it was proscribed in a public debate by Bishop Alexander of Alexandria.

Condemned again, along with his followers, by a synod of approximately one hundred bishops that gathered in Alexandria, Arius addressed a letter to Eusebius of Nicomedia invoking his support. In this document he scolded Alexander for considering the Son co-eternal with the Father and derived from his same substance. Arius also unequivocally affirmed that before being drawn out of nothing, the Son did not exist. Christ, Arius affirmed, was created in the same way as the cosmos, that is, "out of non-existence" (*ex ouk ontōn*). In adopting this phrase, he intended to avoid the materialistic overtones he detected in the commonly used expression "from God" (*ek theou*).[8] The Son, Arius taught, is "neither a part of God nor [deriving] from some underlying substrate" (*oute meros theou oute ex hypokeimenou tinos*). Those phrases expressed an unacceptable understanding of the godhead as a compound substance, capable of being resolved back into its components, or as a shared divine stuff that could be specified into two entities, the Son and the Father.[9]

Arius's definition of the created status of the Son also hinged on the punctiliar (as opposed to continuous) quality of his begetting. Bishop Alexander followed Origen in holding that the Logos was eternally generated from the Father;[10] he differed from his master, on the other hand, in ascribing to the Logos dignity and power equal to God's. By contrast, Arius rejected Origen's doctrine on both scores. To make the Logos co-eternal with God or equally divine, he opined, was tantamount to positing two deities.[11]

In recent decades, scholarship has done away with the image of Arius as the impious, arch-heretical detonator of a global crisis.[12] His religious motives have been recognized by some as lying in such concerns as the conservative upholding of the unique dignity of God the Father for devotional purposes, or the propounding of an exemplarist soteriology.[13] In addition, the identification of theological, exegetical, and philosophical reasons behind his doctrine has allowed scholars to locate his preaching within a web of ongoing debates.[14]

The roots of Arius's theological system have been linked by some to an accentuation of the subordinationism typical of the Origenist tradition. Origen, after all, had sharply marked in his writings the ontological difference between the Father and the Son.[15] Origen also considered that whatever could be said about the Son applied to the Father in a transcendent degree, whereas anything that could be predicated of the Father could be said about the Son only in a relative sense.[16] If Arius could be proven to be a radical epigone of Origen, his bold demotion of the status of the Son of God could be explained.

Critics of this reconstruction have pointed out that Origen's theology, for all its subordinationism, is fundamentally pluralistic and does not specifically aim at emphasizing God's oneness. A competing hypothesis prefers to place Arius in the Antiochene tradition of theological adoptionism and exegetical literalism, putatively embodied by the likes of Paul of Samosata and Lucian of Antioch, who is known to have been Arius's teacher.[17] This solution is not without its own problems. First, Lucian's exegetical and theological views are far from ascertained. Second, Paul's adoptionism can hardly account for a theology, like Arius's, in which God brings about the Son's power simultaneously with his begetting. If Arius's theology is to be considered the product of a literalist exegetical practice, the origins of the latter may be traced back more easily to Peter of Alexandria and to an Alexandrian tradition of opposition to the allegoresis of Clement, Origen, and Dionysius.[18]

Others have scrutinized the philosophical frameworks within which the dispute between Arius and his foes developed. By one interpretation, the Trinitarian controversies led to a divorce between the Platonic tradition and Christian thought. Both the heresiarch and his pro-Nicene opponents agreed that there could be no middle term between the transcendent and the created world; they diverged, instead, over the realm to which the Son should be assigned.[19] According to another reading, the struggle between partisans and opponents of Arius had at its core a divide between Aristotelianism, which empirically derived concepts from concrete individual entities, and Platonism, concerned with pure ideas.[20] Yet other scholars have established various relations between the arguments around Arius's doctrine and middle- and neo-Platonic philosophy.[21]

The First Two Decades of the Debates

Whatever its origins and the appropriate frameworks to interpret it, this local quarrel about the correct terminology to express the generation of Christ soon turned into a global earthquake for Christianity. As a result of his condemnation, Arius began to seek the support of fellow disciples of his teacher Lucian of Antioch (whom he referred to as "Collucianists") elsewhere in the East.[22] Eusebius of Caesarea and his namesake of Nicomedia, responding to the call, mobilized their networks in support of the presbyter harassed by Alexander.[23] After a Palestinian sojourn, probably facilitated by the Caesarean bishop, Arius sought shelter with Eusebius of Nicomedia.[24] Two synods of members of Arius's network, gathered in Bithynia and Palestine, ruled in his favor, taking advantage of the absence of disciplinary regulations for interdiocesan relationships. Soon enough, the radius of epistolary communication on both sides of the dispute was expanded. As in the historical precedent of Paul of Samosata, a local disagreement was given interregional resonance. The conflict between Arius and Alexander was transformed into a problem for a great part of the Christian *oikoumenē* (Christians' inhabited world).

Emperor Constantine, informed of these events, attempted to mediate the dispute. After inviting the two sides to find concord, he requested the intervention of his envoy, Ossius of Corduba.[25] As a result of the latter's inability to bring peace, a council was summoned—by the decision of the emperor or possibly by that of Ossius[26]—to Ancyra in May 325. A different gathering of eastern bishops is very likely to have taken place in Antioch before this convocation was held. If we are to trust the Syriac translation of a Greek document informing us of Ossius's conduction of this synod, the bishops who gathered in the city on the Orontes in late 324 or early 325 condemned Eusebius of Caesarea and other erstwhile allies of Arius's.[27] Possibly alarmed by this outcome, Constantine, who initially might have favored Arius's alliance over the opposing one, decided to switch the location for the ecumenical council from

Ancyra (in Asia Minor) to Nicaea, an episcopal see closer to the interim capital Nicomedia, from where he could better control the assembly.[28]

The emperor offered all bishops the opportunity of traveling for free with the imperial carriage system. Thus, possibly more than 250 Church leaders convened from numerous locales in the Roman East, as well as from the western regions of the empire and from beyond the eastern frontier.[29] According to historical testimonies, Constantine's initial speech at the council was followed by one by the president of the assembly, either Ossius or Eustathius of Antioch.[30] Very little has been handed down about the proceedings of the council itself. A letter by Eusebius of Nicomedia was read, in which the notion of Christ's natural begetting on the part of God was opposed inasmuch as this kind of generation would have made the Son homoousios (an expression commonly translated as "consubstantial") with the Father, with dangerous ditheistic results.

After condemning the views expressed by Eusebius's letter, the council attempted to reach an agreement about a positive doctrinal statement.[31] This task, Athanasius of Alexandria suggests, proved more challenging because of the heterogeneity of the party opposing Arius. Moreover, Arius's allies were reportedly skilled at subtly bending to their own views all the scriptural expressions that the synodal majority put forward in order to express equality between the Son and the Father.[32]

A text was eventually approved by a large coalition of Origenist bishops, led by Alexander of Alexandria, and by the so-called Monarchians, led by Marcellus of Ancyra and Eustathius of Antioch. Eusebius of Caesarea claimed that the council used the creed of his own church as the basis for this text, which would become known as the *Nicaenum*.[33] Whether or not Eusebius should be trusted on this point, the text approved at Nicaea contained a repudiation of several of Arius's own claims.[34] Most famously, the Nicene Creed included the declaration that the Son is homoousios with the Father.

Much ink has been spilled over the origins of the term "homoousios," as well as over its intended meaning in the context of the Nicene Creed.[35] As a technical philosophical term, "ousia," on which the term "homoousios" is built, could assume a wide range of meanings, whose variations went for the most part undetected. Most Christian writers accepted the Platonic contrast between intelligible and sensible substances, rejecting as trivial any attempt to push the inquiry further.[36] Since God's existence was to be taken for granted, when the term "ousia" was used in reference to God it rarely indicated mere existence, a notion that the word *hyparxis* most commonly expressed.[37] Some

Christian authors, such as Alexander of Alexandria and Cyril of Jerusalem, avoided ousia altogether, and referred to hypostasis in a roughly similar sense.[38]

The first occurrence of homoousios in a Christian text is found in the dispute between Dionysius of Rome and his homonym of Alexandria.[39] Meanwhile, the term had encountered some fortune in gnostic literature, receiving the meaning of identity of substance between a variety of entities: generating and generated, creatures generated out of the same substance, and the two partners in a syzygy.[40] The most immediately relevant precedent for the Nicene usage of homoousios is its appearance in the 268 condemnation of Paul of Samosata.[41]

Opinions vary on the proximate sources of the use of homoousios at Nicaea. A common account finds its origins in western theology.[42] Other proposals give credence to Eusebius of Caesarea's claim that the word was inserted in the Nicene Creed solely by the personal order of Constantine,[43] or suggest that Eusebius himself may have had a prominent role in recommending its use to the emperor.[44] One reconstruction credits Alexander of Alexandria for the original promotion of the word with the anti-"Arian" party. Alexander's opponents had tried to tarnish his theological standing by associating him with homoousios, a term that on the occasion of Paul of Samosata's censure had been tied to Monarchian modalism. Much to the surprise of his foes, so the theory goes, Alexander decided to cling to the word by virtue of its ability to prevent Arius and his allies from equivocating.[45] Whatever the origin of the use of the term "homoousios" at Nicaea, its later elevation to the status of a technical gauge of the correct faith proved consequential for the development of the disputes and for the shape of Christian theological discussion more widely.

Whether thanks to the intrinsic appeal of homoousios or to Constantine's intimidating presence, the creed was readily signed by almost all members of the Nicene assembly, including some, like Eusebius of Caesarea, who could have been expected to hold significant theological reservations. Only two bishops from Libya asked to be excused from signing.[46] They were promptly condemned, deposed, and exiled.[47] Shortly after the council, Eusebius of Nicomedia and Theognis of Nicaea were also deposed, this time by Constantine, and exiled to Gaul.[48]

This series of condemnations appeared to have definitively set into place the rejection of Arius's views, and of any accommodation to them, as the orthodox Christian belief in the Roman Empire. Instead, a time of conflict ensued, from which another episcopal majority emerged than the one that had triumphed at Nicaea. This sudden shift is primarily ascribed to a change of heart on Constantine's part. Soon after Nicaea, he began to seek a balance between the orientation expressed by the synod's canons (particularly their anathematisms) and radical forms of subordinationism. The emperor was interested in the formation of a broad ecclesiastical coalition, capable of reining in the more radical wings on both ends of the Trinitarian spectrum. In so doing, he hoped to create the ecclesiastical harmony that the Council of Nicaea had failed to bring about. Through a series of well-calculated episcopal reappointments and depositions, Constantine managed to gain the trust and favor of a wide theologico-ecclesial area of Origenist, limitedly subordinationist eastern bishops.

These Church leaders, though unhappy with the positions of Arius and his allies, were at the same time wary of the homoousios, regarded as akin to Sabellian heresy.[49] In 328 Theognis of Nicaea and Eusebius of Nicomedia, supporters of Arius, were recalled from exile and reinstated as bishops. The anti-Arian champion Athanasius was banned from Alexandria, and his ally Marcellus of Ancyra was condemned as a heretic in Constantinople (336) thanks to the accusations leveled against him by Eusebius of Caesarea. Arius, on the other hand, was rehabilitated on the basis of a confession of faith sent to Constantine (although he died before reentering Alexandria).

Upon Constantine's death (337) the empire was divided between his two sons Constans (who in 340 assumed full power over the western provinces by defeating his brother Constantine II) and Constantius II, in charge of the East. Constantius shared his father's propensity to pursue the unity of the Church. After two decades of ongoing clashes, he concluded that only a centralized and energetic imperial initiative could conclusively settle the controversies and achieve ecclesial unity. To this end he summoned a series of councils aligning with the theological orientation of the Eusebians.[50] The pro-Nicene eastern bishops, who had meanwhile returned home, were forced back into exile in the West.[51]

The Credal Counterpoint of the 340s

From his western exile, Athanasius managed to convince Pope Julius of Rome that their common Origenist enemies in the East were in reality full-fledged "Arians." This feat was to prove rife with negative effects for the relationships between easterners and westerners throughout the remainder of the Trinitarian controversies. Also as a result of Athanasius's maneuvering, in the fall of 340 a Roman council rehabilitated him as well as Marcellus of Ancyra.[52] After the council, Pope Julius wrote a long letter to the Eusebians questioning their behavior.[53] Julius's epistle contains multiple references to the Council of Nicaea. The contexts of all these mentions make it clear that the object to which authority was attached was not the creed the council promulgated, but the excommunications it carried out against Arius and his allies. Nevertheless, the evocation of the number of conciliar members as a source of particular authoritativeness in one of these passages ("So, who is it who is doing dishonor to a council? Is it not those who are setting aside the votes of the three hundred, and who prefer impiety to piety?")[54] makes this letter a witness to the earliest development of a tradition anchoring the faith of the western opponents of the "Eusebians" in the council of 325.

Eusebius of Nicomedia responded to Julius's letter, which accused him and his acolytes of sympathy for the "Arians," by gathering his ecclesiastical alliance in a council held at Antioch in 341, under the presidency of Bishop Flacillus. This synod came to be known also as Dedication council, or as council *in encaeniis*. The Eusebian alliance was the expression of an eastern theological tradition just as distant from the deliberations of Nicaea as it was from the positions of Arius. Its members emphasized the separate subsistence of the Father and the Son, described as hypostaseis. At the same time, their theology eschewed, through a subordinationist configuration of the relationship between the Father and the Son, the ditheistic consequences that would have resulted from coordination between those two divine entities. The ninety-seven bishops at Antioch rejected of course the accusation of Arianism hurled at them by the Roman council, and confirmed the condemnation of Arius's views.

Four formulas of faith have been transmitted in relation to the synod *in encaeniis*.[55] The first, succinct formula is fairly traditional, carrying only the meaningful addition of an anti-Marcellan clause ("remaining also King and God into the ages"):

> For we have been taught since the beginning to believe in one God, the God of the universe, the craftsman and preserver of all things both intellectual and sensible, and in one only-begotten Son of God, who existed before all ages and was along with the Father who had begotten him; through whom also all things came into being, both visible and invis-

> ible; who in the last days, according to the good wish of the Father, came down; and who has taken flesh from the virgin and has fulfilled the Father's whole will [that he] suffer and rise again and ascend into the heavens and sit to the right of the Father and, coming again, judge the living and the dead, remaining also King and God into the ages. And we also believe in the Holy Spirit. And if it is necessary to add, we believe also in the resurrection of the flesh and eternal life.[56]

The formula is preceded by a resolute protestation of independence from Arius, whose ecclesiastical stature the bishops portray in diminutive terms. Rejecting the insinuation that they were followers of the heresiarch, a presbyter,[57] the authors focus on the contents of their own faith, with which, as they claim, his doctrine simply proved to be compatible upon examination:

> We have neither been followers of Arius—for how could we, being bishops, follow a priest?—nor received any other faith than the one handed down since the beginning, but rather, having examined and accepted his faith ourselves, we admitted, rather than followed, him.[58]

The criticized communion with Arius is reduced to a matter of vouchsafing for his belief's conformity with a tradition passed on since apostolic times.

The second formula issued by the Council of Antioch was the most significant and historically consequential of the series of four. It was the official formula of the synod, and was to constitute the basis for credal declarations at the councils of Seleucia (359), Lampsacus (364), and Antiochia of Caria (366).[59] A statement of conformity to the tradition is followed by an exposition of the creed, an argumentative elaboration, and finally some defensive anathematisms. The incipit of the text asserts the alignment of the forthcoming creed with the traditional faith:

> We believe, conformingly to the evangelical and apostolic tradition, in one God, Father almighty, the craftsman, maker, and provider of the universe, from whom [are] all things.[60]

Although the apostles never composed a creed,[61] all the actors in the Trinitarian dispute unfailingly claimed to be founding their doctrine on evangelical and apostolic tradition.[62] According to Arius's words in his *Letter to Alexander*, he had learned his theology from the ancestors (*ek tōn progonōn*).[63] Arius's nemesis Alexander, too, in his own statement of faith, had referred to the apostolic dogmas (*apostolika dogmata*) and accused Arius of deviating from the apostolic canon (*apostolikos kanōn*).[64] The conciliar fathers at Antioch (341) also felt the need to assure their readers about the alignment of their doctrine with the traditional faith.

Claims to conformity with tradition did not limit their references to the apostolic era. As mentioned, Eusebius of Caesarea boasted that the Council of Nicaea used the creed of his own Church as the basis for its text. As Sozomen reports, the Eusebians adduced the second formula of the Council of Antioch of 341 as the creed of Lucian of Antioch.[65] Sozomen is alone, among all authorities who report the text, to add this detail;[66] and even he, who likely draws this piece of information from Sabinus of Heraklea's *Synagogē*, expresses doubts concerning the Eusebians' allegation. Although the formula was in all probability written prior to the time of the council, it seems unlikely that Lucian had originally composed it.[67]

Either way, it is remarkable that the Eusebians felt compelled to present their creed as Lucianic (or to present a Lucianic creed) at the synod. Of course, it is unsurprising that the presentation of a creed as traditional and associated with a martyr would be trusted to lend it prestige. However, in particular in light of Julius's missive, to which the Eusebians were responding at Antioch, one cannot help but notice the resemblance that their gesture—anchoring in the past a newly set-forth conciliar creed—bears to mounting western investment in the *Nicaenum*. As discussed shortly, the reception of the Council of Sardica shows that within the Nicene camp itself this attachment was contested.

The second formula promulgated at Antioch marked a stark distance from the theology of Arius and his followers, and it did so by clearly expressing Christ's divinity. It refrained from equating begetting to creation and defined the Son as a perfect image of the ousia of the Father, an image holding no differences from its model. However, at the moment of expressing belief in the Holy Spirit, a customary citation of Jesus's so-called Great Commission (Matt 28:16–19) allowed the easterners to make an anti-Nicene point they saw as pressing: a distinct hypostasis, they proclaimed, corresponded to each of the three entities named in that verse. Their unity was relegated to mere harmony of will and action:

> And [we believe] in the Holy Spirit, given to the believers for consolation, sanctification, and perfection, as also our Lord Jesus Christ ordered to the disciples, saying: "Go and make disciples of all nations, baptizing them in the name of the Father and of the Son and of the Holy Spirit" (Matt 28:19), namely [in the name] of the Father, who is truly Father,

> of the Son, who is truly Son, and of the Holy Spirit, who is truly Holy Spirit—since the names have not been given superficially and in vain, but rather indicate exactly the particular hypostasis, order, and glory of each of the named, so that they are three things with regard to the hypostasis but one thing only with regard to the harmony.[68]

The blunt affirmation of three hypostaseis was unprecedented thus far in the dispute outside of Arius's own writings (*Letter to Alexander of Alexandria*). The western bishops were going to wince at this mention of three loosely unified hypostaseis.[69]

With the notion of the three hypostaseis secured, the easterners proceeded to produce a few anathematisms. Unlike the argumentative statement about the three hypostaseis, the Antiochene anathematisms were offered not combatively, but defensively. Boilerplate verbiage aside, what was being disavowed were two doctrines—the punctiliar begetting of the Son and his identification as a creature—from which Arius himself had already taken distance:

> Holding then this faith, and holding [it] from the beginning until the end, in the presence of God and of Christ we anathematize every heretical bad opinion. And if anyone teaches contrary to the sound and right faith of the Scriptures, saying that either there is or there has been a time or a season or an age before the Son was begotten, let him be anathema. And if anyone says that the Son is a creature as one of the creatures, or an offspring as one of the offsprings, or a work as one of the works, and not as the divine Scriptures have handed down each of the articles said above, or if he teaches or preaches contrary to what we have received, let him be anathema. For we truly and reverently believe and follow all that has been handed down by the divine Scriptures.[70]

Rather than using this section of the creed to condemn positions held by their opponents, the Antiochene fathers chose to distance themselves from a series of positions with which the westerners were likely to identify them, in good or bad faith. The condemnations were in reality anodyne: already Arius in his confession to Alexander had called Christ a "perfect creature of God, but not as one of the creatures"; and no real actor in the disputes was unwilling to grant that Christ himself was the creator of time. Just like its more aggressive variant, in which the ideas of a real doctrinal adversary were condemned, the form of defensive rhetorical positioning embodied by the anathematisms of the second formula was part and parcel of the polemical ethos that was being forged in the composition of creeds. This new style was soon going to be pervasively adopted by all credal declarations.

The third formula was set forth by Theophronius of Tyana. Though fairly standard in its form, this creed featured two cursory yet sharp remarks about the pre-incarnate subsistence of the Son and the everlastingness of his kingdom. These additions were coherent with the condemnations contained in the creed's anathematisms, which fell on three Monarchian actors (Marcellus, Sabellius, and Paul of Samosata).[71] If it is true, as is commonly held, that in presenting this text Theophronius intended to exculpate himself from accusations of Monarchianism, then both those two theological comments and the anathematisms appended to his creed were here again being used defensively rather than offensively.[72]

The fourth formula of Antioch was strictly speaking not a product of the council, but rather a summary of the second formula. Narcissus of Neronias, Maris of Chalcedon, Theodore of Heraklea, and Mark of Arethusa presented it in 342 to Emperor Constans in Milan (or in Trier). It was going to be issued again by the easterners at Philippopolis (343)[73] and in 351 at the first Council of Sirmium. Its slightly more generic presentation of the Eusebian beliefs was an attempt at mediating with the western clergy and ingratiating the western emperor through milder expressions:

> We believe in One God, Father almighty, creator and maker of all things; from whom all fatherhood in heaven and earth is named. And in His only-begotten Son, our Lord Jesus Christ, who before all ages was begotten from the Father, God from God, Light from Light; through whom all things came into being in the heavens and on earth, the visible ones as well as the invisible ones; who is Word and Wisdom and Power and Life and True Light; who in the last days was made man on our account and was born of the Holy Virgin; who was crucified, died, and was buried; and rose again from the dead on the third day, was taken up into heaven, and sat down at the right of the Father; and is coming at the consummation of the age to judge the living and the dead and to render unto everyone according to his works; whose Kingdom, being indissoluble, endures into the infinite ages; for He shall be seated at the right of the Father, not only in this age but also in the one to come. And in the Holy Spirit, that is, the Paraclete, which, having promised to the apostles, after His ascension to heaven He sent to teach them and remind them

> of all things; through whom also the souls of those who have sincerely believed in Him will be sanctified.[74]

The creed was followed by the anathematisms, which read as follows:

> But those who say that the Son is from nothing or is from another hypostasis and not from God, and that there was a time when he was not, the Catholic Church regards as aliens.[75]

These anathematisms were fairly clear in their disavowal of doctrines consonant with Arius's, although they still left his followers some leeway for equivocation by including the word "time" (*chronos*) in the banned phrase "there was [a time] when he was not."

The divergence between easterners and westerners was bound to manifest itself at Sardica (in Dacia), where in 343 a conciliatory attempt made by Pope Julius, with the support of the western emperor, resulted instead in mutual excommunication between the two factions. While the eastern bishops, gathered in a separate session, confirmed the validity of the decisions of the Antiochene council, their western counterparts published a document that outdid even Nicaea in its Monarchian radicalism. They began by answering in kind the Antiochene assertion of conformity with tradition. With this clarification in place, they reacted vehemently to the Eusebians' affirmation of three divine hypostaseis:

> As for us, this Catholic and apostolic tradition, faith, and profession we have received and learned, [and] this one we maintain: that one is the hypostasis, which the heretics name ousia, of the Father, of the Son, and of the Holy Spirit. And if they asked which one is the hypostasis of the Son, we respond that it is that professed as the Father's only one, and that the Father has never been without the Son, nor the Son without the Father—nor could he be [such], namely Logos not having Spirit.[76]

The assertion that the one divine hypostasis was called ousia by the "heretics," namely the easterners, did not mean that the opponents were assumed to identify the two terms. The target of this statement was, rather, the fact that the easterners identified the unity of God only at the generic level of the ousia, distinguishing instead between multiple hypostaseis. The formulation of this passing condemnation ("which the heretics name ousia") reveals the authors' awareness of the role played by technical terminology. By identifying the hypostasis of the Son with that of the Father, the credal declarations of Sardica made clear its authors' view that the easterners' attachment to the existence of three hypostaseis was the main hindrance on the road toward reconciliation. A change in terminology, it was implicitly suggested, would go a long way toward the regaining of communion. The polemical engagement conducted by means of battling creeds was taking the contenders on a shared quest for acceptable language to describe intra-Trinitarian relations.

As a result of a series of changes within the political landscape,[77] in 344 the Eusebian camp thought it appropriate to make one more attempt at doctrinal agreement with the westerners, an attempt that would maximize areas for potential theological compromise. Thus in 345 an eastern delegation took to Constans in Milan a text promulgated possibly by a council gathered at Antioch the previous year, and known on account of its length as *Long-Lined Exposition* (*Ekthesis makrostichos*).

The first part of the *Exposition* draws very heavily on the fourth Antiochene creed (342), with the addition of some anathematisms contained in the easterners' synodal letter of 343 (designated as "of Philippopolis"), composed after the failure of the negotiations at Sardica. After reproducing the anathematisms, the authors expounded their meaning in seven sections. In a fashion typical of the rhetoric of orthodoxy, the authors positioned themselves as equidistant from opposing blasphemous positions, presenting their doctrine as a middle ground between the extremes of Arianism on the one hand and Monarchianism on the other.

As a whole the document, which defined the relationship between the Father and the Son as one of true generation, made a greater effort to couch the unity between Father, Son, and Holy Spirit in terms that would be satisfactory for the western bishops. The conceptual distinction the Eusebians drew between the three members of the Trinity was pushed to a maximum of compatibility with the westerners' mia-hypostatism (belief in one hypostasis) by completely avoiding the terms "hypostasis" and "ousia." The independent existence of the Son and the Holy Spirit was affirmed, but in a context that reassuringly emphasized the unity of the Father and the Son. Marcellus of Ancyra, the Monarchian theologian par excellence, was condemned alongside "the Jews" and Paul of Samosata.

The *Long-Lined Exposition* displayed a new awareness of the importance that technical terminology was beginning to assume in the dispute. With careful lexical choices, its authors endeavored to assuage the fears of the westerners, who at Sardica had equated with some theoretical coarseness tri-hypostatism (belief in three hypostaseis) with tritheism (belief in three gods):

> Nor, affirming three entities and three persons of the Father and of the Son and of the Holy Spirit according to the Scriptures, do we thereby make out three Gods, because we know the perfect and unbegotten, unbegun and invisible God to be only one, the God and Father of the only-begotten, the only one who has the being from Himself, the only one who grants it without envy to all others.[78]

In the moment it insisted on the triadic nature of God, the *Long-Lined Exposition* used two terms (*pragmata* and *prosōpa*, entities and persons) different from the one (hypostaseis) its inspirers had deployed in the immediately preceding conciliar occasion. The Trinitarian debates were being reconceptualized as a quest for the correct manner of naming the ontological level at which plurality can be observed within God. Without relenting in their insistence on the individuated character of the Son and the Holy Spirit, their response to the westerners' creed of Sardica showed awareness that doctrinal unity depended on mutually agreed-upon lexical choices when talking about God.

Ossius and Protogenes's Letter to Julius

As anticipated earlier, the westerners' Council of Sardica of 343 produced a Monarchian text.[79] It is Sozomen who informs us about the work of the bishops who gathered there:

> They set forth then another statement of faith, more extensive than that of Nicaea, but preserving the same intent and departing only slightly from its words. And so Ossius and Protogenes, who were then the leaders of those from the West convened at Sardica, fearing perhaps that they might be considered by some to make innovations to the decisions of Nicaea, wrote to Julius, and professed to consider these as normative, but that given the need for clarity they had expanded the same [original] intent, so that it may not be possible for Arius's supporters, taking advantage of the brevity of the statement of Nicaea, to lead into strange conclusions those inexperienced in argument.[80]

Sozomen appears to be acquainted with a letter sent by Ossius and Protogenes themselves to Pope Julius of Rome. We are only able to read this letter in the pedestrian Latin retranslation of a Greek version of its original Latin. The

Latin text presents significant obscurities, but its meaning may be understood as follows:

> 1. Ossius and Protogenes to the most beloved brother Julius. 2. We remember and hold onto and retain that rule which contains the catholic faith produced at Nicaea,[81] and all of the present bishops concurred. 3. For three issues were raised: <whether the Son of God comes from the things that are not or from another substance, and [whether he comes] not from God, and> whether there once was when he was not.[82] 4. But since thereafter the disciples of Arius have contrived blasphemies, a certain [specific] rationale[83] has compelled us—so that no one, swayed by those three arguments, may introduce innovations into the [rule of] faith and, falling prey to them, be excluded, and so that [the rule] may become neither expanded nor extended—to expound on the earlier rule while agreeing with it. 5. And so in order[84] to avoid any reprehension, we make this known to your Goodness, most beloved brother: we pronounced that most[85] [of the rule] is firm and fixed but should be formulated more fully with a certain sufficiency of truth, so that all teachers and catechists may be enlightened and the opponents may be confounded and hold onto the catholic and apostolic [rule of] faith.[86]

The episcopal duo was resorting in this missive to a clever ruse by openly appealing to the *stasis* (issue) of letter and intent (*rheton kai dianoia*). The letter of the Nicene Creed required no revision, but its formulaic brevity obscured the original intent, which needed to be elaborated upon in the Sardican creed. No new or modified creed was required: only a longer, hypomnematic explication (that is, one having the nature of a "running exegetic commentary")[87] of the original intention of its authors.

The discussions about Christ's relation to the Father, we learn from the epistle, had led some members of the pro-Nicene alliance to consider coming up with a new formula. This creed would innovate upon or simply replace the *Nicaenum*, an outcome Sozomen in his account renders as an "absurdity" (*atopo*[*s*]). As a result, producing an exposition that would more fully address those theological concerns without generating a new credal document had imposed itself as a necessity to Ossius and Protogenes. Section 5 disavows as undesirable a more comprehensive and prolix (*latior et longior*) formula of faith (*fide*[*s*]), equated with an innovation upon the *Nicaenum* (*ne quis* [. . .] *renovet fidem*).[88] To prevent any inexperienced pro-Nicene from creating a similar document, Ossius, Protogenes, and their pro-Nicene associates resolved to offer an exposition. Sozomen himself, in his account of the letter, mentions the issue of length, although only to remark that the pithiness of the Nicene formulation could offer no answers to the theological questioning of the Arians. The nickname given only two years later to the *Long-Lined Exposition* (345) suggests that the length of a credal document was a significant feature in the evaluation of its appropriateness.

A debate must have unfolded at Sardica as to whether a new document should be written.[89] It is doubtful that the anonymous subjects who had reportedly considered producing a new, longer formula of faith were deviating from standard practice. More likely, they were acting on the grounds of the absence of any precedent indicating that the *Nicaenum* should remain the only formula to be promulgated. In fact, it may well have been their initiative to produce a new formula that originated the fetishization of the *Nicaenum* on the part of the likes of Ossius and Protogenes. The discussions at which the duo's letter hints are the first historical testimony to the idea that the formula of faith composed at Nicaea, called in the letter simply *fides*, might have to be considered the ultimate expression of theological truth. On the other hand, the debate to which Ossius and Protogenes's letter bears witness indicates that Christians were subjecting the practice of producing conciliar documents to scrutiny.

Ossius and Protogenes's letter also points to a circular connection tying theology to creeds, intellectual exchange to the writing of formulas. The Nicene Creed, we are told, had to be written down because three questions had arisen. After its composition, more sophistries and blasphemies made it necessary to write the longer exposition of Sardica: the very Arian sophistries that made the writing of the Sardican document necessary in the eyes of its authors were an unintended outcome of the *Nicaenum*. Like the owl of Minerva, credal statements come along to ratify the reality of—and condense formulaically—an intellectual debate that has already unfolded. Ossius and Protogenes probably expected that the Sardican re-exposition was going to fuel, in turn, further controversy.

At a council summoned to Alexandria in 362, which is discussed more amply in the next chapter, Athanasius of Alexandria would squarely reject the creed of Sardica as an undue addition to the *Nicaenum*, with arguments apparently drawing on documents related to the Sardican council, including Ossius and Protogenes's letter. The *Tome to the Antiochenes*, a document composed by Athanasius at the Council of Alexandria (362), includes a discussion of Trinitarian matters that begins with a disavowal of the Sardican confession:

> 5. 1. And prohibit even the reading or publication of the paper, much talked of by some as having been drawn up concerning the faith at the synod of Sardica. For the synod made no definition of the kind. For whereas some demanded, on the ground that the Nicene synod was defective, the drafting of a creed, and in their haste even attempted it, the holy synod assembled in Sardica was indignant, and decreed that no statement of faith should be drafted, but that they should be content with the faith confessed by the fathers at Nicaea, inasmuch as it lacked nothing but was full of piety, and that it was undesirable for a second creed to be promulgated, lest that drafted at Nicaea should be deemed imperfect, and a pretext be given to those who were often wishing to draft and define a creed. 2. So that if a man propound the above [paper] or any other, stop them, and persuade them rather to keep the peace. For in such men we perceive no motive save only contentiousness. 3. For as to those whom some were blaming for speaking of three hypostaseis, on the ground that the phrase is unscriptural and therefore suspicious, we thought it right indeed to require nothing beyond the confession of Nicaea, but on account of the contention we made inquiry of them [. . .].[90]

The theology of Sardica, to which his ally Marcellus and most of the westerners were attached, had never been particularly dear to Athanasius.[91] Nevertheless, his resolve in asking the Eustathians, his allies, to abjure that theological constellation was a striking departure from the approach that his adherence to the pro-Nicene alliance had forced him to adopt until that point.[92] The doctrines of Sardica, under which only a fraction of the pro-Nicene could comfortably stand, created for Athanasius a problem of association with Monarchianism. Athanasius's intention to co-opt the Meletians into a broader pro-Nicene alliance required that that banner be laid aside, no matter how heavy a burden this might impose on the Eustathians.[93]

Alone among all the members of the Council of Alexandria, Athanasius had partaken in the Sardican synod. He was familiar with the discussions that had taken place there between those who wanted—and, we learn from him, had indeed proceeded—to draft a new creed and those who had opposed this initiative. Athanasius's position, trying to avert the mistake of reading the Sardican document as a substitute for the *Nicaenum*, was aligned with Ossius and Protogenes's.

In light of the tenor of his comments, Athanasius seems to have been acquainted with Ossius and Protogenes's letter. Some of his words in the *Tome* lend support to a proposal for a substantial emendation of the text of that letter, made by the Ballerini brothers.[94] Athanasius writes that

> the holy synod assembled in Sardica was indignant, and decreed that no statement of faith should be drafted, but that they should be content with the faith confessed by the fathers at Nicaea, inasmuch as it lacked nothing but was full of piety, and that it was undesirable for a second creed to be promulgated, lest that drafted at Nicaea should be deemed imperfect, and a pretext be given to those who were often wishing to draft and define a creed.

The text of Ossius and Protogenes's *Letter*, as first reconstructed and translated above, reads:

> But since thereafter the disciples of Arius have contrived blasphemies, a certain [specific] rationale has compelled us—so that no one, swayed by those three arguments, may introduce innovations into the [rule of] faith[95] and, falling prey to them, be excluded, and so that [the rule] may become neither expanded nor extended—to expound on the earlier rule while agreeing with it.

In this rendition, the letter claims that an exposition had been required by the need to avoid the production of a more comprehensive and longer (*latius et longius*) formula of faith on the part of some inexpert pro-Nicene. The emendation suggested by the Ballerini brothers has instead the document itself qualify "the needed exposition" as more inclusive and prolix (*latius et longius*). This longer exposition was necessary in order to prevent the formula of faith from being innovated upon.[96] The passage as amended reads as follows:

> But since thereafter the disciples of Arius have contrived blasphemies, a certain [specific] rationale has compelled us—so that no one, swayed by those three arguments, may introduce innovations into the [rule of] faith—to have their scholium against the Nicene faith excluded, and to have an expanded and extended exposition produced, which agrees with the former.[97]

The Ballerinis' intervention goes too far.[98] In addition, the case for the original presence of the word *scholium* seems thinner than the one that could be made for *scholion*. *Scholion* as a technical Greek word (a *Fremdwort*) never became orthographically and inflectionally naturalized in early Christian Latin.[99] Cicero himself cites the Greek word in transliteration.[100]

The comparison between the Latin text transmitted by the manuscript tradition and the seemingly faithful summary produced by Sozomen might make the first Latin reconstruction given above marginally preferable.[101] Nevertheless, the emendation of *spolium* into *scholion* is attractive in light of intratextual considerations. If *spolium* continues to be read instead ("so that no one, swayed by those three arguments, may introduce innovations into the [rule of] faith and, falling prey to them, be excluded"), it remains somewhat difficult to understand what the hypothetical subject stands at risk of being excluded from.

The reference to a scholium introduces a rhetorically plausible discussion of two competing writing activities: that of the anti-Nicene scholiasts and that of the pro-Nicene expounders of the creed. The term *scholion* is the diminutive of the Greek *scholē*, meaning "occupation" or "study," and denotes a marginal or interlinear annotation on a classical text with explanatory function.[102] From the second century CE, *scholion* came to mean "commentary."[103]

It should be kept in mind that here we are dealing with the Latin version of a Greek translation of a letter originally composed in Latin. Even if the emendation is accepted, it remains unlikely that Ossius and Protogenes would have used the word *scholion* in their original Latin. It is also highly improbable that their opponents would have written glosses on the Nicene Creed, let alone conceptualized them as *scholia*. More likely, the Greek translator rendered a different Latin word, found in the original text, as *scholion*, and the Latin translator transcribed this term into Latin (either out of laziness or in an attempt to preserve the technical value of the term). The word used by Ossius and Protegenes cannot be retrieved, but it likely still had to do with the field of interpretation. Thus, if the emendation by the Ballerinis is maintained, in the imagination of the two pro-Nicene champions the Nicene "scripture" had assumed the status of a text that lent itself to exegesis. In this rendition of the incomplete Latin text of the duo's letter, the intention to prevent the opponents from writing "a scholium against the Nicene faith" rhetorically couches the alternative between orthodoxy and heterodoxy as the opposition between two competing exegetical activities implemented on a scripture (*fides* stands in the text for *scriptura fidei*, the "writ" or statement or rule of faith).

In the text of the *Tome to the Antiochenes*, Athanasius refers to the Sardican document as a *pittakion*, a word meaning "writing table," "leaflet," "note," and "letter." The etymology of the term is unknown. It is ubiquitous (with different spellings and abbreviations) in papyrological documentation, where it seems to indicate, at least sometimes, the papyrus itself.[104] It is very likely that

Athanasius's own use of the word carried negative connotations, as it did in Gelasius's *Syntagm*:

> The holy synod anathematized all these things as well as them [the Arians], not suffering to hear [even] this much of their impious opinion and madness and of their blasphemous words. Rather, they also immediately tore asunder their leaflet (*pittakion*), which they dared to deliver as a load of their impiety.[105]

Also Eusebius of Vercellae, in the Greek translation of his Latin signature of the *Tome to the Antiochenes*, referenced the Sardican creed as a *pittakion*. The Greek text of the bit of his signature (*Tome* 10.3) that is relevant to the discussion of Sardica is riddled with grammatical difficulties. These are persuasively solved by the Latin retroversion proposed by Christoph Schubert, which may be rendered as follows:

> And since for that reason the paper of Sardica is said to be extraneous, lest it appear to have been exposed in addition to the Nicene faith I, too, consent, so that the Nicene faith may not appear to be excluded by it, nor that it [scil. the Sardican paper] be preferred.[106]

The expression *hina mē . . . ekkleiesthai doxē(i)* (back-translated by Schubert as *ne . . . excludi videatur*) is oddly reminiscent of the *ne . . . excludatur* of Ossius and Protogenes's *Letter* (4). Since Athanasius knew the letter of the two bishops, it can be surmised that Paulinus did as well and that he cited it, whether intentionally or unwittingly, at the moment of disavowing the credal value of the statement drafted at Sardica. As would have also been the case with the mention of a scholium if the Ballerinis' emendation is adopted, Athanasius and Paulinus tied a discredited theological posture to a less-than-prestigious literary practice, here with a specific reference to its inferior materiality. Nicaea was not Sardica: a scripture was not a leaflet.

From Milan (345) to Alexandria (362)

As a result of the attempt at reconciliation expressed by the *Long-Lined Expositions* (345), the westerners agreed to condemn Photinus; but the easterners' reported refusal to do the same with Arius halted the negotiations once again. Strife continued. In 346 Constans forced Constantius II (337–361) to authorize Athanasius's return to Alexandria. After Constans's murder (350) and the defeat of the usurper Magnentius (351), Constantius gained control over the whole empire and resolved to unify it religiously. At the councils of Arles (353), Milan (355), and Bézier (356), the western bishops were coerced into again condemning Athanasius. Many bishops faithful to Nicaea were exiled.

Ousted from Alexandria by Constantius, Athanasius fled to one of the monastic communities in the Egyptian countryside. There he was able to devote substantial time to writing. To this period is dated the encyclical letter *To the Bishops of Egypt* (356), in which Athanasius exhorts his fellow bishops not to sign declarations of faith other than that of Nicaea. This was a decisive time for Athanasius's shift toward a staunch and exclusive defense of the *homoousios.*

From the death of Eusebius of Caesarea (339/340) until the early 350s, neither of the theological fronts that were facing one another on the battleground of imperial Christianity—best identified respectively by their anti-"Arian" and anti-Monarchian antagonisms—had made a serious attempt at delving into the doctrinal questions arising from their discussions. This reality was soon to change. In 357 Valens of Musria, Ursacius of Singidunum, and Germinius of Sirmium convened a synod in Sirmium (357), where the position of the Son was starkly subordinated to the Father's, and the doctrine not only of homoousios but even of *homoiousios* (similar according to the ousia) was proscribed. This degree of openness to radical subordinationism was unprecedented in the East, where allegiance to the formula *in encaeniis* of 341 had until then been prevalent.

Those same years saw the rise of the heteroousian movement, spearheaded by Aëtius and Eunomius. Its affiliates had no qualms about proclaiming that the Son's essence (ousia) was different (*heterē*) from God the Father's. After the death of Bishop Leontius, the radical Eusebian Eudoxius of Germanicia ascended to the see of Antioch. He called back from Egypt Aëtius, originally elected deacon by Leontius but then exiled. Aëtius enjoyed in Antioch the favor of the Caesar Constantius Gallus, first cousin of Constantius II. The homoian bishop Eudoxius brought with himself also his disciple Eunomius.

The whole trio—Eudoxius, Aëtius, and Eunomius—was later exiled by decision of a homoiousian council summoned in Sirmium by Constantius II in 358. The reaction against this moderately pro-Nicene backlash was led by Mark of Arethusa, George of Alexandria, and Acacius of Caesarea. The formula their alliance promulgated in Sirmium in 359 proscribed usage of the term "ousia," submitting that Christ was similar (*homoios*) to the Father, and even that was only "according to the Scriptures" (*kata tas graphas*), namely, in no ontologically discrete way. The political alliance Acacius was creating, consequently named "homoian," hoped to impose a solution to the Trinitarian discussions by gaining imperial backing for a diplomatic middle ground between perceived opposite extremes on the Trinitarian spectrum.

To all Christian thinkers invested in the *Nicaenum*, however, the claim of the Son's generic similarity to the Father appeared almost as blasphemous as the radical subordinationism of the heteroousians: if they were similar, they could not be equal. In 359, at the Council of Seleucia, the homoiousians were temporarily able to impose the formula of Antioch (341) on a homoian alliance composed of followers of Acacius and Eudoxius, which was upholding the formula of Sirmium (359). At Ariminum and Nike (359), however, the westerners, gathered in a new council, were compelled to ratify a homoian formula (more on this in Chapter 3). A council gathered in Constantinople in 360 confirmed the decisions of Ariminum, sanctioning the triumph of Acacius and Eudoxius and meting out exile to the homoousians.

The councils of Ariminum (359) and Constantinople (360) dealt significant blows to the heterogeneous camp—composed of homooousians and homoiousians—that opposed radical subordinationism. As Jerome dramatically put it some twenty years after the events, "[T]he whole world groaned and was astonished to find out that it was Arian."[107] But this last anti-Nicene throw of the dice, implemented through coercion, was too little, too late: the gears of the homoiousian reaction had already been set in motion.

After the election of the homoian Eudoxius of Germanicia as a successor, in the see of Antioch, to the cautiously homoian Leontius (344–358), George of Laodicea, an early supporter of Arius's who had progressively shifted toward more broadly acceptable Eusebian postures, had prompted Basil of Ancyra into action by addressing to him an impassioned plea.[108] Basil had convened a council at Ancyra (358), whose lengthy synodal letter had declared the Son "similar according to the ousia" to the Father, and had condemned the homoousios as equivalent to the Sabellian *tautoousios* (a Monarchian expression of self-same being).[109] This new entente had had the effect of splitting the Eusebian alliance, isolating the most subordinationist elements from the rest of the eastern episcopate. A new homoiousian coalition had been shaped. Constantius, worried by the rapid rise of the heteroousians, had lent his ear to the cause of these homoiousian leaders, sanctioning as orthodox the Second Creed of Antioch (341) as reinterpreted through their theology. Eudoxius and some heteroousian bishops were consequently exiled.

Constantius soon had a change of heart, offering his support to Acacius's homoian gambit. But the homoian formula amounted to little more than a political initiative, and the emperor's death in December 361 halted its success. After acceding to the throne, the decidedly anti-Christian emperor Julian[110] issued an edict allowing the exiled bishops to return to their sees.[111] A series of synods were promoted by the pro-Nicene in Gaul (one in particular in 360 or 361 in Paris, where it may have been led by Hilary of Poitiers), Greece, Spain, and Asia Minor. The purpose of these meetings was to regather the forces of the pro-Nicene and concomitantly grant forgiveness to those Christians who had shared communion with their opponents during the years of Constantius's persecution.[112] Different conditions for reconciliation were set depending on the gravity of the returnees' lapsing.

Athanasius was among those pro-Nicene to whom Julian's edict granted the ability to return to their sees. As the next chapter details, in February 362 he hastened back to Alexandria, where pro-Nicene Christians received him with all the honors behooving his revered position of defender of the right faith.[113] Upon his renewed installment within the Alexandrian see, the bishop was faced with the reality of weakened ecclesiastical structures. He proceeded to summon a council in Alexandria to re-array the ecclesiastical landscape of the region, nominate bishops for vacant Egyptian sees, and offer a chance to enter his alliance to those who had joined the ranks of the anti-Nicene during his exile.

The Invention of the *Nicaenum*

After the 325 promulgation of the Nicene Creed, this formula was set aside, half-forgotten for three decades, in particular in the West.[114] The Sardican discussion reported about in the letter of Ossius and Protogenes represents a significant exception to this pattern of oblivion. Hilary testified that he had first heard about the Council of Nicaea as late as 356:

> Though long ago regenerated in baptism, and for some time a bishop [beginning in 350], I never heard of the Nicene Creed until I was going into exile [356], but the Gospels and Epistles suggested to me the meaning of homoousion and homoiousion.[115]

The first occasion for the *Nicaenum* to escape this fate of neglect was the Council of Milan of 355. Following the defeat of the usurper Magnentius in 351, Emperor Constantius was set on harmonizing the empire from the religious standpoint. In order to achieve peace in the Church, he had to convince the western bishops to ratify the condemnation of Athanasius, sanctioned years before by the eastern episcopate. At a council gathered at Arles in 353, all the western bishops (with the exception of Paulinus of Triers), under the pressure of the anti-Nicene Valens of Mursia, confirmed Athanasius's banishment. The Athanasian ally Liberius of Rome, whose legates at the Council of Arles had also defected under pressure, asked Eusebius of Vercellae to accompany Lucifer of Calaris (as well as the deacon Hilary and the presbyter Pancratius) to Milan, to plead with the emperor for the summoning of a new council. Eusebius initially did not intervene at the synod, and Valens, Urascius, and Germinius had an easy time convincing all the westerners (except Lucifer, Hilary, and Pancratius) to condemn Athanasius.

When Eusebius finally resolved to partake in the council, his adversaries denied him admission for ten days. Finally allowed to join, Eusebius refused to sign Athanasius's condemnation before the orthodoxy of all those convened was ascertained. Following Liberius's own suggestion to Constantius, expressed in a letter,[116] Eusebius requested that everybody recognize the Nicene Creed. As Dionysius of Milan was about to sign, Valens interrupted the works of the council by snatching pen and paper away from him. This gesture caused public scandal, leading Constantius to transfer the council to the imperial palace. Dionysius, Lucifer, and Eusebius were eventually exiled.[117]

In the same years in which the legacy of Nicaea underwent contestation at the Council of Milan (355), Athanasius was working to move the Nicene declaration of the Son's consubstantiality with the Father to the center of the debate, where it had never before belonged.[118] Deposed twice consecutively at an Antiochene council (349) and at the First Council of Sirmium (351), Athanasius nevertheless stayed in Alexandria until 356. He was eventually removed from the Egyptian metropolis that same year and subjected to his third exile, the majority of which he spent among the monks of the Egyptian countryside. By speaking about the homoousios in two works composed during this exile—*On the Sentence of Dionysius* (352/353) and the booklets *On the Decrees of the Nicene Synod*, written likely in 355 or the following year[119]—Athanasius impressed an important turn to the whole *oikoumenē*-wide discussions.

On the Decrees was composed in response to a fellow pro-Nicene (possibly Julius of Rome) who had been baffled by his opponents' argument that both the Nicene expression "homoousios" and the notion, also upheld in the creed of Nicaea, that the Son was "from the ousia of the Father" were unscriptural. The ousia language employed by the Council of Nicaea, Athanasius patiently explained, was necessary to defend the validity of actually scriptural titles applied to Christ—such as "Wisdom" (*sophia*), "Power" (*dynamis*), and "Word" (*logos*)—that would have otherwise crumbled under the attacks of the "Arians." The term "homoousios," thus, was employed in order to rule out such explanations of the generation of the Son, as had been proposed by Arius and his followers.[120]

As Ayres notes, homoousios was presented in *On the Decrees* as a complement to the notion that the Son is "from the ousia of the Father," and not as an independent formula designed to contain in itself the essence of the correct faith.[121] "*Homoousios* [was] thus defended," Ayres writes, "not by reference to a detailed understanding of what the term implies in itself, but by arguing that it is an important cipher for other terms and phrases."[122] Several actors at this juncture of the controversies partook in this process of ciphering. As remarked by Barnes, around the year 360 the object of theological debate switched radically and condemned the discussions of the two previous decades to obsolescence. While up to that point the debate had revolved around the question of whether Christ was a creature, thanks to the reconceptualization of the debate brought about by this ciphering the Trinitarian discussion began in earnest.[123]

Athanasius's and Paulinus's likely reliance on Ossius and Protogenes's *Letter to Julius* in the *Tome to the Antiochenes* (362) indicates that Athanasius's readinesss to grant quasi-scriptural status to the creed of Nicaea retrieved the willingness, shown by actors in the 340s, to attribute paramount value to that document. At the same time, the dynamic whose emergence has been witnessed through the distant interaction between the easterners' and the westerners' conciliar documents was brought to a fuller realization through Athanasius's linguistic ciphering. "Homoousios" was retroactively produced as an arbitrary touchstone for correct belief. The creation of this shibboleth imposed a transformation not only on the contents of the Trinitarian debate, but also on the manner of the discussions, which would become increasingly preoccupied with lexical exactitude and with willingness to provide support for one or the other technical term.[124] It is no coincidence that the Athanasian initiative was shortly followed by a proliferation of theological camps identified, by themselves or by their opponents, through one or another signifier (homoians, homoiousians, heteroousians).

In offering a summary of the disputes that occurred in the period between 318 and 362, this chapter has offered a cursory look at changes in the production of conciliar creeds. While these documents were previously composed to satisfy the necessities of a particular community, during the Trinitarian controversies they began to be written in response to each other across the Mediterranean, at times taking on a combative tone. In creeds composed between 340 and 362, a polemical ethos developed through three operations: *logicaliza-*

tion, technicalization, and *formularization*. These conciliar texts logically reconfigured the problem of the status of the Son, originally framed at Nicaea as concerning the manner of his begetting, into an interrogation of his personal subsistence. At the same time, theologians realized that the controversy would be solved only through agreement about how to name that of which there exist three in God. This led to an emphasis on the development of a shared technical terminology as a tool for negotiation. As a result, creeds began to articulate theological truths in formulas capable of attracting universal agreement.

In addition, the creed of the Council of Sardica of 343 has served as a case study for demonstrating that the elevation of creeds to quasi-scriptural status accompanied formularization. Scholarship on the Trinitarian controversies has inquired as to when the creed professed at Nicaea became the golden standard of orthodoxy. While Athanasius of Alexandria is commonly credited with single-handedly carrying out this revolution in the mid-350s, I have proposed that the ratification of the *Nicaenum* as the touchstone of orthodoxy was prepared by changes in conciliar culture that can be traced back to the early 340s.

3 • Theological Labeling

Antioch and Alexandria in the 360s

One and Three Hypostaseis

This chapter focuses on the treatment of the number of hypostaseis in the Council of Alexandria (362), which aimed to address the intellectual and institutional divisions in the Church of Antioch.[1] A study of the workings of this synod still has much to contribute to the history of the evolution of Christian thought. Based on ancient authorities, it is often repeated that the council hosted a confrontation between two Antiochene theologico-ecclesial parties, respectively advocating for the presence of "one hypostasis" and "three hypostaseis" in the godhead. I propose instead that it was Athanasius of Alexandria, the adamant champion of the homoousian faith in the East, who decided to reduce the incompatibility between two theological traditions (Eustathians and Meletians) to a disagreement over the number of hypostaseis.

Athanasius's gesture, involving a significant dose of arbitrariness, exemplified a broader movement toward the creation of expressions that would be easier to recognize, negotiate, and recombine. The distillation of a byword out of a theological style, such as those of the Eustathians and the Meletians, facilitated in turn a lasting shift: the labeling and identification of selves and others in theological discussion. While it is doubtful that the Council of Alexandria "snatched the whole world out of the jaws of Satan,"[2] as Jerome thought it did, it is undeniable that, by bequeathing to theological discussion a labeling mechanism, it constituted a milestone on the road toward the formation of Christian theology as a discursive field.

In order to bring out the importance of the Council of Alexandria in its ecclesiastical-historical context, I offer here an examination of some understudied aspects of its immediate backdrop and workings. In particular, I analyze the significance of an Egyptian gathering that immediately preceded the Council of Alexandria, explore the disciplinary politics involved in the council, and study the Meletians' participation in the council. Through these steps, I aim to prove Athanasius's interest in the reconciliation of Eustathians and Meletians, setting the stage and providing context for my discussion of his rendition of the theological approaches of the two groups in terms of "one hypostasis" and "three hypostaseis."

On November 3, 361, Emperor Constantius II died. On February 9, 362, a decree was published in Alexandria in which the new emperor, Julian, authorized the return of those bishops whom Constantius had exiled. On February 21, Athanasius hastily returned to Alexandria from his third exile. Soon he began to think of ways to exploit the change in imperial power to bring into unity all the Christians who were fond of the *Nicaenum*. The solution of two distinct yet related issues in particular imposed itself as urgent to Athanasius's mind. First, there was the disciplinary question regarding the readmission of clergy who had compromised with "Arianism." Second, Athanasius desired to mend the conflict in the Antiochene Church of pro-Nicene orientation, split between the communities of Meletius and Paulinus.

There remains no synodal letter of the council that Athanasius gathered in Alexandria in 362 in order to solve both these issues.[3] Our only direct evidence for its work is a document—for a long time incorrectly considered its synodal letter—known as *Tome to the Antiochenes*.[4] It was written by Athanasius after the meeting, in collaboration with Eusebius of Vercellae, Asterius of Arabia,[5] and other colleagues, and it was subscribed by twenty-one Church leaders (seventeen bishops and four deacons).

Sent from Alexandria to Antioch, the *Tome* contained detailed instructions for the reconciliation that was to take place. It presents itself as the work of some who had remained in Alexandria after the end of the council proper:

> These things, albeit there was no need to require anything beyond the synod of Nicaea, nor to tolerate the language of contention, yet for the sake of peace, and to prevent the rejection of men who wish to believe aright, we inquired into. And what they confessed, we put briefly into writing, we namely who are left in Alexandria, in common with our fellow ministers, Asterius and Eusebius. For most of us had gone away to our dioceses.[6]

It has been proposed that the council saw two separate moments: a larger session, which discussed the readmission of the *lapsi*, and a smaller one, dealing with the Antiochene situation. In this case, the list of subscribers found at the end of the document (*Tome* 9.3–10.1) would refer only to those "who are left in Alexandria."[7] But the excerpt just cited does not require imagining that the schism at Antioch was only debated by the smaller assembly. It is more likely that the parley about Antioch occurred in the presence of all those convened at Alexandria. Later, a smaller committee of four drafted the *Tome*, which was signed by the twenty-one lingering churchmen.[8]

The *Tome* failed in its effort to bring about peace between the two Antiochene factions. This failure is commonly blamed on the rashness of the Sardinian homoousian bishop Lucifer of Calaris.[9] Recalled by Julian's edict from his exile in the Thebaid (Egypt) along with Eusebius of Vercellae, Lucifer refused to attend Athanasius's synod, to which he sent two delegates instead. He journeyed to Antioch and recruited the help of two fellow bishops to ordain the Eustathian priest Paulinus into the episcopacy.[10] When his representatives brought the *Tome* back to Antioch, Lucifer disavowed their subscriptions to the document, which he found to be too conciliatory.

Eusebius of Vercellae, arriving in Antioch from Alexandria, was reportedly dismayed at Lucifer's action. Unable to mediate between the two factions, Eusebius returned west with nothing to show for his Antiochene foray. The same decree of Julian that had recalled Lucifer from Egypt also allowed Meletius, the foreman of the non-Eustathian pro-Nicene community in Antioch, to return from exile.[11] In 363 Meletius summoned a council to Antioch, which sent to Jovian a creed in which a qualified version of the homoousios was accepted. In that same year Athanasius, after a visit to the emperor, spent time in Antioch, but he and Meletius failed to meet and enter communion.[12] Full reconciliation between the Eustathians and the Meletians was not to be achieved until 482.

The Schism at Antioch

In the Christian community of Antioch, the incessant theological strife of the fourth century had resulted in dramatic institutional division.[13] At some point during the Trinitarian debates the Church witnessed a fivefold split, rent as it was between the homoian, Eustathian, Meletian, Apollinarist, and Luciferian groups. In the early 360s the claimants to the archiepiscopal see were still only three: Euzoius, Paulinus, and Meletius. Each of them had his own set of alliances as well as his share of control over urban masses, churches, and clergy.[14]

Soon after co-presiding over the Nicene council (325), the ardently pro-Nicene champion Eustathius of Antioch, to whose legacy Paulinus's community harkened back, fell victim to the revenge of those opponents he had conspired to bring down at the Council of Nicaea.[15] According to Chrysostom's testimony, when Eustathius was deposed and exiled he begged his acolytes not to precipitate a schism. He asked them instead to retain their faith while continuing to worship in communion with whichever bishops were going to be elected.[16]

The orthodox bishops,[17] ordained by three fellow members of the episcopal ranks, were approved and often appointed by the emperor. They celebrated the liturgy in the cathedral, the octagonal Golden Church dedicated at the time of the synod of 341.[18] Chrysostom's report about Eustathius's irenic plea may be rhetorical plumage. In any event, it is a matter of record that for a while the Eustathians, headed by the priest Paulinus after their eponymous hero's exile, made no autonomous episcopal claims, in spite of worshipping separately from the main assembly. They appear to have de facto recognized the authority of the officially appointed bishops until 343.

The situation changed after the Council of Sardica (343), when an official schism was consummated as a result of the excommunication of Bishop Stephen by a group of western Nicene bishops with whom the Eustathians were in communion.[19] Even then, however, Paulinus was not appointed bishop; his community contented itself with refraining from communicating with Stephen.

Meanwhile, the group supported by the emperor had come to include a growing majority of generically pro-Nicene believers. In spite of their creed, these Christians recognized the authority and attended the liturgical services of the various anti-Nicene who succeeded one another on the episcopal see. They continued to be loyal to the local bishop even under the leaderships of the homoian Leontius (344–357) and of Eudoxius (357–359), who lost Constantius's support after shifting from his erstwhile homoianism into the unabashed denial of similarity between the Father and the Son.

It was not until 360, the year of Meletius's exile following his election as successor to Eudoxius, that the moderate pro-Nicene of Antioch, now galvanized by the heroic resistance of their champion, broke communion with bishops of anti-Nicene ilk, rejecting the leadership of the homoian Euzoius (360–375/6), appointed in lieu of Meletius. In spite of this dissociation, Paulinus's followers still refused to hold communion with the Meletians. The historically persecuted community of Paulinus resented Meletius's record of about-faces, deplored his subscription of the homoian creed at the Council of Constantinople (360), and contested as canonically irregular his ordination in Sebaste (Armenia) performed by bishops tainted by "Arianism."

Thus, as anticipated above, by 360 three separate communities formed in Antioch: the orthodox Church of Euzoius, whose members worshipped in the cathedral; the Meletian group, withdrawn into the apostolic Old Church[20] (or outside of the walls of Antioch)[21] under the leadership of the presbyter Flavian; and the Old Nicene Eustathians, to whom Euzoius had granted the use of a small church inside the town.[22]

In order to address the split internal to the pro-Nicene field, upon the 362 recall of the exiles Eusebius of Vercellae organized in the Thebaid a small-scale non-rigorist ecclesiastical gathering, which preceded the Council of Alexandria. Eusebius's synod may have included members of the homoiousian alliance as well as lapsed pro-Nicene who had reverted to their original views after their deposition at the Council of Constantinople. On December 31, 359, the bishops who had gone on a mission from the Council of Seleucia to Constantius's court at Constantinople had subscribed to the homoian creed of the Council of Ariminum.[23] Now, many of those same bishops who had reportedly been confounded by their own subscription to a heretical formula were again supportive of the deliberations of the Council of Nicaea. Under what conditions could these clergy be reintegrated into the Churches with which Eusebius and Athanasius were in communion?

In its conciliatory orientation toward these lapsed bishops and toward the homoiousians, the Council of the Thebaid laid the groundwork for the attitude of compromise maintained by the Alexandrian gathering that followed a few months later. The attempt at coordinating pro-Nicene of different stripes (homoousians and homoiousians) and immediate backgrounds (*lapsi* and not) initiated by Eusebius was realized more fully—though still ineffectively—by Athanasius in Alexandria. At the same time, by making these overtures to the Meletians, the two councils of 362 precipitated the emergence of a rift between hard-liners and moderates within the Old Nicene alliance.

The Council of the Thebaid

The Egyptian events of 362–363 have generally been read from the viewpoint of the various actors' ecclesiastical strategies, with particular attention paid to Athanasius's own idiosyncrasies and personal antipathies. It is useful, however, to look at the protagonists' views on the issue of the Antiochene episcopacy, particularly from the angle of their disciplinary policies concerning the reintegration of heretics.

Ancient sources offer different stories about the ways in which the Old Nicene exiles began to organize upon their recall from Egypt.[24] Neither Socrates nor Sozomen mentions an official meeting in the Thebaid. Both historians present Eusebius and Lucifer as holding onto a rigorist agenda about the readmission of clergy who had lapsed doctrinally. They also seem to present Athanasius's summoning of the Council of Alexandria as inspired by similar rigorist objectives. Socrates has Lucifer and Eusebius consult about the best ways of preventing the continued violation of ecclesiastical canons and discipline; the pair agree on splitting—Lucifer to Antioch, Eusebius to Alexandria to hold a council with Athanasius.[25] Sozomen's account has Eusebius go to Alexandria "for a restoration and a shared composition of ecclesiastical matters"[26] and to hold a council, in agreement with Athanasius, "for the purpose of securing the doctrines of Nicaea."[27] Lucifer, we are told, traveled instead to Antioch to visit the troubled Church of the city, sending one deacon with Eusebius to Alexandria.

By contrast, Rufinus's account introduces a difference between Eusebius's and Lucifer's programs: the former was inclined to consult with Athanasius, while the latter was more keen to spring into action. Like Socrates and Sozomen, Rufinus makes no mention of an official meeting in the Thebaid (nor, for that matter, of the convocation of a council in Alexandria). He reports instead that Eusebius asked Lucifer to accompany him to Alexandria to confer with Athanasius about the situation of the Church, but the Sardinian bishop decided to travel to Antioch instead, sending his deacons to represent him at Alexandria. Once in Antioch, he hastily ordained the divisive Paulinus, instead of choosing someone agreeable to both factions.[28] We do not know whether Lucifer conveyed to Eusebius his intentions of ordaining Paulinus before leaving the Thebaid. Regardless, their different traveling plans reflect divergent ecclesiastical platforms—which, it can be argued, were eventually realized in the Council of Alexandria and in Paulinus's ordination, respectively.

As we have seen, Rufinus, Socrates, and Sozomen are not informed about an actual council taking place in the Thebaid. The only source providing information about an official meeting prior to the Council of Alexandria is Theodoret. However, scholarship has merged, with virtually no exceptions, his account with those of the other Church historians. Thus, while the historicity of a gathering in the Thebaid is accepted, it is commonly painted as promoting the rigorist intentions Socrates and Sozomen attribute to Eusebius and Lucifer's private confabulations upon their recall from exile.[29]

Yet, if read closely, the terms through which Theodoret characterizes the events in the Thebaid are instructive about the non-rigorist nature of the council:

> But the Italian Eusebius and Hilary, as well as Lucifer, who happened to be the shepherd of the Sardinian island, were staying in the Thebaid, next to Egypt; for Constantius had relegated them. These, meeting with the others of the same mind, declared it necessary to bring the Churches back into harmony. For not only did those of opposite mind besiege them [scil. the churches], but they themselves quarreled with one another. For indeed in Antioch the sound body of the Church was split asunder: those who from the beginning, for the sake of the right worthy Eustathius, had separated from the rest were assembling by themselves; and they who with the admirable Meletius had held aloof from the Arian faction were performing divine service in what is called the Palæa.[30]

The phrase used to describe the meeting (*kata tauton genomenoi*) designates a purposeful coming together. In Theodoret's *Commentary on Isaiah*, the expression indicates the forming of a coalition;[31] elsewhere in *Church History*, Theodoret employs it to describe a reunion of bishops.[32] Thus the meeting in the Thebaid described by him was not the private conversation between Eusebius and Lucifer of which Rufinus, Socrates, and Sozomen speak.

Theodoret is the only source to apprise us of the existence of the Council of the Thebaid. All Rufinus, Socrates, and Sozomen report is a conversation between Eusebius and Lucifer. Since the latter two depend on the former,[33] here we have Rufinus's word against Theodoret's. In writing his *Church History*, Theodoret had at his disposal sources he found in the archives of the Antiochene episcopate. Those included the synodal collections created under Euzoius and Meletius, which preserved imperial and episcopal acts and letters, as well as written and oral testimonies from Meletian bishops such as Eusebius of Samosata and Acacius of Beroea.[34] He also supplemented those materials with information about Antioch drawn from Theodore of Mopsuestia's lost work on Eunomius.[35]

One detail in Theodoret's narrative about the events in the Thebaid suggests that he was using a special Antiochene source for those events, which influenced the course of the schism in Antioch: the addition of one "Italian Hilary" to the Eusebius-Lucifer pair at the beginning of the passage excerpted above. This has been a stumbling block for historians. Armstrong implausibly identified him with the homoian Hilary of Jerusalem.[36] Some saw Theodoret's mention of a Hilary as a mistaken reference to Hilary of Poitiers, allegedly banished by Constantius to the Thebaid and allowed to return by Julian.[37] Yet others identified in this figure the Aquitanian bishop but considered the mention of his presence in the Thebaid a mistake on Theodoret's part.[38] As a result of the Council of Béziers of 356, in fact, the bishop of Poitiers was exiled to Phrygia and, after several travels, was authorized by Constantius to return to Gaul in 360.[39] He had no reason to be in Egypt, and was certainly not relegated there. It is difficult to imagine that Theodoret committed here a blunder of this size.

It is much more likely that the Hilary referenced by Theodoret is the deacon Hilary of Rome, the author of pamphlets ("libelli")[40] on the need to rebaptize those who had received their baptism from heretical clergy.[41] This is the same Hilary who was at some point identified with the elusive Ambrosiaster.[42] In 355 he traveled to Milan with Lucifer of Calaris and the presbyter Pancratius, in order to deliver to Constantius a missive on behalf of Bishop Liberius of Rome.[43] In this letter Liberius besought the gathering of a council that would reexamine the case of Athanasius, whose condemnation issued by the Council of Tyre of 335 had been ratified at the Council of Arles of 353 thanks to the action of Valens of Mursia. Liberius also wrote to Eusebius of Vercellae and Fortunatian of Aquileia asking them to join the delegation in Milan, as we learn from three letters of Liberius to Eusebius contained in an ancient *Life* of the latter.[44]

As a result of the embassy a council did gather in Milan in 355, but it did not go the way Liberius had hoped.[45] Eventually the legates were enjoined to add their signatures to Athanasius's condemnation and were exiled for their refusal.[46] Athanasius informs us also about some gruesome tortures that Hilary had to undergo.[47] Within a span of seven years, Eusebius and Lucifer were transferred to three different locations. Lucifer reached the Thebaid from Germanicia in Syria, via Eleutheropolis in Palestine. Eusebius was banished first to Scythopolis of Palestine, then to Cappadocia, and eventually to the Thebaid.[48] We know Hilary of Rome was deceased by 382[49] but are not informed about the date of his return or death.[50] The sources are also silent about the destination of his exile. It is most likely that he followed Lucifer, with whom he had traveled to Milan, to Palestine, Syria, and eventually Egypt.

Was Theodoret simply speculating about the presence of Hilary of Rome in the Thebaid on the basis of the exile he shared with Lucifer at the Council of Milan? More plausibly, the historian received this bit of information from a particular source that included a narrative of the events immediately preceding Lucifer's—and, most likely, Hilary's—travel to Antioch. From the same source Theodoret may have received his knowledge of the gathering of a small synod proper in the Thebaid.

The nature of the synod can be further investigated. Theodoret names some "others of the same mind" (*alloi homophrones*) with whom Eusebius and Hilary met, resolving to return harmony to a divided Church. If Socrates and Sozomen's narrative is overlaid onto Theodoret's, these subjects will be understood as fellow unfaltering Old Nicene. But Theodoret's phrasing suggests that these need not have been exclusively bishops of Old Nicene persuasion. As much is indicated by the contrastive use, in the following sentence, of the expression "those of an opposite mind" (*hoi tanantia phronountes*), antonymous and cognate to *homophrones*. This phrase is clearly in reference to the anti-Nicene opponents of the aggregate of Old Nicene and non-Old Nicene pro-Nicene Churches.[51] The designation *homophrones* may well have included fellow Nicene of a different kind, to wit, homoiousians.

It stands to reason that, preparing for the launching of a global pro-Nicene campaign, Eusebius and his allies would have wished to also sit down with local homoiousian bishops and with homoiousian exiles. The homoian Council of Constantinople of 360 had deposed a dozen bishops.[52] While some of them had not been removed until a later council, a good number had been exiled. Philostorgius also informs us that the deposed bishops withdrew their signature from the Ariminum creed, reverting to their original homoousian or homoiousian stance.[53] Some of those restored pro-Nicene may well have been exiled to the Thebaid, an area whose imperviousness made it suitable for the relegation of recalcitrant clergy.

It is known that Theodoret constructed in *Church History* an ideological version of the ecclesiastical events of the fourth century, a version that obscured Meletius's Eusebian beginnings and homoian career, and grafted instead his belatedly found Nicene faith onto the unwavering Nicenism of the Eustathians.[54] However, Theodoret's approach toward the historical problem of the Meletians' homoiousianism was not to gloss over the split between the two communities, but rather to downplay its doctrinal significance, depicting it as a petty disagreement over personalities. In the passage referenced above—wherein, I suggest, the homoiousians are qualified as being "of the same mind"—the schism between Eustathians and Meletians is brought to the fore and lamented. The Council of the Thebaid is trustworthily presented as a first attempt at solving a schism perceived as a disgraceful quarrel among siblings.

The irenic agenda of the council promoted by Eusebius of Vercellae found Lucifer of Calaris and his men unwilling to cooperate. As we saw earlier, Rufinus attributes to Eusebius a more reconciling approach toward the pro-Nicene of non-Old Nicene orientation than he does to Lucifer. Theodoret's account similarly seems to allude to a disagreement between Lucifer and Eusebius, and conveys the unviability of a rapprochement:

> The Eusebians and Luciferians strove to find the means of just this union [between Eustathians and Meletians]. Eusebius requested Lucifer to go to Alexandria and consult about this with the great Athanasius, whereas he himself wanted to take up the labor concerning the reconciliation. But Lucifer did not go to Alexandria, and arrived instead at the city of Antioch. Having adduced many arguments for the reconciliation with the ones and the others, and yet seeing that those of Eustathius's party expressed opposition—Paulinus, being a priest, led it—he, acting incorrectly, elected for them Paulinus as bishop.[55]

The departure for Antioch of Lucifer and his coterie—Hilary of Rome and perhaps others—was the product of dissent with Eusebius's proposed conciliatory policies. But what were the exact contents of the opposition of "the Luciferians" to the plan of reconciliation proposed by "the Eusebians"? While a doctrinally motivated hostility to the restoration of relations of communion with the homiousian coalition must have been part of the issue, the events also need to be considered from the often-neglected angle of disciplinary policies. These two reservations—doctrinal and disciplinary—could at times also apply to the same subject, namely, a lapsed homoiousian.

A testimony from Sulpicius Severus instructs us in terms comparable to Rufinus's about Lucifer's disposition toward the disciplinary aspects of the Antiochene schism:

> It is admitted by all that thanks to the intercession of Hilary alone our Gauls have been freed from the sin of heresy. On the other hand, Lucifer, then in Antioch, was of a very different opinion. For he condemned to such an extent those who had been at Ariminum that he even dissociated himself from the communion of those who had received them under the condition of satisfaction or penance. I will not dare to say whether he acted rightly or wrongly.[56]

The reception granted to the lapsed is here to be understood not simply as welcoming them back into the community, but also as their reintegration into the priesthood. In theory, Sulpicius might have been heresiologically projecting the schismatic positions of the western and eastern rigorist communities known as Luciferians (possibly holding no historical connection to Lucifer)[57] onto Lucifer's activity during his short Antiochene stint. Against this possibility stands, however, Sulpicius's epoche concerning Lucifer's posture, to which the ancient historian would have in that case reserved a harsher judgment. Lucifer is known to have polemicized against Hilary of Poitiers after the latter's publication of *On the Synods*, forcing the French bishop to write his *Apologetic Responses*.[58] It appears more likely that Sulpicius intended to record Lucifer and Hilary's actual disagreement on ecclesiastical discipline by highlighting the effects of their respective policies on two different geographic contexts.

Shortly before the Council of the Thebaid, a series of councils summoned in the West had taken tolerant measures regarding the readmission of those who had compromised with homoianism. Seeing the prevalence of rigorist positions, Sulpicius Severus recounts, Hilary of Poitiers "thought that the best thing to be done was to call all back into correction and penance." As a result, "there multiplied the councils in Gaul, and almost all the bishops confessed about their error."[59]

Under Hilary's inspiration, a Gallican council, traditionally referred to as the Council of Paris, took place in 360 or 361. Athanasius in his *Letter to Rufinian* (who was likely a rigorist pro-Nicene) cites a council held by the Greek bishops and one held by the bishops of Spain and Gaul.[60] Basil of Caesarea mentions a letter of Athanasius's in which the Alexandrian justified the conciliatory measures taken with regard to the lapsed by "offering to [him] all the bishops of both Macedonia and Achaea as partakers in this belief."[61]

Liberius of Rome, possibly after consulting with Hilary of Poitiers, was to take a similar initiative in Italy.[62] In the *Letter to Rufinian* Athanasius describes the agenda of the Council of Alexandria of 362 as fully in line with those western episcopal gatherings: "Those who had lapsed and were leaders of impiety," that is, the active promoters of heresy, could be forgiven if they repented, but could not be reintegrated into the priesthood. On the other hand, "those who were not in charge over impiety"—described in another passage of the letter as those who had been forced to accept heresy and acted in the interest of protecting the flock—could be reintegrated into the priesthood after repenting.[63]

As Jerome explained in his *Dialogue between a Luciferian and an Orthodox*, the reason for reinstating the bishops who had lapsed was not that those who had been heretics could be bishops, but rather that those who were being readmitted to the episcopacy were not considered heretics.[64] In short, the designation of "heretic" was being applied by Athanasius and likeminded pro-Nicene, such as Jerome and Eusebius of Vercellae, only to the authors of heretical doctrines or the leaders of heretical groups, and not more broadly to anyone who had held heretical views.

In neither Sulpicius Severus's nor Rufinus's account does Lucifer's rigorist approach draw anything comparable to the Athanasian distinction between "those who have lapsed and were leaders of impiety" and "those who were not in charge over impiety." In 362, the difference between the position of the Old Nicene (among them Athanasius, Eusebius, and perhaps Asterius) and that of their less conciliatory fellow party-members (epitomized by Lucifer and possibly embodied by few others) lay in the amenability to making that distinction. Lucifer coherently stuck to his position after journeying back from Antioch to Italy: in Naples he refused to enter communion with Bishop Zosimus, a repentant signatory of the formula of Ariminum but hardly a significant heretical thinker or influential ecclesiastical player.[65]

Remarkably, the disciplinary disagreement between Athanasius and Lucifer revolved exclusively around the question of the readmission of the clergy. The legitimacy of reintegrating lapsed laypeople was a matter of course for both Church leaders.[66] It was only Hilary, the Roman deacon, who first raised this disciplinary concern, making himself into the posthumous target of Jerome's lampooning. In the *Dialogue between a Luciferian and an Orthodox* Jerome called Hilary a latter-day Deucalion,[67] criticizing in particular Hilary's alleged incoherence: though he had been baptized in a Church that received heretics such as Manicheans or Ebionites, and he himself had received believers who had been baptized by heretics other than "Arians," Hilary now considered the baptism of the "Arians" invalid.[68] Lucifer's disciplinary policies were not as radical as Hilary's. Still, at the council in the Thebaid, or in the discussions that preceded it, his views clashed with those of Eusebius of Vercellae, who promoted an initiative of reconciliation with the homiousians (whether with or without a delegation of the latter being present).

The 384 *Book of Supplications*—a list of grievances sent by the Roman Luciferian priests Faustinus and Marcellinus to Theodosius and Arcadius—has been seen as containing a reference to the council in the Thebaid. This gathering allegedly promulgated, at Eusebius's urging, rigorist regulations about the readmission of the lapsed clergy:[69]

> The bishops execrating these acts of ungodliness, who on account of their faith underwent the punishments of exile or who fled, though physically separated by the distances between the regions, made nonetheless into one in the spirit (*spiritu in unum positi*), through mutual correspondences (*per mutuas litteras*), decree with apostolic vigor (*apostolico*

> *vigore decernunt*) that it is in no way possible to communicate with such bishops, who have betrayed the faith in that way we have reported above, unless they requested the lay communion, bemoaning their acts of ungodliness. But, once Constantius, the protector of the heretics, died, Julian held power alone.[70]

In reality, while the *Book of Supplications* does indicate that some exiled pro-Nicene had made a rigorist determination, the latter cannot be ascribed to the Council of the Thebaid. Whether the phrase "through mutual correspondences" is understood as expressing the means through which the confessors' decree was issued (thus referring to the clause "decree with apostolic vigor") or the tool through which their unity was maintained (modifying the clause "made into one in the spirit"), it is clear that the sentence emphasizes physical dispersal. It could in principle be argued that the geographic distance between the pro-Nicene exiles is being evoked as the state *out of which* they emerged when they supposedly assembled to issue their rigorist decree. But even if this were the case, the timeline established in the *Book* would prevent this gathering from being identified with the synod of the Thebaid. In Faustinus and Marcellinus's narrative the death of Constantius clearly follows the decree of the confessors, whereas all Church historians have the events in the Thebaid unfold as a product of the emperor's demise.

Eusebius of Vercellae's later subscription to the *Tome to the Antiochenes* and his influence over a 363 letter of the Italian bishops disavowing the views of Ariminum[71] suggest that he did not hold extremist views on the matter of reintegrating the lapsed clergy. It is true that the *Letter to Gregory of Elvira*, attributed to Eusebius, voices sympathy for the refusal of this to-be Luciferian champion to communicate "with the hypocrites" (*cum ypocritis*).[72] This text, however, has been proven to be a Luciferian forgery, and has nothing to contribute to knowledge of Eusebius's actual stance.[73]

Historians have often affirmed that Eusebius was in agreement with the course of action that Lucifer was to take. These claims either attribute to Eusebius and Lucifer the intention of undermining Athanasius's activities aimed at reconciliation, or make Athanasius himself into a proponent of a rigorist agenda, who was allegedly in on the plan to consecrate Paulinus.[74] However, even leaving aside Rufinus's mention of Lucifer's disregard for Eusebius's request that he travel to Alexandria, this reconstruction clashes with ancient sources' reports about Eusebius's negative reaction to Lucifer's consecration of Paulinus upon arriving in Antioch, resulting in Lucifer's disgruntlement.[75] Surely Eusebius was acting in Antioch as an emissary of the Alexandrian council; rather than imagining that participation in the synod changed his mind, it is simpler to backdate his tolerant ecclesiastical politics to his time in the Thebaid.

In summary, the small upper-Egyptian synod Eusebius gathered was not a meeting of rigorists. Lucifer left for Antioch in disagreement with its conciliatory spirit, either before or after its celebration. The clergy that did assemble in a synod in the Thebaid laid the groundwork for the Council of Alexandria. Their conference may have also included lapsed pro-Nicene who had reverted to their original views after being deposed at Constantinople in 360, and may even have seen the participation of members of the homoiousian alliance. As such, the council in the Thebaid precipitated the emergence of a consequential rift between hard-liners (those whom Rufinus calls "Luciferians") and moderates (those he dubs "Eusebians," from Eusebius of Vercellae) within the Old Nicene field.

The Disciplinary Action of the Council of Alexandria

Lucifer's elevation of the priest Paulinus to the episcopacy was consistent with his policy on the readmission of the *lapsi* to the priesthood. Meletius could not be reinstated to his episcopal rank because of his serious compromises with "Arianism." Paulinus, who had been shepherding the bishop-less Antiochene community for years, then became the natural candidate for that position. By Athanasius's more complex disciplinary views, instead, the question of Meletius's readmission to the clergy hinged in principle on the assessment of his responsibilities in the spread of heresy, namely on whether he had been a heresiarch or simply a follower of heretical doctrines.

The Athanasian policy on readmission clearly introduced a substantial level of discretion. Some degree of uncertainty must have also been present as to the body which held the responsibility to adjudicate the status of a penitent: Should a bishop be in charge of judging lapsed priests belonging to his own diocese? Should an episcopal committee be formed to establish the terms of a fellow bishop's reintegration? Or should a local, or perhaps general, synod be gathered to decide such matters?

It is reasonable to imagine that the Council of Alexandria saw itself as the appropriate body to adjudicate the readmission to the clergy of Meletius and his acolytes. In order to evaluate the action of this council, it may be helpful to compare its disciplinary workings with those of the Gallican Council of 360 or 361 (traditionally referred to as the "Council of Paris").[76] The poor state of documentation for both councils is similar: in both cases there are no extant conciliar acts, and only a single letter related to a particular aspect of the discussion survives.[77] Nevertheless, the Council of Paris is the only disciplinary synod of this period for which any direct source is available.

The *Epistle of the Council of Paris* presents itself as the Gallican clergy's reply to a (now lost) epistle composed by some eastern bishops and entrusted to Hilary of Poitiers before his return from exile.[78] The easterners' letter must have contained explanations as to why they had given in to their anti-Nicene opponents' pressure to sign the homoian documents of Ariminum and Nike (359). The Gallican bishops begin by thanking God, because "freeing [them] from the error of the world, he now does not even suffer that [they] be added to the inexpiable society of the heretics."[79] They lament the fact that the easterners forced them to refrain from using the word "ousia," which had constituted a bulwark against heresy:

> For the majority of those who were either at Ariminum or at Nike were reduced to silence, under your authority, with regard to the ousia.[80]

This passage, ostensibly casting blame on the easterners for their complicity in Constantius's ruses, has been read as a novel and successful attempt to utilize political circumstances to exercise unhampered conciliar authority beyond the council's regular jurisdiction.[81] While this motive might be accurate, a more complex design emerges from the way the rest of the document deals with the easterners' lack of judgment. After disavowing Monarchian readings of the *Nicaenum* and accepting the idea of Christ's similarity to the Father, the Gallican bishops proceed to absolve themselves for their doctrines:[82]

> Therefore, most beloved ones, since our simplemindedness recognizes from your letter that it was defrauded with regard to the omission of the ousia, [and] that so did even the piousness of those who returned from Ariminum to Constantinople, [and] since the faithful preacher of the Lord's name, our brother Hilary, has reported that not even they [scil. those who had returned from Ariminum to Constantinople], as your zealous letter testifies, could induce those assembled to the condemnation of such great blasphemies, we turn away from all these acts that have been committed inadvertently, through ignorance.[83]

The convoluted syntax of the passage does not detract from the transparency of its logic: the Gallican clergy has been deceived by some easterners who, in turn, had been the object of fraud.[84] These circumstances allow them to turn away from their acts by claiming ignorance and inadvertency.[85] In the continuation of the document they condemn—among others—three groups of people: the main authors of the deceit of Ariminum, whom the easterners had already excommunicated in their letter;[86] a further set of unnamed blasphemers already execrated by the easterners; and those bishops who, whether out of ignorance or impiety (*ignoratione aut impietate*), occupied the sees of exiled brethren.[87]

The workings of the councils of Paris and Alexandria are comparable. In both cases a staunch defender of the Nicene faith (Athanasius in the East and Hilary, "faithful preacher of the Lord's name," in the West), having recently returned from exile, was taking advantage of a novel political scenario (Julian's election in the case of Alexandria, the recent acclamation of Julian as emperor in Paris as a result of a coup in 360 in the case of the Gallican council) to promote the readmission of lapsed pro-Nicene clergy and to explore a homoousian-homoiousian alignment.[88] In both cases the rehabilitation of the lapsed was achieved through the exchange of communion between two communities. Finally, in both cases the establishment of communion required a series of defensive doctrinal elucidations on the part of the two sides.

The comparison with the Council of Paris (360/361) illustrates the possible workings of an episcopal meeting, such as that of Alexandria, meant to achieve reconciliation between two groups that, with some provisos, regarded each other as orthodox. To be sure, in posing some conditions for reconciliation, the *Tome* assumed the central authority of the Old Nicene as the party that the Meletians had the option of rejoining (*Tome* 4.1). The rhetoric of the doctrinal discussion confirms this impression: while the positions of the Eustathians were simply described as being recognized by the Meletians, the Meletians' views had to be officially sanctioned by the fathers gathered at the council (*Tome* 6.1).[89]

Nevertheless, the provisions for rehabilitation established by the *Tome* were in line with the fairly loose conditions upheld by the other councils summoned in the West, as mentioned above. As we have seen, Athanasius himself in his *Letter to Rufinian* described the deliberations of the Council of Alexandria (362) as of a piece with the rulings of those western synods. Scholarly characterizations of the Council of Alexandria as a rigorist gathering, or of the *Tome to the Antiochene* as an adamantly partisan document, appear therefore to be misguided.

We learn from Rufinus that the moderate party was not the only one represented at the council:

> Eusebius meanwhile made his way to Alexandria, where a Council of confessors gathered, few in number but pure in faith and numerous in merits [. . .]. Some fervent spirits thought that no one should be taken back into the priesthood who had in any way stained himself by communion with the heretics. But others in imitation of the apostle sought not what was advantageous to themselves but to the many [. . .].[90]

The Alexandrian deliberations concerning the Antiochene community, encapsulated by the *Tome,* show that out of the confrontation between hard-liners and moderates, the latter emerged as victorious.

Athanasius and the See of Antioch

Characterizations of the *Tome to the Antiochenes* as a rigorist document aim at showing that its only target was inducing the Meletians to join the Eustathians by submitting to harsh disciplinary and doctrinal conditions. However, a reevaluation of the sources for the council and for Athanasius's activity in 362–363 uncovers the synod's conciliatory approach to the disciplinary question of the readmission of lapsed clergy. The *Tome* is best read as a document that aimed for a rapprochement between the two pro-Nicene Antiochene communities. While it is sometimes repeated that the absence of Meletian signatories from the *Tome to the Antiochenes* proves the council's partisan orientation, I argue that envoys of the Meletian alliance may in fact have been in attendance at the council.

Doctrinally, the *Tome* ruled that it was equally legitimate to speak of one or three hypostaseis, as long as "one hypostasis" would not be given a Monarchian meaning (à la Sabellius) or "three hypostaseis" a tritheistic one (à la Arius). The document presents its own treatment of the meaning of "hypostasis" as the product of a negotiation between two ecclesio-theological parties (mia-hypostatic and tri-hypostatic), on whose beliefs an investigation was pursued (*Tome* 5.3–6.4). The mia-hypostatic party, whose positions are scrutinized in *Tome* 6.1–2, is firmly identified with the Eustathians. But at the beginning of the *Tome* Athanasius introduces two groups in quest of reconciliation:

> We are persuaded that being ministers of God and good stewards you are sufficient to order the affairs of the Church in every respect. But since it has come to us, that many (*polloi*) who were formerly separated from us by jealousy now wish for peace, while the most (*pleistoi*) also

having severed their connection with the Arian madmen are desiring our communion [. . .].[91]

The latter group, "the most" who have "severed their connection with the Arian madmen," should be identified with believers leaving Euzoius's community. These subjects do not appear again in the document. The former party, the "many" who "were formerly separated" from Athanasius's communion, are likely to be the members of the tri-hypostatic party, whom later in the document (*Tome* 5.3–4) Athanasius interrogates about their beliefs.[92] In all probability, this party needs also to be identified with those described as gathering at the Old Church of Antioch (*Tome* 3.1; *Tome* 4), and as needing to sever all ties with "Arianism" in order to be received into the fold of the mia-hypostatic, Eustathian community (*Tome* 3.1).[93] But the exact identity of this faction has long been a source of puzzlement. Were they members of the Meletian alliance? The answer to this question largely depends on untangling Athanasius's relationship to the two pro-Nicene claimants to the Antiochene see, Paulinus and Meletius, and to their respective communities.

In one of the earliest studies of the synod of Alexandria, C.B. Armstrong proposed that the council recognized the Eustathians as the only orthodox group, while merely recommending the Meletians' readmission on the most favorable conceivable terms within the boundaries of Old Nicene orthodoxy. Athanasius's position in the *Tome* allegedly differed from Lucifer's rigorist perspective, to which Armstrong also likened Eusebius's, only in that Lucifer and Eusebius were unwilling to accept even this compromise.[94] In Richard Hanson's similar evaluation, not Lucifer but Athanasius himself should be blamed for the failed reconciliation between Eustathians and Meletians: the *Tome*'s conditions showed intransigence toward Meletius and an attempt to insert a wedge between him and his followers.[95] Even more severely, Thomas Elliott construed the *Tome* as a purely sectarian Old Nicene document, through which Athanasius tried to maintain the split in the pro-Nicene community of Antioch.[96]

The question of Athanasius's intentions for the episcopal see of Antioch is central to this debate. Finding an appropriate occupant for this post must surely have been on the council's agenda. The fact that Antioch lay obviously outside of Alexandria's jurisdiction was unlikely to prevent Athanasius from maneuvering to impose a candidate capable of ensuring that the reconciliation promoted in the *Tome* would come to fruition.

The presence of Maximus and Kalemeros as representatives of Paulinus (*Tome* 9.3γ) has been read as a sign that Paulinus had already attained episcopal status by the time of the council. In fact, the canonical rule stated that representatives could be sent by bishops only, and not by mere priests. Armstrong believed that Eusebius and Lucifer had agreed to ordain Paulinus if and only if the Meletians would be amenable to that solution. When the Meletians proved resistant to persuasion, Lucifer decided to ordain Paulinus. Paulinus then sent to Alexandria his emissaries, who tricked the council into believing that reunification had been achieved.

If the *Tome* does not mention that Paulinus should be bishop, Armstrong explained, this was because its authors knew that he had already been consecrated. This reconstruction allowed Armstrong to make sense of the statement that the senders of the document rejoiced at the wish for reconciliation of those who assembled at the Old Church (*Tome* 4).[97] Armstrong also responded to an objection: had Paulinus been considered a bishop at the time of the council, he would have been cited among the addressees of the *Tome* along with the other bishops present at Antioch.[98] However, Armstrong explained, Paulinus, being already the bishop of a party, could not be a member of a conciliatory committee.

This response presents two problems. First, Rufinus, Socrates, and Sozomen all state that Eusebius learned about Paulinus's election only upon reaching Antioch from Alexandria, implying he was not informed of his episcopal status at the council.[99] Second, the phrasing of the valediction implies a distinction between, on the one hand, the relationship tying Lucifer of Calaris to his deacons and, on the other, the link that connects Paulinus to his legates:

> And similarly the other bishops who have come along subscribed, and the two deacons sent by Lucifer (*hoi apostalentes de para men Loukipheros* [. . .] *diakonoi dyo*), bishop of the island of Sardinia, Herennios and Agapetos, beside Paulinus's Maximus and Kalemeros, they themselves deacons.[100]

Herennios and Agapetos are called "the two deacons sent by Lucifer" whereas Maximus and Kalemeros are mentioned simply as being "of Paulinus." The latter designation is compatible with the status of two deacons attending in representation of a bishop-less community, headed by a priest.[101]

Scholarship, whether or not it assumes that Paulinus sent his delegates to Alexandria in his capacity as bishop, has commonly held that Athanasius's long-standing support for Paulinus's candidacy to the Antiochene episcopate was the main hindrance on the road to the Old Nicene's reconciliation with the Meletians.[102] The alliance between Athanasius and Paulinus indeed dated back over fifteen years. In 346 Athanasius, when visiting Antioch, had chosen to communicate with the Eustathians instead of Bishop Leontius, who had been heading a doctrinally heterogeneous community since 344.[103] On that occasion Athanasius had also asked Constantius to guarantee a place of worship to those staunch Nicene dissidents.[104]

On the basis of this evidence, as well as of Basil's *Letter 214* to Count Terentius, it is assumed that at the time of the council (362) Athanasius had definitively recognized Paulinus as the prospective bishop of Antioch. Nevertheless, this assumption makes it impossible to explain Basil's claim, in *Letter 89* to Meletius, that in 363 Athanasius was (still) ready to enter communion with Meletius (who refused).[105] Indeed, the assumption also makes it difficult to explain Athanasius's eagerness to have a rendezvous with Meletius. Given Meletius's stubbornness about his episcopal ambitions, this encounter would have been pointless if Athanasius had already decided about Paulinus's appointment. In reality, Athanasius's long-established communion with Paulinus does not exclude the possibility that he could have been prepared to sacrifice the episcopal ambitions of the Eustathian priest, had the creation of a broad pro-Nicene coalition been on the horizon.

In this regard it ought to be considered that while Paulinus was a mere presbyter, Meletius had already been endowed (however contestedly) with episcopal authority for a long time, and that Athanasius's relatively lax disciplinary policies likely allowed for his readmission to his rank. In spite of Athanasius's friendship with Paulinus, he must have known that the episcopal induction of a priest to the post to which Meletius had staked a claim would no doubt make a reconciliation on "rigorist" terms with the Meletians—the project commonly attributed to Athanasius's intentions—unviable. Moreover, there is no comparing the political personalities of the two churchmen and what they could respectively contribute to the Athanasian initiative of interregional unification of the pro-Nicene: while Meletius was a major ecclesiastical player with global ambitions, Paulinus at this time is not recorded to have even ever left Antioch.[106]

The fait accompli of Lucifer's consecration of Paulinus, with which neither Eusebius of Vercellae nor Athanasius was in agreement, must have played a role in Meletius's growing disinterest in a rapprochement with Athanasius and the Eustathians. The Meletians now had good reasons to consider peace talks over. Working to build an alternative pro-Nicene network to Athanasius's Old Nicene one, Meletius began to actively oppose an agreement with the Alexandrian bishop, working instead on his New Nicene project. Athanasius, on the other hand, only rejected Meletius once the celebration of the Council of Antioch in 363 and Meletius's refusal to confer with him during his Antiochene visit in that same year had made it evident that mending the pro-Nicene schism was not on the Meletian agenda.[107]

After Meletius reentered Antioch thanks to Julian's decree, he summoned there, in October or November 363, a council that affirmed the homoousios with some qualifications.[108] In the third Council of Sirmium (358) and in the Council of Seleucia (359) the homoiousians had repeatedly disavowed the homoousios, in keeping with the eastern tradition that had expressed itself in the Second Creed of Antioch (341). But Athanasius's strategy, undertaken in the mid-350s, of turning the *Nicaenum* into the centerpiece of the controversy had been too successful for Meletius to ignore.[109] At Antioch (363), twenty-four bishops and three priests from Syria, Palestine, and the broader East gave the homoousios an interpretation in accordance with their homoiousian views (arguably along the lines of what Athanasius himself had done, at his most liberal, in *On the Synods*).[110]

Bishops who had subscribed to the deliberations of the Council of Seleucia of 359 (such as Zoilos of Larissa, Eutychios of Eleutheropolis, Peter of Hippo of Palestine, and Arabianos of Antros) and the Council of Constantinople of 360 (churchmen including Eusebius of Samosata, Pelagius of Laodicea, and possibly Acacius of Caesarea) suddenly resolved to recognize the hybrid homoousian/homoiousian declaration promoted by Meletius, which disavowed the competing Old Nicene interpretation of Nicaea.[111]

The tactical squaring of the homoousios with the definition of "similar according to the ousia" (*homoios kat' ousian*) made no real doctrinal sense. In spite of its theoretical inconsistence, the innovative potential of the formula of Antioch (363) was such that it caused a real revolution within the thought system of the homoiousian alliance.[112] The Council of Antioch was hardly a sign of acceptance of Athanasius's offer of unification formulated at Alexandria (362).[113] To the contrary, Meletius's entirely political initiative took advantage of a recrudescence in radical subordinationism to reunite the pro-Nicene field under his aegis, hoping to gain the stamp of approval of the recently enthroned Emperor Jovian.

The Antiochene Events of 363

Two documents apprise us of Athanasius's feelings about the Meletian initiative of 363: the *Letter to Jovian* and the Coptic text "A" of ms. Berolinensis

11,948. Although the two texts record seemingly different sentiments, once the contexts in which they were composed are taken into account their contents can be understood as compatible.

Following the Council of Alexandria, Athanasius had been exiled for a fourth time on October 24, 362, by Julian's order.[114] The news of Julian's death (June 26, 363) was announced in Alexandria on August 9, 363. Shortly thereafter, the information reached Athanasius in his exile. Having secretly passed through Alexandria, Athanasius sailed off on September 6, 363, to meet Jovian in Antioch, eager to sway the emperor in favor of the homoousians. He found him instead in Hierapolis.[115] Possibly at Jovian's own invitation,[116] Athanasius addressed to the emperor a letter on doctrine, signed, as Theodoret informs us, by an episcopal council of fellow Egyptian travelers[117] (which had most likely gathered in Antioch).[118] Athanasius's conference with Jovian was successful: the emperor conceded that he should be reinstated on the see of Alexandria and gave him a document praising his orthodoxy.[119] Athanasius, strengthened in his power, returned to Antioch and eventually (on February 14, 364) to Alexandria.

The success of Athanasius's visit to Jovian is suggested by the failure of competing embassies that visited the emperor after his ascension to the throne. By the time of Athanasius's visit, Jovian had already received the embassy of the heteroousians Candidus and Arrianus,[120] who had reached him in Edessa. The emperor had been deaf to their pleas to refrain from lending support to Athanasius's cause.[121] A later embassy of the homoians of Alexandria, aiming to gain support through four *Petitions* for the episcopacy of their fellow partisan Lucius, met with the emperor's scorn.[122] Also the homoiousians traveled to Jovian, addressing to him in Antioch a booklet with several desiderata: the banishment of "anomoeans" from the Churches, the restoration of the faith of the Council of Seleucia, and the gathering of a new council. They were sent back without a response and implicitly chastised for their contentiousness.[123] Only Athanasius's mission was successful.

In the letter Athanasius delivered to Jovian, he opposed the interpretations of the *Nicaenum* provided by his (unnamed) Meletian opponents:

> This faith then was everywhere in every Church sincerely known and preached. But since now certain who wish to renew the Arian heresy have presumed to set at naught this faith confessed at Nicea by the Fathers, and while pretending to confess it, in fact deny it, misinterpreting the homoousios and themselves blaspheming against the Holy Spirit, in affirming that it is a creature, and came into being as a thing made

by the Son, we hasten as of bounden duty, in view of the injury resulting to the people from such blasphemy, to hand to your Piety the faith confessed at Nicaea; in order that your religiousness may know what has been written with all accuracy, and how far wrong they are who teach contrary to it.[124]

The message's tone toward Meletius's New Nicene alliance was admittedly harsh. The bishop urged the emperor not to place a group that encompassed ex-homoians—such as Acacius of Caesarea and Patrophilus of Scythopolis—in charge of orthodoxy.[125] Athanasius was clearly concerned that Meletius might assume the role of authoritative counselor to Jovian in matters of religious policy that he himself hoped to fulfill. Therefore, he attempted to place Meletius in the worst light possible. The formulations of the text, however, are not per se indicative of an uncompromising refusal of a detente with the Meletians for the sake of Nicaea.

An agreeable attitude toward the Meletians is even more clearly displayed in an Athanasian Coptic fragment, contained in the first part of the second of two surviving leaves of an otherwise lost Coptic codex.[126] This text should perhaps be identified with a fragment of the letter that according to the *Festal Index* Athanasius sent from Antioch (*Festal Letter* 36), or with an attachment to that missive.[127] It is also possible that the message is simply part of the Athanasian correspondence from Antioch.[128] The fragment reads as follows:

> . . . on many [days] . . . your remembrance. Therefore I exhort you: if they publish the writings, do not reproach anybody and do not mock those who at some point spoke while being hostile against us. For this kind of setting-right that has happened is not from you nor from men at all, but rather it is from God that it has happened. And it behooves each one to leave back to God the things that have happened from God, so that, while you appeared considerate, the grace from Him might abundantly fall back upon the Church. I am writing these things to you from Antioch. I have returned from the court, and I have seen the philanthropic king and thanked the Lord of all. Greet each other with a holy kiss [see Rom 16:16]. Those who are with me greet you, above all the bishops who have much suffered with us. I pray that you all be well together, brethren beloved and whom I love.[129]

The first lines preserved express Athanasius's discomfort with the fact that the same people who had been his enemies a short while ago were now about to publish a writing in which they would recant their previous positions. The allusion was likely to the homoiousians of homoian provenance who had partaken in the Council of Antioch (363).[130] Nevertheless, the overall message is fairly irenic toward the Meletians. The letter suggests that Athanasius was hoping for a reconciliation even after the celebration of the Antiochene synod of 363.

It is unknown whether the composition of the letter transmitted in Coptic preceded or followed Meletius's refusal to meet with Athanasius. But even Athanasius's 363 act of communion with the Eustathians, following Meletius's refusal of a meeting, does not need to be confused with a recognition of Paulinus's episcopal authority. When Epiphanius came to Antioch in 374, Paulinus had only the *Tome to the Antiochenes* to show as proof of his communion with Athanasius.[131] This suggests that until his death (373) Athanasius had never produced any written statements in support of Paulinus's episcopacy. The request to mediate with Damasus of Rome that Basil of Caesarea addressed to Athanasius in *Letters 66* and *67* (371) confirms this, as it presupposes that at that late date Athanasius had still not yet officially taken a stance against Meletius, though he persisted in his communion with the Eustathians.

The positions of the *Letter to Jovian* and of Coptic text "A" are a far cry from the views expressed in writings composed in reaction to the Antiochene synodal letter of 363 within less moderate Eustathian milieus, such as the *Refutation of the Hypocrisy of Meletius and Eusebius* and the pseudo-Athanasian *Catholic Epistle*.[132] For example, the *Refutation* rejects the Meletian reinterpretation of the homoousios as "similar according to the substance"; accuses the Council of Antioch of considering the Son created and not begotten; criticizes the historico-philosophical treatise about ousia contained in its document; and alleges that the participants in the synod reduced the Holy Spirit to a creature. None of this theological acrimony surfaces in Athanasius's two writings.

Indeed, the Council of Antioch (363) lent visibility to a rift between moderates (like Athanasius, Eusebius of Vercellae, and to some extent, in light of his subscription of the *Tome*, Paulinus) and radicals (such as Lucifer of Calaris and the authors of the *Refutation* and of *Catholic Epistle*) among the Old Nicene, a rift already precipitated by the Councils of the Thebaid (362) and Alexandria (362).[133] This breach was to come to a head institutionally fifteen years later. When, in 378, Meletius returned from the exile meted out by Valens, Paulinus refused to have him adjoined in the episcopacy. After a controversial ordination of Meletius on the part of his people in a suburban church, the Eustathian and Meletian communities reached an agreement. They pledged that whenever either of the two claimants to the episcopal see, Paulinus and Meletius, would die, none of the six candidates for episcopacy who at the moment appeared viable would make an effort to replace him. Instead, both communities would accept the surviving leader as their own. For a minority of inveterate Eustathians (possibly allied with Lucifer of Calaris) who must have already taken poorly Paulinus's subscription of the *Tome*, this was the last straw. They splintered off from Paulinus's community and created a fifth ecclesiastical party in Antioch, which came to be known as "Luciferian."[134]

This non-conciliatory attitude toward the Meletians extended beyond Antioch. Basil's *Letter* 266 to Athanasius's successor, Peter of Alexandria (373–381), dated to 377–378, testifies to a continued Alexandrian reluctance to communion with the Meletians prior to the Council of Constantinople.[135] A radically philo-Eustathian position can also be observed in the narrative of the Alexandrian *Headless History*, transmitted by the seventh-century *Codex Veronensis LX* (58). This document, dated to the last quarter of the fourth century (and possibly to Peter's episcopal tenure), may be seen as implicitly presenting Paulinus as the legitimate leader of the Antiochene Church as early as 360 (the year of Meletius's replacement by the homoian Euzoius), at a time when no such claim is even historically attested.[136]

In opposition to these sectarian tendencies, the *Letter to Jovian* and the Coptic text "A" show Athanasius in 363 still extending an olive branch to the Meletians, though it is hard to determine with how much conviction or hope. This attitude, I argue, was consistent with Athanasius's disposition toward the party of Meletius displayed in the *Tome to the Antiochenes*.

The Tome to the Antiochenes

Although the *Tome* is primarily a diplomatic document, it does go into some detail about several theological matters, including the status of the Holy Spirit and the presence of a soul in Christ. The portion of the text containing a discussion of Trinitarian matters, and particularly of the number of hypostaseis to be confessed within the godhead, corresponds to chapters 5 and 6 (the beginning of chapter 5 has already been discussed in the previous chapter of this book):

> 5. 1. And prohibit even the reading or publication of the paper, much talked of by some as having been drawn up concerning the Faith at the synod of Sardica. For the synod made no definition of the kind. For whereas some demanded, on the ground that the Nicene synod was de-

fective, the drafting of a creed, and in their haste even attempted it, the holy synod assembled in Sardica was indignant, and decreed that no statement of faith should be drafted, but that they should be content with the Faith confessed by the fathers at Nicaea, inasmuch as it lacked nothing but was full of piety, and that it was undesirable for a second creed to be promulgated, lest that drafted at Nicaea should be deemed imperfect, and a pretext be given to those who were often wishing to draft and define a creed. 2. So that if a man propound the above [paper] or any other, stop them, and persuade them rather to keep the peace. For in such men we perceive no motive save only contentiousness. 3. For as to those whom some were blaming for speaking of three hypostaseis, on the ground that the phrase is unscriptural and therefore suspicious, we thought it right indeed to require nothing beyond the confession of Nicaea, but on account of the contention we made inquiry of them, whether they meant, like the Arian madmen, subsistences foreign and strange, and alien in essence from one another, and that each hypostasis was divided apart by itself, as is the case with creatures in general and in particular with those begotten of men, or like different substances, such as gold, silver, or brass;—or whether, like other heretics, they meant three principles and three gods, by speaking of three hypostaseis. They assured us in reply that they neither meant this nor had ever held it. 4. But upon our asking them "What then do you mean by it, or why do you use such expressions?" they replied, Because they believed in a Holy Trinity, not a Trinity in name only, but existing and subsisting in truth, "both a Father truly existing and subsisting, and a Son truly substantial and subsisting, and a Holy Spirit subsisting and really existing do we acknowledge," and that neither had they said there were three Gods or three principles, nor would they at all tolerate such as said or held so, but that they acknowledged a holy Trinity but one godhead and one principle, and that the Son is coessential with the Father, as the fathers said; while the Holy Spirit is not a creature, nor external, but proper to and inseparable from the ousia of the Father and the Son.

6. 1. Having accepted then these men's interpretation and defense of their language, we made inquiry of those blamed by them for speaking of one hypostasis, whether they use the expression in the sense of Sabellius, to the negation of the Son and the Holy Spirit, or as though the Son were non-substantial, or the Holy Spirit impersonal. 2. But they in their turn assured us that they neither meant this nor had ever held it, but "we

> use the word 'hypostasis' thinking it the same thing to say hypostasis or ousia"; "But we hold that there is one, because the Son is of the ousia of the Father, and because of the identity of nature. For we believe that there is one godhead, and that it has one nature, and not that there is one nature of the Father, from which that of the Son and of the Holy Spirit are distinct." 3. Well, thereupon they who had been blamed for saying there were three hypostaseis agreed with the others, while those who had spoken of one ousia, also confessed the doctrine of the former as interpreted by them. And by both sides Arius was anathematized as an adversary of Christ, and Sabellius, and Paul of Samosata, as impious men, and Valentinus and Basilides as aliens from the truth, and Manicheus as an inventor of mischief. 4. And all, by God's grace, and after the above explanations, agree together that the faith confessed by the fathers at Nicaea is better than the said phrases, and that for the future they would prefer to be content to use its language.[137]

As seen in Chapter 2, in the beginning of the Trinitarian section the document (*Tome* 5.1–2) rejects the formula approved by the western bishops at the Council of Sardica (343). *Tome* 5.3 starts the inquiry into the two ecclesio-theological parties, which continues into the whole of *Tome* 6. At *Tome* 5.3–4 it is ascertained that the tri-hypostatic group conforms to the correct faith, through their disavowal of various heretical interpretations of their fundamental tenet. At *Tome* 6.1–2 a comparable inquiry is made into the positions of the mia-hypostatic faction. These are discovered by the interrogator to be distant from the heretical views attributed to them by their detractors.[138] At *Tome* 6.3–4, agreement between the two parties is reached.[139]

How accurately *Tome* 5–6 records the debate that took place at Alexandria remains an open question. Alberto Camplani has recognized in these sections of the *Tome* the deployment of a proleptic procedure.[140] The document describes the debate not as it occurred at the council, but as Athanasius hoped the two Antiochene parties would conduct it during future negotiations. Even if the summary of the debate in *Tome* 5–6 is proleptic, however, it is unlikely that Athanasius's reconstruction had no historical anchorage in an exchange actually held at the synod. While it is difficult to judge how reliable his account was, there is no reason to doubt the presence of some group opposing the Eustathians at Alexandria.

The *Tome* attributes to the mia-hypostatic party the following statement: "[W]e use the word 'hypostasis' thinking it the same thing to say hypostasis or ousia" (*Tome* 6.2).[141] Luise Abramowski read this affirmation as implying that the tri-hypostatic party (whom she identified with the Meletians) did otherwise, to wit, that they distinguished hypostasis from ousia.[142] As a result, she read in this affirmation a prefiguration *e contrario* of the Cappadocian solution to the Trinitarian crisis, destined to triumph at Constantinople (381) by positing—as the traditional narrative has it—the conceptual and numerical distinction between ousia and hypostasis.[143] Along similar lines, others have read in the doctrinal positions of the Meletians at the Council of Alexandria (362) a prelude to Cappadocian neo-Nicenism, later articulated by Basil of Caesarea in his *Letters 125* (of 373) and *236* (of 376).[144]

Abramowski's inference from the statement in *Tome* 6.2 relies on two unfounded assumptions. The first is that the statement needs to have been made in rhetorical opposition to some other theological posture. It is likelier that it was uttered instead with a generic intent of defense against accusations of Monarchianism.[145] The second assumption is that the theological posture the statement allegedly mirrored has to be unequivocally traced back to one particular group. It is more likely that the *Tome*'s coupling of an implicit three-hypostaseis formula with a mention of homoousios amounted to a diplomatic, atheoretical attempt at patching together two disparate theological positions.[146]

Simonetti suggested that if *Tome* 6 indeed intended to attribute a distinction between ousia and hypostasis to the tri-hypostatic party summoned to Alexandria, as Abramowski suggested, then the latter could not be identified with the Meletian alliance. As seen above, the text of the Council of Antioch (363) was going to bend the homoousios to an understanding of Christ as "similar according to the ousia" of the Father. Since similarity implies numerical distinction, Simonetti reasoned, surely the Meletians counted two separate ousiai (plural of ousia), namely the Father's and the Son's, and the mia-hypostatic party's statement of *Tome* 6.2 could not imply the opposite.[147]

In considering this argument against Abramowski's interpretation, three objections may be raised. First, we do not know whether at the time of the Council of Alexandria the Meletians were already prepared to bring the identity between the homoousios and the homoiousios to its full logical consequences. Second, "similar according to the ousia" can refer to similarity between two entities inasmuch as they share the same ousia:[148] the term "ousia" in the homoiousian formula need not be understood in a numerically discriminating sense. Therefore, the homoiousios can be reconciled with the affirmation of the unity of ousia implied by the distinction between hypostasis and ousia.[149]

Third, and most important, Camplani offers a compelling analysis, different from Abramowski's, of the reason the *Tome* attributed an acknowledgment of the homoousios to the tri-hypostatic party.[150] Athanasius, Camplani explains, was simply recording that group's formal amenability to accepting the *Nicaenum* on the basis of its traditional authoritativeness. The coupling of such acceptance with the clarification that they confessed three undivided and subsistent hypostaseis led Athanasius to translate the Meletians' position into his own theological idiom, phrasing it as an unreserved embrace of (his own interpretation of) the homoousios. The historical Meletian position at Alexandria must have been instead similar to the theology that was to be articulated at Antioch in 363. In summary, although we need to abandon the idea that the second party put forth a Constantinopolitan Creed *avant la lettre,* there is no reason to exclude the presence of a Meletian delegation at the council.

It is undeniable that Athanasius's rendition of the discussion contains at best a great deal of rewriting. The *Tome*'s inquiry into the Eustathians' views includes the characteristically Athanasian expressions *tautotēs tēs physeōs* (identity of nature)[151] and *ek tēs ousias tou patros* (from the ousia of the Father—admittedly already a Nicene phrase). His investigation also shows no occurrence of *prosōpon,* a signature term of the Eustathian alliance that Athanasius preferred to avoid.[152] Similarly, in the discussion of the tri-hypostatic party such typically Athanasian expressions as *enousios* (inherent) and *idion kai adiaireton tēs ousias* (proper and inseparable from the essence) appear.[153] This was not the first time Athanasius reproduced someone else's opinions in his own terms: in *On the Synods,* for example, he had implemented the same procedure while relating the theology of Basil of Ancyra.[154]

Still, during the debate in Alexandria Athanasius, who was acting as *dominus in domo sua,* may have easily induced the parties to take stances in relation to statements that included his preferred theological lexemes. More importantly, Athanasius may have ventriloquized in *Tome* 5–6 the participants in the debate with his own doctrinal vocabulary. The Athanasian idiosyncrasies of the document do not force us to conclude that the bishop fabricated the subjects of the debate, and even less its historical occurrence, out of whole cloth.[155]

The Meletian Signatories

Once the presence of two debating parties at Alexandria is established, the identity of the group opposing the Eustathians remains to be determined. This has proven not to be an easy task. Is it plausible that the council saw the presence of Church leaders of a non-Old Nicene orientation?[156] The possibility has been raised that the second group at Alexandria was composed of ex-homoians from Egypt, who were in communion and doctrinal consonance with the Meletian community of Antioch. These Egyptians might have acted as stand-ins for the Antiochenes. Any non-homoousian Church leaders hailing from Egypt, however, would have been Athanasius's personal local foes.[157] It is easier to imagine that the position of the Meletians was represented by members of that community, about whose precise identity we can only speculate.

The absence of any reference to Meletian envoys in the *Tome* has been seen as a serious impediment for identifying the second party with a Meletian delegation present at the Council of Alexandria. I propose that this obstacle in the documentation is not unsurmountable. Yeum suggested that Athanasius omitted the names of the Meletian participants in the council because in *History of the Arians* he had written that the heterodox should not partake in synods.[158] The point of the conciliatory disciplinary measures adopted by the Council of Alexandria, however, was precisely to readmit into communion those who had previously displayed a heterodox faith. To me it seems preferable to explain the absence of Meletian signatories through an erasure that would have occurred during the Eustathian transmission of the text. As we see later, the textual transmission of the Athanasian corpus is compatible with this hypothesis.

The doctrinal contents of the *Tome* were untroubling for the Eustathians. Paulinus himself had conditionally signed off on the acceptability of the tri-hypostatic definition upon his delegates' arrival in Antioch. In doing so, he had demonstrated that his party, taking distance from Lucifer, was moving in a moderate, nonsectarian direction. The *Tome* as a whole could, and indeed had to, be preserved in the Eustathian archives as an important historical document and a testament to continued synergy with Athanasius. But after Meletius in 363 manifested his persistent refusal of communion with Athanasius, the presumable presence of Meletian signatures in the *Tome* would become problematic for the Eustathians, who in turn refused communion with the Antiochene New Nicene.[159]

The manuscript tradition has transmitted Athanasius's works in a series of collections. Opitz and his collaborators, as well as later scholars, have created order in the massive body of manuscripts transmitting the Athanasian corpus, establishing relationships between different editions and collections of works.[160] In antiquity the Athanasian writings were organized in two big corpora, one apologetic and one doctrinal. The apologetic corpus is attested to only in one textual form, represented by a collection known as *a*, probably produced in Constantinople and dating as far back as the beginning of the fifth century.

The doctrinal corpus is preserved in multiple textual forms, represented by collections *x* (previously known as W) and *y* (previously known as RS) and by tradition *b* (known as a tradition because it does not contain a set group of Athanasian writings). Tradition *b* is also known as the "Antiochene corpus," as it was compiled in the archives of the Eustathian community in Antioch, prior to the mending of the Antiochene schism; its transmission is problematic inasmuch as it is attested with fifth-century Nestorian interpolations and late-fifth-century miaphysite corrections to the latter.[161] Collection *x* dates back to the sixth century, is also of Constantinopolitan origin, and was compiled based on Alexandrian manuscripts. This collection constituted the basis for collection *y*, an attempt, dated to 600–750, at bringing together all of Athanasius's works. Collection *y* introduces into collection *x* elements found in a late-fifth-century miaphysite revision of *b*. Finally, in the twelfth century collection *y* was supplanted by a comprehensive edition produced by Nicolas Doxopater.[162]

The *Tome to the Antiochenes* is transmitted by thirteen different manuscripts, belonging to collections *a* and *y* and to tradition *b*.[163] Ten manuscripts belong to collection *y* (mss. BKAOEFMSHG).[164] Moreover, two manuscripts attesting to the *Tome* may be traced back to tradition *b* (mss. Z and Σ).[165] Ms. Z contains the text of the *Tome* up to 9.3 and presents in the end an aberrant text, whereas ms. Σ contains a Syriac translation of the complete recension of the *Tome*, omitting the mention of the sender. Finally, one manuscript belongs to collection *a* (ms. R).[166]

The *Tome* is extant in three different recensions, for convenience called "brief," "middle," and "long." The brief recension (ms. R) cuts off at 5.3,[167] the middle recension (mss. ZΣ, respectively Greek and Syriac)[168] ends at 9.3, and the long recension (mss. BKAOEFMSHG, all belonging to collection *y*) adds 10.1–11.3. The long recension represents an Alexandrian accretion onto the recension attested by mss. ZΣ (belonging to tradition *b*), a recension on which also ms. R (belonging to collection *a*) depends. Mss. RZΣ (belonging to collection *a* and tradition *b*) are aligned on the one hand, BKAOEFMSHG (belonging to collection *y*) on the other.[169]

Σ does not report the valediction of Athanasius, limiting itself to reporting that of the brethren.[170] Z adds to Athanasius's valediction the signatures of more senders, ten of whom are specified by name.[171] The recension contained in collection *y* adds the subscriptions of the two deacons sent by Lucifer, Herennios and Agapetos, and of Maximos and Kalemeros "of Paulinus";

a mention of the presence of the monks of Apollinarius;[172] and a detailed list of the bishops previously mentioned either as senders (five) or as addressees (seventeen), along with their titles.[173] There follows a Greek translation of the Latin subscription of Eusebius of Vercellae and a copy of Paulinus's subscription. Finally, the valediction of Karterios is appended.[174]

This state of textual transmission enables the supposition that a reference to members of the Meletian alliance was originally contained in the *Tome* and was later removed as the product of a voluntary, ideological scribal omission in the archives of the Eustathian community, after the failure of negotiations between the two communities (363).[175] This hypothesis does not require assuming that there never was an exemplary of the *Tome* independently preserved at Alexandria after the council of 362, whether before or after the receipt of Paulinus's subscription. Whatever may have become of such an original document, the extant Alexandrian recension depends on the Antiochene version, as does the rest of the corpus to which the *Tome* belongs.

Comparable alterations, driven by ideological purposes, of canonical texts of then-recent composition are known to have been performed in Antioch. The Eustathian archives were a site of production of forgeries, with the creation and copying of works such as the pseudo-Athanasian *Catholic Epistle, Great Speech on Faith,* and *Epistolary with Liberius.*[176] Similarly, the reorganizers of the Antiochene archives at the time of Meletius modified the contents of the easterners' creed of Sardica (343) that is reflected both in the Latin and in the Syriac translations of the collection of documents of which this creed was part.[177]

Critics of the notion that the Meletians were present at the Council of Alexandria might point out that the profession of faith of the Council of Antioch (363) accepted only the first two of the four conditions for readmission laid out by the *Tome*: condemnation of the Arian heresy, acceptance of the Nicene Creed (which the council reinterpreted by declaring the homoousios synonymous with homoiousios), censoring of the pneumatomachians (*Tome* 3.1), and denunciation of a bevy of heretics (Sabellius, Paul of Samosata, Valentinus, Basilides, and the Manicheans) (*Tome* 3.3). If Meletian emissaries had subscribed the *Tome,* it could be objected, then they would have reneged on the latter two of the four conditions they had agreed to fulfill at Alexandria.

The Council of Antioch, however, was hardly intended for the ratification and reception of the decisions of the Alexandrian council. Rather, it was an occasion for Meletius to gain centrality on the global ecclesiastical stage in a novel political climate. The pro forma condemnation of by then quasi-irrelevant third-century heretics was not a priority on the Meletian agenda, and the question of the Holy Spirit was an increasingly raging battleground into which it was not expedient for Meletius to enter at that time. Above all, Paulinus's ordination had given the Meletians a pretext to consider the need for dialogue with the Eustathians, to which they would have been bound by their original subscription of the *Tome*, obsolete.

To summarize, in my reading the Council of Alexandria, far from being a rigorist meeting, displayed a moderate orientation in relation both to the question of the readmission of the lapsed clergy and to the reconciliation to be attained between the pro-Nicene of Antioch. There is no evidence that Athanasius ever ceased to court Meletius; in fact, the limited extant evidence (the *Letter to Jovian* and the Coptic text "A") speaks to the contrary. On the other hand, the Meletians need not have lost interest in a possible reconciliation with Athanasius until Lucifer's consecration of Paulinus. For this reason, it can be surmised that, in spite of Athanasius's long-standing allegiance to the Eustathian community, members of the Meletian alliance were in attendance in 362. The absence of their signatures from the *Tome* may be a product of purposeful omission, which could have occurred during the transmission of the document in the Eustathian archives of Antioch. Lucifer's consecration of Paulinus was likely what put an end to Meletian interest in a reunion with the Old Nicene. This reconstruction supports the genuineness of Athanasius's interest in a reconciliation of the schism between Eustathians and Meletians (the "one hypostasis" and "three hypostaseis" parties) at the time of the council.

A Battle of Formulas?

A passage of the *Tome to the Antiochenes* cited above (*Tome* 6.3) approximates an equation between the value of using the formulas "one hypostasis" and "three hypostaseis":

> Well, thereupon they who had been blamed for saying there were three hypostaseis agreed with the others, while those who had spoken of one hypostasis, also confessed the doctrine of the former as interpreted by them.

The equivalence of speaking of one or three hypostaseis is articulated with even greater clarity in Paulinus's subscription of the document:

> I, Paulinus, hold as true what I received from the fathers: that the Father exists and subsists as perfect, the Son subsists as perfect, and the Holy Spirit subsists as perfect. Hence, I accept the foregoing interpretation

> concerning the three hypostaseis, and the one hypostasis or ousia, and those who hold to it. For it is orthodox to hold and confess the Holy Trinity in one divinity.[178]

In actuality, as I argue, the two related formulas into which Athanasius condensed the discord between the Eustathians and Meletians were not representative of the essence of the disagreement between the two groups.[179]

The word "hypostasis," which lay at the center of the discussion in *Tome* 5–6, was not typical of Athanasius's vocabulary. As Xavier Morales has remarked, Athanasius's theology, while influenced by academic logic, worked largely within the matrix of inter- and intra-personal biblical metaphors, such as the Savior being Son (*hyios*) in relation to the Father (*ho patēr*). Athanasius emphasized the limits of the metaphors he used, drawn as they were from the physical cosmos, in relation to the impassibility and indivisibility of divine essence. He repeatedly claimed to reject philosophical vocabulary in favor of exclusively scriptural language or of the scriptural meanings of words that also held a philosophical significance.[180]

In three works attributed to Athanasius the word "hypostasis," is used in a technical sense, to specify the personal subsistence of a member of the Trinity: *On "All Things Have Been Committed to Me by the Father" (Luke 10:22)*;[181] the Coptic text "B" of ms. Berolinensis 11,948;[182] and the *Discourse of Salvation to the Virgins*.[183] However, the relevant passage in the commentary on the Lucan verse is most likely interpolated, and the authenticity of the other two compositions is highly disputed.[184] Evidence for whether Athanasius used the term "hypostasis" specifically to refer to the individuality of Christ remains inconclusive.

A proposal has been made that loyalty to Nicaea or to the mia-hypostatic party forced Athanasius to relinquish tri-hypostatic language.[185] After all, Alexander of Alexandria, for whom Athanasius had served as a deacon, had for similar reasons given up the mention of three hypostaseis in his confession of faith rendered to the Council of Antioch (324). However, Morales's examination of all occurrences of hypostasis (and *hyphistēmi*) in the authentic Athanasian corpus has revealed that the Alexandrian was partial to neither mia- nor tri-hypostatic theology.[186] He occasionally presented his Trinitarian views through one or the other terminological articulation but never pledged allegiance to either.[187]

The usefulness of the categories of mia-hypostatism and tri-hypostatism is debated by scholars.[188] For Lienhard, the dichotomy between one and two (later three) hypostaseis is illuminating of the fourth-century theological debates.[189] Sheltered from the influences of Origen and Tertullian, the mia-hypostatic tradition as described by Lienhard stemmed from an older Monarchian lineage and found its expression at Nicaea and Sardica.[190] Its major exponent was Marcellus of Ancyra.[191] Tri-hypostatic views found expression, instead, at the Council of Antioch of 341. Eusebius of Caesarea came closest to formulating their ideal type, centered on the coexistence of a first principle (the Father) and a subordinated, created second principle (the Son).[192]

Delineating a taxonomy different from Lienhard's, Manlio Simonetti described the mia-hypostatic tradition as a radical strand within the broad theological alliance traditionally called "Monarchian."[193] The theoretical cornerstone of Monarchianism was the defense of the divine monarchy, but its moderate side was averse only to the most divisive outcomes of tri-hypostatic theology, not to tri-hypostatism per se.

A careful reconstruction of the theological personality of Marcellus of Ancyra, the protagonist of the mia-hypostatic tradition, has led to an increasing recognition of the central role played by this Old Nicene champion in the formation of the fourth-century theological mainstream. In particular, a great deal has been gained from the emphasis placed by Lienhard on Marcellus's lasting integration into the ranks of the eastern Old Nicene alliance. By some accounts a "Constantinian" theologian, faithful to the emperor's ecclesio-political project,[194] as late as 371 Marcellus was still in communion with Paulinus, Athanasius, and likeminded bishops in Greece and Macedonia.[195]

For Marcellus, the Father's relationship to the Word resembled that between human beings and their reasoning faculty. Thus, his primary preoccupation with God's monarchy led Marcellus to drastically limit the Son's degree of independent subsistence (though not to reduce it to naught).[196] At the end of his cosmological and economic mission, Christ was to surrender his kingdom to the Father and to dwell in Him as in the beginning. The very inclusion of the Word in Marcellus's Trinitarian account may have been an attempt at a theological update, aimed at coping with the attacks of Origenist thinkers.[197]

In Antioch, several of the theological traits of Marcellus's Monarchianism were shared by the Eustathians. Eustathius, as Chapter 4 shows, upheld the notion of "one hypostasis" of the godhead (although either he or his disciples developed a more complex picture of the Son's subsistence). On the other side, evidence does not support the notion that the "three hypostaseis" phrase was central to the views of Meletius and his partisans.[198] The expression does not appear in Meletius's *Homily on Proverbs 8:22* or in his sermon

On the Sealing of the Sepulcher that has been preserved in Georgian.[199] It is also absent from the *Letter* that the Council of Antioch (363) sent to Jovian.[120] Prior to the synod of 363, the only real objection that the Meletians held regarding the creed of Nicaea concerned not its alleged mia-hypostatism, but the word "homoousios."

There is also no evidence that the number of hypostaseis was central to Eustathian grievances against the Meletians. After the publication of the *Letter* to Jovian, an anonymous author of the Eustathian communion entrusted to the *Refutation of the Hypocrisy of Meletius and Eusebius* his scathing views on that Meletian document. The core of this critique concerns the affirmation of the Son's similarity to the Father:

> The human being was generated in God's resemblance, and [yet] the human being is not God. For that which is similar to something is not the same as that to which it is similar. [. . .] Indeed the Son is not similar to God (since he is God), but rather one and the same [with him], as it has been written: "I and the Father are one" (John 10:30). And [God's own speech] has defined the unity as divinity—not a divinity like that of those who have been fashioned by God, seeing as it has opposed the one kind to the other, as God's speech has it. For he is God not like a human being who is generated in the resemblance of God and is named "God" by resemblance [and] not by nature, having the ousia made similar to God. [. . .] In like manner, then, also he who defines the homoousios as "similar with regard to the ousia" speaks of a different ousia, though one made similar to God. Accordingly, since he does not understand homoousios, he does not appropriately say that it [scil. that which is homoousios] is from the ousia [of that to which it is homoousios] like a human being [is] from the ousia of a human being. But if the Son is not from God like a human being from a human being according to the ousia, but rather by some resemblance—like a statue [is similar] to a human being or like a human being [is similar] to God—it is clear that such a person, though speaking of the homoousios, does not understand the homoousios; for he does not want to understand the homoousios according to the customary usage, that is, in relation to one and the same ousia, but rather against the customary usage.[201]

Nowhere does the *Refutation* contain any mention of the question of the number of hypostaseis. We may deduce that around 362 tri-hypostatism was a concern neither of the Meletians' nor of the Eustathians'.

Interestingly, condemnations of either mia- or tri-hypostatism are also absent from conciliar documents for over a decade prior to the Athanasian revival of the issue of the number of hypostaseis at the Council of Alexandria (362). As shown in Chapter 2, the issue had risen to prominence in the back-and-forth of conciliar documents of the 340s. The First Council of Sirmium (351), however, was the last occasion on which the question of the number of hypostaseis had found its way into a council's declaration. The documents of the 350s that in the past have been understood to harbor opposing condemnations regarding the number of hypostaseis require a different interpretation.

In 359, the westerners summoned by Emperor Constantius II to the Council of Ariminum issued a Latin document to which was appended a list of anathematisms. One of them read as follows:

> If someone speaks of one *persona* or of three separate *substantiae* of the Father, the Son, and the Holy Spirit, and does not confess the one divinity of the perfect Trinity, let it be anathema.[202]

The "one *persona*" heresy condemned is easily identified with some variety of radical Monarchianism: here the word *persona* identifies an ontological level of utmost individuation, a level on which even these pro-Nicene westerners were eager to acknowledge some plurality. By condemning "one *persona*," they were unequivocally conveying their distance from Sabellianism. The opposite denunciation of the "three separate *substantiae*" is more difficult to interpret. Simonetti read this as an explicit attack on the three-hypostaseis doctrine that was widespread in the East.[203] However, while this must have been the theological style the authors of the document meant to condemn, the text's *substantiae* cannot be back-translated into hypostaseis. The main body of the document contained—following a reaffirmation of the validity of the Nicene creed and a proscription of any doctrinal innovation—the following statement:

> We believe it to be clear that nothing must be added to or taken away from all these words [of the *Nicaenum*]. It is decreed that nothing new be undertaken and that the word and entity of *substantia*, placed inside our intellects by many holy writings, retain their validity—an entity, alongside with its word, which the Catholic Church has always confessed and professed with God-inspired doctrine.[204]

What was being defended in this passage, through use of the word *substantia*, was the legitimacy of speaking of ousia. The Second Creed of Sirmium

(357) and (less starkly) the so-called Dated Creed (or Fourth Creed of Sirmium) of May 22, 359, had prohibited use of this word, considered unscriptural, and its cognates. No such ban had been issued on hypostasis. If *substantia* carried the meaning of ousia in the body of the document, it presumably must have also done so in its anathematisms. For these reasons, the possibility has to be ruled out that the westerners at Ariminum specifically attacked the doctrine of the "three hypostaseis." Whatever their understanding was of the distinction between ousia and hypostasis (and it was likely hazy), these fathers' target was the perceived tritheistic outcome of eastern—particularly homoian—theology, which they understood heresiologically as akin to the "three ousiai" formulations found in the works of Eusebius of Caesarea and Narcissus of Neronias, early supporters of Arius.

The westerners' pro-Nicene stance did not carry the day in 359. Their delegation, moved by the emperor to Nike in Thrace and exposed there to the flatteries and threats of the anti-Nicene, resigned to subscribing a Latin declaration quite removed from their beliefs. Theodoret purports to transmit this formula, in a Greek text that coincides almost verbatim with that of the homoian Dated Creed. The only difference between the two is the addition, in the last section of Theodoret's text, of the sentences underlined below, including an attack on mia-hypostatism:

> But as for the term of "ousia," which was naively inserted by the Fathers, and, not being familiar, caused disturbance to the masses, since it is not contained in the Scriptures, we have decided should be removed and that there should be absolutely no mention of ousia for the future, because the Scriptures make absolutely no mention of the ousia of the Father and of the Son. Nor should one hypostasis be spoken of with regard to the *prosōpon* of the Father, Son, and Holy Spirit. But we declare that the Son is like the Father, as also the Holy Scriptures declare and teach. And let all the heresies which have already been previously condemned, and any others which have recently grown up opposed to the creed set out here, be anathema.[205]

We are informed that the Creed of Nike (359) was approved again at Ariminum (359). However, the text of the Creed of Ariminum transmitted in Latin by Jerome is significantly shorter than that of the Creed of Nike reported in Greek by Theodoret. Jerome's text does not include the last section just cited, which contained the disclaimer about ousia and the condemnation of "one hypostasis." His entire text runs as follows:

> We believe in one only true God, Father almighty. We believe in the only-begotten Son of God, who was born from God before all the centuries and before every beginning, alone born only-begotten from the Father alone, God from God, similar to his begetter, the Father, according to the Scriptures, whose birth nobody has known but He Who alone begot him, the Father. Who descended from heaven, was conceived of the Holy Spirit, was born from the Virgin Mary, was crucified by Pontius Pilate, resurrected on the third day, ascended to heaven, is seated to the right of the Father, will come to judge the living and the dead.[206]

In my view, it is distinctly possible that the formula recalcitrantly approved by the western fathers at Nike was the Latin text reported by Jerome as the Creed of Ariminum rather than Theodoret's Greek text (or its Latin model).[207] Vexed and besieged by the homoians, the churchmen could make any number of hermeneutical acrobatics to reconcile the clause "similar according to the Scripture" (shared by Jerome's and Theodoret's documents), which they were forced to sign, with the spirit of the Council of Nicaea. However, it is difficult to conceive that, betraying the very letter of the *Nicaenum*, they would have approved a disavowal of ousia such as the Greek text contains.

Theodoret's version of the formula of Nike is almost identical to the creed of the homoian Council of Constantinople (360) reported by Athanasius. One glaring exception lies in Theodoret's sentence "Nor should one hypostasis be spoken of with regard to the *prosōpon* of the Father, Son, and Holy Spirit."[208] In Athanasius this is transformed into "For nor should hypostasis be spoken of with regard to the Father, Son, and Holy Spirit."[209] What in Theodoret's Creed of Nike (359) was a condemnation of mia-hypostatism, in Athanasius's Creed of Constantinople (360) was a shrewd move to undermine the validity of the homoiousian Creed of Antioch (341), which made use of that term. Hypostasis was thus added to a list of words that should not be uttered when speaking about the Trinity (a list already containing ousia and its cognates).[210] It is more likely that the vector of dependence went from Athanasius's source to Theodoret's than the other way around: the document that Theodoret presents as the Creed of Nike (359) is an anti-mia-hypostatic alteration of the Creed of Constantinople (360) (which in turn was an accretion onto the Dated Creed, from which it differed only in its last section).[211]

In summary, in the past the condemnation of "one hypostasis" in Theodoret's version of the Creed of Nike has been read as a response to the westerners' putative anti-tri-hypostatic anathematism of Ariminum.[212] I propose instead that, first, at Ariminum (359) the westerners never condemned "three hypostaseis"; second, at Nike (359) "one hypostasis" was not mentioned; third, the mention of "one hypostasis" in Theodoret's "Creed of Nike" was the product of an intervention on the Creed of Constantinople (360); fourth and last, talk of hypostasis was banned at Constantinople (360) not in reference to any real-life confrontation between mia- and tri-hypostatic supporters, but to invalidate the basic document of the homoiousian party. If accepted, this reconstruction allows us to appreciate more fully the originality of Athanasius's gesture in the *Tome*. His handling of one and three hypostaseis at the Council of Alexandria (362) can be understood as the intentional resurrection of a problem that, after being prominent in the 340s, had faded into obscurity, last emerging in conciliar documents eleven years prior, at the First Council of Sirmium (351).

The Novelty of the Tome

Mia-hypostatism and tri-hypostatism no doubt existed before their discussion in the *Tome to the Antiochenes*. Nevertheless, prior to 362 these two notions were not yet the stand-ins for the entire theological traditions of the Eustathians and the Meletians into which the *Tome* transformed them. It was Athanasius who reduced the ecclesiastical and theological conflict that was besetting the pro-Nicene field into a confrontation between two related and comparable formulas. Athanasius's genius shines in the *Tome* through his decision to represent the alleged quibbling over the number of hypostaseis as the only obstacle standing in the way of reconciliation between essentially compatible varieties of pro-Nicenism.

Eustathians and Meletians represented two incommensurable traditions of thought. Eustathianism was an idiosyncratically Antiochian tendency: rather than by ardent devotion to the "one hypostasis" formula, the identity of Paulinus's acolytes was marked by adamant loyalty to the memory of their local hero and stalwart defender of Nicaea, Eustathius. Meletius and his followers, on the other hand, belonged to a wider, more cosmopolitan eastern alliance, including bishops of many locales and operating on a broader geo-ecclesiological stage, in cooperation with eastern homoiousian Church leaders.

The difference between these groups—each endowed with its own set of doctrines, practices, and rules for the transmission of knowledge—could hardly be reduced to a dispute over an objective point of disagreement such as the number of hypostaseis. In summarizing their theological trajectories into two formulas, Athanasius harnessed the processes of research for logical and lexical commensurability analyzed in Chapter 2. Once Eustathian and Meletian theologies were both apprehended in terms of hypostasis, they could be reduced to two related and therefore more easily negotiable bywords.

In the narrative of the *Tome*, the thorough questioning of the two parties allowed them to overcome a marginal difference, leading to substantial agreement. The identification of the problem of one versus three hypostaseis as the crux of the divergence between Eustathians and Meletians was no minor sleight of hand. Athanasius gave a fictitious representation (the divergence over the number of hypostaseis) to a real problem (the difference between two theological traditions as a whole) and offered a creative solution—though a formally nonsensical one—by positing the equivalence between one and three hypostaseis.

Though the product of a masterstroke on the part of its author, the *Tome* was of course not a deus ex machina, but rather a document wherein a more diffused dynamic could be observed. It ultimately embodied the transition from the confrontation between geo-cultural theological traditions such as those outlined by Ayres, differing from one another in their epistemological presuppositions and intellectual procedures (what Ayres terms their "theological grammar"), to the global exercise of disagreement over mutually intelligible and recognizable phrases. The theological discipline that was taking shape was based on the expression of different positions operating on the same conceptual level. The phrases into which the traditions were distilled could be more easily represented and negotiated, facilitating processes of identification, labeling, grouping, and contraposition.

These innovations manifested a tendency congruent with Athanasius's moving of the homoousios to the center of the debate with his *On the Decrees of the Nicene Synod* (355/356), and with the development of an emphasis on exactitude (*akribeia*) within the Trinitarian debates. The transformation of Nicaea into the touchstone of orthodoxy around the year 355 imposed new limits on the debate and forced all parties to reckon with its formulation.

Scholars have debated the direction in which influence ran in the theological developments of the 350s. Was the Athanasian privileging of homoousios a reaction to the rising tide of homoianism and to the increased emphasis on the Son's unbegottenness by anti-Nicene theologians?[213] Or, vice versa, was the heteroousian insistence on the precision of language a response to pro-Nicene resolve to focus on the defense of one particular formula? Interestingly, Athanasius appeared to present matters in the latter terms when he self-defensively argued in *On the Decrees* that the "Arians" themselves had created before the pro-Nicene a term (*agen[n]ētos*) that was not scriptural, and which they held up as the standard of correct belief.[214]

According to Richard Vaggione, Athanasius "by allowing some flexibility in technical language [. . .] was able to reach out to Meletius and others who shared a similar narrative theology, and to give homoousios that 'healthful' sense which would allow it to become the symbol of a comprehensive settlement."[215] The laxity in technical language that Athanasius granted in the *Tome* was an expression of the same focus on terminology that produced Eunomius's precision. The events of the 350s and 360s inaugurated a theological climate invested in the generation of signifiers that would allow for the recombination of wide ideological camps and geographically based intellectual traditions.

These processes advanced the Trinitarian debates. As mentioned earlier, the Alexandrian Council has been seen as a crucial turn on the winding path to Constantinople. In particular, the *Tome*'s attribution of the identification of ousia and hypostasis to the Eustathians has been understood as adumbrating, by opposition, the distinction between the two concepts that would be drawn by Basil of Caesarea. Others have countered with good arguments this interpretation of Alexandria (362) as a prefiguration of Constantinople (381). Nonetheless, the *Tome to the Antiochenes*, in spite of the immediate failure to meet its goals, did offer an important contribution to the Trinitarian disputes. During the decade prior to the Council of Alexandria, the notion of hypostasis had been at the margins of the controversy. After the Council of Alexandria (362), this category began to again move to center stage.

As a result, the controversies were reconfigured as a debate about the ontological level on which the bar of Christ's self-standing should be set. Did he possess just a separate *energeia* (as Marcellus believed), a distinct *prosōpon* (à la Eustathius), a different hypostasis (as Eusebians and homoiousians thought), or his own ousia (as claimed by the heteroousians)? This development highlighted the link between the articulation of the Son's individuality and singularity/multiplicity within the godhead. A conversation was sparked about the numerical definition of these technical terms, to wit, whether one or three of each (including hypostaseis) should be confessed.

The disambiguation of ousia and hypostasis in the works of the New Nicene was not a preordained logical outcome driving the course of the controversy. Actors in controversies produce the categories that enable their mutual understanding and eventually the resolution of the dispute. The *Tome* retrieved the question of the number of hypostaseis (which, prominent in the 340s, had lost prominence in the 350s) and connected it to the need for a distinction between hypostasis and ousia. In the Trinitarian controversies, efforts of reconceptualization and lexical clarification of hypostasis sharpened as a result of its selection on the part of Athanasius as a key to solve the Antiochene schism.

4 • Ortholalia

The Negotiation of Formulas in the 370s

Correct Speech in Derogation from Truth

In the first of his *Provincial Letters* (1656), Blaise Pascal offered a fictionalized account of the fierce controversy between the Jansenists and their detractors. The narrator, Louis de Montalte, tells the reader about his attempts to grasp the difference between different ways of conceiving the role of God's grace in human salvation. At first, de Montalte says, he identified the bone of contention in the Jansenist statements that "grace is given to all" and that "grace is effectual and determines our will to do good." Soon, however, he was disabused of this conviction by an anti-Jansenist theologian. The reason the Jansenist Antoine Arnauld was undergoing interrogation at the Sorbonne, the theologian informed him, was his failure to acknowledge "that believers have the power of fulfilling the commandments of God."

But a Jansenist consulted by the narrator denied disagreeing with that affirmation. The anti-Jansenist theologian instructed a by-now-puzzled de Montalte that the Jansenists refused to call that universally bestowed power of fulfilling the commandments "proximate." In that refusal, he explained, lay the crux of the dispute. Nevertheless, in a new questioning of the Jansenists de Montalte learned that the Molinists, the Jansenists' opponents, harbored within their ranks people holding two contrasting interpretations of the "proximity" of that power. One of these conceptions aligned perfectly with the Jansenists' own. As his Jansenist informant put it,

> "So far are [the Molinists] from being united in sentiment that some of them are diametrically opposed to each other. But, being all united in

the design to ruin M. Arnauld, they have resolved to agree on this term 'proximage,' which both parties might use indiscriminately, though they understand it diversely, that thus, by a similarity of language and an apparent conformity, they may form a large body and get up a majority to crush him with the greater certainty."[1]

De Montalte was determined to get to the bottom of this question. Conferring next with a free will advocate, a Molinist disciple of one Monsieur le Moine, de Montalte was told that the "proximate power" of doing something was the same as having "all that is necessary for doing it in such a manner that nothing is wanting to performance." But when he paid a visit to a different, neo-Thomist opponent of the Jansenists, he heard a different story altogether. De Montalte asked his interlocutor:

> "[I]f anything is wanting to that power, do you call it proximate? Would you say, for instance, that a man in the night-time, and without any light, had the proximate power of seeing?" "Yes, indeed, he would have it, in our opinion, if he is not blind." "I grant that," said I; "but M. le Moine understands it in a different manner." "Very true," they replied; "but so it is that we understand it." "I have no objections to that," I said; "for I never quarrel about a name, provided I am apprised of the sense in which it is understood. But I perceive from this that, when you speak of the righteous having always the proximate power of praying to God, you understand that they require another supply for praying, without which they will never pray." "Most excellent!" exclaimed the good fathers, embracing me; "exactly the thing; for they must have, besides, an efficacious grace bestowed upon all, and which determines their wills to pray; and it is heresy to deny the necessity of that efficacious grace in order to pray." "Most excellent!" cried I, in return; "but, according to you, the Jansenists are Catholics, and Monsier le Moine a heretic; for the Jansenists maintain that, while the righteous have power to pray, they require nevertheless an efficacious grace; and this is what you approve. Monsier le Moine, again, maintains that the righteous may pray without efficacious grace; and this is what you condemn." "Ay," said they; "but Monsier le Moine calls that power 'proximate power.'" "How now! fathers," I exclaimed; "this is merely playing with words, to say that you are agreed as to the common terms which you employ, while you differ with them as to the sense of these terms." The fathers made no reply.[2]

De Montalte's exasperated cry ("How now!") in the midst of this excited exchange was an understandable response to the revelation of one of the main devices through which Christian orthodoxy works: ortholalia, or emphasis on terminological correctness.[3] Though rarely discussed as such by ancient Christian authors, the insistence on theological terminology had its roots in late antiquity. The ortholalic device played an integral role in the progressive abandonment of purely zetetic (i.e., inquiry-centered) modes of theological discourse.[4] Harnessing the support of political power, dogmatization led to the late ancient formation of orthodoxy as a stable theoretically and socially operative category.

In times of controversy, formulas used to confess the correct theological opinion can function as more than just a gateway to the truth. They may also serve as an instrument to promote, in disregard of what the debaters know to be the correct belief, the grouping and regrouping of different ecclesiastical parties around a credal statement, with the purpose of contrasting a "heretical" belief. As seen in the previous chapter, the *Tome to the Antiochenes* decreed that speaking of one or three hypostaseis was inconsequential as long as "one hypostasis" would not have a Monarchian meaning, or "three hypostaseis" a tritheistic one. In issuing this proclamation, this document exploited the inclusive power of ortholalia. The two parties were invited to conditionally endorse each other's language by understanding it within their own doctrinal framework. With some provisos, either signifier could be legitimately used without prejudice to truth. Never mind that this solution was devoid of theological substance, as what was signified by the signifier "one hypostasis" was conceptually exclusive of that to which "three hypostaseis" pointed. Just like the Molinists, united despite differences by opposition to Antoine Arnauld, pro-Nicene of different stripes were bound together, at least in Athanasius's wishful imagination, by their opposition to the Eusebians.

This chapter offers a case study in the dynamics of ortholalia. It shows that the reduction of doctrine to formulas, far from enforcing a closure on theological speech, opened up novel types of intellectual exchange. Within a more complexly regulated theological environment, Christian elites' transaction of words still thrived. The dialectical productivity of ortholalia as a discursive device is concretely observed in its effects of reconfiguration on ecclesio-political alliance within the theological debate.

The case study pursued here focuses on the history of effects of a phrase, contained in a fragment attributed to Eustathius of Antioch. The expression under consideration, "subsistent person" (*prosōpon enhypostaton*), offered an innovative terminological solution to a crucial problem: Which degree of substantiality should be attributed to the Son, and how could this degree be correctly expressed? As seen in previous chapters, these were the questions into which the original discussions about Christ's way of being begotten and coeternality to the Father had come to be reformulated. Different actors in the disputes were receptive to the adoption of the phrase *prosōpon enhypostaton*, giving rise to negotiations over the formula and eventually leading to the creation of significant areas of compromise or principled defection between the Old and the New Nicene alliances.[5]

The Theology of Eustathius of Antioch

The expression "subsistent person" is contained in a fragment identified as coming from *Against Photinus* (Fragment 142). In this work, Eustathius or one of his disciples writing in his name had to fend off accusations of polytheism coming from radical Monarchians. Eustathius himself was known as a staunch advocate of the unity of the godhead. Whether or not this fragment was authored by Eustathius, its contents show that his legacy exceeded the defense of "one hypostasis," which the *Tome to the Antiochenes* has handed down as his followers' signature *theologoumenon*.

Born in Side (Pamphylia) sometime between 275 and 300, Eustathius made a name for himself as a confessor during the Diocletianic or Licinian persecutions.[6] He was bishop of Beroea (in Coele Syria, modern-day Aleppo)[7] until a synod led by Ossius called him to succeed Philogonos on the Antiochene see after the latter's death in 324.[8] In 325 he partook in—and possibly presided over—the Council of Nicaea, but in 327–328 he fell victim to the anti-Nicene reaction. In particular, Eusebius of Nicomedia began to scheme against Eustathius, who had contributed to his downfall. Deposed possibly on counts of Sabellianism or, as Athanasius reports, for groundless allegations of immorality,[9] Eustathius was exiled to Thrace and replaced in his see by one of his opponents. Even from exile, Eustathius continued to unwaveringly defend the Nicene homoousios. His Antiochene followers refused for a long time, as seen in the previous chapter, to compromise with the partisans of Meletius.

Eustathius was the author of at least fifteen works in addition to some *Discourses* against Eusebius of Caesarea and a series of *Letters*.[10] His only extant complete writing is the exegetical treatise *On the Belly-Myther of Endor, against Origen*. All of his other compositions are preserved only fragmentarily, excerpted by later authors who cover a chronological span going from John

Chrysostom in the fourth century to Bar ʿEbroyo in the thirteenth.[11] In spite of this poor transmission, Eustathius commanded the interest of many ancient writers of diverse theological orientations.[12] The author who quoted Eustathius most liberally was Theodoret of Cyrrhus, to whom we owe the transmission of forty-one of the excerpts deemed authentic.[13]

Eustathius is remembered in the acts of the second Council of Nicaea (787) as "the unwavering warrior of the true belief and dissolver of the Arian demonic evil."[14] His fame as a staunch advocate of the unity of the godhead and opponent of any sort of theological subordinationism was well deserved.[15] Many of his anti-subordinationist writings date from the years around Nicaea.[16] His influence on the council itself is often cited as great. Sara Parvis credits him for some of the crucial doctrinal points of the *Nicaenum*. These included the expression "begotten, not made" (*gennēthenta ou poiēthenta*),[17] the replacement of the expression "Logos of God" (found in the creed of Eusebius of Caesarea) with "Son of God,"[18] and the substitution of "one Holy Spirit" (*hen pneuma agion*) with "the Holy Spirit" (*to pneuma agion*).[19] Alastair Logan suggested that Eustathius influenced the Council of Nicaea regarding the distinction its creed drew between "begetting" (*gennēma*) and "creature" (*ktisma*).[20]

According to the traditional reading, Eustathius was a Monarchian à la Sabellius, and a conservative element within the pro-Nicene movement.[21] Eustathius's fragments do bear witness to the mia-hypostatic character of his Trinitarian thought. This is the case, for example, with the following passage (preceded by its lemma), cited by Severus of Antioch in his *Letter 3* to Sergius the Grammarian. Here the presentation of the Father-Son dyad is resolved back into the unicity of the hypostasis of the godhead:

> It is time for us to profess also the holy Trinity as (made out) of one hypostasis. For we find that Eustathius of blessed memory, he who was Bishop of Antioch, in the *Commentary on the Ninety-Second Psalm* professed in these terms the Father and the Son to be of one hypostasis:
>
> "While both invisibly work wonders at the very same time, oftentimes the divine Scriptures ascribe the greatness of their action to one, for they on the one hand introduce duality out of singularity, on the other proclaim singularity out of duality, by virtue of the fact that there exists one hypostasis of the godhead."[22]

Some fragments give the impression of a certain lack of dynamicity, typical of Monarchianism, in Eustathius's triadic understanding of the divine. In a passage contained in *On the Belly-Myther of Endor, against Origen*, for example, Eustathius writes:[23]

> But here [scil. in Deut 13:11], presenting the dyad of the Father and of the only-begotten Son, it defined one as the Lord who tests, and the other, alongside this one, [it showed] to be the beloved Lord and God, so as to demonstrate out of a dyad the one divinity and the true theogony.[24]

At the same time, other bits of Eustathius's writing, such as the following Syriac fragment, articulate a cosmogonic role for the Son:

> For if the God-Word[25] took inception from the birth, by passing through the womb of a virgin and wearing the frame of the body, it has been proven true that he came into being from a woman (Gal 4:4). If, however, the Word is God since the beginning beside the Father (see John 1:1–2), and we say that everything came into being through him (see John 1:3), [then] he did not come into being from a woman (Gal 4:4), inasmuch as it is he who is the cause of everything. However, the one who was fashioned in the Holy Spirit came into being from a woman.[26]

In the following passage, drawn from *Against the Ariomaniacs and on the Soul*, Eustathius discusses in no uncertain terms the saving action of "the Child of God":

> Certainly, therefore, in the transgression of the protoplast sin's death fell in, great and fatal. But the child of God, having providently resolved to punish the devil, begetter of death, by means of the human being of the same race, bore that same whole human being after fastening himself to the divine frames, so that [the child of God], having defeated the evil one, might provide incorruptible life.[27]

On the basis of similar passages, Loofs identified in Eustathius's Logos a certain degree of subsistence, due to its soteriological action.[28] It is undeniable that Eustathius did not conceive of the Son as a mere energy or power of the Most High. Nonetheless, Loofs's evaluation might go too far. Between his almost Logos-theological reading and the traditional quasi-Sabellian interpretation of Eustathius's Trinitarianism, Michel Spanneut struck a perceptive middle ground. Spanneut admitted that Eustathius's articulation of the unity of the hypostasis into the action of a duality is a purely "scholastic" movement of thought, by which he appeared to mean a merely logical solution. On the other hand, he emphasized that Eustathius's Christ, called in the extant excerpts "Word," "Son," and "truly begotten," is no mere impersonal attribute of the deity.[29] Fragment 142 from *Against Photinus*, presented below, attests to a theological development consonant with these more personalizing aspects of the Eustathian tendency. This holds true whether the work was authored by Eustathius or one of his followers.[30]

(Pseudo-?)Eustathius of Antioch's Fragment 142

José H. Declerck declared Eustathius's Fragment 142 spurious. Arguments based on chronology,[31] theological contents,[32] and philology have been employed to challenge its Eustathian authorship. The issue is not settled. Of the three kinds of arguments, the most insidious are those based on the resemblance between *Against Photinus* and the abrupt incipit—as well as other bits—of *To the Hellenes*, a treatise attributed to Gregory of Nyssa.[33] Though limited, the parallels between the two texts are striking.[34]

Both the *Sitz-im-Leben* and date of composition of *To the Hellenes* are uncertain.[35] Reinhard Hübner suggested that its extant text form constitutes the abridged version of an original work of Gregory's. In this composition, Hübner proposed, the Nyssen intentionally used Old Nicene terminology and adopted anti-tritheistic postures. He did so to attract the Eustathians toward the Cappadocian pro-Meletian alliance, while covering his flank against accusations of Monarchianism through anti-Photinian rhetoric. The terminological and ideological proximity of the treatise to Old Nicene positions would explain its later Eustathian, possibly pseudo-epigraphic circulation. Indeed, Arianism and Sabellianism, normally anathematized as equally dangerous extremes by Gregory, make no appearance in this treatise.[36] Rudolf Lorenz argued instead that it was Gregory who used *Against Photinus*, a work of Eustathius's which he dated to 344–345.[37] Accused of Sabellianism, Eustathius had felt the need to emphasize the triadic element of his theology; the exile to Thracia and the conflict with Photinus of Sirmium (in nearby Pannonia) had given him an opportunity to do so.[38]

Fragment 142 is cited in the tripartite treatise *Against Damian* written around 588 by the miaphysite patriarch of Antioch Peter of Callinicus (581–591).[39] Shortly after 585, Peter had found himself engaged in a heated polemic against his fellow anti-Chalcedonian (as well as fellow Syrian) Damian, the Coptic Orthodox patriarch of Alexandria (578–605). Damian had been asked to refute a series of chapters composed by tritheistic theologians.[40] Tritheists saw the difference of hypostaseis as corresponding to one of natures, ousiai, and godheads. Faithful to the distinction between first and second ousia that John Philoponus had inherited from Aristotelian thought, tritheist theology saw the divinity that all members of the godhead shared as more of a cognitive construct than a substance of any kind. The *Treatise against the Tri-theists* that Damian of Alexandria composed to rebut the views of these theologians was found deficient in its Trinitarian formulation by Peter of Callinicus, who reacted with a treatise *Against Damian*. This exchange closely resembles that between Eustathius of Antioch and Eusebius of Caesarea in the immediate aftermath of Nicaea.[41] Peter considered Damian a Sabellian, while Damian accused Peter of professing three Gods.[42]

The Eustathian fragment embedded in Peter of Callinicus's argument in *Against Damian* reads as follows:[43]

1. Maurinus, i.e., Photinus, along with his likeminded ones, libels us as though we called the Father, the Son, and the Holy Spirit three Gods, whereby he acts foolishly along with them; for, had we simply said "God and God and God," rightly would they have accused us of declaring three Gods. But if it is the truth and a logical thing for us to call the Father "God," the Son "God," [and] the Holy Spirit "God," nevertheless by [using] the [word] "God" we are not saying three by virtue of division. Even though God is professed of each subsistent person by virtue of their belonging to the one and the very same divine nature, nonetheless in "Father, Son, and Holy Spirit" we recognize a fellowship, a property, and their mutual unity of nature.[44]
2. Therefore if the name of "God" were the marker of a person, [then] by saying three persons, we would by all means also be saying three Gods. But since [the name] is a marker of nature, as it is taken from some property pertaining to a nature like laughter to the human being and barking to the dog—the properties that are said to pertain to natures are markers of natures—we do not say three Gods because we do not say three natures.[45]
3. But if we call "God" each of the persons of the divine nature by virtue of its pertaining to the same nature known [as] the name of God when it is used in the proper sense—"God" not being the marker of a person but belonging to one nature—it is then possible also for the person to be called with this appellation, since it, too, pertains to that nature.[46]
4. For one thing is the person, and another one the nature. Therefore, if divinity pertained to the person, as we profess three persons we would

by all means be saying also three Gods. But, since it pertains to nature, as we profess one nature of the persons, by necessity do we profess that God is only one.[47]

5. If there exists one nature, and divinity pertains to nature, from our professing one nature there follows also that we profess God to be one.[48]
6. As for this nature, whose name is "God," we understand that it always manifests itself in three persons, without being diminished by the absence of a person nor enriched by the addition of a person.[49]

In response to Photinus's accusation of tritheism, the author of the treatise clarified that designating each person as God does not entail a partition within the godhead. The Father, the Son, and the Holy Spirit partake in the same nature (*kyānā, physis*). The nature of the godhead is signified by a name (*šmā, onoma*) and identified based on a set of properties (*dilāyātā, idia*): the name "God" denotes, and divinity inheres to, not each of the persons, but rather the nature they share. When applied to this nature, this name is used in the proper sense (*mārānā ʾit, kyriōs*); when applied to each of the three individual persons (*parṣope qnomāye*), it is still legitimately employed, but only as an appellation (*kunnāyā, prosēgoria*). Each of the three persons is God and may be called such insofar as it shares in the one and same divine nature.

According to Lorenz, the fragment fails to articulate a fully Trinitarian doctrine. The relationship between unity and triadicity is merely entrusted to the eternal manifestation of the one nature of God in three persons. No consideration is given to the unfolding of Christ's action through the history of salvation. The only difference with the views of the Council of Sardica, thus, would lie in the fragment's deployment of a logic of peripatetic origin—whereby each of the persons is reduced to an accident—with the aim of escaping the contrasting accusations of Sabellianism and tritheism.[50] Manlio Simonetti assessed the fragment in a similar way. He felt its conception of *prosōpon* to be consistent with Eustathius's known Monarchianism: the persons are devoid of real substance and identified with signifying properties.[51] In reality this interpretation, based on the passage's mention of a human's laughter and a dog's barking, is unsupported by the text: what the fragment reduces to an individual property is not the difference between the three persons, but the appellation "God" as shared by each of the three persons.[52]

Van Roey back-translated *parṣopā qnomāyā* into *prosōpon hypostatikon* (*persona hypostatica* in Latin), which he described as an anti-Sabellian phrase.[53] In my opinion, *parṣope qnomāye*[54] should be retranslated not into *prosōpa hypostatika*, which would be a *hapax legomenon*, but into the attested expression *prosōpa enhypostata* ("substantial persons").[55] Fragment 142 retains the Eustathian concept of the existence of one sole hypostasis in the godhead. However, in preserving the individuality at the level of the *prosōpon*, the text enriches this entity's substantiality through an adjective built on *qnomā*, meaning "hypostasis" (a meaning it holds, e.g., in the works of Ephrem).[56]

The terminology deployed in Fragment 142 does not directly contradict any of the contents of the certainly genuine fragments we possess of Eustathius's work. Nevertheless, Fragment 142 articulates the substantiality of the three persons of the Christian Trinity in significantly starker terms than anywhere else. This has led to doubts about Eustathius's authorship of the fragment. Its attribution of substantiality to the *prosōpon* is all the more notable—whoever its author is—if we consider its rhetorical context. In a polemic against the radical Monarchian Photinus, the author of the fragment would have been expected to downplay, rather than emphasize, the aspects of Eustathian doctrine that would have exposed him most gravely to accusations of tritheism.

As a product of the ortholalic dynamic displayed by the Council of Alexandria, a novel vocabulary was put in place in Old Nicene milieus. The expression *prosōpon enhypostaton* entered a discussion about the terminological articulation of the relationship between unity and multiplicity within the godhead. Whether this expression came from Eustathius's own quill or was contrived by a fourth-century theologian working within the Eustathian tradition (the fact that from the fifth century on the only theological use of the term *enhypostatos* is Christological as opposed to Trinitarian protects the fragment from suspicions of later fabrications or interpolations), its invention contributed to the creation of a progressive area of compromise within the mia-hypostatic alliance.[57] As we see in the next section, its employment widened the gap between the mia-prosōpic and tri-prosōpic perspectives within this group, while reducing the distance that separated the tri-prosōpic faction from the Meletians. This doctrinal shift resulted in significant institutional reconfiguration.

Prosōpon Enhypostaton

Greek Trinitarianism never gave the term *prosōpon* the perspicuity that Latin theology attributed to *persona*. It might indeed have been the theological usage of *persona* that led to that of *prosōpon*, rather than the other way around.[58] No Trinitarian usage of *prosōpon* is attested with any certainty before the middle of the third century. The first occurrence in a Trinitarian context appears in Origen's *Commentary on the Song of Songs*:

> But those same [mountains] that are called here "high mountains," in the plural, in other [places] are called "high mountain," in the singular, as Isaiah says: "Go up on a high mountain, O you who bring good news to Zion. Raise your voice with strength, you who bring good news to Jerusalem" (Isa 40:9). For that same one which (is understood) there as the Trinity because of the distinction of persons, is here understood as the only God for the unity of substance [*pro unitate substantiae*].[59]

The authenticity of this passage is maintained by some[60] and denied by others, who attribute it to Rufinus because of the seemingly Nicene nature of its phrasing.[61] Unfortunately the excerpt is not preserved among the extant Greek fragments of Origen's *Commentary*. In light of what is known of Rufinus's lax translation practices, and in particular of the liberty with which the Aquileian monk treated the Greek original of the *Commentary on Song of Songs*, skepticism is warranted.[62] The same caution should be applied to a passage of Origen's *Commentary on the Letter to Titus* in which the author censures the mia-prosōpism of the Sabellians, and where *prosōpon* is almost certainly the basis for *persona*.[63]

The works of Clement of Alexandria and others contain the idea that the Logos constitutes God's face inasmuch as it provides a revelation of Him.[64] At other times it is the Holy Spirit that is called a *prosōpon* of God.[65] The first attestation of the word in a specifically binitarian sense goes back to its anti-Monarchian use in Hippolytus's *Against Noëtus*.[66] Tertullian, in *Against Praxeas*, similarly spoke of three *personae*, likely translating the Greek word *prosōpa*.[67] On the opposite end of the Trinitarian spectrum, the Monarchian Callixtus of Rome wrote about God's one *prosōpon*.[68] Hippolytus, Gregory of Nazianzus, John Chrysostom, and John of Damascus all agreed that the Sabellians held mia-prosōpic views; it is likely that Sabellius himself used the expression "one *prosōpon*."[69]

Eusebius of Caesarea is the first to offer greater detail, in reporting that the Sabellians spoke of a tri-prosōpic hypostasis.[70] Prestige considered the phrase a Eusebian gloss and not a citation from Marcellus. Similarly, he saw polemical editorializing rather than faithful citations in Basil of Caesarea's references to the weak tri-prosōpism of the Sabellians, who allegedly acknowledged three *prosōpa* but saw them as theatrical masks.[71] Unlike his fellow Cappadocians, who used *prosōpon* interchangeably with hypostasis, Basil drew a clear distinction between the two terms. At the same time, he located both on the side of plurality (in opposition to ousia, situated on the side of unity): "For it does not suffice to enumerate the differences of persons, but rather it is necessary to confess that each person exists in a true hypostasis."[72] Over the course of Basil's career, a progression of stricture can be observed in his use of the term. He eventually came to see *prosōpon* as contaminated by Sabellianism and in need of qualification, such as the association with perfection or with true subsistence.[73]

According to Prestige there is no evidence for the orthodox discreditation of *prosōpon* at any point: the term was used, contrariwise, as a "non-technical and non-metaphysical expression" for the forms assumed by the divine persons.[74] Simonetti opined otherwise: since the term was never completely detached from its original sense of "appearance," it was perceived as less apt to express subsistence than was hypostasis. Origen's own avoidance of *prosōpon* may indicate a rejection of the concept as denoting too insubstantial a reality.[75] As a result, once hypostasis gained widespread usage as a way to indicate personal subsistence, the plural *prosōpa* began to be used by those looking for a middle ground between mia-prosōpic, mia-hypostatic Sabellianism, on the one hand, and tri-hypostatic Origenism, on the other.[76]

The term "hypostasis," upon which the adjective *enhypostatos* in the formation *prosōpon enhypostaton* is compounded, had been used in writings both philosophical and otherwise for a long time before being taken up by Christian authors.[77] The word makes an appearance in the New Testament (Heb 1:3). Origen introduced it into Christian theology to affirm the separate subsistence of the Father and the Son. He did so in writing against those Christians who were so preoccupied with the defense of the divine monarchy that they denied the substantiality of their respective existence. Origen drew no distinction between hypostasis and ousia. In using the term "hypostasis," he intended to indicate that the Father and the Son are separate not only in thought, but also in actuality.[78] Since then, hypostasis had become part of common theological parlance.

The term *enhypostatos*, understood in dichotomous opposition to *anhypostatos*, would come to assume a central role in Christological discussions during the remainder of late antiquity and the Middle Ages.[79] It may have been Origen himself who coined the term, considering its appearance in fourth-century texts revealing an Origenist influence. Leaving aside texts spuriously attributed to Irenaeus and Origen,[80] the expression is attested in two likely authentic fragments of Origen's works. Only in one of them is *enhypostatos* used in a binitarian technical sense.[81] In this passage, drawn from a catena on Proverbs, Origen distinguishes between the wisdom that is bestowed on believers by the Holy Spirit and true Wisdom, the "subsistent Son and Word of God."[82] Both the sole occurrence of *substantialis* and some of the several occurrences of *substantivus* in the Latin versions of Origen's work are likely translations of *enhypostatos*.[83] In particular, Gleede sees in Origen's reassurance to the effect that "the only-begotten Son of God is His substantially subsistent Wisdom" (*unigenitum filium dei sapientiam eius esse substantialiter subsistentem*) the translation of a phrase containing *enhypostatos*,[84] which would constitute a parallel to the Greek fragment from the catena on Proverbs.[85]

The presence of *enhypostatos* makes unlikely Irenaeus's authorship of a fragment in which Christ is called "veracious type of the Logos *enhypostatos*."[86] However, the term is attested in a binitarian framework in the third-century *Letter of Hymenaeus*, the main source for the deposition of Paul of Samosata,[87] as well as in fourth-century works that place an *enhypostatos logos* alongside or in opposition to the famous pair *endiathetos/prophorikos*.[88] It also appears in Socrates's gloss to a passage of the *Long-Lined Exposition* of Milan (345); the glossator declares the Son "to be *enhypostatos* Word of the Father, and God from God."[89] In all these examples, the adjective seems to safeguard the separate subsistence of the Word.

Meletius used the term *enhypostatos* in the homily that reportedly caused his removal from the Constantinopolitan see and his exile to his native Armenia. Meletius, who was briefly bishop of Sebaste (in Armenia), had partaken as a homoian in the Council of Seleucia (359). Toward the end of 360, Bishop Eudoxius's transfer to Constantinople created a vacancy in Antioch, to whose see Meletius was then consecrated by virtue of Acacius's good offices. However, in 361 he was called to take part, along with Acacius and George of Alexandria, in a session of sermon-tasting for the emperor on *Proverbs* 8:22. Whatever its much-debated theological orientation, Meletius's homily persuaded Constantius to decree the first of his three exiles.[90] The passage of the *Homily on Proverbs 8:22* containing the adjective *enhypostatos* confirms the picture of fairly widespread adoption of the term to indicate the subsistence of Christ as a separate entity.[91]

One characteristic gave *enhypostatos* an edge over the rival and near-synonymous *hyphestōs* (a participle of *hyphistēmi*).[92] The Greek prefix *en* can both retain its literal locative sense (e.g., *engastrios*, "in the womb") and assume a sense of possession (e.g., *entimos*, "having honor"), approximation (e.g., *enereuthēs*, "somewhat red"), or emphasis (e.g., *endēlos*, "very clear"). At times, when used as a prefix with a noun to form an adjective, *en* can hold a variety of meanings deriving from the noun to which the adjective refers (e.g., *enhydros* meaning "water-dwelling" for an animal, "water-rich" for a country, "water-filled" for a container, or "consisting of water" for a stream).[93]

Assuming that the usage of the prefix *en*—as perceived by educated fourth-century Greek readers—in conjunction with the adjective *hypostatos*[94] can be accurately predicted on the basis of the meanings it assumed in most cases, the semasiological diversity of the prefix conferred to *enhypostatos* a certain ambiguity. The adjective could be understood to mean both "nestled within a hypostasis"/"having a hypostasis" and "subsistent"/"hypostatic." The difference between these two acceptations is significant. If each of the three *prosōpa* of the godhead is also a hypostasis in its own right (namely, if *enhypostatos* means subsistent/hypostatic), it becomes difficult to escape a tri-hypostatic outcome. On the contrary, if every *prosōpon* is simply nestled within a hypostasis, it can be conceived that one hypostasis contains all three *prosōpa*, preserving the integrity of mia-hypostatic doctrine.

The description of the Son as a *prosōpon enhypostaton* in the fragment attributed to Eustathius was a product of his refusal to attribute to Christ the status of simply a hypostasis. Tri-hypostatism was clearly not the intended outcome. On the other hand, if *enhypostatos* is simply understood as meaning "nestled within a hypostasis," the adjective adds no degree of subsistence to the existence of the Son. In that case, the author might as well not have bothered qualifying the noun *prosōpon* with this attribute. From a technical viewpoint, then, the innovation implied by the expression *prosōpon enhypostaton* is very untidy. The expression is either incompatible with mia-hypostatic doctrine or superfluous. It is true that linguistic constructs transcend in their usage the semantic limitations of their components: the phrase must have assumed the commonsensical meaning of a somehow "substantial person." At the same time, the logical possibility of the interpretation "nestled within a hypostasis" may have afforded the lexeme a certain degree of amphibology, reducing its perceived riskiness and helping its diffusion.

However, the technical weakness of the expression *prosōpon enhypostaton* was more than just an instance of conceptual vagueness: it was a mirror of the role this phrase played in pro-Nicene discourse. This linguistic coinage corresponded to an area of compromise between the Old and the New Nicene that was emerging in those same years, as testified by the *Tome*'s ortholalic operation described above. For all the *Tome*'s conciliatory rhetoric, no logically sound accommodation was possible between the ideas respectively evoked by the bywords "one hypostasis" and "three hypostaseis." The intersection between the two formulas was but an empty theoretical space. The technically inventive yet theologically meaningless phrase *prosōpon enhypostaton* encapsulated that impossible solution. As shown in the following sections, because of its peculiar semiotic status *prosōpon enhypostaton* lent itself to a series of operations.

Jerome's *Letter 15*: Negotiating a Formula

An important episode in the reception of the phrase *prosōpon enhypostaton* appears in the correspondence of Jerome of Stridon. It is contained in a letter Jerome wrote to Pope Damasus (366–384) at some point between 373 and 377 (*Letter 15*).[95] Sometime at the beginning of the 370s, Jerome's monastic community in Aquileia disbanded. As a result, Jerome decided to make his way from northern Italy to the Holy Land along with some of his eremitic companions.[96] However, he did not reach Jerusalem, the original destination of his pilgrimage. He recounts arriving instead in Syria gravely ill[97] and finding shelter in Antioch at the residence of his friend Evagrius, with whom he may have been traveling eastward. Under Evagrius's patronage, Jerome remained in Antioch for some time (probably between 374 and 375), postponing his journey to Jerusalem and delving into literary, philosophical, and theological studies.[98] A few months after his arrival he entered an ascetic practice outside the city.[99] While at his hermitage, Jerome continued to read and attend to correspondence.[100] He also undertook the study of Hebrew[101] as well as Syriac, which he described as the natives' "quasi-language."[102]

While in Syria, Jerome also deepened his acquaintance with the Trinitarian problems that were tearing apart Christianity in Antioch and in the East more broadly. He must have found it hard to navigate Antioch's complex theologico-ecclesial politics. Although his literary legacy includes a heresiological polemic in defense of his particular version of Trinitarian orthodoxy, Jerome was no great theologian in his own right.[103] On Trinitarian matters his leanings were probably generically Old Nicene, while his sympathies in Antiochene matters must have lain with the Eustathian party. These stances were likely a product of his lifelong familiarity with Old Nicene western clerical circles, and may have been reinforced by his friendship with and patronage by Evagrius, a member of the highly ranked Antiochene family of the Pompeiani.[104] After joining the imperial service, Evagrius received the priestly ordination from Eusebius of Vercellae. Upon Constantius II's death, in 361, he followed Eusebius, who was returning to Italy from his exile. He then spent the next twelve years working in the service of Damasus. Thus, when Evagrius returned to Antioch in 373 or 374, it was only natural for him to join the Eustathian community, despite an impassioned letter from Basil of Caesarea expressing regret at his refusal to enter communion with the Meletians.[105] In due time, at Paulinus's death (388), Evagrius was consecrated as his successor. Jerome himself was eventually to become a partisan of Paulinus, to be ordained by him, and to travel with him and Epiphanius of Salamis to the Council of Constantinople in 380.[106] However, in the mid-370s Jerome was still deferring on the Antiochene schism to Pope Damasus, to whom he repeatedly pledged allegiance.[107]

Jerome's apparent failure to definitively establish communion with the Eustathians may have also had to do with the Meletian affiliation of most ascetics living in the Syrian desert. His cautious nonpartisanship, in any event, was insufficient to shield him from their attacks. The emphasis on ortholalia had repercussions for the interactions between adherents of different communions. As Jerome would later write in a different letter, announcing to the Chalcidian priest Mark his imminent departure from the desert, his Syrian eremitic stint was plagued by theological adversaries. These constantly troubled him for new declarations of faith:

> I am not allowed even a corner of desert. Every day I am demanded to provide an exposition of faith, as though I had been born again without faith. I confess as they want: they are not satisfied. I subscribe: they do not believe. One thing only would satisfy them: that I withdraw from here. I am on the verge of giving up.[108]

The letter belongs to the consulting (*anathetikos*) genre.[109] In light of the lack of any reference in the text to previous acquaintance between the two men, and of the pope's repeated failures to respond to Jerome, it is likely that they had in fact never met.[110] The letter opens with an introduction composed in a highly ornate style. In convoluted prose, Jerome announces his desire to receive advice from the holder of Peter's chair regarding the debates by which Christianity in the east is torn.[111] Next, Jerome succinctly expresses his belief in papal primacy, declaring his absolute loyalty to the bishop of Rome.[112] The last lines of this section introduce the specifics of the theological question on which he is seeking advice. In the letter's third section—which is examined below—Jerome recounts a dispute with the Meletians that exemplifies the problem. In the fourth and last section of the letter Jerome pleads with Damasus to tell him whether he should recognize three hypostaseis. Using sarcastic expressions, Jerome makes no mystery of his aversion to the tri-hypostatic formula but promises to endorse it if sanctioned by the pope.

Damasus left Jerome's missive unanswered. In a new, shorter message addressed to the bishop of Rome (*Letter 16*), sent at a debated date, Jerome again disavowed the claims of the Antiochene episcopal candidates:

> Meletius, Vitalis, and Paulinus claim to cling to you; I could believe it if only one of them stated that; now, either two of them are lying, or all of them. Therefore I beseech your blessedness, by the Lord's cross, by the necessary honor of our faith—the passion—to tell me through your letters with whom I am to hold communion in Syria.[113]

This letter, too, received no reply.[114] Soon after, Jerome, disheartened, resolved to abandon the desert. He announced his imminent departure in the response to the Chalcidian presbyter Mark cited above.

In light of Damasus's support of Paulinus and rejection of Meletius, Jerome's attitude in *Letter 15* has proven difficult to decipher. The contested dating of the letter is often considered critical for interpreting its contents.[115] It is in fact commonly assumed that Jerome's request for guidance may be deemed to be sincere only if his epistle was composed before he received through Evagrius the news of Damasus's recognition of Paulinus, entrusted to the missive *Through My Son* (commonly dated 375)[116] and possibly expressed even earlier in a letter that has not been preserved.[117] The dating of *Letter 15*, in turn, depends on the chronology of Jerome's early post-Aquileian years.[118] A 373 dating for Jerome's arrival at Antioch (as proposed by Greenslade), with his departure for the hermitage dated to the following year, would enable the composition of *Letter 15* prior to the delivery of *Through My Son* (whether the latter is dated to 375 or 376) or at least to Jerome's becoming acquainted with that document.[119]

These attempts at validating Jerome's sincerity by establishing the priority of his composition of *Letter 15* relative to the Antiochene delivery of *Through My Son* rely on the unfounded assumption that prior to reading the pope's declaration Jerome had neither any inkling of Damasus's leanings on the Antiochene schism nor any personal preference on the matter. In reality, since his arrival at Antioch, Jerome had been in the company of Evagrius, whose loyalty to Paulinus must have translated into his own and who, fresh off his mission in Caesarea (374), must have informed Jerome of Damasus's favoring of the presbyter.[120] In whatever year *Letter 15* was composed, Jerome's professed uncertainty about Damasus's position on the Antiochene schism could only be a studied pretense, possibly deployed in coordination with Evagrius (though admittedly a pretense that it would have been harder for him to sustain after the delivery of *Through My Son*). Though fully set in his philo-Eustathian Old Nicenism—he called the Meletian supporters "offspring of the Arians" (*Arrianorum proles*)[121]—and aware of the pope's Eustathian leanings, Jerome thought it best, perhaps out of respect to ecclesiastical hierarchy, to address the pope from a stance of unassuming ignorance.[122]

As anticipated above, in writing to Damasus Jerome bemoaned his plight in the Syrian desert. His heretical adversaries did not leave him alone. One encounter with these doctrinal opponents, described in *Letter 15*, is particularly instructive about the history of the reception of *prosōpon enhypostaton*:

> And since on account of my sins I have come to this wilderness that separates Syria from the border of barbarism, nor can I, since such great expanses divide us, always solicit from your holiness "the holy thing of the Lord," therefore here I follow your colleagues, the Egyptian confessors,[123] and I, small vessel, take refuge under loading boats. I do not know Vitalis, I reject Meletius, I am unaware of Paulinus. Whoever does not gather with you, scatters; that is, whoever is not of Christ is of Antichrist (Matt 12:30). So now—woe is me!—after the Nicene faith, after the Alexandrian decree (of 362)—the west being equally in agreement—a novel expression of three hypostaseis is requested from me, a Roman man, by the Campenses[124] [scil. the Meletians], offspring of the Arians. Which apostles, pray tell, affirmed such things? Which new Paul, master of the gentiles, has taught these doctrines? I ask how they think three hypostaseis can be understood. "Three subsistent persons" [*tres personas subsistentes*], they say. I respond that so do I believe. The meaning does not suffice (for them): they demand the very name, for I know not which venom hides in the syllables. I exclaim: "If somebody does not confess three hypostaseis as three subsistent entities, namely three subsistent persons, may he be anathema," and since I do not proclaim the words, I am judged a heretic. But if somebody, understanding hypostasis as ousia, does not proclaim one hypostasis in three persons, he is a stranger to Christ. And, by virtue of this confession, I am burnt with the branding iron of "unionism" just as much as you.[125]

This passage has been read by some as indicating that Jerome either was unaware or chose to ignore that the *Tome to the Antiochenes*, written by Athanasius and possibly some of his colleagues after the Council of Alexandria

(362), had legitimized the usage of "hypostasis" as a synonym for "person," thereby clearing tri-hypostatic expressions from the charge of heresy and asking both Eustathians and Meletians not to press the matter and engage in logomachies.[126] By contrast, others have recognized in Jerome's attitude toward the Meletians, as expressed in this anecdote, his characteristic intransigence.[127] Yet others portrayed Jerome as lacking a grasp of dogmatic subtleties and contemporaneous theologico-ecclesiastical events.[128] One scholar argued that Jerome's (alleged) failure to abide by the directives of the Council of Alexandria may be understood in light of the minor importance generally held by that gathering at the time.[129]

In my view, far from either purposefully ignoring or even just revealing his ignorance of the decisions of the Alexandrian synod (which he did mention in his epistle),[130] Jerome's retorts to the Meletians are perfectly in line with the resolutions of that council. The ascetic had a firm grasp of the latest conciliatory developments in eastern Old Nicene theology. The *Tome to the Antiochenes* stated that if the tri-hypostatic party (likely identifying the Meletians) abjured tritheism, the mia-hypostatic alliance (almost certainly the Eustathians) would be ready to recognize their triplication of the hypostaseis as legitimate. Personally, Jerome held fast to the equivalence between ousia and hypostasis, and as a result upheld the unicity of God's hypostasis.[131] Nonetheless, he was willing to split the doctrinal difference, so to speak, that separated him from the Meletians: he would accept the notion of three hypostaseis on the condition that hypostasis be understood as synonymous with *persona subsistens*—a phrase that in all likelihood should be back-translated as *prosōpon enhypostaton.*[132]

In their encounter with Jerome, the Meletians demanded that he confess "three hypostaseis." Upon Jerome's request for a clarification, they specified their understanding of "three hypostaseis" as "three subsistent persons." Jerome confessed these very "three subsistent persons" and, when the Meletians pressed him to declare "three hypostaseis," he proclaimed his faith in "three hypostaseis" as coterminous with "three subsistent persons." In other words, Jerome was prepared to push the Eustathian Trinitarian views to their most conciliatory extreme—to the point of recognizing three hypostaseis provided that these would be understood as *prosōpa enhypostata*—for the sake of producing a confession acceptable to the Meletians. Jerome's attitude toward the Meletians was not unlike that of de Montalte's neo-Thomist interlocutor with regard to Monsieur le Moine's "proximate power" in Pascal's *Provincial Letters.* This shared expression would have enabled Jerome to charitably consider the Meletian orthodox, in spite of differing as to the meaning of the phrase.

Jerome repeated the notion of a subsistent person in the letter to the presbyter Mark in which he announced that he was abandoning his hermitage:

> I am called a heretic while I preach the consubstantial trinity; I am accused of Sabellian impiety while I pronounce three *subsistent*, true, integral, and perfect *persons* with unceasing voice. If [I am accused] by the Arians, so be it; if by the orthodox, those who argue with a faith of this kind have ceased to be orthodox. Or, if they prefer, let them condemn me as a heretic with the west, a heretic with Egypt, namely with Damasus and Peter.[133]

The *personae* confessed by Jerome here again should be understood, in the Greek in which his verbal exchanges with the local Meletians likely occurred, not as hypostaseis, but as *prosōpa*. The phrase *subsistentes . . . persona[e]* is in all likelihood a translation of *prosōpa enhypostata.*[134]

From the Old Nicene standpoint, the power of aggregation of the formula *prosōpon enhypostaton* could be extended to nonliteral adherence. While the signifier *prosōpon enhypostaton* itself was still regarded as the minimal litmus test of orthodoxy, more subjects than those confessing the phrase could pass that test. Any signifier that could claim to have as its signified *prosōpa enhypostata* could be legitimately triplicated in speech, including *hypostasis*.

Jerome considered Meletian believers in the triplicity of the hypostaseis orthodox as long as his profession of "three *prosōpa enhypostata*" could be at any point traded back for their "three hypostaseis" confession.[135] In Jerome's report, it was solely the Meletians' show of intransigence that earned them the appellation "offspring of the Arians." They insisted that the tri-hypostatic formula should be uttered without qualification. Only at this request did Jerome balk, fearing that the "three hypostaseis" statement might be understood as "three ousiai."[136]

It can be surmised that Jerome's acceptance of three *prosōpa enhypostata* was representative of broader conciliatory development within the pro-Nicene front in Syria. The locutionary context of *persona[e] subsistentes* in *Letter 15* ("I ask how they think three hypostaseis can be understood. 'Three subsistent persons,' they say. I respond that so do I believe") seems to indicate that the phrase was part of a strategy employed by the Meletians in their debates with members of the Old Nicene alliance in the mid-370s. Meletius's followers knew the members of the Eustathian communion to be susceptible to the appeal of an equivalence between *prosōpon enhypostaton* and hypostasis. As seen from the continuation of the report, they counted on the willingness of the

Old Nicene to accept that equivalence as a stepping stone toward their outright embrace of tri-hypostatism.

The exchange between Jerome and the Meletians makes manifest the dialectical power of ortholalia. At the same time that ortholalia reduced correctness of belief to the appropriateness of one formulaic expression, it also made that expression available for equivalence with an array of competing signifiers. Far from being a mere instrument of closure of the discursive field, the elevation of formulas to the criterion by which the correctness of a subject's faith was judged led to a proliferation of the kinds of operations that could be accomplished within that field.

The Novel Pro-Nicene Front of the 370s

By the mid-370s, the equivalence between *prosōpa enhypostata* and hypostaseis had become sufficiently widespread among at least some quarters of the Old Nicene alliance that homoiousian propaganda could rely on its acceptance in order to promote their tri-hypostatic views. A testimony in this regard comes from Epiphanius. In his *Medicine Chest* (374–377) Epiphanius preserved for posterity knowledge about and excerpts drawn from the works of a great array of Christian heretics. His heresiological activities aside, Epiphanius is better known to readers of ancient Christian literature for his protagonist's role in the second phase of the Origenist controversy and his contributions to the Apollinarist dispute than for his positions on Trinitarian matters. By nobody's account was Epiphanius an ingenious theological mind. Both in *Anchored Discourse*[137] (late 373 or early 374) and in *Medicine Chest* he expressed theological views that lack the originality contained in the systems of Christian *maîtres à penser* like Basil of Caesarea or Athanasius. However, his views provide a glimpse into the way a bishop of a lesser eastern locale with personal ties to Egypt, where Athanasian loyalism was predominant, may have reconciled his ecclesiastical affiliation with an openness to a more substantial understanding of the Trinity.

In his commentary on the *Anchored Discourse*, Oliver Kösters distinguished the theological inclinations of the Old Nicene Epiphanius, author of *the Anchored Discourse*, from those of the New Nicene bishop who wrote the *Medicine Chest*.[138] Not long after Athanasius's death (373), Epiphanius began to undergo a transition from the mia-hypostatic faith to the tri-hypostatic formula propounded by the Meletians. The theoretical basis that allowed him to undergo such a transition, without ever compelling him to cease standing in communion with the Eustathians, remains in need of investigation.

After becoming bishop of Salamis, in 366, Epiphanius communicated with Paulinus, seeking to thwart Meletius's ambitions for the Antiochene episcopate. Epiphanius himself gives us an account of the events that led to this decision. By his own declaration, he chose Paulinus after being shown an autograph Athanasian exemplar of the *Tome to the Antiochenes* carrying the subscription of the Old Nicene claimant. Paulinus's political weakness, in comparison to Meletius's extensive influence in the East, may have also been attractive to the ambitious Cypriot bishop.[139] He later visited Paulinus in Antioch in 376 and as late as 382 journeyed with him to Rome to plead with Damasus in favor of the Eustathian cause.

Epiphanius expounded a boldly mia-hypostatic theology in his *Anchored Discourse*. This was a fairly unsystematic doctrinal letter addressed to the Christians of Syedra in Pamphylia in response to their call for aid against the local pneumatomachians.[140] In sketching a triadic articulation of the divine, Epiphanius feebly rooted it in a theory of names distinguishing between mononyms and homonyms. The distinct names of Father, Son, and Holy Spirit were regarded there as guarantors of the three entities' separate subsistence.[141]

Later, however, Epiphanius had a change of heart about the number of hypostaseis. This is reflected in Basil of Caesarea's *Letter 258* to him, dated to 377. Epiphanius's belief in three hypostaseis is also recorded repeatedly in *Medicine Chest*.[142] In discussing the Marcellans, for example, he criticized their views in the following terms:

> And while the recesses of [Marcellus's] thought are known [only] to God, his pupils and converts, either not knowing his mind or [indeed] reporting his true [ideas], did not want to confess the three hypostaseis, as is the truth, namely that one is the godhead, one the glory, the Trinity which is homoousios and which does not differ in its own glory [. . .].[143]

In *Medicine Chest* Epiphanius also accompanied the expression of one ousia and one hypostasis of the godhead, which he had employed throughout *Anchored Discourse*, with the affirmation of "three subsistent [entities]"[144] and of "three persons [. . .] from the hypostasis that is triple."[145] He used the adjective *enhypostatos* eighteen times in *Anchored Discourse*.[146] As Young Richard Kim indicates, "[H]e seemed to use it as a term to indicate the real, essential existence of the persons of the Trinity, in particular as a foil to Sabellian modalism (in opposition to *anhypostatos/on*)."[147]

Kim emphasizes that through *enhypostatos* Epiphanius intended to instill the notion "that each individual divine person together necessarily comprises one hypostatic God."[148] But in the case of its usage in conjunction with *prosōpon*, the term's primary purpose was not to represent metonymically the whole of the godhead. The phrase was employed, rather, to ensure the substantiality of the three members of the Trinity. Epiphanius's shift toward unconditional acceptance of three hypostaseis—a shift that was to enthuse a homoiousian like Basil—was prepared and enabled by the enhypostatic understanding of the three *prosōpa* that Epiphanius held even during his mia-hypostatic period. Epiphanius's about-face testifies to the success of the propaganda strategy employed by the Meletians. They hoped to overcome the limiting proviso whereby tri-hypostatic language was deemed acceptable, within the progressive eastern mia-hypostatic alliance, only if hypostasis would be understood in the sense of *prosōpon enhypostaton*.

Another occurrence of the technical phrase *prosōpon enhypostaton* appears in a document of the second generation of Marcellan clergy, dating from the same time Epiphanius and Jerome were writing.[149] In 375 eleven pro-Nicene Egyptian bishops were exiled to the Palestinian locale of Sepphoris, whence they sent a letter to the Marcellan clergy of Ancyra. The response of the Ancyran presbyters is preserved by Epiphanius.[150] The document anathematizes some long-held Marcellan teachings. The hostile political circumstances—the New Nicene party had been rapidly gaining ground in response to the imperial empowerment of homoian and, in some locales, even heteroousian leaderships—had required even die-hard mia-hypostatic thinkers to express their theology in an updated terminology. The naming of the persons of the Trinity as subsistent was an integral part of this project.

The letter of the Marcellans from Ancyra contained a profession of faith that condemns those who denied the existence of three subsistent persons in the following terms:

> We condemn [. . .] those who do not say that the holy Trinity consists of three not circumscribable, subsistent, homoousios, co-eternal, and perfect persons.[151]

The adjective *enhypostatos* was used here alongside other ones. Marcellus, however, had fought throughout his life to prevent the godhead from being broken into more than one sole *prosōpon*. It is difficult to imagine that the Ancyran clergy proceeded unthinkingly to attribute substantiality to the *prosōpa* of the various members of the Trinity.[152] "Subsistent" is also the only adjective of the series that clearly goes in the opposite logical direction from a Monarchian defense of God's unity: "homoousios" and "co-eternal" stand as descriptors of the mutual interfusion of the respective *prosōpa* of the Father and the Son, whereas "not circumscribable" and "perfect" are generic expressions of divinity. It is very likely that the formulation contained in this profession of faith was influenced by *prosōpon enhypostaton* as a technical formula. This progressive, conciliatory expression had made its way into the writings of the representatives of one of the most conservative Old Nicene theological outlooks.[153]

By the 360s, the theological alliance that stood behind the banner of Nicaea was composite. Since the Council of Antioch of 363, on the left side of the pro-Nicene spectrum stood the homoiousians. The most compromise-prone Old Nicene, such as Epiphanius, had been led to accept the tri-hypostatic doctrine of that party without any qualification by the equivalence between hypostasis and *prosōpon enhypostaton*. Their more progressive theological stance, open to three *prosōpa enhypostata* and even to their identification with three hypostaseis, was similar to the postures that the Ancyran clergy articulated in response to the Egyptian pro-Nicene.[154] To their immediate right was the diverse Old Nicene camp. Its mainstream, allied with Athanasius, remained at peace with Paulinus's 362 subscription of the *Tome to the Antiochenes*. Further right were the most intransigent Eustathians. Under the influence of Lucifer of Calaris, these had broken communion with Paulinus and rejected any form of rapprochement with the Meletians; similarly rigorist elements also survived elsewhere in the East, such as at Alexandria and Ancyra.

Using the reception of the expression *prosōpon enhypostaton* as a guiding index has allowed us to assay the heterogeneous consistency of the pro-Nicene field, to track its internal dynamics, and to observe the historical consequentiality of its reorganization. The Constantinopolitan settlement of 381, prepared by the Cappadocians' initiative, was the vanishing point toward which the multiple lines that intermeshed within the newly reconfigured pro-Nicene camp led.

In the Trinitarian controversies, ortholalia opened up interstices of engagement between the Old and New Nicene alliances. These rapprochements, made possible by formulaic equivalences, were endowed with both theological and institutional import. The attitude that Pascal's de Montalte frustratedly called "merely playing with words" had its roots in the fourth-century discussions about the Son's relation to the Father. During these exchanges, the set of logical, linguistic, and theoretical operations enabled by the identification of truth with a formula led to a novel organization of the discursive field of Christian theology. The new rules of the theological game, founded in ortholalia, were to regulate Christian ways of teasing out the truth about the divine for centuries to come.

5 • The Ends of Dialogue

كافر همه را به کیش خود پندارد

The unbeliever thinks everyone is of his own faith.
—Persian proverb

It takes a long time to find out which is the bigger nuisance—
the doubter or the believer.
—Wilfred Bion

Dialogue in Late Antiquity

Eusebius has preserved in the *Life of Constantine* a letter sent by the emperor to Alexander of Alexandria and Arius in 324. Coupling respectful phrasings with his unmistakably imperious tone, Constantine asked the two Alexandrian clergymen to put an end to their dissension about trifling matters, so as to restore peace in the Church:

> I call God himself to witness, as I should, the helper in my undertakings and Savior of the Universe, that a twofold purpose impelled me to undertake the duty which I have performed. My first concern was that the attitude toward the Divinity of all the provinces should be united in one consistent view, and my second that I might restore and heal the body of the *oikoumenē* which lay severely wounded. [. . .] But (O best, divine Providence!) what a deadly wound my ears suffered, or rather my very heart, at the news that the division originating among you was much graver than those I had left behind [in Africa], so that your regions, from

> which I had hoped medicine would be supplied to others, were now in greater need of healing. As I considered the origin and occasion for these things, the cause was exposed as extremely trivial and quite unworthy of so much controversy. Being driven therefore to the need for this letter, and addressing myself to that discretion which you have in common, and calling first on the divine Providence to support my action, I offer my modest services as a peaceful arbitrator between you in your dispute. [. . .] But so that I may bring to the attention of your intelligences a slight comparison, you surely know how even the philosophers themselves all agree in one set of principles, and often when they disagree in some part of their statements, although they are separated by their learned skill, yet they agree together again in unity when it comes to basic principle. If this is so, surely it is far more right that we, who are the appointed servants of the great God, should, in a religious commitment of this kind, be of one mind with each other?[1]

In the eyes of the emperor, the identities of the Father and the Son were understandably not an issue over which it was worth rupturing Christian fellowship. The sentiments expressed in this letter are in keeping with the preference for religious consensus that Constantine would demonstrate until his death.[2] This ideal was alternately pursued through the promise of lavish imperial support for those promoting unity and the threat of exile and persecution for the subjects who compromised it. Constantine's successors, including the pagan Julian, shared his interest in building social and political uniformity upon ideological and religious harmony, although the measures they took to achieve that ideal were often less gentle than urbane missives.[3]

One need only think of the 186 BCE *senatus consultum de bacchanalibus*, prohibiting with few exceptions Bacchus festivals throughout Italy, to realize that since republican times the Roman State had consistently manifested little interest in what we would now call freedom of religious expression.[4] In the third century, however, imperial authorities heightened their interest in matters of religious uniformity. Contemporaneous changes in ecclesiastical structures also determined the conditions for limiting free religious expression within the Church itself.[5] Beginning in the fourth century, the identification between an increasingly constrained Church and an empire zealously invested in Christian unity led to the affirmation of state-sanctioned monodoxy, namely, the exclusive legitimation of one opinion concerning religious truth among the social body.[6] As a result, late ancient Roman society experienced widespread religious coercion, particularly at the expense of those Christians dubbed "heretics."

The spread of monodoxy is said to have reached its apogee in the often-referenced late ancient "end of dialogue," embodied by a set of fifth- and sixth-century discursive formations whose genesis is associated with the Christological disputes.[7] Following the establishment of one unquestionable truth about the articulation of the divine-human nature of Christ at the Council of Chalcedon (451), free theological discussion is said to have waned, replaced by the production of florilegia expediently summarizing the truth on a variety of doctrinal topics.[8]

Scholars expressing pessimistic assessments of the state of dialogue in late ancient Christianity have mostly worked with a narrow standard of what constitutes dialogue, going sometimes to the extreme of identifying this concept either with the autohyponymous literary genre—originating with Plato and expressed by such late ancient works as Justin Martyr's *Dialogue with Trypho* and the *Dialogue of Timothy and Aquila*—or with the institution of public debates on philosophical and religious matters.[9] But the shifting and often quite technical rhetorical forms that disagreement took in late antiquity have complex, variable, and above all limited points of contact with the question of the dialogical nature of this era's dominant discourse. Indeed, even leaving aside the fact that the threat of homophony—wherein one selfsame voice governs a seemingly plurivocal exchange—had loomed large on the dialogue form at least from the Platonic writings on, in the post-Nicene era this genre was comfortably put to the service of often censorious theological agendas.[10]

Additionally, an open attitude in philosophical and religious debate was capable of being promoted through multiple intellectual and communication practices, of which the production of literary dialogues (whether in self-standing compositions or embedded in other types of writings) was only one and arguably not the most significant. As Peter Van Nuffelen has observed, free and fair disputation, a mode of intellectual engagement that had its roots in the fierce exchanges of the fourth century, still worked as an ideal in the fifth.[11] Along the same lines, Sébastien Morlet has countered the widespread interpretation of the rise of the florilegium as a sign of obscurantism, remarking that this genre was born out of a need to summarize previous teachings for the purpose of polemical exchange.[12] To be sure, there is no denying that in the fifth and sixth centuries the processes of dogmatization that Christian thought had undergone during the fourth-century Trinitarian controversies culminated in profound changes in the work of Christian intellectuals. Nonetheless, those processes did not lead to an end of dialogue in the theological field, whether ad intra or ad extra, but rather, as seen in the previous chapter, to a redefinition of the rules governing such exchange.[13] Real attempts at curbing debate did exist.[14] But these stood in continuity with similar calls voiced by Christian authors in previous centuries. Late antiquity remained, in the words of Averil Cameron, "a world full of talk."[15]

In this chapter the notion of dialogue is treated, based on the shared connection to the verb *dialegesthai* ("to talk"), as a synonym of dialectic, to be in turn defined simply as the practice of critical and reasoned argumentation by means of questions and answers.[16] As Maingueneau indicates, "[T]he conversational process becomes dialectical inasmuch as it centers around a precise problem defined in a shared fashion and it unfolds among equal partners among whom the word circulates freely, who are moved by a quest for truth, justice, or the common good, and who accept to speak according to explicitly established rules."[17] The following pages, then, focus neither on the institution of real-life public disputations nor on their literary staging or reporting. I wish to examine instead the parting of the ways in relation to the *ends* of dialogue, understood as both the aims of and the constraints placed on the two communities' independent quests for truth through arguments. The question asked here is not whether late ancient Christians and Jews were still "doing dialogue,"[18] be that within their own communities or with each other. Rather, the interrogation centers on whether the processes undergone by rabbinic intellectual culture were compatible with the dogmatic shape acquired by Christianity.

When considering this question, it is tempting to be satisfied with an unqualified negative answer. After all, the Church, enmeshed within imperial structures, manifested a predilection for monodoxy. Rabbinic sources show instead both a pronounced wariness of the Roman Empire—though one coexisting with the representation of frequent dealings with its representatives—and a preference for polydoxy, that is, the upholding, or at least the preservation, of multiple opinions on each subject. Even if accepted, however, this contrast between rabbinic and Christian attitudes alone does not permit us to conclude that the Jews did not partake in the current of intolerance that swept the Mediterranean world in late antiquity. Asserting a putative opposition between a tolerant rabbinic society and an autocratic Christendom, identified by the formula *cogite intrare*,[19] amounts to begging the historical question. The Jewish minority's failure to participate in the atmosphere of state-mandated conformism could equally have been a product of, for example, its relegation to the margins of the political stage after the imperial imposition of Christian beliefs. A different type of probe is necessary.

It is common to see the main line of demarcation between Christianity and Judaism, beginning in ancient times, as lying in the dichotomy between an emphasis on orthodoxy and a concentration on orthopraxy.[20] While Christians—one hears—wearied themselves to find, preserve, and enforce the correct opinion on theological matters, Jews were concerned instead with ensuring observance of the precepts of the Torah. Like most truisms, this characterization holds some verity while being at the same time misleading: Christians and Jews were no doubt invested in safeguarding, respectively, theological truth and covenantal abidance. This fact alone, however, is not particularly illuminating of the manner or reasons that Jews and Christians parted ways. As I argue, the split between the two communities is more fruitfully investigated through the lens of the progressive specification of the intellectual practices through which orthodoxy and orthopraxy were pursued. Pushing the analysis further, I now wish to propose that to apprehend more fully the mutual configuration into which the parting of the ways placed Jews and Christians we ought to bring into relief two more aspects of the question. On the one hand, I intend to discuss rabbis' and theologians' own conceptualizations of those intellectual practices and of their corresponding corporate functions within their respective societies. On the other hand I wish to highlight the broader implications of those conceptualizations for each of the two intellectual communities' dealings with members of the other. In other words, to understand the separation between the rabbinic and theological classes it matters not only what rabbis and theologians did, but also how they conceived of what they were doing and how this affected their outward transactions.

Like the bulk of the account of the parting of the ways pursued in this book, the interpretive supplement proposed in this chapter is at the same time ultimately rooted in the historical efficacy of power and devoted to a more comprehensive exploration of the forms in which power's effects made themselves manifest in the process of separation. As argued in the Introduction, not even watershed moments in the Roman attitude toward Christendom, such as those marked by the so-called Edict of Milan (313) or the Edict of Thessalonica (380), could have produced the parting of the Jewish and Christian ways as though by fiat, through the sheer power of their institutional stabilization of orthodoxy.[21] Nonetheless, the convergence of the Church and the Roman Empire, by placing rabbis and Christian theologians in structurally irreconcilable positions vis-à-vis political power, did cause the two elites to evolve different understandings of their own intellectual activities and distinct self-representations in relation to those. These different identifications, produced as an aftereffect of the constitution of separate intellectual traditions described in the Introduction, fed in turn the process of separation. As argued below, the two intellectual communities reached as a result similarly intolerant ideological outcomes through dissimilar avenues, relying on opposite understandings of their own practices. The answer I propose to the question asked above, then, is that rabbinic Judaism was both capable and incapable, though in different senses, of ideological integration within the late ancient atmosphere of *homonoia* ("one-mindedness") which it was Christendom's historical role to nurture and materially impose in the Roman Empire.[22]

Rabbinic and Patristic Ways of Citing

The analysis in this chapter centers on the principal methods of inquiry of Christian and Jewish literate elites. On the one hand is theology, understood, as it has been in this book, as a discipline practiced by Christian intellectuals in increasingly homogeneous ways and in close relation to institutional power. On the other hand is *talmud* ("study"), the mode of investigation embodied in the discussions contained in the corpora we call the Talmuds.[23] Under primary consideration are the Greek and Latin Christian theological corpus and the Babylonian Talmud. The Bavli, as the latter is also called, presents itself as a commentary on the six orders of the Mishnah, whose compilation is traditionally attributed to Rabbi Judah ha-Nasi in 200–225 CE. The Bavli weaves together sources from the tannaitic period (ca. 10–220 CE)—both passages from the Mishnah and other teachings, known as *barayata* or *beraitot* (singular *baraita*)—and, most prominently, statements by the *amora'im* ("interpreters," singular *amora*) of both Palestinian and Babylonian origin (living ca. 200–500 CE), called *meimrot* (singular *meimra*). These sources are integrated into the commentary on the Mishnah (known as *gemara*) through an anonymous layer called *stam*.[24] The stam provides discursive argumentation (*shaḳla ṿe-ṭarya*), analysis, and framing. It is commonly divided into *sugyot* (singular *sugyah*), self-contained units of discursive analysis largely organized around challenges (*ḳushyot*) and resolutions (*terutsim*).[25]

By comparing the Bavli with theological texts from the Roman Empire, I am treating together bodies of literature that developed in different geocultural and political spheres. Arguably, a more apt comparison would involve either Christian theological texts written in Syriac and the Babylonian

Talmud, or the Greek and Latin theological corpora and the Palestinian Talmud (or Yerushalmi).[26] My decision to pursue instead this course of inquiry is based on several considerations. First, Christian theological literature composed in Syriac, though offering greater geographic overlap with the Bavli, flourished largely after the end of the amoraic period, an important segment of the rabbinic trajectory investigated here. Second, the Palestinian Talmud assumed its ultimate form through the accumulation of literary layers over time.[27] It is true that there seem to be good reasons to nuance the dichotomy between a highly redacted Bavli and a minimalist Yerushalmi. Nevertheless, the Palestinian Talmud, by displaying less systematic redactional or editorial intervention, makes it harder to identify an ideological coherence comparable to the one that may be detected in the anonymous layer of its Babylonian counterpart.[28]

The legitimacy of the comparison is supported by the fact that the rabbinic elites in Palestine and the Sasanian Empire were hardly without contact with one another. This is proven by, among other things, the migration to Babylonia of rabbinic traditions formulated in the Land of Israel, the presence of a fair amount of Babylonian materials in the Yerushalmi, and the Bavli's abundant record of *naḥote'i*, masters "descending" to study from the Land of Israel to Babylonia and then returning to Palestine.[29] A number of the discursive features of the Bavli to which this chapter points are, to an extent occasionally noted here, not just Babylonian (or late Babylonian) but more broadly rabbinic. In any event, it should be emphasized that I do not wish to make a claim about the existence of a meaningful shared historical context for the two models described. This chapter's selection of rabbinic materials is above all retrospectively based on the downstream reverberations of the Bavli on later rabbinic culture (and, from a certain point on, on Jewish culture tout court). The relocation of the Talmudic academies to Baghdad, the capital of the Abbasid Caliphate beginning in 762, along with their institutionalization and their sealing of a fixed literary corpus, led to the prominence of the Babylonian rabbinic heritage as against the Palestinian one beginning in the Geonic period (in the late sixth century) and to the almost complete neglect of the Yerushalmi by worldwide Jewry up to the present day.[30] As a result, the manner of inquiry embodied by the Bavli came to dominate rabbinic self-representations, with lasting effects as well on Christian-Jewish relations. When in medieval times Jews were called on to defend their way of life against Christian theologians in public disputations, it was their allegiance to the Babylonian Talmud they had to justify.

The structuring of a totalizing system of Christian knowledge in the Roman Empire and the progressive construction of its political efficacy have been reconstructed in a valuable body of scholarship.[31] Here I choose to focus neither on those aspects nor on Jewish and Christian forms of political organization or theorization thereof.[32] The question of intolerance is instead reevaluated in this chapter on the basis of an assessment of the political impulses that undergird key discursive operators in the high-cultural literary productions of Jews and Christians. I consider here one aspect of theologians' and rabbis' uses of language and understandings of themselves as actors engaged in its use: the practice of citation (which I treat as synonymous with quotation). For its definition we may rely on the semiotician Stefan Morawski, who described it as "a semantic portion designed to perform a certain function in a new and extraneous semantic structure of a higher order."[33]

As Morawski again writes, "Quotation [. . .] lays bare the fundamental dilemma of every age—choosing between innovation and the duplication of canonized exemplars—and the way in which the past is consciously or unconsciously filtered."[34] The manner in which those who cite deal with the complex link between text and hypotext, between the present of citation and the past of utterance, renders their citational practices an accurate gauge of their own location in the institutional domain.[35] My working assumption here is that the fundamentally disparate ways in which Christian writers of the post-Constantinian period and the editors of the Babylonian Talmud dealt with words inherited from their predecessors are able to shed light on the political facet of their respective textualities.[36]

The main object of reflection is not the two elites' self-representations in relation to their practices of citation.[37] This chapter deals instead with those practices themselves (excepting the sui generis case of scriptural citations) as they emerge visibly in the texts where they gave rise to two habits commonly recognized as pivotal to the theological and Talmudic corpora: on the one hand the device known in studies of Christian literature as the patristic argument (that is, the appeal to earlier theologians to buttress one's opinion) and on the other hand the rabbinic weaving of dicta (sayings) into the stam.

Morawski identifies four basic functions of citation, capable of intermixing in each occurrence: the citation that appeals to authorities, the erudite citation, the stimulative-amplificatory, and the ornamental one. I suggest that Christian theologians' invocation of their predecessors to defend a truth they presented as being under constant siege aligned most closely with the first item in this typology.[38] The Talmud's editors' use of amoraic dicta as a springboard for their discussion—with the aim of celebrating or justifying their own strategies of intellectual production—went instead in the direction of the stimulative-amplificatory function of citation, though occasionally trespassing into the erudite.[39] The Bavli does record plenty of instances of a type of invocation of past statements analogous to the patristic argument: when an amora is reported to have cited an anonymous *mishnah* (a discrete teaching in the Mishnah) and even in some contexts a baraita, the latter are intended to hold authoritative binding force. This manner of citation, however, is encased within the text's stratigraphy. The authoritative citations of tannaitic sources by amoraʾim are still subsumed under the higher-order speech of the stam. In its latest level—whether the latter is understood as the product of a compilatory, editorial, compositional, or redactional gesture—the text of the Talmud interrogates the citation and treats its meaning as multivalent and never settled, in a movement enabling, as seen later through the analysis of a short passage, a revisitation of the past.

The rabbinic literary project had been anthological to a large extent since the second century.[40] Inasmuch as the whole literature of the rabbis was based on the recombination of decontextualized excerpts from conversations carried out across different times and locations, citation had always held a privileged status in the textuality their works embodied and promoted. This situation lent itself since very early on to the manipulation of quotations, visible for example in the Mishnah's free anonymization of positions the Tosefta attributes instead by name.[41]

Such a state of affairs, wherein citation was not only omnipresent but constitutive of the corpus, was incomparable to that of contemporaneous Christian literature, at least before the production of catenae and florilegia. Early Christian authors generally, however, did cite. They referred to Scripture incessantly and inserted into their writings allusions to pagan and Christian works.[42] They infrequently named their attributions, and even more rarely did they mention the titles of the works from which they were borrowing.[43]

Over time, the Christian theological discipline constituted the patristic argument, a distinctive style of citation consisting of "the insertion into a new discursive context of text explicitly attributed to one of the Fathers"[44] for the purposes of buttressing one's position through the voice of a writer of authoritative status. This device was tied to the Christian reverence for tradition (*paradosis*), which second- and third-century Christian authors often spoke of as an uninterrupted chain of transmission going back to Jesus via the apostles. Beginning with Arius and throughout the later Trinitarian controversies, thinkers of all stripes asserted that their doctrines harked back to this apostolic tradition.[45] The deliberations of the Council of Nicaea themselves were based on an understanding of tradition as "the record of the reception of the primary witness in the Church," that witness being Scripture.[46]

The patristic argument, however, was more than a mere appeal to tradition, as it presupposed the representation of the Fathers as a discrete, select, and authoritative collective entity.[47] This representation probably evolved in the fourth century, as few references to "the Fathers" (*hoi pateres*) pre-date it, and in none of them does the term appear to be used in a technical sense.[48] It seems to have been Athanasius who first adopted the expression, through which he designated the totality of the bishops gathered in an ecumenical council.[49] The phrase "Fathers of the Church" (*hoi ekklēsiastikoi pateres*)[50] appears for the first time, with the meaning of "the whole of the representatives of the authentic tradition of the Church,"[51] in the works of Eusebius of Caesarea, in the rhetorical context of a response to Marcellus of Ancyra's critique of Asterius's use of the Fathers.[52]

These occurrences reflect the progressive emergence of a "sense of Patristic authority" that served, as Thomas Graumann writes, "as much to mark identity as to guide theological reasoning."[53] While the Fathers of Nicaea were cited as a collective entity, over time more precise forms of citation arose. During the Trinitarian controvesies the authority of the Fathers began to be mustered by actors of opposite theological leanings in the service of their cause. Thus, the anti-Nicene to whose views the manuscript known as the Bobbio palimpsest attests, for example, collected and mobilized the statements of previous authors in support of their theses.[54] At the same time, the pro-Nicene champion Basil of Caesarea appended to his treatise *On the Holy Spirit* a short florilegium of authorities on matters of liturgical practice.[55] Sometimes the words of the very same Father were pulled in opposite directions, as was the case for the contested legacy of Dionysius of Alexandria (d. ca. 265), vied for by both Athanasius and his opponents.[56] At the culmination of the process that saw the rise of the patristic argument, in the fifth century the notion of "Fathers of the Church" supported as a matter of course the invocation of the authority of individual orthodox bishops.[57]

At some point in his career, Augustine of Hippo (354–430) contrasted the attacks of the Pelagians by developing the notion of an argument based on the consensus of the Fathers, while continuing to reject arguments that drew on the opinion of one individual Father.[58] Augustine's theory of the patristic argument as relying on the consensual authority of Church writers as a corporate entity was akin to the influential formulation found in fifth-century theologian Vincent of Lérin's *Commonitorium* (ca. 434):

> But what if some error should spring up on which no such decree [establishing Church doctrine] is found to bear? Then he must collate and consult and interrogate the opinions of the ancients, of those, namely, who, though living in various times and places, yet continuing in the communion and faith of the one Catholic Church, stand forth acknowledged and approved authorities: and whatsoever he shall ascertain to have been held, written, taught, not by one or two of these only, but by all, equally, with one consent, openly, frequently, persistently, that he must understand that he himself also is to believe without any doubt or hesitation.[59]

Vincent articulated a fundamental distinction between the Fathers—those whose opinions are of a piece with the Church's consensus—and the more inclusive category of ecclesiastical writers.[60] As a result, he expressed reservations about the trustworthiness of authors, such as Origen and Tertullian, whose works he still deemed instructive in some regards.[61] The early-sixth-century *Pseudo-Gelasian Decree* took Vincent's distinction to more extreme consequences by drawing up lists of reliable and unorthodox authors.[62] This distinction gained widespread acceptance, as shown by an episode that occurred in 520. When the African bishop Possessor wrote to Pope Hormisdas (450–523) to inquire about the views on grace of the theologian Faustus of Riez (ca. 410–495), the pontifex made it clear in his reply that Faustus was not to be counted among the Fathers and attached a copy of the *Pseudo-Gelasian Decree*, where Faustus's opinions were regarded with suspicion.[63]

The most consequential outcome of the rise of the patristic argument was perhaps its use during the first session of the Council of Ephesus (431). Here the acts of the council inform us that a florilegium of mostly post-Nicene authors was read out to the assembly at the initiative of Cyril of Alexandria.[64] The place this discursive device had by then gained in arguably the most central institutional practice of the Church—the council—testifies to the status it would soon acquire, becoming a mainstay of theological discourse in the late fifth and sixth centuries.[65]

By adopting the patristic argument as its prime tool of argumentation and decision-making, late ancient Christian theology shaped itself into a discipline endowed with a particular ethos: the recuperation of a truth expressed univocally in the past, but exposed at all times to harmful contestations and misconstruals. Lapses of theological judgment occurred in every generation, requiring Christians to be discerning about the orthodoxy of the authors they cited.

The ethos inspiring the use of amoraic citations in the Talmud was distinctly different, and so was the relationship between human authority and truth on which it drew. As an interpreter and producer of the law, the *talmid ḥakham* (disciple of the sage; plural: *talmidei ḥakhamim*), the privileged agent of rabbinic discourse, entertained a direct relationship with divine authority.[66] The need to establish the *halakhah* (literally the way to walk, or the correct manner of acting in all aspects of day-to-day life) through study constituted the *talmidei ḥakhamim* into spokesmen for the Torah, whose presence was constructed as essential to the functioning of the cultural system in which they were placed.[67]

The rabbis built the Torah as articulating a basic norm that formally established the need to obey God's commandments.[68] However, neither the nature of these precepts nor the way in which they were to be observed was self-evident. As Menachem Elon remarks, "If no Oral Law existed to explain and give content to these legal institutions, it would have been impossible in practice to carry out the provisions that are stated in the scriptural passage."[69] The very possibility of law abidance relied on the explicatory prowess of the sages. The rabbis did not treat Scripture as an event or an act of communication; they focused instead on the meaning conveyed by each sign in relation to their own circumstances.[70] The oral Torah was the elucidation of what God meant to say in a text that not only had left behind the context of the event of its own revelation, but also relegated into the background the contexts of the events it narrated.[71]

Two attitudes toward the oral Torah coexisted in ancient rabbinic thought. By the first understanding, the oral Torah was revealed at the time of the *matan Torah* (the revelation of the law on Sinai) along with its written counterpart. Statements from all generations of rabbis were but expressions of that revelation that were transmitted in a direct line from Sinai. In the other conception, rabbinic dicta concerning the law were considered the product of interpretation of the written Torah.[72] In the sources that display this second attitude, as Elizabeth Shanks Alexander writes, "Oral Torah is not represented as an interpretive supplement that originates at Sinai. Instead, Oral Torah is portrayed as *the actualization of interpretive possibilities already embedded within the text of the written Torah*."[73] Though seemingly contrasting, these two approaches largely coincided in rabbinic ideology: the rabbis' very elucidations of the written Torah were seen as the object of oral revelation on Mount Sinai.

The rabbis acted as though through the production of their explanations they had been performing the work of the Torah. The immutability of Scripture required them to see their own intellectual activities as ever synchronous with the Sinaitic event.[74]

In contrast to this rabbinic self-identification, the fantasy undergirding Christian manners of quoting was that of setting right an authoritative truth that had been corrupted. Theology, as Antoine Compagnon writes, "has as its principle repetition."[75] Despite appearances, this notion is compatible with the fact that at least to some Christians the theological method appeared to consist in the inference of constructs not included in revelation from others that the latter did contain. This process was captured by Marius Victorinus through the expression *de lectis non lecta componere* (to compose from Scripture terms not read there).[76] The theologian's task was recognized to be the iteration of a message already uttered, but only implicitly or imperfectly understood. While the rabbis staged mutually contradictory dicta coming from the past in a polyphonic, synchronous piece that mostly neglected their chronological provenance, Christians used citations to construct an exact diachrony out of whose consistency orthodoxy verifiably arose.[77]

For Morawski, "The quotation which functions by virtue of an authoritative validity accepted by both writer and reader is evidence of both intellectual torpor and emotional-ritual assiduity."[78] If applied to late ancient Christian theologians' use of the patristic argument, this judgment would be ungenerous. There is no doubt that the discursive order to which dogmatization granted entrance was of a different nature than the one preceding it. Nevertheless, despite their practice of the patristic argument and self-representation as guardians of an immutable truth, Christian theologians remained agents of semiotic productivity and theological innovation well past the fifth century. The attribution of truth value to set statements opened the gates for a new type of hermeneutics, based on the interpretation and reconfiguration of the meaning of those assertions. Thus, the tendency to cite conciliar resolutions and patristic authorities as the best way to validate one's theological positions, commonly adduced as an example of the end of dialogue, set instead the premises for new forms of linguistic transactions (a historical dynamic partially explored in Chapter 4). What is more, the Christian "sole opinion" occasionally showed itself as being at odds with itself, revealing further interstices and spaces of internal variation. The restraint of Christian theologians, thus, was not any less intellectually fecund than the exuberance of the rabbis. A productive interplay of difference and continuity occurred both in a system dominated by a certain liberty in the use of the past, such as the one embodied by the rabbinic citational habits, and in one characterized by beholdenness to the ancestors, incarnated by the patristic argument. The difference between the two lay in the gesture that governed the production of meaning: a gesture of opening-up of dialectic in the Talmudic system, and one of closure thereof in the theological discipline.

That from a discourse-analytical viewpoint the disavowal of novelty in Christian theology was precisely the movement through which new ideas emerged does not detract from the fact that the self-representation of its practitioners was pinned on the preservation of an aboriginal content of faith. The already mentioned Vincent of Lérin expressed this fundamental image of theological activities through the theological motto *non nova, nove* (not new ideas, but the old ones told in a new way).[79] Crucially for this chapter's proposal, since it was an original truth that articulated the whole of discourse, no special regard was given to the activities of those performing the necessary duty of explicating the truth anew while having to proclaim nothing new. The retrieval of the integrity of truth that theologians presented themselves as accomplishing made their enterprise, if praiseworthy, hardly divine in their own eyes. While the rabbis' ways of citing ultimately pointed to their self-aggrandizing imagination, quite the contrary was the case for the Christian citational habit. The Christian intellectual guild practiced theology ex officio. The association between the Church and the Roman Empire normalized the profession of Christian theologians and regulated the performance of their expertise in ways unthinkable for the rabbis. Beyond the volatility of imperial support for this or that ecclesio-theological party, theology could count on the institutional backing of the Roman state and had to reckon with its regulating power.

This was a status unknown to the rabbis, whether in the Sasanian or in the Roman Empire. Unlike the study of Torah, theology was constituted into a profession whose legitimacy was a given that did not require of its practitioners self-identificatory investments or social justification. While Church intellectuals knew they were mounting guard over the integrity of God's word, the rabbis conceived of themselves as performing God's work.[80] They expended their labor to grant perpetual efficacy to a revelation outside of history, while theologians were forced to use their knowledge to preserve from corruption a truth historically entrusted to humanity once and for all.

The proliferation of so-called heresies was a bitter reminder for Christian thinkers of the inescapably illusory nature of the stability claimed by faith, elevated to a ground for salvation.[81] Heretics forced theologians continually to question the identity between the object of their faith and the pristine object of God's disclosure. As a result, the genealogies of error drawn by Christian heresiologists located heterodoxy in a historical line that interlocked with the sequence of Christian theologians' remedial interventions to create what Todd Berzon has called "an iterative cycle of orthodox and sectarian contestation."[82] To a sequence of villains learning—or indeed never learning—from one other's mistakes across multiple generations there corresponded a spiritual lineage of champions of an embattled truth, dedicated to restoring its wholeness. The logical unity and theoretical consistency of a persistently resurgent heresy required a perfectly coherent orthodoxy, constituted as the reconstitution of a word originally revealed. But this representation implied the logical priority of heretical corruption to the theological gesture of reinstatement, a dynamic encapsulated by the implicit orthodox formulation, challenged by Walter Bauer, according to which orthodoxy preceded heresy.[83] The mental efforts of Church intellectuals were therefore understood as a denial of the heretical denial of truth. Their theology was a science of the negative, a corrective and accidental enterprise. It is therefore little wonder that its practitioners' main object of self-identification was not their own humble antidotal gesture, but rather the truth that gesture allowed them to emplace anew.

Citing in the Talmud

The citation of dicta from the past, deployed in such a way as to mimic a live discussion, is a sustaining pillar of the Talmud's edifice. At the same time, scholars have come to understand citation as a central device in the strategies of self-representation of the compilers of the Babylonian Talmud, whose identity is the object of extensive debate. From the eleventh until the early twentieth century, the selection and arrangement of the amoraic sources and the composition of the stam were almost unanimously attributed—by traditional and then academic scholars alike—to Rav Ashi (d. 427), Ravina b. Huna (d. 499), or their disciples; the process of instruction was considered concluded by the time of their deaths.[84] This consensus was challenged in the 1930s, when Julius Kaplan argued for a composition in the era of the *savora'im* (reasoners, or sages who lived from the end of the amoraic period until approximately the end of the seventh century) and Abraham Weiss offered the alternative view of an ongoing process of composition of the stam on the part of the amora'im themselves.[85]

Alongside Kaplan's and Weiss's theories of savoraic and continuous amoraic composition there stands, among others, a highly influential proposal first set forth by David Weiss Halivni in 1975 (with considerable evolution in its chronological description).[86] For Halivni, the stam was the product of rabbis working approximately between the demise of Rav Ashi (427) and the advent of the savoraʾim (whom he most recently dated to 650–750). These redactors had little to work with when crafting the gemara. Of the bits of argumentation and dialogue historically produced by earlier sages, only fragments had survived, that is, lone halakhic statements. The editors felt compelled to recapture the argumentation that in the performance of the house of study originally accompanied those prescriptive meimrot attributed by name, an argumentation that was not transmitted over the generations. In this process of recovery of the dialogic context of the halakhic statements, the editors showed a strong preference for dialectic over halakhic decision. By Halivni's theory, the savoraʾim were responsible only for minor editorial changes, such as the arrangement of the contents, the insertion of technical terminology, and interpolations into the text.

Some scholars who sympathize with Halivni's views about the posteriority of the stam's composition to the amoraic traditions it reports have raised doubts about his portrayal of those he called by the Hebrew neologism of *stammaʾim* (authors of the stam) as self-effacing historical actors beholden to an eroded tradition. Shamma Friedman, for example, saw instead in the gemara the product of a creative transformation of materials handed down to the redactors, sometimes aimed at making the meimrot more relevant to their immediate social context.[87] For Friedman, the anonymity of the stam is the result of the identification of its authors—whom he remained reluctant to date or to identify with Halivni's term of stammaʾim—with the activities of their own predecessors, with whose intents the editors perceived no break.

One of the outcomes of locating the redactional layer of the Talmud has been a shift of attention onto the agenda of those responsible for its creation, and at least provisionally away from the exercise of separating the grain of authentic amoraic statements from the chaff of editorial additions. Moulie Vidas, for example, has questioned the tendency shared by both Halivni's and Friedman's accounts to depict the editors as uninterested in marking a distance from the amoraʾim. Instead, he has proposed reading the anonymous layer as the artifice of a group keen on signaling discontinuity with tradition through the orchestration of its sources. The editors, Vidas has argued, sometimes went so far as fabricating the very distinction between the meimrot and the framework in which they encased them.[88] In his reconstruction, the visible layered structure of the text, far from being a function of historical stratification, is a product of textual manufacture. Through the device of citation, the "masters of the Talmud" highlighted their virtuosic ability to innovate through logic and argumentative ingenuity upon past traditions, and as a result the validity of the latter was both retained and undermined. Far from being a mere stratified repository of traditions, the Talmud is presented in this rendition as a stage for its authors' self-representation through citation.

It is easy to recognize that the omnipresent fact of citation as well as the specific citation techniques adopted in the Talmud have a complicating effect on the univocity of its text. Citation formulas, which are only a subset of technical terminology in the Bavli, are perhaps the most conspicuous manifestation of the ubiquitous presence of quotations. Sources are introduced with a citation term, whether they are attributed by name (e.g., "Rabbi X says") or quoted anonymously (e.g., "It was recited"). A battery of introductory formulas precedes statements of any kind.[89] Some specialized phrases introduce the citation of a tannaitic text (sometimes specifically as an objection) or an amoraic halakhah.[90]

The systematic marking-off of quotations through citation formulas exhibits the activity of literary orchestration. As such, it may be seen as effectively historicizing, and therefore relativizing, the validity of the very materials handled.[91] The abridged form in which the Bavli cites battling opinions arguably intensifies this subtle questioning of the contents of the amoraic citations.[92] The shortening further erodes the authoritativeness of the citation by revealing the processes of adaptation the latter had to undergo—including selection, transcription, and stylization—in order to be meaningfully imported into its new context.[93] As a whole, the observable scaffolding left in place by the editors of the stam casts a shadow of doubt on the authoritativeness of the cited statements.[94]

The formulas used to introduce the words of amoraʾim arguably constituted a prominent sign posted by the editors to differentiate between the materials they were handling and those they were composing.[95] The formulas may have been originally associated with the teachings, added at some later point in their transmission, or apposed in the moment of final composition. According to Halivni, they were assigned in the latest stage of production of the Babylonian Talmud.[96] A challenge to this hypothesis has come from Richard Kalmin, who has noticed that in the absence of purely formal determinants the citation formula that accompanies a meimra depends on chronological and geographic factors likely associated with the time and location of the very amoraʾim cited.[97] Some hint about the dating of the formulas might derive from a comparison with their equivalents in the Palestinian Talmud, with which they partly overlap in phraseology. If the formulas were added to both Talmuds around the same time, the Yerushalmi's likely completion in the early fifth century could provide an indication of the time by which amoraic teachings in the Bavli gained theirs.[98] However the chronological question is adjudicated, the adoption and retention of this device in connection to the weaving of statements into the overall literary framework of the Talmud is remarkable for the attention it brings to the stam's performance.

Talmudic scholars have long expressed skepticism about the correctness of the attributions of dicta and about the feasibility of the related task of reconstructing the intellectual biographies of the sages whose names populate the Bavli.[99] The text itself acknowledges at times by means of fixed formulas that some of its attributions are either conjectural or pseudepigraphic. The gemara also admits that the assignation of meimrot to later authorities was a common practice among the amoraʾim.[100] The pervasiveness of Talmudic pseudepigraphy, which goes beyond the cases acknowledged by the Talmud itself, may be connected to fictional amoraic argumentation developed by its editors for literary or didactic purposes, and revealed to us by inconsistencies in the logical flow of the sugyot.[101]

The Bavli's explicit concern with and thematization of the question of citations' correct attributions was the product of a conception of authorship that had undergone significant evolution since the tannaitic era. As Vidas has shown, in tannaitic times the rabbis' limited engagement with the words of their predecessors and the treatment of the latter as tradents—transmitters of tradition, as opposed to authors—of the sayings assigned to them was correlated with a certain amount of textual fluidity: "Since tradition must be binding, but on the other hand it is not bound to any of its specific formulations by specific sages, transmitters may amend it so as to preserve it more faithfully."[102] It was not until the amoraic era that the sages began to see, at least in Palestine, both tannaitic and amoraic statements as originally produced by and expressing the opinions of the rabbis who were recorded as uttering them. The amoraʾim, separating citation from authority, strove to retrieve the original formulation of the dicta, treating rabbinic traditions as texts to be submitted to rational inquiry in their exact formulation.[103] In the Bavli, as Sacha Stern has demonstrated, a "flexible concept of authorship" led the editors to state on occasion that a meimra attributed in a first moment to a sage had actually not been authored by him but was only implicit in his teaching, or that the sage to whom a dictum was attributed was only its tradent and not its originator.[104] Multiple aspects of the literary structure of the Bavli suggest that for this work "rabbinic teachings do not belong to individual rabbis, but rather to some anonymous, collective tradition."[105]

A germane phenomenon, relevant for a survey of rabbinic approaches to the authoritativeness of traditions, concerns variations in the content of the meimrot. Numerous instances of parallel traditions reported with variations are found across the corpus.[106] When it comes to the occurrence of this phenomenon in relation to tannaitic statements, some scholars have speculated that in the time of their creation traditions developed in multiple versions by different schools were committed to writing and preserved in independent recensions. A similar case was made by Eliezer Rosenthal regarding the attestation of different formulations of the selfsame tradition in the Bavli, which Friedman explained instead through its reformulation for purposes of updated relevance or conformance to the opinions of later tradents.[107]

The aggregate of these phenomena makes it clear that, as Friedman writes, "we ought to treat [the meimra] as a distinct literary source and not as a literary quotation of loose talk."[108] In the meimra, in fact, "All we have is a contrived literary rendition of the opinion of an amora, formulated concisely and according to fixed literary models, which were inserted throughout the Talmud [. . .] and so we do not possess '*divrei ha-amoraim*' [the words of the amoraʾim]."[109] More significant for our purposes than this historical consideration is the fact that the Talmud, irrespective of its actual practice, fails even to represent itself as preserving the literal correctness of the citations it adduces. The editors of the Bavli allow with relative insouciance the freedom with which they handle their citations to surface visibly in the text.

An example of this phenomenon may be exhibited through the analysis of a brief sugyah contained in *b.* Ḳiddushin 41a.[110] Here we observe a ruling of Mishnah being gradually subjected to revision in the following centuries, by being first made the object of interpretation in the fourth century—at the height of the amoraic period—and later subverted through a rather uninhibited use of amoraic citations on the part of the editors. This sugyah displays an extreme example of a tendency to use citations as unanchored bits subject to reformulation as well as rearrangement. Although some of the literary phenomena shown by this short passage are not typical of the whole corpus, they sharply manifest the combination of appreciation and liberty with which the editors of the Talmud habitually approached the amoraic citations they handled. Even when they were not busy rewriting as they are observed to do here, they can be seen shifting statements into different argumentative contexts from those to which they originally belonged, or coupling them with meimrot to which they were originally unrelated. In this sense, the following sugyah reveals an impressive sliver of the editors' broader, though often less visible, attitude toward their predecessors. What come to the foreground in the Talmudic citational habit are the performative activities of an intellectual class, not the interest in the preservation of an unchangeable truth such as that which sustains the Christian practice of the patristic argument.

The sugyah under examination is found at the beginning of the second chapter of Ḳiddushin ("Betrothal"), the seventh and last tractate of the order Nashim ("Women"), in the Babylonian Talmud.[111]

> [The Mishnah has taught:] *A man [can] betroth [a woman] by himself or through his agent. A woman [can] be betrothed by herself or through her agent. A man [can] betroth his daughter when she is a young woman by himself or through his agent etc.* [The gemara asks:] Now [that the Mishnah has taught] "through his agent," was it necessary [to also teach] "by himself"? Rav Yosef said: "The *mitsyah* [precept] is more [appropriately performed] by him than through his agent. For [this case is similar to] that of Rav Safra, who would scorch the head [of an animal by himself on the eve of the Sabbath], [and to that of] Rava, who would salt a mullet [by himself on the eve of the Sabbath]." There are some who say that in this [issue] there is also a prohibition, according to what Rav Yehudah said that Rav said. For Rav Yehudah said that Rav said: "A person cannot betroth the woman before seeing her, lest he might see in her something objectionable and she may become repulsive to him. And the Merciful One has said [instead] (Lev 19:18): 'And you shall love your neighbor as yourself.'" And when [the statement] of Rav Yosef was said, it was said with regard to the last clause [of the mishnah]: "A woman can be betrothed by herself or through her agent." Now [that the Mishnah has taught] "through her agent," was it necessary [to also teach] "by herself"? Rav Yosef said: "The mitsyah is more [appropriately performed] by her than through her agent." For [this case is similar to] that of Rav Safra, who would scorch the head [of an animal by himself on the eve of the Sabbath], [and to that of] Rava, who would salt a mullet [by himself on the eve of the Sabbath]." But in this [issue] there is no prohibition, according to what Reish Lakish said. For Reish Lakish said: [Women have a saying:] "It is better to dwell in matrimony than to dwell in an unmarried state."[112]

The mishnah reported here rules on the manners in which a betrothal should be conducted. Instructions for both contracting parties are issued, as well as special indications—irrelevant to the small portion of the gemara's discussion to be examined here—for the case of a father committing his daughter to betrothal. The mishnah teaches that both a man betrothing a woman and a woman being betrothed can engage in the betrothal by themselves or through an agent. However, in principle the ability of a man to betroth a woman in person may be inferred a fortiori from his ability to betroth her through an agent. For this reason, the gemara asks what the mishnah's superfluous mention of the man's own person ("by himself") is meant to teach.[113] In answer to this question, a statement attributed to Rav Yosef, a third-generation amora, is reported, according to which the expression "by himself" is redundantly spelled out to indicate that in-person betrothal is preferable to betrothal by proxy (just like the prepositional phrase "by himself" is given preferential treatment in the order of the sentence relative to "through his agent"). This is in accordance with the general principle whereby every precept is best observed personally rather than through an agent. The example is then reported (drawn from *b.* Shabat 119a) of two fourth-generation amora'im, Rav Safra and Rava, who in tribute to the same principle performed Sabbath preparations by themselves, without availing themselves of any help.[114]

The gemara then proceeds to inform the reader of the opinion of "some who say" (*ika de-ʾamre*) that it is not merely less preferable, but indeed prohibited, for a man to betroth a woman by means of an emissary.[115] We are told that the opinion concerning the prohibition of betrothal by proxy derives from a saying of Rav, cited by Rav Yehudah, according to which a man should not betroth a woman until he has seen her, as he otherwise risks discovering only after the betrothal that something in her repels him, and he might eventually be led to issue her a *geṭ* (divorce document). Somewhat puzzlingly, this outcome is decried as standing at odds with Scripture's commandment to care for one's neighbor's interest as for one's own (Lev 19:18).[116]

The gemara takes note of the apparent contradiction between the statements of Rav Yosef and Rav. If, as Rav Yosef claims, a man's betrothing of a woman through an agent is deemed only less preferable than his doing so by himself, the betrothal by agent must not be disallowed, as Rav instead claims. The redundancy of the syntagm "by himself" cannot possibly be meant to teach the mishnah's preference for in-person betrothal if a man is altogether prohibited from betrothing a woman through an agent. It is to be noted that this logical impossibility is doubly dangerous in that it jeopardizes the establishment of the preferential norm not only regarding the man but also regarding the woman. In Rav Yosef's teaching, in fact, although the interpretation is pinned on the first clause of the mishnah—"A man [can] betroth [a woman] by himself or through his agent"—the validity of the ruling derived from the first clause extends to both the first and the second (and presumably to the third, concerning the man's daughter, as well).

In order for the seeming inconsistency between the opinions of Rav Yosef and Rav to be reconciled, we learn that Rav Yosef's statement was made not about the first clause of the cited mishnah (the *reisha*), concerning a man's ability to betroth a woman, but about the second clause (the *seifa*, a term that can also refer to the last clause), touching on the ways in which a woman is betrothed.[117] What Rav Yosef really said, we are now told, was that the pleonastic prepositional phrase "by herself" in the mishnah's second clause is meant to teach that for the woman the in-person accomplishment of the precept of the betrothal is preferable to its performance by proxy.[118] In the case of the woman, there stands no actual prohibition on betrothal by proxy such as the one derived for the man's betrothal from Rav's words cited by Rav Yehudah. A saying reported by Reish Lakish ("It is better to dwell in matrimony than to dwell in an unmarried state") presumably as popular among women, indicating that a woman will not reject a man after having been betrothed to him, shows in fact that women content themselves with their men no matter what. Therefore, women do not stand at risk of contravening the precept of caring for one's neighbor's interest as for one's own as a result of discovering in them an unpleasant trait.[119] That in-person betrothal is preferable to betrothal through an agent can thus be learned from the redundant preposition with the feminine pronoun ("by herself"). This is said again to be accordant with the general rule that a precept is better observed personally than through a proxy, as also shown by the solicitude of the two masters in their Sabbath preparations.[120]

Whether the expression "And when [the statement] of Rav Yosef was said, it was said with regard to the last clause [of the mishnah]" is attributed to the "some who say" or is presented in the anonymous voice of the stam, its deployment by the editor compels the latter to make a daring philological move. Rav Yosef's meimra contained two occurrences of the masculine pronominal suffix ("by him" and "through his agent"), which had as their referent the man who was the subject of the first clause of the mishnah. Since the woman who is the subject of the second clause requires the use of a feminine pronoun, the only way the referent of the sage's affirmation could have been mistaken was for the meimra itself to have been misreported. Rav Yosef's statement must then be cited in a different form, with the two masculine pronouns converted into the feminine ("by her" and "through her agent"). The amora's dictum is altered before our very eyes.

The expression "when/if . . . was said, it was said with regard to the first/last clause [of the mishnah]" (*ki/i itemar . . . aseifa/areisha itemar*) occurs in multiple passages of the Babylonian Talmud.[121] In some cases, the statement of the amora is simply said to refer to the seifa instead of the reisha, or the other way around, without the need for any emendation of the original meimra.[122] In other cases, however, a reformulation is necessitated in order for the dictum to apply to the new referent.[123] Such is the case in our passage.[124]

The editor of the sugyah was likely working with two statements: one by Rav Yosef, explicitly commenting on the text of the mishnah, and one by Rav Yehudah citing Rav, possibly unrelated to this mishnah in its original utterance.[125] The two sayings may have reached the editor of the sugyah packaged together in one tradition.[126] Rav Yosef's and Rav's statements read respectively as follows: "The mitsṿah is more [appropriately performed] by him than through his agent"[127] and "A person cannot betroth the woman before seeing her, lest he might see in her something objectionable and she may become repulsive to him. And the Merciful One has said [instead] (Lev 19:18): 'And you shall love your neighbor as yourself.'" The editor decided to integrate Rav Yosef's statement with the anecdotal report of the supererogatory Sabbath eve activities of some rabbis portrayed in *b.* Shabat 119a as expressing their respect for the Sabbath by attending personally to its preparations.[128]

Particularly significant for the argument pursued in this chapter is the editor's decision to posit a specious contradiction between the sayings of Rav Yosef and Rav Yehudah citing Rav. These two meimrot were in reality fully compatible for at least two reasons. First, it is perfectly possible for a man to have seen a woman, or to have even known her well, and to still betroth her through an envoy.[129] Second, the "prohibition" announced by the gemara is by necessity one of a light nature. No violation of a Torah commandment is entailed in a betrothal performed through an agent. It is also very likely that even according to those asserting the existence of a "prohibition" of this kind of betrothal, the prohibition applied exclusively a priori, whereas a betrothal by proxy was considered a posteriori valid. Additionally, despite later interpreters' attempts to capture the ḳiddushin under the rubric of "fructification and multiplication" (*periyah u-rviyah*), a Torah precept derived from Gen 1:28, there exists no positive commandment to perform a betrothal.[130] The prohibition that the gemara infers from Rav's words is therefore not a true interdiction, but rather just a strong version of the preference expressed by Rav Yosef.

Artificially opposing Rav Yosef's and Rav's dicta to one another allowed the editor to push the discussion forward: now that Rav's opinion was upheld, Rav Yosef's had to be rescued from incorrectness.[131] In order to do so, as seen above, an amended version of Rav Yosef's statement was provided. One of the outcomes of this way of proceeding was a certain degree of legal uncertainty, as by the end of the sugyah no practical halakhic conclusion is drawn. Nonetheless, as things stand by the close of the discussion, the reader is left with the impression that Rav's opinion is at least temporarily upheld: while a woman can get betrothed by herself (a preferred option) or through an agent, a man can only betroth a woman in person. Remarkably, this state of legal affairs stands in direct contradiction with—or at least represents an important limitation of—the contents of the mishnah, which unquestionably permitted a man to betroth a woman through an envoy. By playing two meimrot against each other and altering with a contrived philological gesture the contents of one of them, our editor not only opened up the text of the mishnah, but allowed the foundation of its provisions to collapse under the weight of the amoraic edifice. This is all the more impressive given the notoriously pragmatic and consequential nature of rabbinic discussions concerning matters related to women.

The editor's craft would be no less conspicuous if he were believed to have inherited, as seems most plausible, not the sole masculine version of Rav Yosef's statement, but rather two separate meimrot, one for the man and one for the woman, and to have staged the discrepancy between Rav's words and the masculine version of Rav Yosef's dictum for the sake of revealing the feminine version only after the coup de théâtre of his philological emendation.[132]

Though not always as extreme as those performed by our editor, manipulations of previous strata were common in the give-and-take of the stam. Although they certainly constituted a qualitative leap, they lay in continuity with the amoraic handling of tannaitic sources as expressed, for example, by the formula "it is defective" (*ḥissorei meḥassera*).[133] Such citational practices bridged two opposite modes of citing, aptly described by Daniel Weidner as "the faithful citation of tradition and the critical citation of philology."[134] As the authority of the handled materials was obliquely questioned in the stam, their contents receded into alethic uncertainty and out of focus while the work of the editors came into the foreground. The activities of the editors of the

Talmud were situated in defiant continuity with the practices that produced the cited materials.[135] The dialectic on which their Talmud was built could not be conceived without the meimrot for whose insertion into the gemara they were responsible: while the stam's talk was meritorious, it could not be sustained without the citations it mobilized. When using an amoraic dictum as the object of their virtuosic operations, the editors relied on its existence to display their skills. As such, the creation of a break with a past utterance also entailed the establishment of a connection with the activity that had produced it. In weaving a thick fabric of citations to exhibit the performance of their work, the editors justified their own strategies of knowledge production as a perfecting continuation of the work of the amoraʾim.[136]

The Chronologies of Jewish and Christian Dialectic

The Bavli's practice of citing amoraic statements embodies a more general rabbinic preference for the validation and transmission of multiple opinions. This tendency is commonly traced back to the Council of Yavneh, allegedly celebrated by Rabban Yohanan ben Zakkai in the first century. Shaye Cohen has argued that this gathering promoted an atmosphere of tolerance and inclusion that was captured in the Mishnah, a document unprecedentedly preserving different opinions on various topics of Jewish law.[137] Taking Cohen's findings farther, Daniel Boyarin has drawn a developmental line from the Yavnean pluralistic ethos in the service of the discovery of truth to the stam's "sensibility of the ultimate contingency of all truth claims, one that goes even beyond the skepticism of the Platonic academy."[138] A series of cross-referencing legendary narratives about Yavneh scattered in the Babylonian Talmud project back into the first century the institutional and discursive reality of fifth- and sixth-century Talmudic academies. This reality implied embrace of a "disputation without telos,"[139] subsumed under the subtly authoritative voice of the literary layer of anonymous authorship known as the stam. Correlated to this aimless debate was a skeptical disavowal not only of rational dialectic, but also of the singularity of religious truth: the redactional layer of the Bavli was "virtually apophatic with respect to the divine mind, its text, and intentions for practice."[140] Thus, Boyarin concludes that "[t]he practice of the Babylonian Talmud [. . .] was constituted through a rejection [. . .] of the desire or hope for 'certain knowledge'"[141] and canonized "unending dissensus as the very essence of the Torah as given at Sinai."[142]

When looking at the Babylonian Talmud, it is hard to dispute that many of its sugyot, especially the most elaborate, manifest a tendency to leave all opinions on any given subject as standing and respectable, avoiding drawing legal conclusion. But is the purpose of complex sugyot really to determine that truth cannot be identified?[143] Or is it, as others have proposed, to defend the intelligence of the amora'im and the internal consistency of the legal system each of them upheld?[144] Many theories have been set forth to explain the interminable proliferation of debate in the Talmud. The recent development of an interpretive strand attuned to the detection of subtle argumentative-prescriptive "tendencies" behind the seemingly inconclusive give-and-take of a certain number of sugyot stands as a note of caution against an assessment of the Bavli's enterprise as aiming overall at a gleeful dismantlement of any and all truth claims.[145] The Talmud's promotion of endless dialectic is undeniable.[146] But the semiotic fabric of the Bavli is still best characterized, with Sergey Dolgopolski's felicitous phrase, as a "well-structured uncertainty."[147] My reading of the rabbinic idealization of dialectic, then, privileges a different aspect from Boyarin's renditions of a skeptical or apophatic epistemology.[148] The extreme appreciation of discussion was tied not to a hermeneutical commitment to the contingency or non-existence of truth, but to the rabbis' investment in the celebration or justification of their own intellectual activities.[149]

The continued existence of the rabbis as a social group critically depended on their ability to protract their disputations. Dialectic virtuosity being the hallmark of a successful rabbi, a stage was needed on which he could continue projecting his competence. The investment in the social practices of the house of study was fully integrated within rabbinic ideology, to which Torah study was central since the tannaitic period.[150] It was also linked to the amoraic redefinition of the rabbi as a scholar and to the professionalization of the rabbinical class, which had a correlate in the elevation of the study of Torah to a status superior to all other pious activities.[151] Even the amoraic insistence on the oral nature of Torah instruction was meant to emphasize the requirement for mediation of tradition by a master: the activities of the house of study needed to endure.[152]

In his investigations of the Talmudic penchant for dialectic, primarily based on haggadic passages, Boyarin has set the emergence of this phenomenon in a chronological parallel with rising Christian dogmatism. In rabbinic culture, the elevation of hermeneutic indeterminacy to a religious ideal coincided with the creation of long-lived institutions, including the formation of the Yeshiva, the composition of the Talmud, and the valuing of study as worship. Among the various narratives Boyarin has discussed is the famous story of the oven of Akhnai. In a dispute with the sages about the purity of an oven, the second-generation tanna Rabbi Eliezer successfully invoked in support of his position a series of preternatural occurrences and, eventually, the manifestation of a heavenly voice. His preference for revealed divine knowledge over the rules of Talmudic dialectic cost Eliezer his affiliation to the rabbinic community. Boyarin compared this ideological rendition to a legend about the Council of Nicaea found in the *Church History* of Rufinus (d. 411).[153] This fifth-century Christian tale constitutes a variation on the theme, found in four ancient authors, of a debate with a pagan philosopher reportedly held at Nicaea.[154] In Rufinus's version, the pagan rhetorician, who could not be defeated by skilled ecclesiastical dialecticians, was silenced by an unlearned Christian confessor. While Christians dealt with lack of unity within the community by demonizing perceived theological sophistry, Boyarin concluded from the comparison, the rabbis handled disagreement by divinizing dialectic. The two tendencies evolved contemporaneously, in the fifth and sixth centuries, and both discredited a fair and rational dialogue aimed at achieving the truth, privileging instead apophatic simplicity in the service of hierarchy and authority.

Any attempt at pinpointing a clear timeline for the emergence of rabbinic discursive formations is bound to clash against a large number of unknowns. Additionally, the lack of a shared immediate geo-cultural and political context between the Bavli and the Latin and Greek theological corpus makes the search for parallel timelines largely futile. Nonetheless, a focus on halakhic as opposed to haggadic materials in the Talmud and a reassessment of crucial passages in ancient ecclesiastical histories together reveal the inception of the citational habits described in this chapter, and of the discursive formations they encase, at a significantly earlier time—the fourth century—than the period on which Boyarin's examination of its full development has focused.

Boyarin's chronology emphasizes the break between the attitudes toward dialectic held by the amora'im (akin to the Yerushalmi's) and by the Bavli's editors.[155] And indeed, the differences between the amoraic intellectual project and that of the stam are undeniable. While dialectical argument was central to the editors' scholarly undertaking, even late amora'im were still invested in the establishment of halakhah.[156] Even so, the production of dialectic as a critical feature of the textuality of the stam was the end point of a historical process that had begun in the fourth century, when the ideal of legal prescriptiveness was beginning to decline.

Three facts—pertaining to a domain that straddles the issue of citation and the broader hermeneutical question of dialectic—support the conclusion that this ideal was progressively relinquished in the fourth century.[157] First, as David Kraemer has demonstrated, the first four generations of amora'im (ca.

230–350) show an evolution from the concise and prescriptive style of the Mishnah and of *midrash halakhah* (legal interpretation) to the highly argumentative, logical, and self-reflexive statements attributed to the fourth-generation amora'im Abaye and Rava.[158] This period exhibits a steady increase in the use of argumentation as compared with prescriptiveness and in the recourse to meta-discursivity.[159] It is likely that Rava was involved in the formulation of pedagogical procedures and in the promotion of a more theoretical and speculative manner of learning, with an emphasis on the reasoned explanation of the law that led to the recording of entire discussions.[160] Second, despite the default tendency in Babylonia to deliberate on halakhic matters exclusively based on the pronouncements of authoritative rabbis of previous generations, among later amora'im the authority of their amoraic forefathers was relativized.[161] Whereas second- and third-generation amora'im saw any challenge to the authority of first-generation amora'im as preposterous, such reactions were much less frequent among amora'im of the fourth and fifth generations (ca. 320–370).[162] Third, fifth-generation amora'im (ca. 350–370) sometimes opined that in disputes between early amora'im no final position could be established, and represented the positions of those predecessors as all valid.[163]

There is no denying that it was the later composers of the Bavli who converted dialectic into the paramount form of rabbinic discourse.[164] The competitive, status-driven culture of the rabbinic academies of Babylonia fostered admiration for the dialectician able to manipulate truth by constructing hypothetical cases and mastering the objection-and-solution format.[165] However, the editors' relative disinterest in legal ruling and their elevation of dialectic to an end to itself was the conclusion of a longer trajectory. While these phenomena fully came to fruition in the sixth century, their burgeoning lends itself to be dated to the early fourth.

Similarly, the appeal to the Fathers was already inchoately developed during the fourth-century Trinitarian controversies. An episode reported by Socrates in *Church History* instructs us about the status to which the authority of the pre-Nicene Fathers had risen by the end of these theological disputes. Emperor Theodosius, forced by "Arian" grievances over the Constantinopolitan settlement of 381 to summon a new council at Constantinople in 383, sought to promote a discussion between the different parties:

> Not long afterwards in the month of June, under the same consulate, the bishops of every sect arrived from all places: the emperor, therefore, sent for Nectarius the bishop, and consulted with him on the best

> means of freeing the Christian religion from dissensions, and reducing the Church to a state of unity. "The subjects of controversy," said he, "ought to be fairly discussed, that by the detection and removal of the sources of discord, a universal agreement may be effected." Hearing this proposition Nectarius fell into uneasiness, and communicated it to Agelius, bishop of the Novatians, inasmuch as he entertained the same sentiments as himself in matters of faith. This man, though eminently pious, was by no means competent to maintain a dispute on doctrinal points; he therefore proposed to refer the subject to Sisinnius, his reader, as a fit person to manage a conference. Sisinnius, who was not only learned, but possessed of great experience, and was well informed both in the expositions of the sacred Scriptures and the principles of philosophy, being convinced that disputations, far from healing divisions, usually create heresies of a more inveterate character, gave the following advice to Nectarius: knowing well that the ancients have nowhere attributed a beginning of existence to the Son of God, conceiving him to be co-eternal with the Father, he advised that they should avoid dialectic warfare and bring forward as evidences of the truth the testimonies of the ancients. "Let the emperor," said he, "demand of the heads of each sect, whether they would pay any deference to the teachers who were in agreement before the division in the Church [*tōn pro tēs diaireseōs en tē ekklēsia prosarmosantōn didaskalōn*]; or whether they would repudiate them, as alienated from the Christian faith. If they reject their authority, then let them also anathematize them: and should they presume to take such a step, they would themselves be instantly thrust out by the people, and so the truth will be manifestly victorious. But if, on the other hand, they are not willing to set aside the ancients [*tous archaious*], it will then be our business to produce their books, by which our views will be fully attested." Nectarius having heard these words of Sisinnius, hastened to the palace, and acquainted the emperor with the plan which had been suggested to him; who at once perceiving its wisdom and propriety, carried it into execution with consummate prudence.[166]

Graumann has argued that this passage contains elements of historical embellishment and has hypothesized that the Church historian drew on a local Novatian source that celebrated Sisinnius. His skepticism, however, goes too far in its denial of historicity to the appeal to the patristic argument recorded in the passage. Graumann identifies what he calls a "parenthesis" in the set of clauses represented by the words "knowing well that the ancients have nowhere attributed a beginning of existence to the Son of God, conceiving him to be co-eternal with the Father."[167] He sees the "parenthesis," corresponding to the words "conceiving him to be co-eternal with the Father," as the product of an interpolation by Socrates, as allegedly shown by the ignorance these words reveal about the state of Trinitarian debate.[168] Sisinnius, as a competent theologian, would have known that attempts to use the pre-Nicene Fathers as a benchmark of orthodoxy made earlier during the controversies had proven ineffective. Graumann hints that Sisinnius's very reference to the Fathers as "witnesses" rather than "decisive judges" signals awareness of the historical ineffectualness of arguments invoking the opinions of pre-Nicene Fathers. Moreover, the scholar argues, Sisinnius would have known that the temporality of the Son's existence had ceased to be a point of contention between pro- and anti-Nicene many decades earlier.[169] The characterization of the Son as "co-eternal" (*sunaïdion*) to the Father, a typically Origenian construct, is thus claimed to be more appropriately read as the product of Socrates's boundless admiration for Origen than as Sisinnius's own view.[170] As a result of this analysis, Graumann hypothesizes that the Novatian source that lionized the Constantinopolitan reader attributed to him a generic reference to the need for the pro-Nicene to argue for their position based on its fidelity to tradition.[171] It is to this account that Socrates latched on, in his alleged construction of the fantasy of a fourth-century invocation of the patristic argument, based on Sisinnius's equally fictional reasoning to the effect "that the ancients have nowhere attributed a beginning of existence to the Son of God."

Graumann's account presents some contradictions. First, the hypothesis of an interpolation presupposes that the remainder of the report about Sisinnius's motivations (the set of clauses beyond the alleged parenthesis) belonged to a report grounded in some historical source. This assumption is incompatible with the thesis, advocated by Graumann, that the very act for which those motivations were adduced, that is, the proposal of the patristic test, was Socrates's own invention. Second, the notion that the reference to the Fathers as mere "witnesses" indicates awareness of the weakness of the patristic argument is hard to reconcile with the proposal that the very introduction of the patristic test into the narrative was the ideologically laden work of Socrates's hand. Third, and most important, the scheme attributed to Sisinnius is presented in *Church History* precisely as a tactic to allow Nectarius and Agelius's parties to eschew the debate (*dialexis*) imagined by Theodosius. If Socrates's presentation of Sisinnius's plan to submit the various sects to a test of patristic conformity is replaced with his allegedly historical suggestion that his fellow partisans generically reference tradition during the debate, the whole structure of Socrates's story comes undone and the very reason for the Novatian source's preservation of Sisinnius's role in it is nullified.

It is indeed likely that there existed a Novatian source for this episode. It is known that Socrates had sympathies for the Novatian movement, whose moral rigor and dogmatic orthodoxy he admired, and that he recruited the help of a Novatian informer, the priest Auxanon. It is also likely that the motives adduced for Sisinnius's formulation of his proposal—expressed in the set of clauses in which Graumann identified a parenthesis—were either Socrates's or his source's fabrication. Socrates himself, after all, does not include the justification for Sisinnius's suggestion in the direct speech he places in his mouth. But there seems to be no compelling reason to deny the veracity of the report that Sisinnius's proposal involved an appeal to the authority of the Fathers.[172]

The argument that such an appeal is nowhere else attested to until the Council of Ephesus (431) amounts of course to a mere petition of principle.[173] In fact, Rufinus of Aquileia informs us about a different trace of the emergence of a novel regime of patristic textuality in a Roman episcopal reunion held just one year before the Council of Constantinople of 383:

> When discussions were being held on the matter of reconciling the followers of Apollinarius, Bishop Damasus commissioned a certain friend of his, a presbyter and an extremely eloquent man who regularly performed such duties for him, to draw up a statement of the Church's faith which those who wished to be reconciled would have to subscribe. In devising a form of words for the incarnation of our Lord, this man found it necessary to use the phrase "*homo dominicus.*" The Apollinarians took offense at the expression and began to attack it as a novelty. The deviser set about defending himself, answering their objections from the authority of the ancient writings of catholic men. Now it happened that to one of those who were complaining of the novelty of the expression he showed the phrase in question occurring in a work by Bishop Athanasius.[174]

The criterion of orthodoxy invoked in this Roman synod is not, as in its near-contemporaneous Council of Constantinople (383), willingness to express generic doctrinal agreement with ancient authors who remain (at least in *Church History*) unnamed. It is instead verbatim adherence to the formula demonstrably proclaimed by one named writer of high repute. Admittedly, in the episode reported by Rufinus this new formation is still observed in its embryonic state: Damasus is said to have produced the patristic prooftext for his formula only in response to the Apollinarist protests. But the joint power of Socrates's and Rufinus's reports makes it hard to deny that in the early Theodosian era the tendency to quote earlier writers and synodal documents, sporadically observed during the Trinitarian controversies, was sharpening into a coherent habit commanding institutional sway. Although the theological mechanism of appeal to orthodox writers of previous generations would not assume clearer contours until the fifth century, it was already operative in the last quarter of the fourth century.

The Parted Ways of Intolerance

Thus far this chapter has argued that the Jewish and the Christian traditions initiated in the fourth century a rethinking of their approach to dialectic as embodied in their respective citational habits, and that in both cases these approaches found their full fledging and achieved a stable form by the sixth century. While in Christian writings citations were embedded in a mechanism—the patristic argument—favorable to claims based on authority, in the Bavli citation was a crucial tool in the establishment of the stam's predilection for dialectic give-and-take.[175] These different citational habits reveal politically consequential differences between Jewish and Christian intellectuals' conceptions of their respective standings. Christian theologians' expertise in the Christianized Roman Empire required them to expound a truth that it was the empire's own role to police. The rabbis' processual truth, on the other hand, amounted to the unfolding of their own hermeneutical methods. Thus, the self-identifications of Christian theologians and Jewish sages revolved around different aspects of their processes of intellectual production: respectively the object and the fact of their own labor. This state of matters had profound effects on the two intellectual elites' implicit views of the polity. While the theologians identified the object of their belief with political rationality, the rabbis located that principle squarely in their operations.

Two divergent paths to intolerance unfolded out of the Jewish and Christian traditions as a result. Theologians staked claims to a hidden, superior rationality that led to the establishment of monodoxy—intolerance toward diversity of ideas—as central to Christian discourse. The rabbis justified instead their own socialized forms of learning as the site of the constantly renewed manifestation of divine reason. In doing so, they set up what may be called "monology"—defined as the toleration of one sole manner of speaking, a product of their agreement to disagree—as a device of methodological intolerance.[176] The story of Elisha ben Abuyah analyzed in Chapter 1 is emblematic in this regard. It was not Elisha's recourse to foreign *theologoumena* but his participation in an alien manner of speaking that determined his exclusion from the rabbinic forum, resulting in—rather than being caused by—his violation of orthopraxis. A similar preoccupation may be evinced from the narrative about the ousting of Rabbi Eliezer in the story of the oven of Akhnai.[177] Unwilling—not unlike Elisha—to subscribe to the practices of the rabbinic community, Eliezer was excommunicated.

The monological and monodox forms of intolerance respectively generated by the Jewish and Christian intellectual traditions were not exactly antithetical, but rather asymmetrical. The intolerant paradigm embodied by the Talmud—its exclusionary inclusivity—was predicated on granting a license of rationality to the bearers of all viewpoints so long as these were formulated within the bounds of rabbinic modes of learning.[178] By relinquishing the ground of the "correct opinion," the rabbis tended to center their activities as a worthy manifestation of their corporate existence. This staging had as its inadvertent result an inconspicuous totalitarian reflex, arising out of the sphere of intellectual practice but inevitably pervading the whole discursive system. The Christian model of intolerance—its inclusionary exclusivity—revolved instead around the acceptance of one sole opinion, but one continuously accessible to the rational insight of all human beings. Theologians' rigid insistence on right belief, with their attendant demureness about the inherent value of their work, had as a correlate the nurturing of a certain universalistic impulse deriving from the domain of credence. This impulse, also mostly removed from sight, was destined, for better or worse, to have unexpected historical effects on western modernity.[179]

Both groups' approaches to intra-communal pluralism tended, each in its own way, toward intolerance. For the rabbis, however, the question of the polis posed itself only adventitiously, and less urgently than for their Christian counterparts. This was not only a product of the rabbinic elite's comparatively trivial political responsibilities, no matter their geographic location. Seeing their social group as an organic totality embodying divine reason, Jewish sages were only marginally preoccupied with imposing a firm hand on the polity outside the walls of the academy and beyond the fellowship of the *ḥaverim*, the faithful Jewish allies of the rabbinic movement. Though with important distinctions and gradations between Palestinian and Babylonian Judaism—and in Babylonia between amoraic and later times—the *ʿammei ha-ʾarets* (Jewish commoners) against whom the sages occasionally voiced their invectives for failing to observe halakhah with sufficient care were to them but a de-politicized, fitfully bothersome afterthought.[180]

The rabbis' totalitarian urge did not extend to Jewish society because they had succumbed to the temptation of organically structuring the house of study itself as an accomplished totality. The authoritarian proclivities of Christian intellectuals, instead, were on full display since their own professional activities were not conceived as in themselves articulating political meaning. This state of affairs had important consequences for the encounter between the already-parted Jewish and Christian ways. Once the separation was consummated, the two intellectual traditions paid one another disproportionate degrees of attention. The continued existence of Judaism represented a greater historical conundrum and theoretical challenge for Christianity than the other way around.[181] As many have argued, rabbinic identity was articulated in opposition to various figures of otherness—including the sectarian *minim*, with whom Christians were probably lumped—but never in specific relation to Christianity.[182]

To be sure, Jewish and Christian elites engaged in many forms of dialogue, and traces of their conversations remain visible in rabbinic literature.[183] The Bavli contains materials that testify to the percolation into rabbinic culture of—and to some rabbinic interaction with—Christian theological and exegetical constructs.[184] But precisely the fact that the rabbis on occasion broke their otherwise deafening silence about Christians, while never casting them as protagonists in their representations of otherness, may act as a corrective to conspiratorial assessments of "the most thunderous silence in Jewish history."[185] The rabbis were as wary of Christians as they were of other forms of social life that eluded their normative instincts. Nevertheless, they appeared hardly as concerned with Christians' existence as the metaphor of two siblings vying for supremacy, common in the scholarly conversation on the parting of the ways, would have us expect. Although the scriptural heritage shared by Jews and Christians objectively thrust their literate elites into competition for the legacy of biblical Israel, the prevalent lack of direct engagement with Christianity found in the late ancient Jewish corpus suggests that opposition to this tradition was not a fundamental aspect of rabbinic identity formation.[186]

The asymmetry described above between Jewish and Christian attitudes toward their own activities allows us better to understand this puzzling state of intercommunal relations. To the rabbinic monological mind, Christian theologians appeared to be unengaged in the appropriate practice, the dialectic typical of Talmudic discussion. Placed outside the correct order of speech, Church intellectuals were naturally precluded from partaking in discursive reason. As such, the rabbis saw interlocution with them as inherently unproductive. Contrarily, to the monodox eyes of Christian theologians, the troublesome element of Jewish historical persistence was not the rabbis' refusal to engage in the practices of the Church's thinking body, which Christians themselves did not invest with particular value, but rather their failure to believe the truth of revelation. But as subjects recalcitrant to the acceptance of orthodox belief, the Jews also retained their potential ability to attain it. A universally available insight into divine rationality continued to be within reach for them, had they only desired or been graced to accede to it. Hence the interest the Jews never ceased to elicit in Christians: even when other actors occupied them, the specter of Judaism lingered in Church writers' peripheral vision, its fate ever ready to be mobilized against heresy. Throughout late antiquity, Christians did not tire of lavishing these estranged siblings with unwanted attention, whether to convert them, reprimand them, or use them as a foil in their own theological battles.[187]

Conclusion

While Christianity and Judaism stand today as two discrete traditions, scholars agree that considerable effort was needed to sever them in ancient times. But how and when that process of separation took place has been the subject of endless debate. Over the past century, models for configuring ancient Christian-Jewish relations have shifted from early historiographies inspired by supersessionist theology; to the view, predominant in the second half of the twentieth century, of a definitive parting of the ways occurring as early as the first or second century CE; to the present emphasis on the absence of historical evidence for an early separation, epitomized by the hyperbole of "the ways that never parted."

Some of the problems historians face in modeling Christian-Jewish relations in antiquity—with their obscure and shape-shifting dynamics of filiation, difference, and congruity—are curiously reminiscent of those raised in the fourth century by the arcane theological issues tackled by the likes of Arius, Athanasius, and Basil. Were Judaism and Christianity the same, discrete, or caught in some more complex articulation of identity and otherness? And if they made up one entity, how could their conspicuously different manifestations be accounted for and described? Did a Jewish religion ever stand independently from Christianity before the child tradition interpellated it into existence?

Answers to these questions in contemporary scholarship surpass in diversity and theoretical resourcefulness even the solutions those Trinitarian thinkers and their colleagues offered to their own conundrums. The evidence for the Christian-Jewish parting has been reinterpreted a myriad of times. Giving one more turn to the historiographic screw, this book examines the role played by the fourth-century Trinitarian controversies in the late ancient estrangement between Jews and Christians. I propose that new partitions emerged in Judeo-Christianity thanks to the novel practices that Christians developed during those debates to express their ideas about God.

It was hardly the views about Christ articulated during the Trinitarian disputes that caused the Christian-Jewish continuum to break: based on the background of Second Temple Judaism, none of the theological options explored by Christians would have caused particular scandal to a contemporaneous Jew on account of its articulation of divine reality. Nevertheless, by definitively and cohesively disengaging from earlier modes of inquiry and argumentation that functioned as bridges between the proto-rabbinic and proto-Christian intellectual elites, the production of a theological field on the part of believers in Jesus was largely responsible for the separate constitution of Christianity and Judaism as intellectual traditions.

The fourth-century transformations in Christian ways of discussing God were certainly grounded in profound mutations in the status of Christians in the Roman Empire. However, the reference to the political does not offer a sufficient explanation for the new discursive order of theology and the separation between Jews and Christians. A denser description is called for. Investigating the late ancient emergence of a Christian rhetoric, Averil Cameron wrote that "it is still useful to ask how Christians, the quintessential outsiders as they appeared to men like Nero, Pliny, Tacitus and Suetonius, talked and wrote themselves into a position where they spoke and wrote the rhetoric of Empire. For it is perfectly certain that had they not been able to do this, Constantine or no Constantine, Christianity would never have become a world religion."[1] I submit that if Christians had not begun to talk and write about the divine in the way they did during the Trinitarian controversies, Constantine or no Constantine, Christianity would not have stood as a separate intellectual tradition.

The core of this work contains a chronological narrative about the Trinitarian controversies, combining thematic overviews with more focused case studies. Rather than providing a new comprehensive account of the whole theological landscape of the fourth century, I have chosen to approach the subject through samplings of less-leafed-through pages of the corpus, sometimes capable of yielding nuances neither thematized in antiquity nor perceived in contemporary scholarship. The limited time bracket of the reconstruction pursued by these chapters, corresponding to the period from the reign of Constantine through that of Jovian, accords with the goal to trace the inception, rather than the full fledging, of a particular style of intellectual inquiry. This central section of the book does not include an exhaustive description of the steps that contributed to the emergence of theology. Rather, it highlights observable moments, with the aim of seizing three important gestures performed by Christian intellectuals: the placing of increasing emphasis on conciliar creeds, the recombination of geo-cultural traditions of debate, and the development of a specialized set of rules for doctrinal discussion.

This account is bookended by a discussion of broader discursive formations in Christian and rabbinic self-understandings. In particular, I attend in the last chapter to a description of the effects that the specification of the intellectual practices of the Christians had on the self-understanding of Jewish and Christian literate leaderships. Of course, both the chronology of these repercussions and the dynamics activated varied from one locale to another (dramatically so between Rome and the regions outside the Roman Empire). For this work, I have chosen to represent these effects in something approximating an ideal form, abstracting from those variations. After the parting, a fundamental asymmetry installed itself in the relationship between the two communities. Christian theologians, enamored with the exclusive truthfulness of their belief, endeavored to bring a recalcitrant Jewry under its saving power. The rabbis, on their part, focused as they were on the unshared legitimacy of their own practices for knowledge production, remained unmoved by those calls and uninterested in interlocution with actors who appeared placed in a mistaken order of discourse.

Abbreviations

CCSG	Corpus Christianorum. Series Graeca
CCSL	Corpus Christianorum. Series Latina
CSCO	Corpus Scriptorum Christianorum Orientalium
CSEL	Corpus Scriptorum Ecclesiasticorum Latinorum
GCS	Die Griechischen Christlichen Schriftsteller der ersten drei Jahrhunderte
PG	Patrologiae cursus completus. Series Graeca
PL	Patrologiae cursus completus. Series Latina
PLS	Patrologiae cursus completus. Series Latina. Supplementum
PTS	Patristische Texte und Studien
SC	Sources Chrétiennes
TU	Texte und Untersuchungen zur Geschichte der Altchristlichen Literatur

Notes

Introduction

1. For the details of this reconstruction, in which Quartodecimanism is distinguished from Protopaschism, see Daunoy, "La question"; Grumel, "Le problème"; Visonà, "Ostern"; DelCogliano, "The Promotion." On ancient controversies concerning Easter see Lohse, *Das Passafest*; Huber, *Passa und Ostern*; Cantalamessa, Lienhard, and Quigley, *Easter*; Ó Cróinín and Warntjes, *The Easter Controversy*; Mosshammer, *The Easter Computus*, 109–316.

2. See Sozomen, *Historia ecclesiastica* 1.16. The decision of the Council of Arles of 314 is discussed in Optatus of Milevis, *De schismate Donatistarum*, App. 4; ed. Ziwsa, *S. Optati Milevitani libri VII*, 207; reported in Turner, *Ecclesiae Occidentalis monumenta*, I, 384.

3. See Theodoret of Cyrrhus, *Historia ecclesiastica* 1.9. See also Socrates of Constantinople, *Historia ecclesiastica* 1.9. The text adduced as a second reason the need for uniformity within the Church. A similar sentiment is expressed by Constantine in a letter to the churches reported in Eusebius's *Life of Constantine*: see McCarthy, "The Council of Nicaea," 191 (and on Eusebius's testimony about the Paschal workings of the council in his treatise *On Easter* see ibid., 190). On the Paschal discussions at Nicaea see also Gwynn, "Reconstructing the Council of Nicaea," 102–103. McCarthy (191) rightly underlines the instrumental nature of the references to Judaism in this debate.

4. On the paschal question at Nicaea see Duchesne, "La question de la Pâque." On the impact of the dispute see Petersen, "Eusebius and the Paschal Controversy."

5. In recent decades these debates have been more commonly referred to as "Trinitarian," in a shift away from the heritage of heresiological practices, as well as in recognition of the relatively marginal role that the figure of Arius occupied in the intellectual landscape of all those eastern Christian thinkers—in some historical accounts called

"Eusebians"—who fought against the coalition that had emerged victorious from the Council of Nicaea (325): see, e.g., Hanson, *The Search*, xvii–xviii. On the Eusebians (οἱ περί Εὐσέβιον) as an Athanasian construct see Gwynn, *The Eusebians.* On Athanasius's construction of "Arianism," see Gwynn, "Christian Controversy." On the dating of Arius's earliest activities see Simonetti, *La crisi ariana*, 26, n. 1; Hanson, *The Search*, 129–138; Ayres, *Nicaea and Its Legacy*, 15–16 and n. 14. On the chronology of the earlier phase of the Trinitarian debates and its literary testimonies see Brennecke, Heil, Stockhausen, and Wintjes, *Athanasius Werke. Dritter Band. Erster Teil. 3. Lieferung*, xix–xxxii.

6. For an introduction to the notion of "discourse" see Maingueneau, *Discours et analyse du discours*, 17–29.

7. See Cameron, "Jews and Heretics." See also Shepardson, "Christian Division"; Shepardson, "'Exchanging Reed for Reed'"; Shepardson, "Defining the Boundaries"; Shepardson, *Anti-Judaism*; Laird, "John Chrysostom," 134–136; Burrus, "Hailing Zenobia."

8. See Gen 25:24. See also A. Segal, *Rebecca's Children*; Capes, *Israel's God.* Some scholars have attended to an excavation of the unspoken motives underlying the creation of the historiographic consensus on the parting of the ways. In a nutshell, the notion of two sibling traditions rising out of the ashes of the Second Temple allows Christians and Jews to posit, respectively, their continuity with Judaism and their priority to Christianity, while—reassuringly for both contemporary Jewry and Christendom—guarding the supposed difference between the two entities: see, e.g., Becker and Reed, "Introduction," 16. That this may well be so does not eliminate the potential explanatory power of the model.

9. See Reed, "'Jewish Christianity' after the 'Parting of the Ways'"; Yuval, *Two Nations.* On the various terminologies through which different models of ancient Christian-Jewish relations are captured see Gabrielson, "Parting Ways."

10. See, e.g., Gager, *The Origins of Anti-Semitism*; M. Taylor, *Anti-Judaism*; Wilson, *Related Strangers*; Lieu, *Image and Reality*; Paget, "Anti-Judaism"; Fredriksen and Irshai, "Christian Anti-Judaism"; Auwers, Burnet, and Luciani, *L'antijudaïsme des Pères.*

11. See Boyarin, "Rethinking Jewish Christianity." On Jewish Christianity see, among an immense number of studies, Paget, "Jewish Christianity"; Paget, "The Definition"; Jackson-McCabe, *Jewish Christianity Reconsidered*; Crone, "Jewish Christianity and the Qurʾān (Part One)"; Crone, "Jewish Christianity and the Qurʾān (Part Two)"; Reed, *Jewish-Christianity and the History of Judaism*; Jackson-McCabe, *Jewish Christianity: The Making.*

12. Neusner, *The Three Stages*, 77. For subsequent uses of the expression see Boyarin, "Semantic Differences," 66, n. 4. The notion that "[t]hough neither were born in this century, yet both [Judaism and Christianity] owe more to its outstanding leaders than to any other similar group of contemporaries, and both are to this day, in many ways, fourth century religions" is found as early as 1934 in Parkes, *The Conflict*, 155. For

an argument in favor of considering Christianity and Judaism two religions born in the fourth century see Ruether, "Judaism and Christianity."

13. See Boyarin, *Dying for God*, 18: "It seems reasonable to surmise that it was not until the fourth century, when Christianity became the hegemonic religion of the Empire and Christian 'orthodoxy' was set, that rabbinic Judaism solidified and emerged in its own orthodoxy and hegemony, as Judaism *tout court*."

14. As shown by the critical reception of Le Goff, *Les intellectuels au Moyen Âge* (originally published in 1957), the application of the noun "intellectual" (and of the associated adjective), coined as late as the nineteenth century, to pre-modern phenomena is not unproblematic (for the volume's reception see the essays collected in *Il comportamento dell'intellettuale*, particularly the "Introduction" as well as Le Goff's "Introduction" to the 1985 edition). Discarding the eighth- to ninth-century Carolingian renaissance as a restricted, courtly phenomenon, Le Goff saw in the flourishing of studies in Paris and Chartres in the twelfth century the first affirmation of a class of urban intellectuals, "those making a profession of thinking and of teaching their thought." In the thirteenth century, the universities where those teachers gathered would develop their own scholastic methods, organize their material practices, and affirm their institutional power vis-à-vis secular and ecclesiastical authorities. My adoption of the word "intellectuals" does not entail pre-dating the rise of the intelligentsia in European culture. The question as to whether this class of educated Christian thinkers in late antiquity constituted a social group with which high-medieval and later intellectuals were in objective sociological continuity is best adjudicated by others. See also Asor Rosa, "Intellettuali"; Tabacco, "Gli intellettuali del medioevo" (in particular 7–38). On the application of the term "intellectuals" to Christian writers see Markschies, "Intellectuals and Church Fathers"; Markschies, "Preface"; Ayres and Ward, "Introduction and Acknowledgments," 1–2; Yadin-Israel, "Christian, Jewish, and Pagan Authority" (referring to the historical discussion of the term "intellectual" in Collini, *Absent Minds*). On early Christain "intellectuals" see also Secord, "Julius Africanus"; Secord, *Christian Intellectuals*.

15. Outside the Roman Empire "Arianism" was widespread among the Goths: see Simonetti, *Studi sull'arianesimo*; Simonetti, "Arianesimo latino"; Luiselli, "Dall'arianesimo dei Visigoti."

16. See Lim, *Public Disputation*, 149–182.

17. Along with this divergence there came the development of strikingly different relationships to the Hellenic philosophical tradition. While Greek philosophical concepts and terminology largely underlay, and to a certain degree enabled, the speculations about the divine of Christian theologians (see Zachhuber, *The Rise of Christian Theology*, for the effects of this encounter in post-Chalcedonian times), Jewish interpreters between Philo of Alexandria (first century BCE to first century CE) and Saadia Gaon (ninth to tenth century CE) eschewed any systematic use of philosophy: see Krei-

sel, "Philosophical Interpretations," 92–120. This important aspect is excluded from my treatment, which privileges the formal facets of the emergence of the Christian intellectual traditions over a scrutiny of the threads that contributed to its formation.

18. For a definition of binitarianism see Bucur, "'Early Christian Binitarianism.'" See also Hurtado, "The Binitarian Shape"; Boyarin, "The Gospel of the Memra."

19. To reconstruct this discussion, mostly conducted between Daniel Boyarin, Menahem Kister, and Peter Schäfer, see Boyarin, "The Parables of Enoch"; Boyarin, "Daniel 7"; Boyarin, *The Jewish Gospels*; Schäfer, *The Jewish Jesus*; Boyarin, "Shuv le-ʿinyian shetei reshuyot"; Kister, "'Panim be-fanim'"; Schäfer, "Metatron in Babylonia"; Kister, "Meṭaṭron ṿe-haʾel"; Schäfer, *Two Gods in Heaven*.

20. The theme of divine sonship was also taken up in early medieval Jewish reflection and later Kabbalistic thought: see Idel, *Ben*.

21. This consensus was largely solidified by the publication of Boyarin, *Border Lines*. For the reception of this fundamental work see, amid the abundant literature, the review essays contained in Burrus, Kalmin, Lapin, and Marcus, "Boyarin's Work" and Boyarin's response in "Twenty-Four Refutations." For a succinct exposition of the evidence for the Second Temple background of New Testament Christology see J.D.G. Dunn, *The Parting of the Ways*, 241–270.

22. For recent work on the category of religion as it relates to late antiquity see Nongbri, *Before Religion*, with further bibliographical references.

23. Admittedly, monotheistic ideas may also be found in late ancient religious phenomena unrelated to the Jewish field and dubbed "pagan" by Christians. However, my examination does not rely on a phenomenological typology, but rather it holds elite social actors as its ultimate historical reference. In recent years a mounting corpus of scholarship has dealt with the question of pagan monotheism: see Athanassiadi and Frede, *Pagan Monotheism*; Mitchell and Van Nuffelen, *Monotheism between Christians and Pagans*; Mitchell and Van Nuffelen, *One God*; Van Nuffelen, "Beyond Categorisation"; Ahmed, Fürst, Gers-Uphaus, and Klug, eds. *Monotheistische Denkfiguren* (see also the more dated but fundamental Erik Peterson, *Heis theos*). The label "pagan monotheism" has come to be applied to non-Christian and non-Jewish expressions of "belief in the powers of a unique, supreme divinity, though not necessarily to the exclusion of all other gods," a belief that is said to have "underpinned most forms of religion in the Roman world of the fourth and fifth centuries A.D." (Mitchell and Van Nuffelen, *Monotheism between Christians and Pagans*, 1). Sharp critiques of this model have been offered, sometimes with good arguments: see, e.g., Sfameni Gasparro, "Monoteismo pagano"; Cerutti, "Unità del divino"; Cerutti, "Monoteismo pagano?"; and several of the contributions collected in Guittard, *Le monothéisme*. See also the pugnacious review of the volume edited by Mitchell and Van Nuffelen contained in Wells, "Spotting an Elephant."

24. The reasons for this tension might have as much to do with an intrinsic logic of monotheism as with the origins of its Jewish variety (a problem irrelevant to my discus-

sion), whether such origins be sought in the Canaanite context of pre-exilic Israelite religion or, as Assmann has it, in Egyptian culture; see, e.g., Assmann, *Of God and Gods.*

25. See Kraemer, "Concerning the Theological Assumptions of the Yerushalmi," 355–356.

26. *B.* ʿAvodah zarah 3b. On God in rabbinic Judaism see Mottolese, *Dio nel giudaismo rabbinico.*

27. See, e.g., MacMullen, "Sfiducia nell'intelletto." On the role of literature in fourth-century Roman society see Lançon, "Militia philosophorum"; Van Hoof and Van Nuffelen, "The Social Role"; Vessey, "Literary History." On fourth-century theological works as literature see Dihle, *Greek and Latin Literature,* 539–553.

28. 383 is the year of the presentation of four faith declarations to Emperor Theodosius by Bishops Nectorius, Eunomius, Demophilus, and Eleusios (respectively, an orthodox, a heteroousian, a homoian, and a Macedonian). On this occasion also Palladius and Wulfila appeared at the imperial court. R. Williams, *Arius,* 48–61, has provided an argument in favor of a complete reshuffling of the chronological order of the earliest documents of the Trinitarian controversies; by his account, *Of One Body* would be as late as 325. This document has been commonly assumed to be the work of Alexander himself; for a dissenting opinion attributing it to Athanasius see Stead, "Athanasius' Earliest Written Work."

29. For several insights on the new "order of books" inaugurated by the Christian fourth century see Vessey, "The Forging of Orthodoxy."

30. This theory was recently articulated most sharply in Boyarin, *Judaism* (relying partly on Nirenberg, *Anti-Judaism*). On Jewish religion as a modern invention see Batnitzky, *How Judaism Became a Religion.* See also Barton and Boyarin, *Imagine No Religion.* For a summary of Boyarin's views on the parting of the ways see Marcheselli, "Daniel Boyarin."

31. On the participation of lay masses in the theological debates of the fourth century see MacMullen, "The Historical Role"; McLynn, "Christian Controversy and Violence"; Lyman, "*Lex Orandi*"; Perrin, "À propos de la participation des fidèles"; Perrin, "The Limits"; Ullucci, "What Did He Say?"; Perrin, Civitas confusionis; Tannous, *The Making of the Medieval Middle East,* 11–43.

32. In their exchanges and occasional confrontations, such cultural elements as lore, narratives, epistemological assumptions, and "ways of knowing"—on which see Chin and Vidas, *Late Ancient Knowing*—could be freely transacted, borrowed, and contested. These instances of continued engagement between literate subjects, which continue to be the object of important studies, lie outside the scope of my account. Select recent examples of the extremely vast literature on the topic include Kister, "Allegorical Interpretations"; Monnickendam, *Jewish Law*; Bar-Asher Siegal, *Jewish-Christian Dialogues.*

33. MacIntyre, *After Virtue,* 222.

34. Asad, *The Idea,* 14.

35. As Markschies, *Christian Theology*, 5–19, indicates, for some time Christian thinkers eschewed the application of the terms θεολογία (theology), θεόλογος/θεολόγος (theologian), and θεολογεῖν (to theologize) to their own reflexive activities. Those terms had in fact long designated in the Greek-speaking world the activities of those who composed, or cultically recited, mythological teachings and hymns about the gods. The close Platonic association of the word θεολογία, however, may be credited for its progressive adoption on the part of Christian authors, starting with Justin Martyr. Beginning in the late third century, the semantic field of θεολογία came to point to a reflection on intra-divine relations, in the wake of Clement of Alexandria's and, above all, Origen's usage. In a fragment of a treatise that may have been authored by Hippolytus, θεολογεῖν is used to refer to words that have as their object Jesus's divinity. In Didymus the Blind's *Commentary on Zacharias*, θεολογία refers to a discussion of divine nature as opposed to speech about its economic unfolding—a distinction retained in Eusebius of Caesarea's theorization, whereby theology was turned into a subdiscipline of philosophy. Around the time of Eusebius, θεολογία also began to designate Christian thought pursued against the heretics and with the dogmatic validation of a council. This terminological exploration is only of marginal interest to this study, as a focus on authors' conscious lexical choices in the representation of their own intellectual labor risks casting a shadow on the concretions, symptomatic of wider changes, that emerge from their texts. On θεολογία and related terms in early Christian literature see also Stiglmayr, "Mannigfache Bedeutung"; Kattenbusch, "Die Entstehung"; Whaling, "The Development" (all cited by Markschies).

36. See Markschies, *Christian Theology*, 4. The distinction is first made in Assmann, *The Search for God*, 10–12.

37. See Ayres, "Irenaeus," 155–163.

38. Laudan, *Progress and Its Problems*, 80–81. These metaphysical and methodological dimensions, Laudan explained (81), are often closely intertwined. Laudan's theories about the workings of science were first offered in *Progress and Its Problems* with the aim of addressing deficiencies in the work of Thomas Kuhn (1922–1996) and Imre Lakatos (1922–1974). Although philosophers of science typically blend in their elaborations the descriptive problem (how to identify units of knowledge) and the evaluative question (how to assess scientific progress and rationally to compare different programs) here only the first aspect of their debates is of strict relevance. In his famed *The Structure of Scientific Revolutions* (1962, republished with a postscript in 1970), Kuhn had identified scientific paradigms—defined rather inconsistently (see Shapere, review of Kuhn, *The Structure of Scientific Revolutions*)—as the basic unit of science. Paradigms for Kuhn provide scientists with their problems as well as with insights about how these can be solved. During periods of "normal science," paradigms are deemed unchangeable, but loss of confidence in them due to the proliferation of anomalies results in crisis and in the replacement of a paradigm with a new one. Lakatos, partly reacting to the Kuhnian attack on traditional philosophy of science, identified the building block of the scien-

tific edifice not in a paradigm (or in the theories that fall under its umbrella) but in a research program (see above all Imre Lakatos, "Falsification"). The research program is founded on a hard core of unfalsifiable and unchangeable assumptions (a negative heuristic) and on a protective belt of ancillary hypotheses, capable of being altered as the result of the refutation of a theory under the guidance of a positive heuristic, also contained in the program's core. Unlike Lakatos's research programs, Laudan's research traditions are capable of different and contradictory formulations over their typically long lives, their evolution being a result of a modification in their hard core (see Laudan, *Progress and Its Problems*, 78–79 and 96–100). They all generate theories, both contemporaneous and successive to one another, and often mutually inconsistent ones (see ibid., 78–79). The relationship between a research tradition and its constituent theories, however, is not one of entailment, in either direction. Rather, research traditions serve to limit their constituent theories' domain of application, generate conceptual problems for them, provide a heuristic for their construction, and rationalize or justify them (see ibid., 86–92).

39. These include "empiricism and nominalism in philosophy, voluntarism and necessitarianism in theology, behaviorism and Freudianism in psychology, utilitarianism and intuitionism in ethics, Marxism and capitalism in economics" (Laudan, *Progress and Its Problems*, 78).

40. On the fact that councils were not an ever-present institution see Ayres, *Nicaea and Its Legacy*, 85. On the functioning of the early councils see MacMullen, *Voting about God*. On the expansion of the institute of the council during the fourth century see Graumann, "The Conduct of Theology," 542–543, and on its decision-making processes see Graumann, "Theologische Diskussion." It is worth noticing that in the fourth century synods increasingly became assemblies of one ecclesiastical group claiming to represent the whole Church.

41. See Jaeger, "La preuve judiciaire," 522–529.

42. Boltanski, *The Making of a Class*, 34. Boltanski describes in relation to his object a two-stage process, which he surmises "may well be a paradigm for a more general set of social processes" (31): the first step involves objectification and institutionalization, the second the acquisition of a distinctive identity. Boltanski finds it "necessary to analyze not only the organizational process that created [the group] but also the concomitant symbolic process of group definition" (34). This task is sketched, though in a different analytical mode than the one envisioned by Boltanski, as far as the Christian and Jewish leaderships are concerned, in Chapter 5 of the present book.

43. Ibid., 145. Boltanski speaks of the representation of the group as having to be understood in three senses: in the sense of the definition of what distinguishes the group from other groups (with effects of alterations of the whole semantics of society); in the psychological sense of a "representation" of where the group stands in the minds of its members and of others; and in the sense of "a stylized image that helps to establish the sort of collective belief in its existence that the group must command before it

can claim social recognition" (34–35). The process of ecclesiastical institutionalization had been favored by the rise of monoepiscopacy in the third century. On this phenomenon see Bremmer, *The Rise of Christianity*, 66; Camplani, "Le trasformazioni"; Stewart, *The Original Bishops*; Urciuoli, *Servire due padroni*, 133–136. On the relationship between the rise of monoepiscopacy and the constitution of Christian archives see Camplani, "Setting a Bishopric."

44. The notion of "discursive field" is introduced in Maingueneau, *Sémantique de la polémique*, 15. A discursive field is heterogeneous, containing "*dominant* and *dominated* positionings, *central* and *peripheral* ones" (Maingueneau, *La philosophie*, 31, italics in the original; Maingueneau, "Champ discursif").

45. The notion of "positioning" has been privileged in recent decades in discourse analysis over that of "discursive formation" (*formation discursive*), first elaborated by Michel Foucault and then developed within an Althusserian framework—and imported into the discipline—by Michel Pêcheux: see Maingueneau, "Positionnement," 454; Maingueneau, "Formation discursive," 270. "Positioning" can refer both to an identity and to the operation that allows a speaker to achieve and maintain that identity, an ambiguity pointing to the fact that identities can only be preserved through ceaseless effort: see Maingueneau, "Positionnement," 453.

46. See Maingueneau, "Positionnement," 454.

47. Making discourse a primary object of investigation in the study of ancient literary corpora aids in moving beyond the age-worn debate between textualists and contextualists in intellectual history, by questioning the very existence of a difference between an inside and an outside of the text. As Maingueneau writes (*La philosophie*, 12), "[T]o think in terms of discourse means to associate intimately language (more broadly the semiotic resources available in a society), communicational activity, and knowledge (the different types of knowing, individual or collective, mobilized in the construction of the sense of enunciations)." Discourse analysis, thus, examines "neither the textual workings nor the situation of communication, but rather that which ties them through an enunciation device deriving both from the verbal and the institutional" (14). By relating "utterances to communication devices, to the norms of an activity, to the groups that draw from it their legitimacy" (16), discourse analysis evidences how any act of enunciation "must be carried out at the same time in the world that it builds and in the world wherein it is built, which is deployed as a device of legitimation for the situation of enunciation from which [the act of enunciation] claims to arise" (17).

48. The notion of "constituting discourse" was first introduced in Cossutta and Maingueneau, "L'analyse des discours constituants." The idea is further developed in Maingueneau, "Analyzing Self-Constituting Discourses"; Maingueneau, "Constituant (discours —)"; Maingueneau, *La philosophie*.

49. Maingueneau, "Analyzing Self-Constituting Discourses," 183.

50. See ibid., 197.

51. Discursive fields are produced within the inter-discourse. The latter, strictly speaking, is itself "a discursive space, *a whole of discourses* (belonging to the same discursive field or to distinct ones) entertaining relations of mutual delimitation" (Maingueneau, "Interdiscours," 324, italics in the original). The inter-discourse logically precedes the discourses by which it is formed. The priority of the inter-discourse relative to discourse is an axiom of French discourse analysis, asserted above all by Michel Pêcheux: the ideological subjection (*assujettissement*) of the subject can only be achieved by discursive formations insofar as the inter-discourse dominates them, since it is in the inter-discourse that the constitution of objects and their relations, adopted by subjects in their discourse, occurs (see ibid., 324–325).

52. For example, although theological terminology was rarely the subject of intense discussion in homiletic or catechetical literature, it was integrated into works belonging to those genres in a way that allowed it to govern their expositions of the scriptural text (which were otherwise formally comparable to the expositions that had been conducted in previous centuries).

53. For a recent example see Tannous, *The Making of the Medieval Middle East*, 85–198, where the legacy of the Council of Chalcedon (451) is explored.

54. Exceptions include Lyman, "A Topography of Heresy"; Burrus, *Begotten, Not Made*; Lim, *Public Disputation*; Galvão-Sobrinho, *Doctrine and Power*. Among the most noticeable historico-theological works on the Trinitarian controversies of the recent two decades are Ayres, *Nicaea and Its Legacy* and Anatolios, *Retrieving Nicaea*. For a survey of different trends in Anglophone scholarship on early Christianity see Cameron, "Patristics and Late Antiquity." See also Vessey, "'La patristique.'"

55. Symbolum Nicaenum; ed. Kelly, *Early Christian Creeds*, 215. I am leaving the term *ousia* untranslated because the understanding of its meaning, on which an English translation depends, was a matter of contention and the subject of important shifts during the Trinitarian controversies themselves. Translations such as "essence" or "substance" are often encountered.

56. Symbolum Nicaenum; ed. Kelly, *Early Christian Creeds*, 216.

57. See Zahn, *Marcellus von Ancyra*, 87; Harnack, *Lehrbuch*, II, 262–264; Loofs, "Das Nicänum," 68. Harnack proposed that the Cappadocian reinterpretation of the Nicene formula, derived from homoiousian theology, was a reaction to the subordinationist theology of the homoians and heteroousians: see Harnack, *Lehrbuch der Dogmengeschichte*, II, 251–253. On the homoiousian theologico-ecclesial alliance see Löhr, *Die Entstehung*; Löhr, "A Sense of Tradition." For a clear formulation (and contestation) of the traditional historiographic model see Brennecke, "Erwägungen," 241. For a refutation of the theory that the Nicene homoousios was understood at Constantinople in a homoiousian sense see Ritter, *Das Konzil von Konstantinopel*, 270–293; see also Dinsen, *Homoousios*; Hanson, *The Search*, 190–202. For a synthetic evaluation of the course of the Trinitarian controversies see Hanson, "The Doctrine of the Trinity."

Lienhard, "*Ousia* and *Hypostasis*," 103, questions the notion that the parallel usage of ousia and hypostasis in the Nicene Creed indicates their synonymousness. On ousia and hypostasis see also Prestige, *God in Patristic Thought*, 179–196. On the relationship between the use of the two terms at the Council of Antioch of 268 and in the councils of the 340s see Giulea, "Antioch 268 and Its Legacy."

58. A variation on this reconstruction suggests that it was the philosophical distinction between ousia and hypostasis that had been lost: only Basil of Caesarea's understanding of ousia as an Aristotelian secondary substance (δευτέρα οὐσία: see Aristotle, *Categoriae* 5), mediated through his rival Eunomius's retrieval of the dichotomy, led to a solution (see Morales, *La théologie trinitaire*, 22).

59. Such narratives are compatible with a triumphalist conception of the evolution of doctrine that has been lastingly dominant, if at times concealed under a cloak of historicism, in the historiography of Christian theology. As recently as 1975, for example, Aloys Grillmeier referred to the Chalcedonian formula—which would import a temporary cessation of hostilities in the fifth-century Christological controversies—as a "hidden entelechy" (*Christ in Christian Tradition*, I, 548). Similar accounts describe the unfolding of Christian thought in its first few centuries as a providentially driven sequence of twists and turns, inevitably culminating in the eventual orthodox formulations. At the same time, they celebrate the orthodox doctrinal achievement as the elaboration most adequately seizing the spirit of the original content of faith, though partly rewriting its letter with the aim of contrasting the threat of heresy. For a critique of this approach see Daley, "Christ and Christologies." On this topic see also Reiser, "An Essay"; Reiser, "Dogma and Heresy"; R. Williams, "Does It Make Sense"; Boyarin, "Beyond Judaisms," 351, n. 80. See also McGuckin, "Il lungo cammino," 41.

60. See Prestige, *God in Patristic Thought*, 211–213.

61. This was not a mere interpretive sleight of hand: the vague phrasing of the anathema was at the very least capacious enough to contain this understanding. See Stead, *Divine Substance*, 241–242.

62. See de Halleux, "'Hypostase' et 'Personne,'" 317.

63. See, e.g., Simonetti, "«Persona»," 534, and the sharply contrasting words of de Halleux, "'Hypostase' et 'Personne,'" 317, n. 5.

64. De Halleux himself concedes, however, that soon enough the Old Nicene alliance would interpret the Nicene Creed and its anathema in such a way as to view ousia and hypostasis as synonymous, whereas the New Nicene would distinguish between the two. For accounts that follow de Halleux see Hanson, *The Search*, 198–207; Zachhuber, "The Antiochene Synod," 88. For a definition of Old and New Nicene see note 67 below.

65. The results of this scholarship are summarized in Behr, "The Question of Nicene Orthodoxy."

66. De Régnon, *Études*. See Coakley, "Re-thinking Gregory," 432–436; Hennessy, "An Answer." See M.R. Barnes, "De Régnon Reconsidered."

67. In contrast to Barnes's tripartite distinction between Old, New, and pro-Nicenism, Ayres distinguishes only the label of "old Nicene" from that of "pro-Nicene"; he defines the latter as "a constantly developing theology with at least two significant phases between 360 and 380" (Ayres, "Nicaea and Its Legacy: An Introduction," 143). The concept of New Nicenism, coined by Loofs ("Jungnicänismus") and soon adopted by Cavallera ("néonicénisme"), became commonplace in the historiography of the early twentieth century: see Loofs, *Leitfaden*, 139–141; Cavallera, *Le schisme d'Antioche*, 303–305 (cited in Markschies, "Was ist lateinischer »Neunizänismus«?," 74, nn. 4 and 7, respectively). See also M.R. Barnes, "One Nature, One Power." I use the term "Old Nicene" in reference to the Eustathians and to all those in communion with them; "pro-Nicene" for any subjects expressing support for the Council of Nicaea of 325 (in whichever manner this creed was understood); and "New Nicene" for members of the alliance formed by Meletius at the Council of Antioch of 363. For a history of the pro-Nicene movement see DelCogliano, "The Emergence of the Pro-Nicene Alliance."

68. These four positions are the theologies of "the true Wisdom" (Alexander of Alexandria and Athanasius), "the One Unbegotten" (the "Eusebians"), "the undivided Monad" (Marcellus of Ancyra), and "a Son born without division" (western theologians).

69. Ayres, *Nicaea and Its Legacy*, 43.

70. Ibid., 236. In their responses to *Nicaea and Its Legacy*, Christopher Beeley and John Behr both argued, though from diverging positions and with regard to different aspects of the book's argumentation, that Ayres, eager to mend the alleged split between East and West, had glossed over important differences in ways of discussing the godhead (for example, by applying readings fit for Latin theologians, in particular Augustine, to eastern Greek writers, especially the Cappadocian fathers): see Beeley, "Divine Causality"; Behr, "Response to Ayres." See also the critique of Ayres's treatment of the Latin West in Beckwith, Review of Ayres, *Nicaea and Its Legacy*.

71. See Coakley, "Introduction: Disputed Questions," 138. See, however, the repudiation of a similar approach in Ayres and Radde-Gallwitz, "Doctrine of God."

72. This approach is influenced by the social-constructivist enterprise of the sociology of scientific knowledge, which over the last half century has also become increasingly attuned to the impact of local factors on scientific thought. Historical works on modern science have adopted the insights provided by such models: see, e.g., Schaffer and Shapin, *Leviathan and the Air-Pump*, in particular 3–21 and 332–344. For a treatment of the relationship between epistemic shifts and the structuring of a new order of books in the Theodosian era see Mark Letteney's forthcoming monograph *The Christianization of Knowledge*.

73. Ayres, *Nicaea and Its Legacy*, 1.

74. Ibid., 11. For a definition of the three criteria categorizing actors as pro-Nicene see ibid., 236. For examples of writings fulfilling this definition see ibid., 98–99. Ayres, "A Response," provides supplementary explanations about this author's perspective on culture.

75. Ayres, *Nicaea and Its Legacy*, 236 and 274–278.

76. See Newman, *The Arians of the Fourth Century*. On Newman's treatment of the Antiochene vs. Alexandrian school divide in relation to the Trinitarian disputes see King, *Newman and the Alexandrian Fathers*, 70–126.

77. Simonetti, *La crisi ariana*; Hanson, *The Search*.

1. A Tale of Two Heretics

1. On late ancient Christian heresiology see Simon, "From Greek Hairesis"; Le Boulluec, *La notion d'hérésie*; Cameron, *Christianity*; Desjardins, "Bauer and Beyond"; Cameron, "How to Read Heresiology"; Boyarin, "Hybridity and Heresy"; K. King, "Social and Theological Effects" (as well as other essays in Iricinschi and Zellentin, *Heresy and Identity*); Thomassen, "What Is Heresy"; Berzon, *Classifying Christians*. On Jewish heresiology see S. Cohen, "A Virgin Defiled"; Martin Goodman, "The Function"; Kats, "The Rabbinic Response," 287–294; Burns, "The Relocation of Heresy"; Schremer, "Beyond Naming"; Cohn, "Heresiology"; Bar-Asher Siegal, *Jewish-Christian Dialogues*, 1–42; den Dulk, "'One Would Not Consider Them Jews'"; Klawans, *Heresy*.

2. There is no lack of scholarship on the figure of Elisha ben Abuyah: see, e.g., Graetz, *Gnosticismus und Judenthum*, 62–71; Bin Gurion, "ʿErekh Aḥer"; Finkelstein, *Akiba*, 163–164 and 253–256; Hyman, *Sefer toldot tannaʾim*, 155–157; Stroumsa, "Aḥer"; Halperin, *The Merkabah*, 167–177; Halperin, *The Faces of the Chariot*, 31–37; Liebes, *Ḥeṭʾo shel Elishaʿ*; Goshen-Gottstein, "Four Entered Paradise Revisited," 114–119 and 126–129; Goshen-Gottstein, *The Sinner*; Arad, *Meḥallel shabat*, 244–245. Treatments of the Acher sugyah in *b.* Ḥagigah 15a can be found in Rubenstein, "Elisha ben Abuya"; Rubenstein, *Rabbinic Stories*, 229–244; Rubenstein, *Talmudic Stories*, 64–104 (based on Rubenstein, "Elisha ben Abuya"); Goshen-Gottstein, *The Sinner*, 89–124; Beʾeri, *Yatsa le-tarbut raʿah*, 105–171; Swartz, "Jewish Visionary Tradition," 219; Rovner, "Structure and Ideology"; Grossberg, "Between 3 Enoch"; Boyarin, "The Quest."

3. *T.* Ḥagigah 2:3: ארבעה נכנסו לפרדס בן עזאי ובן זומא אחר ור׳ עקיבא אחד הציץ ומת אחד הציץ ונפגע אחד הציץ וקיצץ בנטיעות ואחד עלה בשלום וירד בשלום בן עזאי הציץ ומת עליו הכתוב אומ׳ יקר בעיני ה׳ המותה לחסידיו בן זומא הציץ ונפגע עליו הכתוב אומ׳ דבש מצר׳ אכול דייך וגו׳ אלישע הציץ וקיצץ בנטיעות עליו הכתוב אומר אל תתן את פיך לחטיא את בשרך; ed. Lieberman, II, 381. Trans. adapted from Rubenstein, *Talmudic Stories*, 65, in turn based on Goshen-Gottstein, "Four Entered Paradise Revisited," 76–77.

4. Van der Heide, "Midrash and Exegesis," 52. Modern scholars have continued to debate the referents of those descriptions and quotations: see, e.g., Scholem, *Jewish Gnosticism*, 14–20; Urbach, "Ha-mesorot"; Fischel, *Rabbinic Literature*, 1–34.

5. Rubenstein, *Talmudic Stories*, 264.

6. For a translation of the expression *hahu gavra* as first-person singular pronoun see E. Melamed, "Lishana maʿalyah," 132 [= *ʿIyunim*, 276].

7. אחר קיצץ בנטיעות עליו הכתוב אומר אל תתן את פיך לחטיא את בשרך מאי היא חזא מיטטרון דאתיהבא ליה רשותא למיתב למיכתב זכוותא דישראל אמר גמירא דלמעלה לא הוי לא ישיבה ולא תחרות ולא עורף ולא עיפוי שמא חס ושלום שתי רשויות הן אפקוהו למיטטרון ומחיוהו שיתין פולסי דנורא אמרו ליה מאי טעמא כי חזיתיה לא קמת מקמיה איתיהיבא ליה רשותא למימחק זכוותא דאחר יצתה בת קול ואמרה שובו בנים שובבים חוץ מאחר אמר הואיל ואיטריד ההוא גברא מההוא עלמא ליפוק ליתהני בהאי עלמא נפק אחר לתרבות רעה נפק אשכח זונה תבעה אמרה ליה ולאו אלישע בן אבויה את עקר פוגלא ממישרא בשבת ויהב לה אמרה אחר הוא. The more or less arbitrary partition of the story into lettered units is mine, for the purpose of referring to these units later.

8. *Hekhalot* literature is a fluid collection of Hebrew and Aramaic mystical texts from late antiquity and the early Middle Ages. For a helpful introduction to *3 Enoch* (ed. Odeberg) in the context of Hekhalot literature see P. Alexander, "3 (Hebrew Apocalypse of) Enoch," 223–253.

9. A completely different narrative is presented in *y.* Ḥagigah 2:1 (77b).

10. The phrase *shetei reshuyot* was first systematically investigated in A. Segal, *Two Powers in Heaven* (where *b.* Ḥagigah 15a is treated in pages 60–67). Recent treatments of the topic include (very selectively) A. Segal, "'Two Powers in Heaven'"; Schremer, "Midrash"; McGrath, *The Only True God*, 81–96; Schäfer, *The Jewish Jesus*; Kister, "'Panim be-fanim;'" Grossberg, "One God, Two Powers."

11. Because I focus on the ideological features of the version of the story contained in *b.* Ḥagigah 15a, I avoid discussing questions of priority between the Babylonian Talmud and *3 Enoch* (see Schäfer, *Synopse*, sections 20, 338–339, 344–346, 671–673) that have largely occupied scholars. Among those who attribute priority to the version contained in the Babylonian Talmud are Urbach, "Ha-mesorot"; P. Alexander, "3 Enoch." For the claim that *3 Enoch* contains materials that are earlier than the Babylonian Talmud see Morray-Jones, "Hekhalot Literature"; Deutsch, *Guardians of the Gate*, 48–77; Boyarin, "Two Powers in Heaven"; Boyarin, "Beyond Judaisms"; Klaus, "Jewish Mysticism." D. Septimus, "Ḥeṭʾo shel Meṭaṭron," offers a comparison between the various versions of the story in different sources. Schäfer, *The Jewish Jesus*, 130, assumes a common source. See also Boustan, "Rabbinization," 494 and 499–450. The sugyah in *b.* Ḥagigah 15a is also transmitted by different Babylonian Talmud manuscripts with great textual variation. Kister, "Meṭaṭron," 64–67, and Goshen-Gottstein, *The Sinner*, 277–283, are among the studies providing variants. As selectively discussed in this chapter, several scholars who have dealt with this text have speculated about its original form. These treatments were typically based on a limited number of manuscripts and on the examination of only the most significant macro-variants in the text. While there is value in the hypotheses those scholars formulated, an attempt at reconstructing an Urtext (or even just an original narrative) of this pericope must consider its multiple variants, of unequal significance, across the whole extant manuscript tradition. It remains in any event debatable whether such an effort should be undertaken at the scale of a sugyah, without considering—at least as relevant contextual information—textual

variation at the level of the chapter or of the treatise. Since this task cannot be pursued here, my study does not set out to solve text-critical problems. Rather than reconstructing a hypothetical original text that does not correspond to any extant one, the discussion is based on the standard print (Vilna) text. Other versions are briefly cited when relevant.

12. I prefer to translate למיכתב (in the clause דאתיהבא ליה רשותא למיתב למיכתב contained in *b*) as a further purpose clause subordinated to the purpose clause למיתב rather than as an asyndeton connecting two coordinated purpose clauses, which is how it has been generally translated ("to sit and to write down"): the sole, specified purpose of Metatron's sitting was to write down the merits of Israel. On this למיתב see Y.N.H. Epstein, *Meḥḳarim*, 337.

13. In relation to the legitimacy of celestial sitting, Menachem Kister has recently identified two different trends within rabbinic literature (Kister, "Meṭaṭron," 82). One claims that no sitting whatsoever is permitted in heaven, while another considers that select non-divine figures are allowed to sit, whether because of their status or because of the function they perform. If Kister's conclusions are accepted, the contents of the sugyah within the framework I have proposed could be logically reduced to a demonstration of the risks involved in applying a traditional teaching aligning with the former, more restrictive line of thought to a mystical vision of the heavens (where the latter, more permissive custom is followed).

14. See Schäfer, *The Origins*, 224.

15. This struggle is sometimes understood as taking place entirely within rabbinic and para-rabbinic circles (e.g., by Boyarin), and other times as a form of engagement with actual outsiders.

16. It has been claimed that the original narrative recounted Elisha's lapse into binitarianism simply as an outcome of his encounter with the angel, without any reference to the latter's sitting. The Vilna text, which contains the sitting, is identical to the text of the Pesaro 1514 print and the Venice 1521 print. Ms. München Bayerische Staatsbibliothek Hebr. 95 omits Metatron's sitting. Mss. München Bayerische Staatsbibliothek Hebr. 6; Oxford Bodleian Opp. Add. Fol. 23 (366); E = BL 400 (Harley 5508); Göttingen 3; Biblioteca Apostolica Hebr. 134 (with a necessary emendation of חזא in חדא); Vaticana Biblioteca Apostolica Hebr. 171; and Spanish print 1480 qualify the permission to sit and write as being granted one hour a day. Ms. Cambridge T-S F2 (1) 204 extends the permission to three hours a day. This section (*b*) contains further variants. P. Alexander, "3 Enoch," 62–63 (followed by Boyarin, "The Quest"), sees as adventitious the presence of the traditional teaching concerning behaviors that are inappropriate in the heavenly realm. According to Alexander the original narrative is the version carried by ms. München Bayerische Staatsbibliothek Hebr. 95. Here Elisha's slip into mistaken belief is simply a result of a vision of the glowing appearance of Metatron. Although this is possible, the supporting argument presented in P. Alexander, "3 Enoch," 62, n. 23, seems unconvincing, because the lectio חזא מ[י]

טטרון דא[י]תיהיבא ליה רשותא (a phrasing that according to him switches the focus from Metatron's sitting to his appearance) is also carried by versions of the text that do specify that Metatron was sitting while writing the merits of Israel, making that into the origin of Elisha's blasphemy: Spanish print 1480; Pesaro 1514 print; Venice print 1521; Vilna print; and mss. München Bayeriche Staatsbibliothek Hebr. 6; Oxford Bodleian Opp. Add. Fol. 23 (366); BL 400 (Harley 5508); Göttingen 3; Vaticanus Biblioteca Apostolica Hebr. 171; Oxford – Bodl. Heb. D. 63 (2826) 31–32. According to Alexander, at a later stage the author of the text in ms. Vaticanus Biblioteca Apostolica Hebr. 134 tried to make sense of this narrative, in which Metatron's fault remains unexplained, by seizing on the mention of sitting in the quotation introduced by the *gemire/gemiri* and identifying his sin with that action. Alexander deemed ms. Vaticanus Biblioteca Apostolica Hebr. 134 to have a text preferable to the one received by the Vilna edition because, while presenting a *lectio facilior* from the prosodic standpoint, it offers a *lectio difficilior* from the ideological point of view (why would standing be proscribed when it appears to be what Metatron should have done?). In Alexander's reconstruction, precisely because the mention of standing in the teaching as quoted in ms. Vaticanus Biblioteca Apostolica Hebr. 134 made the story contradictory, it was suppressed in the manuscript used by the editors. P. Alexander, "3 Enoch," 60–61, also proposed that, before being integrated into the narrative of ms. Munich 95, the teaching introduced by *gemire/gemiri* was simply meant as a denial of the notion that God and the angels could possess body parts or be capable of passion (see also Boyarin, "Beyond Judaisms," 347 and n. 68, on a proposal by Michal Bar-Asher Siegal). It is indeed difficult to deny the compelling evidence suggesting that the motif of sitting plays an important part in the mistaken perception of Metatron's status as unduly elevated in this narrative; Enoch, a scribe and a witness of God's judgment in Jubilees 4:23, is portrayed as sitting down in heaven writing in 2 Enoch 23:4–6. Building on Alexander's proposal, Boyarin, in "The Quest", speculatively reconstructed the text of this section of the proto-sugyah as reading: "He saw that Metatron had been given sovereignty [רשות] to sit and write the good deeds of Israel. Perhaps, God forbid, there are two sovereignties [שתי רשויות]!" This allows Boyarin to bring *b. Ḥagigah* 15a and *3 Enoch* together to the point of ideological consonance and to claim that sitting is central to the story of the apotheosis of Metatron, without having to jettison Alexander's theory about the extrinsic origin of the teaching introduced by *gemire/gemiri*.

17. The meaning that the editors of *b. Ḥagigah* 15a sought to shape clearly differs both from that conveyed by the short anti-anthropomorphic list contained in the traditional teaching and from the original sense of the Elisha narrative prior to the alleged insertion of that list. Their interest in the teaching might have correlated more to its ability to be credibly presented as traditional (through the preface *gemire/gemiri* and other features) and incorporated into their ideological construction.

18. See D.W. Halivni, "Reflections," 105. In *b. Menaḥot* 62b the word is explained by Rashi as tantamount to "from Sinai" (*mi-Sinai*), a phrase that may in turn be equiva-

lent to the expression "a law (given) to Moses on Sinai" (*halakhah le-Mosheh mi-Sinai*). This latter category, as C. Hayes, "*Halakhah le-Moshe mi-Sinai*," explains, is applied to a law that does not require logical justification and that, because of its authoritativeness, is most often not subject to debate. Halivni has argued that the equivalence between *gemire/gemiri* and *halakhah le-Mosheh mi-Sinai* is not always operative, adducing multiple examples of usages of *gemire/gemiri* in which no halakhic implication can be detected. Nevertheless, he seems to have worked with a fairly narrow definition of *halakhah le-Mosheh mi-Sinai*: as Hayes, "*Halakhah le-Moshe mi-Sinai*," 115, n. 95, has demonstrated, this expression can appear in haggadic contexts as well. The equivalence between *gemire/gemiri* and *halakhah le-Mosheh mi-Sinai* is therefore not yet fully disproven. Be that as it may, it is not necessary for our purposes to determine exactly whether, in attributing a *gemire/gemiri* to a tanna, our sugyah specifically understood it as *halakhah le-Mosheh mi-Sinai*.

19. In the parallel to our sugyah contained in *Merkavah Rabah* (ed. Schäfer, *Synopse*, section 672) the expression *gemire/gemiri* is replaced by *shanu ḥakhamim* ("our teachers have taught"), the Hebrew equivalent of a phrase that in the Talmud has the role of introducing a tannaitic teaching (a mishnah or a teaching from the Tosefta). Further research might explain the reasons that led the *ba'al ha-sugyah* to present theological discourse in the form of the product of the application of a traditional teaching to theosophical speculations on the part of a sage of the tannaitic era. This editorial choice, I venture very tentatively, might reflect an intention of mild erosion of the authoritativeness of a mode of inquiry based on the rote repetition of traditional teachings, set up in parallel to the marginalization of mystical journeys observed above. Further explanations might include tensions between the *ba'alei talmud* ("masters of Talmud") and the *ba'alei mishnah* ("masters of the mishnah"), or simply *tanna'im* ("reciters"), contemporary to them; as well as the possible links, explored in Vidas, *Tradition*, between such reciters and the producers and transmitters of *Hekhalot*-like literature containing the kind of cosmological, apocalyptic, and theosophical contents that find their way into the second chapter of tractate Ḥagigah.

20. ועל רוחות מאי רוחות אמר אביי זעפא ואמר אביי גמירי דזעפא בליליא לא הוי והא קא חזינן דהוי ההוא דאתחולי בימּמא ואמר אביי גמירי דזעפא תרתי שעי לא קאי לקיים מה שנאמר לא תקום פעמים צרה והא קא חזינן דקאי דמפסיק ביני ביני.

21. This was already the interpretation of some *rishonim* (eleventh- through fifteenth-century rabbis and *posḳim*, or legal decisors): see, e.g., Ḥananel ben Ḥushiel, commentary ad loc. (ח"ו שיש עליו [= על מיטטרון] דין אלא להראות לאלישע שיש לו אדון), and Todros ben Joseph Abulafia, *Sefer otsar ha-kavod*, ad loc. (כך הראה לו אל אלישע אחר לפי דעתו ומחשבתו המכוערת כדי להודיע לו שאין אלא רשות אחד בלבד).

22. See *t.* Kipurim 4:6–8 (ed. Lieberman, II, 251–252); *Mekhilta de-Rabi Yishma'el*, Yitro 7 (ed. Horovitz and Rabin, 228); *Avot de-Rabi Natan* (version A) 29 (ed. Schechter, 88); *y.* Yoma 8:8 (45b–c); *y.* Sanhedrin 10:1 (27c); *y.* Shevu'ot 1:9 (33b); *b.* Yoma 86a.

In a loose sense, this might be considered a rabbinic comparandum for the Gospels' declaration of the unpardonability of blasphemy against the Holy Spirit (Mark 3:29 and parallels). On *yissurim* see Wolf, "Suffering and Sacrifice."

23. As in the well-known tale of the oven of Akhnai, reported in *b.* Bava metsiʿa 59b and referenced in *b.* Ḥullin 44a. See Kühn, *Offenbarungsstimmen*, 369–375; Bockmuehl, *Revelation and Mystery*, 107–108; Rubenstein, *Talmudic Stories*, 34–63. For a survey of tannaitic materials see Costa, "Littérature apocalyptique" and for one of Talmudic materials see Costa and Ohali, "Littérature apocalyptique."

24. On rabbinic conceptualizations of repentance see Schechter, *Some Aspects*, 293–343; Urbach, *The Sages*, 462–471; Urbach, "Redemption and Repentance"; Petuchowski, "The Concept of 'Teshuvah'"; Ber, "ʿAl maʿaśei kaparah"; Naiweld, *Les antiphilosophes*, 95–127; Kiel, "The Systematization of Penitence"; Kiel, "Penitential Theology"; Bar-Asher Siegal, "Ethics and Identity Formation."

25. Balberg, "Bein heṭroṭopyah le-ʾutopyah," 200.

26. [a] אַל־תִּתֵּן אֶת־פִּיךָ לַחֲטִיא אֶת־בְּשָׂרֶךָ
[b] וְאַל־תֹּאמַר לִפְנֵי הַמַּלְאָךְ כִּי שְׁגָגָה הִיא
[c] לָמָּה יִקְצֹף הָאֱלֹהִים עַל־קוֹלֶךָ וְחִבֵּל אֶת־מַעֲשֵׂה יָדֶיךָ

Other textual forms of the sugyah quote Qoh 5:5 in its entirety.

27. See Borowitz, *The Talmud's Theological Language-Game*, 130–132.

28. The link with the mention of a *malʾakh*, raised—with a different interpretation—in P. Alexander, "3 Enoch," 56, encourages the exploration of other passages in rabbinic literature containing exegeses of Qoh 5:5b in reference to angelic creatures. See also the broader discussion ibid.

29. This position is antithetical to the one expressed in Arad, *Meḥallel shabat*, 288. The original meaning of the phrase "cut the shoots" is debated in scholarship, with many commentators reading it as a metaphor for Elisha's severing his own connection with the people of Israel (an image curiously resonant of the root imagery in Rom 11) and others seeing in it an allusion to the dismantling of the rabbinic "safeguard around the Torah" (*seyag la-Torah*), built in order to protect it against trespasses (*m.* Avot 1:1). For various interpretations see Neumark, *Geschichte*, I, 93; Marmorstein, *Religionsgeschichtliche Studien*, II, 68; Scholem, *Jewish Gnosticism*, 16, n. 6, and 127; Urbach, "Ha-mesorot," 14; Schäfer, "New Testament," 27–28; Mopsik, *Le Livre hébreu d'Hénoch*, 30–37; Abrams, "The Boundaries," 293–296; Goshen-Gottstein, *The Sinner*, 92. For an overview of theories regarding the question of which exact heresy constituted Elisha's deviant belief see the critical history of scholarship in Klaus, "Jewish Mysticism," 101–104.

30. See Rubenstein, *Talmudic Stories*, 71.

31. See Job 14:7–9 and Dan 4:11–12:23.

32. Grossberg, "Between 3 Enoch," 120. The contents of the article are also found in Grossberg, *Heresy*, 176–192.

33. Grossberg, "Between 3 Enoch," 119. For Grossberg's definition of orthopraxy see Grossberg, "Orthopraxy."

34. Grossberg, "Between 3 Enoch," 137.

35. Grossberg, ibid., 121, cites the treatment of the figure of Metatron in *3 Enoch* contained in Schäfer, *The Origins*, 324–327.

36. See A. Segal, *Two Powers in Heaven*, 61, n. 4; P. Alexander, "3 Enoch," 57; Morray-Jones, "Hekhalot Literature," 30; Deutsch, *Guardians of the Gate*, 55 (cited in Grossberg, "Between 3 Enoch," 120, n. 9).

37. Grossberg, "Between 3 Enoch," 125–126.

38. Ibid., 127.

39. Ibid., 130.

40. Boyarin, "The Quest."

41. Schäfer, "Metatron in Babylonia," 37.

42. According to Boyarin, "The Quest," Metatron in *b.* Ḥagigah 15a is never debased, but only made the object of heavenly theatrics for the purpose of ensuring that humankind make no more mistakes about divine sovereignty.

43. See *b.* Shabat 73a.

44. Exod 35:33; see also Exod 35:32 (וְלַחְשֹׁב מַחֲשָׁבֹת) and Exod 35:34 (וְחֹשְׁבֵי מַחֲשָׁבֹת). See *b.* Shabat 49b; *b.* Beitsah 13b. See R. Hacohen, "Melekhet maḥashevet"; Nebenzahl, "Melekhet maḥashevet." See also Kafri, "Mitʿaseḳ"; Rosilio, "Bi-gdar din mitʿaseḳ"; Olmi, "Mitʿaseḳ."

45. See also Maimonides, *Mishneh Torah, Hilkhot shabat* 1.2–4.

46. See Teuber, "Melakhah ke-darkah."

47. See, e.g., *b.* Shabat 29b; *b.* Pesaḥim 25b; *b.* Nazir 42a; *b.* Bava ḳamma 44b. The concept of *davar she-ʾeino mitkayyein* applies to any Torah prohibition, not just to Sabbath regulations. See Motti Goodman, "Din davar she-ʾeino mitkayyein"; Sternberg, "Davar she-ʾeino mitkayyein"; Tal, "Davar she-ʾeino mitkayyein"; Elias, "Davar she-ʾeino mitkayyein"; Gur, "Rabi Shimʿon ve-Rabi Yehudah." The need for an action forbidden by the Torah to be intentional in order for it to be sanctionable mi-deʾoraita—as per the opinion of Rabbi Shimon—finds an exception in the case in which the unintended outcome is known to be inevitable (according to the principle of *pesiḳ reisha*, referring to he who "cut the head" of a chicken on the Sabbath not in order to kill it, but to let his child play with the head: this person is considered liable for the unintended killing, which could be predicted with certainty). Rabbi Shimon's opinion, which condones mi-deʾoraita those actions from which an unintentional and uncertain outcome forbidden by the Torah might derive (while sanctioning them mi-derabanan), contrasts with the less lenient view of Rabbi Judah, who sanctions them mi-deʾoraita (in all cases according to Yom Tovben Avraham Asevilli, commentary on *b.* Yoma 34b; only in cases of Sabbath regulations according to Tosafot on *b.* Shabat 41b). On *pesiḳ reisha* see Rabinovitch, "Be-ʿinyan pesiḳ reisha"; Fruman, "Modeh Rabi Shimʿon"; Stav, "Pesiḳ reisha"; Geltzer, "'Pesiḳ reisha'"; Tal, "Melakhah she-hi ḳerovah"; Tal, "Pesiḳ reisha bi-

de-rabanan"; Salmon, "Melakhah"; Heber, "Be-din eino mitkayyein"; Twik, "Pesiḳ reisheh." The notion of *pesiḳ reisha* finds further specification through the case described as *pesiḳ reisha de-la niḥa leh* (referring to one who "cut the head [of a chicken] without benefiting from it": see *b.* Shabat 103a). On *pesiḳ reisha de-la niḥa leh* see Z. Melamed, "Be-gidrei pesiḳ reisha"; Stav, "Pesiḳ reisha de-la niḥa leh."

48. The reading of rabbinic literature on the topic inspires some confusion. See, e.g., Yechiel Michel Epstein, *'Arukh ha-shulḥan, Yoreh de'ah, Hilkhot shabat* 242.20, where the notion of thoughtful work is reduced to the question of intention, with references to cases treated in *b.* Bava ḳamma 26b. On intentional acts on the Sabbath see Maimonides, *Mishneh Torah, Sefer Zemanim, Hilkhot shabat* 1.5.8–12; for his sources see Karo, *Magid Mishneh*, ad loc.; Vidal of Tolosa, *Magid Mishneh*, ad loc.; Abraham ben Moses de Boton, *Leḥem Mishneh*, ad loc. See also Lifschitz, "Melekhet maḥshevet."

49. See Yanir, "Melakhah she-'einah tserikhah le-gufah"; Z. Melamed, "Be-gidrei pesiḳ reisha"; Kalmanson, "Melakhah she-'einah tserikhah le-gufah"; Tal, "Melakhah she-'einah tserikhah le-gufah"; Bamberger, "Melakhah she-'einah tserikhah le-gufa"; Segelman, "Melakhah she-'einah tserikhah le-gufah."

50. See S. Rosenberg, "Be-gidrei meḳalḳel"; Neria, "Melekhet maḥashevet"; Bamberger, "Melakhah."

51. *M.* Ḥagigah 1:8: התר נדרים פורחים באויר ואין להם על מה שיסמכו הלכות שבת וחגיגות ומעילות כהררים תלוים בסערה מקרא ממועט והלכות [מרובות] הדינים והעבדות והטהרות והטמאות והעריות יש להם על מה שייסמכו הן הן גופי תורה. Both the text and the translation of the mishnah are taken (and the latter slightly adapted) from Bar-Asher Siegal, "Mountains Hanging by a Strand?" The translation of the gemara is mine. For the establishment of this new text of the mishnah see ibid., 244–255.

52. D.W. Halivni. *Meḳorot u-msorot: Be'urim ba-Talmud. Massekhet Yoma-Ḥagiga*, 590–593. See also Roth, "*Gufei Torah*," 210–214.

53. Jaffee, *Torah in the Mouth*, 86. On the parallel of this passage in the Tosefta (*t.* Ḥagigah 1.9) see Hirshman, "Torah in Rabbinic Thought," 901.

54. See *b.* Shabat 73b.

55. See *b.* Shabat 93b: "One who carries out a dead person on a bed is liable, and similarly (one who carries out) an olive-bulk of a dead person and an olive-bulk of a carcass and a lentil-bulk of a creeping animal is liable. And (for) Rabbi Shimon he is exempt" (המוציא [. . .] את המת במטה חייב וכן כזית מן המת וכזית מן הנבלה וכעדשה מן השרץ חייב ורבי שמעון פוטר).

56. *B.* Ḥagigah 10b: הלכות שבת מיכתב כתיבן לא צריכא לכדר' אבא דאמר רבי אבא החופר גומא בשבת ואין צריך אלא לעפרה פטור עליה כמאן כרבי שמעון דאמר מלאכה שאינה צריכה לגופה פטור עליה אפילו תימא לרבי יהודה התם מתקן הכא מקלקל הוא מאי כהררין התלויין. בשערה מלאכת מחשבת אסרה תורה ומלאכת מחשבת לא כתיבא.

57. See Tosafot on *b.* Shabat 94a, s.v. את המת.

58. Rashi interprets the gemara's eventual concession to the mishnah that the notion of thoughtful work is not written in the Torah as referring to the derivation of this

category by a mere *heḳesh* between two verses: Exod 35:2, שֵׁשֶׁת יָמִים תֵּעָשֶׂה מְלָאכָה וּבַיּוֹם הַשְּׁבִיעִי יִהְיֶה לָכֶם קֹדֶשׁ שַׁבַּת שַׁבָּתוֹן לַיהוָה כָּל הָעֹשֶׂה בוֹ מְלָאכָה יוּמָת ("For six days work shall be done, but on the seventh day you will have a holy [day of] complete rest for the Lord. Anyone who does any *work* on that day will certainly die," italics mine), and Exod 35:33, וּבַחֲרֹשֶׁת אֶבֶן לְמַלֹּאת וּבַחֲרֹשֶׁת עֵץ לַעֲשׂוֹת בְּכָל מְלֶאכֶת מַחֲשָׁבֶת ("[. . .] in cutting stones to be set, in wood carving and in executing every kind of thoughtful *work*").

59. Hayes, "*Halakhah le-Moshe mi-Sinai*," 115, n. 95 (the hyperbole in *b*. Ḥagigah 10b is admittedly muted). On this set of issues see also Hayes, "Rabbinic Contestations of Authority."

60. See *b*. Shabat 141a.

61. We can also observe here in its embryonic phase Acher's paradoxical memorialization in Talmudic sources. The hagiographical cycle that follows the narrative of *b*. Ḥagigah 15a, containing an abundance of tales about his post-lapsarian period, portrays him as tragically belonging to the rabbinic community even as an excommunicated outcast; moreover, though going to the grave unrepentant, he is granted—to the heavenly voice's chagrin, one may assume—the possibility of repentance by Rabbi Meir (*b*. Ḥagigah 15a) and forgiven post mortem thanks to Rabbi Yochanan's intercession (*b*. Ḥagigah 15b).

62. Ms. Oxford Bodleian Opp. Add. fol. 23 (366) and the manuscript used by the Spanish print of 1480: שידע כבודי ומרד בי ("who knew My honor and rebelled against me"). Of the two, only the latter reports the story of the radish.

63. God's utterance is in Gen 2:17: וּמֵעֵץ הַדַּעַת טוֹב וָרָע לֹא תֹאכַל מִמֶּנּוּ כִּי בְּיוֹם אֲכָלְךָ מִמֶּנּוּ מוֹת תָּמוּת ("But of the tree of knowledge of good and evil you shall not eat, for on the day you eat from it you will certainly die"). Eve's report is contained in Gen 3:3: וּמִפְּרִי הָעֵץ אֲשֶׁר בְּתוֹךְ הַגָּן אָמַר אֱלֹהִים לֹא תֹאכְלוּ מִמֶּנּוּ וְלֹא תִגְּעוּ בּוֹ פֶּן תְּמֻתוּן ("'But as for the fruit of the tree in the middle of the garden'—God said—'do not eat of it, *nor touch it*, lest you die,'" italics mine).

64. *Bereshit Rabah* 19:3; ed. Albeck and Theodor, 172: ומפרי העץ אשר בתוך הגן הה"ד אל תוסף על דבריו פן יוכיח בך ונכזבת תני ר' חיא שלא תעשה את הגדר יותר מן העקר שלא יפל ויקצץ את הנטיעות. See *Avot de-Rabi Natan* (version A) 1 (ed. Schechter, 3). For rabbinic passages expressing similar ideas see *t*. Shabat 1:16–17; *y*. Shabat 1:4 (3c).

65. See, e.g., Issachar Berman ben Naphtali ha-Kohen, *Mattenot kehunnah*, ad loc. See also Abraham bar Asher, *Or ha-śekhel*, ad loc.

66. Rabbi Hiyya's failure to use the word *seyag* (safeguard) to refer to the rabbinic hedge might be noteworthy in this regard. This was in fact the standard expression, integrated in the phrase *seyag la-Torah* ("a safeguard around the Torah"), to describe the multiplication of self-professedly rabbinic decrees for the aim of protecting an untransgressible legal core: see Stein, "The Concept of 'Fence'"; Cook, "The Law of Moses"; Panken, *The Rhetoric of Innovation*, 247–314; Hidary and Osborne, "Fence." See also some insights in Twersky, "Make a Fence around the Torah." Arguably, had the statement meant to refer generically to the need to keep mi-derabanan legislation within its due proportions, the word *seyag* could have been used.

67. Although *ʿiḳḳar* is admittedly not the word used in *b.* Ḥagigah 15a to describe the radish, the verb used for its uprooting is the cognate *ʿaḳar*, "to uproot," thus framing the radish itself as a root.

68. I see no need to speculate here about relationships of textual dependence.

69. See Sirinelli, *Les vues historiques*; Momigliano, "Pagan and Christian Historiography"; Momigliano, "The Origins of Ecclesiastical Historiography"; Cameron, "Eusebius of Caesarea."

70. Burrus, "Rhetorical Stereotypes" saw the description of Paul's conduct as that of a bad rhetorician.

71. On the ecclesiastical dimension of the dispute see Josef Rist, "Cyprian von Karthago"; Slootjes, "Bishops and Their Position of Power"; Camplani, "Le trasformazioni," 102–108 and 113. As suggested by Camplani, "L'*Esposizione XIV*," Aphrahat's *Demonstration 14*, though composed further to the east, could be read as testifying to similar tensions continuing into the fourth century. The gradual emergence of centralizing forms of ecclesial organization is consistent with developments observed in the *Teaching of the Apostles*, a fourth-century Syrian document that goes beyond Ignatius of Antioch's ecclesiology in programmatically casting the bishop as a king ruling in solitude over his community: see Mueller, *L'ancien testament*; Pérès, "The 'Episcopos'"; Mueller, "The Ancient Church Order Literature." A comparable perspective also emerges from the fourth-century redactional stratum of the *Pseudoclementines*, another work of Syrian origin. Here the episcopal office is cast in the mold of human and divine monarchy as well as gubernatorial authorities, a development that according to Pouderon, "L'évêque" finds its *Sitz im Leben* in the ecclesiastical reality of fourth-century Antioch. On the emergence of monarchical episcopal leadership within presbyterial governance structures in the *Pseudoclementines* see Bobertz, "The Development."

72. Eusebius of Caesarea, *Historia ecclesiastica* 7.27.2. On Paul's Christology see Réville, "La christologie"; Lawlor, "The Sayings of Paul of Samosata"; Lawlor, "The Sayings of Paul of Samosata: Additional Notes"; Galtier, "L'*homoousios*"; Loofs, *Paulus von Samosata*"; Soden, "Neue Forschungen"; Riedmatten, *Les actes* (along with the substantial assessment in Chadwick's review thereof); Sample, *The Messiah*; Sample, "The Christology"; Brennecke, "Zum Prozess"; de Navascués Benlloch, "El fr. 37"; Lang, "The Christological Controversy"; Uríbarri Bilbao, "Trasfondo escriturístico." See also Harnack, "Die Reden."

73. Eusebius, *Historia ecclesiastica* 7.27–30.

74. The *Letter of Hymenaeus* (or *Letter of the Six Bishops*), the fragments of the transcript of the debate between Paul and Malchion, and the fragments of the synodal letter reported by Eusebius and later *florilegia* are the only sources recognized as authentic in de Navascués Benlloch, *Pablo de Samosata*. On the ancient historiography of Paul and on the sources for the reconstruction of the events of the synod see Bardy, "La lettre"; Bardy, *Paul de Samosate*; Schwartz, *Eine fingierte Korrespondenz*; Bardy, "Le Concile d'Antioche (379)"; Richard, "Malchion"; Burke, "Eusebius"; Hübner, "Die

Hauptquelle." On Paul of Samosata see Scheidweiler, "Paul von Samosata"; Downey, *A History*, 263–264 and 310–315; Fischer, "Die antiochenischen Synoden"; Simonetti, "Paolo di Samosata"; Simonetti, "Per la rivalutazione"; Grillmeier, "Neue Fragmente"; Perrone, "L'enigma"; Stead, "Marcel Richard on Malchion"; Simonetti, "Eresia e ortodossia"; Simonetti, "Sulla corrispondenza."

75. The fragments of the synodal letter are edited in de Navascués Benlloch, *Pablo de Samosata*, 78–84.

76. See Dionysius's letter to Stephen, apud Eusebius, *Historia ecclesiastica*, 7.4.1.

77. On the affair of the two Dionysii see Simonetti, *Studi*, 273–297; Abramowski, "Dionysius von Rom"; Morales, *La théologie trinitaire*, 25–31.

78. On geo-ecclesiology see Blaudeau, *Alexandrie et Constantinople*; Blaudeau, "Between Petrine Ideology and Realpolitik."

79. This was a milestone on the road to the declaration, made at Nicaea in 325, of the superiority of the episcopal see of Antioch (although only at Chalcedon, in 451, was an exact description of its jurisdiction provided). The ramifications of this development can be witnessed in the fifth-century *Teaching of Addai*, where, as noticed by Griffith, "The *Doctrina Addai*," Edessene Church leaders were offered an alliance with the Antiochene and Roman episcopates against the rising political and ecclesiastical power of Constantinople. The *Teaching* shows Edessa as positioned in a web of alliances punctuating the ecclesiastical and political landscape of the fourth century.

80. Eusebius, *Historia ecclesiastica* 7.30.18–19: Τοῦ δὴ οὖν Παύλου σὺν καὶ τῇ τῆς πίστεως ὀρθοδοξίᾳ τῆς ἐπισκοπῆς ἀποπεπτωκότος, Δόμνος, ὡς εἴρηται, τὴν λειτουργίαν τῆς κατὰ Ἀντιόχειαν ἐκκλησίας διεδέξατο. ἀλλὰ γὰρ μηδαμῶς ἐκστῆναι τοῦ Παύλου τοῦ τῆς ἐκκλησίας οἴκου θέλοντος, βασιλεὺς ἐντευχθεὶς Αὐρηλιανὸς αἰσιώτατα περὶ τοῦ πρακτέου διείληφεν, τούτοις νεῖμαι προστάττων τὸν οἶκον, οἷς ἂν οἱ κατὰ τὴν Ἰταλίαν καὶ τὴν Ῥωμαίων πόλιν ἐπίσκοποι τοῦ δόγματος ἐπιστέλλοιεν. οὕτω δῆτα ὁ προδηλωθεὶς ἀνὴρ μετὰ τῆς ἐσχάτης αἰσχύνης ὑπὸ τῆς κοσμικῆς ἀρχῆς ἐξελαύνεται τῆς ἐκκλησίας.

81. On Aurelian's removal of Paul and the nomination of the "house of the church" see Milburn, "Ο ΤΗΣ ΕΚΚΛΗΣΙΑΣ ΟΙΚΟΣ"; Mohrmann, "Les dénominations," 158–159.

82. Eusebius, *Historia ecclesiastica* 7.13.2; cited in Clarke, "Third-Century Christianity," 647.

83. See, e.g., Chadwick, *The Early Church*, 115.

84. See Millar, "Paul of Samosata," 14–16; de Navascués Benlloch, *Pablo de Samosata*, 205–208.

85. See Homo, *Essai*, 96–97; Barone-Adesi, *L'età della "lex Dei,"* 43–45.

86. This does not imply that Eusebius was unaware of the form of the rescript.

87. Eusebius, *Historia ecclesiastica* 7.30.20; ed. Bardy, II, 219; trans. adapted from *NPNF2* I, 316. On Aurelian as a persecutor see Hurley, "Some Thoughts."

88. On the intermesh between Christian identity and the Roman Empire see Cameron, *Christianity*.

89. The ethno-national interpretation of the events is favored in Bardy, *Paul de Samosate*, 249–262; Daniélou and Marrou, *Nouvelle histoire*, 247; H. Grégoire, *Les persécutions*, 59–60. See also Downey, *A History*, 309. Skepticism about this interpretation is expressed by Loofs, *Paulus von Samosata*, 34; Alföldi, "The Crisis," 178, n. 1; Millar, "Paul of Samosata"; Chadwick, *The Church*, 166 (despite the different reading conveyed in Chadwick, *The Early Church*, 114–115). Bardy, *La question*, 19, expressed a more cautious opinion than in his 1961 study on Paul. See also Perrone, "L'enigma," 282–284.

90. On *ducenarii* see Pflaum, *Les procurateurs*, 236–255; Pflaum, *Les carrières procuratoriennes*, II, 950–951 and passim (see all references ibid., III, 1282); A. Jones, *Studies*, 23 and 41; A. Jones, *The Later Roman Empire*, II, 525, 578, 583, and 599. According to Millar, "Paul of Samosata," 13, the letter only accused Paul of posing as a *ducenarius*, a position he never occupied. Stommel, "Bischofsstuhl," 55, considered and rejected this possibility. Jacques, *Rom und das Reich*, I, 386, considers that Paul's title was merely honorary and was bestowed upon him as a result of his friendship with Zenobia. Paul's role as a *ducenarius* is fully accepted by Urciuoli, *Servire due padroni*, 316–319. On the political facet of the affair see also Baldini, "Il ruolo di Paolo di Samosata," 59–77; Norris, "Paul of Samosata"; Teja, "Pablo de Samosata"; John Rist, "Paul von Samosata."

91. On Zenobia see Berutti, "Zenobia"; Hanslik and Wegenast, "Zenobia"; Teixidor, "Antiquités sémitiques"; Wieber, "Die Augusta aus der Wüste"; Hartmann, *Das palmyrenische Teilreich*; Yon, "Zénobie et les femmes de Palmyre"; Bussi, "Zenobia/Cleopatra"; Zahran, *Zenobia*; Bravo Castañeda, "Otra reina en Roma"; Burgersdijk, "Zenobia's Biography"; Breytenbach, "A Queen for All Seasons"; Lippold, "Rolle und Bild"; Ratti, "Malalas"; Kissel, "Palmyra"; Pastor Muñoz and Pastor Andrés, "Zenobia"; Winsbury, *Zenobia of Palmyra*; Girotti, "I ritratti di Zenobia"; Molinier Arbo, "Zénobie"; P. Jones, "Rewriting Power"; McInnes-Gibbons, "The Clash for Civilisation"; Molinier Arbo, "Femmes de pouvoir"; Hidalgo de la Vega, "Zenobia, reina de Palmira"; Andrade, *Zenobia*.

92. Athanasius, *Historia Arianorum ad monachos* 71.1; ed. Opitz, *Athanasius Werke. Zweiter Band. 5. Lieferung*, 221–222; trans. *NPNF2* IV, 296.

93. Philastrius, *Diversarum haereseon liber* 36(64).2; ed. Heylen, 244.

94. Gainsaying Philastrius's claim, Epiphanius of Salamis, *Adversus haereses* 65.2.5, affirms that the only difference between Paul's followers and the Jews is the former's failure to observe the Sabbath and to practice circumcision.

95. Chrysostom, *In Ioannem Homiliae* 8.1; ed. PG 59, 66. Chrysostom refers to Paul of Samosata in the same work also at *In Ioannem Homiliae* 4.1; ed. PG 59, 47.

96. Theodoret, *Haereticarum fabularum compendium* 2.8.1; ed. Bieler and Gleede, 114.

97. Pseudo-Athanasius of Alexandria, *Fragmentum* (= *Fragmentum Magni Athanasii*); ed. PG 26, 1293B.

98. Pseudo-Paul of Samosata, *Ad Zenobiam* (apud Pamphilus the Theologian, *Capitulorum diversorum seu dubitationum solutio de recta erga Christum religione*); ed. De-

clerck, 132. Pamphilus's work was partially edited by Mai, but the fragments attributed to Paul of Samosata are not included in his edition; they were retrieved and published, based on ms. Athon., Vatopedi 236, only by Declerck. On Pamphilus see Richard, "Léonce et Pamphile"; Declerck, "Encore une fois"; Hainthaler, *Christ in Christian Tradition*, 129–150.

99. See Grillmeier, "Neue Fragmente"; De Navascués, *Pablo de Samosata*, 53–55. Declerck at first considered the fragments authentic ("Deux nouveaux fragments") but later expressed himself more cautiously about their attribution ("Encore une fois," 204, n. 17).

100. Photius, *Bibliotheca* 265; ed. Henry, VIII, 60; ed. Bianchi, Canfora, and Schiano, 858. See also the suggestion about the origin of this entry in Bianchi, Canfora, and Schiano, *Fozio. Biblioteca*, 1193–1194. I do not see how this passage can be taken to mean, as Stoneman, *Palmyra*, 152, suggests, that Longinus converted Zenobia to Judaism.

101. Michael the Syrian, *Chronicon* 6.8; ed. Ibrahim, 119. As the angle brackets in the translation indicate, the Syriac text in the beginning of the passage reported is defective and has been reconstructed by Chabot, I, 196, in the apparatus.

102. Grigorios Bar ʿEbroyo, *Chronicon*; ed. Abbeloos and Lamy, I, 58.

103. Grigorios Bar ʿEbroyo, *Historia compendiosa dynastiarum*, 7; ed. Ṣāliḥānī, ١٢٩; ed. Pococke, III, 129.

104. Eusebius of Caesarea, *Historia ecclesiastica* 7.27–30.

105. Nikephoros Kallistos Xanthopoulos, *Historia ecclesiastica* 6.27; ed. PG 145, 1181.

106. *Y.* Terumot 8:10 (46b): זעיר בר חיננא איתציד בספסופה סלק רבי אימי ורבי שמואל מפייסה עלוי אמרה להון זנביה מלכתא יליף הוא ברייכון עבד לכון ניסין מעשיקין ביה עלל חד סרקיי טעין חד ספסר אמר לון בהדא ספסירא קטל בר ניצור לאחוי ואישתיזיב זעיר בר חיננא; ed. Guggenheimer, 315. Different translations have been proposed: see Schwab, 107; Avery-Peck, 419–420; Guggenheimer, 315; Neusner, *Narrative and Document*, II, 125; Appelbaum, "The Rabbis," 542; Andrade, *Zenobia*, 181–182.

107. For interpretations of the story see Smallwood, *The Jews*, 532; Hartmann, *Das palmyrenische Teilreich*, 330; Appelbaum, "The Rabbis," 542–543. See also Avi-Yonah, *The Jews of Palestine*, 125–127.

108. See Cumont, *Les religions orientales*, 367, n. 59.

109. See Dittenberger, *Orientis Graeci inscriptiones*, I, 207 (nr. 129) = Frey, *Corpus inscriptionum iudaicarum*, II, 374–376 (nr. 1449).

110. See Frey, *Corpus inscriptionum iudaicarum*, II, 67–68 (nr. 820).

111. On the complex mosaic of religions at Palmyra see Gawlikowski, "Les dieux de Palmyre"; Kaizer, *The Religious Life*; Kaizer, "Man and God," 179–191; Kaizer, "From Zenobia to Alexander"; Kubiak, "Des 'dieux bons'"; Kaizer, "Patterns of Worship."

112. See Millar, "Paul of Samosata," 13.

113. For this theme in relation to rabbinic literature see Kister, "Plucking on the Sabbath."

114. See Herrmann, "*Massekhet Hagigah*," 246.

115. For overviews of this topic see Maier, *Jesus von Nazareth*; Schäfer, *Jesus in the Talmud.*

116. *B.* ʿAvodah Zarah 10b.

117. In uncensored editions of *b.* Yoma 77a.

118. See Kiel, "Reimagining Enoch"; Herrmann, "Jewish Mysticism in Byzantium," 107–108, proposed that the negative judgment received by Jesus in the Babylonian Talmud, which agrees with the Sasanian context of the composition of the work, constitutes the basis for this Talmud's negative interpretation of Metatron.

2. Credal Culture: The Trinitarian Debates, 318–362

1. *Regulae definitionum contra haereticos prolatae* 1; ed. Parmentier, 233. The duplication of the phrase "something that is neither born nor made" (*quod neque natum neque factum est*) is in the text.

2. See Hanson, "Dogma and Formula."

3. See Kelly, *Jerome: His Life*, 30. On early creeds see also Kinzig, *Faith in Formulae*, I, 1–28; Edwards, "The Creed," 135–144.

4. The question of the relationship between duality and unity in the divine was articulated already by Origen of Alexandria, *Conversatio cum Heraclide* 2: "We must treat this matter carefully, and point out in what respect [the Father and the Son] are two and in what respect these two are one God" (ed. Scherer, 58).

5. On the shift, through the Trinitarian controversies, to an intellectual environment in which theological truth is captured by formulas see Hanson, "Dogma and Formula."

6. On the dating of Arius's earliest activities see Simonetti, *La crisi ariana*, 26, n. 1; Hanson, *The Search*, 129–138; Ayres, *Nicaea and Its Legacy*, 15–16 and n. 14. On the chronology of the earlier phase of the Trinitarian debates and the literary testimonies to this stage of the discussion see Brennecke, Heil, Stockhausen, and Wintjes, *Athanasius Werke. Dritter Band. Erster Teil. 3. Lieferung*, xix–xxxii.

7. It should be remarked that the Council of Nicaea, in declaring that the Son was begotten, not made, condemned the use of the verb ποιέω, not of the verb κτίζω.

8. See de Halleux, "'Hypostase' et 'Personne,'" 317.

9. Arius's affirmation that Christ was created "out of non-existence" ran counter to a philosophical commonplace that may be traced back to Parmenides: nothing can come into being from nothing. Theorists of self-production and self-generation had challenged this notion, but their objections could hardly apply to the Son of God. Arius's doctrine remained therefore both theologically and philosophically problematic. That might be why he felt the need to qualify the expression with implicit reliance on the Aristotelian distinction between different types of causality. He explained that the expression "out of non-existence" applies to the Son's generation only insofar as his material cause is concerned. Christ is instead "from God" (ἐκ θεοῦ) with regard to his efficient cause, inasmuch as he is created by his will (βούλημα) and volition (θέλημα).

To use the distinction affirmed in Plato, *Timaeus* 41B, God was for Arius Christ's maker but not his begetter. This note draws on Stead, "The Word 'from Nothing.'" On God as a Father in early Christian theology see Widdicombe, *The Fatherhood of God.*

10. Origen, *De principiis* 4.4.1.

11. The opposite formula (οὐκ ἦν ὅτε οὐκ ἦν) is attested in Origen, *De principiis* 1.2.9 ("non est autem quando non fuerit") (see also Origen, *De principiis* 4.4.1) and Origen, *Commentarius in Epistulam ad Romanos* 1.7.4 ("non erat quando non erat"). A philosophical precedent for the disagreement between Arius and Alexander over the generation of the Son in or outside of time has been identified in intra-Platonist discussions about the creation of the world. Plato, *Timaeus* 38B–39, made time dependent on the motion of the heavenly bodies, thus making a creation in time virtually impossible. Since time was commonly understood by Christians as having been created through the Son, a comparable problem arose for Arius and anybody else who might have had an interest in claiming that the Son's creation had occurred in time. The second-century Platonist philosopher Atticus had solved this difficulty by affirming that before the creation of time as we know it, measured through astronomical units, there existed an indefinite extension of immeasurable time. Arius believed he had overcome the problem by similarly avoiding usage of chronological language and proclaiming that "there once was when he was not" (ἦν ποτε ὅτε οὐκ ἦν), as opposed, e.g., to affirming that "there was *a time* when he was not" (ἦν πότε χρόνος ὅτε οὐκ ἦν). His adversaries, however, were not particularly impressed with this lexical trick. The slight intervening gap that Arius posited could in fact only be conceptually translated in chronological terms. To the mind of Arius's opponents, his very use of the aorist tense (ὑπῆρξεν) of the verb ὑπάρχω (to come into being) to express the Son's coming into existence gave away his view that the generation of the Logos was not an eternal accompaniment to the Father's being. Be this as it may, a God who had not been eternally Father posed an additional philosophical difficulty for Arius. On the "Arian" avoidance of the term χρόνος see Athanasius of Alexandria, *Oratio I contra arianos* 13.1; 14.7. On these matters see Meijering, "Ἦν ποτε ὅτε οὐκ ἦν ὁ Υἱός"; Meijering, "Die Diskussion über den Willen"; Stead, "The Platonism of Arius"; Löhr, "Arius Reconsidered (Part 1)"; Löhr, "Arius Reconsidered (Part 2)."

12. See Wiles, "Attitudes to Arius."

13. See Lorenz, *Arius judaizans*; Gregg and Groh, *Early Arianism*. See also the history of reception of Arianism in Wiles, *Archetypal Heresy*.

14. See Lyman, "Arius and Arians"; Lyman, "Arius and Arianism."

15. On Origen's Trinitarian theology see Harl, *Origène*; Nemeshegyi, *La paternité de Dieu*; Rius-Camps, *El dinamismo trinitario*. On Origen and Arius see Pollard, "Logos and Son in Origen"; Pollard, "The Origins of Arianism." On Origen's subordinationism see Rius-Camps, "¿Subordinacionismo en Orígenes?" For a non-subordinationist reading of Origen's theology see Ramelli, "Cristo-Logos in Origene"; Ramelli, "Origen's Anti-Subordinationism." On the role of subordinationism in the Trinitarian controversies see Simonetti, "Dal subordinazionismo all'egalitarismo." On Arius as himself not

interested primarily in the subordination of the Father to the Son see R. Williams, "The Logic of Arianism"; R. Williams, "The Son's Knowledge of the Father." See also Widdicombe, *The Fatherhood of God.*

16. Origen of Alexandria, *Commentarius in Evangelium Ioannis* 13.151.

17. Pollard, "Logos and Son"; Pollard, "The Origins of Arianism." The latter proposal echoes the association of Arius's teaching to the heresy of Paul of Samosata made among others by Alexander of Alexandria, *Epistula ad Alexandrum Constantinopolitanum* 9.

18. See Wiles, "In Defence of Arius." On scriptural exegesis in the Trinitarian controversies see Pollard, "The Exegesis of Scripture."

19. Ricken, "Nikaia als Krise." See also Ricken, "Die Logoslehre des Eusebios"; Ricken, "Das Homousios von Nikaia"; Ricken, "Emanation und Schöpfung"; Ricken, "Zur Rezeption der platonischen Ontologie." The basic view of Ricken has been taken up by Robertson, *Christ as Mediator,* 97–136. For an interesting theological take on the question of the role of Greek philosophy at (and around) the Council of Nicaea see Welte, "Die Lehrformel von Nikaia."

20. See the reconstruction of these scholarly positions in Wolfson, "Philosophical Implications."

21. For this debate see, e.g., Stead, "The Platonism of Arius"; Barnard, "What Was Arius' Philosophy?"; R. Williams, "The Logic of Arianism"; Mortley, "The Alien God in Arius"; Stead, "Philosophy in Origen and Arius." By one account, Arius's stance on the generation of the Son emerged from postures taken in intra-Platonist debates about God's creation of the world. In Alexandrian doctrinal discussions pre-dating Arius's intervention, Christians applied to Christ Plato's teaching concerning the generation of the world in order to stress the unity and indivisibility of God against the Valentinian and Manichaean doctrine of prolation (προβολή), Stoic conceptions of material divinity, and the speculations of Stoicizing Platonists such as Plutarch. In Plato, *Timaeus* 28C, the demiurge is in fact notoriously called father (πατήρ) and maker (ποιητής) of all things. These two expressions were commonly understood as respectively referring to the demiurge's relationship to rational beings and to the rest of creation. As a result of exegetical discussions of this passage (discussions to which witness is borne, e.g., by Plutarch, *Quaestiones platonicae* 2), Platonically-minded thinkers (pagan and Christian alike) had split opinions over the origin of the cosmos: see Stead, "Philosophy."

22. Arius received support in Libya (Secondus of Ptolemais and Theonas of Marmarica), Phoenicia (Paulinus of Tyre and Gregory of Berytus), Palestine (Eusebius of Caesarea), Bithynia (Maris of Chalcedon, Theognis of Nicaea, and Eusebius of Nicomedia), Phrygia (Theodotus of Laodicea), Cilicia (Athanasius of Anazarbus, Anthony of Tarsus), and Cappadocia (Asterius the Sophist).

23. On the theology of Eusebius of Caesarea see Berkhof, *Die Theologie*; Weber, *Archè*; Farina, "La teologia di Eusebio"; Luibhéid, *Eusebius.* On the theological views of Eusebius of Nicomedia see Luibhéid, "The Arianism of Eusebius"; Stead, "Athanasius' Earliest Written Work."

24. It may be there that Arius composed his dogmatic work, the *Banquet*. On this work see Stead, "The *Thalia* of Arius"; Simonetti, "Ancora sulla datazione"; Metzler, "Ein Beitrag zur Rekonstruktion"; Pardini, "Citazioni letterali dalla «ΘΑΛΕΙΑ»"; Camplani, "Studi atanasiani."

25. On Ossius see De Clercq, *Ossius of Cordova*; Ayán, Crespo, Polo, and González, *Osio de Córdoba*; Reyes Guerrero, *El siglo*. On Ossius's importance for the implementation of Constantine's religious policies, especially in relation to Nicaea, see Aiello, "Ossio e la politica religiosa"; Vilella Masana, "Constantino y Osio."

26. See S. Fernández, "Who Convened the First Council."

27. See Schwartz, "Zur Geschichte des Athanasius, VI"; Schwartz, "Zur Geschichte des Athanasius, VII"; Nau, "Littérature canonique syriaque"; Harnack, "Die angebliche Synode"; Seeberg, *Die Synode von Antiochien*; Cross, "The Council of Antioch"; Nyman, "The Synod at Antioch"; Chadwick, "Ossius of Cordova"; Holland, "Die Synode von Antiochien"; Simonetti, *La crisi ariana*, 38–41; R. Williams, *Arius*, 58–59; Hanson, *The Search*, 146–151; Logan, "Marcellus of Ancyra"; Strutwolf, *Die Trinitätstheologie*, 31–44; Brennecke, Heil, Stockhausen, and Wintjes, *Athanasius Werke. Dritter Band. Erster Teil. 3. Lieferung*, xxxiv–xxxvi; Brennecke and Heil, "After a Hundred Years."

28. On Constantine's debated early theological proclivities in the dispute that opposed Arius to Alexander of Alexandria see Elliott, "Constantine's Preparations." On his behavior at Nicaea see Dainese, "Costantino a Nicea"; Drake, "The Elephant in the Room." On Licinius's involvement in the controversy see Van Dam, "Imperial Fathers." On Constantine's attitude after Nicaea see Elliott, "Constantine." On Constantine's role in the Trinitarian disputes more generally see López Kindler, "Constantino y el arrianismo." See also Aiello, "Costantino e i vescovi di Roma." On the role played by Constantine's "theological" legacy among his successors see Aiello, "Costantino 'eretico.'"

29. On the number of participants see Dossetti, *Il simbolo di Nicea*; Fernández Hernández, "Los sinodales de Nicea"; Grant, "Religion and Politics."

30. On the presidency of the council see Chadwick, "Ossius of Cordova"; Fernández Hernández, "Los presidentes."

31. See Stead, "«Eusebius» and the Council of Nicea."

32. See Athanasius of Alexandria, *De decretis Nicaenae synodi* 19–20.

33. See Loofs, "Das Nicänum."

34. See the discussion in Simonetti, *La crisi ariana*, 83–84; Hanson, *The Search*, 163–166.

35. In light of this debate, I have avoided providing a univocal English translation for the word, opting instead for using the Greek term throughout. For a history of "homoousios" see Prestige, *God in Patristic Thought*, 197–218.

36. See Stead, *Divine Substance*. In his examination, influenced by analytical philosophy, Stead identified seven dimensions and four modes of reference jointly constituting an ideal grid of possible meanings of ousia, based on varying valences of the verb "to be" (εἶναι), from which this noun derives (some of the twenty-eight slots

remain empty, while some others are hardly distinguishable from an adjacent one). On the origins of the homoousios, its pre-Nicene history, and its utilization at Nicaea see Ortiz de Urbina, "L'*homoousios* preniceno"; Stead, "Homoousios"; Tuilier, "Le sens du terme ὁμοούσιος"; Stead, "The Significance of the Homoousios"; Stead, "«Homoousios»"; Dinsen, *Homoousios*; Bienert, "Das vornicaenische ὁμοούσιος"; Ritter, "Zum homoousios von Nizäa"; Simonetti, "Ancora su *Homoousios*"; Bartolozzi, "L'ὁμοούσιος niceno." On the use of ousia and hypostasis in the Platonic tradition, in relation to its Trinitarian appropriation, see Corrigan, "Οὐσία and ὑπόστασις."

37. On ὕπαρξις see Glucker, "The Origin of ὑπάρχω."

38. They did so either out of fear that the term "ousia" would be understood in its sense of "stuff"; as a result of a perceived need to harmonize their theological language with the Latin use of *substantia*; or out of wariness of the non-scriptural nature of this usage of the word. The saying contained in Plato, *De republica* 509B, to the effect that the idea of the good is "beyond being" (ἐπέκεινα τῆς οὐσίας) might have also been influential upon this Christian reticence, although Plato's statement was interpreted in a variety of ways—including as "beyond material substance," "beyond created substance," and "beyond intelligible substance." For a denial that the idea of the good transcended the realm of being in Plato see Baltes, "Is the Idea of the Good Beyond Being?" (for a rebuttal of Baltes's thesis, see Damschen and Ferber, "Is the Idea of the Good Beyond Being?").

39. It is likely that the passage attributed to Origen in which "homoousios" is used in a Trinitarian context is not authentic, as argued by Hanson, "Did Origen Apply." Edwards, "Did Origen Apply," believes instead in the authenticity of the passage.

40. See Ptolemy the Gnostic, *Epistula ad Floram*, apud Epiphanius of Salamis, *Adversus haereses* 33.7.8; Irenaeus of Lyons, *Adversus haereses* 1.5.1; 1.5.5.

41. See Galtier, "L'*homoousios*"; Prestige, *God in Patristic Thought*, 201–209; Dalmau, "El *homoousios* y el Concilio"; Brennecke, "Zum Prozess"; de Navascués Benlloch, *Pablo de Samosata*.

42. Summarized in Stead, *Divine Substance*, 250–251.

43. See Beatrice, "The Word 'Homoousios,'" claiming that the use of the term "homoousios" at the Council of Nicaea derived from Constantine's Hermetic background.

44. See Ramelli, "Origen's Anti-Subordinationism," 48–49; Ramelli, "Origen, Eusebius, the Doctrine of *Apokatastasis*."

45. See M.R. Barnes, "The Fourth Century," 49. According to Brennecke, "Zum Prozess," the idea that Paul was condemned because of his use of ὁμοούσιος was a polemical invention of the homoiousians aimed at denouncing the creed of Nicaea as heretical.

46. Secundus of Ptolemais and Theonas of Marmarica. Arius was probably not at the council.

47. Arius was proably sent to Illyria. On his exile see T.D. Barnes, "The Exile and Recalls."

48. On the reasons and circumstances of these depositions see Hanson, *The Search*, 173–174.

49. Ancient sources blame Constantine's about-face on the influence of some of his female relatives at the imperial court. Although Helena, Constantia, and Basilina did favor the Eusebians over the Nicene (partly because of family connections), it is unlikely that they were behind Constantine's change of heart. See Athanasius of Alexandria, *Historia Arianorum ad monachos* 5.6; Philostorgius, *Historia ecclesiastica* 2.12; Ammianus Marcellinus, *Res Gestae* 22.9.4; Rufinus of Aquileia, *Historia ecclesiastica* 1.9; 1.12; Socrates of Constantinople, *Historia ecclesiastica* 1.25; Sozomen, *Historia ecclesiastica* 2.27; Theodoret of Cyrrhus, *Historia ecclesiastica* 2.3.

50. See Simonetti, "Dibattito trinitario," 7–13; Segneri, *Atanasio. Lettera agli Antiocheni*, 16–30. See also Simonetti, "L'imperatore arbitro."

51. On the religious politics of Constantius II see Tietze, *Lucifer von Calaris*; Zurutuza, "La intolerancia religiosa."

52. On the date of the council see Fernández Hernández, "La primera intervención," 440.

53. The letter is reported by Athanasius of Alexandria, *Apologia secunda contra arianos* 20–36. It is edited and translated in Thompson, *The Correspondence of Pope Julius I*, 38–81.

54. Pope Julius I, *Epistula II*; ed. Thompson, 44; trans. Thompson, 45.

55. On the creeds of the Dedication council see Tetz, "Die Kirchweihsynode von Antiochien"; Fernández Hernández, "Dos alternativas orientales."

56. Athanasius of Alexandria, *De synodis Arimini in Italia et Seleucia in Isauria* 22.2–7; ed. Martin and Morales, 248. The First Creed of Antioch (341) is also reported by Socrates of Constantinople, *Historia ecclesiastica* 2.10.4–8 (ed. Maraval and Périchon, II, 42). It is also edited in Hahn and Hahn, *Bibliothek der Symbole*, 183–184; Brennecke, Heil, Stockhausen, and Wintjes, *Athanasius Werke. Dritter Band. Erster Teil. 3. Lieferung*, 149–150. For interpretations of this creed see Simonetti, *La crisi ariana*, 154–155; Bethune-Baker, *An Introduction*, 172; Kelly, *Early Christian Creeds*, 266.

57. See Athanasius of Alexandria, *Apologia secunda contra Arianos* 21–35.

58. Athanasius of Alexandria, *De synodis Arimini in Italia et Seleucia in Isauria* 22.3; ed. Martin and Morales, 248. The creed is also edited in Brennecke, Heil, Stockhausen, and Wintjes, *Athanasius Werke. Dritter Band. Erster Teil. 3. Lieferung*, 149–150.

59. Sozomen, *Historia ecclesiastica* 4.22.9–10; 6.7.5; 6.12.4.

60. Athanasius of Alexandria, *De synodis Arimini in Italia et Seleucia in Isauria* 23.2; ed. Martin and Morales, 250. The Second Creed of Antioch (341) is also reported by Socrates of Constantinople, *Historia ecclesiastica* 2.10.10–18 and (in Latin) by Hilary of Poitiers, *De synodis, seu De fide Orientalium* 29–30; ed. PL 10, 502–504. It is also edited in Hahn and Hahn, *Bibliothek der Symbole*, 184–186; Brennecke, Christof, Heil, Stockhausen, and Wintjes, *Athanasius Werke. Dritter Band. Erster Teil. 3. Lieferung*, 146–147.

61. See Kelly, *Early Christian Creeds*, 1–29.

62. See Simonetti, "La tradizione."

63. Arius, *Epistula ad Alexandrum Alexandrinum*; apud Athanasius of Alexandria, *De synodis Arimini in Italia et Seleuciae in Isauria* 16.2; ed. Martin and Morales, 226. The letter is not reported in *De synodis* in its entirety: the ending is only carried by Epiphanius of Salamis, *Adversus haereses* 69.8.5. The letter as a whole is edited in Hans-Georg Opitz, *Athanasius Werke. Dritter Band. Erster Teil. 1. Lieferung*, 12–13.

64. Arius, *Epistula ad Alexandrum Alexandrinum* 45; 66.

65. Sozomen, *Historia ecclesiastica* 3.5.8–9; 6.12.4; Athanasius of Alexandria, *De synodis Arimini in Italia et Seleucia in Isauria* 23.2–10; Socrates of Constantinople, *Historia ecclesiastica* 2.10.10–18; Hilary of Poitiers, *De synodis, seu De fide Orientalium* 29–30.

66. Among the ancient authorities that do not report the text but only talk about it, the formula is also presented as Lucian's in a pseudo-Athanasian dialogue, in Philostorgius's *Church History*, and, in dependence on the latter, in the *Passion of St. Artemius*: see Pseudo-Athanasius of Alexandria, *De sancta Trinitate dialogus III* 1.2.15; Philostorgius, *Historia ecclesiastica* 8.8; *Passio Sancti Artemii* 70.

67. See Bardy, *Recherches sur Saint Lucien*, 85–132; Simonetti, *La crisi ariana*, 158, n. 54; Simonetti, "Le origini dell'arianesimo," 328, n. 33; Brennecke, *Hilarius von Poitiers*, 10–16; Löhr, *Die Entstehung*, 10–16; Brennecke, "Lukian von Antiochien," 187–189.

68. Athanasius of Alexandria, *De synodis Arimini in Italia et Seleucia in Isauria* 23.5–6; ed. Martin and Morales, 252.

69. For an interpretation of the second formula of Antioch see Kelly, *Early Christian Creeds*, 270–271.

70. Athanasius of Alexandria, *De synodis Arimini in Italia et Seleucia in Isauria* 23.7–10; ed. Martin and Morales, 252; trans. adapted from Kelly, *Early Christian Creeds*, 269–270.

71. The Third Creed of Antioch (341) is found in Athanasius of Alexandria, *De synodis Arimini in Italia et Seleucia in Isauria* 24.2–5. It is also edited in Hahn and Hahn, *Bibliothek der Symbole*, 186–187; Brennecke, Heil, Stockhausen, and Wintjes, *Athanasius Werke. Dritter Band. Erster Teil. 3. Lieferung*, 143–144.

72. On the possible background of Theophronius's presentation of his creed see Kelly, *Early Christian Creeds*, 267–268. The circumstance of a bishop having to prove his orthodoxy through a short formula is peculiar and was reproduced on the occasion of the presentation of a creed on the part of Hilary of Poitiers at the Council of Seleucia (359).

73. Socrates of Constantinople, *Historia ecclesiastica* 2.20.9, gives this location, whereas Sozomen, *Historia ecclesiastica* 3.11.4–9, locates the composition at Sardica (more credibly according to Simonetti, *La crisi ariana*, 172, n. 27).

74. Athanasius of Alexandria, *De synodis Arimini in Italia et Seleucia in Isauria* 25.2–4; ed. Martin and Morales, 256–258. The Fourth Creed of Antioch (341) is also reported by Socrates of Constantinople, *Historia ecclesiastica* 2.18.3–6. It is also edited in Hahn and Hahn, *Bibliothek der Symbole*, 187–188.

75. Athanasius of Alexandria, *De synodis Arimini in Italia et Seleucia in Isauria* 25.5; ed. Martin and Morales, 258.

76. Theodoret of Cyrrhus, *Historia ecclesiastica* 2.8.39–40; ed. Bouffartigue, Canivet, Martin, Pietri, and Thélamon, I, 368–370. The Westerners' Creed of Sardica is also edited in Hahn and Hahn, *Bibliothek der Symbole*, 188–190; Brennecke, Heil, Stockhausen, and Wintjes, *Athanasius Werke. Dritter Band. Erster Teil. 3. Lieferung*, 206–212.

77. On these developments see Simonetti, *La crisi ariana*, 187–189.

78. Athanasius of Alexandria, *De synodis Arimini in Italia et Seleucia in Isauria* 26.4.1; ed. Martin and Morales, 262. The *Long-Lined Exposition* is also reported by Socrates of Constantinople, *Historia ecclesiastica* 2.19.3–28 (ed. Maraval and Périchon, II, 72–82). It is also edited in Hahn and Hahn, *Bibliothek der Symbole*, 192–196; Brennecke, Heil, Stockhausen, and Wintjes, *Athanasius Werke. Dritter Band. Erster Teil. 3. Lieferung*, 270–277.

79. For interpretations of this text see Hall, "The Creed of Sardica"; Ulrich, *Die Anfänge*, 59–87.

80. Sozomen, *Historia ecclesiastica* 3.12.5–6; ed. Grillet, Festugière, and Sabbah, II, 108.

81. Thompson chooses to translate instead: "We keep in mind, hold to, and retain the document produced at Nicaea that contains the catholic faith," making *factam aput Niceam* depend on *scripturam* rather than on *fidem*.

82. Some editions, such as mine, provide all three questions; others provide none of them, and others just the third (these differences are irrelevant to my discussion here). On these three questions see Thompson, *The Correspondence of Pope Julius I*, 93, n. 2.

83. Thompson and Tetz understand *ratio quaedam* as "reason itself"; Brennecke as "a reasonable foresight."

84. Tetz's reconstruction, detaching the words *priori consentientes* ("agreeing with the former [faith]") from this sentence and placing them at the start of the next one, does not allow for the ambiguity of the direct object that is present in the *Athanasius Werke* edition. Either placement preserves the pro-Nicene rhetoric of the letter.

85. Brennecke and Ayán read "previous things" (*priora*) for Tetz's and Thompson's "many things" (*pluria*).

86. Re-edition of Ossius Cordobensis and Protogenes Serdicensis, *Epistula ad Iulium papam*, based on ms. Verona, Biblioteca Capitolare, LX (tenth century at the latest) + Rome, Biblioteca Casanatense, 378 (A.III.24) (second half of the eighth century) (see Lowe, *Codices Latini Antiquiores*, IV, nr. 416 and 510 and Supplementum): *Dilectissimo fratri Iulio Osius et Protogenes. Meminimus et tenemus et habemus illam scripturam quae continet catholicam fidem factam aput Niceam et consenserunt omnes qui aderant episcopi. Tres enim questiones motae sunt* <. . .> *quod* [the ms. has *quad*] *erat quando non erat. Sed quoniam post hoc discipuli Arrii blasphemias* [the ms. has *blasphemiae*] *conmoverunt ratio*

quaedam coegit ne quis ex illis tribus argumentis circumventus renove{n}t fidem et excludatur eorum spolium et ne fia<t> latior et longior exponere priori consentientes. Ut igitur nulla reprehensio fiat haec significamus tuae bonitati frater dilectissime: plura placuerunt firma esse et fixa et haec plenius cum quadam sufficientia veritatis dictari ut omnes docentes et caticizantes clarificentur et {p}repugnantes obruantur et teneant catholicam et apostolicam fidem (I wish to thank Zlatko Pleše for his contribution of this text). Previous editions of the text include the one by Girolamo and Pietro Ballerini in PL 56, 839–840; Turner, *Ecclesiae Occidentalis monumenta*, I/2, 644; Tetz, "'Ante omnia de sancta fide et de integritate veritatis,'" 247–248; Brennecke, Heil, Stockhausen, and Wintjes, *Athanasius Werke. Dritter Band. Erster Teil. 3. Lieferung*, 231–232; Thompson, *The Correspondence of Pope Julius I*, 95–97; Ayán, Crespo, Polo, and González, *Osio de Córdoba*, 30–33 (aiming at improving Turner's rendition). The *Athanasius Werke* Latin text does not seem to comport with its editors' German rendition of it (Brennecke, Heil, Stockhausen, and Wintjes, *Athanasius Werke. Dritter Band. Erster Teil. 3. Lieferung*, 231–232).

87. Montinari, "Hypomnema," 814.

88. The edition of Tetz, "'Ante omnia de sancta fide et de integritate veritatis,'" 247–248, has the letter express a different idea: "But because the disciples of Arius have since then stirred blasphemies, a certain reason compelled [us]—lest anyone, deceived by those three arguments, should remove the faith, and (so that) their [scil. Arius's disciples'] spoil be excluded, and lest an impiety [might occur]—to offer an exposition more amply and more extensively" (*Sed quoniam post hoc discipuli Arrii blasphemias conmoverunt, ratio quaedam coegit, (ne quis ex illis tribus argumentis circumventus re<m>ove<a>t fidem et excludatur eorum spolium et nef<as>) lati<us> et longi<us> exponere*). In this reconstruction, the authors of the document decided to offer an exposition that they themselves considered more inclusive and prolix (*latius et longius exponere*) in order to prevent the formula of faith from being set aside (*ne quis* [. . .] *removeat fidem*) or—as per another, only slightly divergent reconstruction (Thompson, *The Correspondence of Pope Julius I*, 96)—rejected (*ne quis* [. . .] *rennuerit fidem*).

89. Patricio de Navascués, "Osio en Sárdica (343)," 394, interprets the verb *meminimus* ("we remember") in *Letter* 2 as a reference to the Arians, and *tenemus* ("we hold on") as an allusion to the well-intentioned Nicene who could fall into the temptation of renewing the faith. This interpretation might contain a slight overreading.

90. Athanasius of Alexandria, *Tomus ad Antiochenos* 5.3–4; ed. Segneri, 88; trans. adapted from *NPNF2* IV, 484. I regret that, because of the production times of this book, the 2021 French translation and commentary of the *Tome to the Antiochenes* prepared on the basis of the text of the *Athanasius Werke* by Annick Martin and Xavier Morales for Sources Chrétiennes (see the List of Editions of Ancient Sources) has appeared in print and become available to me too late to be able to be referenced in my discussion.

91. See Tetz, "Über nikäische Orthodoxie," 204.

92. This is especially true if, as some claim, Athanasius had undersigned the creed of the westerners at Sardica.

93. See Segneri, *Atanasio. Lettera agli Antiocheni*, 122–127.

94. PL 56, 839–840, n. *e*.

95. I take *fides* to be a shorthand for *scriptura fidei* (the "writ" or statement or rule of faith), in Greek πίστεως γραφή, the same expression used by Sozomen, *Historia ecclesiastica* 3.12.5.

96. This is the general sense of the text also in the parsing of Tetz, "'Ante omnia de sancta fide et de integritate veritatis'" and Thompson, *The Correspondence*.

97. *Ratio quaedam coegit (ne quis ex illis tribus argumentis circunventus renovet fidem) ut excludatur eorum scholium adversus Nicaenam fidem, et fiat latior et longior expositio priori consentiens.*

98. The brothers Girolamo and Pietro Ballerini marked the whole passage, from *et excludatur* to *consentien[te]s*, as "depravatus" and "mutilus." As a result, they supplemented *adversus Nicaenam fidem* and replaced *exponere* with *expositio*, the initial *et* with *ut*, and *consentientes* with *consentiens*. The addition of the paraphrastic phrase *adversus Nicaenam fidem* is certainly to be rejected: *eorum*, which clearly refers to Arius's disciples, is sufficient to convey the anti-Nicene nature of the alleged scholium. If the emendation is to be accepted, it must be tamed into a text reading as follows: *Ratio quaedam coegit (ne quis ex illis tribus argumentis circunventus renovet fidem) ut excludatur eorum scholium, et fiat latior et longior expositio priori consentiens* ("But since thereafter the disciples of Arius have contrived blasphemies, a certain [specific] rationale has compelled us—so that no one, swayed by those three arguments, may introduce innovations into the [rule of] faith—to have their scholium excluded, and to have an expanded and extended exposition produced, which agrees with the former").

99. See, e.g., Montana, "The Making," where the word "scholium" is never mentioned.

100. Cicero, *Ad Atticum* 16.7.3.

101. Sozomen's sentence "They set forth then another statement of faith, more extensive than that of Nicaea, but preserving the same intent and departing only slightly from its words" corresponds to sentence 2 in the *Letter*, "We remember and hold onto and retain that rule which contains the catholic faith produced at Nicaea, and all of the present bishops concurred," with Sozomen's πίστεως γραφὴν corresponding to Ossius and Protogenes's *scripturam* and *fidem* (*Letter*, 2). Sozomen's phrase "fearing perhaps that they might be considered by some to make innovations to the decisions of Nicaea" corresponds to "so that no one, swayed by those three arguments, may introduce innovations into the [statement of] faith" (*Letter*, 4). Sozomen's phrase "and professed to consider these as normative, but that given the need for clarity they had expanded the same [original] intent" corresponds to "we pronounced that most [of the rule] is firm and fixed but should be formulated more fully with a certain sufficiency of truth" (*Letter*, 5).

102. On σχόλιον see Dyck and Glock, "Scholien."

103. See Epictetus, *Dissertationes ab Arriano digestae* 3.21.6; Galen, *Commentarius in Hippocratis De medici officina librum* 3.1.18. Jerome of Stridon, *Epistula praefatoria ad Homilias Origenis in Ezechielem*, divided Origen's exegetical writings into tomes (or commentaries), homilies, and scholia. Clement's *Hypotyposeis* (as well as other Christian writings later than the letter under discussion) were considered scholia.

104. See the apparatus in the edition of P.Gen. 62 at http://papyri.info/ddbdp/c.ep.lat;;227 [retrieved on October 29, 2021]. The word πιττάκιον also indicated the list of members of a society, the πιττακιάρχης being its chairman.

105. Gelasius of Cyzicus, *Syntagma* 26.3; ed. Hansen (2002), 83.

106. Athanasius of Alexandria, *Tomus ad Antiochenos* 10.3: Καὶ ἐπειδὴ ἔξωθεν λέγεται τὸ τῆς Σαρδικῆς πιττάκιον ἕνεκεν τοῦ μὴ παρὰ τὴν ἐν Νικαίᾳ πίστιν δοκεῖν ἐκτίθεσθαι, καὶ ἐγὼ συγκατατίθεμαι, ἵνα μὴ ἡ ἐν Νικαίᾳ πίστις διὰ τούτου ἐκκλείεσθαι δόξῃ, μήτε εἶναι προκομιστέον; ed. Segneri, 100. I translate here, however, the retroversion proposed by Christoph Schubert in "Ein wiedergewonnenes Schreiben": *et quoniam extraneum dicitur Serdicae pittacium ea causa, ne praeter Nicaenam fidem videatur expositum esse, et ego adsentior, ne Nicaena fides per hoc excludi videatur nec esse praeferendum*. Schubert himself translates: "Und da nun die Vereinbarung von Serdica deswegen als, nicht zu rezipieren bezeichnet wird, damit es nicht den Anschein habe, sie sei über den Glauben von Nizäa hinaus aufgestellt, so stimme auch ich dem zu, damit es nicht den Anschein habe, der Glaube von Nizäa sei durch sie ausgeschlossen oder sie sei vorzuziehen." I find a translation highlighting the material preferable to Schubert's "Vereinbarung" ("agreement") for *pittacium* (the likely Latin reconstruction given Athanasius's use).

107. Jerome of Stridon, *Altercatio Luciferiani et orthodoxi* 19; ed. Canellis, 158.

108. The letter, also addressed to Macedonius of Constantinople, Cecropius of Nicomedia, and Eugene of Nicaea, is reported in full in Sozomen, *Historia ecclesiastica* 4.13.

109. On the importance of the events of 358 see Simonetti, *La crisi ariana*, 348–350.

110. On Julian's religious politics see Fatti, *Giuliano a Cesarea*. See also Elm, *Sons of Hellenism*.

111. *Historia acephala Athanasii* 8.10.

112. See Sulpicius Severus, *Chronica* 2.45; Athanasius of Alexandria, *Epistula ad Rufinianum*; Basil of Caesarea, *Epistula CCIV* 6; Basil of Caesarea, *Epistula CCLI* 4; Socrates of Constantinople, *Historia ecclesiastica* 3.10.

113. On the chronology of Athanasius's return to Alexandria see Barnard, "Athanasius and the Emperor Jovian."

114. Evidence is also lacking that the creed was ever deployed in a liturgical context (including during that period): see Gavrilyuk, "The Legacy of the Council of Nicaea," 335. On the reception of Nicaea up to 360 see S. Parvis, "The Reception of Nicaea." See also G.D. Dunn, "Catholic Reception," 347–349.

115. Hilary of Poitiers, *De synodis, seu De fide Orientalium* 91; ed. PL 10, 545.

116. Hilary of Poitiers, *Fragmenta historica*, Series A, VII, 6; ed. Feder, 92–93.

117. According to Brennecke, *Hilarius von Poitiers*, 164–181, Liberius in the letter mentioned in the text was referring not to the Nicene Creed but to its Sardican interpretation. Hilary's account of Eusebius's proposal of the Nicene Creed at the Council of Milan was, in Brennecke's view, an ex post reconstruction following the Council of Sirmium of 357, where the homoousios was banned. Simonetti, "Eusebio nella controversia ariana," 177–179 rejects Brennecke's reconstruction.

118. See Ayres, "Athanasius' Initial Defense."

119. The dating of *On the Sentence of Dionysius* is debated: for a later dating (357/360) see Heil, *Athanasius von Alexandrien*, 22–35. The 352/353 dating is found in T.D. Barnes, *Athanasius and Constantius*, 111 and 198–199.

120. See Anatolios, *Athanasius: The Coherence of His Thought*, 89–90.

121. See Ayres, *Nicaea and Its Legacy*, 141–142.

122. Ibid., 142–143. See also Ayres, "Athanasius' Initial Defense."

123. See T.D. Barnes, *Athanasius and Constantius*, 132.

124. For a comparable methodological stance see the "Preface" in Boys-Stones, *Post-Hellenistic Philosophy*.

3. Theological Labeling: Antioch and Alexandria in the 360s

1. On the Council of Alexandria see Socrates of Constantinople, *Historia ecclesiastica* 3.7; Sozomen, *Historia ecclesiastica* 5.12.3–5; Rufinus of Aquileia, *Historia ecclesiastica* 10.29–30. On the reports of the various Church historians on the Council of Alexandria see Duval, "La place," 283–284. The council is dated by Martin, *Athanase d'Alexandrie*, 543, n. 4, to a date between February 24 and March 31, 362; by Tetz, "Über nikäische Orthodoxie," 196, to April; by Simonetti, *La crisi ariana*, 395, to May; by Karmann, *Meletius von Antiochien*, 186, to the spring or early summer; by Camplani, *Atanasio di Alessandria. Lettere festali*, 633, to the summer. See Segneri, *Atanasio. Lettera agli Antiocheni*, 53, n. 96.

2. Jerome of Stridon, *Altercatio Luciferiani et orthodoxi* 20; ed. Canellis, 146.

3. Tetz, "Ein enzyklisches Schreiben," sees the so-called *Catholic Epistle* as (the first part of) the synodal letter of Alexandria. The authenticity of the *Catholic Epistle* is accepted by Yeum, *Die Synode von Alexandrien*, 15–17; Gemeinhardt, "Der *Tomus*," 178. For Amidon, *The Church History*, 57, n. 41, Rufinus read the *Catholic Epistle* or some version of it. Camplani, "Atanasio e Eusebio," 219–226, considers the work a Eustathian/Marcellan forgery. On the *Catholic Epistle* see also Morales, *La théologie trinitaire*, 365–374; Gemeinhardt, "Epistula catholica"; Karmann, *Meletius von Antiochien*, 181–184; Duval, "La place," 285, n. 14.

4. Athanasius of Alexandria, *Tomus ad Antiochenos*. The *Tome to the Antiochenes* is cited as "epistula ad Antiochenos" or "ad Antiochenos epistula" in Peter of Alexandria, *Epistula ad episcopos Aegyptios fidei causa exules*, apud Facundus of Hermiane, *Pro defen-*

sione trium capitulorum 11.2.1 and 11.2.4. For the indirect tradition see Brennecke, Heil, and Stockhausen, *Athanasius Werke. Zweiter Band. Erster Teil. 8. Lieferung*, lxxxviii. On the *Tome* see Pasté, "Del simbolo «Quicumque»"; Simonetti, *La crisi ariana*, 360–370; Morales, *La théologie trinitaire*, 376–389; Segneri, *Atanasio. Lettera agli Antiocheni*; Martin, Review of Segneri, *Atanasio*.

5. Mistakenly recorded as "of Petra": see Martin, *Athanase d'Alexandrie*, 543, n. 4.

6. Athanasius of Alexandria, *Tomus ad Antiochenos* 9.1; ed. Segneri, 96; trans. adapted from *NPNF2* IV, 485–486.

7. See Tetz, "Über nikäische Orthodoxie," 196 (along with Joannou, *Die Ostkirche*, 136, cited in Tetz, "Über nikäische Orthodoxie," 196, n. 7). Karmann, *Meletius von Antiochien*, 171, speaks of two sessions of the council, though conceding (172) that the Antiochene schism might have been discussed also in the former of the two. For Yeum, *Die Synode*, 16, the second session was run by a committee charged by the plenary council.

8. See Simonetti, "Ancora sul concilio," 8–10.

9. See Theodoret of Cyrrhus, *Historia ecclesiastica* 3.5; Rufinus of Aquileia, *Historia ecclesiastica* 10.27; Socrates of Constantinople, *Historia ecclesiastica* 3.9; Sozomen, *Historia ecclesiastica* 5.12. On Lucifer and his theology see Krüger, *Lucifer Bischof von Calaris*; Marcello, *La posizione di Lucifero;* Zedda, "La dottrina"; Simonetti, "Appunti"; Opelt, "Formen der Polemik"; Diercks, "Luciferi Calaritani," i–cxxxi; Piras, "Kritische Bemerkungen"; Simonetti, "Lucifero di Cagliari"; Gastoni, "La battaglia antiariana"; Ulrich, *Die Anfänge*, 217–230; Corti, *Lucifero di Cagliari*; López, "El cisma luciferiano"; Canellis, "Écrire contre l'Empereur"; Whiting, *Christian Communities*; Cibis, *Lucifer von Calaris*.

10. The ordination of Paulinus is narrated in Theodoret of Cyrrhus, *Historia ecclesiastica* 3.2; Socrates of Constantinople, *Historia ecclesiastica* 3.9; Sozomen, *Historia ecclesiastica* 5.12; Rufinus of Aquileia, *Historia ecclesiastica* 1.27. See also Jerome of Stridon, *Chronicon, ad annuum Romanorum XXXVI*; ed. Helm, 242; trans. Donalson, 50.

11. The chronology of Meletius's return is unclear. See Socrates of Constantinople, *Historia ecclesiastica* 3.9.3; Sozomen, *Historia ecclesiastica* 5.13.3; Theodoret of Cyrrhus, *Historia ecclesiastica* 3.4.2. The *Chronicon Paschale* dates the death of Eustathius, the return of Meletius, and the overtaking of the Old Church all to 362: "Meletius too, who had been demoted for impiety and other evils, returned to Antioch and seized the Old Church, when those of the clergy who had already been legally demoted by the holy synod also ran to join him"; ed. Dindorf, I, 547–548; trans. adapted from Whitby and Whitby, 37–38.

12. For a summary of the events see Devreesse, *Le patriarcat d'Antioche*, 17–38.

13. On Antioch in this period see Liebeschuetz, *Antioch*. On the schism of Antioch see Cavallera, *Le schisme*; Devreesse, *Le patriarcat d'Antioche*, 17–38; Barker, *The Meletian Schism*; Spoerl, "The Schism at Antioch"; Guillén Pérez, "El patriarcato de Antioquía," 329–335; Ward, *The Schism at Antioch*; Morales, *La théologie trinitaire*, 357–395; Martin,

"Antioche ou la difficile unité"; Segneri, *Atanasio. Lettera agli Antiocheni*, 36–67; Martin, Review of Segneri, *Atanasio*; Chadwick, *The Church in Ancient Society*, 415–432.

14. Gwynn, "Archaeology," 243–245, claims that religious reality on the ground in Antioch may have been more irenic than the sources would have us believe. On the spatial dimension of religious controversy in Antioch see Shepardson, *Controlling Contested Places*.

15. See Chadwick, "The Fall."

16. See John Chrysostom, *Laudatio S. patris nostri Eustathii Antiocheni* 4.

17. I use the word "orthodox" in the context of the Trinitarian controversies exclusively to indicate a position or community bolstered by imperial power at the time in question.

18. This church stood on the island in the river Orontes. See Downey, *A History of Antioch*, 342–345.

19. For a novel rendition of the chronology of Antiochene bishops in the time leading up to the Council of Sardica see de Navascués Benlloch, "La *communio*," 854–855.

20. See Theodoret of Cyrrhus, *Historia ecclesiastica* 2.32.11; 3.4.3. Socrates of Constantinople, *Historia ecclesiastica* 2.44.5–7, and Sozomen, *Historia ecclesiastica* 4.28.9–10, do not specify the location. It is unclear whether the Meletians retained the use of the Old Church during Meletius's exile or only after his return: see Simonetti, *La crisi ariana*, 362, n. 25.

21. See Socrates of Constantinople, *Historia ecclesiastica* 3.9.

22. See Socrates of Constantinople, *Historia ecclesiastica* 5.1.3.

23. On this council see D.H. Williams, "The Council of Ariminum."

24. On the council in the Thebaid see Armstrong, "The Synod of Alexandria," 206–209; Simonetti, *La crisi ariana*, 359 (who sees it as a mere colloquy between Lucifer and Eusebius); Yeum, *Die Synode von Alexandrien*, 27–32 (with a similar reading).

25. Socrates of Constantinople, *Historia ecclesiastica* 3.5–6.

26. Sozomen, *Historia ecclesiastica* 5.12.1; ed. Grillet, Festugière, and Sabbah, III, 148.

27. Sozomen, *Historia ecclesiastica* 5.12.1; ed. Grillet, Festugière, and Sabbah, III, 148.

28. Rufinus of Aquileia, *Historia ecclesiastica* 10.28.3.

29. See, e.g., Armstrong, "The Synod of Alexandria," 208–209.

30. Theodoret of Cyrrhus, *Historia ecclesiastica* 3.4.2–3: Εὐσέβιος δὲ καὶ Ἱλάριος οἱ ἐκ τῆς Ἰταλίας καὶ Λουκίφερ ὁ Σαρδῶ τὴν νῆσον ποιμαίνειν λαχὼν ἐν τῇ Θηβαίων τῇ πρὸς Αἴγυπτον διῆγον· ἐκεῖ γὰρ αὐτοὺς ὁ Κωνστάντιος ἐξωστράκισεν. Οὗτοι σὺν τοῖς ἄλλοις ὁμόφροσι κατὰ ταὐτὸν γενόμενοι χρῆναι τὰς ἐκκλησίας ἔλεγον εἰς μίαν συναγαγεῖν συμφωνίαν. Οὐ γὰρ μόνον αὐτὰς οἱ τἀναντία φρονοῦντες ἐπολιόρκουν, ἀλλὰ καὶ αὐταὶ πρὸς ἑαυτὰς ἐστασίαζον. Καὶ γὰρ ἐν Ἀντιοχείᾳ διχῇ τὸ ὑγιαῖνον σῶμα τῆς ἐκκλησίας διῄρητο· οἵ τε γὰρ ἐξ ἀρχῆς Εὐσταθίου χάριν τοῦ πανευφήμου τῶν ἄλλων ἀποκριθέντες καθ' ἑαυτοὺς συνηθροίζοντο, καὶ οἱ μετὰ Μελετίου τοῦ θαυμασίου τῆς Ἀρειανικῆς

συμμορίας χωρισθέντες ἐν τῇ καλουμένῃ Παλαιᾷ τὰς λειτουργίας ἐπετέλουν τὰς θείας; ed. Bouffartigue, Canivet, Martin, Pietri, and Thélamon, II, 108–110.

31. Theodoret of Cyrrhus, *Commentarii in Esaïam*, 17.14: "We have already said before how those people, *having come together* [κατὰ ταὐτὸν γενόμενοι], both killed and took captive many thousands among them" (προειρήκαμεν δὲ ἤδη ὡς πολλὰς αὐτῶν μυριάδας οὗτοι κατὰ ταὐτὸν γενόμενοι καὶ κατηκόντισαν καὶ αἰχμαλώτους ἀπήγαγον); ed. Guinot, II, 120. Guinot (II, 121) translates: "se coalisèrent."

32. Theodoret of Cyrrhus, *Historia ecclesiastica* 2.33.2: "'I cannot,' said the admirable Eusebius, 'give up the common deposit before all those who have entrusted it (to me) *have gotten together* [κατὰ ταυτὸν γένοιντο]'"; ed. Bouffartigue, Canivet, Martin, Pietri, and Thélamon, I, 496.

33. Martin, "Athanase d'Alexandrie," 542, n. 4. On Socrates's self-avowed (see Socrates of Constantinople, *Historia ecclesiastica* 2.1) dependence on Rufinus of Aquileia see Walraff, *Der Kirchenhistoriker Sokrates*, 186–189. On Sozomen's dependence on both Rufinus and Socrates see Schoo, *Die Quellen*; Jeep, *Quellenuntersuchungen*, 188. More broadly on the relationships between the three historians see Leppin, "The Church Historians (I)," 219–254.

34. See Martin, "L'Église d'Antioche," 483.

35. See L. Parmentier, *Theodoret Kirchengeschichte*, xci–xcv. In general, Theodoret used Rufinus or the latter's likely main source, the lost *Church History* of Gelasius of Caesarea: see Güldenpenning, *Die Kirchengeschichte*, 26–39; Rauschen, *Jahrbücher der christlichen Kirche*, 559–563; L. Parmentier, *Theodoret Kirchengeschichte*, lxxxiv–lxxxvi. On the debated relationship between Rufinus's and Gelasius's works see Schamp, "Gélase ou Rufin," 360–390; Van Deun, "The Church Historians," 156–167; Marasco, "The Church Historians (II)," 284–288; Marinides, Stutz, and Wallraff, *Gelasius of Caesarea*, xxx–xxxvii. Theodoret also occasionally used Socrates (see Güldenpenning, *Die Kirchengeschichte*, 39–41) and Sabinus of Heraklea (see Güldenpenning, *Die Kirchengeschichte*, 59–61), but not Sozomen, who wrote after Theodoret. Theodoret used the anonymous homoian source of the 360s called by Burgess *Antiochene Continuation of Eusebius* (ed. Bidez, *Philostorgius Kirchengeschichte*, 179–222), considered by Battifol the work of an Arian historian and possibly used by Philostorgius himself: see Güldenpenning, *Die Kirchengeschichte*, 49–56; Battifol, "Un historiographe"; Burgess, *Studies*. For the dating of this source to the 360s see Gwatkin, *Studies of Arianism*, 219–224; Brennecke, *Studien zur Geschichte der Homöer*, 114–157. On Philostorgius see Marasco, "The Church Historians (II)," 257–284.

36. Armstrong, "The Synod of Alexandria," 348. On Hilary of Jerusalem see Hanson, *The Search*, 399; 401.

37. L. Parmentier, *Theodoret Kirchengeschichte*, 387, s.v. Ἱλάριος. This onomastic entry has remained unaltered in the two further editions of Theodoret's *Church History* published in the same series: see Scheidweiler, *Theodoret Kirchengeschichte*, 405; Hansen, *Theodoret Kirchengeschichte*, 387.

38. See Bouffartigue, Canivet, Martin, Pietri, and Thélamon, *Théodoret de Cyr. Histoire ecclésiastique*, II, 109, n. 3.

39. See Sulpicius Severus, *Vita sancti Martini Turonensis* 7.1; ed. Fontaine, I, 266. See also Sulpicius Severus, *Chronica* 2.42.1–2; 2.45.2–4; ed. Senneville-Grave, 322; 328–332; ed. Parroni, 99; 102. On Hilary's exile and its motivations see Wilmart, "Les 'Fragments Historiques'"; D.H. Williams, "A Reassessment"; Smulders, *Hilary of Poitiers' Preface*, 126–131; Ménard, "Exil et déploiement d'une théologie." On Hilary's presentation of his own exile see T.D. Barnes, "Hilary of Poitiers on His Exile"; Barry, "Heroic Bishops"; Barry, *Bishops in Flight*, 18–20. On Hilary's return from exile to Gaul see Duval, "Vrais et faux problèmes." Hilary's return is mentioned in Sulpicius Severus, *Chronica* 2.45; *Altercatio Heracliani laici cum Germinio episcopo sirmiensi* (*initio*).

40. Jerome of Stridon, *Altercatio Luciferiani et orthodoxi*, 27; ed. Canellis, 196.

41. On Hilary of Rome see Cavallera, *Saint Jérôme*, 56–57; Pérez Mas, *La crisis luciferiana*, 45–51, 183–186, 267–275, and 361–363. See also Jörg Rüpke, *Fasti sacerdotum*, 716, s.v. "Hilarius" (entry n. 1898), with references to ancient sources for his activity; Pietri and Pietri, *Prosopographie chrétienne*, I, 985–986 (s.v. "Hilarius 1"); Pietri, "Appendice prosopographique," 386. The possibility of this identification is raised in Pérez Mas, *La crisis luciferiana*, 126. Jerome mentions Hilary in *Altercatio Luciferiani et orthodoxi*, 21; 25; 26 (twice); 27 (ed. Canellis [SC], 172, 189, 192, 194, and 197) and, along with Lucifer and Pancratius, in Lucifer, *De regibus apostaticis*, 5 (ed. Diercks, 145). Hilary of Rome is also mentioned in Hilary of Poitiers, *Apologetica responsa* 5 (ed. Durst, 438).

42. See PL 35, 2007–2008; PL 17, 43. Langen, *De commentariorum in epistulas Paulinas qui Ambrosii et Quaestionum biblicarum quae Augustini nomine feruntur scriptore dissertatio*, 5, and Krüger, *Lucifer Bischof von Calaris*, 88, rejected this theory. Souter, *A Study of Ambrosiaster*, 175, denied the possibility of Ambrosiaster being a deacon. For the debate about the identity of Ambrosiaster see Bruyn, Cooper, and Hunter, *Ambrosiaster's Commentary*, xxiv–xxv; Hunter, "Presidential Address."

43. *Epistula legatorum*, apud Hilary of Poitiers, *Fragmenta historica*, Series A, VII; ed. Feder, 89–93; ed. Bischoff, Bulhart, Heylen, Hoste, and Wilmart, *Eusebius Vercellensis*, 120.

44. Ed. Bischoff, Bulhart, Heylen, Hoste, and Wilmart, *Eusebius Vercellensis*, 120–123. On the letters see Saxer, "Fonti storiche," 123–124; Simonetti, "Eusebio di Vercelli," 156–157. On the *Life* see R. Grégoire, "Agiografia e storiografia."

45. The sources for the Council of Milan of 355 are Rufinus of Aquileia, *Historia ecclesiastica* 10.20; Socrates of Constantinople, *Historia ecclesiastica* 2.36; Sozomen, *Historia ecclesiastica* 4.9, Theodoret of Cyrrhus, *Historia ecclesiastica* 2.15; Lucifer of Calaris, *Moriundum esse pro Dei Filio* 1; Athanasius, *Historia Arianorum ad monachos* 31–34; 76 (ed. Opitz, 199–202; 224–226); Hilary of Poitiers, *Liber I ad Constantium* 8 (on the eclectic nature of this tripartite text, of which chapter 8 constitutes the third part, see Wilmart, "L'*Ad Constantium*"; Wickman, "Shaping Church-State Relations," 287, n. 1; Wickham, *Hilary of Poitiers: Conflicts*, xxvi; D. Williams, "The Anti-

Arian Campaigns," 9, n. 11). On the Council of Milan see Müller, "Die Synode von Mailand."

46. No explicit mention is made of the exile of the presbyter Pancratius. More clergymen were exiled at the council than just the Roman delegates. The names of the exiles of 355 are provided varyingly by different sources: Socrates of Constantinople, *Historia ecclesiastica* 2.36.3–5 and 2.37.1, has Paulinus of Trier, Dionysius of Alba, and Eusebius; Sozomen, *Historia ecclesiastica* 4.9.3, mentions Dionysius of Alba, Eusebius of Vercellae, Paulinus of Trier, Rhodanos (of Toulouse), and Lucifer; Theodoret of Cyrrus, *Historia ecclesiastica* 2.15.4, cites Liberius, Paulinus, Dionysius, Lucifer, and Eusebius; Jerome of Stridon, *Chronicon, ad annuum Romanorum XVIII*, mentions Lucifer of Calaris, Dionysius of Milan, Pancratius the Roman priest, and Hilarius the deacon. Rufinus of Aquileia, *Historia ecclesiastica* 10.21, has Dionysius, Eusebius, Paulinus, Rhodianus, Lucifer, and Hilary. Hilary of Poitiers, *Liber I ad Constantium* 2, makes mention of Paulinus, Eusebius, Lucifer, and Dionysius. The Dionysius of Alba cited by Socrates of Constantinople and Sozomen is identified with Dionysius of Milan by Pierre Maraval in Maraval and Périchon, *Socrates de Constantinople. Histoire ecclésiastique*, II, 161, n. 4, and by Grillet, Festugière, and Sabbah, *Sozomène. Histoire ecclésiastique*, II, 218, n. 3. On the exile of Dionysius of Milan see Paredi, "L'esilio in Oriente." Amidon, *The Church History*, 53, n. 33, identifies the Hilary cited by Rufinus with Hilary of Poitiers; since Rhodanius was exiled at the Council of Béziers of 356, where also Hilary was exiled, this is probably correct. Paulinus of Trier (mentioned by Socrates of Constantinople, Sozomen, Theodoret, and Rufinus) had already been exiled at the Council of Arles. On the exile of the pro-Athanasians in 355 see also the other sources provided in Helm, *Die Chronik des Hieronymus*, 450, nr. 240a; 181–189. On the exiles of the council of 355 see Van Nuffelen, "Arius, Athanase, et les autres," 155; Ménard, "L'exil, enjeu de la sainteté," 241–242.

47. Athanasius of Alexandria, *Historia Arianorum ad monachos* 41.1–2 (ed. Hans-Georg Opitz, *Athanasius Werke. Zweiter Band. 5. Lieferung*, 205–206). Here the name of the presbyter accompanying Hilary is not Pancratius but Eutropius.

48. On the exiles of Eusebius of Vercellae see Simonetti, "Eusebio nella controversia Ariana," 159–162 (in particular 159, n. 62); Studer, "Eusebio," 185–187; Meloni, "Eusebio di Vercelli," 345–351; Müller, "Die Synode von Mailand."

49. See Jerome of Stridon, *Altercatio Luciferiani et orthodoxi* 21.

50. The mention of one Hilary in Jerome of Stridon, *Chronicon, ad annuum Romanorum XXII* ("Hilary returned to Gaul after he had offered his book on his own behalf to Constantius at Constantinople" [*Hilarius cum aput Constantinopolim libru pro se Constantio porrexisset, ad Gallias redit*]; ed. Helm, 241; trans. Donalson, 49), just like that contained in Jerome of Stridon, *Chronicon, ad annuum Romanorum XXIII* ("Gaul—through the agency of Hilary—condemned the treacheries of the falsehood of Ariminium" [*Gallia per Hilarium Ariminensis perfidiae dolos damnat*]; ed. Helm, 242; trans. Donalson, 50), is mistakenly referred to Hilary the deacon in Helm, *Die Chronik*

des Hieronymus, 266. For correct identifications of this Hilary as Hilary of Poitiers see Donalson, 81, n. 241g; 82, n. 242a; Jeanjean and Lançon, *Saint Jérôme, Chronique*, 92, n. *I*; 96, n. *a* (as well as, seemingly, Helm's own apparatus ad loc.).

51. The transition καὶ γὰρ ("and in fact") indicates that the Antiochene schism is an example of the discord described in the previous sentence, which is therefore nothing but the rift between Old Nicene and non-Old Nicene pro-Nicene.

52. Macedonius of Constantinople, Eustathius of Sebaste, Eleusius of Cyzicus, Basil of Ancyra, Heortasius of Sardis, Dracontius of Pergamus, Silvanus of Tarsus, Sophronius of Pompeiopolis in Paphlagonia, Elpidius of Satala, Neonas of Seleucia, Ciryl of Jerusalem, and the newly elected bishop of Antioch Anianus (Sozomen 4.24–25; Socrates of Constantinople 2.42; Theodoret of Cyrrhus, *Historia ecclesiastica* 2.27–28; *Chronicon Paschale* (ed. Dindorf, I, 542); Epiphanius of Salamis, *Adversus haereses* 73.23.4). On the actions of the Council of Constantinople see also Athanasius of Alexandria, *De synodis Arimini in Italia et Seleucia in Isauria* 30; Basil of Caesarea, *Adversus Eunomium* 1.2.

53. Philostorgius, *Historia ecclesiastica* 5.1.

54. See n. 13 in Chapter 4 below.

55. Theodoret of Cyrrhus, *Historia ecclesiastica* 3.4.6–3.5.2: Τῆσδε τῆς συναφείας οἱ περὶ τὸν Εὐσέβιον καὶ Λουκίφερα πόρον ἐπεζήτουν εὑρεῖν· καὶ Λουκίφερα μὲν ὁ Εὐσέβιος τὴν Ἀλεξάνδρειαν ἠξίου καταλαβεῖν καὶ Ἀθανασίῳ τῷ μεγάλῳ περὶ τούτου κοινώσασθαι, αὐτὸς δέ γε τὸν περὶ τῆς συμβάσεως ἤθελεν ἀναδέξασθαι πόνον. αλλ' ὁ Λουκίφερ εἰς μὲν τὴν Ἀλεξάνδρειαν οὐκ ἀφίκετο, τὴν Ἀντιόχου δὲ πόλιν κατέλαβε. Πολλοὺς δὲ περὶ συμβάσεως λόγους καὶ τούτοις κἀκείνοις προσενεγκών, εἶτα ἰδὼν ἀντιλέγοντας τοὺς τῆς Εὐσταθίου συμμορίας (ἡγεῖτο δὲ ταύτης Παυλῖνος πρεσβύτερος ὤν), ἐχειροτόνησεν αὐτοῖς, οὐκ εὖ γε ποιῶν, τὸν Παυλῖνον ἐπίσκοπον; ed. Bouffartigue, Canivet, Martin, Pietri, and Thélamon, II, 110–112.

56. Sulpicius Severus, *Chronica*, 2.45; ed. Senneville-Grave, 330; ed. Parroni, 102–103. On the section of Sulpicius's *Chronica* devoted to the Trinitarian controversies and on its sources see Ghizzoni, *Sulpicio Severo* 222–229; Zecchini, "Latin Historiography," 335–338.

57. See Simonetti, "Appunti"; Simonetti, "Lucifero di Cagliari"; Pérez Mas, *La crisis luciferiana*. For Lucifer's own views on penance, see also Todde, *Peccato e prassi*.

58. See Smulders, "Two Passages," 240–243.

59. Sulpicius Severus, *Chronica* 2.45; ed. Senneville-Grave, 330; ed. Parroni, 102.

60. See Athanasius, *Epistula ad Rufinianum*; ed. Joannou, 78. Given what Athanasius says in a later part of the letter (79, lines 17–21), it seems likely that Rufinian was a pro-Nicene who had hesitations about establishing communion with lapsed clergy. On the difficult identification of Rufinian see Stockhausen, "Epistula ad Rufinianum," 236. On the dating of *To Rufinian* see Joannou, *Discipline générale antique*, 61; Martin, *Athanase d'Alexandrie*, 547; Camplani, "Atanasio e Eusebio," 199.

61. Basil of Caesarea, *Epistula CCIV* 6: τούτου τοῦ δόγματος κοινωνούς μοι παρεχομένου τούς τε τῆς Μακεδονίας καὶ τῆς Ἀχαΐας ἐπισκόπους ἅπαντας; ed. Deferrari,

II, 170. Since this is also the text of PG 32, 753B (and Courtonne, 179, where no mention of a variant is found in the apparatus), Schaff's translation—supposedly based on PG—of "Asia" for Ἀχαΐα in *NPNF2* IV, 245, is probably a misprint. On the transmission of *Letter 204* see Fedwick, *Bibliotheca*, 514–515. In light of the details provided by Basil about the provenance of the bishops who agreed with Athanasius, it seems that the Alexandrian's letter in Basil's possession, whether or not it was directly addressed to Basil, should not be identified with his *Letter to Rufinian* (Stockhausen, "Epistula ad Rufinianum," 235, expresses the opposite opinion). I am also unable to find in the *Letter to Rufinian* the mention of a Roman or Italian council to which Stockhausen (236–237) refers twice.

62. See Liberius, *Epistula ad catolicos episcopos Italiae*, apud Hilary of Poitiers, *Fragmenta historica*, Series B, IV, 1; ed. Feder, 156–157. On Hilary's stop in Rome see Sulpicius Severus, *Vita sancti Martini Turonensis* 6.7 (ed. Fontaine, 266). See also Fontaine, *Sulpice Sévère*, 606–607; Simonetti, *La crisi ariana*, 356, n. 7; Duval, "Vrais et faux problèmes," 263, nn. 4–7; 274–275. From a letter of Pope Siricius we learn that Liberius sent out decrees forbidding the rebaptizing of Arians: see Siricius, *Epistula ad Himerium Tarraconensem* 2; ed. Coustant, 624–625; ed. PL 13, 1133–1134. In the letter *Olim et ab initio* (ed. Hinschius) Liberius sympathizes with Athanasius and the Egyptian bishops assembled in a synod. Thompson, *The Earliest Papal Correspondence*, 43, considers this epistle spurious.

63. Athanasius, *Epistula ad Rufinianum*; ed. Joannou, 78.

64. Jerome of Stridon, *Altercatio Luciferiani et orthodoxi* 20.

65. See Faustinus and Marcellinus, *Libellus precum* 63; ed. Günther, 23–24; ed. Simonetti, 375; ed. Canellis, 166.

66. This seems to be the reality to which the statement about Lucifer in Jerome of Stridon, *Altercatio Luciferiani et orthodoxi* 20 (ed. Canellis, 170) refers: "Let me only say one thing, which is established also in the present: that he differs from us in words, not in actions, since he receives also those who have received baptism from the Arians."

67. Jerome of Stridon, *Altercatio Luciferiani et orthodoxi* 26: *Deucalion orbis* (literally "Deucalion of the world"); ed. Canellis, 192. Jerome used against the Luciferians the argument used by Cyprian, whose writings he read, against his adversaries: see Battifol, "Les sources de l'*Altercatio*"; Duval, "Saint Jérôme devant le baptême," 145–180. Jerome in the *Dialogue between a Luciferian and an Orthodox* notes that Hilary acknowledged in his *libelli* that Popes Julius (337–352), Mark (336), Silvester (314–335), and all older bishops have admitted heretics to penance. The mention of all three immediate predecessors of Liberius, but not of Liberius himself, allows us to surmise that the *libelli* were written explicitly against Liberius, after the latter's *Letter to the Catholic Bishops of Italy*: see Battifol, "Les sources de l'*Altercatio*," 99. On Jerome's *Altercatio*, its dating, and its sources see Grützmacher, "Die Abfassungszeit," 1–8; Voss, "Vernachlässigte Zeugnisse," 161; Rebenich, *Hieronymus und sein Kreis*, 99, n. 473, and 138, n. 689;

Canellis, "La composition du Dialogue," 247–288; Jeanjean, *Saint Jérôme et l'hérésie,* 21–26; Canellis, "Saint Jérôme et les Ariens," 155–194; Duval, "Saint Jérôme devant le baptême."

68. Jerome of Stridon, *Altercatio Luciferiani et orthodoxi,* 26–27; ed. Canellis, 192–197.

69. Pérez Mas, *La crisis luciferiana,* 126–127.

70. Faustinus and Marcellinus, *Libellus precum* 50–51; ed. Günther, 20; ed. Simonetti, 372; ed. Canellis, 156.

71. *Epistula episcoporum Italiae ad episcopos Inlyrici,* apud Hilary of Poitiers, *Fragmenta historica,* Series B, IV, 2; ed. Feder. See Meslin, *Les Ariens d'Occident,* 328.

72. Pseudo-Eusebius of Vercellae, *Epistula ad Gregorium Illiberitanum*; ed. Feder, 46.

73. The opposite is asserted in Müller, "Die Synode von Mailand," 163–181. See Saltet, "La formation," 228–230; Saltet, "Fraudes littéraires," 326; Wilmart, "L'*Ad Constantium,*" 297; Chapman, "The Contested Letters," 326–328; Simonetti, *La crisi ariana,* 234, n. 50; Hanson, *The Search,* 508, n. 2; Simonetti, "Eusebio di Vercelli"; Simonetti, "Scritti di e attribuiti a Eusebio di Vercelli," 453–456; Simonetti, "Lucifero di Cagliari," 293. The authenticity of the letter is taken for granted instead by Feder, *Studien zu Hilarius,* I, 64–66; Bardy, "Faux et frauds," 16; Duval, "Vrais et faux problèmes," 267, n. 65; D.H. Williams, *Ambrose of Milan,* 50–52.

74. For the former view, see Armstrong, "The Synod of Alexandria"; for the latter see Elliott, "Was the «Tomus ad Antiochenos» a Pacific Document?"

75. Elliott, "Was the «Tomus ad Antiochenos» a Pacific Document?," 3, understandably has to enigmatically reduce Lucifer's anger to his being "upset *by something* after Eusebius' arrival" (italics mine).

76. On the Council of Paris see Brennecke, *Studien zur Geschichte der Homöer,* 87; Simonetti, *La crisi ariana,* 357; Feder, *Studien zu Hilarius,* I, 62–64; Meslin, *Les Ariens d'Occident,* 292 and 328. For the possibility that the council was not held in Paris see Brennecke, Heil, Müller, Stockhausen, and Wintjes, *Athanasius Werke,* 584. The council is dated to the summer of 360 by Feder, *Studien zu Hilarius,* 63. On proposals for dating the council see Borchardt, *Hilary of Poitiers' Role,* 178–179, nn. 1, 2, 5, 6, and 7. For a balanced evaluation of the dating (abstaining from any definitive proposal) see Duval, "Vrais et faux problèmes," 265–266, n. 63. According to Brennecke, *Studien zur Geschichte der Homöer,* 87, n. 1, Julian might have been present at the council. Duval, "Vrais et faux problèmes," 264, ponders the question, while T.D. Barnes, *Athanasius and Constantius,* 288, n. 12 (with reference to 226–228), rejects this hypothesis.

77. It is unclear whether the letter of the Gallican bishops to their eastern colleagues is to be considered a synodal letter (as Feder, *Studien zu Hilarius,* 62, and Borchardt, *Hilary of Poitiers' Role,* 178, believe).

78. It is difficult to guess which eastern community had entrusted Hilary with the letter, since the route of his return from exile—including whether it was by land or

sea—is far from ascertained, except for his likely stop in Rome: see Duval, "Vrais et faux problèmes," 263 and nn. 45 and 46. However, the contents of the letter to which the Gallican clergy are responding seem to suggest that an eastern synod had gathered, of which we are not informed by any other source.

79. *Epistula synodi Parisiensis (ca. 360)*, apud Hilary of Poitiers, *Fragmenta historica*, Series A, I, 1; ed. Feder, 43; ed. Gaudemet, 92.

80. *Epistula synodi Parisiensis (ca. 360)*, apud Hilary of Poitiers, *Fragmenta historica*, Series A, I, 1; ed. Feder, 43–44; ed. Gaudemet, 92.

81. Moore, *A Sacred Kingdom*, 59–60 (in a chapter based on Moore, "The Spirit of the Gallican Councils").

82. On the doctrinal contents of the document see Hefele, *Histoire des conciles*, 960, n. 1; Simonetti, *La crisi ariana*, 356–358; Hanson, *The Search*, 465–466; Wickham, *Hilary of Poitiers*, 12.

83. *Epistula synodi Parisiensis (ca. 360)*, apud Hilary of Poitiers, *Fragmenta historica*, Series A, I, 4: *Itaque, carissimi, cum ex litteris uestris in usiae silentio fraudem se passam simplicitas nostra cognoscat, etiam pietatem eorum, qui de Arimino Constantinopolim reuerterunt, conuentos, sicut epistola uestra contenta testatur, neque eos ad tantarum blasphemiarum damnationem potuisse compellere, fidelis dominici nominis praedicator frater noster Hilarius nuntiaverit, nos quoque ab his omnibus, quae per ignorantiam perpere gesta sunt, referimus*" ed. Feder, 45; Gaudemet, 96 (Guademet inserts a comma between *praedicator* and *frater*). The sentence, no matter how its syntax is parsed, presents difficulties. My translation differs significantly from those of Gaudemet, 97; Wickham, *Hilary of Poitiers*, 94; Brennecke, Heil, Müller, Stockhausen, and Wintjes, *Athanasius Werke. Dritter Band. Erster Teil. 4. Lieferung*, 584.

84. The translation in Brennecke, Heil, Müller, Stockhausen, and Wintjes, *Athanasius Werke*, 584, has the *simplicitas* of the Gallican bishops recognize the *pietatem eorum, qui de Arimino Constantinopolim reuerterunt*. This solution, which would have *cognoscat* separately support an infinitive clause and a direct object, though being grammatically correct, seems at odds with the overall rhetorical emphasis of the sentence, which lies on the deceit that men of good faith have suffered rather than on the intrinsic piety of the delegation of the Council of Ariminum.

85. The translation of *refero* plus the preposition *a* as "to turn away from" seems to me preferable both to Gaudemet's "prendre acte de" and to the German translators' "berichten von." My reading is here consistent with that of Wickham, *Hilary of Poitiers*, 94 ("to draw away from").

86. These are Auxentius, Ursacius, Valens, Gaius, Megasius, and Justinus.

87. The logic that allows the Gallican bishops to perform their self-absolution involves two gestures: establishing communion with another subject in need of release from guilt and distinguishing between some worthy and others unworthy of fellowship. In the mirror of the Gallicans' letter, we may observe a similar gesture being

performed by the easterners in their original communication: they themselves had offered recognition to their fellow lapsed clergy in Gaul, while condemning others whose behavior they saw as beyond the pale. Something similar was happening in Italy in the same years. Liberius in his *Letter to the Catholic Bishops* told his colleagues that they should readmit the *lapsi* into communion. The pope was speaking *pro domo sua*: he himself, while exiled, had signed the condemnation of Athanasius. The Italian bishops, in turn, responded with a letter addressed to their colleagues of the Illyricum, disavowing the decisions of Ariminum and condemning Valens and Ursacius: see *Epistula episcoporum Italiae ad episcopos Inlyrici*, apud Hilary of Poitiers, *Fragmenta historica*, Series B, IV, 2; ed. Feder. On Liberius and his correspondence see Altaner and Stuiber, *Patrologie*, 354.

88. For a discussion of the chronological implications of the absence from the *Letter* of any reference to Julian's recent acclamation see Duval, "Vrais et faux problèmes," 264–266.

89. My reading of this circumstance is opposite to that of Segneri, *Atanasio. Lettera agli Antiocheni*, 140, according to whom this was an attempt on Athanasius's part to balance the burden of the disciplinary requests imposed on the Meletians. See also Tetz, "Über nikäische Orthodoxie," 206–207; Yeum, *Die Synode*, 94; Karmann, *Meletius von Antiochien*, 235.

90. Rufinus of Aquileia, *Historia ecclesiastica* 10.29; ed. Mommsen, Schwartz, and Winklemann, 991; trans. Amidon, 36.

91. Athanasius, *Tomus ad Antiochenos* 1.1; ed. Segneri, 80; trans. adapted from *NPNF2* IV, 483.

92. See Segneri, *Atanasio. Lettera agli Antiocheni*, 108–109.

93. See Karmann, *Meletius von Antiochien*, 117; 185, n. 102; 221–225; 228, n. 179; 233, n. 189; Tetz, "Über nikäische Orthodoxie," 205–206; Simonetti, "Il concilio di Alessandria," 53–59.

94. See Armstrong, "The Synod of Alexandria," 247–355.

95. See Hanson, *The Search*, 644–653. Leroux, "Athanase," 145–156, expresses a similar position.

96. See Elliott, "Was the «Tomus ad Antiochenos» a Pacific Document?," 7–8. For an antithetical view see Fairbairn, "The Sardican Paper." Elliott's position was anticipated in part by Leroux, "Athanase," 151–154.

97. A similar reconstruction is provided in Krüger, *Lucifer Bischof von Calaris*, 51; Diercks, *Luciferi Calaritani Opera*, xxx.

98. Eusebius of Vercellae, Lucifer of Calaris, Asterius of Petra, Cymatius of Paltos, and Anatolius of Beroea. The group of five bishops is treated as an episcopal committee by Lietzmann, *Geschichte*, III, 269; Tetz, "Über nikäische Orthodoxie," 197 and passim; Yeum, *Die Synode*, 16.

99. See Simonetti, *La crisi ariana*, 371, n. 53.

100. Athanasius, *Tomus ad Antiochenos* 9.3y; ed. Segneri, 96–98.

101. Admittedly, it could be imagined that, although Lucifer ordained Paulinus prior to the departure of Maximus and Kalemeros, the Council of Alexandria, informed of the ordination, preferred to refer to him in an ambiguous way in order not to compromise reconciliation. However, the report about Eusebius's dismay in learning about the ordination upon his arrival in Antioch makes it much more probable that Paulinus was ordained after the two deacons had already left. Athanasius did not have to agree with the ordination.

102. See, e.g., Brennecke, *Studien zur Geschichte der Homöer*, 178; Karmann, *Meletius von Antiochien*, 415–416; 418, n. 164; 468.

103. See Athanasius, *Apologia secunda contra Arianos* 51–57; *Historia Arianorum ad monachos* 21–23; Sozomen, *Historia ecclesiastica* 3.20.4.

104. Rufinus of Aquileia, *Historia ecclesiastica* 1.20; Sozomen, *Historia ecclesiastica* 3.20; Theodoret of Cyrrhus, *Historia ecclesiastica* 2.12; Socrates of Constantinople, *Historia ecclesiastica* 2.23 (who extends Athanasius's request to every city where there was a non-Arian Christian community).

105. Basil of Caesarea, *Epistula LXXXIX*. Basil's *Letter 258* to Epiphanius alleges that it was because of "the malice of advisors" (κακίᾳ συμβούλων) that Meletius and Athanasius were unable to achieve communion when the latter visited Antioch and sought a rapprochement: see Basil of Caesarea, *Epistula CCLVIII*; ed. Deferrari, II, 42. It is more likely that with that expression Basil had in mind Meletians (as suggested by Cavallera, *Le schisme d'Antioche*, 122 and 127–128, n. E) than Eustathians (as proposed by Martin, *Athanase d'Alexandrie*, 585, n. 153). The Antiochene schism is discussed in Basil's correspondence also in *Epistulae LVII, LXVIII, CXX, CXXIX, CXXXIX, CCVIII,* and *CCXIV*.

106. He only went abroad in 382, traveling to the Roman synod that recognized his authority.

107. This reconstruction is compatible with the one offered in Zachhuber, "The Antiochene Synod," 90. One argument Zachhuber uses in support of his proposal, however, seems objectionable: he emphasizes that Basil of Caesarea makes no mention of Lucifer's ordination of Paulinus as an impediment to reconciliation between Athanasius and Meletius in his *Letter 258* to Epiphanius and *Letter 89* to Meletius. To recall an act that must have been the cause of much fury for the Meletians, however, would have been counterproductive to Basil's aim of effecting a reconciliation between Meletius and Athanasius. See also Greenslade, *Schism in the Early Church*, 158 and 303.

108. On the dating of the council see Zachhuber, "The Antiochene Synod," 84.

109. Athanasius of Alexandria, *De decretis Nicaenae synodi*; Athanasius of Alexandria, *De synodis Arimini in Italia et Seleucia in Isauria*. On the dating of *On the Decrees* see Heil, "De decretis Nicaenae synodi," 211. On the dating of *On the Synods* see Heil, "De synodis Arimini in Italia et Seleucia in Isauria," 222.

110. See Morales, *La théologie trinitaire*, 318. The text of the Meletians' confession to Jovian is preserved in Socrates of Constantinople, *Historia ecclesiastica* 3.25.10–18; and

Sozomen, *Historia ecclesiastica* 6.4.7–10 (with some differences in the names of the signatories).

111. Socrates of Constantinople, *Historia ecclesiastica* 3.25.6–19. See Sozomen, *Historia ecclesiastica* 6.4.6–11; Hieronymus, *Chronicon, ad annuum Romanorum XXXVII.* In probable dependence on the *Synagogē* of the homoiousian Sabinus of Herakles, Socrates sees those bishops' motives as merely opportunistic. On Socrates's dependence on Sabinus's *Synagogē* see Zachhuber, "The Antiochene Synod," 84.

112. The profession of faith is preserved by Socrates of Constantinople, *Historia ecclesiastica* 3.25.10–18 (Socrates found it in Sabinus's *Synagogē*). For a commentary on the text see Orbe and Simonetti, *Il Cristo,* 254–255 and 586. See also Segneri, *Atanasio. Lettera agli Antiocheni,* 64, n. 118.

113. Simonetti, "Ancora sul concilio," 16–18, reads instead the Council of Antioch as a sign that Meletius preferred not to reject the call to harmony of the Council of Alexandria altogether.

114. On Athanasius's exiles see T.D. Barnes, "The Exile," 109–129. On the dates of the exile see Albert and Martin, *Histoire «acéphale»,* 69–101.

115. *Historia acephala Athanasii* 4.4 (ed. Albert and Martin, 152–154); *Index festale* 35 (ed. Albert and Martin, 264). See Socrates of Constantinople, *Historia ecclesiastica* 3.21.17; Ammianus Marcellinus, *Res Gestae* 25.10.4. Jovian was in Edessa on September 27, 363, and in Antioch on October 22, 363. According to Sozomen, *Historia ecclesiastica* 6.5.1, Athanasius did join Jovian in Antioch.

116. See Brennecke, *Studien zur Geschichte der Homöer,* 171, n. 81. Sozomen, *Historia ecclesiastica* 6.5.1, reports the rumor that Athanasius himself had made contact of his own accord with the emperor. Jovian's letter, if it ever existed, is lost. See Brennecke, *Studien zur Geschichte der Homöer,* 171, n. 81.

117. Athanasius, *Epistula ad Iovianum de fide,* apud Theodoret of Cyrrhus, *Historia ecclesiastica* 4.3; ed. Brennecke, Heil, and Stockhausen, *Athanasius Werke. Zweiter Band. Erster Teil. 8. Lieferung,* 352–356. The authenticity of the text is disputed by Brennecke, *Studien zur Geschichte der Homöer,* 171, n. 83, but not by Martin, *Athanase d'Alexandrie,* 578–582. Stockhausen, "Athanasius in Antiochien," 96 and 101, dates the text to October 363; Zachhuber, "The Antiochene Synod," 97, dates it to December 363 or January 364. See Epiphanius of Salamis, *Adversus haereses* 68.11.3; Gregory of Nazianzus, *Oratio* 21.33; Rufinus of Aquileia, *Historia ecclesiastica* 11.1; Socrates of Constantinople, *Historia ecclesiastica* 3.24.2; Theodoret of Cyrrhus, *Historia ecclesiastica* 4.2.4–5. For Zachhuber, "The Antiochene Synod," 89, the contents of the synodal letter of the Meletian Council of Antioch of 363, with their combination of "similar according to the ousia" (ὅμοιος κατ᾽οὐσίαν) and "from the ousia of the Father" (ἐκ τῆς οὐσίας τοῦ πατρός), were also acceptable for Athanasius, and created a link with Athanasius of Alexandria, *De synodis Arimini in Italia et Seleucia in Isauria* 41. The use of the expression ἐκ τῆς οὐσίας τοῦ πατρός—a concept that, though accepted by first-generation "Eusebians," had subse-

quently been rejected by the anti-Nicene of the 340s and 350s—was the remarkable sign of a Nicene reorientation of the Meletians. Morales, *La théologie trinitaire*, 78, similarly argues that, in shaping the solution that would be adopted at Constantinople, the Cappadocians, though certainly drawing on homoiousian and Meletian tendencies, found substantial inspiration in Athanasius's balanced theological approach. Ayres, *Nicaea and Its Legacy*, 221, criticizes Drecoll, *Die Entwicklung der Trinitätslehre*, on the issue of Basil's trajectory from homoiousianism to "neo-Nicenism," and sides rather with Simonetti, "Dal nicenismo al neonicenismo," and Sesboüé, *Saint Basile et la Trinité*, who claim Basil's substantial independence from Athanasius. See also Hübner, "Basilius von Caesarea und das *Homoousios*"; Ayres, *Nicaea and Its Legacy*, 187–221.

118. See Camplani, "Atanasio e Eusebio," 233–234, contra Barnard, *Studies*, 231–240.

119. Jovian, *Epistula ad Athanasium*; ed. Brennecke, Heil, and Stockhausen, *Athanasius Werke. Zweiter Band. Erster Teil. 8. Lieferung*, 357. See *Historia acephala Athanasii* 4.4; Socrates of Constantinople, *Historia ecclesiastica* 3.24; Epiphanius of Salamis, *Adversus haereses* 68.11.3; Rufinus of Aquileia, *Historia ecclesiastica* 2.1. See also Barnard, "Athanasius and the Emperor Jovian"; Martin, *Athanase d'Alexandrie*, 576 and n. 121; Lenski, *Failure of Empire*, 237. The authenticity of Jovian's letter is questioned in Schwartz, "Zur Kirchengeschichte," 166, n. 3 [= Schwartz, *Gesammelte Schriften*, IV, 50, n. 2; and Brennecke, *Studien zur Geschichte der Homöer*, 171, n. 82; but it is affirmed by T.D. Barnes, *Athanasius and Constantius*, 159 and 290, n. 49. If the letter is authentic, Jovian's decision should be seen not as a specifically pro-Old Nicene resolution, but as part of a broader initiative whereby those bishops whom Constantius had banned and who had not come back to their sees during Julian's reign were being granted a right to return: see Brennecke, *Studien zur Geschichte der Homöer*, 178–181. On Jovian's religious policies see Wirth, "Jovian: Kaiser und Karikatur"; Marcos, "Emperor Jovian's Law."

120. See Philostorgius, *Historia ecclesiastica* 8.2. Candidus and Arrianus had recently been named bishops respectively of Lydia and Ionia by Aetius and Eunomius.

121. See Philostorgius, *Historia ecclesiastica* 8.6.

122. *Historia acephala Athanasii* 4.7; Epiphanius of Salamis, *Adversus haereses* 68.11.4; Socrates of Constantinople, *Historia ecclesiastica* 3.4.2; Sozomen, *Historia ecclesiastica* 6.5.2 (which reports that the homoian candidate was not Lucius but the eunuch Probatianus). See also *Historia ecclesiae alexandrinae* 5.75; ed. Orlandi, I, 52 (Coptic); 68–69 (Latin). The *Petition Made in Antioch to Emperor Jovian by Lucius, Bernicianus, and Some Other Arians against Athanasius, Bishop of Alexandria* is preserved in an appendix to Athanasius's *Letter to Jovian*; ed. Brennecke, Heil, and Stockhausen, *Athanasius Werke. Zweiter Band. Erster Teil. 8. Lieferung*, 357–361. On its authenticity see Martin, *Athanase d'Alexandrie*, 588–589.

123. See Socrates of Constantinople, *Historia ecclesiastica* 3.25.2–4; Sozomen, *Historia ecclesiastica* 6.4.3–5. Socrates calls this party "Macedonians" and mentions as signatories of the "booklet" (βιβλίον) Basil of Ancyra, Silvanus of Tarsus, Sophronios of

Pompeiopolis, Pasinikos of Zela, Leontius of Comane, Callicratus of Claudioupolis, and Theophilos of Castabala. The relative chronology of the Athanasian, homoiousian, heteroousian, and homoian embassies is unclear.

124. Athanasius, *Epistula ad Iovianum de fide* 1.6; ed. Brennecke, Heil, and Stockhausen, *Athanasius Werke. Zweiter Band. Erster Teil. 8. Lieferung*, 353–354; trans. adapted from *NPNF2* IV, 567–568.

125. See Brennecke, Heil, and Stockhausen, *Athanasius Werke. Zweiter Band. Erster Teil. 8. Lieferung*, 353, commentary on lines 12–15; Martin, *Athanase d'Alexandrie*, 579–582; Camplani, *Atanasio di Alessandria*, 488, n. 1; T.D. Barnes, *Athanasius and Constantius*, 160; Segneri, *Atanasio. Lettera agli Antiocheni*, 116–120.

126. Ms. Staatliche Museen zu Berlin, Preussischer Kulturbesitz, Agyptisches Museum und Papyrussammlung 11,948. For a record of the papyrus (number 108404 on www.trismegistos.org [last accessed on October 30, 2021]), dated by Camplani, "Atanasio e Eusebio," 230, to the fifth to sixth century and likely found in Hermopolis/El-Ashmunein, see Beltz, "Katalog," 111. The fragment was edited by Pieper, "Zwei Blätter," 74, and again by Lefort, *Lettres*, 69–71 (xiii, n. 34, provides a description and a fourth- to fifth-century dating). Lefort, incorrectly considering the document lost, limited himself to emending Pieper's edition based on the latter's reproduction of the text.

127. See *Index festale* 36.

128. Arguments against this being a festal letter or a post-scriptum thereto were originally advanced by Camplani, *Le lettere festali di Atanasio*, 105 and Camplani, "Atanasio e Eusebio," 231. Martin, *Athanase d'Alexandrie*, 587, n. 163, wrote in favor of the identification with *Festal Letter 36*. Camplani, *Atanasio di Alessandria*, 485, later accepted that this could be an attachment to *Festal Letter 36*.

129. Athanasius, *Epistula festalis XXXVI* (?): . . ϩⲛ̣ϩⲁϩ ⲛ̄ . [.] . [. .] . [. .] ⲡ̣ⲉⲧⲛ̄ⲣ̄ⲡⲙⲉⲉ[ⲩ]ⲉ· ϯⲡ̣ⲁⲣⲁⲕⲁⲗ̣ⲉⲓ ϭⲉ [ⲙ̄]ⲙⲱⲧⲛ ⲉϣⲱⲡ̣ⲉ ⲉ̣ⲩϣⲁⲛⲧⲉϭⲛⲉⲥϩⲁï ⲉⲃⲟⲗ· ⲙ̣̄ⲡ̣ⲣ̣̄ⲛⲟϭⲛⲉϭ ⲛ̄ⲗⲁⲁⲩ· ⲟⲩⲇⲉ ⲙ̄ⲡⲣ̄ⲥⲱⲃⲉ ⲛ̄ⲥⲁ ⲛⲉⲛⲧ̣ⲁ̣ⲩϣⲁϫⲉ ⲛ̄ⲟⲩⲟⲩⲟⲉⲓϣ ⲉ̣ⲩϯⲟⲩⲃⲏⲛ· ⲡⲉ̣[ïⲥ]ⲟⲟ̣ϩⲉ ⲅⲁⲣ ⲛ̄ⲧⲉïⲙⲓⲛ̣[ⲉ ⲛ̄]ⲧ̣ⲁ̣ϥϣⲱⲡ̣ⲉ ⲛ̄ⲟⲩⲉⲃⲟ̣ⲗ ⲛ̄ϩⲏ̣ⲧ̣[ⲧ]ⲏⲩⲧⲛ̄ ⲁⲛ ⲡⲉ· ⲟⲩⲇⲉ ⲛ̄ⲟ̣[ⲩ]ⲉⲃⲟⲗ ϩⲛ̄ⲣⲱⲙⲉ ⲁⲛ̣ ⲡⲉ [ⲉⲡ]ⲧⲏⲣϥ̄· ⲁⲗⲗⲁ ⲛ̄ⲧⲁϥ[ϣ]ⲱⲡⲉ ⲉⲃⲟⲗ ϩⲓⲧⲙ̄ⲡ̣ⲛⲟⲩ[ⲧⲉ] ⲁⲩⲱ ⲥⲡⲣⲉⲡⲓ ⲛ̄ⲛ̣ⲉ̣[ϩ]ⲃⲏⲩⲉ ⲉⲛⲧⲁⲩϣⲱ̣ⲡⲉ ⲉⲃⲟⲗ ϩⲓⲧⲙ̄ⲡⲛⲟ̣ⲩ̣ⲧⲉ ⲉⲧⲣⲉⲟⲩⲟⲛ̣ ⲛ̣ⲓⲙ̣ ⲕⲁⲁⲩ ⲟⲛ ⲙ̄ⲡⲛⲟ̣ⲩⲧⲉ ϫⲉⲕⲁⲥ ⲉⲁⲧⲉⲧⲛ̄ⲟⲩⲱⲛϩ ⲉⲃ̣ⲟ̣ⲗ̣ ⲛ̄ⲉⲩⲅⲛⲱⲙⲱ̣ⲛ ⲉ[ⲣⲉ]ⲧⲉⲭⲁⲣⲓⲥ ⲉⲃ̣ⲟⲗ ϩ̣ⲓ̣ⲧ[ⲟⲟ]ⲧϥ̄ ⲛⲁϣ̣ⲱ̣ⲡ̣ⲉ̣ ⲟⲛ ⲉϩⲟ̣ⲩⲛ̣ [ⲉⲧ]ⲉⲕⲕⲗⲏⲥⲓⲁ ⲉⲡⲉ[ϩ]ⲟⲩⲟ· ⲛ̣ⲁï ⲇⲉ ϯⲥϩⲁï ⲙ̄ⲙⲟⲟⲩ ⲛ̣ⲏⲧⲛ̄ [ⲉ]ⲃⲟⲗ ϩⲛ̄ⲧⲁ(ⲛ)ⲧⲓⲟⲭⲓⲁ· ⲁïⲕⲟⲧ̄ⲧ̄ ⲉⲃⲟⲗ ϩⲙ̄ⲡⲕⲟⲙⲓⲧⲁⲧⲟⲛ· ⲁⲩⲱ ⲁïⲛⲁⲩ ⲉⲡⲙⲁïⲣⲱⲙⲉ ⲛ̄ⲣ̄ⲣⲟ ⲁⲩⲱ ⲁïϯⲉⲟⲟⲩ ⲙ̄ⲡϫⲟⲉⲓⲥ ⲙ̄ⲡⲧⲏⲣϥ̄ ⲁⲥⲡ[ⲁ]ⲍ̣ⲉ ⲛ̄ⲛⲉⲧⲛ̄ⲉⲣⲏⲩ ϩⲛ̄ⲟ̣[ⲩⲡ]ⲓ ⲉⲥⲟⲩⲁⲁⲃ· ⲥⲉϣⲓⲛ[ⲉ] ⲉⲣⲱⲧⲛ̄ ⲛ̄ϭⲓⲛⲉ̣ⲧ̣ⲛ̄ⲙ̄ⲙⲁï· ⲙⲁⲗⲓⲥⲧⲁ ⲛ̄[ⲉ]ⲡⲓⲥⲕⲟⲡⲟⲥ ⲉⲛⲧⲁⲩ[ϣ̄ⲡ̄]ϩⲓⲥⲉ ⲛ̄ⲙ̄ⲙⲁⲛ ⲉⲡⲉ[ϩⲟⲩ]ⲟ· ϯϣⲗⲏⲗ ⲉⲧⲣⲉⲧ[ⲛ̄ⲟⲩ]ϫⲁï ϩⲓⲟⲩⲥⲟⲡ ⲛⲉⲥⲛⲏ[ⲩ] ⲙ̄ⲙⲉⲣⲓⲧ ⲁⲩⲱ ⲉϯⲟⲩ[ⲁ]ϣⲟⲩ; ed. Camplani.

130. See T.D. Barnes, *Athanasius and Constantius*, 160; Camplani, *Atanasio di Alessandria*, 485.

131. See Epiphanius of Salamis, *Adversus haereses* 77.20.5–8. See Zachhuber, "The Antiochene Synod," 100.

132. The *Refutation* may have been authored by Eugene the Deacon or Evagrius of Antioch (the Latin translator of Athanasius's *Life of Anthony*). See Gemeinhardt, "Refutatio hypocriseos"; Karmann, *Meletius von Antiochien*, 426–452; Stockhausen, "Athanasius in Antiochien," 94 and 102. Hübner, *Die Schrift des Apollinarius*, 284, n. 12, attributes the text to Apollinarius; Karmann, *Meletius von Antiochien*, 430–432, tentatively accepts Apollinarius's authorship. For a history of the transmission of the *Refutation* see Stockhausen, "Die pseud-athanasianische *Disputatio contra Arium*," 139.

133. On Paulinus's use of the *Tome to the Antiochenes* in the 370s see Bergjan, "From Rivalry to Marginalisation," 33–39.

134. See Socrates of Constantinople, *Historia ecclesiastica* 5.5; Sozomen, *Historia ecclesiastica* 7.3. A different version of the events is related by Theodoret of Cyrrhus, *Historia ecclesiastica* 5.3.9–20. For an analysis of the reliability of the various accounts see Martin, "Antioche ou la difficile unité." See also Cavallera, *Le schisme d'Antioche*, 232–234.

135. Basil of Caesarea, *Epistula CCLXVI* 2. See Deferrari and Way, *Saint Basil: The Letters*, II, 250, n. 1. Although Peter had been designated by Athanasius as his own successor, Athanasius harbored different feelings toward Meletius in 363.

136. *Historia acephala Athanasii* 2.7; ed. Albert and Martin, 146–148. See Annick Martin's remarks in Albert and Martin, *Histoire «acéphale»*, 64–65. The role of Meletius in this narrative remains ambiguous.

137. Athanasius of Alexandria, *Tomus ad Antiochenos* 5–6; ed. Segneri, 86–90; trans. adapted from *NPNF*2 IV, 484–485.

138. For a detailed summary of different analyses of the theological exposition of this section see Segneri, *Atanasio. Lettera agli Antiocheni*, 136–138.

139. Amidon, "Paulinus' Subscription," 74, effectively captures the diplomatic logic of the *Tome*: "[T]he two parties at variance used each the other's preferred language to subscribe a document which endorsed the language of both as compatible within the doctrinal framework of the creed of one of them."

140. Camplani, "Atanasio e Eusebio," 215. See also Morales, *La théologie trinitaire*, 383; Gemeinhardt, "Tomus ad Antiochenos," 229.

141. Ὑπόστασιν μὲν λέγομεν ἡγούμενοι ταὐτὸν εἶναι εἰπεῖν ὑπόστασιν καὶ οὐσίαν.

142. Lienhard, "Did Athanasius Reject Marcellus?," 76, interprets that it was the Meletians who identified hypostasis and ousia.

143. Abramowski, "Trinitarische und christologische Hypostasenformeln," 41–45. As evidence for the claim that the Meletians at the synod were already familiar with the distinction between ousia and hypostasis, Abramowski adduced the fact that the formula was known to Marius Victorinus. Victorinus (275–363) offered in *Against Arius* his Trinitarian interpretation of the being-living-thinking triad. In doing so, he produced two statements that indubitably show acquaintance with a formulaic expression of the distinction between ousia and hypostasis. See Marius Victorinus, *Adversus Arium*

2.4: "and therefore it was said: 'from one substance there exist three subsistences'" ("et ideo dictum est: *de una substantia tres subsistentias esse*"; ed. Hadot and Henry, I, 408); Marius Victorinus, *Adversus Arium* 3.4: "and that is thus said by the Greeks: 'there exist the three hypostaseis from one ousia'" ("idque a Graecis ita dicitur: ἐκ μιᾶς οὐσίας τρεῖς εἶναι τὰς ὑποστάσεις"; ed. Hadot and Henry, I, 450). The second book of *Against Arius* was completed in 361 and the third in 362: see Hadot, *Marius Victorinus: Recherches*, 278–280. On Marius Victorinus's Trinitarian theology see Voelker, "An Anomalous Trinitarian Formula"; Voelker, *The Trinitarian Theology of Marius Victorinus*; Erismann, "Identité et ressemblance." According to Hadot, in utilizing the formula "three hypostaseis from one ousia" Victorinus was handling and repurposing a homoiousian source. Alternative explanations for Victorinus's acquaintance with the formula are provided in Hübner, "Zur Genese der trinitarischen Formel," 131, n. 40 (contra his solution see Gemeinhardt, "Apollinaris of Laodicea," 290, n. 26); Simonetti, "All'origine della formula."

144. See Karmann, *Meletius von Antiochien*, 231–232; 283–305; 298–300.

145. See also Camplani, "Atanasio e Eusebio," 205.

146. Simonetti, "Il concilio di Alessandria"; Simonetti, "Genesi e sviluppo," 172.

147. Simonetti, "Il concilio di Alessandria," 357.

148. See Zachhuber, "The Antiochene Synod," 89.

149. This conclusion can be logically reconciled, despite appearances, with the fact that the Council of Antioch also surprisingly considered the Son as "from the ousia of the Father" (ἐκ τῆς οὐσίας τοῦ πατρὸς), a statement contained in the Nicene Creed and consistently rejected by the anti-Nicene in the 340s and 350s. See Karmann, *Meletius von Antiochien*, 377.

150. Camplani, "Atanasio e Eusebio," 210–211.

151. See Athanasius of Alexandria, *Oratio III contra arianos* 22.1; ed. Metzler and Savvidis, 332; ed. Bara, Dîncă, Kannengiesser, Metzler, and Savvidis, 344; trans. *NPNF2* IV, 405. The similar expression τῶν οὐσίων . . . ταυτότης (identity of ousiai) is found in Athanasius of Alexandria, *De synodis Arimini in Italia et Seleucia in Isauria* 53.2; ed. Martin and Morales, 356.

152. See Simonetti, "Il concilio di Alessandria," 356, nn. 9 and 10; Morales, *La théologie trinitaire*, 382 and 388. In contrast to Marcellus of Ancyra, who referred to the Father and the Son as being "one and the same thing, one person" (ἓν καὶ τὸ αυτό, ἓν πρόσωπον), the Eustathians used πρόσωπον as a key term to express multiplicity in the godhead. Basil of Caesarea had heavily attacked the three πρόσωπα preached by Sabellianism, presenting them as a crypto-Jewish device (see Basil of Caesarea, *Epistula CCX* 3). Athanasius, who was attempting to defuse polemics concerning the number of hypostaseis, had no use for another term that, used to express triplicity, would lead to similar contention.

153. For ἐνούσιος see Athanasius of Alexandria, *Oratio II contra arianos* 2.5 (ed. Metzler and Savvidis, 179; ed. Bara, Dîncă, Kannengiesser, Metzler, and Savvidis, 22); Atha-

nasius of Alexandria, *De synodis Arimini in Italia et Seleucia in Isauria* 41.8 (ed. Martin and Morales, 322). For ἴδιον καὶ ἀδιαίρετον τῆς οὐσίας see Athanasius of Alexandria, *De decretis Nicaenae synodi* 23.2 (τῆς τοῦ πατρὸς οὐσίας ἴδιον . . . γέννημα) (ed. Opitz, 19); *De sententia Dionysii* 24.3 (ἴδιον καὶ ἀδιαίρετον τῆς τοῦ πατρὸς οὐσίας) (ed. Opitz, 64). All parallels cited in Camplani, "Atanasio e Eusebio," 206–207.

154. See Camplani, "Atanasio e Eusebio," 207, n. 43; S. Fernández, "Criterios."

155. Of the opposite opinion is Segneri, *Atanasio. Lettera agli Antiocheni*, 138.

156. On the list of signatories to the *Tome* see Martin, *Athanase d'Alexandrie*, 493–495; 546, n. 9; Camplani, "Atanasio e Eusebio," 200–201.

157. Zachhuber, "The Antiochene Synod of AD 363," 93, argues that these might have been local bishops of generically Nicene orientation; contra this proposal see Camplani, "Atanasio e Eusebio," 212.

158. Yeum, *Die Synode*, 84, n. 372. See Athanasius, *Historia Arianorum ad monachos* 36.

159. The proposal of an alteration of the text of the *Tome to the Antiochenes* stands or falls independently from the validity of a similar suggestion that has been made regarding the Christological materials contained in *Tome* 7. These passages have been related to the presence of Apollinarist emissaries mentioned in *Tome* 8, which has puzzled more than one reader: see, e.g., Tetz, "Über nikäische Orthodoxie," 218, n. 72; Yeum, *Die Synode*, 117. The Christological remarks of *Tome* 7 constituted a novelty in the theology of Athanasius, who had never dealt before in such detail with the question of Christ's soul. Reginald Weijenborg proposed that the whole manuscript tradition of the *Tome* derives from a corrupt version of the text, in which the Christological section had been interpolated by Apollinarists after Athanasius's death (373) (see Weijenborg, "De authenticitate"; Weijenborg, "Apollinaristic Interpolations"). Weijenborg's conclusion was based on the alleged dependence of three passages of *Tomus* 7 on later letters of Athanasius to Maximus and Epictetus (after 369) and on the *Third Oration against the Arians*. The interpolation would have occurred prior to Paulinus's clarification to Epiphanius, which contains excerpts from that chapter. Tetz, "Über nikäische Orthodoxie," 211, n. 54, refuted Weijenborg's thesis by showing that a citation of the Christological section (*Tome* 7.1) is contained in Eugene the Deacon's *Exposition of Faith to Athanasius*, dated to 371: the Marcellans would not have dared to use an interpolated text of Athanasius's in a text addressed to Athanasius himself. Segneri, *Atanasio. Lettera agli Antiocheni*, 143, further contradicted Weijenborg's claim by pointing to Paulinus's clarification in *Tome* 11, which quotes verbatim from *Tome* 7 and was composed when the *Tome* had first reached Antioch, in 362. For a detailed discussion of the Christological section of the *Tome* see Segneri, *Atanasio. Lettera agli Antiocheni*, 141–157.

160. On the editions of Athanasius's works see Stockhausen, "Praefatio," xi–cxii; T.D. Barnes, "The New Critical Edition"; Camplani, Review of Brennecke, Heil, and Stockhausen, *Athanasius Werke. Zweiter Band. Erster Teil. 8. Lieferung*; Camplani, Review of Brennecke, Heil, Stockhausen, and Wintjes, *Athanasius Werke. Dritter Band.*

Erster Teil. 3. Lieferung. For Latin and Syriac translations see Brennecke and Stockhausen, "Die Edition der »Athanasius Werke«"; Stockhausen, "Textüberlieferung."

161. See Opitz, *Untersuchungen zur Überlieferung,* 190–203. Lebon, Review of Hans-Georg Opitz, *Untersuchungen zur Überlieferung*; and Bizer, *Studien zu pseudathanasianischen,* 257–258, expressed skepticism about Opitz's theses concerning this tradition. On the genesis of this collection in the Eustathian community see Tetz, "Zur Theologie des Markell"; Tetz, "Les écrits «dogmatiques»," 181–188. Latin versions of Athanasius's works also depend on tradition *b.*

162. See Stockhausen, "Praefatio," xi–lxviii.

163. Surveyed in Opitz, *Untersuchungen,* passim.

164. Ms. B = Basilensis Graecus A III, 4 (13th century); ms. K = Athous Vatopediou 5/6 (14th century); ms. A = Ambrosianus I 59 sup., 464 (13th–14th centuries); ms. O = Scorialensis Graecus X II 11, 371 (13th–14th centuries); ms. E = Scorialensis Graecus Ω III 15, 548 (12th–13th centuries); ms. F = Laurentianus San Marco 695 (13th century); ms. M = Marcianus Graecus 49 (13th century); ms. S = Parisinus Coislinianus Graecus 45 (12th century); ms. H = Laurentianus Pluteus IV 20 (13th century); ms. G = Laurentianus Pluteus IV 23 (10th–11th centuries).

165. Ms. Z = Vaticanus Graecus 1,431 (11th century); ms. Σ = BL Or. 8606/Biblioteca Ambrosiana fr. 46 [A 296 inf.] (copied in Edessa in 723). See Karl Pinggéra, "Syrische Tradition," 398.

166. Ms. R = Parisinus Graecus 474 (11th century).

167. Its model was probably complete: see Segneri, *Atanasio. Lettera agli Antiocheni,* 71, n. 134.

168. The Syriac version gives a faithful rendition of the Antiochene Greek recension; ed. Thomson. On this version see also Stockhausen, "Praefatio," xlix. On the Syriac corpus of Athanasius's works see Opitz, "Das syrische Corpus."

169. See Stockhausen, "Praefatio," xxv–xxvi.

170. ܫܐܠܘ ܒܫܠܡܐ ܕܟܠܗܘܢ ܐܚܐ ܗܢܘܢ ܕܥܡܟܘܢ. ܫܐܠܝܢ ܒܫܠܡܟܘܢ ܐܚܐ ܗܠܝܢ ܕܥܡܢ ("Send greetings to all those brethren who are with you. These brethren that are with us send greetings"); ed. Thomson, 37.

171. Agathos, Ammonios, Agathodaimon, Drakontios, Hermaion, Markos, Theodoros, Andreas, Paphnoutios, (another) Markos, and the others. This list of bishops corresponds to entries five (Agathos) through fifteen (Markos) mentioned in the "Prologue" to the *Tome,* with the exception of number nine (Adelphios) and the addition of the expression "and the rest" (καὶ οἱ λοιποί).

172. See *Tome* 9.3γ: Παρῆσαν δὲ καί τινες Ἀπολλιναρίου τοῦ ἐπισκόπου μονάζοντες, παρ' αὐτοῦ εἰς τοῦτο πεμφθέντες ("And there were present some monks of Apollinarius the bishop, sent from him for this").

173. See *Tome* 10.1–2. Eusebius and Asterius are both senders in Alexandria and addressees in Antioch. Rufinus's version of the events only reports the names of Athanasius, Asterius, and Eusebius, along with a mention of "those who were with" Asterius:

see Rufinus of Aquileia, *Historia ecclesiastica* 10.30. Duval, "La place," 290, suggests that Rufinus was using an official document, which he decided not to cite in its entirety but only for the names that interested him.

174. For an exhaustive discussion of the signatures see Segneri, *Atanasio. Lettera agli Antiocheni*, 165–169.

175. The same might have happened to a mention of Meletius himself in the *Tome* (whose lack vis-à-vis two mentions of Paulinus constitutes, admittedly, a difficulty for my argument that Athanasius was genuinely interested in a reconciliation with the Meletians).

176. On the *Catholic Epistle* see above, note 3 in this chapter. On the *Great Speech on Faith* (also known as *Letter to the Antiochenes* [= *CPG* 2803]) see Lebon, "Le *sermo maior*"; Schwartz, "Der s. g. Sermo maior," 61, Scheidweiler, "Wer ist der Verfasser"; Tetz, "Zur Theologie des Markell von Ankyra II"; Simonetti, "Su alcune opere attribuite di recente a Marcello d'Ancira"; Tetz, "Markellianer und Athanasios"; Simonetti, "Ancora sulla paternità." On the *Letter to Liberius* (also known as *Against the Theopaschites* [= *CPG* 2805]) see Tetz, "Zur Theologie des Markell von Ankyra III," attributing it to Marcellus; Brennecke, Heil, Stockhausen, and Wintjes, *Athanasius Werke. Dritter Band. Erster Teil. 3. Lieferung*, 590, attributing it to the Eustathians; Vinzent, Review of Kinzig, *Neue Texte und Studien*, 1288, attributing it to Liberius himself.

177. See Camplani, "Fourth-Century Synods," 68; Camplani, "Setting a Bishopric," 252–265. See also Camplani, "Lettere episcopali," 148–149. The Latin text is preserved in *Codex Veronensis* LX (58), ff. 78b–79b; ed. Girolamo Ballerini and Pietro Ballerini, *Disquisitiones* (PL 56, 854–856). On this manuscript see E. Schwartz, "Über die Sammlung," 1–23; Telfer, "The Codex Verona"; Field, *On the Communion*, passim. The Syriac text is preserved in several manuscripts (ms. Bibliothèque nationale de France syr. 62, ff. 182–183; mss. Mardin, Library of the Residence of the Archbishopric 309, 310, 320 [modern copy]; ms. *Vaticanus Borgianus* syr. 148) and edited in Schulthess, *Die syrischen Kanones*, 167–168.

178. Athanasius, *Tomus ad Antiochenos* 11.2; ed. Segneri, 100; trans. Amidon, "Paulinus' Subscription," 53, n. 1.

179. Dörrie, "Ὑπόστασις," 36, has claimed that the agreement proclaimed by the *Tome* was the end point of a long history of referential ambiguity for the term "hypostasis." Athanasius was allegedly able to stabilize the sense of hypostasis by privileging its meaning of "realization" over that of "reality" (81–82). This outcome was tantamount to a rejection of the Sardican understanding of hypostasis as "reality," influenced by the common Latin translation "*substantia*" (see Dörrie, "Ὑπόστασις," 78).

180. See Morales, *La théologie trinitaire*, 41–46.

181. See ibid., 46–58.

182. See ibid., 58–64.

183. See ibid., 65–67.

184. On Coptic text "B" see Camplani, "Atanasio e Eusebio," 235–239.

185. See Abramowski, "Trinitarische und christologische Hypostasenformeln," 41.

186. Morales, *La théologie trinitaire*, 77, contra Brennecke, "Zum Prozess," 288, according to whom Athanasius was a mia-hypostatic thinker.

187. Morales, *La théologie trinitaire*, 387.

188. The helpfulness of these categories for understanding the Trinitarian controversies is questioned by Ayres, *Nicaea and Its Legacy*, 41, n. 1, and defended by S. Parvis, "Joseph Lienhard," passim.

189. See Lienhard, Contra Marcellum: *Marcellus of Ancyra*, 38. On the soteriological consequences of the divide see 41–42; 45. Lienhard's reinterpretation of the Trinitarian controversies is articulated across a long series of publications: see Lienhard, "Marcellus of Ancyra"; Lienhard, Contra Marcellum: *The Influence of Marcellus*; Lienhard, "The 'Arian' Controversy"; Lienhard, "Acacius of Caesarea's *Contra Marcellum*"; Lienhard, "Basil of Caesarea"; Lienhard, "Did Athanasius Reject Marcellus?," Lienhard, Contra Marcellum: *Marcellus of Ancyra*; Lienhard, "*Ousia* and *Hypostasis*"; Lienhard, "Two Friends of Athanasius." See also Vinzent, "Athanasius und Markell."

190. Lienhard, "*Ousia* and *Hypostasis*," 109.

191. On Marcellus see Seibt, *Die Theologie des Markell*; Hanson, *The Search*, 217–235; Vinzent, *Markell von Ankyra*; Pollard, "Marcellus of Ancyra"; Logan, "Marcellus of Ancyra and the Councils"; Logan, "Marcellus of Ancyra on Origen"; Logan, "Marcellus of Ancyra, Defender." See also Ayres, *Nicaea and Its Legacy*, 62; 66. It should be remarked that, although Marcellus rejected the Alexandrian doctrine of three hypostaseis, no text of Marcellus's is extant in which he asserts the existence of one hypostasis.

192. See Lienhard, Contra Marcellum: *Marcellus of Ancyra*, 28–46 (approximately the same as Lienhard, "The 'Arian' Controversy").

193. See Simonetti, "«Persona» nel dibattito cristologico."

194. Seibt, "Ein *argumentum*"; Seibt, *Die Theologie des Markell*. See the substantial evaluation in Simonetti, Review of Seibt, *Die Theologie des Markell*.

195. See T.D. Barnes, *Athanasius and Constantius*, 93 and n. 39 (289). As Lienhard has demonstrated in "Did Athanasius Reject Marcellus?" and "Two Friends," it is very likely that Athanasius never formally rejected Marcellus. Athanasius and Marcellus met possibly as early as 335 (Council of Tyre) and with certainty by 341 (Council of Rome). Their mediated communion was secured by the shared communion with the Eustathians. On Marcellus's theology see S. Fernández, "¿Crisis arriana o crisis monarquiana en el siglo IV?," 204–206.

196. See Ayres, *Nicaea and Its Legacy*, 62–63. Stead, *Divine Substance*, 228, remarks that Marcellus's example can be understood on the basis of the Platonic doctrine that the rational part of the soul equals the true person, but its stringency is not complete inasmuch as reason does not exhaust a person's existence. For Hanson, *The Search*, xix, to the contrary, Marcellus's theology "could quite properly be called Sabellian." Sa-

bellius, however, had modified the erstwhile Monarchian view that the Father and the Son are one and the same, by claiming that the Father had become Son. Unlike other Monarchians, Marcellus theorized a two-staged prolation of God's Word. After dwelling dormant in the Father, the Word was set forth to create the cosmos. The two-λόγοι theory, originally a grammatical and psychological doctrine deriving from Stoic philosophy, had become part of common intellectual parlance through the mediation of Philo of Alexandria. Christian theologians from the second century on had adopted it with varied outcomes as an alternative to the eternal generation of the Son. While Clement of Alexandria, *Stromateis* 5.6.3, and Origen of Alexandria, *Commentarius in Evangelium Ioannis* 1.24.151, had lamented the Monarchian use of this theory, Marcellus embraced it. According to M.R. Barnes, *The Power of God*, 137, Marcellus adopted from Galen the technical terminology (δύναμις/ἐνέργεια) that he employed to distringuish between the Logos as a faculty and as an activity of God. Strutwolf, *Die Trinitätstheologie*, 183–187, argues that Eusebius, Marcellus's main rival, also held a variety of two-λόγοι theology. On the two λόγοι see Pohlenz, "Die Begründung"; Pohlenz, *Die Stoa*, II, 21–22; Mühl, "Der λόγος ἐνδιάθετος"; Chiesa, "Le problème du langage," 314; Orbe, "Orígenes y los monarquianos"; Matelli, "ΕΝΔΙΑΘΕΤΟΣ e ΠΡΟΦΟΡΙΚΟΣ"; Labarriére, "*Logos endiathetos*"; Panaccio, *Le discours intérieur*, 53–93; Edwards, "Clement of Alexandria"; Achard, "Philosophie antique"; Manetti, "«Lógos endiáthetos»." On the two λόγοι in Philo see Wolfson, *The Philosophy of the Church Fathers*, I, 177; Wolfson, *Philo*, 226–240; 253–261; 287–289.

197. See Simonetti, *La crisi ariana*, 66. Similarly, Ayres, *Nicaea and Its Legacy*, 62, believes that Marcellus's thought underwent an evolution after his composition of *Against Asterius*, which was excerpted extensively by Eusebius of Caesarea.

198. See Zachhuber, "The Antiochene Synod," 93.

199. Meletius of Antioch, *De sigillatione sepulcri*; ed. Kim. The homily on Proverbs 8:22 is preserved by Epiphanius of Salamis, *Adversus haereses* 73.29–33.

200. This latter circumstance is admittedly less indicative, given that the emperor would have been presumed by the writers of the document to have little use for a detailed explanation of the subtleties of their theological position.

201. *Refutatio hypocriseos Meletii et Eusebii* 1–6; ed. PG 28, 85A–B; ed. Stockhausen, 675–677.

202. *Damnatio blasphemiae Arrii*; ed. Duval, 11.

203. See Simonetti, *La crisi ariana*, 318.

204. Hilary of Poitiers, *Fragmenta Historica*, Series A, IX, 1, 3; ed. Feder, 95–96.

205. Theodoret of Cyrrhus, *Historia ecclesiastica* 2.21.7; ed. Bouffartigue, Canivet, Martin, Pietri, and Thélamon, I, 432; trans. adapted from Hanson, *The Search*, 380.

206. Jerome of Stridon, *Altercatio Luciferiani et orthodoxi* 18; ed. Canellis, 146.

207. Simonetti, *La crisi ariana*, 322, n. 19, entertained this possibility, though without adducing arguments.

208. Theodoret of Cyrrhus, *Historia ecclesiastica* 2.21.7: Μήτε μὴν δεῖν ἐπὶ προσώπου Πατρὸς καῖ Υἱοῦ καὶ ἁγίου Πνεύματος μίαν ὑπόστασιν ὀνομάζεσθαι; ed. Bouffartigue, Canivet, Martin, Pietri, and Thélamon, I, 432; ed. Brennecke, Heil, Müller, Stockhausen, and Wintjes, *Athanasius Werke. Dritter Band. Erster Teil. 4. Lieferung*, 473.

209. Athanasius of Alexandria, *De synodis Arimini in Italia et Seleucia in Isauria* 30.9: Καὶ γὰρ οὐδὲ ὀφείλει ὑπόστασις περὶ πατρὸς καῖ υἱοῦ καὶ ἁγίου πνεύματος ὀνομάζεσθαι; ed. Martin and Morales, 288.

210. The Greek translation of a Latin text could also be invoked, without detriment to my general argument, to surmise that the target of either Athanasius's text or Theodoret's (or both) was not the notion of (one) hypostasis but that of (one) *substantia*.

211. I am unable to speculate about the circumstances of this alteration.

212. As does Simonetti, *La crisi ariana*, 339.

213. See, e.g., Kopecek, *A History of Neo-Arianism*, 143–144.

214. On the role of ἀγέν[ν]ητος in the Trinitarian controversy and on the graphic confusion between ἀγένητος and ἀγέννητος see Prestige, "Ἀγέν[ν]ητος and γεν[ν]ητός," 486–496; Lebreton, "Ἀγέννητος dans la tradition"; Prestige, "Ἀγέν[ν]ητος and Cognate Words." See also Hanson, *The Search*, 202–207; M. Parmentier, "Rules of Interpretation," 268.

215. Vaggione, *Eunomius of Cyzicus*, 285. Vaggione writes (300) that "[w]ith the departure of the unifying hand of the state, the non-Nicene jurisdictions found it increasingly difficult to articulate the *positive* sense in which they believed the Son to be like the Father—some said it was in the will, others in the nature, still others in a shared capacity to create. For Eunomius these positions shared only one thing in common: they all led sooner or later to homoousios. The practical result for Eunomius and his followers was that they were forced to become more explicitly sectarian: they refused to accept either the baptism or the ordination of most other non-Nicene" (italics in the original). See also ibid., 330.

4. Ortholalia: The Negotiation of Formulas in the 370s

1. Pascal, *The Provincial Letters*, 147.

2. Ibid., 150–151.

3. For a different, confessional understanding of "ortholalia" as a form of hypocrisy see Espín, "Ortholalia."

4. On the use of ζητεῖν (in frequent combination with γυμνάζειν to indicate a particular type of theological investigation) see Perrone, "Der formale Aspekt der origeneischen Argumentation"; Graumann, *Die Kirche der Väter*, 134–137.

5. I have found the idea that Fragment 142, attributed to Eustathius, affected the Eustathian theologico-ecclesial alliance after 362 also in Lorenz, "Die Eustathius von Antiochien zugeschriebene Schrift," 121.

6. Jerome of Stridon, *De viris illustribus* 85; Athanasius of Alexandria, *Historia Arianorum ad monachos* 4.1. Bardenhewer, *Geschichte der altkirchlichen Literatur,* 230–232, remains an important collection of ancient authorities about Eustathius.

7. Theodoret of Cyrrhus, *Historia ecclesiastica* 1.3. See Spanneut, *Recherches,* 13–23.

8. The historical details are murky. See Burgess, *Studies,* 183–190.

9. See Chadwick, "The Fall," 27–35 (who places the deposition in 326); Simonetti, *La crisi ariana,* 104–107; T.D. Barnes, "Emperors and Bishops," 53–75; Hanson, "The Fate of Eustathius," 171–179; Burgess, *Studies,* 191–196; T.D. Barnes, "The Date of the Deposition"; P. Parvis, "Constantine's *Letter to Arius*"; S. Parvis, *Marcellus of Ancyra,* 101–107. For a different assessment of the chronology of Eustathius's life and deposition see Fernández Hernández, "La deposición del obispo"; Fernández Hernández, "Las consecuencias de la deposición."

10. Eustathius of Antioch, *De Engastrimytho contra Origenem* (composed between 312 and 324); *Contra Ariomanitas et de anima* (61 excerpts; composed after 325); *In inscriptiones titulorum* (3 excerpts); *In illud: Dominus creavit me initium viarum suarum (Prov 8:22)* (17–20 excerpts; composed after 325); *In inscriptiones Psalmorum graduum* (2–3 excerpts); *Commentarius in Ps. 92* (5 excerpts); *Contra Arianos* (7 excerpts); *De fide contra arianos* (4 excerpts; this could be the same work as the previous one: see Declerck, *Eustathii Antiocheni, patris Nicaeni, Opera,* ccclxxxvi); *Epistula ad Alexandrum Alexandrinum (De Melchisedech)* (5 excerpts; composed before 324); *De temptationibus* (1 excerpt; composed possibly before the break of the Trinitarian controverseis); *Oratio coram tota Ecclesia in: Verbum caro factum est (Ioh. 1,14)* (1 excerpt in two languages); *Secunda oratio coram tota Ecclesia* (1 excerpt); *De Hebraismo* (1 excerpt); *In Ioseph* (2 excerpts); *In Samaritanam* (1 excerpt). See Declerck, *Eustathii Antiocheni, patris Nicaeni, Opera,* ccclxxxvi.

11. See Spanneut, *Recherches*; Declerck, *Eustathii Antiocheni, patris Nicaeni, Opera,* ccclxxxvi. Declerck's new edition of Eustathius's extant works, containing a total of one hundred and fifty-five excerpts, adds sixty-two fragments to those contained in Michel Spanneut's 1948 collection. Eight of the new items are in Syriac, thus bringing the total count of the Syriac excerpts, edited and translated in Declerck's volume by Lucas Van Rompay, to twenty-five. The Syriac excerpts from works by Eustathius of Antioch edited by Declerck (*Eustathii Antiocheni, patris Nicaeni, Opera*) are nr. 65, 80*, 81*, 84*, 88, 92, 93, 94*, 109, 110, 111, 112, 113 (‡ *imo*), 117 (‡), 118 (‡), 119 (‡ *b*), 124*, 125*, 126*, 134 (†), 142 (†; ‡ *b* and *c*), 143* (†), 153 (†), 154 (†), 155 (†). Asterisks (*) mark those excerpts that are newly edited and were not present in Spanneut, *Recherches*; obelisks (†) indicate the fragments declared spurious by Declerck; and the diesis sign (‡) is apposed to fragments declared spurious by Sellers, *Eustathius of Antioch.*

12. The excerpts transmitted under Eustathius's name are found in forty-two different sources. Between the sixth and eighth centuries Eustathius's authority was invoked

against a wide array of perceived heresies. At least seventeen of the sources reporting Eustathius's excerpts were composed during the fifth century and are quoted by dyophysite, orthodox, and miaphysite writers alike.

13. Eustathius's prominence in Theodoret's writings is no happenstance: Eustathius helped Theodoret find his way out of a historiographic predicament in which his ecclesiastical allegiance placed him. As a result of the ecclesiastical struggles that he began to face in 448, Theodoret turned to the history of the Church of Antioch during the Trinitarian controversies as a source of inspiration for his own organization of the episcopacy. The outcome of this historiographic effort is preserved in his *Church History* (449), narrating the history of the Antiochene episcopate from the inception of the Arian crisis until the year 428. The work's narrative identifies the orthodox tradition of Antioch with Meletius. However, this bishop's initial election as a homoian to the Antiochene episcopal see posed a problem to Theodoret: How could he justify that Meletius had come to accept the Nicene homoousios only as late as 363, years after his consecration? Theodoret solved this by counterfactually placing Meletius directly within the Eustathian tradition. The communion the Meletians had eventually gained in 414 with the Eustathians, a group that had adamantly upheld the homoousios at a time when Meletius was overtly battling it, allowed Theodoret to bridge a decades-long gap in his own Antiochene community's record of orthodoxy. Eustathius's crucial role in this reconstruction probably accounts both for the authority to which he rose in Theodoret's *Church History* and for the abundance of his citations in Theodoret's other writings. On these issues see Camplani, "Atanasio e Eusebio"; Martin, "Antioche aux IVe et Ve siècle"; Martin, "L'Église d'Antioche."

14. *Acta concilii nicaeni secundi* 6: Εὐστάθιος ὁ εὐσταθὴς πρωτόμαχος τῆς ὀρθοδόξης πίστεως, καὶ τῆς Ἀρειανῆς κακοδαιμονίας καταλύτης; ed. Mansi, XIII, 265C.

15. For overall evaluations of Eustathius's theology see Cartwright, *The Theological Anthropology*; Burn, *S. Eustathius of Antioch;* Sellers, *Eustathius of Antioch*; Sellers, *Two Ancient Christologies*; Gericke, *Marcell von Ancyra*.

16. See Declerck, *Eustathii Antiocheni, patris Nicaeni, Opera*, cccxc.

17. S. Parvis, *Marcellus of Ancyra*, 60.

18. Ibid., 86.

19. Ibid., 90. See the negative opinion expressed by Simonetti, "Un libro recente," 108, on S. Parvis's claims.

20. See Logan, "Marcellus of Ancyra," 436, n. 41.

21. This is the position of, e.g., Zoepfl, "Die trinitarischen und christologischen Anschauungen."

22. Eustathius of Antioch, *Commentarius in Ps. 92*: ܥܠܬܐ ܗܝ ܠܝ܆ ܕܐܦ ܐܬܬܠܬܦܘܬܐ ܡܢܝܬܐ܆ ܕܐܢܫ ܡܘܡܬܐ ܢܐܡܪ. ܡܛܠ ܕܡܫܝܚܐ ܠܗܘ ܕܒܗܘܢܐ ܠܦܠܛܘܢܝܐ ܐܘܣܛܐܬܝܘܣ܆ ܗܘ ܕܗܘܐ ܐܦܝܣܩܘܦܐ ܕܐܢܛܝܘܟܝܐ܆ ܕܡܘܕܝܢܐ ܕܗܝܡܢܘܬܐ ܕܬܠܡܝܕܐ ܘܬܐܡܪ܆ ܠܐܠܗܐ ܘܠܒܪܢܫܐ ܕܐܢܫ ܡܘܡܬܐ ܐܬܬܠܡܘܢ܆ ܒܟܠܗܐ ܗܠܝܢ ܐܡܪ ܕܬܐܪܣܘܢ ܡܢ <ܒܪ> ܒܗ ܒܪ ܒܗ ܗܕܝܢ ܬܫܡܫܬܐ ܠܐ ܡܬܚܫܚܢܘܬܐ. ܗ̇ܝ ܕܝܢ ܢܦܫܗ ܒܒܪܐ ܕܗܠܝܢ.

ܠܚܕ ܕܝܢ ܩܢܘܡ ܡܫܬܥܝܢ܆ ܗܢܘܢ ܟܬܒܐ ܐܠܗܝܐ ܕܬܪܝܢܘܬܐ ܟܕ ܡܢ ܚܕܝܘܬܐ ܡܥܠܝܢ. ܠܚܕܝܘܬܐ ܕܝܢ ܡܢ ܬܪܝܢܘܬܐ ܡܟܪܙܝܢ. ܒܗ̇ ܕܚܕ ܩܢܘܡܐ ܐܝܬܘܗܝ ܕܐܠܗܘܬܐ ܀; ed. Declerck, 156–157, Fragment 88 (= Spanneut, *Recherches*, 38 = Cavallera, *S. Eustathii, episcopi Antiocheni in Lazarum, Mariam et Martham homilia christologica*, Fragment 9). Schwartz, "Der s. g. Sermo maior," 61, back-translates the second part (from ܬܪܝܗܘܢ on) as follows: Οἱ δύο μὲν ἐν ταυτῷι θαυματουργοῦσιν ἀοράτως, ταύτην δὲ τὴν μεγαλουργίαν αὐτῶν ἑνὶ [δὲ] πολλάκις ἀνατιθέασιν αἱ θεῖαι γραφαί, τὴν δυάδα μὲν ἐκ μονάδος εἰσάγουσαι, τὴν δὴ μονάδα ἐκ δυάδος κηρύττουσαι, καθὸ μία ἡ τῆς θεότητος ὑπόστασις.

23. Any reference to "Arianism" is missing from this work, suggesting that its composition preceded the inception of the Trinitarian controversies.

24. Eustathius of Antioch, *De engastromytho* 24; ed. Declerck, *Eustathii Antiocheni, patris Nicaeni, Opera*, 49–50.

25. For this translation of the expression ὁ θεός λόγος see Behr, "Response to Ayres," 148.

26. Eustathius of Antioch, *In inscriptiones titulorum*; ed. Declerck, *Eustathii Antiocheni, patris Nicaeni, Opera*, 137 (Fragment 65b). There is a Greek version of this fragment, which may be translated as follows: "If indeed the Word received a beginning of the generation since the moment he, having passed through the motherly womb, bore the bodily frames, he gave proof that he was born of a woman (Gal 4:4). If, however, the Word was also God from above beside the Father, and [if] we say that everything came into being through him, then he was not born of a woman who [permanently] exists and is the cause of all the originated [beings]. However, he came into being from a woman who was placed in the womb of the virgin mother by the Holy Spirit"; ed. Declerck, 136 (Fragment 65a).

27. Eustathius of Antioch, *Contra Ariomanitas et de anima*; ed. Declerck, 85–86 (Fragment 22b). The term "Ariomaniacs" (Ἀρειομανῖται) was coined based on Ἀρειμανής, "belligerent," "Ares-possessed" (see Simonetti, "Ariomaniti").

28. Loofs, *Nestorius and His Place*, 108–110; Loofs, *Paulus von Samosata*, 295–310; Loofs, *Theophilus von Antiochien*, passim.

29. Spanneut, "La position théologique," 222.

30. As proposed, e.g., by Spanneut, *Recherches*, 82–83.

31. The chronological arguments in favor of and against the authenticity of the fragment appear to elide one other. I recount here in their broad outlines the arguments against Eustathius's authorship that are based on the presumption of his early death (for a detailed reconstruction of various scholars' positions see Declerck, *Eustathii Antiocheni, patris Nicaeni, Opera*, cclxxxiv–cclxxxv, on which my outline depends). Cavallera, *S. Eustathii, episcopi Antiocheni in Lazarum, Mariam et Martham homilia christologica*, 95, and Cavallera, *Le schisme d'Antioche*, 66, laid out some of the chronological arguments for incompatibility. Those were accepted, among others, by Sellers, *Eustathius of Antioch*, 66–67, and Spanneut, *Recherches*, 82–83. The name of

Photinus, who was refuted in the work from which Fragment 142 derives, appears in the ancient sources for the first time—and does so as the object of a condemnation, alongside the name of Marcellus of Ancyra—in the *Long-Lined Exposition* of 345. It is thus unlikely, it is argued, that Photinus emerged as a protagonist in the Trinitarian debates any earlier than the 340s. In addition, Eustathius's name does not appear among those of the exiles—such as Asclepias of Gaza, Marcellus of Ancyra, Lucius of Adrianopolis, and Paul of Constantinople—recalled by Constantine II in 337 or 338 (see Simonetti, *La crisi ariana*, 136–139). Similarly, when at the Council of Sardica (343) Athanasius, Marcellus, and Asclepias were reestablished in their episcopal sees, Eustathius's name is again nowhere to be found in the sources. The absence of his name is all the more noteworthy because of his good relations with Ossius of Corduba, who presided over the synod, and of Sardica's proximity to the place of Eustathius's exile, whichever of the options for the latter is chosen (see Declerck, *Eustathii Antiocheni, patris Nicaeni, Opera*, cclxxxiv–cclxxxv, n. 445). Furthermore, the encyclical letter of the Eusebians summoned to Philippopolis around the same time as the westerners were gathering at Sardica seems to refer to Eustathius's career as being over (see Declerck, *Eustathii Antiocheni, patris Nicaeni, Opera*, cclxxxv–cclxxxvi, nn. 446–447). Finally, a passage of Athanasius's *History of the Arians* (ca. 358) appears to treat Eustathius as long gone (Athanasius of Alexandria, *Historia Arianorum ad monachos* 4.1: Εὐστάθιός τις ἦν ἐπίσκοπος τῆς Ἀντιοχείας, ἀνὴρ ὁμολογητής). Nevertheless, as anticipated above in this note, these arguments are largely inconclusive, as a comparable number of points of equal weight may be made against the notion that by 340 Eustathius had already died. First, no mention is made anywhere in the sources of the fact that the Eustathian community headed until 362 by the priest Paulin lacked a bishop: this would only be explicable if Eustathius was alive somewhere. As Schwartz suggested, Eustathius might have died in 361, immediately prior to the election of Meletius to the Antiochene see. This possibility seems to be supported by the turn of phrase used by Theodoret of Cyrrhus, *Historia ecclesiastica* 3.4.5, in describing Meletius's appointment: πρὸ γὰρ τῆς Μελετίου χειροτονίας Εὐσταθίου τετελευτηκότος (which, as Declerck writes, is admittedly not a definitive indication of the amount of time that elapsed between the two events: see Declerck, *Eustathii Antiocheni, patris Nicaeni, Opera*, cclxxxviii, n. 459). Second, when Athanasius of Alexandria, *Apologia de fuga sua* 3.3, mentions the demise of Lucius of Adrianopolis he makes no mention of Eustathius's death. Third, John Chrysostom, *Laudatio S. patris nostri Eustathii Antiochaeni* 4 (ed. PG 50, 604), refers in admiring terms to Eustathius's incessant performance of pastoral activities, despite his inability to recover his see, until Meletius's enthronement (although this passage might also be read as referring to the posthumous efficacy of Eustathius's teachings or as part of Chrysostom's overall attempt to draw a strong connection between Eustathius and Meletius) (see Declerck, *Eustathii Antiocheni, patris Nicaeni, Opera*, cclxxxviii, n. 460*bis*). Fourth, Socrates of Constantinople, *Historia ecclesiastica* 4.14.3–4, and in dependence on him Sozomen, *Historia* *ecclesiastica* 4.13.2, among others, report that Eustathius was recalled by Jovian and hid in Constantinople. There in 370 he allegedly ordained Evagrius. Persecuted anew by the anti-Nicene, he was exiled by Valens to Vize, in eastern Thrace (see Declerck, *Eustathii Antiocheni, patris Nicaeni, Opera*, cclxxxix). Fifth and last, Theodorus Lector affirms that Eustathius's relics were returned to Antioch under Patriarch Callandion (479–484/485), one hundred years after Eustathius's death, which would then be placed around 380.

32. Michel Spanneut, *Recherches*, 82, contended that the terminological distinction between "person," "nature," and "property" found in the fragment is too evolved to be Eustathius's. Robert Victor Sellers, *Eustathius of Antioch*, 56 and 66–67, expressed a similar reservation about the distinction between nature and person. Given the precious little we possess of Eustathius's work, and the fragmentary form in which most of it is attested, these claims seem inconclusive. Moreover, denying the Eustathian authorship of Fragment 142 on the basis of its contents seems to mistake for tri-hypostatic the tri-prosōpic but mia-hypostatic theology conveyed by this passage.

33. The full title of *To the Hellenes* runs in the most reliable manuscripts as follows: "How, Saying That There are Three Persons in the Godhead, We Do Not Say Three Gods: To the Hellenes from Common Concepts" (πῶς τρία πρόσωπα λέγοντες ἐν τῇ θεότητι οὔ φαμεν τρεῖς θεούς. πρὸς τοὺς Ἕλληνας ἀπὸ τῶν κοινῶν ἐννοιῶν). Since the 1958 publication of the edition by Müller, based on eight manuscripts, five more fragments of the work have come to light. Since these, to my knowledge, have not yet been collated, it is impossible to determine whether they are going to change our understanding of the text. Considering these circumstances, any speculations about the resemblance between Gregory's work and the Eustathian fragments must be treated as provisional. See Leemans, "Logic and the Trinity," 112–114.

34. None of the parallels include the expression whose reception I investigate in this chapter. Declerck, ccxciii–ccxcviii, presented a comparison of the Greek of *To the Hellenes* with the French translation of the Syriac of Eustathius's fragment rather than with the Syriac itself. The parallels are concentrated in the incipit of *To the Hellenes* (Gregory of Nyssa, *Ad Graecos ex communibus notionibus*); ed. Müller, 19–33.

35. A dating around 388 is proposed by Daniélou, Review of Müller, *Gregorii Nysseni Opera*, 614–615; May, "Die Chronologie des Lebens," 58–59. Hübner, "Gregor von Nyssa," established a link between this work and the Antiochene ecclesiastical developments of 379, the year of the Meletian council that paved the way for the Council of Constantinople. Hübner meant to lend support to his thesis that Gregory of Nyssa and the Old Nicene alliance were ideologically and politically much closer than previously assumed. His argument relied on the one hand on the contents of the Marcellan *Exposition of Faith of the Deacon Eugene of Ancyra* (dated to 371 by Tetz, "Markellianer und Athanasios von Alexandrien"), read as expressing Old Nicene availability to engage in doctrinal dialogue with the Meletians. On the other hand, Hübner emphasized Gregory's recorded contacts with the Marcellans (Gregory of Nyssa, *Epistula V*

2) and his attempts to produce harmony at a council to be gathered in Ancyra that Basil of Caesarea opposed (Basil of Caesarea, *Epistula C*). Hübner's account equated mia-hypostatism with the community of Marcellus of Ancyra, excluding from consideration mia-hypostatic thinkers of different stripes such as Eustathius. See Leemans, "Logic and the Trinity."

36. See Ziegler, *Les petits traités*, 141.

37. Lorenz, "Die Eustathius von Antiochien zugeschriebene Schrift gegen Photin," 121–124.

38. Fragment 142 was also originally considered the work of Eustathius by Zachhuber, "Gregor von Nyssa und das Schisma." He raised the possibility that *To the Hellenes* might be a later reworking of an original treatise by Eustathius, made by his pupils. These would have attempted to pass off their adaptation as Gregory's in order to boost their own orthodox credentials. Zachhuber eventually revised this opinion based on what he saw as clear markers of the Nyssen's authorship, mostly identified in something akin to a literary *Stimmung*. Zachhuber also analyzed the structure of the work: in the first part (1.1–23.3) Gregory cites Eustathian fragments to refine and expand their contents, so as to craft an acceptable theological compromise; in the second part (23.4–28.8) he addresses three questions that have been raised about his speech; in the conclusion (28.9–29.3) he rebuts an objection. Throughout the work, according to Zachhuber, Gregory deals with Eustathian materials in a rudimentary manner, to the point that *To the Hellenes* can be read as a slightly amended draft of an oral presentation, aimed at bringing peace between the Eustathian and Meletian communities. Gregory's use of a work by Eustathius appeared outlandish to Declerck, *Eustathii Antiocheni, patris Nicaeni, Opera*, ccxcvii, since as inspired a theologian as Gregory would have been above recycling unexceptional literary materials. Declerck preferred to envision a later author who used fragments of Gregory's *To the Hellenes* in a writing published pseudoepigraphically as Eustathius's. It has been demonstrated, however, that in writing *On the Christian Mode of Life* Gregory repurposed the so-called Messalian *Great Letter* (attributed to Macarius or to Simeon of Mesopotamia): see Staats, *Gregor von Nyssa und die Messalianer*; Staats, *Makarios-Symeon, Epistola Magna*. No matter how talented an author Gregory was, if he did appropriate some of the contents of *Against Photinus* he was not deploying this technique for the last time.

39. Peter of Callinicus, *Tractatus contra Damianum* 3.40–42. Assemani and Assemani, *Bibliothecae apostolicae Vaticanae codicum manuscriptorum catalogus*, I/III, 66–68, were the first to remark on the presence of Eustathian citations in Peter's *Against Damian*. The first edition of Fragments 142b and 142c, drawn from the indirect tradition of a Syriac Trinitarian florilegium contained in a manuscript from the quondam British Museum (ms. BL Add. 14,532, f. 132v; the same florilegium is contained in mss. BL Add. 12,155, BL Add. 14,533, and BL Add. 14,538), was published by Cowper, *Syriac Miscellanies*, 60, along with an opaque English translation. In 1883 Jean-Pierre-Paulin

Martin published the Syriac text and a Latin translation of the two fragments in Jean Baptiste Pitra, *Analecta sacra*, II, 212 (texts) and 442 (translations) (Declerck Fragment 142b = Martin Fragment V; Declerck Fragment 142c = Martin Fragment VI). See also Jean Baptiste Pitra, *Analecta sacra*, II, xxvi. Cavallera, *S. Eustathii, episcopi Antiocheni in Lazarum, Mariam et Martham homilia christologica*, 96, mistook part of the passage edited by Cowper, which belonged to Damian of Alexandria's own voice in the *Many-Lined Letter*, for a third fragment, and edited it separately. Lorenz, "Die Eustathius von Antiochien zugeschriebene Schrift gegen Photin," consulting mss. Vaticanus Syrus 108 and Berolinensis Sachau 201, was able to rectify this mistake and to understand that Fragment 142b and Fragment 142c were parts of a longer citation (= Fragment 142a). He published the latter as a whole text for the first time, thus providing the broader context from which the author of the Syriac Trinitarian florilegium had drawn his authorities. Lorenz also added the previously unpublished Fragment 143 and produced a German translation of both Fragment 142a (translated at 112–113) and Fragment 143. A Latin translation of Fragment 142a is offered in Van Roey, "Le traité contre les Trithéites," 234. Through Van Roey's partial reconstruction of Peter's *Against Damian* it was also possible to learn that it had been not Peter, but Damian himself, quoted by Peter, who had originally cited Eustathius's *Against Photinus*. Damian had quoted Eustathius in at least two loci: the *Treatise against the Tritheists* (where he assembled Fragment 142a, Fragment 142b, and Fragment 142c) and the *Many-Lined Letter* (Πολύστιχος ἐπιστολή, carrying Fragment 143 and some lines of Fragment 142c) (= CPG 7245 and CPG 7246.1 respectively). Fragment 142a = Damian of Alexandria, *Tractatus adversus tritheistas* 5, apud Peter of Callinicus, *Tractatus contra Damianum* 3.40.130–160; Fragment 142b = Damian of Alexandria, *Tractatus adversus tritheistas* 5, apud Peter of Callinicus, *Tractatus contra Damianum* 3.40.171–178; Fragment 142c = Damian of Alexandria, *Epistula prolixa*, apud Peter of Callinicus, *Tractatus contra Damianum* 3.40.62–67; 3.40.119–124; 3.43.26–31; 3.43.33–38; Damian of Alexandria, *Tractatus adversus tritheistas* 5, apud Peter of Callinicus, *Tractatus contra Damianum* 3.40.179–184. A history of the editions of the fragments is told in Declerck, *Eustathii Antiocheni, patris Nicaeni, Opera*, cviii–cix; cxxviii–cxxix; cclxxxiii–clxxxiv.

40. On Damian see R. Ebied, "Peter of Antioch"; Blaudeau, "Le voyage"; Orlandi, "Papiro di Torino 63."

41. See Socrates of Constantinople, *Historia ecclesiastica* 1.23; Sozomen, *Historia ecclesiastica* 2.18.

42. The crisis brought about a thirty-year schism between the orthodox churches of Antioch and Alexandria, which ended only in 616, by the joint initiative of Athanasius I Gammolo, Patriarch of Antioch, and Pope Anastasius of Alexandria.

43. I have divided the passage (edited by Lucas Van Rompay in Declerck, *Eustathii Antiocheni, patris Nicaeni, Opera*, 200–201) into sections that follow the subdivision of Fragment 142a into Fragment 142b, Fragment 142c, and other sections not covered by

either of these two fragments, and I have tagged anew each section and subsection. A French translation is offered by Lucas Van Rompay (ibid.).

44. ܚܫܡ ܠܝ ܗܟܝܠ ܠܡ ܡܪܢܘܣܘܬܗ ܐܘ ܒܝܬ ܦܪܢܣܘܬܗ ܒܡ ܬ̈ܪܝܢ ܗܢ ܒܝܬܗ. ܐܝܟ ܡܢ ܕܬܠܬܐ ܐ̈ܠܗܐ ܐܡܪܝܢ ܠܐܒܐ ܘܠܒܪܐ ܘܠܪܘܚܐ ܩܕܝܫܐ. ܒܪ ܦܘܪܫ ܚܫܒܢܘܗܝ ܓܝܪ. ܐܠܐ ܠܘ ܟܢܫ ܐܡܪܝܢ ܗܘܝܢ ܥܡܫܟܚܢܘܬܐ: ܐܠܗܐ ܘܐܠܗܐ ܘܐܠܗܐ. ܒܐܝܢܐ ܕܝܢ ܓܝܪ ܗܘܘ ܠܝ ܕܬܠܬܐ ܐ̈ܠܗܐ ܐܡܪܝܢ ܗܘܝܢ. ܐܢ ܕܝܢ ܫܪܝܪܬܐ ܐܝܬܘܗܝ ܘܐܢܦ̈ܐ ܕܐܡܪܝܢ: ܠܐܒܐ ܐܠܗܐ: ܠܒܪܐ ܐܠܗܐ: ܠܪܘܚܐ ܩܕܝܫܐ ܐܠܗܐ. ܐܠܐ ܠܗ ܒܗ̇، ܕܐܠܗܐ ܐܠܗܐ ܬܠܬܐ ܒܦܘܠܓܐ ܐܡܪܝܢ. ܐܦ ܥܠ ܟܠ ܚܕ *ܦܪ̈ܨܘܦܐ ܡܘܡܚܝܢܐ* ܐܠܗܐ ܡܬܬܐܡܪܐ. ܒܗ̇، ܕܚܕ ܐܝܬܘܬܗܘܢ ܘܡܠܬܗ ܒܪ ܕܡܠܬܗ ܕܚܝܠܐ ܐܠܗܐ. ܐܠܐ ܒܗ̇، ܕܐܒܐ ܘܒܪܐ ܘܪܘܚܐ ܩܕܝܫܐ. ܡܬܬܐܡܪܝܢ ܐܫܘܝܘܬܐ ܘܕܠܝܠܬܐ ܘܫܘܝܘܬܗܘܢ ܒܚܝܠܬܐ ܕܐܠܗܘܬ ܚܕܐ; ed. Declerck, 199–200, Fragment 142, lines 1–11 (= Fragment 142a.α).

45. ܫܡܐ ܗܟܝܠ ܕܐܠܗܐ. ܐܢ ܡܢ ܡܫܘܕܥܢܐ ܐܝܬܘܗܝ، ܗܘܐ ܕܦܪ̈ܨܘܦܐ. ܒܪ ܬܠܬܐ ܦܪ̈ܨܘܦܐ ܐܡܪܝܢ ܡܢ ܟܠܦܪܘܣ ܘܬܠܬܐ ܐ̈ܠܗܐ ܐܡܪܝܢ ܗܘܝܢ. ܡܛܠ ܕܝܢ ܕܡܫܘܕܥܢܐ ܕܟܝܢܐ ܐܝܬܘܗܝ. ܒܪ ܡܢ ܕܝܠܝܘܬܐ ܡܕܡ ܕܥܠ ܟܝܢܐ ܐܝܬܘܗܝ ܡܬܢܣܒ. ܐܝܟܢܐ ܕܥܠ ܒܪܢܫܐ ܡܢ ܓܚܟܘܬܐ: ܥܠ ܟܠܒܐ ܕܝܢ ܢܒܚܘܬܐ: ܕܝܠܝܘܬܐ ܕܝܢ ܕܟܝ̈ܢܐ ܐܝܬܝܗܝܢ ܡܬܐܡܪ̈ܢ ܡܫܘ̈ܕܥܢ ܠܟܝ̈ܢܐ. ܬܠܬܐ ܐ̈ܠܗܐ ܠܐ ܐܡܪܝܢ. ܡܛܠ ܕܠܘ ܬܠܬܐ ܟܝ̈ܢܐ ܐܡܪܝܢ; ed. Declerck, 200, Fragment 142, lines 11–18 = Fragment 142b (= Fragment 142a.β) = Spanneut, *Recherches*, Fragment 83 = Cavallera, *S. Eustathii, episcopi Antiocheni in Lazarum, Mariam et Martham homilia christologica*, Fragment 80. Schwartz, "Der s. g. Sermo maior," 60, back-translates as follows: Εἰ οὖν τὸ θεός ὄνομα δηλωτικὸν ἦν προσώπου, τρία λέγοντες πρόσωπα πάντως ἂν εἴπομεν καὶ τρεῖς θεούς· ἐπειδὴ <δὲ> δηλωτικὸν φύσεώς ἐστι τὸ ἀπὸ ἰδιώματός τινος ἐπὶ φύσεως ὄντος λαμβανόμενον, ὡς ἐπ' ἀνθρώπου μὲν γέλως, ἐπὶ κυνὸς δὲ ὑλαγμός, τὰ δὲ τῶν φύσεων ὄντα ἰδιώματα λέγεται δηλωτικὰ φύσεων, τρεῖς θεοὺς οὐ λέγομεν, διότι οὐ τρεῖς φύσεις λέγομεν.

46. ܐܢ ܕܝܢ ܥܠ ܚܕ ܡܢ ܦܪ̈ܨܘܦܐ ܕܟܝܢܐ ܐܠܗܐ ܐܠܗܐ ܐܡܪܝܢ: ܒܗ̇، ܕܕܝܠܗ ܕܟܝܢܐ ܐܝܬܘܗܝ: ܕܗ̇ܘ ܕܫܡܐ ܕܐܠܗܐ ܒܪ ܡܬܢܟܪܝܘܬ ܡܬܬܐܡܪ ܡܬܬܘܣܦ. ܠܗ ܒܪ ܐܠܗܐ ܡܫܘܕܥܢܐ ܐܝܬܘܗܝ، ܕܦܪ̈ܨܘܦܐ. ܐܠܐ ܐܝܬܘܗܝ، ܕܚܕ ܟܝܢܐ. ܡܫܡܫ ܕܝܢ ܕܒܗܘܢ ܒܟܝܢܐ ܢܛܝܪܐ ܐܦ ܦܪ̈ܨܘܦܐ. ܒܗ̇، ܕܐܦ ܕܟܝܢܐ ܗ̇ܘ ܐܝܬܘܗܝ،; ed. Declerck, 200, Fragment 142, lines 18–23 (= Fragment 142a.γ).

47. ܐܚܪܢܐ ܡܢ ܓܝܪ ܐܝܬܘܗܝ، ܦܪ̈ܨܘܦܐ. ܐܚܪܢܐ ܕܝܢ ܟܝܢܐ. ܐܢ ܗܟܝܠ ܕܦܪ̈ܨܘܦܐ ܗ̇ܘ، ܕܐܠܗܐ ܐܝܬܘܗܝ ܗܘܬ. ܒܪ ܬܠܬܐ ܦܪ̈ܨܘܦܐ ܐܡܪܝܢ. ܡܢ ܟܠܦܪܘܣ ܘܬܠܬܐ ܐ̈ܠܗܐ ܐܡܪܝܢ ܗܘܝܢ. ܡܛܠ ܕܝܢ ܕ<ܚ>ܕ ܟܝܢܐ ܐܝܬܘܗܝ. ܒܕ<ܐ ܚܕ ܟܝܢܐ ܐܡܪܝܢ ܕܦܪ̈ܨܘܦܐ. ܡܢ ܐܢܢܩܐ ܕܚܕ ܒܠܚܘܕ ܐܝܬܘܗܝ، ܐܠܗܐ ܐܡܪܝܢ; ed. Declerck, 200, Fragment 142, lines 23–27 = Fragment 142c (= Fragment 142a.δ) = Spanneut, *Recherches*, Fragment 84 = Cavallera, *S. Eustathii Episcopi Antiocheni in Lazarum, Mariam et Martham homilia christologica*, Fragment 80(2). Schwartz, "Der s. g. Sermo maior," 61, retroverts as follows: Ἕτερον μέν ἐστι πρόσωπον, ἕτερον δὲ φύσις. εἰ ἄρα προσώπου τὸ θεός ἦν, τρία λέγοντες πρόσωπα πάντως ἄν ἔιπομεν καὶ τρεῖς θεούς· ἐπεὶ δ' ὅτι μία ἡ φύσις λέγομεν τῶν προσώπων, ἀναγκαίως ὅτι εἷς μόνον ὁ θεός.

48. ܐܢ ܕܝܢ ܚܕ ܟܝܢܐ ܡܢ ܐܝܬܘܗܝ،: ܕܟܝܢܐ ܕܝܢ ܗ̇ܘ، ܕܐܠܗܐ. ܢܦܩܐ ܠܗ̇، ܕܢܐܡܪ ܚܕ ܟܝܢܐ. ܗ̇ܘ، ܕܚܕ ܐܠܗܐ ܐܝܬܘܗܝ، ܢܐܡܪ܀; ed. Declerck, 200, Fragment 142, lines 27–29 (= Fragment 142a.ε).

49. ܗܢܐ ܕܝܢ ܟܝܢܐ ܕܐܝܬܘܗܝ، ܫܡܐ ܐܠܗܐ. ܕܬܠܬܝܗܘܢ ܦܪ̈ܨܘܦܐ ܠܥܠ ܡܢ ܡܫܟܚܐ ܡܫܬܟܚܝܢ. ܒܪ ܠܐ ܡܬܦܪܫ ܒܡܫܘܕܥܘܬܐ ܕܦܪ̈ܨܘܦܐ. ܘܠܐ ܡܫܬܘܬܦܢ ܒܡܫܘܕܥܘܬܐ ܕܦܪ̈ܨܘܦܐ; ed. Declerck, 201, Fragment 143).

50. Lorenz, "Die Eustathius von Antiochien zugeschriebene Schrift gegen Photin," 121 and passim. Lorenz sees this application of Aristotelian categories to the problem

of unity vs. triadicity in God as a first step on the road that would later be traveled by the Cappadocians.

51. Simonetti, *La crisi ariana*, 73.

52. These examples were scholastic: Porphyry in *Isagoge* had used human laughter and the neighing of horses as an example of the ἴδιον; barking was discussed by Porphyry in his *Commentary* on the Categories of Aristotle; and laughing, barking, and neighing were later used as instances of ἴδια by Ammonius and the sixth-century author commonly known as Elias: see Lorenz, "Die Eustathius von Antiochien zugeschriebene Schrift gegen Photin," 118 and nn. 51 and 52.

53. Van Roey, "Le traité contre les Trithéites," 234–235.

54. Lorenz, "Die Eustathius von Antiochien zugeschriebene Schrift," 12, translates as "einzelne Persone[n]"; Lucas Van Rompay, in Declerck, *Eustathii Antiocheni, patris Nicaeni, Opera*, 200, translates as "personne[s] hypostatique[s]."

55. Halleux, "'Hypostase' et 'Personne,'" 335, proposes πρόσωπα ὑφεστῶτα.

56. The term *qnomā* can acquire in Ephrem different meanings: "concrete thing" or "person"; "material substance"; and "true essence" of something. Later East-Syriac Christology would use the adjective *qnomāyā*, based on the noun *qnomā*, to describe the two *kyāne* (natures) of Christ, united under one *parsopā*: see, e.g., Giwargis, *Epistula ad Minam*; ed. Chabot, 236. For seventh-century East-Syrians a *kyānā* needs its *qnomā*, whereas two *kyāne qnomāye* can be united under one *parsopā*.

57. Indirect evidence that at a later stage the Old Nicene might have held less insubstantial an opinion of the Son may be gleaned also from Socrates of Constantinople, *Historia ecclesiastica* 1.23, where the author declares not to understand what Eustathius's feud with Eusebius of Caesarea might have been about considering that they both saw the Son as ἐνυπόστατος and ἐνυπάρχων: "Because of these circumstances, they both wrote arguments as if against adversaries, and, though both declaring that the Son of God is subsistent (ἐνυπόστατον) and existent, and confessing that God is one in three hypostaseis, they could not—I do not know how—agree with one another, and therefore did not manage in any way to remain at peace" (Διὰ ταῦτα ἕκαστοι ὡς κατὰ ἀντιπάλων τοὺς λόγους συνέγραφον· ἀμφότεροί τε λέγοντες ἐνυπόστατόν τε καὶ ἐνυπάρχοντα τὸν υἱὸν εἶναι τοῦ θεοῦ, ἕνα τε θεὸν ἐν τρισὶν ὑποστάσειν εἶναι ὁμολογοῦντες, ἀλλήλοις οὐκ οἶδ' ὅπως συμφωνῆσαι οὐκ ἴσχυον· καὶ διὰ ταῦτα ἡσυχάζειν οὐδενὶ τρόπῳ ἠνείχοντο). Of course, this passage should not be taken at face value. It is nearly impossible that Eustathius ever spoke except condemningly of three hypostaseis. However, this citation might capture a historical kernel about the openness of the Eustathian tradition to the affirmation of a certain individualizing discreteness of the Father and the Son. More specifically, the use of ἐνυπόστατος might well derive from employment of the word in the expression πρόσωπον ἐνυπόστατον.

58. On the issue of the legal origins of Tertullian's use of *persona* see Prestige, *God in Patristic Thought*, 159.

59. Origen, *Commentarius in Canticum* 3.43 (on *Song* 2:9); ed. Fürst and Strutwolf, 376; ed. Barbàra.

60. Prestige, *God in Patristic Thought*, 94; 161–162.

61. Simonetti, *Origene. Commento al Cantico dei Cantici*, 239, n. 256. On the commentary in general see J.C. King, *Origen on the* Song of Songs; Perrone, "'The Bride at the Crossroads.'"

62. See Scott, *Origen and the Life of the Stars*, 168–172; Limone, "I nomi dell'amore"; Prinzivalli, "A Fresh Look."

63. See Prestige, *God in Patristic Thought*, 161.

64. Clement of Alexandria, *Paedagogus* 1.7.57.2.

65. See, e.g., Cyril of Alexandria, *Thesaurus de sancta et consubstantiali Trinitate*; ed. PG 75, 577.

66. Hippolytus, *Contra Noëtum* 14. On the authorship and dating of this work see Simonetti, *Ippolito. Contro Noeto*, 17–139; Cerrato, *Hippolytus between East and West*, 72–96 and passim.

67. See Bethune-Baker, *An Introduction*; Rankin, "Tertullian's Vocabulary"; Ribas Alba, *Persona*, 304–312. An account of the polysemy of *persona* in *Against Praxeas* is found in Evans, *Adversus Praxean liber*, 46–50.

68. Apud Pseudo-Hippolytus, *Refutatio omnium haeresium* (= *Philosophoumena*) 10.27.4. On Callixtus's theology see Ronald E. Heine, "The Christology of Callistus"; Vogt, "Die Trinitätslehre des Papstes Kalixt I"; Prinzivalli, "Callisto I, santo," 240–242.

69. See Simonetti, "Sabellio e il sabellianismo," 24, n. 70. On πρόσωπον in relation to Sabellianism see Bethune-Baker, *An Introduction*, 233–235; Prestige, *God in Patristic Thought*, 160–161.

70. Eusebius of Caesarea, *De ecclesiastica theologia* 3.6.4; ed. Klostermann and Hansen, 164.

71. See Prestige, *God in Patristic Thought*, 161. Milano, *Persona in teologia*, 56, similarly reads this as a *reductio ad absurdum*.

72. Οὐ γὰρ ἐξαρκεῖ διαφορὰς προσώπων ἀπαριθμήσασθαι, ἀλλὰ χρὴ ἕκαστον πρόσωπον ἐν ὑποστάσει ἀληθινῇ ὑπάρχον ὁμολογεῖν. Basil of Caesarea, *Epistula CCX* 5; ed. Deferrari, III, 210.

73. Lucian Turcescu, "Prosōpon and Hypostasis in Basil."

74. Prestige, *God in Patristic Thought*, 162.

75. See Simonetti, "«Persona» nel dibattito cristologico," 531–532.

76. Simonetti, "Sabellio," 24.

77. On the history of hypostasis see Prestige, *God in Patristic Thought*, 163–177; Dörrie, "'Υπόστασις," 35–74; Hammerstaedt, "Der trinitarische Gebrauch"; Hammerstaedt, "Das Aufkommen"; Hammerstaedt, "Hypostasis"; Thümmel, "Logos und Hypostasis"; Ramelli, "*Hebrews* and Philo"; Limone, "Il contributo di Origene." On hypostasis in the Trinitarian controversies see Abramowski, "Trinitarische und christologische

Hypostasenformeln"; Milano, *Persona in teologia*, 91–103; Simonetti, "«Persona» nel dibattito cristologico"; Zachhuber, "Basil and the Three-Hypostases Tradition"; Zachhuber, "Individuality and the Theological Debate."

78. Origen of Alexandria, *Contra Celsum* 8.12; 8.14; 8.67. See Dörrie, "'Υπόστασις," 76–78; Hammerstaedt, "Der trinitarische Gebrauch"; Hammerstaedt, "Hypostasis," 1004–1008; Zachhuber, "Individuality," 96. Origen of Alexandria, *Commentarius in Evangelium Ioannis* 2.10.75, speaks of τρεῖς ὑποστάσεις (ed. Blanc, I, 254).

79. While ἀνυπόστατος appeared in non-Christian writings, ἐνυπόστατος did not: see Gleede, *The Development*, 12–13.

80. Ibid., 13–14.

81. The other fragment (from an otherwise lost *Letter to Photius and Andrew* by Origen), in which ἐνυπόστατος is used doxologically, is contained in Origen, *Adnotationes in Deuteronomium* (on Deut 16:20); ed. PG 17, 28B (cited in Gleede, *The Development*, 15).

82. Origen, *Expositio in Proverbia* 88; ed. PG 17, 185B: Ἐνυπόστατος Υἱὸς καὶ Λόγος τοῦ Θεοῦ (cited in Gleede, *The Development*, 15).

83. Gleede, *The Development*, 16. *Substantivus* occurs in Origen, *De principiis* 1.7.1; *substantialis* in Ambrose of Milan, *Expositio Evangelii secundum Lucam* 1.5.61; both cited in Gleede, *The Development*, 16, n. 36.

84. Origen, *De principiis* 1.2.2.

85. It could be asked if a disciple of the anti-Origenist Eustathius (who, e.g., in *On the Belly-Myther of Endor, against Origen*, interpreting Saul's consultation with a witch in *1 Samuel*, had attacked the Alexandrian exegete for allegorizing on all occasions except the one at hand: see Verheyden, "Origen," and Verheyden, "Eustathius of Antioch") would not have abhorred a term with Origenist roots. However, ἐνυπόστατος was very liberally employed by Epiphanius, who was no admirer of Origen (see Epiphanius of Salamis, *Adversus haereses* 63–64 and *Ancoratus* 54–55; 62–63; 87; see also E.A. Clark, *The Origenist Controversy*, 86–104). This indicates that the memory of the Origenian provenance of ἐνυπόστατος was lost at some point. The same may be said for Jerome (on whose anti-Origenism see ibid., 121–151), though his use of the expression is much more limited.

86. Irenaeus of Lyons, *Fragmenta*: τοῦ ἐνυποστάτου Λόγου τύπος ἀψευδής; ed. PG 7, 1240C. See Grant, "The Fragments," 213 (cited in Gleede, *The Development*, 13).

87. See Schwartz, "Eine fingierte Korrespondenz," 46; de Navascués Benlloch, *Pablo de Samosata*, 214–248.

88. See Gleede, *The Development*, 26–29. For the condemnation of ἐνδιάθετος/προφορικός λόγος in the fourth century see Gleede, 39.

89. Ibid., 30. The term is missing from the Athanasian tradition of the text.

90. The following two, under Valens, were ordered in 365 and 369. According to Simonetti, "Melezio di Antiochia," 3190, given the conformity of Meletius's sermon to

the homoian creed of Ariminium (359), an administrative or disciplinary pretext must have been adduced for his exile. For interpretations of the sermon see Dünzl, "Die Absetzung"; Karmann, *Meletius von Antiochien*, 65–134; Daley, "The Enigma of Meletius," 132–133. See also Brennecke, *Studien*, 66–81; Hihn, "The Election and Deposition"; S. Kim, "And They Sealed."

91. Meletius of Antioch, *Homilia in Proverbia 8:22*, apud Epiphanius of Salamis, *Adversus haereses* 73.31.6–7; ed. Holl, III, 306–307; trans. Williams, II, 477.

92. The expression πρόσωπον ὑφεστώς appears in a treatise composed by Basil of Ancyra to expound the contents of the synodal letter of the Council of Ancyra (358) and to qualify his acceptance of the compromise between homoiousians and homoians reached at the fourth Council of Sirmium of the same year. The synodal letter of Ancyra established at the same time the distinction between the Father, the Son, and the Holy Spirit and their similarity according to the substance. In this treatise, reported in Epiphanius of Salamis, *Adversus haereses* 73.12–22, Basil traced back the distinction between the hypostaseis of the Father, the Son, and the Holy Spirit to their being respectively self-caused, generated by the Father, and subsisting from the Father through the Son; at the same time, he argued that the three constitute one godhead, one kingdom, and one principle. Basil writes (apud Epiphanius of Salamis, *Adversus haereses*, 73.16.1–4): "The easterners, as I said, call the individualities of subsistent persons [προσώπων ὑφεστώτων] 'hypostaseis.' They do not mean that the three hypostaseis are three first principles, or three Gods, for they condemn anyone who speaks of three Gods. Nor do they call the Father and the Son two Gods; they confess that the godhead is one, and that it encompasses all things through the Son, in the Holy Spirit. [But] though they confess one godhead, dominion, and first principle, they still acknowledge the persons in an orthodox manner through the individualities of the hypostaseis"; ed. Holl, III, 288–289; trans. adapted from Williams, II, 461. Basil reassures here his presumably Old Nicene readers about the orthodoxy of those easterners who "call the individualities of subsistent persons [πρόσωπα ὑφεστώτα] 'hypostaseis'" while at the same time acknowledging that these are not three first principles. If πρόσωπον ὑφεστώς is taken to be a near-synonym of πρόσωπον ἐνυπόστατον, the argument is then not unlike that later used by the Meletians in their encounter with Jerome (see below). Simonetti, *La crisia ariana*, 264, n. 24, noticed that the use of πρόσωπον was unusual at the time Basil was writing. This letter is widely considered to be a document written by Basil of Ancyra and George of Laodicea: see Cavalcanti, *Studi eunomiani*, 6–7; Kopecek, *A History of Neo-Arianism*, I, 115–116; Simonetti, *La crisi ariana*, 259–266. On this treatise see also Hanson, *The Search*, 366–371; Morales, *La théologie trinitaire*, 36–39; Fairbairn, "The Synod of Ancyra (358)"; Stockhausen, "Der Brief der Synode von Ankyra."

93. Gleede, *The Development*, 11; Schwyzer, *Griechische Grammatik*, 456–457 (as cited by Gleede).

94. Both the orthographies ὑπόστατος and ὑποστατός are attested.

95. *Letter 15* is one of six letters of Jerome's addressed to Damasus: 15, 16, 18 (a commentary on Isa 6 composed at a previous time but dedicated to the Pope when Jerome was in Rome), 20, 21, and 36. Damasus addressed Jerome in *Letters* 19 and 35 of Jerome's epistolary collection. On the correspondence of the two men, with a particular focus on *Letters* 35 and 36, see Cain, "In Ambrosiaster's Shadow." On Damasus see Morison, "An Unacknowledged Hero"; Pietri, "Damase évêque de Rome"; Carletti, "Damaso I, santo"; Ghilardi and Pietri, "Damaso."

96. On this journey see Eduard Ortuño Córcoles, "Jerónimo en Antioquía."

97. Jerome of Stridon, *Epistula III* 3.1; ed. Hilberg, I, 14.

98. On Evagrius see Cavallera, *Saint Jérôme,* 153–154; 158–162; 300–301.

99. This was either in the desert outskirts of Chalcis-on-Belus (Qenneshrin) or on an estate Evagrius possessed in Maronia, along the road that connects Chalcis to Antioch. See Rebenich, *Hieronymus und sein Kreis,* 85–90. Jerome's Syrian asceticism began in the second half of 375. The Syrian chronology established by Cavallera, *Saint Jérôme,* 14–15, is restated by Scourfield, "Jerome, Antioch, and the Desert," contra Kelly, *Jerome,* 46; see also Jay, "Jérôme." The rigor of Jerome's ascetic practice has been questioned: see Kelly, *Jerome,* 45–56; Rebenich, *Hieronymus und sein Kreis,* 85–98; Clausi, "*O rerum quanta mutatio!,*" 124. Cain, *The Letters of Jerome,* 135, suggests to the contrary that Jerome practiced a radical form of asceticism.

100. *Letters* 2–17 were composed from the Syrian hermitage. This bundle of letters, at the exclusion of *Letter* 14, constitutes according to Cain, *The Letters of Jerome,* 17, a carefully constructed propagandistic collection, aimed at promoting the author's image. The idea of a highly intentional authorial self-presentation in Jerome's correspondence, which Cain holds concerning the whole of Jerome's correspondence, is found also in Vessey, "Jerome's Origen."

101. On Jerome's knowledge of Hebrew see Rebenich, "Jerome: The *Vir Trilinguis*"; Kamesar, *Jerome,* 1–26; Graves, *Jerome's Hebrew Philology*; D. King, "*Vir Quadrilinguis?*"

102. Jerome of Stridon, *Epistula VII* 2; ed. Hilberg, I, 27: *Hic enim aut barbarus seni sermo discendus est aut tacendum est.* The evaluation of Jerome's knowledge of Aramaic and Syriac in D. King, "*Vir Quadrilinguis?,*" makes only passing references to his stay in the Syrian desert.

103. The majority of Jerome's theological activity happened in tight connection with the exegesis of Scripture and had as its object the question of grace: see the studies in the fourth section of Ayroulet and Canellis, *L'exégèse de saint Jérôme.* It is no happenstance that in the ninety pages devoted to Jerome by the *Dictionnaire de théologie catholique* his Trinitarian or Christological thought makes almost no appearance; see Forget, "Jérôme (Saint)." It was very likely Jerome's limited theological stature that eventually induced Cavallera to refrain from writing the announced second volume of his monograph on the saint, which was supposed to be devoted to theological doctrine: see Cavallera, *Saint Jérôme*; Force, "La deuxième partie."

104. See M.H. Williams, *The Monk and the Book*, 39, n. 39. On the *curiales* turning into Church leaders in the fourth century see McLynn, "*Curiales* into Churchmen."

105. See Basil of Caesarea, *Epistula CLVI* 3. See Cavallera, *Le schisme d'Antioche*, 153–162; Rebenich, *Hieronymus und sein Kreis*, 72; Rebenich, *Jerome*, 15 and n. 19.

106. According to Rousseau, "Jerome as Priest," 187–188, Jerome's "acceptance of ordination at the hands of the orthodox Paulinus of Antioch in the late 370s must have appeared pig-headed and partisan, especially when he clearly had no intention of submitting himself to the authority of a particular bishop."

107. For further details about the context in which *Letter 15* was composed see Fiano, "Splitting the Difference," 64–71.

108. Jerome of Stridon, *Epistula XVII* 3; ed. Hilberg, I, 72: *Non mihi conceditur unus angulus heremi. Cotidie exposcor fidem, quasi sine fide renatus sum. Confiteor, ut volunt: non placet. Subscribo: non credunt. Unum tantum placet, ut hinc recedam. Iam iam cedo.* Clausi, "*O rerum quanta mutatio!*," 140, n. 54, speculates that the expression *non mihi conceditur unus angulus heremi* might be reminiscent of the image conveyed by the famous words found in Athanasius's *Life of Anthony*, "[T]he desert was made a city" (ἡ ἔρημος ἐπολίσθη; Athanasius of Alexandria, *Vita Antonii* 14; ed. Bartelink, 174).

109. On Jerome's *Letter 15* as an example of his rhetoric see also Jeanjean, "Saint Jérôme entre polémique et hérésiologie," 144. The letter is analyzed in detail in Conring, *Hieronymus als Briefschreiber*, 198–215, and discussed in Reutter, *Damasus, Bischof von Rom*, 22–23.

110. Mierow believes otherwise; see Lawler and Mierow, *The Letters of St. Jerome*, 210, n. 1. See also Lawler, "Jerome's First Letter to Damasus," 549, n. 7; Conring, *Hieronymus als Briefschreiber*, 200, n. 274. On the further correspondence of Damasus and Jerome see Nautin, "Le premier échange épistolaire," arguing that the Damasian epistles are in reality Jeromian forgeries.

111. On Jerome's concern for ecclesiastical unity in this section see Hamblenne, "Jérôme et le clergé du temps," 365, n. 18.

112. On Jerome's deferential attitude toward Damasus and on his notion of papal primacy in *Letters 15* and *16* see Conring, *Hieronymus als Briefschreiber*, 209–212; Diefenbach, "*Una Petri sedes.*"

113. Jerome of Stridon, *Epistula XVI* 2; ed. Hilberg, I, 69: *Meletius, Vitalis atque Paulinus tibi haerere se dicunt: possem credere, si hoc unus adsereret; nunc aut duo mentiuntur aut omnes. Idcirco obtestor beatitudinem tuam per crucem domini, per necessarium fidei nostrae decus, passionem:* [. . .] *ut mihi litteris tuis, apud quem in Syria debeam communicare, significes.* Clausi, "*O rerum quanta mutatio!*" 137–138, analyzes this letter in relation to Jerome's ascetic ideal. On Jerome's relation to the Church of Antioch see Hamblenne, "Jérôme et le clergé du temps," 361–363 and n. 16.

114. See Conring, *Hieronymus als Briefschreiber*, 199, n. 272.

115. Cavallera, *Saint Jérôme*, II, 16, and Lawler, "Jerome's First Letter," 548, date *Letter 15* to 376. Previously, however, Lawler and Mierow, *The Letters of St. Jerome*, 196, had warned that its current dating, along with that of other letters, relied on the somewhat debated chronology of Jerome's sojourn in the desert. Cain, *The Letters of Jerome*, 210, dates *Letter 15* to "around 377," providing no additional explanation. Conring, *Hieronymus als Briefschreiber*, 202, dates it to 376/377.

116. M.H. Williams, *The Monk*, 274, dates the arrival of *Through My Son* to Antioch to 376. Accordingly, she dates *Letter 15* to the summer of 375, and *Letter 16* to the spring of 376 (274–276).

117. Greenslade, *Early Latin Theology*, 305–306.

118. On this chronology see Cavallera, *Saint Jérôme*, 12–20; Rebenich, *Hieronymus*, 86; Kelly, *Jerome*, 52–56; M.H. Williams, *The Monk*, 273–276.

119. Greenslade considers Damasus's failure to respond to Jerome's *Letter 15* as potential proof of its 374–375 dating, on the conjecture that the pope either remained undecided as to which community to support or assumed that Jerome would hear about the decision contained in *Through My Son* before he would be able to receive whatever personal response Damasus might draft. The main obstacle to this reconstruction is the fact that *Letter 15* treats Vitalis as a fourth contestant vying for the episcopacy in Antioch, while Apollinaris did not ordain Vitalis bishop until 375. But since Vitalis's activities obviously predated his ordination, it is conceivable that Jerome simply mentioned him as the leader of an ecclesiastical faction. Greenslade's solution is similar to the one proposed by J. Taylor, "St Basil the Great," 263, according to whom "Jerome's letters are proof that at the time when he wrote them no clear sign of Roman favour had been accorded to any of the rival claimants to the see of Antioch, or at least none had yet become known to the ascetics of Chalcis."

120. A somewhat similar position is expressed by Lawler, "Jerome's First Letter," 551. Kelly, *Jerome*, 57, writes that Jerome had refused to take sides in the Antiochene dispute; against this interpretation see M.H. Williams, *The Monk and the Book*, 40, n. 40.

121. Jerome of Stridon, *Epistula XV* 5.1; ed. Hilberg, I, 64.

122. There is no telling whether Jerome had till then avoided taking an outwardly recognizable and definitive stance in favor of communion with the Eustathians, possibly because of the Meletian affiliation of most ascetics living in the Syrian desert. If this was the case, his cautious nonpartisanship proved in any event insufficient to shield him from the attacks of those hermits, as demonstrated by his letter to Mark.

123. These are the Egyptian pro-Nicene exiled by Valens in 373, who were going to return to their sees thanks to Gratian's decree in 378: see Conring, *Hieronymus als Briefschreiber*, 204, n. 286.

124. Both Labourt, *Saint Jérôme*, 47, and Cavallera, *Saint Jérôme*, 53, render *campenses* as "campagnards"; Bardy, "St. Jerome and Greek Thought," 88, similarly translates it as "peasants." The study by Jülicher, "Campenses," 1443, provides support

for this reading. Similarly, according to Freemantle, "[t]he Meletians were so called because, denied access to the churches of the city, they had to worship in the open air outside the walls" (*NPNF2* VI, 19, n. 4). See also the remarks in Labourt, *Saint Jérôme*, 164. Downey, *A History*, 411 and n. 83, explains instead that the nickname comes from the military area (*campus*) across the Orontes near which the Meletians had been reduced to celebrating their services.

125. Jerome of Stridon, *Epistula XV* 2.2–3.2; ed. Hilberg, I, 64–65: *Et quia pro facinoribus meis ad eam solitudinem conmigraui, quae Syriam iuncto barbariae fine determinat, nec possum sanctum domini tot interiacentibus spatiis a sanctimonia tua semper expetere, ideo hic collegas tuos Aegyptios confessores sequor et sub onerariis nauibus parua nauicula delitesco. Non noui Vitalem, Meletium respuo, ignoro Paulinum. quicumque tecum non colligit, spargit, hoc est, qui Christi non est, antichristi est. Nunc igitur—pro dolor!—post Nicenam fidem, post Alexandrinum iuncto pariter occidente decretum trium ὑποστάσεων ab Arrianorum prole, Campensibus, nouellum a me, homine Romano, nomen exigitur. Qui ista, quaeso, apostoli prodidere? Quis nouus magister gentium Paulus haec docuit? Interrogamus, quid tres hypostases posse arbitrentur intellegi: "Tres personas subsistentes" aiunt. Respondemus nos ita credere: non sufficit sensus, ipsum nomen efflagitant, quia nescio quid ueneni in syllabis latet. Clamamus: "Si quis tres hypostases ut tria ἐνυπόστατα, hoc est ut tres subsistentes personas, non confitetur, anathema sit" et, quia uocabula non edicimus, heretici iudicamur. Si quis autem hypostasin usian intellegens non in tribus personis unam hypostasin dicit, alienus a Christo est et sub hac confessione uobiscum pariter cauterio unionis inurimur.*

126. See Lawler, "Jerome's First Letter," 548.

127. See Pépin, "Attitudes d'Augustin," 299, n. 69. Similar readings of this episode are offered in Kelly, *Jerome*, 53–54; Simonetti, "«Persona» nel dibattito cristologico," 537–538; Jeanjean, *Saint Jérôme et l'hérésie*, 19; Jeanjean, "Saint Jérôme face à l'exercice du pouvoir épiscopal," 181–182. On this passage see also Gemeinhardt, "Apollinaris of Laodicea," 286. On Jerome's heresiological polemics and his engagement with theology see Duval, "Saint Jérôme devant le baptême"; Jeanjean, *Saint Jérôme et l'hérésie*; Canellis, "Saint Jérôme et les Ariens"; Fürst, "Hieronymus," 180; Jeanjean, "Saint Jérôme entre polémique et hérésiologie."

128. See Grützmacher, *Hieronymus*, I, 270 (cited in Conring, *Hieronymus als Briefschreiber*, 208, n. 299); Greenslade, *Early Latin Theology*, 306.

129. See Conring, *Hieronymus als Briefschreiber*, 208, n. 299.

130. Jerome of Stridon, *Epistula XV* 5.1.

131. See Jerome of Stridon, *Epistula XV* 4–5.

132. In principle, the alternative possibility exists of seeing *persona subsistens* as a rendition of πρόσωπον ὑφεστώς.

133. Jerome of Stridon, *Epistula XVII* 2.2: ed. Hilberg, I, 71: *Hereticus vocor homousiam praedicans trinitatem; Sabellianae inpietatis arguor tres subsistentes, veras, integras*

perfectasque personas indefessa voce pronuntians. Si ab Arrianis, merito; si ab orthodoxis, qui huiusmodi arguunt fidem, esse orthodoxi desierunt aut, si eis placet, hereticum me cum occidente, hereticum com Aegypto, hoc est cum Damaso Petroque, condemnent. Balavoine, "La rhétorique polémique," examines closely the rhetoric of *Letter 17* (which she dates to 377) and concludes that throughout this composition Jerome worked hard at establishing his ethos of a "cultivated yet ill-treated defender of Christian orthodoxy" (paragraph 1).

134. It could be argued that the technical nature of the use of the phrase is diluted by the fact that *subsistentes* is used alongside two more adjectives; but *veras* and *integras* can also be understood as epexegetical expansions on *subsistentes*, used to illustrate the full meaning of the technical term.

135. This expansion of the bounds of orthodoxy was achieved through the creation of a metaphoric field. A metaphor arises—according to one theory—when a signifier ceases to refer to the signified to which it is commonly linked and assumes as its referent a different signifier (which takes up the status of signified). In the metaphor implicitly set up by the Meletian propagandists, the signifier "hypostasis" no longer pointed to a hypostasis, but to the signifier "πρόσωπον ἐνυπόστατον." They demanded that Jerome wholly accept this process of substitution of one signifier for another. He, on his part, refused out of concern that memory of the elided signified πρόσωπον ἐνυπόστατον might be resultingly lost. If that occurred, the signifier "hypostasis" would then become available for any other signified to attach itself to it, including the signifier "ousia."

136. The exchange represents both Jerome and the Meletians as lacking an understanding of the concept of hypostasis per se: the former flattens the term onto the notion of person, while the latter are suspected of flattening it onto the concept of ousia (and if they branded Jerome as a Monarchian on account of his confession, they were guilty as charged).

137. On the meaning of the title Ἀγκωρυτός see Kösters, *Die Trinitätslehre*, 107.

138. See Kösters, *Die Trinitätslehre*, passim. On Epiphanius's staunch homoousianism, at least at this point in his career, see Fairbairn, "The Synod of Ancyra"; Y.R. Kim, *Epiphanius of Cyprus*, 88–90.

139. Pourkier, *L'hérésiologie*, 443.

140. See Epiphanius of Salamis, *Ancoratus* 6.5.

141. See Epiphanius of Salamis, *Ancoratus* 6.8; 8.4. See also Kösters, *Die Trinitätslehre*, 121–129; 332–347.

142. Epiphanius of Salamis, *Adversus haereses* 25.6.4; 69.80.3; 72.1.3; 73.34.2; 73.36.4; 78.24.5.

143. Epiphanius of Salamis, *Adversus haereses* 72.1.3; ed. Holl, III, 255: καὶ τὰ μὲν κρύφια τῆς ἐννοίας θεῷ ἔγνωσται, οἱ δὲ ἀπ' αὐτοῦ γεγονότες καὶ κατηχηθέντες, ἢ τὴν ἐκείνου ἔννοιαν ἀγνοοῦντες ἢ [μὴ] τὰ ἐκείνου ἀληθῆ διηγούμενοι, οὔτε τὰς τρεῖς

ὑποστάσεις ὁμολογεῖν ἤθελον, ὡς ἔχει ἡ ἀλήθεια, ὅτι μία ἐστὶν ἡ θεότης, μία δοξολογία, ὁμοούσιος οὖσα ἡ τριὰς καὶ οὐδὲν διαλλάττουσα τῆς ἰδίας δόξης [. . .].

144. Epiphanius of Salamis, *Ancoratus* 67.4: τρία ἐνυπόστατα; ed. Holl, 82.

145. Epiphanius of Salamis, *Ancoratus* 67.7: τρία πρόσωπα [. . .] ἐξ ὑποστάσεως οὔσης τριττῆς; ed. Holl, 82.

146. Epiphanius of Salamis, *Ancoratus* 25.2; 31.3; 34.8; 35.1; 36.4; 38.2; 39.3; 39.4; 39.5; 39.6; 54.5; 55.8; 67.7; 68.2; 83.4. In *Medicine Chest* the adjective ἐνυπόστατος appears fifty-six times.

147. Y.R. Kim, *Epiphanius of Cyprus*, 131, n. 132. See also A. Jacobs, *Epiphanius of Cyprus*, 189–190.

148. Y.R. Kim, *Epiphanius of Cyprus*, 131.

149. The occurrences discussed in this chapter exhaust all those I have been able to find in Christian literature from the fourth century.

150. On this letter see Lienhard, "*Ousia* and *Hypostasis*," 116–117.

151. Epiphanius of Salamis, *Adversus haereses* 72.11.5: ἀναθεματίζοντες [. . .] τοὺς μὴ λέγοντας τὴν ἁγίαν τριάδα τρία πρόσωπα ἀπερίγραφα καὶ ἐνυπόστατα καὶ ὁμοούσια καὶ συναΐδια καὶ αὐτοτελῆ; ed. Holl, III, 266.

152. It should also be considered, however, that Marcellus's theology was largely hypothetical: like Origen, Marcellus held a distinction between ecclesiastical teaching and theological research. Given the fragmentary state of his works, it is difficult to ascertain whether a particular statement was pronounced by him as doctrine or as a hypothesis. The Synodal Letter of the Westerners' Council of Sardica (343) accuses the adversaries of "pretend[ing] that those statements that Marcellus set down, he put forward as already proven" (apud Hilary of Poitiers, *Fragmenta historica*, Series B, II, 1.6; ed. Feder, 117).

153. Lienhard, "The 'Arian' Controversy," 437, sees in this letter a document of the mia-hypostatic party and an exception to the loss of significance that the categories of mia-hypostatic and dyo- (or tri-)hypostatic theology underwent after 361.

154. I would consider Jerome, Athanasius, and possibly Vitalis (after his conversion from Meletianism to Old Nicenism) exponents of this tendency.

5. The Ends of Dialogue

1. Eusebius of Caesarea, *Vita Constantini* 2.64–65.1; 2.68.1–2; 2.71.2 (see also the parallel in Socrates of Constantinople, *Historia ecclesiastica* 1.7); ed. Bleckmann and Schneider, 292; 294–296; 298–300; trans. adapted from Cameron and Hall, 116–118. The letter is considered a forgery by Battifol, *La paix constantinienne*, 315–317; Pietras, *Concilio di Nicea*, 194–198. Its authenticity, however, is accepted by most: see, e.g., Simonetti, *La crisi ariana*, 35–37; Drake, "Constantine," 5; Camplani, "Il Cristianesimo in Egitto," 872a; Elliott, "Constantine's Preparations," 127–128; T.D. Barnes, *Constantine and Eusebius*, 212–213; T.D. Barnes, *Constantine: Dynasty, Religion and Power*, 120;

Cameron and Hall, *Eusebius. Life of Constantine,* 250–252; Lenski, *Constantine and the Cities,* 40, 58, and 265; Drake, "The Elephant in the Room," 118–119. According to Hall, "Some Constantinian Documents," 87–89, the letter, though the work of Constantine, was composed for the Council of Antioch of 325, and not sent to Arius and Alexander; S. Parvis, *Marcellus of Ancyra,* 77, n. 172, sees the letter as addressing a large eastern audience but not specifically the Council of Antioch.

2. See Barone Adesi, "La libertà religiosa." On Constantine's adoption of and views about Christianity see Girardet, *Der Kaiser und sein Gott.* On the relationship between the Christian emperors and the episcopate during the Trinitarian controversies see Just, *Imperator et episcopus.*

3. On the role of emperors, e.g., in summoning and directing the outcome of councils see Brennecke, "Synode als Institution." On imperial authorities and religious politics and legislation in late antiquity see Girardet, *Kaisertum.*

4. On the place of religion in the Roman Empire see Ando, *The Matter of the Gods.*

5. See Lim, "Christians"; Athanassiadi, *Vers la pensée unique.* See also Athanassiadi, "Christians and Others"; Cleve, "The Triumph of Christianity."

6. The term "monodoxie" is used by Athanassiadi, *La lutte,* passim.

7. The circumstance that language be treated technically is not a necessary condition for dogmatization: forms of dogmatization exist wherein linguistic technicalization plays no role. On the state's subservience to the Church in the fifth century as evidenced by repressive anti-heretical legislation see Acerbi, "Intolerancia." On tolerance and intolerance in the fifth-century Roman Empire see also Canella, *Il peso della tolleranza,* 181–210 (and 211–218 on the situation in the western post-Roman kingdoms). Discussions of tolerance and intolerance in late antiquity have mainly focused on two issues. On the one hand, the question is asked as to whether those terms are anachronistic when applied to an epoch that did not possess such notions either lexically or conceptually. On the other hand, scholars have found it important to establish whether the constraints on religious freedoms observable in the late ancient Roman Empire confirm that monotheisms are, as Jan Assmann insists, inherently coercive and exclusionary: see Assmann, "Monotheism"; Assmann, *The Price of Monotheism;* Mimouni, "Il monoteismo." Van Nuffelen, *Penser la tolerance,* has shown the similarity of Christian and pagan arguments in favor of both religious freedom and religious coercion (see also the review of that volume in Canella, "Lo sviluppo"). On these topics see Sfameni Gasparro, "Religious Tolerance"; Kahlos, *Forbearance and Compulsion;* Marcos, "De la convivencia"; Zecchini, "Religione pubblica"; Wendy Mayer, "Religious Conflict"; Marcos, "Current Perspectives"; Kahlos, *Religious Dissent.* Drake, in "Lambs into Lions" and *Constantine,* argues that politics, and not theology, was at the root of increasing religious coercion. The conversation about the end of dialogue in late antiquity has been animated to a large extent by prescriptive ideals. Whatever their nature—which seems to range from the Popperian project of an open society to the

more utopian notes of Bakhtinian dialogism, passing through Habermas's notion of the public sphere—these often-unspoken ideological commitments rarely contribute clarity to the exchanges.

8. On florilegia see Schermann, *Die Geschichte*; Chadwick, "Florilegium"; Richard, "Les florilèges"; Mühlenberg, "Griechische Florilegien"; Allen and van Roey, *Monophysite Texts*; ter Haar Romeny, "Les Pères grecs"; T. Fernández, "La tendencia compilatoria"; Ebied and Fiori, *Florilegia Syriaca*.

9. On late ancient Christian dialogues see Rigolio, *Christians in Conversation*, 1–38.

10. See ibid., 12.

11. See Van Nuffelen, "The End of Open Competition?," 159. See also Engels and Van Nuffelen, "Religion and Competition."

12. Morlet, "L'Antiquité," 419.

13. A similar idea is expressed in Graumann, "Authority and Doctrinal Normation," 38, in relation to the canonization of the Nicene Creed at the Council of Ephesus (431).

14. See Lim, *Public Disputation*, 182–229.

15. Cameron, *Dialoguing*, 23. On the long trajectory of orthodoxy in Byzantium see Cameron, *Byzantine Matters*, 87–111.

16. See Plato, *Cratylus* 390C. See also Brunschwig, "Introduction," ix–xiv; Lalande, *Vocabulaire*, I, 225–227, s.v. "Dialectique."

17. Maingueneau, "Dialectique."

18. See Goldhill, "Why Don't Christians Do Dialogue?"

19. This is the master's injunction, uttered to the servant, to compel people to enter the house, in Jesus's Parable of the Banquet (Luke 14:23). For its interpretation see Augustine of Hippo, *Epistula XCIII ad Vincentium* 2.5; ed. PL 33, 323. On Augustine's attitude toward dialogue see G. Clark, "Can We Talk?"

20. See Benoît and Simon, *Le judaïsme*, 55–56.

21. Polymnia Athanassiadi and Rebecca Lyman have proposed, with different arguments, locating the late ancient drive toward monodoxy within a broader cultural climate, in which the Platonic predilection for unity found institutional embodiment in the actions of political and ecclesiastical leaderships within the Roman Empire: see Lyman, "Natural Resources"; Athanassiadi, "The Creation"; Lyman, "Hellenism." For a reconstruction of a political philosophy of Neoplatonism see O'Meara, *Platonopolis*; O'Meara, "The Transformation." See also Dillon, "Orthodoxy"; MacMullen, "The Search." Although a contextualization of the monodox drive within the broader intellectual landscape of the Roman Empire must remain outside the bounds of this book, Athanassiadi's and Lyman's proposals contain a promising path forward for exploring the construction of orthodoxy beyond the domain of power, seeking a deeper integration between a history of ideas and imperial political history in this period.

22. The word ὁμόνοια is found repeatedly in Constantine's *Letters*. See references and a discussion in Macmullen, *Constantine*, passim.

23. See Bacher, *Die exegetische Terminologie*, II, 234–235.

24. The Babylonian Talmud also contains discussions that do not include any tannaitic or amoraic source or that do not mark their sources as such: see Elman, "The World of the 'Sabboraim.'" On the question of the late composition of the stam see the nuanced position of Y. Brody, "Setam ha-Talmud," and the response contained in Friedman, "'Al titmah ʿal hosafah she-nizkar bah shem amora.'"

25. Vidas, *Tradition*, 28, defines the sugyah as "a carefully planned literary construct"; see also L. Jacobs, "The Talmudic *Sugya*." The division of the text of the Talmud into sugyot was accomplished later than the time when the Talmud was redacted; the borders between sugyot are relative and fluid. On the development of the sugyah see Weiss, *Ha-Talmud ha-bavli*; Weiss, *ʿAl ha-yetsirah ha-sifrutit*, 1–75; Y.N.H. Epstein, *Mevoʾot le-sifrut ha-ʾamoraʾim*, 9–144; C. Albeck, *Mavo la-Talmudim*, 576–596; Weiss, *Meḥkarim ba-Talmud*, passim. On Weiss's views see Feldblum, "The Talmud." Brodsky, "From Disagreement," has proposed that a combination of the genres of progymnasmata and of Roman legal scholia (the latter investigated by Catherine Hezser in "The Codification" and "Roman Law") explains—though not by mere influence but through a dynamic of "Creolization"—the rise of the genre of Talmud as first practiced in Greco-Roman Palestine and then further developed in the Babylonian Talmud.

26. Among the abundant literature on the relationship between Judaism and Syriac Christianity, see Becker, "The Comparative Study"; Becker, "Polishing the Mirror"; and the contributions collected in Butts and Gross, *Jews and Syriac Christians*.

27. See Moscovitz, "The Formation and Character," 672.

28. See D.W. Halivni, *Midrash, Mishnah, and Gemara*, 142, n. 16; Hayes, *Between the Babylonian and Palestinian Talmuds*, 185–186, contra Neusner, *The Documentary Foundation*. On the stam of the Yerushalmi see also D.W. Halivni, *The Formation*, 193–196. Rubenstein, "Some Structural Patterns," 309, suggests seeing the difference in editing between the Bavli and the Yerushalmi as a matter of degree and not of kind.

29. On the migration of traditions see Y.N.H. Epstein, *Mevoʾot le-sifrut ha-ʾamoraʾim*, 312–314; Florsheim, "Sugyot bavliot" (both cited in A. Gray, *A Talmud in Exile*, 3, n. 6); and the studies collected in Ilan and Nikolski, *Rabbinic Traditions*. On the *naḥoteʾi* see M.M. Schwartz, "As They Journeyed from the East"; Redfield, "Redacting Culture"; Redfield, "When X Arrived, He Said"; Redfield, "Traveling Rabbis"; Kiperwasser, *Going West*, 6–7.

30. See R. Brody, *The Geonim of Babylonia*; Kraemer, *A History of the Talmud*, 179–184. For a more cautious opinion about the standing of the Yerushalmi in Geonic times see Rustow, *Heresy*, 17–23. The study of the Yerushalmi might now be on the cusp of a revival.

31. See above all Cameron, *Christianity*; Cameron, "The Cost of Orthodoxy." See also Brown, *Power and Persuasion*; Grafton and Williams, *Christianity*. On the role of the Jews in the Christian Empire see A. Jacobs, *Remains of the Jews*, 21–54.

32. On the political views of the Mishnah see Neusner, *Rabbinic Political Theory.*

33. Morawski, "The Basic Functions of Quotation," 691. Morawski also defines quotation as "the literal reproduction of a verbal text of a certain length [. . .] wherein what is reproduced forms an integral part of some work and can easily be detached from the new whole in which it is incorporated" (ibid.). For literature in various theoretical veins about quoting see Compagnon, *La seconde main;* Regier, *Quotology;* Finnegan, *Why Do We Quote?;* Morson, *The Words of Others.*

34. Morawski, "The Basic Functions of Quotation," 691–692.

35. On the political implications of citation see Giorgio Agamben's discussion of Walter Benjamin in the essay "The Melancholy Angel" (in Agamben, *The Man without Content,* 64–72).

36. On the possibility of doing "Talmudic history" in general in light of the redactional problems of the Talmud see Schremer, "Stammaitic Historiography." On a germane issue see Goldenberg, "Is the Talmud a Document?"

37. By self-representations with regard to citational practices I am referring, for the rabbinic side, to such passages as the discussion in *m.* ʿEduyot 1:4–6 about the reporting of the minority opinion or the statement in *y.* Sheḳalim 2:5 (47a) according to which if a sage's ruling is mentioned his lips whisper in the grave.

38. Morawski, "The Basic Functions of Quotation," 692, holds the same view.

39. Morawski, ibid., 694, describes the stimulative-amplificatory citation as "a kind of 'surgical appliance' doing duty for a part of [the investigator's] argument, or as a springboard for speculations in the same vein, or finally as a reinforcement of the terms in which he poses his problems or the answer which he advances." A further distinction between the theological and Talmudic citations, which does not detract from the commonality of the two operations, lies in the fact that the amoraic quotation constitutes a great part of the material out of which the text of the Bavli is woven, whereas if the patristic citation were eliminated from the theological treatises in which it is set forth, the text, with the necessary adjustments, would still stand (this is of course not true of catenae and florilegia).

40. According to Hirshman, *The Stabilization of Rabbinic Culture,* 5, "[A]ll of rabbinic literature is anthological." On the anthological character of the Mishnah and the Babylonian Talmud see respectively Elman, "Order, Sequence, and Selection"; E. Segal, "Anthological Dimensions." On the transmission of the Mishnah see Y.N.H. Epstein, *Mavo le-nosaḥ ha-Mishnah,* II, 673–706; Lieberman, *Hellenism in Jewish Palestine,* 83–99; A. Rosenthal, "Le-masoret girsat ha-Mishnah." On the transmission of the Yerushalmi see Moscovitz, "Sugyot muḥlafot"; Moscovitz, "Sugyot maḳbilot"; Moscovitz, "The Formation and Character." On the transmission of the Bavli see Y.N.H. Epstein, *Mevoʾot le-sifrut ha-ʾamoraʾim,* 140–141; E. Rosenthal, "Toldot ha-nosaḥ"; R. Brody, "Sifrut ha-geʾonim"; Friedman, "Le-hithayyut shinnuyei ha-girsaʾot"; Kalmin, "The Formation and Character." Goldberg, "Der verschriftete Sprechakt," proposed to read the whole of rabbinic literature as a weaving of speech-acts (see also Goldberg, "Entwurf," 3–5).

On midrash as a montage of scriptural quotes see Neusner and Green, *Writing with Scripture*. On rabbinic citations see also Ebach, "Das Zitat als Kommunikationsform."

41. The extensive problems related to the manner of transmission and composition of the early rabbinic corpus have significant consequences for our understanding of the treatment of citations in tannaitic works. The question of the role of orality in the transmission of the texts is particularly difficult. A concise summary of the debate on whether and when the Mishnah was written down may be found in E. Alexander, "The Orality of Rabbinic Writing," 50–51. Among the many theories proposed, it is worth mentioning the one advocated by Sussman, "'Torah she-be-ʿal peh,'" 228–238, according to which the Mishnah was composed orally and only written down over the period between the fifth and the eighth centuries.

42. Early Christian writers inherited their citation techniques from Greco-Roman literature (Greek verbs that designate citing include ἀνακαλεῖν, ἐπάγεσθαι, εἰσφέρειν, and παρατίθεσται). Non-Christian Latin and Greek writers did not make use of citation formulas, relying instead on dynamic semiotic processes to announce that a quote was coming, and without always reproducing their sources verbatim: see Behrendt, "Die Markierung von Zitaten." For an example of the integration of pagan citations in a Christian writing see Gosserez, "Citations païennes." Irenaeus in his anti-Gnostic polemic referenced the writings of several Christian authors. Pseudo-Hippolytus in his *Refutation* was the first to refer to the authority of earlier ecclesiastical writers, such as Irenaeus, with apparent doctrinal intent. The anonymous treatise *Against Artemon* appeals to the authority of various Christian authors to prove the divinity of Christ. See Longosz, "Argument patrystyczny," 197 (I wish to thank Susan Cook Summer for her translation of this article from Polish); Hadot, "Patristique," 4.

43. On the phenomenon of allusion (as opposed to citation) in late ancient poetry see Pelttari, *The Space That Remains*, 126–160. Christians are credited with the invention of grouped citations, of which Eusebius's *Church History*, the *Apophthegmata patrum*, and the genre of the cento constitute examples: see Gain, "Citations isolées." See also Vianès, "Des ossements dispersés"; Bureau, "Texte composé, texte composite."

44. Vessey, "The Forging of Orthodoxy," 500. Vessey's definition does not include the intention behind the act, which I am supplying.

45. See Simonetti, "La tradizione"; Hanson, *The Search*, 872; Longosz, "La tradizione" (a summary of Longosz, *De auctoritate traditionis*).

46. Person, *The Mode of Theological Decision Making*, 220.

47. On the development of the patristic argument see P.T.R. Gray, "'The Select Fathers'"; Dolbeau, "La formation du Canon des Pères"; Rothschild, "Au fondement de la notion de «Pères»"; Meunier, "L'autorité des «Pères»."

48. See Clement of Alexandria, *Stromateis* 1.1.3; Alexander of Jerusalem, *Epistula ad Origenem*, apud Eusebius of Caesarea, *Historia ecclesiastica* 6.14.9; Dionysius of Alexandria, *Epistula III ad Philemonem presbyterum Romanum*, apud Eusebius of Caesarea, *Historia ecclesiastica* 7.7.5. For a pessimistic view about the historical use of the pre-

fourth-century dossier on the patristic argument see de Halleux, "Pourquoi les Églises ont-elles besoin," 512.

49. See Meunier, "Genèse de la notion de «Pères de l'Église»," 318–321. Meunier explains that it was not until the Council of Ephesus of 431 CE that members of a council would apply the phrase "the Fathers" to themselves (323).

50. Greek adjectives in this period could be treated as functional replacements for the genitive of the noun on which they were based. Thus, οἱ ἐκκλησιαστικοί πατέρες (literally "the ecclesiastical Fathers") was equivalent to οἱ πατέρες τῆς ἐκκλησίας ("the Fathers of the Church").

51. Morlet, "Aux origines de l'argument patristique?"

52. Eusebius of Caesarea, *De ecclesiastica theologia* 1.14. On the role of references to the Fathers in Eusebius's polemic against Marcellus see Morlet, "Aux origines de l'argument patristique?"; Graumann, *Die Kirche der Väter*, 23–71.

53. See Graumann, "The Conduct of Theology," 540.

54. See the discussion of Paulinus of Tyre and Athanasius of Anazarbus in Graumann, *Die Kirche der Väter*, 88–92.

55. Basil of Caesarea, *De spiritu sancto* 72–74; see Graumann, *Die Kirche der Väter*, 200–231; Graumann, "The Conduct of Theology," 550; Price, "Conciliar Theology," 2. As noted by Graumann, here Basil's claim to tradition is generic and tied not only to his mention of past authorities but also to an invocation of liturgical custom.

56. See Graumann, "The Conduct of Theology," 549–550.

57. The citation of an auctoritas (with whichever function) was hardly a Christian invention in Greco-Roman literature: see Calame, "Modes de la citation," which identifies the auctoritas as part of a quadripartite typology of citation (alongside *excerptum*, *mutatio*, and *traditio*) in a work, the *Theognidea*, composed as early as the sixth century BCE. The late ancient Christian development of lists of auctoritates was fully integrated in a trans-confessional trend wherein the summarization and convenient presentation of knowledge in the form of collections, doxographies, and epitomes was privileged: see Hadot, "Patristique," 7; Graumann, *Die Kirche der Väter*, 5–6 and nn. 7, 8, and 9.

58. See Rebillard, "A New Style of Argument." Previous examinations of Augustine's development of the patristic argument include Maschio, "L'argomentazione patristica."

59. Vincent of Lérins, *Commonitorium* 3.4(8); ed. Demeulenaere, 150; trans. adapted from *NPNF2* XI, 132–133. This was in line with Vincent's famous understanding of what is "truly and properly Catholic" (*vere propieque catholicum*) as "that which was believed everywhere, always, by all" (*quod ubique, quod semper, quod ab omnibus creditum est*): see Vincent of Lérins, *Commonitorium* 2.5(6); ed. Demeulenaere, 149. On the ideological novelty embodied by Vincent's *Commonitorium* see Sieben, *Die Konzilsidee der Alten Kirche*, 149–170; Vessey, "La pastristique," 443–444.

60. See Amann, "Pères de l'Église," 1194. The notion of "ecclesiastical writer" is first found in Jerome of Stridon, *De viris illustribus*, Prologue; Jerome of Stridon, *Epistula CXII Ad Augustinum* 3.

61. Vincent of Lérins, *Commonitorium* 17–18.

62. Pseudo-Gelasius of Cyzicus, *De libris recipiendis et non recipiendis.*

63. Bishop Possessor, *Epistula ad Hormisdam* (*Collectio Avellana* 230); ed. PL 63, 489; ed. Günther, 695–696. Hormisdas, *Epistula LXX ad Possessorem Episcopum* (*Collectio Avellana* 231); ed. PL 63, 490–493; ed. Günther, 696–700. See Gennaro and Glorie, *Scriptores Illyrici minores*, xxxvi; Chadwick, *The Church in Ancient Society*, 652.

64. See Mansi, *Sacrorum conciliorum nova et amplissima collectio*, IV, 1183–1196. The florilegium included quotes by Peter of Alexandria, Athanasius, Julius of Rome (in reality an Apollinarist forgery: see Amann, "Pères de l'Église," 1193), Felix of Rome (also an Apollinarist forgery: see ibid.), Theophilus of Alexandria, Cyprian, Ambrose, Gregory of Nazianzus, Basil of Caesarea, Gregory of Nyssa, and, in a different document (Doc. 75 of the *Athenian Collection*), Atticus of Constantinople and Amphilochius of Iconium. On the patristic argument at Ephesus see Meunier, "Genèse de la notion," 324–326; Graumann, *Die Kirche der Väter*, 255–419. On the patristic argument in Cyril of Alexandria see Madoz, "El Concilio de Éfeso"; du Manoir de Juaye, *Dogme et spiritualité*, 454–490; Nacke, *Das Zeugnis der Väter*. See also the "triangulation" of references to the Fathers, Scripture, and councils discussed in relation to the Council of Ephesus in Graumann, "Authority and Doctrinal Normation," 21 and passim. On the development of the patristic argument see also Price, "Conciliar Theology."

65. On the use of the patristic argument from the sixth century on see Lang, "Patristic Argument" (on the sixth century); O'Connell, "The «Patristic Argument»" (on the ninth century).

66. See Naiweld, *Les antiphilosophes*, 148–156.

67. While the Christian project of conversion of the self to God required that the truth about each of the two poles in the relationship—the divine and the human—be known, reflection on those aspects was of no major significance to the rabbinic movement. Late ancient rabbinic Judaism was keen on regulating human activities and ensuring the correct conduct of human subjects not primarily by converting or even curbing the subject's drives but by multiplying limitations on their expression. The sensual and fundamentally amoral nature of the individual, represented by the *yetser ha-ra*ʿ (evil inclination), was left unreformed. The manifestations of that amorality were instead limited thanks to a robust legal structure preventing it from unraveling in the world of praxis. See Maghen, "The Baffling Coexistence"; Novick, "Etiquette and Exemplarity in Judaism"; Rosen-Zvi, *Demonic Desires*, passim. The rabbinic law did not require individuals to discover their inherent, divinely bestowed rationality in order to act virtuously; instead, it demanded that they appropriate and interiorize a law with which they were constitutively in conflict. No harmony between the human subject

and the law was conceivable, but only an ever-precarious conformation of the former to the latter. Whatever the eudaemonistic benefits that observance of the law could grant, those were never presented as a rationale for obedience. In fact, possibly in reaction to Hellenistic philosophies and to the development of Christian asceticism, late ancient rabbis purposefully radicalized a positive, exterior, authoritarian image of the divine law: see Naiweld, *Les antiphilosophes* (and Naiweld, "Au commencement"). For another reading of the relationship between rabbinic law and the self see Hoffmann Libson, *Law and Self-Knowledge.*

68. On rabbinic conceptions of the law see Hayes, *What's Divine about Divine Law?*, 166–370.

69. Elon, *Jewish Law*, I, 200–201.

70. On rabbinic understandings of Scripture's act of communication see Arnold Goldberg, "Rede und Offenbarung."

71. The literary features of the Hebrew Bible itself might not be without responsibility in eliciting this manner of reading from the rabbis. See Eric Auerbach's well-known essay "Odysseus' Scar" (in Auerbach, *Mimesis*, 3–23).

72. See Samely, *Forms*, 108. In the Bavli this exegetical effort is extended to the Mishnah, whose status during the amoraic period became such that scriptural modes of exegesis (although not of all of Rabbi Ishmael's rules) could be applied to it: see Avinoam Cohen, "Biḳoret hilkhatit," 334; Henshke, "Abaye ṿe-Rava," 193; Elman, "Progressive *Derash*," 231–232.

73. E. Alexander, "The Orality of Rabbinic Literature," 42 (italics in the original).

74. See Goldberg, "The Rabbinic View," 155–156. Jewish sages inherited *midrash* (interpretation) from the second-century founders of their movement. Midrash was a discursive strategy aimed at elevating the Torah to a cosmological, epistemological, and ontological principle (see Naiweld, "The Discursive Machine," 415). The hermeneutics of the rabbis did not deal with the empirical reality mirrored by the Torah, but rather constituted its linguistic universe into their empirical world: see Goldberg, "The Rabbinic View," 154; Levy, "Rabbinic Philosophy of Language," 194–195; Naiweld, "La littérature rabbinique classique"; Boyarin, "Midrash and the 'Magic Language.'" Lacking an interest in the world reflected in Scripture, the rabbis read the Torah within the horizon of their present, without assigning to the time elapsed since the matan Torah any hermeneutical, let alone text-critical, value: see Samely, "Text and Time," 146. On the relationship between rabbinic discussion, memory, and retrieval of truth see Brodsky, "The Democratic Principle."

75. Compagnon, *La seconde main*, 158. This definition is applied by Compagnon to what he calls "theologal" (rather than "theological") discourse, defined as "the discourse of the discourse of God" (172).

76. Marius Victorinus, *Adversus Arium* 2.7; ed. Hadot and Henry, I, 414; trans. Clark, 208. See Henry, "The 'Adversus Arium' of Marius Victorinus," 51; Hadot, "*De lectis non lecta componere.*"

77. For a philosophical conceptualization of the role of temporality in the Talmud see Dolgopolski, *The Open Past.* On rabbinic time more broadly see Kaye, *Time in the Babylonian Talmud*; Gribetz, *Time and Difference.*

78. Morawski, "The Basic Functions of Quotation," 692–693.

79. Against an understanding of late ancient Christian theology as iterative see Brox, "Zur Berufung auf 'Väter,'" 285.

80. Incidentally, this assessment of Christian theology is compatible with at least some contemporary Christian understandings; see, e.g., the definition of Trinitarian doctrine as "superstructure" built "in order to safeguard [. . .] truth" in Hanson, "The Transformation of Images," 278.

81. See Naiweld, "Qu'est-ce qu'une culture sans foi?"

82. Berzon, *Classifying Christians,* 340. On heresy as a category constitutive of the identity of the Jesus movement see Lettieri, "L'eresia originaria e le sue alterazioni. I"; Lettieri, "L'eresia originaria e le sue alterazioni. II."

83. On the logical and chronological succession of heresy and orthodoxy see Boyarin, *Border Lines,* 3.

84. The exception is constituted by the instances in which the *rishonim* (eleventh-through- fifteenth-century rabbis and *poseḳim,* or legal decisors) showed awareness of the savoraic or geonic origin of parts of the Bavli: see Spiegel, "Leshonot perush."

85. Kaplan, *The Redaction*; Weiss, *Ha-Talmud ha-Bavli.* C. Albeck, "Le-ʿarikhat ha-Talmud ha-Bavli"; C. Albeck, *Mavo la-Talmudim,* 579–596, expressed similar ideas, but with different arguments. For a fuller history of studies see Neusner, *The Formation*; Tenenblatt, *Ha-Talmud ha-Bavli*; Kalmin, *The Redaction.*

86. See D.W. Halivni, *Meḳorot u-msorot: Beʾurim ba-Talmud. Massekhet Yoma-Ḥagiga*; D.W. Halivni, *Meḳorot u-msorot: Beʾurim ba-Talmud. Massekhet ʿEruvin-Pesaḥim*; D.W. Halivni, *Midrash, Mishnah, and Gemara,* 76–104; D.W. Halivni, *Meḳorot u-msorot: Beʾurim ba-Talmud. Massekhet Shabat*; D.W. Halivni, *Meḳorot u-msorot: Beʾurim ba-Talmud. Massekhet Bava ḳamma*; D.W. Halivni, *Meḳorot u-msorot: Beʾurim ba-Talmud. Massekhet Bava metsiʿa*; D.W. Halivni, *Meḳorot u-msorot: Beʾurim ba-Talmud. Massekhet Bava batra*; the abridged translation of the latter item in D.W. Halivni, "Aspects of the Formation"; and its full, annotated translation in D.W. Halivni, *The Formation.* See also Rubenstein, "Translator's Introduction"; Rubenstein, "Criteria," 417, n. 1. Halivni originally proposed that the redaction by the stammaʾim happened mainly between Rav Ashi's demise and the end of the fifth century. After moving the terminus ad quem of stammaitic activities to the middle of the sixth century, he later envisioned a continued stammaitic redaction between the middle of the sixth and the middle of the eighth century. For a different hypothesis see the three-source theory set forth by Hauptman in *Development* and "Sheloshet ha-markivim."

87. Friedman, "Pereḳ ha-ʾishah rabah," 278–321. See in particular the methodology (301–308) that would allow one to separate the stam from the amoraic layer (anticipated by Klein in "Gemara and Sebara" and "Gemara Quotations in Sebara"). Friedman ap-

plied his critical program to one chapter of the Bavli in his work *Talmud ʿarukh*. See also Friedman, "Uncovering Literary Dependencies," 36–39.

88. For Vidas the "masters of the Talmud" responsible for these operations were in competition with the tannaʾim (repeaters). These tannaʾim were not the homonymous protagonists of the Mishnah or the Tosefta, but those sages, living in the amoraic period, who focused on recitation and faithful transmission of meimrot. Several Talmudic sugyot speak negatively of this group.

89. According to Goldberg, "Zitat und Citem," 96, the introductory formulas are a part of a "citeme" (*Citem*), the smallest textual unit that can be recognized as a citation and is capable of being understood by itself, without the need for any co-text (defined, in contradistinction from context, as the textual framework of the literary unit). Goldberg (ibid.) distinguished the citeme from the citation (*Zitat*). The former is to be understood as a literary form, the latter as the "expression of a known or unknown historical person or group of people ('the Rabbis')."

90. Some formulas (such as *she-neʾemar, talmud lomar*, or *di-khtiv*) are used specifically for scriptural quotations. Examples of formulas for tannaitic quotations include *tanu rabanan, tanya, tanya nami hakhi, tenan hatam, de-tanya, tenan, ta shmaʿ, amar mar, ḳa-tanaʾei* (for objections: *itteiveh, ṿe-ha-tanya, ṿe-ha-tenan*); for amoraic halakhah: *itemar*. Other formulas introduce statements made at the level of the stam (e.g., *u-rminhu, tiyuvta, bi-shlama, teiḳu*), while yet others have a meta-discursive function, indicating the type of argument that is being produced (e.g., *gufa, ḳushya, teiruts*). These formulas could evolve over time: see Friedman, "Uncovering Literary Dependencies," 39.

91. See Samely, *Forms*, 100–102. Samely sees this historicization as empty or merely formal, since the Talmud rarely invites the reader to relativize in light of the intellectual disposition or the biography of a particular rabbi.

92. See Samely, ibid., 105. On the semiotic status of abridged citations see also Goldberg, "Zitat und Citem," 98.

93. See Samely, *Forms*, 102. Samely hypothesizes that historically speaking this process might have occurred prior to the moment of compilation of the Talmud, at a stage in which the statements of different sages might have been rephrased in a particular stylistic mold—such as the argumentative form—in order to be recorded.

94. While a citation is only possible insofar as part of its original context is carried along by the cited material, the cited statement needs to lose its context to rise to absolute validity. Even if purely formal, this excerption of some context, while granting intelligibility to the citation, also exposes it to the doubt that its contents were only valid in the context of the utterance to which they originally belonged.

95. Amoraic citation formulas include *amar X amar Y* (X said, Y said), *amar X mishum Y* (X said in the name of Y), *amar X mishmei de-Y* (with the same meaning as the preceding example), and *hakhi amar X* (thus said X). Combinations of these formulas are also found, such as *amar X amar Y amar Z* (X said, Y said, Z said), *X amar, hakhi*

amar Y (X said, thus said Y), *X amar, hakhi amar Y amar Z* (X said, thus said Y, Z said), or *hakhi amar X mishum Y* (thus said X in the name of Y). Generally speaking, the first three generations of amora'im (ca. 230–320) used the formula *amar X amar Y* (X said, Y said), whereas the fourth and fifth generations (fourth century) tended to use the formula *amar X mishum/mishmei de-Y* (X said in the name of Y): see Kalmin, *Sages, Stories, Authors, and Editors,* 127–140. In the formula *amar X amar Y* scholars have typically seen a hierarchical relationship (most often of master and disciple), with the quoting rabbi being subject to the authority of the quoted. A direct chain of transmission is also commonly assumed: see B. Cohen, "Citation Formulae," 25.

96. See D.W. Halivni, *Midrash, Mishnah, and Gemara,* 98–99, claiming that all technical terminology derives from the savoraic layer (the same position previously held by Klein, "Gemara and Sebara," 85–90). See also Weiss, *Le-ḥeḳer ha-Talmud,* 64–70.

97. See Kalmin, "Quotation Forms"; Kalmin, *Sages, Stories, Authors, and Editors,* 127–140; B. Cohen, "Citation Formulae." On amoraic attributions see Kraemer, *The Mind of the Talmud,* 20–26.

98. See Kalmin, *Sages, Stories, Authors, and Editors,* 139.

99. On these questions see Green, "What's in a Name?"; Kraemer, "On the Reliability"; Kraemer, *The Mind of the Talmud,* 20–25; L. Jacobs, "How Much"; Elman, *Authority and Tradition,* 22–23.

100. See Bacher, *Tradition und Tradenten,* 524–533; C. Albeck, *Mavo la-Talmudim,* 523–556; D.W. Halivni, "Safḳei de-gavrei"; S. Stern, "Attribution and Authorship," 47 (see 33–38 for the distinction between conjectural and pseudepigraphic attribution).

101. See Kraemer, *The Mind of the Talmud,* 87–90; S. Stern, "Attribution and Authorship," 41–42; Hayes, *Between the Babylonian and Palestinian Talmuds,* 14–15; Rovner, "Pseudepigraphic Invention," 11–19.

102. Vidas, *The Rise of Talmud.*

103. Ibid.

104. S. Stern, "The Concept of Authorship," 183. According to Stern "the Bavli's decision to adopt, almost deliberately, an ambivalent, self-contradictory view of authorship must be related to the context of a specific ideology, which holds the difficult balance between the authority of a monolithic Torah from Sinai on the one hand, and that of individual rabbinic teachers on the other" (189).

105. S. Stern, "The Concept of Authorship," 187.

106. In the words used by Katzoff, "Nine at Once," 40, n. 3, to summarize Yaakov Nahum Epstein's position, Epstein distinguished between three types of variations: "variations between manuscripts of a particular fixed-text work, presumably caused by errors in transmission oral, or written"; "variations in a single tradition as presented in separate works, presumably the result of deliberate changes [or] reworking of content"; and "variations between manuscripts of a single work whose text was not yet fixed, changes peculiar to oral transmission of works."

107. E. Rosenthal, "Toldot ha-nosaḥ"; Friedman, "Le-hithayyut shinnuyei ha-girsaʾot," 67–77; Friedman, "Keitsad medaḳdeḳin?"; Friedman, "Uncovering Literary Dependencies."

108. Friedman, "Pereḳ ha-ʾishah rabah," 309.

109. Ibid., 309 (trans. from Gafni, "The Modern Study of Rabbinics," 50).

110. I am grateful to Erez DeGolan for pointing me to this passage and to its significance.

111. *B.* Ḳiddushin 41a: האיש מקדש בו ובשלוחו האשה מתקדשת בה ובשלוחה האיש מקדש את בתו כשהיא נערה בו ובשלוחו גמ׳ השתא בשלוחו מקדש בו מיבעיא אמר רב יוסף מצוה בו יותר מבשלוחו כי הא דרב ספרא מחריך רישא רבא מלח שיבוטא איכא דאמרי בהא איסורא נמי אית בה כדרב יהודה אמר רב דאמר רב יהודה אמר רב אסור לאדם שיקדש את האשה עד שיראנה שמא יראה בה דבר מגונה ותתגנה עליו ורחמנא אמר ואהבת לרעך כמוך וכי איתמר דרב יוסף אסיפא איתמר האשה מתקדשת בה ובשלוחה השתא בשלוחה מיקדשא בה מיבעיא אמר רב יוסף מצוה בה יותר מבשלוחה כי הא דרב ספרא מחריך רישא רבא מלח שיבוטא אבל בהא איסורא לית בה כדר״ל דאמר ר״ל טב למיתב טן דו מלמיתב ארמלו.

112. This is the translation of the saying טב למיתב טן דו מלמיתב ארמלו provided by Sokoloff, *A Dictionary*, 508. The expression appears also in *b.* Yevamot 118b; *b.* Ketubot 75a; *b.* Ḳiddushin 7a; *b.* Bava ḳamma 111a. Jastrow, *Dictionary*, 540–541, translates instead טן דו as "in grief." Kiel, "Cognizance of Sin," 327, n. 22, considers it a "Middle Persian-Aramaic amalgamated expression" and explains, citing Shai Secunda, that טן דו "is a Persian loanword that connotes 'togetherness' or 'in matrimony,' but literally means 'two bodies'" (for further references see Sokoloff, *A Dictionary*, 508). On this phrase see also Ahdut, *Maʿamad ha-ʾishah*, 220, n. 102; Schremer, *Zakhar u-nḳevah*, 258, n. 100.

113. It is common for both the Bavli and the Yerushalmi to identify *yitturei lashon* (linguistic pleonasms) in the text of the Mishnah. See Elman, "Progressive *Derash*," 230–231.

114. Since Rav Safra and Rava are later than Rav Yosef by one generation, it is extremely likely that the latter's statement did not historically include a mention of the two sages. It still cannot be excluded that the editor, in disregard of this fact, intended to attribute the report of the anecdote about the two rabbis to Rav Yosef.

115. In the Bavli the expression *ika de-ʾamre* (there are some who say)—to which are germane *ve-ʾamre lah* (and [some] say it) and *ika de-matne lah* ("there are some who teach it")—normally introduces either a divergent opinion relative to, or a different version of, one that has just been produced (see Weiss, *Le-ḥeḳer ha-Talmud*, 221–260). Brodsky, "From Disagreement to Talmudic Discourse," 176, n. 8, points out a parallel with the Middle Persian technical term "ast kē ēdon gowēd." According to Klein, "Gemara and Sebara," 82, "[I]n all cases where the Talmud records alternative versions these are to be regarded as different expansions of the same, or very nearly the same, underlying text." Moreover, "[T]wo versions introduced by a form of אמר will usually be built round the same original text. With תני there will be either slight textual difference or the whole passage will be given a different context. It is important to observe

that all textual differences must be slight, even though the halakhic consequences of the difference may be considerable (ibid., 82–83, n. 44)." Friedman, *Le-Toratam shel tanna'im*, 197, writes: "Nowadays research shows that the concept 'there are some who say' presents two sources of unequal value. One of the two is identified as original, whereas the other appears reworked." The phrase in our sugyah, then, is not simply used to bring in as relevant to the discussion an opinion originally uttered with no connection to the sugyah's own topic. To the contrary, the "some who say" expressed their opinion about the very issue under debate here. Two interpretations are possible for the use of the expression in our context: (*a*) The "some who say" claim that Rav Yosef argued for the undesirability of betrothal by proxy based not on the first but on the second clause of the mishnah: the object of the correction is then the report about Rav Yosef's words (later instantiated in the formula "And when [the statement] of Rav Yosef was said, it was said with regard to the last clause [of the mishnah]"). (*b*) The "some who say" provide not a correction of the report about Rav Yosef's statement but an answer to the gemara's question ("[W]as it necessary [to also teach] 'by himself'?") alternative to Rav Yosef's, and they argue that it is possible to derive from the expression "by himself" not only a preference for in-person betrothal but indeed a prohibition of betrothal by proxy. Within the framework of this second possibility, it seems impossible to decide whether (*b1*) the editor intended to present everything that follows the words "There are some who say" (up to and including the saying reported by Reish Lakish) as constituting those people's affirmation; or (*b2*) the words attributed to "some who say" end at the citation from Leviticus and contain only the mention of the prohibition along with the citation of Rav's meimra from which it was derived. By this reading, the "some who say" would be opining that betrothal by proxy is not just less preferable than in-person betrothal but a priori prohibited. Outside the citation of their opinion (whether presented as direct or indirect), the gemara would then be stating in the voice of the stam that that opinion is still capable of being reconciled with Rav Yosef's conviction about the mere preferability of in-person betrothal, as he learned the latter not from the first clause of the mishnah but from the second. In spite of appearances, no insight into which of these two interpretations (*b1* or *b2*) is preferable can be derived from the fact that the sugyah is built through a clear parallelism between two sections (separated by the sentence "And when what [was said by] Rav Yosef was said, it was said about the latter part [of the Mishnah]"). The parallelism relies on a tripartite structure: [(1) to האיש מקדש בו ובשלוחו האשה מתקדשת בה ובשלוחה האיש מקדש את בתו
כשהיא נערה בו ובשלוחו there corresponds האשה מתקדשת בה ובשלוחה (both citations from the mishnah); (2) to השתא בשלוחו מקדש בו מיבעיא אמר רב יוסף מצוה בו יותר מבשלוחו כי הא דרב ספרא
השתא בשלוחה מיקדשא בה מיבעיא אמר רב יוסף there corresponds מחריך רישא רבא מלח שיבוטא
מצוה בה יותר מבשלוחה כי הא דרב ספרא מחריך רישא רבא מלח שיבוטא (both answers by Rav Yosef to the gemara's question about the cited bit of the Mishnah, followed by a citation of the habits of Raf Savra and Rava); (3) to איכא דאמרי בהא איסורא נמי אית בה כדרב יהודה אמר רב

דאמר רב יהודה אמר רב אסור לאדם שיקדש את האשה עד שיראנה שמא יראה בה דבר מגונה ותתגנה עליו אבל בהא איסורא לית בה כדר"ל דאמר ר"ל טב למיתב there corresponds ורחמנא אמר ואהבת לרעך כמוך טן דו מלמיתב ארמלו (both statements regarding the presence or absence of a prohibition followed by an amoraic source). As mentioned, this structure is reconcilable with both possible presentational intentions (*b1* and *b2*). For a significantly different reading of the contents of this sugyah see Weiss, *Le-ḥeḳer ha-Talmud*, 289–291. See also S. Albeck, *Yesodot*, 211.

116. Toward the end of the sugyah, we learn that the woman does not stand at risk of failing to observe this precept because women tend to prefer staying betrothed to a man they dislike rather than remaining alone. Since a woman cannot issue a geṭ (even though a rabbinical court can force a man to issue a geṭ to a woman at her request), the fact that the precept of caring for one's neighbor's interest as for one's own is presented as in principle applicable to the woman seems to indicate that the concern Leviticus 19:18 is understood to express by the "some who say" mentioned in the gemara is specifically the safeguarding of the loving bond of the married couple (which makes the geṭ undesirable) rather than the mere avoidance of the woman's humiliation (whose perpetration might be construed in theory as a failure to care for the interest of one's neighbor). This is curious, since Leviticus 19:18 is never invoked in the Bavli as the basis for the institution of marriage (see B. Epstein, *Ḥamishah ḥumshei Torah*, ad loc.).

117. The distinction between the reisha and the seifa of the mishnah is commonly used in the gemara to discuss the exact referent of both tannaitic and amoraic statements: see, e.g., *b.* Beraḥot 18a; *b.* Shabat 146b; *b.* Shabat 150b; *b.* Ketubot 12a; *b.* Ketubot 72b; *b.* Giṭṭin 86a; *b.* Ḳiddushin 46a; *b.* Ḳiddushin 65a; *b.* Bava ḳamma 75b; *b.* Bava metsiʿa 30a; *b.* Bava batra 87b; *b.* Zevaḥim 11b; *b.* Bekhorot 13b; *b.* Niddah 68a.

118. Later commentators explain that the precept the gemara mentions in relation to the woman is one she is mandated to fulfill only if she is going to have intercourse with a man. See Horowitz, *Sefer ha-miknah*, 86.

119. It should be noted that while in principle the gemara could have been read as saying that the legal opinion about the impermissibility of the betrothal by agent for a man, introduced by the "some who say," is merely congruent with—rather than derived from—Rav's statement, the fact that the permissibility of using an agent for the woman is explained through her unlikelihood to reject a man after having been betrothed to him indicates that this would be a misreading. The statement by Reish Lakish is cited here from *b.* Yevamot 118b: see Aminoah, *ʿArikhat massekhet Ḳiddushin*, 138–139 and n. 6.

120. It can be presumed that according to this new rendition of Rav Yosef's statement the phrase "by himself" could not be omitted by the mishnah from the first clause, since that omission would have resulted in lack of uniformity, compelling a misleading contrastive interpretation of the omission of the self's mention for the man and its mention for the woman. It is immaterial whether the disfavor of the use of an

agent derived from the second clause of the mishnah is considered limited to the case of the woman (whereas the man's use of an agent would fall under the prohibition derived from Rav's words) or is seen as extending also to the case of the man but is overridden there by the prohibition derived from Rav's words.

121. The expression *ki/i* [. . .] *itemar aseifa/areisha itemar* ("when/if [. . .] was said, it was said with regard to the first/last clause [of the mishnah]") in the Bavli may be compared with the phrase *emor de-vatra/sofa*, used in the Yerushalmi, on which see Moscovitz, *Ha-ṭerminologyah*, 74–76. Given the way in which the gemara proceeds, the phenomenon whereby the reference of a meimra is switched from the seifa to the reisha, rather than the other way around, is rarer; such uncommon cases are marked with an asterisk in the following notes.

122. E.g., *b.* Beitsah 13b; *b.* Bava batra 24b; *b.* Bava batra 88b (with the inconsequential elision of the first two words of the scriptural citation reported in the meimra); *b.* Niddah 55a. *B.* Menaḥot 70b is a particular case because the formula is seemingly applied to a discussion and not to a meimra.

123. E.g., *b.* Sukah 35b; *b.* Ketubot 15b*; *b.* Ketubot 18b*; *b.* Yevamot 104b; *b.* Bava ḳamma 56a; *b.* Me῾ilah 13b. The occurrences in *b.* Bava ḳamma 114a and *b.* Niddah 11b have a more ambiguous status. In both cases, it is unclear how far the statements attributed to the amora (Rav Ashi in the former, Rav Yehudah citing Shemuel in the latter) are meant to extend. If they are understood as being limited to the words לא שנו אלא לסטים עובד כוכבים and לא שנו אלא לטהרות respectively, then the reformulations found in the two sugyot (into לא שנו אלא עכו"ם and לא שנו אלא באשה עסוקה בטהרות) are unnecessary for the purpose of the statement's application to the seifa. To the contrary, if the quotations of Rav Ashi's and Shemuel's statements are understood as extending past those few words, the reformulations found in the gemara are to be seen as logically necessary. It should also be said that while sometimes in the Bavli the repetition of a citation introduced by the formula *ki/i itemar* [. . .] *aseifa/areisha itemar* contains a logically unnecessary reformulation, suggesting a generally casual attitude toward the verbatim reporting of meimrot (see, e.g., *b.* Yoma 85a* and possibly also *b.* Bava ḳamma 114a and *b.* Niddah 11b), this does not detract from the noteworthiness of cases in which alterations take place that are functional to the stamma's agenda.

124. This use of the formula, in which the report of the meimra is corrected, is close in its effects to the gemara's deployment of the distinct formula *i itemar hakhi itemar* ("if it was said, it was said thus": e.g., *b.* Sukah 33b; *b.* Sotah 9a), sometimes used to salvage an amora's statement, through the fiction of an emendation, from an otherwise irrefutable objection raised against it. On *i itemar hakhi itemar* see C. Albeck, *Mavo la-Talmudim*, 662–664.

125. It should be noted that the issue of the quantity of meimrot of Rav Yosef on this subject inherited by the editor of the sugyah is distinct both from the question concerning how many were ever recorded and from the inquiry into the number of statements, if any, Rav Yosef historically made about the subject.

126. Aminoah, *'Arikhat massekhet Ḳiddushin,* 137–139, believes this source to have been produced at the academy of Pumbedita. In Aminoah's reconstruction the Pumbeditan source contained two statements by Rav Yehudah citing Rav (one according to which a man cannot betroth a woman before seeing her and another, appearing later, with which we are not concerned here) and of two statements by Rav Yosef (one according to which the mitsyah is more appropriately performed by the man than by his agent and another according to which it is more appropriately performed by the woman than by her agent).

127. It is very unlikely that Rav Yosef's original statement skipped over the first clause of the mishnah and was pinned on the second clause.

128. Aminoah, *'Arikhat massekhet Ḳiddushin,* 138, proposes that the editor was working in Mahoza, as he selected the Mahozite rabbis Rav Safra and Rava from a longer series of amora'im of various origins. See also the additional reasoning for the Mahozite origin of the sugyah provided ibid., 138–139. The second occurrence of the anecdote in ms. Munich 95 and both occurrences in ms. Oxford Oppenheim 248 (367) identify the rabbi who scorched the head of an animal as Rav Yosef. The second occurrence in some manuscripts may identify him as Rav Ḥisda. Both Rav Yosef and Rav Ḥisda appear in the string of examples given in *b.* Shabat 119a.

129. See Tosafot, ad loc.

130. On betrothal as conducive to the fulfillment of the precept of periyah u-rviyah see Asher ben Jehiel on *b.* Ketubot 1.12. Maimonides, *Hilkhot ishut* 1.2, seems to consider betrothal a precept from the Torah in and of itself.

131. On the use of literary artifice in the organization of the sugyot see L. Jacobs, "Evidence"; L. Jacobs, Review of Weiss, *Le-ḥeḳer ha-Talmud*; L. Jacobs, "Further Evidence."

132. Although much more work would be required to corroborate this hypothesis, the contrived nature of this sugyah and its hinging on a reformulation involving the alteration of the grammatical gender in a citation might not be without relation to its position at the opening of the second chapter of the tractate. The initial sugyot of the first chapter of Bavli tractates are famously highly orchestrated, and they often foreground linguistic or grammatical issues (on this focus see Elman, "The World of the 'Sabboraim,'" 383–385). Weiss, *Ha-yetsirah shel ha-savora'im,* 10, argued that these sugyot are almost all of savoraic origin, an origin to which Sherira bar Hanina in his famous *Letter* (ed. Lewin) in the tenth century had already traced the first sugyah of *Ḳiddushin*: see Y.N.H. Epstein, *Mevo'ot le-sifrut ha-'amora'im,* 610–615; Avinoam Cohen, "Le-'ofiyah shel ha-halakhah" (and on Sherira's *Letter* see R. Brody, *The Geonim of Babylonia,* 20–25; R. Brody, "Epistle of Sherira Gaon"). For studies of initial sugyot of Bavli tractates see, e.g., L. Jacobs, "Further Evidence"; Fuchs, "'Arikhatah u-mgamatah shel sugyiat ha-petiḥah"; Rubenstein, *Talmudic Stories,* 212–242; Avinoam Cohen, "Beginning Gittin/Mapping Exile"; Vidas, *Tradition,* 23–44; Wasserman, *Jews, Gentiles, and Other Animals,* 36–73; Fonrobert, "The Place of Shabbat." For studies of initial sugyot

of chapters other than the first in a Bavli tractate see Friedman, "Pereḳ ha-ʾishah rabah"; Shustri, "Me-ʾagadah le-halakhah." On the peculiarities of Bavli tractates' first chapters see also L. Jacobs, "Further Evidence," 68, n. 1.

133. On this formula see Y.N.H. Epstein, *Mavo le-nosaḥ ha-Mishnah*, I, 595–673; Bigman, "Ḥissorei meḥassera"; Segelman, "Ḥissorei meḥassera"; Sofer, "Ḥissorei—mi ḥasserah?"

134. Weidner, "Reading Gerschom Scholem," 230.

135. This is consonant with Goldberg's remark that although the text of the Bavli contains many voices, it ultimately does not say anything that those he calls its "producers" (*Hersteller*) do not want it to say: see Goldberg, "Die Zerstörung," 207. A similar idea is expressed in Boyarin, *Socrates and the Fat Rabbis*. For Boyarin, however, the function of Goldberg's *Hersteller* is performed by the *stamma* (anonymous editor) of the sugyah, whose centralizing authorial voice quells his sources' polyphony. This stamma's labor for Boyarin is overlayed by the stamma of the Talmud through the insertion of grotesque, comical, incongruous bits of narrative. For critical engagements with this argument see Wimpfheimer, "The Dialogical Talmud"; Z. Septimus, "Revisiting the Fat Rabbis"; Burrus, "Socrates, the Rabbis and the Virgin"; Becker, "Positing a 'Cultural Relationship.'"

136. In this sense, the operation of the rabbis is comparable, with all due distinctions, to the one that can be seen at play in Athenaeus of Naucratis's *Deipnosophists*: see Jacob, "La citation comme performance."

137. S. Cohen, "The Significance of Yavneh."

138. Boyarin, *Border Lines*, 153. See also Boyarin's works "A Tale of Two Synods"; "One Church; One Voice"; "The Yavneh-Cycle"; "Anecdotal Evidence"; "The Christian Invention of Judaism"; *Border Lines* (particularly 151–201); "Dialectic and Divination." Boyarin's argument is developed coherently—and with some overlaps and repetitions—through this set of publications, but most fully in *Border Lines*, into which some of these studies are incorporated and reworked. Therefore, I treat here the discussions contained in the various publications as a whole while directing all specific references to *Border Lines*. Fraade, "Rabbinic Polysemy," offers a critique of Boyarin's reconstruction based on the assessment that pluralism and polysemy may be found already in tannaitic literature. Chronological distinctions between the tannaitic era and later times must be acknowledged (despite, e.g., the parallel in *t.* Sotah 7:11–12 for the statement of *b.* Ḥagigah 3b to the effect that "[the different opinions] were all given by one shepherd"). Similarly, although the generic ethos attributed to Yavneh by Cohen finds expression in formulations that may be retrieved also in the Yerushalmi (see, e.g., the parallel for *b.* ʿEruvin 13b in *y.* Yevamot 1:6 [3b]), variance must be recognized between the degrees of appreciation for legal pluralism displayed by the Palestinian amoraʾim and by the later redactors of the Babylonian Talmud: see Hidary, *Dispute for the Sake of Heaven* (and, on differences on the related issue of the

importance attributed to judicial conformity to the law, Ben-Menahem, *Judicial Deviation*, 86–98).

139. Boyarin, *Border Lines*, 161.

140. Ibid., 152.

141. Ibid., 151.

142. Ibid., 170–171.

143. See Kraemer, *The Mind of the Talmud*, 103–104 and 126.

144. See Elman, "Argument for the Sake of Heaven," 273–277.

145. This approach is expounded in Kahana, *"Mi-penei tikkun ha-ʿolam,"* 14–19. See also Sabato, *Talmud Bavli massekhet Sanhedrin perek shelishi*.

146. The issue of the Talmud's dialectic needs to be disambiguated from at least two others: judicial pluralism (defined as the toleration of conflicting solutions to a legal question) and polysemy. An additional distinction, cutting across all these three categories, should be made between the corpus's practice and its thematization thereof. There are of course significant links and ample overlaps between the conclusions to be drawn from a differential analysis of the contents of the resulting six areas of inquiry. See also the distinctions regarding this set of issues made in Kiel, "Reinventing Yavneh," 582, n. 20. For a sample of the extremely vast literature on midrashic polysemy see D. Stern, "Midrash and Indeterminacy"; Halbertal, *People of the Book*, 53–62; Yadin-Israel, "The Hammer on the Rock"; Boyarin, "De/re/constructing Midrash"; Levinson, "Aḥat diber Elohim"; Fraade, "Rabbinic Polysemy" (particularly the conceptual distinctions drawn at 3–4); Boyarin, "Socrates and the Fat Rabbis." On various aspects of halakhic dialectic see L. Jacobs, *The Talmudic Argument*; Naeh, "ʿAśeh libekha ḥadrei ḥadarim"; Fisch, *Rational Rabbis*; Hidary, "Right Answers Revisited"; Hidary, *Dispute for the Sake of Heaven*, passim; Hidary, "The Agonistic Bavli"; Fraade, "'A Heart of Many Chambers'"; Hidary, *Rabbis and Classical Rhetoric*, passim. On judicial pluralism in the Talmud see Ben-Menahem, "Is There Always"; Ben-Menahem, "Interpretive Essay," 17–36"; Ben-Menahem, *Judicial Deviation*; Hayes, "Legal Truth," 80. See Wimpfheimer, *Narrating the Law*, for an argument—relevant to the distinction between polysemy and judicial pluralism—in favor of breaking down the dichotomy between narrative and law. By analyzing the discursive ramifications of textual practices adopted in the pursuit of legal discourse, rather than in narrative exegesis, I am choosing to focus on one aspect central to rabbinic ideology.

147. Dolgopolski, *Other Others*, 13. Dolgopolski's inquiry into the political dimension of the Bavli's semiotic universe uncovers the Talmudic give-and-take as rooted not in intersubjectivity but in interpersonality (11). Dolgopolski differentiates between "logical argumentation," described as "[t]he default position for the intersubjective response to disagreement," and "the rhetorical-dialectical form of argument," defined as "[t]he default position for the interpersonal response to disagreement." In the former, "rhetorical and dialectical forms" are "no more than tolerated deviations." The latter,

typical of the Talmud, instead "helps strengthen the initial arguments of both parties, making their reinforced positions totally dependent on the success of mutual self-refutation" (62). See also Dolgopolski, "*Tosafot Gornish* Post-Kant." For a philosophical understanding of the Talmud's (or rather of talmud's) agreement to disagree see Dolgopolski, *What Is Talmud?*

148. Levy, "Rabbinic Philosophy of Language," 185, n. 41, similarly rejects a mystical understanding of rabbinic language in favor of the notion of a philosophy of language preoccupied with the human dimension of dialogue (but see ibid., 196, n. 73).

149. Hayes, *Between the Babylonian and Palestinian Talmuds*, 199, n. 44, expresses reservations about drawing conclusions for ideological formations from literary forms when it comes to the Talmud, since the structuring of those formations is at least partly dependent on the accumulation of materials over time. The editors, Hayes explains, might well have been disposed to argue in similar ways to the tanna᾽im in their academies, but the multiple layers of literary materials they handled imposed on them the performance of a different literary task. Hayes prefers to assert more prudently that "the Bavli and the Mishnah reveal to us very different aspects of the worlds of those that produced them. In other words, we as readers undergo very different intellectual experiences when we study the various texts." I am largely sympathetic with this cautionary note and recognize that not every literary product, and perhaps no literary product, can be read as the mirror of one identifiable ideological formation. I remain interested, however, in the ideological productivity of the textualities I am describing. My sole reservation regarding Hayes's warning concerns her characterization of time as "intellectually neutral" (ibid.), a position that if brought to its radical consequences risks de-historicizing ideology and turning it into an entity only accessible in a pure and intentional form, in relation to which material disturbances must be tuned out. In my view, material conditions (including such time-dependent factors as the number of literary sources a generation of writers found on its hands) are not accidental to ideological formations, but rather the stuff out of which those formations are always produced.

150. On Torah study see Hirshman, "Torah in Rabbinic Thought," 907–913. On the ascetic dimension of this practice see Satlow, "And on the Earth You Shall Sleep"; Diamond, "Holy Men and Hunger Artists"; Kiel, "Study versus Sustenance." On Oral Torah see also Safrai, "Oral Torah"; D.W. Halivni, *Revelation Restored*, 54–74. For a review of the rabbinic sources that articulate the ideology of Oral Torah see D. Rosenthal, "Torah she-be-ʿal peh ṿe-Torah mi-Sinai." On orality in midrash see Fraade, "Literary Composition."

151. See Vidas, *The Rise of Talmud.*

152. This ideological insistence conflicts with evidence showing that teaching was in fact conducted in a not purely oral environment. See Jaffee, *Torah in the Mouth*, 140–152 (as well as Jaffee, "Writing and Rabbinic Oral Tradition"). See also E. Alexander, *Transmitting Mishna*; E. Alexander, "The Orality of Rabbinic Literature." Yuval,

"The Orality," sees the ideology of orality as related to self-definition vis-à-vis Christian practices of writing.

153. Rufinus of Aquileia, *Historia ecclesiastica* 10.3.

154. An analysis of the legend is found in Lim, *Public Disputation*, 182–216, on which Boyarin, *Border Lines*, 167–168, relies.

155. Yet Boyarin, *Border Lines*, 170, dates the oven of Akhnai narrative to the fourth or fifth century.

156. The later amoraʾim shared this interest with the redactors of the Yerushalmi, their near-contemporaries: see Kraemer, "Concerning the Theological Assumptions of the Yerushalmi," 362–364. Zellentin, *Rabbinic Parodies*, 9–10 and n. 34, argues that the Yerushalmi and Palestinian literature in general are more polysemic than the Bavli because they do not remove ambiguity through the overbearing voice of the stam. Some savoraʾim nurtured a distinct interest in halakhah: see B. Cohen, *For Out of Babylonia*.

157. On the legitimacy of a diachronic reading of the Bavli see Hayes, *Between the Babylonian and Palestinian Talmuds*, 11–13.

158. The reported exchanges of Abaye and Rava might be fictional: see Kalmin, *Sages, Stories, Authors, and Editors*, 175–192.

159. The first two generations of amoraʾim (ca. 230–290) still expressed themselves in a way that has been described as "apodictic," and with the intention of prescribing halakhah (for the meaning and history of the concept of apodicticity in the context of the Talmud see Kalmin, "The Post-Rav Ashi Amoraim," 168–170 and n. 40). Argumentation in these first two generations was limited and extremely concise, being mostly embodied by use of the expression *itteiveh* ("he replied to him," indicating a difficulty raised against an amora based on a tannaitic source) and by a measly count of three objections introduced by the formula *matḳif leh* (he raises an objection to him), and it referred not yet to fellow amoraʾim, as would be the case later, but to tannaitic sources. The phrase *itteiveh*, especially in the cases of discussions involving Rabbi Yochanan or Reish Lakish, might have to be attributed to the stammaitic layer. The transition from the second (ca. 250–290) to the third generation (ca. 290–320) of amoraʾim saw the development of an interest in the explanatory justification of, and in reflection on, apodictic statements. Argumentative dicta also proliferated in the third generation, including some built exclusively on logic in lieu of authoritative statements. By the fourth amoraic generation (ca. 320–350), apodictic meimrot were reduced to only approximately twice as many as argumentative ones. The majority of the apodictic statements preserved from this point on contained explanations. Additionally, self-reflexivity and rhetoric began to take as their object no longer solely apodicticity, but also argumentation itself. This trajectory was furthered, though without major changes, from the fifth generation (ca. 350–370) on. Granted, these features may partly be the product of the selectivity of later preservation. However, the steady progression in the manifestation of these trends suggests the historicity of a diminution of interest in the production of apodictic halakhic statements and of a growth of interest in the exercise of argumenta-

tive skills. See Kraemer, *Stylistic Characteristics*, and the summary of the key conclusions of this work in his *The Mind of the Talmud*, 26–49. Kraemer's results are largely compatible with the characterization of the different styles of the various amoraic generations in Kalmin, *The Redaction* (see ibid., 5, for a distinction between "prescriptive," "interpretative or explanatory," and "argumentational" teachings). Kalmin's methodology and in particular his extrapolations concerning the redactional history of the Bavli have been challenged by some critics: see Neusner's and Aminoah's Reviews of Kalmin's *Sages, Stories, Authors, and Editors*.

160. Hirshman, *The Stabilization of Rabbinic Culture*, 115. See also Moscovitz, *Talmudic Reasoning*, 354.

161. On the Babylonian tendency to which this development ran counter see Avinoam Cohen, "ʿAl maṭbeʿa ha-lashon"; E.B. Halivni, *Kelalei pesaḳ ha-halakhah ba-Talmud*, 98, 108–112, 124–126.

162. See Kalmin, *Sages, Stories, Authors, and Editors*, 52–54. Admittedly, the seeming loss in efficacy of the principle of authority appears to contrast with the fact that while some second- and third-generation amoraʾim considered that the first-generation amora Rav could legitimately disagree with the opinions of the tannaʾim, no later amora thought the same about him (see ibid., 44, n. 1). A more complete analysis appears to be required, which would differentiate between various relationships of authority, such as those of different generations of amoraʾim to the tannaʾim vs. those of different generations of amoraʾim to earlier amoraʾim.

163. Kalmin, *Sages, Stories, Authors, and Editors*, 49.

164. See D.W. Halivni, *Midrash, Mishnah, and Gemara*, 76–92; Rubenstein, "The Thematization of Dialectics"; Rubenstein, *The Culture*, 39–53.

165. See Rubenstein, *The Culture*, 22–23. See also Gafni, "The Modern Study of Rabbinics," 54, on the distinction between leadership in the Yerushalmi, premised on traditional authority, and in the Bavli, drawing on knowledge of Torah and ingenuity. For an analysis of what is presented as the Bavli's self-critique in relation to late rabbinic scholastic tendencies see Wolf, "Haven't I Told You?"

166. Socrates of Constantinople, *Historia ecclesiastica* 5.10.6–15; ed. Maraval and Périchon, III, 174–178: Οὐκ εἰς μακρὰν δὲ μετὰ ταῦτα παρῆσαν οἱ πανταχόθεν πάσης θρησκείας ἐπίσκοποι, κατὰ τὴν αὐτὴν ὑπατείαν, τῷ Ἰουνίῳ μηνί. Μεταπεμψάμενος οὖν ὁ βασιλεὺς Νεκτάριον τὸν ἐπίσκοπον, ἐκοινολογεῖτο πρὸς αὐτὸν, τίς ἂν γένοιτο μηχανὴ ὅπως ἂν μὴ διαφωνοίη ὁ Χριστιανισμὸς, ἀλλ᾽ ἑνωθῇ ἡ ἐκκλησία: ἔλεγέν τε δεῖν γυμνασθῆναι τὸ χωρίζον τὰς ἐκκλησίας ζήτημα, τήν τε διαφωνίαν ἐκποδὼν ποιήσαντας, ὁμοφωνίαν ταῖς ἐκκλησίαις ἐργάσασθαι. Τοῦτο ἀκούσας ὁ Νεκτάριος ἐν φροντίσιν ἦν: καὶ μεταστειλάμενος τὸν τηνικαῦτα τῶν Ναυατιανῶν ἐπίσκοπον Ἀγέλιον, ὡς κατὰ τὴν πίστιν ὁμόφρονα, φανερὰν αὐτῷ τὴν τοῦ βασιλέως καθίστησι γνώμην. Ὁ δὲ τὰ μὲν ἄλλα ἦν εὐλαβὴς, σύστῆναι δὲ λόγοις περὶ τοῦ δόγματος οὐκ ἰσχύων, ἀναγνώστην ὑπ᾽ αὐτῷ Σισίννιον ὄνομα πρὸς τὸ διαλεχθῆναι προεβάλλετο. Σισίννιος δὲ ἀνὴρ ἐλλόγιμος καὶ πραγμάτων ἔμπειρος, ἀκριβῶς τε εἰδὼς τὰς τῶν ἱερῶν γραμμάτων ἑρμηνείας καὶ τὰ

φιλόσοφα δόγματα, συνεῖδεν ὡς αἱ διαλέξεις οὐ μόνον οὐχ ἑνοῦσι τὰ σχίσματα, ἀλλὰ γὰρ καὶ φιλονεικοτέρας τὰς αἱρέσεις μᾶλλον ἀπεργάζονται: καὶ διὰ τοῦτο τοιάνδε τινὰ συμβουλὴν τῷ Νεκταρίῳ ὑπέθετο. Εὖ ἐπιστάμενος ὡς οἱ παλαιοὶ ἀρχὴν ὑπάρξεως τῷ Υἱῷ τοῦ Θεοῦ δοῦναι ἀπέφυγον, κατειλήφεισαν γὰρ αὐτὸν συναΐδιον τῷ Πατρὶ, συμβουλεύει φυγεῖν μὲν τὰς διαλεκτικὰς μάχας, μάρτυρας δὲ καλέσειν τὰς ἐκδόσεις τῶν παλαιῶν: καὶ πεῦσιν παρὰ τοῦ βασιλέως τοῖς αἱρεσιάρχαις προσάγεσθαι, "πότερον λόγον ποτε ποιοῦνται τῶν πρὸ τῆς διαιρέσεως ἐν τῇ ἐκκλησίᾳ προσαρμοσάντων διδασκάλων, ἢ ὡς ἀλλοτρίους τοῦ Χριστιανισμοῦ παρακρούονται. Εἰ μὲν γὰρ τούτους ἀθετοῦσιν, οὐκοῦν ἀναθεματίζειν αὐτοὺς τολμάτωσαν: καὶ εἰ τοῦτο τολμῆσαι ποιήσωσιν, ὑπὸ τοῦ πλήθους ἐξελαθήσονται. Καὶ τούτου γενομένου, προφανὴς ἔσται ἡ νίκη τῆς ἀληθείας. Εἰ δὲ μὴ παρακρούονται τοὺς ἀρχαίους τῶν διδασκάλων, ἡμέτερόν ἐστι τὸ παρασχεῖν τὰς βίβλους τῶν παλαιῶν, δὶ ὧν ἡ παῤ ἡμῶν δόξα μαρτυρηθήσεται." Ταῦτα ἀκούσας παρὰ τοῦ Σισιννίου ὁ Νεκτάριος δρομαῖος ἐπὶ τὰ βασίλεια χωρεῖ: γνωρίζει δὲ τῷ βασιλεῖ τὰ συμβεβουλευμένα αὐτῷ. Ὁ δὲ ἁρπάζει τὴν γνώμην, καὶ σοφῶς τὸ πρᾶγμα μετεχειρίσατο; trans. adapted from *NPNF2* II, 122–123. The story has a parallel in Sozomen, *Historia ecclesiastica* 7.12, which depends on Socrates's account.

167. Εὖ ἐπιστάμενος ὡς οἱ παλαιοὶ ἀρχὴν ὑπάρξεως τῷ Υἱῷ τοῦ Θεοῦ δοῦναι ἀπέφυγον, κατειλήφεισαν γὰρ αὐτὸν συναΐδιον τῷ Πατρὶ.

168. Graumann, "The Synod of Constantinople," 162. The Greek text of the purported parenthesis is κατειλήφεισαν γὰρ αὐτὸν συναΐδιον τῷ Πατρὶ.

169. Ibid., 176.

170. Ibid., 161–162.

171. Ibid., 165–166. The historicity of the entire episode is denied by Walraff, "Il «sinodo di tutte le eresie»"; Walraff, *Der Kirchenhistoriker Sokrates*, 275–281. I engage here only with Graumann's arguments because his own denial is more qualified than Walraff's. The story's veracity is not doubted by Salaverri, "El argumento de tradición patrística," 111; du Manoir de Juaye, "L'argumentation patristique," 445–447; Rebillard, "A New Style of Argument," 562, n. 15.

172. On this episode see also Simonetti, *La crisi ariana*, 552, n. 78.

173. See Walraff, "Il «sinodo di tutte le eresie»," 279; Walraff, *Der Kirchenhistoriker Sokrates*, 277, where the argument is made that the report of Sisinnius's proposal constitutes Socrates's attempt at constructing an etiology for the patristic argument.

174. Rufinus, *De adulteratione librorum Origenis* 13; ed. Simonetti, 7–17, 15; trans. adapted from Vessey, "The Forging of Orthodoxy," 498. The quite extraordinary continuation of the episode, not strictly relevant for my argument, is analyzed by Vessey (497–505).

175. Practiced through shaḳla ṿe-ṭarya across the Bavli, dialectic is also famously theorized in numerous passages. The locus classicus for its thematization is perhaps *b.* ʿEruvin 13b (a passage whose contents are also referenced in *b.* Giṭṭin 6b). Here the Talmud famously recounts that at the end of a three-year dispute between the houses of

Shammai and Hillel, a heavenly voice declared, "These and these are [both] the words of the living God, but the halakhah follows the house of Hillel." The text interprets the decision as a reward for the kindness and humility of Hillel's disciples, who retained memory of the rulings of the house of Shammai and mentioned their opponents' deliberations before theirs. This passage has been variously interpreted as meaning, inter alia, that both sets of opinions are legitimate although they do not both constitute a valid legal solution (Ben-Menahem, "Is There Always," 168); that truth is not the exclusive prerogative of any one position (Kraemer, *The Mind of the Talmud*, 139–148); and that the deficiency of the human mind finds a dispute where God only sees unity (Elman, "The World of the 'Sabboraim,'" 383–395; see also D. Stern, *Midrash and Theory*, 32–33, for a similar interpretation in relation to the *derashah*, or scriptural exposition, contained in *b.* Ḥagigah 3a–3b). Perhaps fittingly, approval of dialectic is not univocally shared across the Babylonian Talmud: elsewhere (e.g., in *b.* Sanhedrin 88b) disagreement is treated as a symptom of religious decline.

176. The rabbis' methodological intolerance was still capable of accommodating multiple pragmatic approaches, as demonstrated, e.g., by Reish Lakish's citation of a proverb in the sugyah reported above.

177. Boyarin, *Border Lines*, 166–171. This story (reported in *b.* Bava metsiʿa 59b and referenced in *b.* Ḥullin 44a) may well be the most written-about Talmudic passage in English-language scholarship. For one hermeneutic take and bibliographic references see Rubenstein, *Talmudic Stories*, 34–63. Boyarin, *Socrates and the Fat Rabbis*, 222–230, also treats this episode.

178. On the limited character of rabbinic inclusivism see Boyarin, *Border Lines*, 153; Hidary, *Dispute for the Sake of Heaven*, 36.

179. The opposition between the totalitarian urge of the Jewish tradition and the universalist drive of the Christian side is expectably also an asymmetrical one: at the antipodes of totalitarianism one arguably finds democracy, not universalism; and the opposite of the latter is not totalitarianism, but particularism. Since, as argued, the political impulses of the two traditions originated from different aspects of the intellectual act (its fact for rabbinic Judaism, its content for Christian theology), it can be argued that their political effects pertain correspondingly to two distinct, though obviously related, facets of political existence, namely a social praxis and a rational ideal.

180. The classical study on the *ʿammei ha-ʾarets* is Oppenheimer, *The ʿAm Ha-ʾarets*. See also S. Stern, *Jewish Identity*, 87–138; Kalmin, *The Sage*, 27–50; Rubenstein, *The Culture*, 123–142; Miller, *Sages and Commoners*. On the social standing of the rabbis see Neusner, *A History of the Jews*, 126–130. While many hostile statements about the *ʿammei ha-ʾarets* attributed to Palestinian rabbis are found in *b.* Pesaḥim 49b, Wald, *Pereḳ Ellu ʿovrin*, 211–239, demonstrated that those reflect a distinctly Babylonian interest. On differences between the Bavli and the Yerushalmi with regard to this subject see Kalmin, "The Formation and Character," 849–850. For a conceptualization of the

relationship between rabbis and non-rabbis in second-century Palestine see Schremer, "The Religious Orientation."

181. See Lieu, "History and Theology," 88.

182. See Bakhos, "Figuring (Out) Esau"; Schremer, *Brothers Estranged.* Although both Bakhos and Schremer were writing about the Palestinian context, their insights can be extrapolated to a large extent to rabbinic literature more generally. In my view, although the fact that Jewish polemic about minim arose approximately at the same time (in the second and third century) as Christian heresiology likely indicates (as per Boyarin, *Border Lines*, 5–6 and 27–28) participation in a shared discourse, it does not necessarily suggest that the Christians were the exclusive or even privileged object of anti-minim rhetoric.

183. See Boyarin, *Border Lines*; Yuval, *Two Nations.*

184. See, e.g., Kalmin, "'Manasseh Sawed Isaiah with a Saw of Wood'"; Kalmin, "The Function and Dating"; M. Rosenberg, "Penetrating Words"; Bar-Asher Siegal, *Jewish-Christian Dialogues.*

185. See Boyarin, *Dying for God*, 20 (itself a citation from an unnamed source).

186. See Naiweld, "The Not So Significant Other." Similar conclusions about the marginality of Christians to the preoccupations of the rabbis have been reached by Shinan, *Aggadatam shel meturgemanim*, II, 345–352; Goldenberg, "Did the Amoraim See"; Visotzky, *Golden Bells and Pomegranates*, 154–172; all cited in M.H. Hacohen, *Jacob & Esau*, 80, n. 72.

187. See, e.g., Van Rompay, "A Letter of the Jews"; Cameron, "Flights of Fancy." See also Cameron, *Dialoguing in Late Antiquity*, passim.

Conclusion

1. Cameron, *Christianity*, 14.

Editions of Ancient Sources

Acta concilii nicaeni secundi
Ed. Giovan Domenico Mansi, *Sacrorum conciliorum nova et amplissima collectio*, 31 vols., Florence: Antonius Zatta, 1759–1798, vol. 12 (cols. 951–1154), vol. 13 (cols. 1–496).
Altercatio Heracliani laici cum Germinio episcopo sirmiensi
Ed. PLS 1, pp. 345–350.
Ambrose of Milan
Expositio Evangelii secundum Lucam
Ed. Marc Adriaen, *Sancti Ambrosii Mediolanensis Opera IV* (CCSL 14), Turnhout: Brepols, 1957, pp. 1–400.
Ammianus Marcellinus
Res Gestae
Ed. Liselotte Jacob-Karau, Wolfgang Seyfarth, and Ilse Ulmann, *Rerum gestarum libri qui supersunt*, 2 vols., Leipzig: B. G. Teubner, 1978.
Aristotle
Categoriae
Ed. Lorenzo Minio-Paluello, *Aristotelis categoriae et liber de interpretatione* (Scriptorum classicorum bibliotheca Oxoniensis), Oxford: Oxford University Press, 2008.
Athanasius of Alexandria
Apologia secunda contra arianos
Ed. Hanns Christof Brennecke, Uta Heil, Annette von Stockhausen, and Angelika Wintjes, eds., *Athanasius Werke. Dritter Band. Erster Teil. 3. Lieferung*, Berlin: De Gruyter, 2007, pp. 87–120 [= 1–43.4]; Hanns Christof Brennecke, Uta Heil, Christian Müller, Annette von Stockhausen, and Angelika Wintjes, eds., *Athanasius Werke. Dritter Band. Erster Teil. 4. Lieferung*, Berlin: De Gruyter, 2014, pp. 121–160 [= 43.5–80.3]; Hanns Christof Brennecke, Uta Heil, and Annette von Stockhausen,

eds., *Athanasius Werke. Dritter Band. Erster Teil. 5. Lieferung*, Berlin: De Gruyter, 2014, pp. 161–168 [= 81–90.3].

De decretis Nicaenae synodi

Ed. Hans-Georg Opitz, *Athanasius Werke. Zweiter Band. Erster Teil. 1. Lieferung*, Berlin: De Gruyter, 1935, pp. 1–45.

De sententia Dionysii

Ed. Hans-Georg Opitz, *Athanasius Werke. Zweiter Band. Erster Teil. 1. Lieferung*, Berlin: De Gruyter, 1935, pp. 46–67.

De synodis Arimini in Italia et Seleucia in Isauria

Ed. and trans. Annick Martin and Xavier Morales, *Athanase d'Alexandria. Lettre sur les synodes* (SC 563), Paris: Les Éditions du Cerf, 2013.

Epistula ad Rufinianum

Ed. and trans. Périclès-Pierre Joannou, *Discipline générale antique* (Pontificia commissione per la redazione del codice di diritto canonico orientale 9), 3 vols. in 4, Grottaferrata: Tipografia Italo-Orientale S. Nilo, 1962–1964, vol. 2, pp. 76–80.

Ed. and trans. Annick Martin and Xavier Morales, *Tome aux Antiochiens, lettres à Rufinien, à Jovien et aux Africains*, (SC 622), Paris: Les Éditions du Cerf, 2021, pp. 65–127.

Epistula ad Serapionem

Ed. and trans. Joseph Lebon, *Athanase d'Alexandrie, Lettres à Sérapion sur la divinité du Saint-Esprit* (SC 15), Paris: Les Éditions du Cerf, 1947.

Epistula festalis XXXVI (?)

Ed. and trans. Alberto Camplani, "Atanasio e Eusebio tra Alessandria e Antiochia (362–363). Osservazioni sul *Tomus ad Antiochenos*, l'*Epistula catholica* e due fogli copti (edizione di Pap. Berol. 11948)," in Enrico Dal Covolo, Renato Uglione, and Giovanni Maria Vian, eds., *Eusebio di Vercelli e il suo tempo* (Biblioteca di scienze religiose 133), Rome: Libreria Ateneo Salesiano, 1997, pp. 191–246, 242–243.

Historia Arianorum ad monachos

Ed. Hans-Georg Opitz, *Athanasius Werke. Zweiter Band. 5. Lieferung*, Berlin: De Gruyter, 1935, pp. 183–200; *Athanasius Werke. Zweiter Band. 6. Lieferung*, Berlin: De Gruyter, 1935, pp. 201–230.

Oratio I contra Arianos

Ed. Karin Metzler and Kyriakos Savvidis, *Athanasius Werke. Erster Band. Erster Teil. 2. Lieferung*, Berlin: De Gruyter, 1998, pp. 109–175.

Ed. and trans. Adriana Bara, Lucian Dîncă, Charles Kannengiesser, Karin Metzler, and Kyriakos Savvidis, *Athanase d'Alexandrie. Traités contre les Ariens* (SC 598–599), 2 vols., Paris: Les Éditions du Cerf, 2019, vol. 1.

Oratio II contra Arianos

Ed. Karin Metzler and Kyriakos Savvidis, *Athanasius Werke. Erster Band. Erster Teil. 2. Lieferung*, Berlin: De Gruyter, 1998, pp. 177–260.

Ed. and trans. Adriana Bara, Lucian Dîncă, Charles Kannengiesser, Karin Metzler, and Kyriakos Savvidis, *Athanase d'Alexandrie. Traités contre les Ariens* (SC 598–599), 2 vols., Paris: Les Éditions du Cerf, 2019, vol. 2, pp. 14–275.

Oratio III contra Arianos

Ed. Karin Metzler and Kyriakos Savvidis, *Athanasius Werke. Erster Band. Erster Teil. 3. Lieferung*, Berlin: De Gruyter, 1998, pp. 305–381.

Ed. and trans. Adriana Bara, Lucian Dîncă, Charles Kannengiesser, Karin Metzler, and Kyriakos Savvidis, *Athanase d'Alexandrie. Traités contre les Ariens* (SC 598–599), 2 vols, Paris: Les Éditions du Cerf, 2019, vol. 2, pp. 276–487.

Tomus ad Antiochenos

Ed. Robert W. Thomson, *Athanasiana Syriaca* (CSCO 273. Scriptores syri 119), 4 vols. in 8, Louvain: Secrétariat du Corpus SCO, 1967, vol. 2.3, pp. 30–37.

Ed. and trans. Angelo Segneri, *Atanasio. Lettera agli Antiocheni. Introduzione, testo, traduzione e commento*, Bologna: Edizioni Dehoniane, 2010.

Ed. and trans. Annick Martin and Xavier Morales, *Tome aux Antiochiens, lettres à Rufinien, à Jovien et aux Africains*, (SC 622), Paris: Les Éditions du Cerf, 2021.

Vita Antonii

Ed. Gerhard J.M. Bartelink, *Athanase d'Alexandrie. Vie d'Antoine* (SC 400), Paris: Les Éditions du Cerf, 1994.

Athanasius of Alexandria (Pseudo-)

De sancta Trinitate dialogus III

Ed. PG 28, cols. 1201–1249.

Fragmentum (= *Fragmentum Magni Athanasii*)

Ed. PG 26, cols. 1293–1294.

Oratio IV contra arianos

Ed. Markus Vinzent, *Pseudo-Athanasius, Contra Arianos IV. Eine Schrift gegen Asterius von Kappadokien, Eusebius von Cäsarea, Markell von Ankyra und Photin von Sirmium*, Leiden: Brill, 1996.

Augustine of Hippo

Epistula XCIII ad Vincentium

Ed. PL 33, cols. 321–347.

Avot de-Rabi Natan

Ed. Sinyur Zalman Schechter, *Avot de-Rabi Natan*, London: D. Nutt; Vienna: Ch.D. Lippe; Frankfurt am Main: D. Kauffmann, 1887.

Basil of Caesarea

Adversus Eunomium

Ed. PG 29, cols. 497–669, 672–768.

De spiritu sancto

Ed. and trans. Benoît Pruche, *Sur le Saint-Esprit*, 2nd ed. (SC 17 bis), Paris: Les Éditions du Cerf, 1968.

Epistulae

Ed. PG 32, cols. 219–1112.

Ed. and trans. Roy Joseph Deferrari, *Saint Basil: The Letters* (Loeb Classical Library 190, 215, 243, 270), 4 vols., London: W. Heinemann, 1926–1943.

Ed. and trans. Yves Courtonne, *Saint Basile. Lettres* (Collection des universités de France), 3 vols., Paris: Les Belles lettres, 1957–1966.

Ed. and trans. Roy Joseph Deferrari and Agnes C. Way, *Saint Basil: Letters* (Fathers of the Church 13, 28), 2 vols., Washington, DC: Catholic University of America Press, 2008.

Bereshit Rabah

Ed. Hanoch Albeck and Julius Theodor, *Midrash Bereshit Rabah* (3 vols.), Berlin: Tsevi Hirsh Itsḳovsḳi, 1903–1936.

Chronicon Paschale

Ed. Ludwig August Dindorf, *Chronicon Paschale* (Corpus Scriptorum Historiae Byzantinae 16, 17), 2 vols., Bonn: Weber, 1832.

Trans. Mary Whitby and Michael Whitby, *Chronicon Paschale 284–628 AD* (Translated texts for historians. Latin series 7), Liverpool: Liverpool University Press, 1989.

Cicero

Ad Atticum

Ed. David Roy Shackleton Bailey, *M. Tulli Ciceronis Epistulae ad Atticum*, 2 vols., Stuttgart: Teubner, 1987.

Clement of Alexandria

Paedagogus

Ed. and trans. Marguerite Harle, Henri-Irénée Marrou, Chantal Matray, and Claude Mondésert, *Le pédagogue* (SC 70, 108, 158), 3 vols., Paris: Les Éditions du Cerf, 2008.

Stromata

Ed. Ludwig Früchtel, Otto Stählin, Ursula Treu, *Clemens Alexandrinus* (GCS 12, 17, 39, 52), 4 vols., Berlin: De Gruyter, 2011–2015, vol. 2. pp. 3–518; vol. 3. pp. 1–102.

Trans. John Ferguson, *Stromateis, Books 1–3* (Fathers of the Church 85), Washington, DC: Catholic University of America Press, 1991.

Cyril of Alexandria

Thesaurus de sancta et consubstantiali Trinitate

Ed. PG 50, cols. 9–656.

Damnatio blasphemiae Arrii

Ed. Yves-Marie Duval, "Une traduction latine inédite du Symbole de Nicée et une condamnation d'Arius à Rimini: Nouveau fragment historique d'Hilaire ou pièces des Actes du concile?," *Revue Bénédictine* 82 (1972): pp. 7–25.

Dionysius of Alexandria

Epistulae

Ed. Charles L. Feltoe, *The Letters and Other Remains of Dionysius of Alexandria*, Cambridge: University Press; New York: Macmillan, 1904.

Trans. Charles L. Feltoe, *St. Dionysius of Alexandria: Letters and Treatises*, London: Society for Promoting Christian Knowledge; New York: Macmillan, 1918.

Didymus the Blind

Commentarii in Zacchariam

Ed. and trans. Louis Doutreleau, *Didyme l'Aveugle sur Zacharie* (SC 83, 84, 85), 3 vols., Paris: Les Éditions du Cerf, 1962.

3 Enoch

Ed. and trans. Hugo Odeberg, *3 Enoch or the Hebrew Book of Enoch*, 2nd ed., Cambridge: Cambridge University Press, 1928.

Trans. Philip S. Alexander in James H. Charlesworth, *The Old Testament Pseudepigrapha*, 2 vols., Garden City, NY: Doubleday, 1983–1985, vol. 1, pp. 223–315.

Epictetus

Dissertationes ab Arriano digestae

Ed. Heinrich Schenkl, *Dissertationes ab Arriano digestae*, Stuttgart: Teubner, 1965.

Epiphanius of Salamis

Adversus haereses

Ed. Karl Holl, *Epiphanius* (GCS 25, 31, 37, Neue Folge 4), 4 vols., Leipzig: J.C. Hinrichs, 1915–2006, vol. 1, pp. 151–464; vol. 2; vol. 3.

Trans. Frank Williams, *The Panarion of Epiphanius of Salamis* (Nag Hammadi and Manichaean Studies 63, 79), 2 vols., Leiden: Brill, 2009–2013.

Ancoratus

Ed. Karl Holl, *Epiphanius* (GCS 25, 31, 37, Neue Folge 4), 4 vols., Leipzig: J.C. Hinrichs, 1915–2006, vol. 1, pp. 1–149.

Epistula episcoporum Italiae ad episcopos Inlyrici

Ed. Alfred Leonhard Feder, *S. Hilarii episcopi Pictaviensis opera. Pars 4: Tractatus mysteriorum. Collectanea antiariana parisina (Fragmenta historica) cum appendice (Liber I ad Constantium). Liber ad Constantium imperatorem (Liber II ad Constantium). Hymni. Fragmenta minora. Spuria* (CSEL 65), Vienna: F. Tempsky, 1916, pp. 158–159.

Epistula synodi Parisiensis (c. 360)

Ed. Alfred Leonhard Feder, *S. Hilarii episcopi Pictaviensis opera. Pars 4: Tractatus mysteriorum. Collectanea antiariana parisina (Fragmenta historica) cum appendice (Liber I ad Constantium). Liber ad Constantium imperatorem (Liber II ad Constantium). Hymni. Fragmenta minora. Spuria* (CSEL 65), Vienna: F. Tempsky, 1916, pp. 43–46.

Ed. and trans. Jean Gaudemet, *Conciles Gaulois du IVe siècle* (SC 241), Paris: Les Éditions du Cerf, 1977, pp. 92–98.

Eugenius of Ancyra

Expositio fidei (dubious attribution)

Ed. PG 25, cols. 199–208.

Eusebius of Caesarea

De ecclesiastica theologia

Ed. Erich Klostermann and Günther Christian Hansen, *Gegen Marcell. Über die kirchliche Theologie. Die Fragmente Marcells*, 2nd ed. (GCS 14. Eusebius Werke 4), Berlin: Akademie-Verlag, 1972, pp. 61–182.

Historia ecclesiastica

Ed. and trans. Gustave Bardy, *Histoire ecclésiastique* (SC 31, 41, 55, 73), 4 vols., Paris: Les Éditions du Cerf, 1952–1960.

Ed. Theodor Mommsen, Eduard Schwartz, and Friedhelm Winkelmann, *Die Kirchengeschichte*, 2nd ed. (GCS N.F. 6. Eusebius Werke 2), 3 vols., Berlin: Akademie-Verlag, 1999, vol. 1, vol. 2 (pp. 509–904).

Vita Constantini

Ed. and trans. Bruno Bleckmann and Horst Schneider, *De vita Constantini = Über das Leben Konstantins* (Fontes Christiani 83), Turnhout: Brepols, 2007.

Trans. Averil Cameron and Stuart G. Hall, *Life of Constantine*, Oxford: Clarendon Press and Oxford University Press, 1999.

Eusebius of Vercellae (Pseudo-)

Epistula ad Gregorium Illiberitanum

Ed. Alfred Leonhard Feder, *S. Hilarii episcopi Pictaviensis opera. Pars 4: Tractatus mysteriorum. Collectanea antiariana parisina (Fragmenta historica) cum appendice (Liber I ad Constantium). Liber ad Constantium imperatorem (Liber II ad Constantium). Hymni. Fragmenta minora. Spuria* (CSEL 65), Vienna: F. Tempsky, 1916, pp. 46–47.

Eustathius of Antioch

De engastromytho

Ed. José H. Declerck, *Eustathii Antiocheni, patris Nicaeni, Opera quae supersunt omnia* (CCSG 51), Turnhout: Brepols; Louvain: Louvain University Press, 2002, pp. 1–60.

Fragmenta

Ed. Michel Spanneut, *Recherches sur les écrits d'Eustathe d'Antioche* (Mémoires et travaux 55), Lille: Facultés catholiques, 1948, pp. 94–131.

Ed. José H. Declerck, *Eustathii Antiocheni, patris Nicaeni, Opera quae supersunt omnia* (CCSG 51), Turnhout: Brepols; Louvain: Louvain University Press, 2002, pp. 61–208.

Facundus of Hermiane

Pro defensione trium capitulorum

Ed. and trans. Jean-Marie Clément, Anne Fraïsse-Bétoulières, and Roel Vander Plaetse, *Dèfense des trois chapitres (à Justinien)* (SC 471, 478, 479, 484, 499), 4 vols. in 5, Paris: Les Éditions du Cerf, 2002–2006.

Faustinus and Marcellinus

Libellus precum

Ed. Otto Günther, *Epistulae imperatorum pontificum aliorum inde ab A. CCCLVII usque ad a. DLIII datae avellane quae dicitur collectio* (CSEL 35), 1 vol. in 2, Vienna: E. Tempsky, 1895–1898, vol. 1.1, pp. 5–44.

Ed. Manlio Simonetti in Vinzenz Bulhart, *Gregorii Iliberritani episcopi quae supersunt* (CCSL 69), Turnhout: Brepols, 1967, pp. 359–392.

Ed. and trans. Aline Canellis, *Supplique aux empereurs: Libellus precum et lex Augusta. Précédé de Faustin, confession de foi* (SC 504), Paris: Les Éditions du Cerf, 2006, pp. 106–236.

Galen

Commentarius in Hippocratis De medici officina librum

Ed. Karl Gottlob Kühn, *Claudii Galeni opera omnia*, 20 vols., Leipzig: C. Cnobloch, 1821–1833, vol. 18/2, pp. 629–925.

Gelasius of Cyzicus

Syntagma

Ed. Günther Christian Hansen, *Anonyme Kirchengeschichte (Gelasius Cyzicenus, CPG 6034)* (GCS N.F. 9), Berlin: De Gruyter, 2002.

Ed. and trans. Günther Christian Hansen, *Anonymus von Cyzicus. Historia ecclesiastica = Kirchengeschichte* (Fontes Christiani 49), 2 vols., Turnhout: Brepols, 2008.

Gelasius of Cyzicus (Pseudo-)

De libris recipiendis et non recipiendis

Ed. Ernst von Dobschütz, *Das Decretum Gelasianum de libris recipiendis et non recipiendis* (TU 3.8.4/38.4), Leipzig: J.C. Hinrichs, 1912.

Giwargis I, Catholicos

Epistula ad Minam

Ed. and trans. Jean-Baptiste Chabot, *Synodicon orientale, ou, Recueil de synodes nestoriens*, Paris: Imprimerie nationale, 1902, pp. 227–245 (Syriac), pp. 490–514 (French).

Gregory of Nazianzus

Orationes

Ed. PG 35, cols. 395–1252; 36, cols. 10–664.

Gregory of Nyssa

Ad Graecos ex communibus notionibus (dubious attribution)

Ed. Friedrich Müller, *Gregorii Nysseni Opera. III/1. Opera dogmatica minora*, Leiden: Brill, 1958, pp. 17–33.

Trans. Thierry Ziegler, *Les petits traités trinitaires de Grégoire de Nysse: Témoins d'un itinéraire théologique (379–383)*, Ph.D. dissertation. Strasbourg: Université de Strasbourg, 1987, pp. 2–19.
Trans. Hermann Josef Vogt, "Die Schrift 'Ex communibus notionibus' des Gregor von Nyssa," *Theologische Quartalschrift* 171 (1991): pp. 204–218, 204–211.
Trans. Claudio Moreschini, *Opere di Gregorio di Nissa* (Classici delle religioni 4), Turin: Unione tipografica-Editrice torinese, 1992, pp. 1887–1909.
Trans. Daniel F. Stramara, "Gregory of Nyssa, *Ad Graecos 'How It Is That We Say There Are Three Persons in the Divinity But Do Not Say There Are Three Gods'* (To the Greeks: Concerning the Commonality of Concepts)," *Greek Orthodox Theological Review* 41 (1996): pp. 375–391.
Epistulae
Ed. Giorgio Pasquali, *Gregorii Nysseni Opera. VIII/2. Epistulae*, Leiden: Brill, 1959.
Trans. Anna M. Silvas, *Gregory of Nyssa: The Letters* (Vigiliae Christianae. Supplements 83), Leiden: Brill, 2007.
De instituto christiano
Ed. Werner Jaeger in Virginia Woods Callahan, John P. Cavarnos, and Werner Jaeger, eds., *Gregorii Nysseni Opera. VIII/1. Opera ascetica*, Leiden: Brill, 1952, pp. 41–89.
Trans. Virginia Woods Callahan, *Ascetical Works* (The Fathers of the Church 58), Washington, DC: Catholic University of America Press, 1967, pp. 125–158.

Grigorios Bar ʿEbroyo

Chronicon
Ed. and trans. Jean-Baptiste Abbeloos and Thomas Joseph Lamy, *Chronicon ecclesiasticum quod e codice musei Britannici descriptum conjuncta opera ediderunt*, 3 vols., Louvain: Peeters, 1872–1877.
Historia compendiosa dynastiarum
Ed. and trans. Edward Pococke, *Tārīkh mukhtaṣar al-duwal = Historia compendiosa dynastiarum*, 3 vols., Oxford: Henricus Hall Academiae Typographus, 1663.
Ed. Anṭūn Ṣāliḥānī, *Tārīkh mukhtaṣar al-duwal*, Beirut: Al-Maṭbaʿah al-Kāthūlīkīyah lil-Ābāʾ al-Yasūʿīyīn, 1890.

Hilary of Poitiers

Apologetica responsa
Ed. and trans. Michael Durst, *Hilaire de Poitiers. Lettre sur les synodes* (SC 621), Paris: Les Éditions du Cerf, 2021.
De synodis, seu De fide Orientalium
Ed. PL 10, cols. 479–546.
Fragmenta historica
Ed. Alfred Leonhard Feder, *S. Hilarii episcopi Pictaviensis opera. Pars 4: Tractatus mysteriorum. Collectanea antiariana parisina (Fragmenta historica) cum appendice (Liber I ad Constantium). Liber ad Constantium imperatorem (Liber II ad Constantium). Hymni. Fragmenta minora. Spuria* (CSEL 65), Vienna: F. Tempsky, 1916, pp. 41–97.

Liber I ad Constantium

Ed. Alfred Leonhard Feder, *S. Hilarii episcopi Pictaviensis opera. Pars 4: Tractatus mysteriorum. Collectanea antiariana parisina (Fragmenta historica) cum appendice (Liber I ad Constantium). Liber ad Constantium imperatorem (Liber II ad Constantium). Hymni. Fragmenta minora. Spuria* (CSEL 65), Vienna: F. Tempsky, 1916, pp. 179–187.

Ed. Bernhard Bischoff, Vinzenz Bulhart, F. Heylen, Anselm Hoste, and André Wilmart, *Eusebius Vercellensis, Filastrius Brixiensis, Hegemonius (Ps.), Isaac Iudaeus, Archidiaconus Romanus, Fortunatianus Aquileiensis, Chromatius Aquileiensis Opera quae supersunt; Diversorum hereseon liber; Adversus haereses; Opera quae supersunt; De reconciliandis paenitentibus; Commentarii in evangelia; Opera quae supersunt* (CCSL 9), Turnhout: Brepols, 1957.

Ed. and trans. André Rocher, *Hilaire de Poitiers. Contre Constance* (SC 334), Paris: Les Éditions du Cerf, 1987.

Hippolytus

Contra Noëtum

Ed. and trans. Manlio Simonetti, *Contro Noeto* (Biblioteca patristica 35), Bologna: EDB, 2000.

Hippolytus (Pseudo-)

Refutatio omnium haeresium (= *Philosophoumena*)

Ed. Miroslav Marcovich, *Refutatio omnium haeresium* (PTS 25), Berlin: De Gruyter, 1986.

Historia acephala Athanasii et Index festale

Ed. and trans. Micheline Albert and Annick Martin, *Histoire «acéphale» et index syriaque des lettres festales d'Athanase d'Alexandrie* (SC 317), Paris: Les Éditions du Cerf, 1985.

Historia ecclesiae alexandrinae

Ed. and trans. Tito Orlandi, *Storia della Chiesa di Alessandria* (Testi e documenti per lo studio dell'antichità 17, 31), 2 vols., Milan: Istituto editoriale cisalpino, 1968–1970.

Hormisdas, Pope

Epistula LXX ad Possessorem Episcopum

Ed. PL 63, cols. 490–493.

Ed. Otto Günther, *Epistulae imperatorum pontificum aliorum inde ab A. CCCLVII usque ad a. DLIII datae avellane quae dicitur collectio* (CSEL 35), 2 vols., Vienna: E. Tempsky, 1895–1898, vol. 2, pp. 696–700.

Irenaeus of Lyons

Adversus haereses

Ed. and trans. Louis Doutreleau and Adelin Rousseau, *Irénée de Lyon. Contre les hérésies* (SC 100, 152, 153, 210, 211, 263, 264, 293, 294), 10 vols., Paris: Les Éditions du Cerf, 2002–2013.

Fragmenta

Ed. PG 7, cols. 1223–1264.

Jerome of Stridon

Altercatio luciferiani et orthodoxi

Ed. and trans. Aline Canellis, *S. Hieronymi Presbyteri Opera. III. Opera polemica. 4. Altercatio Luciferiani et orthodoxi* (CCSL 79B), Turnhout: Brepols, 2000.

Ed. and trans. Aline Canellis, *Débat entre un luciférien et un orthodoxe = Altercatio luciferiani et orthodoxi* (SC 473), Paris: Les Éditions du Cerf, 2003.

Chronicon

Ed. Rudolf Helm, *Die Chronik des Hieronymus: Hieronymi Chronicon*, 2nd ed. (GCS 47. Eusebius Werke 7), Berlin: Akademie-Verlag, 1956.

Ed. and trans. Malcolm Drew Donalson, *A Translation of Jerome's Chronicon with Historical Commentary*, Lewiston, NY: Mellen University Press, 1996.

De viris inlustribus

Ed. Ernest Cushing Richardson, *Hieronymus liber De viris illustribus. Gennadius liber De viris inlustribus* (TU 14.1a), Leipzig: J.C. Hinrichs, 1896, pp. 1–56.

Epistulae

Ed. Isidorus Hilberg, *Sancti Eusebii Hieronymi Epistulae*, 2nd ed. (CSEL 54, 55, 56.1, 56.2), 3 vols. in 4, Vienna: Verlag der Österreichischen Akademie der Wissenschaften, 1996.

Ed. and trans. Thomas Comerford Lawler and Charles Christopher Mierow, *The Letters of St. Jerome* (Ancient Christian Writers 33), New York: Newman Press, 1963.

Epistula praefatoria ad Homilias Origenis in Ezechielem

Ed. and trans. Willem Adolf Baehrens, *Origenes Werke* (GCS 2, 3, 6, 10, 22, 29, 30, 33, 35, 38, 40, 41, 49), 13 vols. in 14, Leipzig: J.C. Hinrichs, 1899–1955, vol. 8, pp. 318–319.

John Chrysostom

In Ioannem Homiliae

Ed. PG 59, cols. 23–482.

Laudatio S. patris nostri Eustathii Antiochaeni

Ed. PG 50, cols. 597–606.

Jovian, Emperor

Epistula ad Athanasium

Ed. Hanns Christof Brennecke, Uta Heil, and Annette von Stockhausen, *Athanasius Werke. Zweiter Band. Erster Teil. 8. Lieferung*, Berlin: De Gruyter, 2006, p. 357.

Julius I, Pope

Epistulae

Ed. and trans. Glen L. Thompson, *The Correspondence of Pope Julius I* (Library of Early Christianity 3), Washington, DC: Catholic University of America Press, 2015.

Liberius, Pope

Epistula ad catolicos episcopos Italiae

Ed. Alfred Leonhard Feder, *S. Hilarii episcopi Pictaviensis opera. Pars 4: Tractatus mysteriorum. Collectanea antiariana parisina (Fragmenta historica) cum appendice*

(Liber I ad Constantium). Liber ad Constantium imperatorem (Liber II ad Constantium). Hymni. Fragmenta minora. Spuria (CSEL 65), Vienna: F. Tempsky, 1916, pp. 156–157.

Liberius, Pope (Pseudo-)

Olim et ab initio

Ed. Paul Hinschius, *Decretales Pseudo-Isidorianae et Capitula Angilrammi*, Leipzig: B. Tauchnitz, 1863, 476–478.

Lucifer of Calaris

De regibus apostaticis

Ed. Gerardus Frederik Diercks, *Luciferi Calaritani opera quae supersunt* (CCSL 8), Turnhout: Brepols, 1978, pp. 133–161.

Moriundum esse pro Dei Filio

Ed. Gerardus Frederik Diercks, *Luciferi Calaritani opera quae supersunt* (CCSL 8), Turnhout: Brepols, 1978, pp. 263–300.

Lucius, Bernicianus, et al.

Petitio ad Iovianum imperatorem

Ed. Hanns Christof Brennecke, Uta Heil, and Annette von Stockhausen, *Athanasius Werke. Zweiter Band. Erster Teil. 8. Lieferung*, Berlin: De Gruyter, 2006, pp. 357–361.

Marius Victorinus

Adversus Arium

Ed. and trans. Pierre Hadot and Paul Henry, *Marius Victorinus. Traités théologiques sur la Trinité* (SC 68, 69), 2 vols., Paris: Les Éditions du Cerf, 1960, vol. 1, pp. 188–603.

Trans. Mary T. Clark, *Marius Victorinus: Theological Treatises on the Trinity*, Washington, DC: Catholic University of America Press, 1981.

Mekhilta de-Rabi Ishma'el

Ed. H. Saul Yisrael Horovitz and Avraham Rabin, *Mekhilta de-Rabbi Yishma'el*, Frankfurt am Main: J. Kauffmann, 1931.

Meletius of Antioch

De sigillatione sepulcri

Ed. and trans. Sergey Kim, "And They Sealed the Stone with the Seal of the Unit: A Georgian Homily of Meletius of Antioch from the Holy Week Cycle (CPG 3425–7)," *Le Muséon: Revue d'études orientales* 123 (2019): pp. 415–441.

Merkavah rabah

Ed. Peter Schäfer, *Synopse zur Hekhalot-Literatur* (Texte und Studien zum Antiken Judentum 2), Tübingen: J.C.B. Mohr, 1981.

Michael the Syrian

Chronicon

Trans. Jean-Baptiste Chabot, *Chronique de Michel le Syrien, patriarche jacobite d'Antioche (1166–1199)*, 4 vols., Paris: Ernest Leroux, 1899–1910.

Ed. Gregorios Yuhanna Ibrahim, *The Edessa-Aleppo Syriac Codex of the Chronicle of Michael the Great*, Piscataway, NJ: Gorgias Press, 2009.

Nikephoros Kallistos Xanthopoulos

Historia ecclesiastica

Ed. PG 145 (cols. 560–1332), 146 (cols. 9–1273), 147 (cols. 9–448).

Optatus of Milevis

De schismate Donatistarum

Ed. Karl Ziwsa, *S. Optati Milevitani Libri VII* (Corpus scriptorum ecclesiasticorum Latinorum 26), Vienna: F. Tempsky, 1893.

Origen of Alexandria

Adnotationes in Deuteronomium

Ed. PG 17, cols. 23–36.

Commentarius in Canticum

Ed. and trans. Manlio Simonetti, *Commento al Cantico dei Cantici*, Rome: Città nuova editrice, 1976.

Ed. and trans. Maria Antonietta Barbàra, *Commentario al Cantico dei cantici*, Bologna: Edizioni Dehoniane, 2005.

Ed. and trans. Alfons Fürst and Holger Strutwolf, *Origenes. Werke mit deutscher Übersetzung. IX/1. Der Kommentar zum Hohelied*, Berlin: De Gruyter; Freiburg: Herder, 2016.

Commentarius in Epistulam ad Romanos

Ed. and trans. Theresia Heither, *Commentarii in Epistulam ad Romanos = Römerbriefkommentar* (Fontes Christiani 2), 5 vols., Freiburg im Breisgau: Herder, 1990–1996.

Commentarius in Evangelium Ioannis

Ed. PG 14, cols. 21–830.

Ed. and trans. Cécile Blanc, *Commentaire sur saint Jean* (SC 120, 157, 222, 290, 385), 5 vols., Paris: Les Éditions du Cerf, 1966–1992.

Contra Celsum

Ed. and trans. Marcel Borret, *Contre Celse* (SC 132, 136, 147, 150, 227), 5 vols., Paris: Les Éditions du Cerf, 1967–1976.

Conversatio cum Heraclide

Ed. and trans. Jean Scherer, *Entretien d'Origène avec Héraclide* (SC 67), Paris: Les Éditions du Cerf, 1960.

De principiis

Ed. and trans. Herwig Görgemanns and Heinrich Karpp, *Origenes vier Bücher von den Prinzipien*, Darmstadt: Wissenschaftliche Buchgesellschaft, 1976.

Expositio in Proverbia

Ed. PG 17, cols. 161–252.

Ossius of Cordoba and Protogenes of Sardica

Epistula ad Iulium papam

Ed. PL 56, cols. 839–840.

Ed. Cuthbert Hamilton Turner, *Ecclesiae Occidentalis monumenta iuris antiquissima. Canonum et conciliorum Graecorum interpretationes latinae*, 2 vols. in 9, Oxford: Clarendon Press, 1899–1939, vol. 1, part 2, 644.

Ed. Martin Tetz, "'Ante omnia de sancta fide et de integritate veritatis': Glaubensfragen auf der Synode von Serdika (342)," *Zeitschrift für die neutestamentliche Wissenschaft und die Kunde der älteren Kirche* 76 (1985): pp. 243–269.

Ed. and trans. Juan José Ayán, Manuel Crespo, Jesús Polo, and Pilar González, *Osio de Córdoba: Un siglo de la historia del cristianismo. Obras, documentos conciliares, testimonios* (Biblioteca de Autores Cristianos 712), Madrid: Biblioteca de Autores Cristianos, 2013.

Pamphilus the Theologian

Capitulorum diversorum seu dubitationum solutio de recta erga Christum religione

Ed. Angelo Mai, *Nova Patrum Bibliotheca*, 9 vols., Rome: 1844–1888, II, 595–653.

Paul of Samosata (Pseudo-)

Ad Zenobiam

Ed. and trans. José H. Declerck, "Deux nouveaux fragments attribués à Paul de Samosate," *Byzantion: Revue internationale des études byzantines* 54 (1984): pp. 116–140.

Peter of Callinicus

Tractatus contra Damianum

Ed. and trans. Rifaat Y. Ebied, Albert Van Roey, and Lionel R. Wickham, *Petri Callinicensis patriarchae Antiocheni Tractatus contra Damianum* (CCSG 29, 32, 35, 54), 4 vols., Turnhout: Brepols; Louvain: Louvain University Press, 1994–2003.

Philastrius of Brescia

Diversarum haereseon liber

Ed. Bernhard Bischoff, Vinzenz Bulhart, F. Heylen, Anselm Hoste, and André Wilmart, eds., *Eusebius Vercellensis, Filastrius Brixiensis, Hegemonius (Ps.), Isaac Iudaeus, Archidiaconus Romanus, Fortunatianus Aquileiensis, Chromatius Aquileiensis Opera quae supersunt. Diversorum hereseon liber. Adversus haereses. Opera quae supersunt. De reconciliandis paenitentibus. Commentarii in evangelia. Opera quae supersunt* (CCSL 9), Turnhout: Brepols, 1957, pp. 217–324.

Philostorgius

Historia ecclesiastica

Ed. Joseph Bidez, *Philostorgius Kirchengeschichte mit dem Leben des Lucian von Antiochien und den Fragmenten eines Arianischen Historiographen* (GCS 21), Leipzig: J.C. Hinrichs, 1913.

Passio Sancti Artemii

Ed. PG 115, cols. 1160–1264.

Photius

Bibliotheca

Ed. and trans. René Henry, *Bibliothèque*, 9 vols., Paris: Les Belles lettres, 1959–1991.

Ed. and trans. Nunzio Bianchi, Luciano Canfora, and Claudio Schiano, *Fozio. Biblioteca*, Pisa: Edizioni della Normale, 2016.

Plato

Cratylus

Ed. and trans. Harold North Fowler, *Plato in Twelve Volumes. IV. Cratylus, Parmenides, Greater Hippias, Lesser Hippias* (Loeb Classical Library 167), Cambridge, MA: Harvard University Press, 1926, pp. 1–191.

De republica

Ed. and trans. Chris Emlyn-Jones and William Preddy, *Plato V and VI. Republic* (Loeb Classical Library 237, 276), 2 vols., Cambridge, MA: Harvard University Press, 2013.

Timaeus

Ed. and trans. Robert Gregg Bury, *Plato. Timaeus. Critias. Cleitophon. Menexenus. Epistles* (Loeb Classical Library 234), Cambridge, MA: Harvard University Press, 2014, pp. 1–253.

Plutarch

Quaestiones platonicae

Ed. and trans. Harold F. Cherniss, *Plutarch. Moralia. XIII/1* (Loeb Classical Library 427), Cambridge, MA: Harvard University Press, 1976.

Possessor, Bishop

Epistula ad Hormisdam

Ed. PL 63, col. 489.

Ed. Otto Günther, *Epistulae imperatorum pontificum aliorum inde ab A. CCCLVII usque ad a. DLIII datae: Avellana quae dicitur collectio* (CSEL 35), 2 vols., Vienna: E. Tempsky, 1895–1898, vol. 2, pp. 695–696.

Ptolemy the Gnostic

Epistula ad Floram

Ed. and trans. Gilles Quispel, *Ptolémée. Lettre à Flora*, 2nd ed. (SC 24 bis), Paris: Les Éditions du Cerf, 1966.

Refutatio hypocriseos Meletii et Eusebii

Ed. PG 28, cols. 85–88.

Ed. and trans. Annette von Stockhausen, in Hanns Christof Brennecke, Uta Heil, and Annette von Stockhausen, eds., *Athanasius Werke. Dritter Band. Erster Teil. 5. Lieferung*, Berlin: De Gruyter, 2014, pp. 674–678.

Regulae definitionum contra haereticos prolatae

Ed. Martien F.G. Parmentier, "Rules of Interpretation Issued against the Heretics (CPL 560)," *Journal of Eastern Christian Studies* 60 (2008): pp. 231–273.

Rufinus of Aquileia

De adulteratione librorum Origenis

Ed. Manlio Simonetti, *Tyrannius Rufinus. Opera* (CCSL 20), Turnhout: Brepols, 1991, pp. 7–17.

Historia ecclesiastica

Ed. Theodor Mommsen, Eduard Schwartz, and Friedhelm Winkelmann, *Die Kirchengeschichte*, 2nd ed. (GCS N.F. 6. Eusebius Werke 2), 3 vols., Berlin: Akademie-Verlag, 1999, vol. 2, pp. 957–1040.

Trans. Philip R. Amidon, *The Church History of Rufinus of Aquileia. Books 10 and 11*, New York: Oxford University Press, 1997.

Sherira bar Hanina

Epistula

Ed. Benjamin Manasseh Lewin, *Iggeret rav Sherira Ga'on: Mesudderet bi-shnei nusḥa'ot, nosaḥ Sefarad ṿe-nosaḥ Tsarfat, 'im ḥillufei ha-girsa'ot mi-kol kitvei-haṿad ṿe-ḳiṭ'ei ha-"Genizah" she-ba-'olam*, Haifa: [s.n.] 1921 (repr: Jerusalem: Major, 1962).

Siricius, Pope

Epistula ad Himerium Tarraconensem

Ed. Pierre Coustant, *Epistolae Romanorum pontificum et quae ad eos scriptae sunt a. S. Clemente I usque ad Innocentium III, quotquot reperiri poruerunt seu novae sue diversis in locis sparsim editae. I. Ab anno Christi 67 ad annum 440*. Paris: Delatour and Coustelier, 1721.

Ed. PL 13, cols. 1131–1148.

Socrates of Constantinople

Historia ecclesiastica

Ed. and trans. Pierre Maraval and Pierre Périchon, *Socrate de Constantinople. Histoire ecclésiastique* (SC 477, 493, 505, 506), 4 vols., Paris: Les Éditions du Cerf, 2004–2007.

Sozomen

Historia ecclesiastica

Ed. and trans. Bernard Grillet, André-Jean Festugière, and Guy Sabbah, *Sozomène. Histoire ecclésiastique* (SC 306, 418, 495, 516), 4 vols., Paris: Les Éditions du Cerf, 1983–2008.

Sulpicius Severus

Chronica

Ed. and trans. Ghislaine de Senneville-Grave, *Chroniques* (SC 441), Paris: Les Éditions du Cerf, 1999.

Ed. Piergiorgio Parroni, *Sulpicii Severi Chronica* (CCSL 63), Turnhout: Brepols, 2017.

Vita sancti Martini Turonensis

Ed. Jacques Fontaine, *Sulpice Sévère. Vie de Saint Martin* (SC 133, 134, 135), 3 vols., Paris: Les Éditions du Cerf, 1967–1969.

Talmud Yerushalmi. Massekhet Terumot

Ed. and trans. Heinrich W. Guggenheimer, *The Jerusalem Talmud. First order, Zeraim. Tractates Terumot and Mas'erot* (Studia Judaica 21), Berlin: De Gruyter, 2002.

Trans. Moïse Schwab, *Le Talmud de Jérusalem. III. Traités Troumoth, Maasseroth, Maasser schéni, Ḥalla, Orla, Biccurim*, Paris: Maisonneuve, 1879.

Trans. Alan J. Avery-Peck, *The Talmud of the Land of Israel: A Preliminary Translation and Explanation*. Vol. 6, *Terumot*, Chicago: University of Chicago Press, 1988.

Tertullian

Adversus Praxean

Ed. and trans. Ernest Evans, *Adversus Praxean liber = Tertullian's Treatise against Praxeas*, London: SPCK, 1948.

Theodoret of Cyrrhus

Commentarii in Esaïam

Ed. and trans. Jean-Noël Guinot, *Théodoret de Cyr. Commentaire sur Isaïe* (SC 276, 295, 315), 3 vols., Paris: Les Éditions du Cerf, 1980–1984.

Haereticarum fabularum compendium

Ed. PG 83, cols. 355–556.

Ed. Jonathan Bieler and Benjamin Gleede, *Unterscheidung von Lüge und Wahrheit. Abriss über die üblen Märchen der Häretiker Zusammenfassung der göttlichen Lehrsätze. Anhang: Pseudo-Theodoret, Gegen Nestorius an Sporakios* (GCS 26), Berlin: De Gruyter and Berlin-Brandenburgische Akademie der Wissenschaften, 2020.

Historia ecclesiastica

Ed. Léon Parmentier, *Theodoret Kirchengeschichte* (GCS 19), Leipzig: J.C. Hinrichs, 1911.

Ed. Léon Parmentier and Felix Scheidweiler, *Theodoret Kirchengeschichte* (GCS 44), 2nd ed., Berlin: Akademie-Verlag, 1954.

Ed. Günther Christian Hansen, *Theodoret Kirchengeschichte* (GCS N.F. 5), 3rd ed., Berlin: Akademie-Verlag, 1998.

Ed. and trans. Jean Bouffartigue, Pierre Canivet, Annick Martin, Luce Pietri, and Françoise Thélamon, *Théodoret de Cyr. Histoire Ecclésiastique* (SC 501, 530), 2 vols., Paris: Les Éditions du Cerf, 2009.

Tosefta

Ed. Saul Lieberman, *The Tosefta according to the Codex Vienna, with Variants from Codices Erfurt, London, Genizah Mss. and Editio Princeps (Venice 1521) together with*

References to Parallel Passages in Talmudic Literature and a Brief Commentary, 2 vols., New York: Jewish Theological Seminary of America, 1962.

Vincent of Lérins

Commonitorium

Ed. Roland Demeulenaere, *Foebadius. Victricius. Leporius. Vincentius Lerinensis. Evagrius. Rubricius* (CCSL 64), Turnhout: Brepols, 1985, pp. 145–195.

Bibliography

Abramowski, Luise. "Dionysius of Rome († 268) and Dionysius of Alexandria († 264/5)." Pages 1–35 in Luise Abramowski, *Formula and Context: Studies in Early Christian Thought*. Collected Studies Series 365. Brookfield, VT: Variorum, 1992. [= Translation of "Dionysius von Rom († 268) und Dionysius von Alexandrien († 264/5) in den arianischen Streitigkeiten des 4. Jahrhunderts." *Zeitschrift für Kirchengeschichte* 93 (1982): 240–272.]

———. "Trinitarische und christologische Hypostasenformeln." *Theologie und Philosophie* 54 (1979): 38–49.

Abrams, Daniel. "The Boundaries of Divine Ontology: The Inclusion and Exclusion of Meṭaṭron in the Godhead." *Harvard Theological Review* 87 (1994): 291–321.

Acerbi, Silvia. "Intolerancia dogmática en el siglo V: Un estudio de la legislación imperial anti-herética (CTh. XVI, 5, 66—C.I. I, I, 3—ACO II, III, 3)." Pages 127–144 in *Libertad e intolerancia religiosa en el Imperio romano*. Edited by José Fernández Ubiña and Mar Marcos. 'Ilu. Revista de Ciencias de las Religiones. Anejo 18. Madrid: Publicaciones Universidad Complutense de Madrid, 2007.

Achard, Martin. "Philosophie antique: *Logos endiathetos* et théorie des *lekta* chez les Stoïciens." *Laval Théologique et Philosophique* 57 (2001): 225–233.

Agamben, Giorgio. *The Man without Content*. Translated by Georgia Albert. Stanford, CA: Stanford University Press, 1999 [= Translation of *L'uomo senza contenuto*. Milano: Rizzoli, 1970].

Ahdut, Eliyahu. *Ma'amad ha-'ishah ha-yehudiyah be-Vavel bi-tḳufat ha-Talmud*. Ph.D. dissertation. Jerusalem: Hebrew University, 1999.

Ahmed, Luise, Alfons Fürst, Christian Gers-Uphaus, and Stefan Klug, eds. *Monotheistische Denkfiguren in der Spätantike*. Tübingen: Mohr Siebeck, 2013.

Aiello, Vincenzo. "Costantino e i vescovi di Roma. Momenti di un problematico incontro." Pages 203–218 in *Costantino I. Enciclopedia costantiniana. Sulla figura e l'immagine dell'imperatore del cosiddetto Editto di Milano, 313–2013*. Rome: Istituto dell'Enciclopedia Treccani, 2013.

———. "Costantino 'eretico'. Difesa della 'ortodossia' e anticostantinianesimo in età teodosiana." *Atti dell'Accademia romanistica costantiniana* 9 (1993): 55–84.

———. "Ossio e la politica religiosa di Costantino." Pages 261–274 in *Costantino I. Enciclopedia costantiniana. Sulla figura e l'immagine dell'imperatore del cosiddetto Editto di Milano, 313–2013*. Rome: Istituto dell'Enciclopedia Treccani, 2013.

Albeck, Chanoch. "Le-ʿarikhat ha-Talmud ha-bavli." Pages 1–12 in *Sefer zikaron le-ʾAsher Gulʾak ṿe-li-Shmuʾel Ḳlain za"l*. Jerusalem: Ḥevrah le-hotsaʾat sefarim ʿal yad ha-Universiṭah ha-ʿIvrit, 1942.

———. *Mavo la-Talmudim*. Tel Aviv: Devir, 1969.

Albeck, Shalom. *Yesodot be-dinei ha-mamonot ba-Talmud*. Ramat Gan: Bar Ilan University Press, 1994.

Albert, Micheline, and Annick Martin. *Histoire «acéphale» et index syriaque des lettres festales d'Athanase d'Alexandrie*. SC 317. Paris: Les Éditions du Cerf, 1985.

Alexander, Elizabeth Shanks. "The Orality of Rabbinic Literature." Pages 38–57 in *The Cambridge Companion to the Talmud and Rabbinic Literature*. Edited by Charlotte Elisheva Fonrobert and Martin S. Jaffee. Cambridge: Cambridge University Press, 2007.

———. *Transmitting Mishnah: The Shaping Influence of Oral Tradition*. Cambridge: Cambridge University Press, 2006.

Alexander, Philip S. "3 Enoch and the Talmud." *Journal for the Study of Judaism* 18 (1987): 40–68.

———. "3 (Hebrew Apocalypse of) Enoch." Pages 223–315 in vol. 1 of *The Old Testament Pseudepigrapha*. Edited by James H. Charlesworth. 2 vols. Garden City, NY: Doubleday, 1983.

Alföldi, András. "The Crisis of the Empire (A.D. 249–270)." Pages 175–231 in *Cambridge Ancient History*, vol. 12, *The Imperial Crisis and Recovery, A.D. 193–324*. 2nd ed. Edited by Frank Ezra Adcock, John Bagnell Bury, and Stanely Arthur Cook. Cambridge: Cambridge University Press, 1939.

Allen, Pauline, and Albert van Roey, eds. *Monophysite Texts of the Sixth Century*. Orientalia Lovaniensia Analecta 56. Leuven: Peeters, 1994.

Altaner, Berthold, and Alfred Stuiber. *Patrologie. Leben, Schriften und Lehre der Kirchenväter*. 9th ed. Freiburg: Herder, 1978.

Amann, Émile. "Pères de l'Église." Columns 1192–1215 in vol. 12.1 of *Dictionnaire de théologie catholique*. 15 vols. Paris: Letouzey et Ané, 1903–1950.

Amidon, Philip R. *The Church History of Rufinus of Aquileia. Books 10 and 11*. New York: Oxford University Press, 1997.

———. "Paulinus' Subscription to the «Tomus ad Antiochenos»." *Journal of Theological Studies* 53 (2002): 53–74.

Aminoah, Noah. *ʿArikhat massekhet Ḳiddushin ba-Talmud ha-Bavli: Siddur, ʿarikhah, girsaʾot shel gemara, yaḥasei sugyot, Bavli Yerushalmi*. Tel Aviv: Beit-ha-sefer le-madaʿei ha-Yahadut ʿal shem Ḥayim Rozenberg, Universiṭat Tel Aviv: 1976/1977.

———. Review of Richard Lee Kalmin, *Sages, Stories, Authors, and Editors in Rabbinic Babylonia*. *Jewish Quarterly Review* 84 (1993–1994): 283–288.

Anatolios, Khaled. *Athanasius: The Coherence of His Thought*. London: Routledge, 1998.

———. *Retrieving Nicaea: The Development and Meaning of Trinitarian Doctrine*. Grand Rapids, MI: Baker Academic, 2011.

Ando, Clifford. *The Matter of the Gods: Religion and the Roman Empire*. Berkeley: University of California Press, 2008.

Andrade, Nathanael P. *Zenobia: Shooting Star of Palmyra*. New York: Oxford University Press, 2018.

Appelbaum, Alan. "The Rabbis and Palmyra: A Case Study on (Mis-)Reading Rabbinics for Historical Purposes." *Jewish Quarterly Review* 101 (2011): 527–544.

Arad, Mordechai. *Meḥallel shabat be-farhesya: Munaḥ talmudi u-mashmaʿuto ha-hisṭorit*. New York: Jewish Theological Seminary of America, 2009.

Armstrong, C.B. "The Synod of Alexandria and the Schism at Antioch in A.D. 362." *Journal of Theological Studies* 22 (1921): 206–221, 247–355.

Asad, Talal. *The Idea of an Anthropology of Islam*. Washington, DC: Center for Contemporary Arab Studies, Georgetown University, 1986.

Asor Rosa, Alberto. "Intellettuali." Columns 801–827 in vol. 7 of *Enciclopedia*. 16 vols. Turin: Einaudi, 1979.

Assemani, Stephanus Evodius, and Joseph Simonius Assemani, eds. *Bibliothecae apostolicae Vaticanae codicum manuscriptorum catalogus in tres partes distributus, in quarum prima orientales, in altera graeci, in tertia latini, italici aliorumque Europaeorum idiomatum codices*. Rome: Typographia Linguarum Orientalium, 1759.

Assmann, Jan. "Monotheism and Its Political Consequences." Pages 141–159 in *Religion and Politics: Cultural Perspectives*. Edited by Bernhard Giesen and Daniel Šuber. International Studies in Religion and Society 3. Leiden: Peeters, 2005.

———. *Of God and Gods: Egypt, Israel, and the Rise of Monotheism*. Madison: University of Wisconsin Press, 2008.

———. *The Price of Monotheism*. Stanford, CA: Stanford University Press, 2010.

———. *The Search for God in Ancient Egypt*. Translated by David Lorton. Ithaca, NY: Cornell University Press, 2001. [= Translation of *Ägypten. Theologie und Frömmigkeit einer frühen Hochkultur*. Stuttgart: Kohlhammer, 1984.]

Athanassiadi, Polymnia. "Christians and Others: The Conversion Ethos of Late Antiquity." Pages 23–48 in *Conversion in Late Antiquity: Christianity, Islam, and Beyond; Papers from the Andrew W. Mellon Foundation Sawyer Seminar, University of Oxford, 2009–2010*. Edited by Neil McLynn, Arietta Papaconstantinou, and Daniel L. Schwartz. Burlington, VT: Ashgate, 2015.

———. "The Creation of Orthodoxy in Neoplatonism." Pages 271–291 in *Philosophy and Power in the Graeco-Roman World: Essays in Honour of Miriam Griffin*. Edited by Gillian Clark and Tessa Rajak. Oxford: Oxford University Press, 2002.

———. *La lutte pour l'orthodoxie dans le platonisme tardif: De Numénius à Damascius.* Âne d'or 25. Paris: Les Belles lettres, 2006.

———. *Vers la pensée unique: La montée de l'intolérance dans l'Antiquité tardive.* Paris: Les Belles lettres, 2010.

Athanassiadi, Polymnia, and Michael Frede, eds. *Pagan Monotheism in Late Antiquity.* Oxford: Clarendon, 1999.

Auerbach, Eric. *Mimesis: The Representation of Reality in Western Literature.* Translated by Willard R. Trask. Princeton, NJ: Princeton University Press, 1953 [= Translation of *Mimesis. Dargestellte Wirklichkeit in der abendländischen Literatur.* Bern: A. Francke, 1946].

Auwers, Jean-Marie, Régis Burnet, and Didier Luciani, eds. *L'antijudaïsme des Pères: Mythe et (ou) réalité. Actes du colloque de Louvain-la-Neuve, 20–22 mai 2015.* Paris: Bauchesne, 2017.

Avery-Peck, Alan J. *Terumot.* Vol. 6 of *The Talmud of the Land of Israel: A Preliminary Translation and Explanation.* 35 vols. Chicago: University of Chicago Press, 1988.

Avi-Yonah, Michael. *The Jews of Palestine.* New York: Schocken Books, 1976.

Ayán, Juan José, Manuel Crespo, Jesús Polo, and Pilar González. *Osio de Córdoba: Un siglo de la historia del cristianismo. Obras, documentos conciliares, testimonios.* Madrid: Biblioteca de Autores Cristianos, 2013.

Ayaso Martínez, José Ramón. "Espacios de libertad en el judaísmo rabínico clásico." Pages 13–25 in *Libertad e intolerancia religiosa en el Imperio romano.* Edited by José Fernández Ubiña and Mar Marcos. 'Ilu. Revista de Ciencias de las Religiones. Anejo 18. Madrid: Publicaciones Universidad Complutense de Madrid, 2007.

Ayres, Lewis. "Athanasius' Initial Defense of the Term Ὁμοούσιος: Rereading the *De Decretis.*" *Journal of Early Christian Studies* 12 (2004): 337–359.

———. "Irenaeus and the 'Rule of Truth': A Reconsideration." Pages 145–163 in *The Rise of the Early Christian Intellectual.* Edited by Lewis Ayres and H. Clifton Ward. Arbeiten zur Kirchengeschichte 139. Berlin: De Gruyter, 2020.

———. *Nicaea and Its Legacy: An Approach to Fourth-Century Trinitarian Theology.* Oxford: Oxford University Press, 2004.

———. "Nicaea and Its Legacy: An Introduction." *Harvard Theological Review* 100 (2007): 141–144.

———. "A Response to the Critics of Nicaea and Its Legacy." *Harvard Theological Review* 100 (2007): 159–171.

Ayres, Lewis, and Andrew Radde-Gallwitz. "Doctrine of God." Pages 864–885 in *The Oxford Handbook of Early Christian Studies.* Edited by Susan Ashbrook Harvey and David G. Hunter. Oxford: Oxford University Press, 2008.

Ayres, Lewis, and H. Clifton Ward. "Introduction and Acknowledgments." Pages 1–5 in *The Rise of the Early Christian Intellectual.* Edited by Lewis Ayres and H. Clifton Ward. Arbeiten zur Kirchengeschichte 139. Berlin: De Gruyter, 2020.

Ayroulet, Élie, and Aline Canellis, eds. *L'exégèse de saint Jérôme.* Memoires du Centre Jean Palerne 42. Saint-Étienne: Publications de l'Université de Saint-Étienne, 2018.

Bacher, Wilhelm. *Die exegetische Terminologie der jüdischen Traditionsliteratur.* 2 vols. Leipzig: J.C. Hinrichs, 1905.

———. *Tradition und Tradenten in den Schulen Palästinas und Babyloniens.* Leipzig: G. Fock, 1914.

Bakhos, Carol. “Figuring (Out) Esau: The Rabbis and Their Others.” *Journal of Jewish Studies* 58 (2007): 250–262.

Balavoine, Émilie. “La rhétorique polémique dans la lettre 17 de Jérôme.” *Exercices de rhétorique* 14 (2020). Published open-access March 18, 2020, at http://journals.openedition.org/rhetorique/950. Retrieved October 30, 2021.

Balberg, Mira. “Bein heṭroṭopyah le-ʾutopyah: Ḳeriʾah bi-shnei sipurei masaʿ el zonot u-v-ḥazarah.” *Meḥḳerei Yerushalayim be-sifrut ʿivrit* 22 (2008): 191–213.

Baldini, Antonio. “Il ruolo di Paolo di Samosata nella politica culturale di Zenobia e la decisione di Aureliano ad Antiochia.” *Rivista di storia dell’antichità* 5 (1975): 59–77.

Ballerini, Girolamo, and Pietro Ballerini. *Disquisitiones de antiquis collectionibus et collectoribus canonum in Opera Leonis magnis.* Venice, 1753. Reprinted in PL 56.

Baltes, Matthias. “Is the Idea of the Good in Plato’s *Republic* Beyond Being?” Pages 3–25 in *Studies in Plato and the Platonic Tradition: Essays Presented to John Whittaker.* Edited by Mark Joyal. Aldershot, UK: Ashgate, 1997. [= Pages 351–371 in Matthias Baltes, *Dianoémata. Kleine Schriften zu Platon und zum Platonismus.* Stuttgart: B.G. Teubner, 1999.]

Bamberger, Ittay. “Melakhah she-ʾeinah tserikhah le-gufah u-mḳalḳel.” *Mi-beit midrashenu—Shabat* (2010–2011): 264–270.

Bardenhewer, Otto. *Geschichte der altkirchlichen Literatur.* Vol. 3, *Das vierte Jahrhundert mit Ausschluss der Schriftsteller syrischer Zunge.* Freiburg im Breisgau: Herder Verlagshandlung, 1912.

Bardy, Gustave. “Faux et frauds littéraires dans l’antiquité chrétienne.” *Revue d’Histoire Ecclésiastique* 32 (1936): 5–23, 275–302.

———. “La lettre des six évêques à Paul de Samosate.” *Recherches de Science Religieuse* 16 (1916): 17–33.

———. *La question des langues dans l’église ancienne.* Paris: Beauchesne, 1948.

———. “Le Concile d’Antioche (379).” *Revue Bénedictine* 45 (1933): 196–213.

———. *Paul de Samosate: Étude historique.* Études et Documents 4. Louvain: Spicilegium Sacrum Lovaniense and E. Champion, 1923.

———. *Recherches sur Saint Lucien d’Antioche et son école.* Paris: Gabriel Beauchesne et ses fils, 1936.

———. “St. Jerome and Greek Thought.” Pages 83–112 in *A Monument to Saint Jerome: Essays on Some Aspects of His Life, Works, and Influence.* Edited by Francis Xavier Murphy. New York: Sheed & Ward, 1952.

Barker, Celia B. *The Meletian Schism at Antioch.* M.A. thesis. Durham, UK: Durham University, 1974.

Barnard, Leslie W. “Athanasius and the Emperor Jovian.” Pages 384–389 in *Studia Patristica XXI: Papers Presented to the Tenth International Conference on Patristic Stud-*

ies Held in Oxford 1987. Second Century: Tertullian to Nicaea in the West, Clement of Alexandria and Origen, Athanasius. Edited by Elizabeth Anne Livingstone. Louvain: Peeters, 1989.

———. *Studies in Athanasius' Apologia Secunda.* Europäische Hochschulschriften. Reihe 23, 467. Bern: Peter Lang, 1992.

———. "What Was Arius' Philosophy?" *Theologische Zeitschrift* 28 (1972): 110–117.

Barnes, Michel René. "De Régnon Reconsidered." *Augustinian Studies* 26 (1995): 51–79.

———. "The Fourth Century as Trinitarian Canon." Pages 47–67 in *Christian Origins: Theology, Rhetoric, and Community.* Edited by Lewis Ayres and Gareth Jones. London: Routledge, 1998.

———. "One Nature, One Power: Consensus Doctrine in Pro-Nicene Polemic." Pages 205–223 in *Studia Patristica XXIX: Historica, Theologica et Philosophica, Critica et Philologica; Papers Presented at the Twelfth International Conference on Patristic Studies Held in Oxford 1995.* Edited by Elizabeth Anne Livingstone. Louvain: Peeters, 1997.

———. *The Power of God: Δύναμις in Gregory of Nyssa's Trinitarian Theology.* Washington, DC: Catholic University of America Press, 2001.

Barnes, Timothy David. *Athanasius and Constantius: Theology and Politics in the Constantinian Empire.* Cambridge, MA: Harvard University Press, 1993.

———. *Constantine and Eusebius.* Cambridge, MA: Harvard University Press, 1981.

———. *Constantine: Dynasty, Religion and Power in the Later Roman Empire.* Chichester, UK: Wiley-Blackwell, 2011.

———. "The Date of the Deposition of Eustathius of Antioch." *Journal of Theological Studies* 51 (2000): 150–160.

———. "Emperors and Bishops, A.D. 324–344: Some Problems." *American Journal of Ancient History* 3 (1978): 53–75.

———. "The Exile and Recalls of Arius." *Journal of Theological Studies* 60 (2009): 109–129.

———. "Hilary of Poitiers on His Exile." *Vigiliae Christianae* 46 (1992): 129–140.

———. "The New Critical Edition of Athanasius' *Defence before Constantius.*" *Zeitschrift für Antikes Christentum* 11 (2007): 378–401.

Barone Adesi, Giorgio. *L'età della "lex Dei."* Pubblicazioni dell'Istituto di diritto romano e dei diritti dell'Oriente mediterraneo 71. Naples: Jovene, 1992.

———. "Libertà religiosa e convivenza delle religioni nell'editto di Milano e negli indirizzi legislativi costantiniani." Pages 11–40 in *Da Costantino a oggi: La libera convivenza delle religioni. Atti del Seminario interdisciplinare nel 1700° anniversario dell'Editto di Milano organizzato dai dottorati di ricerca in "Diritti e istituzioni" e in "Diritto, persona e mercato" del Dipartimento di giurisprudenza dell'Università degli studi di Torino (Torino, 24 ottobre 2013).* Edited by Giovanni Zuanazzi. Quaderni del Dipartimento di giurisprudenza dell'Università di Torino 2. Naples: Editoriale scientifica, 2015.

Barry, Jennifer. *Bishops in Flight: Exile and Displacement in Late Antiquity*. Oakland: University of California Press, 2019.

———. "Heroic Bishops: Hilary of Poitiers' Exilic Discourse." *Vigiliae Christianae* 70 (2016): 1–20.

Bartolozzi, Giuseppe. "L'ὁμοούσιος niceno: Alcune considerazioni." *Augustinianum* 53 (2013): 375–392.

Barton, Carlin A., and Daniel Boyarin. *Imagine No Religion: How Modern Abstractions Hide Ancient Realities*. New York: Fordham University Press, 2016.

Batnitzky, Leora Faye. *How Judaism Became a Religion: An Introduction to Modern Jewish Thought*. Princeton, NJ: Princeton University Press, 2011.

Battifol, Pierre. *La paix constantinienne et le catholicisme*. 5th ed. Paris: Lecoffre, 1929.

———. "Les sources de l'*Altercatio Luciferiani et Orthodoxi* de St Jérôme." Pages 97–113 in *Miscellanea geronimiana. Scritti varii pubblicati nel XV centenario della morte di San Girolamo*. Edited by Vincenzo Vannutelli. Rome: Tipografia Poliglotta Vaticana, 1920.

———. "Un historiographe anonyme arien du IVe siècle." *Römische Quartalschrift* 9 (1895): 57–97.

Beatrice, Pier Franco. "The Word 'Homoousios' from Hellenism to Christianity." *Church History* 2 (2002): 243–272.

Becker, Adam H. "The Comparative Study of 'Scholasticism' in Late Antique Mesopotamia: Rabbis and East Syrians." *Association of Jewish Studies Review* 34 (2010): 91–113.

———. "Polishing the Mirror: Some Thoughts on Syriac Sources and Early Judaism." Pages 897–915 in vol. 2 of *Envisioning Judaism: Studies in Honor of Peter Schäfer on the Occasion of His Seventieth Birthday*. Edited by Ra'anan S. Boustan, Klaus Herrmann, Reimund Leicht, Annette Yoshiko Reed, and Giuseppe Veltri. Tübingen: Mohr Siebeck, 2013.

———. "Positing a 'Cultural Relationship' between Plato and the Babylonian Talmud: Daniel Boyarin's *Socrates and the Fat Rabbis* (2009)." *Jewish Quarterly Review* 101 (2011): 255–269.

Becker, Adam H., and Annette Yoshiko Reed. "Introduction: Traditional Models and New Directions." Pages 1–33 in *The Ways That Never Parted: Jews and Christians in Late Antiquity and the Early Middle Ages*. Edited by Adam H. Becker and Annette Yoshiko Reed. Tübingen: Mohr Siebeck, 2003.

Beckwith, Carl L. Review of Ayres, *Nicaea and Its Legacy: An Approach to Fourth-Century Trinitarian Theology*. *Journal of Early Christian Studies* 13 (2005): 398–400.

Beeley, Christopher. "Divine Causality and the Monarchy of God the Father in Gregory of Nazianzus." *Harvard Theological Review* 100 (2007): 199–214.

Be'eri, Nurit. *Yatsa le-tarbut ra'ah: Elisha' ben Avuyah, 'Aḥer.'* Tel Aviv: Yedi'ot aḥaronot, 2007.

Behr, John. "The Question of Nicene Orthodoxy." Pages 15–27 in *Byzantine Orthodoxies: Papers from the Thirty-sixth Spring Symposium of Byzantine Studies, University of Durham, 23–25 March 2002*. Edited by Augustine M.C. Casiday and Andrew Louth. Society for the Promotion of Byzantine Studies Publications 12. Aldershot: Ashgate, 2006.

———. "Response to Ayres: The Legacies of Nicaea, East and West." *Harvard Theological Review* 100 (2007): 145–152.

Behrendt, Anja. "Die Markierung von Zitaten in Theorie und Praxis am Beispiel von Cicero, *Fam.* 13,15." Pages 111–134 in *Fremde Rede—Eigene Rede: Zitieren und verwandte Strategien in antiker Prosa*. Edited by Alexandra Binternagel and Ute Tischer. Bern: Lang, 2010.

Beltz, Walter. "Katalog der koptischen Handschriften der Papyrus-Sammlung der Staatlichen Museen zu Berlin (Teil I)." *Archiv für Papyrusforschung und verwandte Gebiete* 26 (1978): 57–119.

Ben-Menahem, Hanina. "Interpretive Essay." Pages 1–42 in *Controversy and Dialogue in the Jewish Tradition: A Reader*. Edited by Hanina Ben-Menahem, Neil S. Hecht, and Shai Wosner. Publications of the Institute of Jewish Law, Boston University School of Law 31. London: Routledge, 2005.

———. "Is There Always One Uniquely Correct Answer to a Legal Question in the Talmud?" *Jewish Law Annual* 6 (1987): 164–175.

———. *Judicial Deviation in Talmudic Law: Governed by Men, Not by Rules*. Chur, Switzerland: Harwood Academic, 1991.

Benoît, André, and Marcel Simon. *Le judaïsme et le christianisme antique: D'Antiochus Epiphane à Constantin*. Nouvelle Clio. L'histoire et ses problèmes 10. Paris: Presses universitaires de France, 1968.

Ber, Moshe. "ʿAl maʿaśei kaparah shel baʿalei teshuvah be-sifrut Ḥazal." *Tsion* 46 (1981): 159–181. [= Pages 216–238 in Moshe Ber, *Ḥakhmei ha-Mishnah ve-ha-Talmud. Hagutam, poʿalam u-manhigutam*. Edited by Raphael Yankelevitz, Emmanuel Friedheim, and Daniel Sperber. Ramat Gan: Bar Ilan University Press, 2011.

Bergjan, Silke-Petra. "From Rivalry to Marginalisation: *Tomus ad Antiochenos* and the Paulinus Group in Antioch." Pages 19–39 in *Dealing with Difference: Christian Patterns of Response to Religious Rivalry in Late Antiquity and Beyond*. Edited by Geoffrey D. Dunn and Christine Shepardson. Studien und Texte zu Antike und Christentum 129. Tübingen: Mohr Siebeck, 2021.

Bergmann, Ari. *Halevy, Halivni, and the Oral Formation of the Babylonian Talmud*. Ph.D. dissertation. New York: Columbia University, 2014.

Berkhof, Hendrikus. *Die Theologie des Eusebius von Caesarea*. Amsterdam: Uitgeversmaatschappij Holland, 1939.

Berutti, Girolamo. "Zenobia, regina di Palmira, e il dominio romano sul deserto siriano." *Romana. Rivista dell'Istituto Interuniversitario Italiano* (1941): 393–394.

Berzon, Todd S. *Classifying Christians: Ethnography, Heresiology, and the Limits of Knowledge in Late Antiquity*. Oakland: University of California Press, 2016.

Bethune-Baker, James Franklin. *An Introduction to the Early History of Christian Doctrine to the Time of the Council of Chalcedon*. London: Methuen, 1903.

Bianch, Nunzio, Luciano Canfora, and Claudio Schiano. *Fozio. Biblioteca*. Pisa: Edizioni della Normale, 2016.

Bidez, Joseph, *Philostorgius Kirchengeschichte mit dem Leben des Lucian von Antiochien und den Fragmenten eines Arianischen Historiographen*. GCS 21. Leipzig: J.C. Hinrichs, 1913.

Bienert, Wolfgang A. "Das vornicaenische ὁμοούσιος als Ausdruck der Rechtgläubigkeit." *Zeitschrift für Kirchengeschichte* 90 (1979): 151–175.

Bigman, David. "Ḥissorei meḥassera ɣe-ʾika de-ʾamre: ʿIyun be-hiɣɣatsrut girsah ḥalufit be-divrei amora." *Maʿagalim* 8 (2012/2013): 17–28.

Bin Gurion, Yosef. "ʿErekh Aḥer (eize leḳuṭim)." *Ha-Goren: Meʾasef le-ḥokhmat Yiśraʾel* 8 (1911/1912): 76–83.

Bizer, Christoph. *Studien zu pseudathanasianischen Dialogen der Orthodoxos und Aëtios*. Ph.D. dissertation. Bonn: Bizer, 1970.

Blaudeau, Philippe. *Alexandrie et Constantinople (451–491). De l'histoire à la géo-ecclésiologie*. Bibliothèque des écoles françaises d'Athènes et de Rome 327. Rome: École Française de Rome, 2006.

———. "Between Petrine Ideology and Realpolitik: The See of Constantinople in Roman Geo-Ecclesiology (449–536)." Pages 364–384 in *Two Romes: Rome and Constantinople in Late Antiquity*. Edited by Lucy Grig and Gavin Kelly, Oxford: Oxford University Press, 2015.

———. "Le voyage de Damien d'Alexandrie vers Antioche puis Constantinople (579–580), motivations et objectifs." *Orientalia Christiana Periodica* 63 (1997): 333–361.

Bobertz, Charles A. "The Development of Episcopal Order." Pages 183–211 in *Eusebius, Christianity, and Judaism*. Edited by Harold W. Attridge and Gohei Hata. Detroit: Wayne State University Press, 1992.

Bockmuehl, Markus N.A. *Revelation and Mystery in Ancient Judaism and Pauline Christianity*. Wissenschaftliche Untersuchungen zum Neuen Testament 2. Reihe 36. Tübingen: Mohr Siebeck, 1990.

Boltanski, Luc. *The Making of a Class: Cadres in French Society*. Cambridge: Cambridge University Press and Éditions de la Maison des Sciences de l'Homme, 1987. [= Translation of *Les cadres: La formation d'un groupe* sociale. Paris: Les éditions de minuit, 1982.]

Borchardt, Carl F.A. *Hilary of Poitiers' Role in the Arian Struggle*. 2nd ed. Dordrecht: Springer Science and Business Media, 1966.

Borowitz, Eugene B. *The Talmud's Theological Language-Game: A Philosophical Discourse Analysis*. Albany: State University of New York Press, 2006.

Bouffartigue, Jean, Pierre Canivet, Annick Martin, Luce Pietri, and Françoise Thélamon, eds. *Théodoret de Cyr. Histoire Ecclésiastique*. 2 vols. SC 501, 530. Paris: Les Éditions du Cerf, 2009.

Boulnois, Marie-Odile. "Les Pères de l'Église et l'hellénisme. Définitions et points de repère." Pages 13–20 in *Les Chrétiens et l'hellénisme. Identités religieuses et culture grecque dans l'Antiquité tardive*. Edited by Arnauld Perrot. Études de littérature ancienne 20. Paris: Rue d'Ulm, 2012.

Boustan, Ra'anan S. "Rabbinization and the Making of Early Jewish Mysticism." *Jewish Quarterly Review* 101 (2011): 482–501.

Boyarin, Daniel. "Anecdotal Evidence: The Yavneh Conundrum, 'Birkat Hamminim,' and the Problem of Talmudic Historiography." Pages 1–35 in vol. 2 of *The Mishnah in Contemporary Perspective*. Edited by Alan J. Avery-Peck and Jacob Neusner. 2 vols. Leiden: Brill, 2006.

———. "Beyond Judaisms: Meṭaṭron and the Divine Polymorphy of Ancient Judaism." *Journal for the Study of Judaism in the Persian, Hellenistic, and Roman Period* 41 (2010): 323–365.

———. *Border Lines: The Partition of Judaeo-Christianity*. Philadelphia: University of Pennsylvania Press, 2007.

———. "The Christian Invention of Judaism: The Theodosian Empire and the Rabbinic Refusal of Religion." *Representations* 85 (2004): 21–57. [= Pages 150–177 in *Religion: Beyond a Concept*. Edited by Hent de Vries. New York: Fordham University Press, 2008.]

———. "Daniel 7, Intertextuality, and the History of Israel's Cult." *Harvard Theological Review* 105 (2012): 139–162.

———. "De/re/constructing Midrash." Pages 299–322 in *Current Trends in the Study of Midrash*. Edited by Carol Bakhos. Leiden: Brill, 2006.

———. "Dialectic and Divination in the Talmud." Pages 217–241 in *The End of Dialogue in Antiquity*. Edited by Simon Goldhill. Cambridge: Cambridge University Press, 2008.

———. *Dying for God: Martyrdom and the Making of Christianity and Judaism*. Stanford, CA: Stanford University Press, 1999.

———. "The Gospel of the Memra: Jewish Binitarianism and the Prologue to John." *Harvard Theological Review* 94 (2001): 243–284.

———. "Hybridity and Heresy: Apartheid Comparative Religion in Late Antiquity." Pages 339–358 in *Postcolonial Studies and Beyond*. Edited by Matti Bunzl, Antoinette Burton, Jed Esty, Suvir Kaul, and Ania Loomba. Durham, NC: Duke University Press, 2005.

———. "Is Metatron a Converted Christian?" *Judaïsme Ancien/Ancient Judaism* 1 (2013): 13–62.

———. *The Jewish Gospels: The Story of the Jewish Christ*. New York: New Press, 2012.

———. *Judaism: The Genealogy of a Modern Notion*. New Brunswick, NJ: Rutgers University Press, 2018.

———. "Midrash and the 'Magic Language': Reading without Logocentrism." Pages 131–139 in *Derrida and Religion: Other Testaments*. Edited by Kevin Hart and Yvonne Sherwood. London: Routledge, 2005.

———. "One Church; One Voice: The Drive towards Homonoia in Orthodoxy." *Religion and Literature* 33 (2001): 1–22.

———. "The Parables of Enoch and the Foundation of the Rabbinic Sect: A Hypothesis." Pages 53–72 in *"The Words of a Wise Man's Mouth Are Gracious" (Qoh 10,12): Festschrift for Günter Stemberger on the Occasion of His 65th Birthday*. Edited by Mauro Perani. Berlin: De Gruyter, 2005.

———. "The Quest of the Historical Meṭaṭron." Kent Shaffer Lectures, Yale Divinity School, New Haven, CT: March 8–10, 2016.

———. "Rethinking Jewish Christianity: An Argument for Dismantling a Dubious Category (To Which Is Appended a Correction of My *Border Lines*)." *Jewish Quarterly Review* 99 (2009): 7–36.

———. "Semantic Differences; or, 'Judaism'/'Christianity.'" Pages 65–85 in *The Ways That Never Parted: Jews and Christians in Late Antiquity and the Early Middle Ages*. Edited by Adam H. Becker and Annette Yoshiko Reed. Tübingen: Mohr Siebeck, 2003.

———. "Shuv le-ʿinyian shetei reshuyot ba-Mekhilta." *Tarbits. Rivʿon le-madaʿei ha-Yahadut* 81 (2012/2013): 87–101.

———. *Socrates and the Fat Rabbis*. Chicago: University of Chicago Press, 2009.

———. "A Tale of Two Synods: Nicaea, Yavneh, and Rabbinic Ecclesiology." *Exemplaria: Medieval, Early Modern, Theory* 12 (2000): 21–42.

———. "Twenty-Four Refutations: Continuing the Conversations." *Henoch: Studies in Judaism and Christianity from Second Temple to Late Antiquity* 28 (2006): 30–45.

———. "Two Powers in Heaven; or, The Making of a Heresy." Pages 331–370 in *The Idea of Biblical Interpretation: Essays in Honor of James L. Kugel*. Edited by Hindy Najman and Judith H. Newman. Leiden: Brill, 2003.

———. "The Yavneh-Cycle of the Stammaim and the Invention of the Rabbis." Pages 237–289 in *Creation and Composition: The Contribution of the Bavli Redactors (Stammaim) to the Aggada*. Edited by Jeffrey L. Rubenstein. Texte und Studien zum antiken Judentum 114. Tübingen: Mohr Siebeck, 2005.

Boys-Stones, George R. *Post-Hellenistic Philosophy: A Study of Its Development from the Stoics to Origen*. Oxford: Oxford University Press, 2001.

Bravo Castañeda, Gonzalo. "Otra reina en Roma: Zenobia de Palmira." *Gerión* 22, número extra 8 (2004): 81–93.

Bremmer, Jan N. *The Rise of Christianity through the Eyes of Gibbon, Harnack, and Rodney Stark*. Groningen: Barkhuis, 2010.

Brennecke, Hanns Christof. "Bischofsversammlung und Reichssynode. Das Synodalwesen im Umbruch der konstantinischen Zeit." Pages 35–53 in *Einheit der Kirche in vorkonstantinischer Zeit. Vorträge gehalten bei der Patristischen Arbeitsgemeinschaft, 2.–4. Januar 1985 in Bern*. Edited by Fairy von Lilienfeld and Adolf Martin Ritter. Oikonomia 25. Erlangen: Lehrstuhl für Geschichte und Theologie des christlichen Ostens, 1989. [= Pages 25–48 in Hanns Christof Brennecke, *Ecclesia est in re publica. Studien zur Kirchen- und Theologiegeschichte im Kontext des Imperium Romanum*. Edited by Uta Heil, Annette von Stockhausen, and Jörg Ulrich. Arbeiten zur Kirchengeschichte 100. Berlin: De Gruyter, 2007.]

———. "Erwägungen zu den Anfängen des Neunizänismus." Pages 241–257 in *Oecumenica et Patristica: Festschrift für Wilhelm Schneemelcher zum 75. Geburtstag*. Edited by Wolfgang A. Bienert, Damaskinos Papandreou, and Knut Schäferdiek. Stuttgart: Kohlhammer, 1989.

———. *Hilarius von Poitiers und die Bischofsopposition gegen Konstantius II. Untersuchungen zur 3. Phase des Arianischen Streites (337–361)*. PTS 26. Berlin: De Gruyter, 1984.

———. "Lukian von Antiochien in der Geschichte des arianischen Streites." Pages 170–192 in *Logos. Festschrift für Luise Abramowski zum 8. Juli 1993*. Edited by Hanns Christof Brennecke, Ernst Ludwig Garsmück, and Christoph Markschies. Beihefte zur Zeitschrift für die neutestamentliche Wissenschaft und die Kunde der älteren Kirche 67. Berlin: De Gruyter, 1993.

———. *Studien zur Geschichte der Homöer. Der Osten bis zum Ende der homöischen Reichskirche*. Beiträge zur Historischen Theologie 73. Tübingen: J.C.B. Mohr Siebeck, 1988.

———. "Synode als Institution zwischen Kaiser und Kirche in der Spätantike. Überlegungen zur Synodalgeschichte des 4. Jahrhunderts." Pages 19–50 in *Die Synoden im trinitarischen Streit: Über die Etablierung eines synodalen Verfahrens und die Probleme seiner Anwendung im 4. und 5. Jahrhundert*. Edited by Uta Heil and Annette von Stockhausen. TU 177. Berlin: De Gruyter, 2017.

———. "Zum Prozess gegen Paul von Samosata: Die Frage nach der Verurteilung des Homoousios." *Zeitschrift für die neutestamentliche Wissenschaft und die Kunde der älteren Kirche* 75 (1984): 270–290.

Brennecke, Hanns Christof, and Uta Heil. "After a Hundred Years: On the Discussion about the Synod of Antioch 325; A Reply to Holger Strutwolf." *Zeitschrift für Kirchengeschichte* 123 (2012): 95–113.

Brennecke, Hanns Christof, Uta Heil, Christian Müller, Annette von Stockhausen, and Angelika Wintjes, eds. *Athanasius Werke. Dritter Band. Erster Teil. 4. Lieferung*. Berlin: De Gruyter, 2014.

Brennecke, Hanns Christof, Uta Heil, and Annette von Stockhausen, eds. *Athanasius Werke. Zweiter Band. Erster Teil. 8. Lieferung*. Berlin: De Gruyter, 2006.

Brennecke, Hanns Christof, Uta Heil, Annette von Stockhausen, and Angelika Wintjes. *Athanasius Werke. Dritter Band. Erster Teil. 3. Lieferung*. Berlin: De Gruyter, 2007.

Brennecke, Hanns Christof, and Annette von Stockhausen. "Die Edition der »Athanasius Werke«." Pages 151–171 in *Erlanger Editionen. Grundlagenforschung durch Quelleneditionen: Berichte und Studien*. Edited by Helmut Neuhaus. Erlanger Studien zur Geschichte 8. Erlangen: Palm & Enke, 2009.

Breytenbach, Margaretha M. "A Queen for All Seasons: Zenobia of Palmyra." *Akroterion: Tydskrif vir die Klassieke in Suid-Afrika/Akroterion: Journal for the Classics in South Africa* 50 (2005): 51–66.

Brodsky, David. "The Democratic Principle Underlying Jewish Law: Moving beyond Whether It Is So to How and Why It Is So." Pages 51–71 in *Is Judaism Democratic? Reflections from Theory and Practice throughout the Ages*. Edited by Leonard J. Greenspoon. Studies in Jewish Civilization 29. West Lafayette, IN: Purdue University Press, 2018.

———. "From Disagreement to Talmudic Discourse: Progymnasmata and the Evolution of a Rabbinic Genre." Pages 173–231 in *Rabbinic Traditions between Palestine and Babylonia*. Edited by Ronit Nikolsky and Tal Ilan. Leiden: Brill, 2014.

Brody, Robert. "Epistle of Sherira Gaon." Pages 253–264 in *Rabbinic Texts and the History of Late-Roman Palestine*. Edited by Philip Alexander and Martin Goodman. Proceedings of the British Academy 165. Oxford: Oxford University Press, 2010.

———. *The Geonim of Babylonia and the Shaping of Medieval Jewish culture*. New Haven, CT: Yale University Press, 1998.

———. "Sifrut ha-geʾonim ṿe-ha-ṭeḳsṭ ha-talmudi." Pages 237–303 in vol. 1 of *Meḥḳerei Talmud. Kovets meḥḳarim ba-Talmud u-v-tḥumim govlim*. 3 vols. in 4. Edited by David Rosenthal and Yaakov Sussmann. Jerusalem: Magnes, 1990.

Brody, Yerachmiel. "Setam ha-Talmud ṿe-divrei ha-ʾamoraʾim." *Iggud: Mivḥar maʾamarim be-madʿei ha-yahadut* 1 (2005): 213–232.

Brown, Peter. *Power and Persuasion in Late Antiquity: Towards a Christian Empire*. Madison: University of Wisconsin Press, 1992.

Brox, Norbert. "Zur Berufung auf 'Väter' des Glaubens." Pages 42–67 in *Heuresis. Festschrift für Andreas Rohracher, 25 Jahre Erzbischof von Salzburg*. Edited by Thomas Michels. Salzburg: Otto Müller, 1969. [= Pages 271–296 in Norbert Brox, *Das Frühchristentum. Schriften zur historischen Theologie*. Edited by Franz Dünzl, Alfons Fürst, and Ferdinand R. Prostmeier. Freiburg: Herder, 2000.]

Brunschwig, Jacques. "Introduction." Pages vii–cxliii in vol. 1 of *Aristote. Topiques*. Edited by Jacques Brunschwig. 2 vols. Paris: Les Belles lettres, 1967–2007.

Bruyn, Theodore S. de, Stephen A. Cooper, and David G. Hunter, eds. *Ambrosiaster's Commentary on the Pauline Epistles: Romans*. Writings from the Greco-Roman World 41. Atlanta: SBL, 2017.

Bucur, Bogdan. "'Early Christian Binitarianism': From Religious Phenomenon to Polemical Insult to Scholarly Concept." *Modern Theology* 27 (2011): 102–120.

Bureau, Bruno. "Texte composé, texte composite: Le mécanisme de la citation et sa function dans quelques commentaires de psaumes de Cassiodore." Pages 225–262 in Hôs ephat', dixerit quispiam, *comme disait l'autre. Mécanisme de la citation et de la mention dans les langues de l'Antiquité*. Edited by Christian Nicolas. Recherches & Travaux. Hors-série 15. Grenoble: Ellug—Université Stendhal, 2006.

Burgersdijk, Diederik. "Zenobia's Biography in the «Historia Augusta»." *Talanta: Proceedings of the Dutch Archaeological and Historical Society* 36–37 (2004): 139–151.

Burgess, Richard W. *Studies in Eusebian and Post-Eusebian Chronography*. Vol. 2, *The "Continuatio Antiochiensis Eusebii": A Chronicle of Antioch and the Roman Near East during the Reigns of Constantine and Constantius II, AD 325–350*. Series Historia. Einzelschriften 135. Stuttgart: Franz Steiner, 1999.

Burke, John. "Eusebius on Paul of Samosata: A New Image." *Klēronomia: Periodikon dēmosieuma tou Patriarchikou Hidrymatos Paterikōn Meletōn* 7 (1975): 8–20.

Burn, Andrew E. S. *Eustathius of Antioch*. London: Faith Press, 1926.

Burns, Joshua Ezra. "The Relocation of Heresy in a Late Ancient Midrash, or: When in Rome, Do as the Romans." *Jewish Studies Quarterly* 19 (2012): 129–147.

Burrus, Virginia. *Begotten, Not Made: Conceiving Manhood in Late Antiquity*. Stanford, CA: Stanford University Press, 2000.

———. "Hailing Zenobia: Anti-Judaism, Trinitarianism, and John Henry Newman." *Culture and Religion: An Interdisciplinary Journal* 3 (2002): 163–177.

———. "Rhetorical Stereotypes in the Portrait of Paul of Samosata." *Vigiliae Christianae* 43 (1989): 215–225.

———. "Socrates, the Rabbis and the Virgin: The Dialogic Imagination in Late Antiquity." Pages 457–474 in *Talmudic Transgressions: Engaging the Work of Daniel Boyarin*. Edited by Charlotte Elisheva Fonrobert, James Adam Redfield, Ishay Rosen-Zvi, Aharon Shemesh, and Moulie Vidas. Supplements to the Journal for the study of Judaism 181. Leiden: Brill, 2017.

Burrus, Virginia, Richard Kalmin, Hayim Lapin, and Joel Marcus. "Boyarin's Work: A Critical Assessment." *Henoch: Studies in Judaism and Christianity from Second Temple to Late Antiquity* 28 (2006): 7–30.

Bussi, Silvia. "Zenobia/Cleopatra. Immagine e propaganda." *Rivista italiana di numismatica e scienze affini* 104 (2003): 261–268.

Butts, Aaron Michael, and Simcha Gross, eds. *Jews and Syriac Christians: Intersections across the First Millennium*. Tübingen: Mohr Siebeck, 2020.

Cain, Andrew. "In Ambrosiaster's Shadow: A Critical Re-Evaluation of the Last Surviving Letter Exchange between Pope Damasus and Jerome." *Revue d'Études Augustiniennes et Patristiques* 51 (2005): 257–277.

———. *The Letters of Jerome: Asceticism, Biblical Exegesis, and the Construction of Christian Authority in Late Antiquity*. Oxford: Oxford University Press, 2009.

Calame, Claude. "Modes de la citation et critique de l'intertextualité: Jeux énonciatifs et pragmatiques dans les «Théognidéa»." Pages 221–241 in *La citation dans l'Antiquité: Actes du colloque du PARSA Lyon, ENS LSH, 6–8 novembre 2002*. Edited by Catherine Darbo-Peschansk. Grenoble: Millon, 2004.

Cameron, Averil. *Byzantine Matters*. Princeton, NJ: Princeton University Press, 2014.

———. *Christianity and the Rhetoric of Empire: The Development of Christian Discourse*. Sather Classical Lectures 55. Berkeley: University of California Press, 1991.

———. "The Cost of Orthodoxy." *Church History and Religious Culture* 93 (2013): 339–361.

———. *Dialoguing in Late Antiquity*. Hellenic Studies 65. Washington, DC: Center for Hellenic Studies, 2014.

———. "Eusebius of Caesarea and the Rethinking of History." Pages 71–88 in *Tria corda. Scritti in onore di Arnaldo Momigliano*. Edited by Emilio Gabba. Biblioteca di Athenaeum 1. Como: New Press, 1983.

———. "Flights of Fancy: Some Imaginary Debates in Late Antiquity." Pages 385–406 in *Christians Shaping Identity from the Roman Empire to Byzantium: Studies Inspired by Pauline Allen*. Edited by Geoffrey Dunn and Wendy Mayer. Supplements to Vigiliae Christianae 132. Leiden: Brill, 2015.

———. "How to Read Heresiology." *Journal of Medieval and Early Modern Studies* 33 (2003): 471–492.

———. "Jews and Heretics: A Category Error?" Pages 345–360 in *The Ways That Never Parted: Jews and Christians in Late Antiquity and the Early Middle Ages*. Edited by Adam H. Becker and Annette Yoshiko Reed. Tübingen: Mohr Siebeck, 2003.

———. "Patristics and Late Antiquity: Partners or Rivals?" *Journal of Early Christian Studies* 28 (2020): 283–302.

Cameron, Averil, and Stuart G. Hall. *Life of Constantine*. Oxford: Clarendon Press and Oxford University Press, 1999.

Camplani, Alberto. *Atanasio di Alessandria. Lettere festali. Anonimo. Indice delle lettere festali*. Milan: Paoline Editoriale Libri, 2003.

———. "Atanasio e Eusebio tra Alessandria e Antiochia (362–363). Osservazioni sul *Tomus ad Antiochenos*, l'*Epistula catholica* e due fogli copti (edizione di Pap. Berol. 11948)." Pages 191–246 in *Eusebio di Vercelli e il suo tempo*. Edited by Enrico Dal Covolo, Renato Uglione, and Giovanni Maria Vian. Biblioteca di scienze religiose 133. Rome: Libreria Ateneo Salesiano, 1997.

———. "Fourth-Century Synods in Latin and Syriac Canonical Collections and their Preservation in the Antiochene Archives (Serdica 343 CE–Antioch 325 CE)." Pages 61–72 in *Cultures in Contact: Transfer of Knowledge in the Mediterranean Context; Selected Papers*. Edited by Sofía Tollaras Tovar and Juan Pedro Monferrer-Sala. Series Syro-Arabica 1. Beirut: Centre de Documentation et de Recherches Arabes Chrétiennes and Oriens Academic, 2013.

———. "Il cristianesimo in Egitto prima e dopo Costantino." Pages 863–882 in *Costantino I. Enciclopedia costantiniana. Sulla figura e l'immagine dell'imperatore del cosiddetto Editto di Milano, 313–2013*. Rome: Istituto dell'Enciclopedia Treccani, 2013.

———. *Le lettere festali di Atanasio di Alessandria. Studio storico-critico*. Rome: C.I.M., 1989.

———. "L'*Esposizione XIV* di Afraate: Una retorica antiautoritaria nel contesto dell'evoluzione istituzionale della Chiesa siriaca." Pages 191–235 in *Storia e pensiero religioso nel Vicino Oriente. L'età bagratide—Maimonide—Afraate*. Edited by Carmela Baffioni, Rosa Bianca Finazzi, Anna Passoni Dell'Acqua, and Emidio Vergani. Milan: Biblioteca Ambrosiana and Bulzoni, 2014.

———. "Le trasformazioni del cristianesimo orientale: Monoepiscopato e sinodi (II–IV secolo)." *Annali di Storia dell'Esegesi* 23 (2006): 67–114.

———. "Lettere episcopali, storiografia patriarcale e letteratura canonica: A proposito del *Codex veronensis LX (58)*." *Rivista di storia del cristianesimo* 3 (2006): 117–164.

———. Review of Hanns Christof Brennecke, Uta Heil, Annette von Stockhausen, and Angelika Wintjes, *Athanasius Werke. Dritter Band. Erster Teil. 3. Lieferung. Adamantius: Journal of the Italian Research Group on Origen and the Alexandrian Tradition* 14 (2008): 659–663.

———. Review of Hanns Christof Brennecke, Uta Heil, and Annette von Stockhausen, eds. *Athanasius Werke. Zweiter Band. Erster Teil. 8. Lieferung. Adamantius: Journal of the Italian Research Group on Origen and the Alexandrian Tradition* 14 (2008): 656–659.

———. "Setting a Bishopric/Arranging an Archive: Traces of Archival Activity in the Bishopric of Alexandria and Antioch." Pages 231–272 in *Manuscripts and Archives: Comparative Views on Record-Keeping*. Edited by Alessandro Bausi, Christian Brockmann, Michael Friedrich, and Sabine Kienitz. Studies in Manuscript Cultures 11. Berlin: De Gruyter, 2018.

———. "Studi atanasiani: Gli *Athanasius Werke*, le ricerche sulla *Thalia* e nuovi sussidi bibliografici." *Adamantius: Journal of the Italian Research Group on Origen and the Alexandrian Tradition* 7 (2001): 115–130.

Canella, Tessa. *Il peso della tolleranza. Cristianesimo antico e alterità*. Storia 86. Brescia: Morcelliana, 2017.

———. "Lo sviluppo teologico cristiano dell'idea di tolleranza: A margine di un recente volume di Peter Van Nuffelen." *Adamantius: Journal of the Italian Research Group on Origen and the Alexandrian Tradition* 24 (2018): 493–505.

Canellis, Aline. "Écrire contre l'Empereur . . . Le *De Athanasio* de Lucifer de Cagliari." Pages 153–171 in *Écrire contre. Quête d'identité, quête de pouvoir dans la littérature des premiers siècles chrétiens*. Edited by Françoise Vinel. Strasbourg: Presses universitaires de Strasbourg, 2012.

———. "La composition du *Dialogue contre les Lucifériens* et du *Dialogue contre les Pélagiens* de saint Jérôme. À la recherche d'un canon de l'*altercatio*." *Revue des Études Augustinienne* 43 (1997): 247–288.

———. "Saint Jérôme et les Ariens: Nouveaux éléments en vue de la datation de l'«Altercatio Luciferiani et Orthodoxi»?" Pages 155–194 in *Les chrétiens face à leurs adversaires dans l'Occident latin du IVe siècle: Actes des journées d'études du GRAC, Rouen, 25 avril 1997 et 28 avril 2*. Edited by Jean-Michel Poinsotte. Publications de l'Université de Rouen 297. Mont-Saint-Aignan: Publications de l'Université de Rouen, 2001.

Cantalamessa, Raniero, Joseph T. Lienhard, and Jason M. Quigley, eds. *Easter in the Early Church: An Anthology of Jewish and Early Christian Texts*. Collegeville, MN: Liturgical Press, 1993.

Capes, David B., ed. *Israel's God and Rebecca's Children: Christology and Community in Early Judaism and Christianity; Essays in Honor of Larry W. Hurtado and Alan F. Segal*. Waco, TX: Baylor University Press, 2007.

Carletti, Carlo. "Damaso I, santo." Pages 349–372 in vol. 1 of *Enciclopedia dei Papi*. 3 vols. Rome: Istituto della Enciclopedia Italiana Treccani, 2000.

Cartwright, Sophie. *The Theological Anthropology of Eustathius of Antioch*. Oxford: Oxford University Press, 2015.

Cavalcanti, Elena. *Studi eunomiani*. Orientalia Christiana Analecta 202. Rome: Pontificum Institutum Orientalium Studiorum, 1976.

Cavallera, Ferdinand. *Le schisme d'Antioche (IVe et Ve siècle)*. Paris: Alphonse Picard et fils, 1905.

———. *Saint Jérôme, sa vie et son œuvre*. Études et documents 1. Louvain: Spicilegium sacrum Lovaniense and Champion, 1922.

———. *S. Eustathii Episcopi Antiocheni in Lazarum, Mariam et Martham homilia christologica nunc primum e codice Gronoviano edita cum commentario de fragmentis Eustathianis accesserunt fragmenta Flaviani I Antiocheni*. Paris: Alphonse Picard et fils, 1905.

Cerrato, J.A. *Hippolytus between East and West: The Commentaries and the Provenance of the Corpus*. Oxford: Oxford University Press, 2002.

Cerutti, Maria Vittoria. "Monoteismo pagano? Elementi di tipologia storica." *Adamantius: Journal of the Italian Research Group on Origen and the Alexandrian Tradition* 15 (2009): 307–330.

———. "Unità del divino e unicità del principio: Aspetti della rappresentazione dell'altro." *Annali di scienze religiose* 8 (2003): 179–195.

Chabot, Jean-Baptiste. *Chronique de Michel le Syrien, patriarche jacobite d'Antioche, 1166–1199*. 4 vols. Paris: Ernest Leroux, 1899–1910.

Chadwick, Henry. *The Church in Ancient Society: From Galilee to Gregory the Great*. Oxford: Oxford University Press, 2001.

———. *The Early Church*. 4th ed. Harmondsworth, UK: Penguin, 1973.

———. "The Fall of Eustathius of Antioch." *Journal of Theological Studies* 49 (1948): 27–35.

———. "Florilegium." Pages 1131–1160 in vol. 7 of *Reallexikon für Antike und Christentum. Sachwörterbuch zur Auseinandersetzung des Christentums mit der antiken Welt*. 29 + 1 vols. Edited by Theodor Klauser. Stuttgart: Anton Hiersemann, 1950–.

———. "Ossius of Cordova and the Presidency of the Council of Antioch 325." *Journal of Theological Studies* N.S. 9 (1958): 292–304.

———. Review of Henri de Riedmatten, *Les actes du procès de Paul de Samosate: Étude sur la christologie du 3e au 4e siècle*. *Journal of Theological Studies* N.S. 4.1 (1953): 91–94.

Chapman, J. "The Contested Letters of Pope Liberius: 13. The Forger and His Work." *Revue Bénédictine* 27 (1910): 325–352.

Chiesa, M. Curzio. "Le problème du langage intérieur chez les Stoïciens." *Revue internationale de philosophie* 45 (1991): 301–321.

Chin, C. Michael, and Moulie Vidas, eds. *Late Ancient Knowing: Explorations in Intellectual History*. Oakland: University of California Press, 2015.

Chronister, Andrew C. "Augustine and Patristic Argumentation in His Anti-Pelagian Works: Change or Continuity?" *Augustiniana* 64 (2014): 187–226.

Cibis, Anna Theresa. *Lucifer von Calaris. Studien zur Rezeption und Tradierung der heiligen Schrift im 4. Jahrhundert*. Studien zur Geschichte und Kultur des Altertum 1.28. Paderborn: Schöningh, 2014.

Clark, Elizabeth Ann. *The Origenist Controversy: The Cultural Construction of an Early Christian Debate*. Princeton, NJ: Princeton University Press, 1992.

Clark, Gillian. "Can We Talk?" Pages 117–135 in *The End of Dialogue in Antiquity*. Edited by Simon Goldhill. Cambridge: Cambridge University Press, 2008.

Clarke, Graeme. "Third-Century Christianity." Pages 589–671 in *The Cambridge Ancient History. Second Edition*. Vol. 12, *The Crisis of Empire, A.D. 193–337*. Edited by Alan K. Bowman, Averil Cameron, and Peter Garnsey. Cambridge: Cambridge University Press, 2005.

Clausi, Benedetto. "*O rerum quanta mutatio!* Città e deserto nell'ideologia ascetica e nella scrittura epistolare di Gerolamo." Pages 123–163 in *La città. Frammenti di storia dall'antichità all'età contemporanea. Atti del Seminario di studi (Università della Calabria, 16–17 novembre 2011)*. Edited by Marina Intrieri and Paolo Siniscalco. Rome: Aracne, 2013.

Cleve, Robert L. "The Triumph of Christianity: Religion as an Instrument of Control." Pages 530–542 in *Forms of Control and Subordination in Antiquity*. Edited by Doi Masaoki and Yuge Tory. Leiden: Brill, 1988.

Coakley, Sarah. "Introduction: Disputed Questions in Patristic Trinitarianism." *Harvard Theological Review* 100 (2007): 125–138.

———. "Re-thinking Gregory of Nyssa: Introduction—Gender, Trinitarian Analogies, and the Pedagogy of *The Song*." *Modern Theology* 18 (2002): 431–443.

Cohen, Aryeh. "Beginning Gittin/Mapping Exile." Pages 69–112 in *Beginning/Again: Toward a Hermeneutics of Jewish Texts*. Edited by Aryeh Cohen and Shaul Magid. New York: Seven Bridges, 2002.

Cohen, Avinoam. "ʿAl maṭbeʿa ha-lashon 'lo shemiʿa li ke-lomar lo sevira li' ba-Talmud ha-bavli." *Tarbits. Rivʿon le-madaʿei ha-Yahadut* 53 (1984–1985): 467–472.

———. "Biḳoret hilkhatit le-ʿumat biḳoret sifrutit be-sugiyot ha-Talmud (pereḳ ba-hithayyut ha-shikhvatit shel ha-Bavli)." *Asupot* 3 (1989/1990): 331–339.

———. "Le-ʾofiyah shel ha-halakhah ha-savoraʾit: Sugyat ha-Bavli reish Ḳiddushin u-masoret ha-Geʾonim." *Dinei Israel* 24 (2006/2007): 161–214.

———. *Ravina ve-ḥakhmei doro: ʿIyunim be-seder ha-zemanim shel amoraʾim aḥaronim be-Vavel*. Ramat Gan: Bar Ilan University Press, 2001.

Cohen, Barak Shlomo. "Citation Formulae in the Babylonian Talmud: From Transmission to Authoritative Traditions." *Journal of Jewish Studies* 70 (2019): 24–44.

———. *For Out of Babylonia Shall Come Torah and the Word of the Lord from Nehar Peqod: The Quest for Babylonian Tannaitic Traditions*. Leiden: Brill, 2017.

———. "Rav Sheshet le-ʿumat Rav Naḥman: Shetei shiṭot parshaniyot li-mḳorot tannaʾyim." *Hebrew Union College Annual* 76 (2005): 11–32.

Cohen, Shaye J.D. "The Significance of Yavneh: Pharisees, Rabbis, and the End of Jewish Sectarianism." *Hebrew Union College Annual* 55 (1984): 27–53. [= Pages 44–69 in Shaye J.D. Cohen, *The Significance of Yavneh and Other Essays in Jewish Hellenism*. Tübingen: Mohr Siebeck, 2010.]

———. "A Virgin Defiled: Some Rabbinic and Christian Views on the Origins of Heresy." *Union Seminary Quarterly Review* 36 (1980): 1–11. [= Pages 534–547 in Shaye J.D. Cohen, *The Significance of Yavneh and Other Essays in Jewish Hellenism*. Tübingen: Mohr Siebeck, 2010.]

Cohn, Naftali S. "Heresiology in the Third-Century Mishnah: Arguments for Rabbinic Legal Authority and the Complications of a Simple Concept." *Harvard Theological Review* 108 (2015): 508–529.

Collini, Stefan. *Absent Minds: Intellectuals in Britain*. Oxford: Oxford University Press, 2006.

Compagnon, Antoine. *La seconde main, ou le travail de la citation*. Paris: Éditions du Seuil, 1979.

Conring, Barbara. *Hieronymus als Briefschreiber: Ein Beitrag zur spätantiken Epistolographie*. Studien und Texte zu Antike und Christentum 8. Tübingen: Mohr Siebeck, 2001.

Cook, Johann. "The Law of Moses as a Fence and a Fountain." Pages 280–288 in *Sense and Sensitivity: Essays on Reading the Bible in Memory of Robert Carroll*. Edited by Alastair G. Hunter and Phillip R. Davies. Sheffield, UK: Sheffield Academic Press, 2002.

Corrigan, Kevin. "Οὐσία and ὑπόστασις in the Trinitarian Theology of the Cappadocian Fathers: Basil and Gregory of Nyssa." *Zeitschrift für antikes Christentum* 12 (2008): 114–134.

Corti, Giuseppe. *Lucifero di Cagliari: Una voce nel conflitto tra Chiesa e impero alla metà del IV secolo 2004*. Studia patristica Mediolanensia 24. Milan: Vita e pensiero, 2004.

Cossutta, Frédérique, and Dominique Maingueneau. "L'Analyse des discours constituants." *Langages* 117 (1995): 112–125.

Costa, José. "Littérature apocalyptique et Judaïsme rabbinique: Le problème de la bat qol." *Revue des études juives* 169 (2010): 57–96.

Costa, José, and Avigail Ohali. "Littérature apocalyptique et Judaïsme rabbinique: Le problème de la bat qol (deuxième partie)." *Judaïsme Ancien/Ancient Judaism* 6 (2018): 83–174.

Cowper, Benjamin Harris. *Syriac Miscellanies; or Extracts Relating to the First and Second General Councils, and Various Other Quotations, Theological, Historical, & Classical*. London: Williams and Norgate, 1861.

Crone, Patricia. "Jewish Christianity and the Qurʾān (Part One)." *Journal of Near Eastern Studies* 74 (2015): 225–253.

———. "Jewish Christianity and the Qurʾān (Part Two)." *Journal of Near Eastern Studies* 75 (2016): 1–21.

Cross, Frank Leslie. "The Council of Antioch in 325 A.D." *Church Quarterly Review* 128 (1939): 49–76.

Cumont, Franz Valery Marie. *Les religions orientales dans le paganisme romain*. Paris: Ernest Leroux, 1906.

Dainese, Davide. "Costantino a Nicea: Tra realtà e rappresentazione letteraria." Pages 405–417 in *Costantino prima e dopo Costantino/Constantine before and after Constantine*. Edited by Giorgio Bonamente, Noel Lenski, and Rita Lizzi Testa. Munera. Studi storici sulla Tarda Antichità 35. Bari: Edipuglia, 2012.

Daley, Brian E. "Christ and Christologies." Pages 886–905 in *The Oxford Handbook of Early Christian Studies*. Edited by Susan Ashbrook Harvey and David G. Hunter. Oxford: Oxford University Press, 2008.

———. "The Enigma of Meletius of Antioch." Pages 128–150 in *Tradition and the Rule of Faith in the Early Church: Essays in Honor of Joseph T. Lienhard*. Edited by R. Rombs. Washington, DC: Catholic University of America Press, 2010.

Dalmau, José María. "El *homoousios* y el Concilio de Antioquía de 268." *Miscelánea Comillas. Revista de ciencias humanas y sociales* 34 (1960): 324–340.

Damschen, Gregor, and Rafael Ferber. "Is the Idea of the Good beyond Being? Plato's 'epekeina tês ousias" Revisited (Republic, 6, 509b8–10)." Pages 197–203 in *Second Sailing: Alternative Perspectives on Plato*. Edited by Mika Kajava, Debra Nails, Eero Salmenkivi, and Harold Tarrant. Espoo, Finland: Wellprint Oy, 2015.

Daniélou, Jean. Review of Friedrich Müller, *Gregorii Nysseni Opera dogmatica minora, Pars I*. *Gnomon* 31 (1959): 612–615.

Daniélou, Jean, and Henri-Irénée Marrou. *Nouvelle histoire de l'Église*. Vol. 1, *Des origines à Saint Grégoire le Grand*. Paris: Éditions du Seuil, 1963.

Daunoy, Fernard. "La question pascale au Concile de Nicée." *Échos d'Orient* 24 (1925): 424–444.

Declerck, José H. "Deux nouveaux fragments attribués à Paul de Samosate." *Byzantion. Revue internationale des études byzantines* 54 (1984): 116–140.

———. "Encore une fois Léonce et Pamphile." Pages 199–216 in *Philohistôr. Miscellanea in honorem Caroli Laga septuagenarii*. Edited by Antoon Schoors and Peter Van Deun. Orientalia Lovaniensia Analecta 60. Louvain: Peeters, 1994.

———. *Eustathii Antiocheni, patris Nicaeni, Opera quae supersunt omnia*. CCSG 51. Turnhout: Brepols; Louvain: Louvain University Press, 2002.

De Clercq, Victor Cyril. *Ossius of Cordova: A Contribution to the History of the Constantinian Period*. Washington, DC: Catholic University of America Press, 1954.

Deferrari, Roy Joseph, and Agnest C. Way, eds. *Saint Basil: The Letters*. Fathers of the Church 13, 28. 2 vols. Washington, DC: Catholic University of America Press, 2008.

de Halleux, André. "'Hypostase' et 'Personne' dans la formation du dogme trinitaire (ca 375–381)." *Revue d'histoire ecclésiastique* 79 (1984): 311–369 and 623–670. [= Pages 113–214 in André de Halleux, *Patrologie et œcuménisme: Recueil d'études*. Bibliotheca Ephemeridum theologicarum Lovaniensium 93. Louvain: Louvain University Press, 1990.]

Dekoninck, Ralph, Janine Desmulliez, and Myriam Watthee-Delmotte. "Introduction." Pages 5–8 in *Controverses et polémiques religieuses: Antiquité—temps modernes*. Edited by Ralph Dekoninck, Janine Desmulliez, and Myriam Watthee-Delmotte. Paris: L'Harmattan, 2007.

DelCogliano, Mark. "The Emergence of the Pro-Nicene Alliance." Pages 256–281 in *The Cambridge Companion to the Council of Nicaea*. Edited by Young Richard Kim. Cambridge: Cambridge University Press, 2021.

———. "The Promotion of the Constantinian Agenda in Eusebius of Caesarea's 'On the Feast of Pascha.'" Pages 39–68 in *Reconsidering Eusebius: Collected Papers on Literary, Historical and Theological Issues*. Edited by Sabrina Inowlocki and Claudio Zamagni. Vigiliae Chrisitanae Supplements 107. Leiden: Brill, 2011.

den Dulk, Matthijs. "'One Would Not Consider Them Jews': Reassessing Jewish and Christian 'Heresy.'" *Journal of Early Christian Studies* 27 (2019): 353–381.

de Régnon, Théodore. *Études de théologie positive sur la Sainte Trinité*. Paris: Victor Retaux, 1892.

Desjardins, Michel. "Bauer and Beyond: On Recent Scholarly Discussions of Αἵρεσις in the Early Christian Era." *Second Century: A Journal of Early Christian Studies* 8 (1991): 65–82.

Deutsch, Nathaniel. *Guardians of the Gate: Angelic Vice Regency in Late Antiquity*. Leiden: Brill, 1999.

Devreesse, Robert. *Le patriarcat d'Antioche depuis la paix de l'Église jusqu'à la conquête arabe*. Paris: Gabalda, 1945.

Diamond, Eliezer. *Holy Men and Hunger Artists: Fasting and Asceticism in Rabbinic Culture*. Oxford: Oxford University Press, 2004.

Diefenbach, Steffen. "Una Petri sedes. Hieronymus und der päpstliche Primat." Paper delivered at Girolamo e Roma. Convegno internazionale in occasione del XVI centenario della morte, Sapienza University of Rome, Universität Konstanz, and Insistutum Pastristicum Agustinianum, Rome, September 30–October 3, 2019.

Diercks, Gerardus Frederik. *Luciferi Calaritani opera quae supersunt*. CCSL 8. Turnhout: Brepols, 1978.

Dihle, Albrecht. *Greek and Latin Literature of the Roman Empire: From Augustus to Justinian*. London: Routledge, 1994.

Dillon, John M. "Orthodoxy and Eclecticism: Middle Platonists and Neo-Pythagoreans." Pages 103–125 in *The Question of "Eclecticism." Studies in Later Greek Philosophy*. Edited by John M. Dillon and Anthony Arthur Long. Berkeley: University of California Press, 1988.

Dinsen, Frauke. *Homoousios: Die Geschichte des Begriffs bis zum Konzil von Konstantinopel (381)*. Th.D. dissertation. Kiel: Christian-Albrechts-Universität zu Kiel, 1976.

Dittenberger, Wilhelm. *Orientis Graeci inscriptiones selectae. Supplementum sylloges inscriptionum graecarum*. 2 vols. Leipzig: S. Hirzel, 1903.

Dolbeau, François. "La formation du Canon des Pères, du IVe au VIe siècle." Pages 17–39 in vol. 1 of *Les réceptions des Pères de l'Église au Moyen Âge. Le devenir de la tradition ecclésiale. Congrès du Centre Sèvres—Facultés jésuites de Paris (11–14 juin 2008). Actes*. 2 vols. Edited by Rainer Berndt and Michel Fédou. Archa verbi. Subsidia 10. Münster: Aschendorff Verlag, 2013.

Dolgopolski, Sergey. *The Open Past: Subjectivity and Remembering in the Talmud*. New York: Fordham University Press, 2013.

———. *Other Others: The Political after the Talmud*. New York: Fordham University Press, 2018.

———. "*Tosafot Gornish* Post-Kant: The Talmud as Political Thought." Pages 74–105 in *Talmudic Transgressions: Engaging the Work of Daniel Boyarin*. Edited by Charlotte Elisheva Fonrobert, James Adam Redfield, Ishay Rosen-Zvi, Aharon Shemesh, and Moulie Vidas. Supplements to the Journal for the Study of Judaism 181. Leiden: Brill, 2017.

———. *What Is Talmud? The Art of Disagreement*. New York: Fordham University Press, 2009.

Donalson, Malcolm Drew. *A Translation of Jerome's* Chronicon *with Historical Commentary*. Lewinston, NY: Mellen, 1996.

Dörrie, Heinrich. "Υπόστασις. Wort- und Bedeutungsgeschichte." *Nachrichten der Akademie der Wissenschaften zu Göttingen. Philologisch-Historische Klasse* 3 (1955): 35–92. [= Pages 13–69 in Heinrich Dörrie, *Platonica Minora*. Munich: Wilhelm Fink, 1976.]

Dossetti, Giuseppe L. *Il simbolo di Nicea e di Costantinopoli. Edizione critica*. Testi e ricerche di scienze religiose 2. Rome: Herder, 1967.

Downey, Glanville. *A History of Antioch in Syria: From Seleucus to the Arab Conquest*. Princeton, NJ: Princeton University Press, 1961.

Drake, Harold Allen. "Constantine and Consensus." *Church History: Studies in Christianity and Culture* 64 (1995): 1–15.

———. *Constantine and the Bishops: The Politics of Intolerance*. Baltimore: Johns Hopkins University Press, 2000.

———. "The Elephant in the Room: Constantine at the Council." Pages 111–132 in *The Cambridge Companion to the Council of Nicaea*. Edited by Young Richard Kim. Cambridge: Cambridge University Press, 2021.

———. "Lambs into Lions: Explaining Early Christian Intolerance." *Past and Present* 153 (1996): 3–36.

Drecoll, Volker Henning. *Die Entwicklung der Trinitätslehre des Basilius con Cäsarea. Sein Weg vom Homöusianer zum Neonizäner*. Göttingen: Vandenhoeck & Ruprecht, 1996.

Drobner, Hubertus R. *Lehrbuch der Patrologie*. 3rd ed. Frankfurt am Main: Peter Lang, 2011.

Duchesne, Louis. "La question de la Pâque au Concile de Nicée." *Revue des questions historiques* 28 (1880): 5–42.

Dudzik, Pavel. "Nicene Terminology Defended by Athanasius of Alexandria in «De decretis Nicaenae synodi» and the Possible Influence of Eusebius' «Epistula ad Caesarienses»." *Vox Patrum. Antyk chrześcijański* 61 (2014): 123–135.

Dunn, Geoffrey D. "Catholic Reception of the Council of Nicaea." Pages 347–367 in *The Cambridge Companion to the Council of Nicaea*. Edited by Young Richard Kim. Cambridge: Cambridge University Press, 2021.

Dunn, James D.G. *The Partings of the Ways between Christianity and Judaism and Their Significance for the Character of Christianity*. London: SCM, 2006.

Dünzl, Franz. "Die Absetzung des Bischofs Meletius von Antiochien 361 n. Chr." *Jahrbuch für Antike und Christentum* 43 (2000): 71–93.

Durand, Georges M. de. "Pères de l'Église." Pages 893–895 in *Dictionnaire critique de théologie*. Edited by Jean-Yves Lacoste. Paris: Presse Universitaire de France, 1998.

Duval, Yves-Marie. "La place et l'importance du Concile d'Alexandrie ou de 362 dans l'*Histoire de l'Église* de Rufin d'Aquilé." *Revue d'Études Augustiniennes et Patristique* 47 (2001): 283–302.

———. "Saint Jérôme devant le baptême des hérétiques. D'autres sources de l'*Altercatio Luciferiani et Orthodoxi*." *Revue des Études Augustinienne* 14 (1968): 145–180.

———. "Vrais et faux problèmes concernant le retour d'exil d'Hilaire de Poitiers et son action en Italie en 360–363." *Athenaeum: Studi Periodici di Letteratura e Storia dell'Antichità* 48 (1970): 251–275.

Dyck, Andrew, and Andreas Glock. "Scholien." Pages 209–214 in vol. 11 of *Der neue Pauly: Enzyklopädie der Antike*. Edited by Hubert Cancik and Helmuth Schneider. Stuttgart: Verlag J.B. Metzler, 2001.

Ebach, Jürgen Hiob. "Das Zitat als Kommunikationsform. Beobachtungen, Anmerkungen und Fragestellungen am Beispiel biblischen und rabbinischen Zitierens." Pages 27–84 in Jürgen Hiob Ebach, *Gott im Wort. Drei Studien zur biblischen Exegese und Hermeneutik*. Neukirchen-Vluyn: Neukirchener Verlag, 1997.

Ebied, Bishara, and Emiliano Fiori, eds. *Florilegia Syriaca: Mapping a Knowledge-Organizing Practice in the Syriac World*. Vigiliae Christianae Supplements 179. Leiden: Brill, 2023.

Ebied, Rifaat Y. "Peter of Antioch and Damian of Alexandria: The End of a Friendship." Pages 277–282 in *A Tribute to Arthur Vööbus: Studies in Early Christian Literature and Its Environment, Primarily in the Syrian East*. Chicago: Lutheran School of Theology at Chicago, 1977.

Edwards, Mark Julian. "Clement of Alexandria and His Doctrine of the Logos." *Vigiliae Christianae* 54 (2000): 159–171.

———. "The Creed." Pages 135–157 in *The Cambridge Companion to the Council of Nicaea*. Edited by Young Richard Kim. Cambridge: Cambridge University Press, 2021.

———. "Did Origen Apply the Word *Homoousios* to the Son?" *Journal of Theological Studies* 49 (1989): 658–670.

Elias, Tzadok. "Davar she-ʾeino mitkayyein u-mlakhah she-ʾeinah tserikhah le-gufah." *Meorenu* 12 (2014/2015): 141–149.

Elliott, Thomas George. "Constantine and 'the Arian Reaction after Nicaea.'" *Journal of Ecclesiastical History* 43 (1992): 169–194.

———. "Constantine's Preparations for the Council of Nicaea." *Journal of Religious History* 17 (1992–1993): 127–137.

———. "Was the «Tomus ad Antiochenos» a Pacific Document?" *Journal of Ecclesiastical History* 58 (2007): 1–8.

Elm, Susanna. *Sons of Hellenism, Fathers of the Church: Emperor Julian, Gregory of Nazianzus, and the Vision of Rome*. Berkeley: University of California Press, 2012.

Elman, Yaakov. "Argument for the Sake of Heaven. *The Mind of the Talmud*: A Review Essay." *Jewish Quarterly Review* 84 (1993–1994): 261–282.

———. *Authority and Tradition: Toseftan baraitot in Talmudic Babylonia*. New York: Yeshiva University Press; Hoboken, NJ: Ktav, 1994.

———. "Order, Sequence, and Selection: The Mishnah's Anthological Choices." Pages 53–80 in *The Anthology in Jewish Literature*. Edited by David Stern. New York: Oxford University Press, 2004.

———. "Progressive *Derash* and Retrospective *Peshat*: Non-Halakhic Considerations in Talmud Torah." Pages 189–287 in *Modern Scholarship in the Study of Torah: Contributions and Limitations*. Edited by Shalom Carmy. Northvale, NJ: Jason Aronson, 1996.

———. "The World of the 'Sabboraim': Cultural Aspects of Post-Redactional Additions to the Bavli." Pages 383–415 in *Creation and Composition: The Contribution of the Bavli Redactors (Stammaim) to the Aggada*. Edited by Jeffrey L. Rubenstein. Texte und Studien zum antiken Judentum 114. Tübingen: Mohr Siebeck, 2005.

Elon, Menachem. *Jewish Law: History, Sources, Principles*. Translated by Bernard Auerbach and Melvin J. Sykes. 4 vols. Philadelphia: Jewish Publication Society, 1994.

Engels, David, and Peter Van Nuffelen. "Religion and Competition in Antiquity: An Introduction." Pages 9–44 in *Religion and Competition in Antiquity*. Edited by David Engels and Peter Van Nuffelen. Collection Latomus 343. Brussels: Éditions Latomus, 2014.

Epstein, Barukh Halevi. *Ḥamishah ḥumshei Torah ʿim ḥamesh megilot: Torah temimah*. 5 vols. Vilnius: Re'em, 1902.

Epstein, Yaakov Nachum Halevi. *Mavo le-nosaḥ ha-Mishnah: Nosaḥ ha-Mishnah ve-gilgulav l-imei ha-ʾamoraʾim ha-rishonim ve-ʿad defusei Yom-Ṭov Lipman Heler*. 2 vols. 3rd ed. Jerusalem: Magnes, 2000.

———. *Meḥḳarim be-sifrut ha-Talmud u-vi-lshonot shemiyot*. 3 vols. in 4. Jerusalem: Magnes, 1983–1991.

———. *Mevo'ot le-sifrut ha-'amora'im: Bavli v-Irushalmi.*. Tel Aviv: Magnes, 1962.

Erismann, Christophe. "Identité et ressemblance: Marius Victorinus, théologien et lecteur d'Aristote." *Les Études philosophiques* 101 (2012): 181–190.

Espín, Orlando. "Ortholalia." Column 993 in *An Introductory Dictionary of Theology and Religious Studies.* Edited by Orlando Espín and James B. Nickoloff. Collegeville, MN: Liturgical Press, 2007.

Evans, Ernest. *Adversus Praxean liber = Tertullian's Treatise against Praxeas.* London: SPCK, 1948.

Fairbairn, Donald. "The Sardican Paper, Antiochene Politics, and the Council of Alexandria (362): Developing the «Faith of Nicaea»." *Journal of Theological Studies* 66 (2015): 651–678.

———. "The Synod of Ancyra (358) and the Question of the Son's Creaturehood." *Journal of Theological Studies* N.S. 64 (2013): 111–136.

Farina, Raffaele. "La teologia di Eusebio e la 'svolta di Nicea.'" *Salesianum* 27 (1965): 666–671.

Fatti, Federico. *Giuliano a Cesarea. La politica ecclesiastica del principe apostata.* Studi e testi tardoantichi 10. Rome: Herder, 2009.

Feder, Alfred Leonhard. *Studien zu Hilarius von Poitiers.* Sitzungsberichte der Akademie der Wissenschaften in Wien. Philosophisch-Historische Klasse 162.4, 166.5, 169.5. 3 vols. Vienna: Alfred Hölder, 1910–1913.

Fedwick, Paul Jonathan. *Bibliotheca basiliana universalis: A Study of the Manuscript Tradition of the Works of Basil of Caesarea.* Vol. 1, *The Letters.* Turnhout: Brepols, 1993.

Feldblum, Meyer S. "The Talmud: Abraham Weiss's Views." Pages 88–125 in *Essential Papers on the Talmud.* Edited by Michael Chernick. New York: New York University Press, 1994.

Fernández, Samuel. "¿Crisis arriana o crisis monarquiana en el siglo IV? Las críticas de Marcelo de Ancira a Asterio de Capadocia." Pages 203–208 in *Studia Patristica LXV: Papers Presented at the Sixteenth International Conference on Patristic Studies held in Oxford 2011.* Vol. 14, *Clement of Alexandria: The Fourth-Century Debates.* Edited by Markus Vinzent. Louvain: Peeters, 2013.

———. "Criterios para interpretar los textos sinodales según el *De synodis* de Atanasio." *Scripta theologica* 49 (2017): 9–30.

———. "Who Convened the First Council of Nicaea: Constantine or Ossius?" *Journal of Theological Studies* 71 (2000): 196–211.

Fernández, Tomás. "La tendencia compilatoria en época de controversia teológica." *Maia: Rivista di Letterature Classiche* 66 (2014): 157–171.

Fernández Hernández, Gonzalo. "Dos alternativas orientales al credo niceno de 325 expuestas al sínodo de la Dedicación (Antioquía, 341)." *Antigüedad y cristianismo: Monografías históricas sobre la Antigüedad tardía* 18 (2001): 425–427.

———. "La deposición del obispo Asclepas de Gaza." *Studia Historica. Historia Antigua* 13–14 (1995): 401–404.

———. "La primera intervención sinodal del occidente cristiano en la disputa arriana del siglo IV: El Concilio Romano de 340." *Carthaginensia. Revista de estudios e investigación* 25 (2009): 439–443.

———. "Las consecuencias de la deposición del Obispo Eustacio de Antioquía en el bienio 331–332 de la Era Cristiana." *Estudios Humanísticos. Geografía, Historia y Arte* 19 (1997): 41–44.

———. "Los presidentes del concilio de Nicea de 325." *Habis* 39 (2008): 309–316.

———. "Los sinodales de Nicea." *Antigüedad y cristianismo: Monografías históricas sobre la Antigüedad tardía* 11 (1994): 401–403.

Fiano, Emanuel. "Splitting the Difference: Jerome and the Schism of Antioch in His Letter 15." *Sacris Erudiri: A Journal of Late Antique and Medieval Christianity* 59 (2021): 61–81.

Field, Lester L. *On the Communion of Damasus and Meletius. Fourth-Century Synodal Formulae in the Codex Veronensis LX.* Studies and texts 145. Toronto: Pontifical Institute of Mediaeval Studies, 2004.

Finkelstein, Louis. *Akiba: Scholar, Saint and Martyr.* Cleveland: Meridian, 1962.

Finnegan, Ruth. *Why Do We Quote? The Culture and History of Qutation.* Cambridge: Open Book, 2011.

Fisch, Menachem. *Rational Rabbis: Science and Talmudic Culture.* Bloomington: Indiana University Press, 1997.

Fischel, Henry A. *Rabbinic Literature and Greco-Roman Philosophy: A Study of Epicurea and Rhetorica in Early Midrashic Writings.* Leiden: Brill, 1973.

Fischer, Joseph Anton. "Die antiochenischen Synoden gegen Paul von Samosata." *Annuarium Historiae Conciliorum* 18 (1986): 9–30.

Florsheim, Joel. "Sugyot Bavliot b-Irushalmi Neziḳin." *Sinai* 120 (1997–1998): 53–85 and 161–181.

Fonrobert, Charlotte Elisheva. "The Place of Shabbat: On the Architecture of the Opening Sugya of Tractate Eruvin (2a–3a)." Pages 437–454 in *Strength to Strength: Essays in Appreciation of Shaye J.D. Cohen.* Brown Judaic Studies 363. Providence, RI: Brown Judaic Studies, 2018.

———. *Sulpicii Severi Chronica.* SC 133. Paris: Les Éditions du Cerf, 1967.

Force, Paul. "La deuxième partie du 'Saint Jérôme' du Père Cavallera." *Chronique. Institut Catholique de Toulouse* 2 (1986): 12–18.

Forget, Jacques. "Jérôme (Saint)." Columns 894–983 in vol. 8.1 of *Dictionnaire de théologie catholique.* 15 vols. Paris: Letouzey et Ané, 1903–1950.

Fraade, Steven D. "'A Heart of Many Chambers': The Theological Hermeneutics of Legal Multivocality." *Harvard Theological Review* 108 (2015): 113–128.

———. "Literary Composition and Oral Performance in Early Midrashim." *Oral Tradition* 14 (1999): 33–51.

———. "Rabbinic Polysemy and Pluralism Revisited: Between Praxis and Thematization." *AJS Review* 31 (2007): 1–40.

Fredriksen, Paula, and Oded Irshai. "Christian Anti-Judaism: Polemics and Policies." Pages 977–1034 in *The Cambridge History of Judaism*. Vol. 4, *The Late Roman-Rabbinic Period*. Edited by Steven T. Katz. Cambridge: Cambridge University Press, 2006.

Frey, Jean-Baptiste. *Corpus inscriptionum iudaicarum: Recueil des inscriptions juives qui vont du IIIe siècle avant Jésus-Christ au VIIe siècle de notre ère*. 2 vols. Sussidi allo studio delle antichità cristiane 1 and 3. Vatican City: Pontificio istituto di archeologia cristiana, 1936–1952.

Friedman, Shamma Yehudah. "'Al titmah ʿal hosafah she-nizkar bah shem amora': Shuv le-meimrot ha-ʾamoraʾim u-stam ha-Talmud be-sugyot ha-Bavli." Pages 135–157 in *Melekhet maḥashevet: Ḳovets maʿamarim be-nośʾe ʿarikhah ṿe-hitpatḥut shel ha-sifrut ha-Talmudit*. Edited by Aharon Amit and Aharon Shemesh. Ramat Gan: Bar Ilan University Press, 2011.

———. "Keitsad medaḳdeḳin? ʿIyun be-shinnuyei ha-grasot shel ha-Talmud ha-Bavli le-regel hofaʿat y"g kerakhim shel 'Diḳduḳei sofrim ha-shalem.'" *Tarbits* 68 (1998/1999): 129–162.

———. "Le-hithaṿṿut shinnuyei ha-girsaʾot ba-Talmud ha-Bavli." *Sidra* 7 (1990/1991): 67–102.

———. *Le-Toratam shel tannaʾim: Asupat meḥḳarim metodologiyim ṿe-ʿiyuniyim*. Jerusalem: Mosad Byaliḳ, 2013.

———. "Pereḳ ha-ʾishah rabah ba-Bavli, be-tsiruf mavo kelali ʿal derekh ḥeḳer ha-sugyah." Pages 277–441 in *Meḥḳarim u-mḳorot. Meassef le-maddaʿei ha-Yahadut*. Edited by Haim Zalman Dimitrovsky. Analecta Judaica 1. New York: Jewish Theological Seminary and Ktav, 1977.

———. *Talmud ʿarukh: Pereḳ ha-śokher et ha-ʾumanin. Bavli Bava metsiʿa pereḳ shishi: Mahadurah ʿal derekh ha-meḥḳar ʿim perush ha-sugyot*. 2 vols. Jerusalem: Beit ha-midrash le-rabanim be-Ameriḳah, 1990–1996.

———. "Uncovering Literary Dependencies in the Talmudic Corpus." Pages 35–57 in *The Synoptic Problem in Rabbinic Literature*. Edited by Shaye J.D. Cohen. Brown Judaic Studies 326. Providence, RI: Brown University Press, 2000.

Fruman, Yehudah. "Modeh Rabi Shimʿon bi-fsiḳ reisha ṿe-lo yamut." *Mi-meʿayan Meḥolah* 9 (2000/2001): 7–40.

Fuchs, Uziel. "ʿArikhatah u-mgamatah shel sugyiat ha-petiḥah le-massekhet Bava batra." *Sidra* 33 (2007/2008): 83–105.

Fürst, Alfons. "Hieronymus: Theologie als Wissenschaft." Pages 168–183 in *Theologen der christlichen Antike: Eine Einführung*. Edited by Wilhelm Geerlings. Darmstadt: Wissenschaftliche Buchgesellschaft, 2002.

Gabrielson, Timothy A. "Parting Ways or Rival Siblings? A Review and Analysis of Metaphors for the Separation of Jews and Christians in Antiquity." *Currents in Biblical Research* 19 (2021): 178–204.

Gafni, Isaiah. "The Modern Study of Rabbinics and Historical Questions: The Tale of the Text." Pages 41–61 in *The New Testament and Rabbinic Literature*. Edited by Reimund Bieringer, Florentino García Martínez, Didier Pollefeyt, and Peter Tomson. The New Testament and Rabbinic Literature 136. Leiden: Brill, 2010.

Gager, John G. *The Origins of Anti-Semitism: Attitudes toward Judaism in Pagan and Christian Antiquity*. Oxford: Oxford University Press, 1983.

Gain, Benoît. "Citations isolées et citations groupées dans la littérature chrétienne des premiers siècles." Pages 179–190 in Hôs ephat', dixerit quispiam, *comme disait l'autre. Mécanisme de la citation et de la mention dans les langues de l'Antiquité*. Edited by Christian Nicolas. Recherches & Travaux. Hors-série 15. Grenoble: Ellug—Université Stendhal, 2006.

Galtier, Paul. "L'*homoousios* de Paul de Samosate." *Recherches de Science Religieuse* 12 (1922): 30–45.

Galvão-Sobrinho, Carlos R. *Doctrine and Power: Theological Controversy and Christian Leadership in the Later Roman Empire*. Berkeley: University of California Press, 2014.

Gastoni, Luciano Maria. "La battaglia antiariana di Lucifero e il suo coinvolgimento in alcuni scismi del tempo." Pages 169–185 in *La Sardegna paleocristiana tra Eusebio e Gregorio Magno: Atti del Convegno nazionale di studi, Cagliari, 10–12 ottobre 1996*. Edited by Attilio Mastino, Giovanna Sotgiu, and Natalino Spaccapelo. Cagliari: Pontificia Facoltà Teologica della Sardegna, 1999.

Gaudemet, Jean. *Conciles Gaulois du IVe siècle*. SC 241. Paris: Les Éditions du Cerf, 1977.

Gavrilyuk, Paul L. "The Legacy of the Council of Nicaea in the Orthodox Tradition: The Principle of Unchangeability and the Hermeneutic of Continuity." Pages 327–346 in *The Cambridge Companion to the Council of Nicaea*. Edited by Young Richard Kim. Cambridge: Cambridge University Press, 2021.

Gawlikowski, Michal. "Les dieux de Palmyre." *Aufstieg und Niedergang der römischen Welt II,18,4*. (1990): 2605–2658.

Geltzer, Aron. "'Pesiḳ reisha': Biṭṭul toda'at ha-yaḥid." *Ma'aliyot* 24 (2003/2004): 42–51.

Gemeinhardt, Peter. "Apollinaris of Laodicea: A Neglected Link of Trinitarian Theology between East and West?" *Zeitschrift für Antikes Christentum* 10 (2006): 286–301.

———. "Der *Tomus ad Antiochenos* (362) und die Vielfalt orthodoxer Theologien im 4. Jahrhundert." *Zeitschrift für Kirchengeschichte* 117 (2006): 169–196.

———. "Epistula catholica." Pages 226–228 in *Athanasius-Handbuch*. Edited by Peter Gemeinhardt. Tübingen: Mohr Siebeck, 2011.

———. "Refutatio hypocriseos Meletii et Eusebii." Pages 348–350 in *Athanasius-Handbuch*. Edited by Peter Gemeinhardt. Tübingen: Mohr Siebeck, 2011.

———. "Tomus ad Antiochenos." Pages 228–235 in *Athanasius-Handbuch*. Edited by Peter Gemeinhardt. Tübingen: Mohr Siebeck, 2011.

Gennaro, Salvatore, and François Glorie, eds. *Scriptores Illyrici minores*. CCSL 85. Turnhout: Brepols, 1972.

Gericke, Wolfgang. *Marcell von Ancyra, der Logos-Christologe und Biblizist, sein Verhaltnis zur Antiochenischen Theologie und zum Neuen Testament*. Theologische Arbeiten zur Bibel-, Kirchen- und Geistesgeschichte 10. Halle: Akademischer Verlag, 1940.

Ghellinck, Joseph de. "Diffusion, utilisation et transmission des écrits patristiques." *Gregorianum* 14 (1933): 356–400.

Ghilardi, Massimiliano, and Charles Pietri. "Damaso." Pages 1325–1329 in vol. 1 of *Nuovo Dizionario Patristico e di Antichità cristiane*. Edited by Angelo Di Berardino. Genoa: Marietti, 2006–2008.

Ghizzoni, Flaminio. *Sulpicio Severo*. Pubblicazioni dell'Istituto di lingua e letteratura latina dell'Università degli studi di Parma 8. Parma: Università degli Studi di Parma, 1983.

Girardet, Klaus Martin. *Der Kaiser und sein Gott. Das Christentum im Denken und in der Religionspolitik Konstantins des Grossen*. Berlin: De Gruyter, 2010.

———. *Kaisertum, Religionspolitik und das Recht von Staat und Kirche in der Spätantike*. Bonn: Habelt, 2009.

Girotti, Beatrice. "I ritratti di Zenobia nella «Historia Augusta»: Tra simbologia e «inventio»." Pages 195–209 in *Oggetti-simbolo: produzione, uso e significato nel mondo antico*. Edited by Isabella Baldini Lippolis and Anna Lina Morelli. Ornamenta 3. Bologna: Ante Quem, 2011.

Giulea, Dragoş Andrei. "Antioch 268 and Its Legacy in the Fourth-Century Theological Debates." *Harvard Theological Review* 2 (2018): 192–215.

Gleede, Benjamin. *The Development of the Term* Ἐνυπόστατος *from Origen to John of Damascus*. Leiden: Brill, 2012.

Glucker, John. "The Origin of ὑπάρχω and ὕπαρξις as Philosophical Terms." Pages 1–23 in *Hyparxis e hypostasis nel Neoplatonismo: Atti del I Colloquio internazionale del Centro di ricerca sul neoplatonismo, Università degli studi di Catania, 1–3 ottobre 1992*. Edited by Francesco Romano and Daniela Patrizia Taormina. Lessico Intellettuale Europeo 64. Florence: Olschki, 1994.

Goldberg, Arnold. "Der verschriftete Sprechakt als rabbinische Literatur." Pages 123–141 in *Schrift und Gedächtnis. Archäologie der literarischen Kommunikation I*. Edited by Aleida Assmann and Jan Assmann. Munich: Wilhelm Fink, 1983. [= Pages 1–21 in Arnold Goldberg, *Rabbinische Texte als Gegenstand der Auslegung. Gesammelte Studien II*. Edited by Peter Schäfer and Margarete Schlüter. Texte und Studien zum antiken Judentum 73. Tübingen: Mohr Siebeck, 1999.]

———. "Die Zerstörung von Kontext als Voraussetzung für die Kanonisierung religiöser Texte im rabbinischen Judentum." Pages 201–211 in *Kanon und Zensur. Archäologie der literarischen Kommunikation II*. Edited by Aleida Assmann and Jan Assmann. Munich: Wilhelm Fink, 1987. [= Pages 413–425 in Arnold Goldberg, *Mystik und Theologie des rabbinischen Judentums. Gesammelte Studien I*. Edited by Peter Schäfer and Margarete Schlüter. Tübingen: Mohr Siebeck, 1997.]

———. "Entwurf einer formanalytischen Methode für die Exegese der rabbinischen Traditionsliteratur." *Frankfurter Judaistische Beiträge* 5 (1977): 1–41. [= Pages 50–79 in Arnold Goldberg, *Rabbinische Texte als Gegenstand der Auslegung. Gesammelte Studien II*. Edited by Peter Schäfer and Margarete Schlüter. Texte und Studien zum antiken Judentum 73. Tübingen: Mohr Siebeck, 1999.]

———. "The Rabbinic View of Scripture." Pages 153–166 in *A Tribute to Geza Vermes: Essays on Jewish and Christian Literature and History*. Edited by Philip R. Davies and Richard T. White. Sheffield, UK: JSOT, 1990. [= Pages 230–241 in Arnold Goldberg, *Rabbinische Texte als Gegenstand der Auslegung. Gesammelte Studien II*. Edited by Peter Schäfer and Margarete Schlüter. Tübingen: Mohr Siebeck, 1999.] [= Translation of "Die Schrift der rabbinischen Schriftausleger." *Frankfurter Judaistische Beiträge* 15 (1987): 1–15.]

———. "Rede und Offenbarung in der Schriftauslegung Rabbi Aqibas." *Frankfurter Judaistische Beiträge* 8 (1980): 66–75. [= Pages 337–350 in Arnold Goldberg, *Mystik und Theologie des rabbinischen Judentums. Gesammelte Studien I*. Edited by Peter Schäfer and Margarete Schlüter. Tübingen: Mohr Siebeck, 1997.]

———. "Zitat und Citem. Vorschläge für die descriptive Terminologie der Formanalyse rabbinischer Texte." *Frankfurter Judaistische Beiträge* 6 (1978): 23–26. [= Pages 96–98 in Arnold Goldberg, *Rabbinische Texte als Gegenstand der Auslegung. Gesammelte Studien II*. Edited by Peter Schäfer and Margarete Schlüter. Texte und Studien zum antiken Judentum 73. Tübingen: Mohr Siebeck, 1999.]

Goldenberg, Robert. "Did the Amoraim See Christianity as Something New?" Pages 293–302 in *Pursuing the Text: Studies in Honor of Ben Zion Wacholder on the Occasion of His Seventieth Birthday*. Edited by John Kampen and John C. Reeves. Journal for the Study of the Old Testament Supplement Series 184. Sheffield, UK: Sheffield Academic Press, 1994.

———. "Is the Talmud a Document?" Pages 3–10 in *The Synoptic Problem in Rabbinic Literature*. Edited by Shaye J.D. Cohen. Brown Judaic Studies 326. Providence, RI: Brown University Press, 2000.

Goldhill, Simon. "Why Don't Christians Do Dialogue?" Pages 1–11 in *The End of Dialogue in Antiquity*. Edited by Simon Goldhill. Cambridge: Cambridge University Press, 2008.

Goodman, Martin. "The Function of *Minim* in Early Rabbinic Judaism." Pages 501–510 in vol. 1 of *Geschichte-Tradition-Reflexion, Festschrift für Martin Hengel zum 70. Geburstag*. 3 vols. Edited by Hubert Cancik, Hermann Lichtenberger, and Peter Schäfer. Tübingen: Mohr Siebeck, 1996. [= Pages 163–174 in Martin Goodman, *Judaism in the Roman World: Collected Essays*. Ancient Judaism and Early Christianity 66. Leiden: Brill, 2007.]

Goodman, Motti. "Din davar she-ʾeino mitkayyein." *Orot ʿEtsion* 9 (1985/1986): 47–53.

Goshen-Gottstein, Alon. "Four Entered Paradise Revisited." *Harvard Theological Review* 88 (1995): 69–133.

———. *The Sinner and the Amnesiac: The Rabbinic Invention of Elisha ben Abuya and Eleazar Ben Arach*. Stanford, CA: Stanford University Press, 2000.

Gosserez, Laurence. "Citations païennes dans les paraphrases bibliques préfacielles de Prudence." Pages 209–223 in Hôs ephat', dixerit quispiam, *comme disait l'autre. Mécanisme de la citation et de la mention dans les langues de l'Antiquité*. Edited by Christian Nicolas. Recherches & Travaux. Hors-série 15. Grenoble: Ellug—Université Stendhal, 2006.

Graetz, Heinrich. *Gnosticismus und Judenthum*. Krotoszyn: B.L. Monasch, 1846.

Grafton, Anthony, and Megan Williams. *Christianity and the Transformation of the Book: Origen, Eusebius, and the Library of Caesarea*. Cambridge, MA: Harvard University Press, 2006.

Grant, Robert M. "The Fragments of the Greek Apologists and Irenaeus." Pages 179–234 in *Biblical and Patristic Studies in Memory of R.P. Casey*. Edited by J. Neville Birdsall and Robert W. Thomson. Freiburg im Breisgau: Herder, 1963.

———. "Religion and Politics at the Council at Nicaea." *Journal of Religion* 55 (1975): 1–12.

Graumann, Thomas. "Authority and Doctrinal Normation in Patristic Discourse: The Nicene Creed at the First Council of Ephesus." Pages 20–38 in *A Celebration of Living Theology: A Festschrift in Honour of Andrew Louth*. Edited by Leonard Alde and Justin A. Mihoc. London: Bloomsbury Academic, 2014.

———. "The Conduct of Theology and the 'Fathers' of the Church." Pages 539–555 in *A Companion to Late Antiquity*. Edited by Philip Rousseau. Oxford: Blackwell-Wiley, 2009.

———. *Die Kirche der Väter: Vätertheologie und Väterbeweis in den Kirchen des Ostens bis zum Konzil von Ephesus (431)*. Beiträge zur historischen Theologie 118. Tübingen: Mohr Siebeck, 2002.

———. "The Synod of Constantinople, AD 383: History and Historiography." *Millennium: Jahrbuch zu Kultur und Geschichte des Ersten Jahrtausends n. Chr.* 7 (2010): 133–168.

———. "Theologische Diskussion und Entscheidung auf Synoden. Verfahrensformen und -erwartungen." Pages 51–82 in *Die Synoden im trinitarischen Streit: Über die Etablierung eines synodalen Verfahrens und die Probleme seiner Anwendung im 4. und 5. Jahrhundert*. Edited by Uta Heil and Annette von Stockhausen. TU 177. Berlin: De Gruyter, 2017.

Graves, Michael. *Jerome's Hebrew Philology: A Study Based on His Commentary on Jeremiah*. Leiden: Brill, 2007.

Gray, Alyssa. *A Talmud in Exile: The Influence of Yerushalmi Avodah Zarah on the Formation of Bavli Avodah Zarah*. Brown Judaic Studies 342. Providence, RI: Brown Judaic Studies, 2005.

Gray, Patrick Terrell R. "'The Select Fathers': Canonizing the Patristic Past." Pages 21–36 in *Studia Patristica XXIII: Papers Presented to the Tenth International Confer-*

ence on Patristic Studies Held in Oxford 1987; Late Greek Fathers, Latin Fathers after Nicaea, Nachleben of the Fathers. Edited by Elizabeth A. Livingstone. Leuven: Peeters, 1989.

Green, William Scott. "What's in a Name? The Problematic of Rabbinic 'Biography.'" Pages 77–96 in *Approaches to Ancient Judaism: Theory and Practice*. Edited by William Scott Green. Missoula, MT: Scholars' Press, 1978.

Greenslade, Stanley Lawrence. *Early Latin Theology: Selections from Tertullian, Cyprian, Ambrose, and Jerome*. The Library of Christian Classics 5. Philadelphia: Westminster, 1956.

———. *Schism in the Early Church*. London: SCM, 1953.

Gregg, Robert C., and Denis E. Groh. *Early Arianism: A View of Salvation*. London: SCM, 1981.

Grégoire, Henri. *Les persécutions dans l'Empire romain*. 2nd ed. Brussels: Palais des Académies, 1964.

Grégoire, Réginald. "Agiografia e storiografia nella *Vita antiqua* di Eusebio di Vercelli." Pages 187–200 in *La Sardegna paleocristiana tra Eusebio e Gregorio Magno: Atti del Convegno nazionale di studi, Cagliari, 10–12 ottobre 1996*. Edited by Attilio Mastino, Giovanna Sotgiu, and Natalino Spaccapelo. Cagliari: Pontificia Facoltà Teologica della Sardegna, 1999.

Gribetz, Sarit Kattan. *Time and Difference in Rabbinic Judaism*. Princeton, NJ: Princeton University Press, 2020.

Griffith, Sidney. "The Doctrina Addai as a Paradigm of Christian Thought in Edessa in the Fifth Century." *Hugoye* 6 (2003): 269–292.

Grillet, Bernard, André-Jean Festugière, and Guy Sabbah, eds. *Sozomène. Histoire ecclésiastique*. 4 vols. SC 306, 418, 495, 516. Paris: Les Éditions du Cerf, 1983–2008.

Grillmeier, Aloys. *Christ in Christian Tradition*. 2nd ed. Atlanta: John Knox, 1975.

———. "Neue Fragmente zu Paul von Samosata?" *Theologie und Philosophie* 65 (1990): 392–394.

Grossberg, David M. "Between 3 Enoch and Babylonian Talmud Hagigah: Heresiology and Orthopraxy in the Ascent of Elisha ben Abuyah." Pages 117–139 in *Hekhalot Literature in Context: Between Byzantium and Babylonia*. Edited by Ra'anan S. Boustan, Martha Himmelfarb, and Peter Schäfer. Tübingen: Mohr Siebeck, 2013.

———. *Heresy and the Formation of the Rabbinic Community*. Texts and Studies in Ancient Judaism 168. Tübingen: Mohr Siebeck, 2017.

———. "One God, Two Powers, and the Rabbinic Rejection of Subordinationism." *Journal for the Study of Judaism* 53 (2021): 405–436.

———. "Orthopraxy in Tannaitic Literature." *Journal for the Study of Judaism* 41 (2010): 517–561.

Grumel, Venance. "Le problème de la date pascale aux IIIe et IVe siècles. L'origine du conflit: Le nouveau cadre du comput juif." *Revue d'études byzantines* 18 (1960): 163–178.

Grützmacher, Georg. "Die Abfassungszeit der *Altercatio Luciferiani et Orthodoxi* des Hieronymus." *Zeitschrift für Kirchengeschichte* 21 (1901): 1–8.

———. *Hieronymus. Eine biographische Studie zur alten Kirchengeschichte.* Studien zur Geschichte der Theologie und der Kirche 6.2, 10.1–2. Leipzig: Dieterich, 1901–1908.

Guillén Pérez, María Gloria. "El patriarcato de Antioquía: Una somera introducción." Pages 327–378 in *Romanización y Cristianismo en la Siria Mesopotámica*. Edited by Antonino González Blanco and Gonzalo Matilla Séiquer. Antigüedad y Cristianismo 15. Murcia: Universidad de Murcia, Servicio de Publicaciones, 1998.

Guittard, Charles, ed. *Le monothéisme: Diversité, exclusivisme ou dialogue? Association européenne pour l'étude des religions (EASR), Congrès de Paris, 11–14 septembre 2002.* Paris: Éditions Non Lieu, 2010.

Güldenpenning, Albert. *Die Kirchengeschichte des Theodoret von Kyrrhos: Eine Untersuchung ihrer quellen.* Halle: Max Niemeyer, 1889.

Gur, Menachem. "Rabi Shimʿon ṿe-Rabi Yehudah—bein ideʾal le-reiʾalyah." *Ḳol be-ramah* 28 (2015/2016): 355–360.

Gwatkin, Henry Melvill. *Studies of Arianism: Chiefly Referring to the Character and Chronology of the Reaction Which Followed the Council of Nicæa.* 2nd ed. London: Deighton Bell, 1900.

Gwynn, David Morton. "Archaeology and the «Arian Controversy» in the Fourth Century." Pages 229–263 in *Religious Diversity in Late Antiquity*. Edited by Susanne Bangert and David Morton Gwynn. Late Antique Archaeology 6. Leiden: Brill, 2010.

———. "Christian Controversy and the Transformation of Fourth-Century Constantinople." Pages 206–220 in *Religious Practices and Christianization of the Late Antique City (4th–7th Cent.)*. Edited by Aude Busine. Religions in the Graeco-Roman World 182. Leiden: Brill, 2015.

———. *The Eusebians: The Polemic of Athanasius of Alexandria and the Construction of the "Arian Controversy."* Oxford: Oxford University Press, 2007.

———. "Reconstructing the Council of Nicaea." Pages 90–110 in *The Cambridge Companion to the Council of Nicaea*. Edited by Young Richard Kim. Cambridge: Cambridge University Press, 2021.

Hacohen, Malachi Haim. *Jacob & Esau: Jewish European History between Nation and Empire*. New York: Cambridge University Press, 2018.

Hacohen, Reʾem. "Melekhet maḥashevet ba-sheviʿit." *Gullot. Ḥiddushei Torah be-veit midrashenu* 3 (1994/1995): 47–59.

Hadot, Pierre. "*De lectis non lecta componere* (Marius Victorinus, *adversus Arium* II 7): raisonnement théologique et raisonnement juridique." Pages 209–220 in *Studia Patristica 1: Papers Presented to the Second International Conference on Patristic Studies Held at Christ Church, Oxford, 1955. Part 1.* Edited by Kurt Aland and Frank Leslie Cross. TU 63. Berlin: Akademie-Verlag, 1957. [= Pages 53–64 in Pierre Hadot, *Études de patristique et d'histoire des concepts*. L'âne d'ôr 34. Paris: Les Belles lettres, 2010.]

———. *Marius Victorinus: Recherches sur sa vie et ses oeuvres*. Paris: Études Augustiniennes, 1971.

———. "Patristique." Columns 638–643 in vol. 17 of *Encyclopedia universalis*. 18 vols. Paris: Encyclopaedia Universalis, 1996. [= Pages 3–25 in Pierre Hadot, *Études de patristique et d'histoire des concepts*. L'âne d'ôr 34. Paris: Les Belles lettres, 2010.]

Hadot, Pierre, and Paul Henry, eds. *Marius Victorinus. Traités théologiques sur la Trinité I*. SC 68. Paris: Les Éditions du Cerf, 1960.

Hahn, August, and Georg Ludwig Hahn, eds. *Bibliothek der Symbole und Glaubensregeln der alten Kirche*. Breslau: E. Morgenstern, 1897.

Hainthaler, Theresia. *Christ in Christian Tradition*. Vol. 2, part 3, *The Churches of Jerusalem and Antioch from 451 to 600*. Oxford: Oxford University Press, 2013.

Halbertal, Moshe. *People of the Book: Canon, Meaning, and Authority*. Cambridge, MA: Harvard University Press, 1997.

Halivni, David Weiss. "Aspects of the Formation of the Talmud." Pages 339–360 in *Creation and Composition: The Contribution of the Bavli Redactors (Stammaim) to the Aggada*. Edited and translated by Jeffrey L. Rubenstein. Texte und Studien zum antiken Judentum 114. Tübingen: Mohr Siebeck, 2005.

———. *The Formation of the Babylonian Talmud*. Introduced, translated, and annotated by Jeffrey L. Rubenstein. Oxford: Oxford University Press, 2013. [= Translation of *Meḳorot u-msorot: Be'urim ba-Talmud: Massekhet Bava batra*. Jerusalem: Magnes, 2007.]

———. *Meḳorot u-msorot: Be'urim ba-Talmud. Massekhet Bava batra*. Jerusalem: Magnes, 2007.

———. *Meḳorot u-msorot: Be'urim ba-Talmud. Massekhet Bava ḳamma*. Jerusalem: Magnes, 1993.

———. *Meḳorot u-msorot: Be'urim ba-Talmud. Massekhet Bava metsi'a*. Jerusalem: Magnes, 2003.

———. *Meḳorot u-msorot: Be'urim ba-Talmud. Massekhet 'Eruvin-Pesaḥim*. Jerusalem: Jewish Theological Seminary, 1982.

———. *Meḳorot u-msorot: Be'urim ba-Talmud. Massekhet Shabat*. Jerusalem: Jewish Theological Seminary, 1982.

———. *Meḳorot u-msorot: Be'urim ba-Talmud. Massekhet Yoma-Ḥagiga*. Jerusalem: Jewish Theological Seminary, 1975.

———. *Midrash, Mishnah, and Gemara: The Jewish Predilection for Justified Law*. Cambridge, MA: Harvard University Press, 1986.

———. "Reflections on Classical Jewish Hermeneutics." *Proceedings of the American Academy for Jewish Research* 62 (1996): 21–127.

———. *Revelation Restored: Divine Writ and Critical Responses*. Boulder, CO: Westview Press, 1997.

———. "Safḳei de-gavrei." *Proceedings of the American Academy for Jewish Research* 46–47 (1979–1980): 67–83.

Halivni, Ephraim Betzalel. *Kelalei pesaḳ ha-halakhah ba-Talmud*, Lod, Israel: Makhon Haberman le-meḥḳerei sifrut, 1998.

Hall, Stuart G. "The Creed of Sardica." Pages 173–184 in *Studia Patristica XIX: Papers Presented to the Tenth International Conference on Patristic Studies Held in Oxford 1987; Historica, Theologica, Gnostica, Biblica et Apocrypha*. Edited by Elizabeth A. Livingstone. Leuven: Peeters, 1989.

———. "Some Constantinian Documents in the *Vita Constantini*." Pages 86–104 in *Constantine: History, Historiography, and Legend*. Edited by Samuel N.C. Lieu and Dominic Montserrat. New York: Routledge, 1998.

———. "Pourquoi les Églises ont-elles besoin aujourd'hui d'une théologie patristique?" Pages 511–525 in *Les Pères de l'Eglise au XXe siècle: Histoire, littérature, théologie. L'aventure des Sources chrétiennes*. Paris: Éditions du Cerf, 1997, 511–525.

Halperin, David J. *The Faces of the Chariot: Early Jewish Responses to Ezekiel's Vision*. Texte und Studien zum Antiken Judentum 16. Tübingen: J.C.B. Mohr (Paul Siebeck), 1988.

———. *The Merkabah in Rabbinic Literature*. American Oriental Series 62. New Haven, CT: American Oriental Society, 1980.

Hamblenne, Pierre. "Jérôme et le clergé du temps. Idéaux et réalités." *Augustinianum* 37 (1997): 351–410.

Hamman, Adalbert. "Père—Père de l'Église." Columns 1992–1993 in vol. 2 of *Dictionnaire encyclopédique du christianisme ancien*. 2 vols. Edited by Angelo Di Berardino and François Vial. Paris: Les Éditions du Cerf, 1990.

Hammerstaedt, Jürgen. "Das Aufkommen der philosophischen Hypostasisbedeutung." *Jahrbuch für Antike und Christentum* 35 (1992): 7–11.

———. "Der trinitarische Gebrauch des Hypostasisbegriffs bei Origenes." *Jahrbuch für Antike und Christentum* 34 (1991): 12–20.

———. "Hypostasis." Pages 986–1035 in vol. 16 of *Reallexikon für Antike und Christentum. Sachwörterbuch zur Auseinandersetzung des Christentums mit der antiken Welt*. 29 vols. and 1 suppl. Edited by Ernst Dassman, Theodor Klauser, and Georg Schöllgen. Stuttgart: A. Hiersemann, 1994.

Hansen, Günther Christian. *Theodoret Kirchengeschichte*. 3rd ed. GCS N.F. 5. Berlin: Akademie-Verlag, 1998.

Hanslik, Rudolf, and Klaus Wegenast. "Zenobia, Herrscherin von Palmyra." Columns 1–8 in vol. 19 of the Second Series of *Paulys Realencyclopädie der classischen Altertumswissenschaft*. Munich: Alfred Druckenmüller Verlag, 1972.

Hanson, Richard Patrick Crosland. "Did Origen Apply the Word *Homoousios* to the Son?" Pages 293–303 in *Epektasis. Mélanges patristiques offerts à Jean Daniélou*. Edited by Jacques Fontaine and Charles Kannengiesser. Paris: Beauchesne, 1972. [= Pages 53–70 in Richard Patrick Crosland Hanson, *Studies in Christian Antiquity*. Edinburgh: T&T Clark, 1985.]

———. "The Doctrine of the Trinity Achieved in 381." *Scottish Journal of Theology* 36 (1983): 41–57. [= Pages 233–252 in Richard Patrick Crosland Hanson, *Studies in Christian Antiquity*. Edinburgh: T&T Clark, 1985.]

———. "Dogma and Formula in the Fathers." Pages 169–184 in *Studia Patristica XII: Papers Presented to the Sixth International Conference on Patristic Studies Held in Oxford, 1971*. Edited by Elizabeth A. Livingstone. TU 115. Berlin: Akademie-Verlag, 1975. [= Pages 298–318 in Richard Patrick Crosland Hanson, *Studies in Christian Antiquity*. Edinburgh: T&T Clark, 1985.]

———. "The Fate of Eustathius of Antioch." *Zeitschrift für Kirchengeschichte* 95 (1984): 171–179.

———. *The Search for the Christian Doctrine of God: The Arian Controversy 318–381*. Edinburgh: T&T Clark, 1988.

———. "The Transformation of Images in the Trinitarian Theology of the Fourth Century." Pages 97–116 in vol. 1 of *Studia Patristica XVII: Papers Presented to the Eighth International Conference on Patristic Studies, Oxford 1979*. 3 vols. Edited by Elizabeth A. Livingstone. New York: Pergamon, 1982. [= Pages 253–278 in Richard Patrick Crosland Hanson, *Studies in Christian Antiquity*. Edinburgh: T&T Clark, 1985.]

Harl, Marguerite. *Origène et la fonction révélatrice du Verbe Incarné*. Collection Patristica Sorbonensia 2. Paris: Éditions du Seuil, 1958.

Harnack, Adolf von. "Die angebliche Synode von Antiochien im Jahre 324/5." *Sitzungsberichte der Königlich Preussischen Akademie der Wissenschaften zu Berlin. Philologisch-Historische Klasse* (1908): 477–491; (1909): 401–425.

———. "Die Reden Paulus von Samosata an Sabinus (Zenobia?) und seine Christologie." *Sitzungsberichte der Preussischen Akademie der Wissenschaft. Philosophische-Historische Klasse* 22 (1924): 130–151.

———. *Lehrbuch der Dogmengeschichte*. 4th ed. 2 vols. Tübingen: J.C.B. Mohr, 1909–1910.

Hartmann, Udo. *Das palmyrenische Teilreich*. Stuttgart: Steiner, 2001.

Hauptman, Judith. *Development of the Talmudic Sugya: Relationship between Tannaitic and Amoraic Sources*. Lanham, MD: University Press of America, 1988.

———. "Sheloshet ha-markivim ha-yesodiyim shel ha-sugyiah: Ha-setam, ha-meimra, ṿe-ha-barayita." Pages 27–38 in *Melekhet maḥashevet: Ḳovets maʿamarim be-nośe ʿarikhah ṿe-hitpatḥut shel ha-sifrut ha-Talmudit*. Edited by Aharon Amit and Aharon Shemesh. Ramat Gan: Bar Ilan University Press, 2011.

Hayes, Christine. *Between the Babylonian and Palestinian Talmuds: Accounting for Halakhic Difference in Selected Sugyot from Tractate Avodah Zarah*. New York: Oxford University Press, 1997.

———. "*Halakhah le-Moshe mi-Sinai* in Rabbinic Sources: A Methodological Case Study." Pages 61–118 in *The Synoptic Problem in Rabbinic Literature*. Edited by Shaye J.D. Cohen. Brown Judaica Series 326. Atlanta: Scholars, 2000.

———. "Legal Truth, Right Answers and Best Answers: Dworkin and the Rabbis." *Diné Israel. Studies in* Halakhah *and Jewish Law* 25 (2008): 73–121.

———. "Rabbinic Contestations of Authority." *Cardozo Law Review* 28 (2006): 123–141.

———. *What's Divine about Divine Law? Early Perspectives*. Princeton, NJ: Princeton University Press, 2015.

Heber, Simcha. "Be-din eino mitkayyein u-fsiḳ reisheh." *Binot* 2 (2013/2014): 60–75.

Hefele, Karl-Joseph von. *Histoire des conciles d'après les documents originaux*. Vol. 1, part 2. Paris: Letouzey et Ané, 1907.

Heil, Uta. *Athanasius von Alexandrien:* De Sententia Dionysii. PTS 52. Berlin: De Gruyter, 1999.

———. "De decretis Nicaenae synodi." Pages 210–214 in *Athanasius-Handbuch*. Edited by Peter Gemeinhardt. Tübingen: Mohr Siebeck, 2011.

———. "De synodis Arimini in Italia et Seleucia in Isauria." Pages 221–226 in *Athanasius-Handbuch*. Edited by Peter Gemeinhardt. Tübingen: Mohr Siebeck, 2011.

Heine, Ronald E. "The Christology of Callistus." *Journal of Theological Studies* N.S. 49 (1998): 56–91.

Helm, Rudolf. *Die Chronik des Hieronymus: Hieronymi Chronicon*. GCS 47. Eusebius Werke 7. Berlin: Akademie-Verlag, 1956.

———. *Die Chronik des Hieronymus*. 3rd ed. Berlin: Akademie-Verlag, 1984.

Hennessy, Kristin. "An Answer to de Régnon's Accusers: Why We Should Not Speak of 'His' Paradigm." *Harvard Theological Review* 100 (2007): 179–197.

Henry, Paul. "The 'Adversus Arium' of Marius Victorinus, the First Systematic Exposition of the Doctrine of the Trinity." *Journal of Theological Studies* 1 (1950): 42–55.

Henshke, David. "Abaye ṿe-Rava: Shetei gishot le-Mishnat ha-tannaʾim." *Tarbits. Rivʿon le-madaʿei ha-Yahadut* 49 (1980): 187–193.

Herrmann, Klaus. "Jewish Mysticism in Byzantium: The Transformation of Merkavah Mysticism in *3 Enoch*." Pages 85–116 in *Hekhalot Literature in Context: Between Byzantium and Babylonia*. Edited by Ra'anan S. Boustan, Martha Himmelfarb, and Peter Schäfer. Tübingen: Mohr Siebeck, 2013.

———. "*Massekhet Hagigah* and Reform Judaism." Pages 245–268 in *A Feminist Commentary on the Babylonian Talmud: Introduction and Studies*. Edited by Tal Ilan, Tamara Or, Dorothea M. Salzer. Christiane Steuer, and Irina Wandrey. Tübingen: Mohr Siebeck, 2007.

Hezser, Catherine. "The Codification of Legal Knowledge in Late Antiquity: The Talmud Yerushalmi and Roman Law Codes." Pages 581–642 in vol. 1 of *The Talmud Yerushalmi and Graeco-Roman Culture*. Edited by Catherine Hezser and Peter Schäfer. Texts and Studies in ancient Judaism 71, 79, and 93. Tübingen: Mohr Siebeck, 1998–2003.

———. "Roman Law and Rabbinic Legal Composition." Pages 144–163 in *The Cambridge Companion to the Talmud and Rabbinic Literature*. Edited by Charlotte Elisheva Fonrobert and Martin S. Jaffee. Cambridge: Cambridge University Press, 2007.

Hidalgo de la Vega, María José. "Zenobia, reina de Palmira: Historia, mito y tradiciones." *Florentia Iliberritana: Revista de estudios de antigüedad clásica* 28 (2017): 79–104.

Hidary, Richard. "The Agonistic Bavli: Greco-Roman Rhetoric in Sasanian Persia." Pages 137–164 in *Shoshannat Yaakov: Jewish and Iranian Studies in Honor of Yaakov Elman*. Edited by Shai Secunda and Steven Fine. Leiden: Brill, 2012.

———. *Dispute for the Sake of Heaven: Legal Pluralism in the Talmud*. Brown Judaic Studies 353. Providence, RI: Brown University Press, 2010.

———. *Rabbis and Classical Rhetoric: Sophistic Education and Oratory in the Talmud and Midrash*. Cambridge: Cambridge University Press, 2018.

———. "Right Answers Revisited: Monism and Pluralism in the Talmud." *Diné Israel: Studies in* Halakhah *and Jewish Law* 26–27 (2009–2010), 229–255.

Hidary, Richard, and William R. Osborne. "Fence." Columns 1159–1162 in *Encyclopedia of the Bible and Its Reception*. Vol. 8. Berlin: de Gruyter, 2014.

Hihn, Oliver. "The Election and Deposition of Meletius of Antioch: The Fall of an Integrative Bishop." Pages 357–374 in *Episcopal Elections in Late Antiquity*. Edited by Shawn W.J. Keough, Johan Leemans, Carla Nicolaye, and Peter Van Nuffelen. Arbeiten zur Kirchengeschichte 119. Berlin: De Gruyter, 2011.

Hirshman, Marc G. *The Stabilization of Rabbinic Culture, 100 C.E.–350 C.E.: Texts on Education and Their Late Antique Context*. Oxford: Oxford University Press, 2009.

———. "Torah in Rabbinic Thought: The Theology of Learning." Pages 889–924 in *The Cambridge History of Judaism*. Vol. 4, *The Late Roman-Rabbinic Period*. Edited by Steven T. Katz. Cambridge: Cambridge University Press, 2006.

Hoffmann Libson, Ayelet. *Law and Self-Knowledge in the Talmud*. Cambridge: Cambridge University Press, 2018.

Holland, Davis L. "Die Synode von Antiochien (324/25) und ihre Bedeutung für Eusebius von Caesarea und das Konzil von Nizäa." *Zeitschrift für Kirchengeschichte* 81 (1970): 163–181.

Homo, Léon, *Essai sur le règne de l'empereur Aurélien (270–275)*. Bibliothèque des Écoles Françaises d'Athènes et de Rome 89. Paris: Albert Fontemoing, 1904.

Horowitz, Pinchas Halevi. *Sefer ha-miknah*. Ofibakh: Zvi Hirsch, 1801.

Huber, Wolfgang. *Passa und Ostern. Untersuchungen zur Osterfeier der alten Kirche*. Beihefte zur Zeitschrift für die neutestamentliche Wissenschaft und die Kunde der älteren Kirche 35. Berlin: Töpelmann, 1969.

Hübner, Reinhard M. "Basilius von Caesarea und das *Homoousios*." Pages 70–91 in *Christian Faith and Greek Philosophy in Late Antiquity: Essays in Tribute to George Christopher Stead in Celebration of His Eightieth Birthday, 9th April 1993*. Edited by Lionel R. Wickham, Caroline P. Bammel, and Erica C.D. Hunter. Leiden: Brill, 1993.

———. "Die Hauptquelle des Epiphanius (*Panar. Haer* 65) über Paulus von Samosata: Ps. Athanasius, *Contra Sabellianos*." *Zeitschrift für Kirchengeschichte* 90 (1979): 55–74.

———. *Die Schrift des Apollinarius von Laodicea gegen Photin (Pseudo-Athanasius, contra Sabellianos) und Basilius von Caesarea*. PTS 30. Berlin: De Gruyter, 1989.

———. "Gregor von Nyssa und Markell von Ankyra." Pages 199–229 in *Écriture et culture philosophique dans la pensée de Grégoire de Nysse. Actes du colloque de Chevetogne (22–26 septembre 1969)*. Edited by Marguerite Harl. Leiden: Brill, 1971.

———. "Zur Genese der trinitarischen Formel bei Basilius von Caesarea." Pages 123–156 in *Für euch Bischof—mit euch Christ. Festschrift für Friedrich Kardinal Wetter zum siebzigsten Geburtstag*. Edited by Peter Neuner and Manfred Weitlauff. St. Ottilien: EOS Verlag, 1998.

Hunter, David G. "Presidential Address: The Significance of Ambrosiaster." *Journal of Early Christian Studies* 17 (2009): 1–26.

Hurley, Patrick R. "Some Thoughts on the Emperor Aurelian as 'Persecutor.'" *Classical World: A Quarterly Journal on Antiquity* 106 (2012–2013): 75–89.

Hurtado, Larry Weir. "The Binitarian Shape of Early Christian Worship." Pages 187–213 in *The Jewish Roots of Christological Monotheism: Papers from the St. Andrews Conference on the Historical Origins of the Worship of Jesus*. Edited by James R. Davila, Gladys S. Lewis, and Carey C. Newman. Leiden: Brill, 1999.

Hyman, Aaron. *Sefer toldot tanna'im ṿe-'amora'im: mesudar 'a[l] p[i] a[lef] b[eit] 'im be'urim ṿe-girsa'ot shonot*. Jerusalem: Ḳiryah ne'emanah, 1964.

Idel, Moshe. *Ben: Sonship and Jewish Mysticism*. London: Continuum; Jerusalem: Shalom Hartman Institute, 2007.

Il comportamento dell'intellettuale nella società antica. Pubblicazioni dell'Istituto di filologia classica e medievale 67. Genoa: Università di Genova, Facoltà di lettere, Istituto di filologia classica e medievale, 1980.

Ilan, Tal, and Ronit Nikolski. *Rabbinic Traditions between Palestine and Babylonia*. Leiden: Brill, 2014.

Iricinschi, Eduard, and Holger M. Zellentin, ed. *Heresy and Identity in Late Antiquity*. Texts and Studies in Ancient Judaism 119. Tübingen: Mohr Siebeck, 2008.

Jackson-McCabe, Matt. *Jewish Christianity: The Making of the Christianity-Judaism Divide*. New Haven, CT: Yale University Press, 2020.

———, ed. *Jewish Christianity Reconsidered: Rethinking Ancient Groups and Texts*. Minneapolis: Fortress, 2007.

Jacob, Christian. "La citation comme performance dans les «Deipnosophistes» d'Athénée." Pages 147–174 in *La citation dans l'Antiquité: Actes du colloque du PARSA Lyon, ENS LSH, 6–8 novembre 2002*. Edited by Catherine Darbo-Peschansk. Grenoble: Millon, 2004.

Jacobs, Andrew. *Epiphanius of Cyprus: A Cultural Biography of Late Antiquity*. Oakland: University of California Press, 2016.

———. "Jews and Christians." Pages 169–185 in *The Oxford Handbook of Early Christian Studies*. Edited by Susan Ashbrook Harvey and David G. Hunter. Oxford: Oxford University Press, 2008.

———. *Remains of the Jews: The Holy Land and Christian Empire in Late Antiquity*. Stanford, CA: Stanford University Press, 2004.

Jacobs, Louis. "Evidence of Literary Device in the Babylonian Talmud." *Journal of Jewish Studies* 3 (1952): 157–162.

———. "Further Evidence of Literary Device in the Babylonian Talmud." Pages 60–69 in *Studies in Talmudic Logic and Methodology*. London: Valentine, 1961.

———. "How Much of the Babylonian Talmud Is Pseudepigraphic?" Pages 6–17 in Louis Jacobs, *Structure and Form in the Babylonian Talmud*. Cambridge: Cambridge University Press, 1991. [= Revised version of "How Much of the Babylonian Talmud Is Pseudepigraphic?" *Journal of Jewish Studies* 28 (1977): 45–59.]

———. Review of Abraham Weiss, *Le-ḥeḳer ha-Talmud*. *Journal of Jewish Studies* 7 (1956): 114–117.

———. *The Talmudic Argument: A Study in Talmudic Reasoning and Methodology*. Cambridge: Cambridge University Press, 1984.

———. "The Talmudic *Sugya* as a Literary Unit." *Journal of Jewish Studies* 24 (1974): 119–126.

Jacques, François. *Rom und das Reich in der hohen Kaiserzeit: 44 v. Chr.–260 n. Chr.* 2 vols. Stuttgart: B.G. Teubner, 1998–2001.

Jaeger, Hasso. "La preuve judiciaire d'après la tradition rabbinique et patristique." Pages 415–594 in *Recueils de la Société Jean Bodin. Tome XVI. La preuve (antiquité)*. Brussels: Les Éditions de la Librairie Encyclopédique, S.P.R.L., 1965.

Jaffee, Martin S. "Rabbinic Authorship as a Collective Enterprise." Pages 17–37 in *The Cambridge Companion to the Talmud and Rabbinic Literature*. Edited by Charlotte Elisheva Fonrobert and Martin S. Jaffee. Cambridge: Cambridge University Press, 2007.

———. *Torah in the Mouth: Writing and Oral Tradition in Palestinian Judaism, 200 BCE–400 CE*. Oxford: Oxford University Press, 2001.

———. "Writing and Rabbinic Oral Tradition: On Mishnaic Narrative, Lists and Mnemonics." *Journal of Jewish Thought and Philosophy* 4 (1995): 123–146.

Jastrow, Marcus. *A Dictionary of the Targumim, the Talmud Babli and Yerushalmi, and the Midrashic Literature with an Index of Scriptural Quotations*. 2 vols. London: Luzac; New York: G.P. Putnam, 1903.

Jay, Pierre. "Jérôme auditeur d'Apollinaire de Laodicée à Antioche." *Revue d'Études Augustiniennes et Patristique* 20 (1974): 36–41.

Jeanjean, Benoît. "Saint Jérôme entre polémique et hérésiologie (du portrait à charge à l'hérésiologie dans l'«Aduersus Heluidium», l'«Aduersus Iouinianum» et le «Contra Vigilantium»)." Pages 143–153 in *Les chrétiens face à leurs adversaires*. Edited by Jean-Michel Poinsotte. Publications de l'Université de Rouen 297. Mont-Saint-Aignan: Publications de l'Université de Rouen, 2001.

———. *Saint Jérôme et l'hérésie*. Paris: Institut d'Études Augustiniennes, 1999.

———. "Saint Jérôme face à l'exercice du pouvoir épiscopal. Du respect dû à l'évêque à la mise en cause de son autorité dans le *Contre Jean de Jérusalem*." Pages 179–202 in *Les Pères de l'Église et le pouvoir: Une Église profondément transformée. L'impact de la faveur impériale sur l'exercice ecclésial du pouvoir. Actes du VIe colloque de La Rochelle, 6, 7 et 8 septembre 2013*. Edited by Pascal-Grégoire Delage, André Giudicelli, and Bernard Housset, 179–202. Royan: CaritasPatrum, 2014.

Jeanjean, Benoît, and Bertrand Lançon, eds. *Saint Jérôme, Chronique: Continuation de la chronique d'Eusèbe, années 326–378. Suivie de quatre études sur les chroniques et chronographies dans l'antiquité tardive (IVe–VIe siècles)*. Rennes: Presses universitaires de Rennes, 2004.

Jeep, Ludwig. *Quellenuntersuchungen zu den griechischen Kirchenhistorikern*. Leipzig: Tuebner, 1884.

Joannou, Périclès-Pierre, *Die Ostkirche und die Cathedra Petri im 4. Jahrhundert*. Stuttgart: A. Hiersemann, 1972.

———. *Discipline générale antique*. Vol. 2, *Les canons des synodes particuliers (IVe–IXe s.)*. Pontificia commissione per la redazione del codice di diritto canonico orientale 9.2. Grottaferrata: Tipografia Italo-Orientale S. Nilo, 1962.

Jones, Arnold Hugh Martin. *Studies in Roman Government and Law*. Oxford: B. Blackwell, 1960.

———. *The Later Roman Empire, 284–602: A Social, Economic, and Administrative Survey*. 3 vols. Oxford: Basil Blackwell, 1964.

Jones, Prudence. "Rewriting Power: Zenobia, Aurelian, and the *Historia Augusta*." *Classical World: A Quarterly Journal on Antiquity* 109 (2015): 221–233.

Jülicher, Adolf. "Campenses." Column 1443 in *Realenzyklopädie der klassischen Altertumswissenschaft. Band III. Halbband 6. Campanus ager-Claudius*. Stuttgart: J.B. Metzler, 1899.

Just, Patricia. *Imperator et episcopus: Zum Verhältnis von Staatsgewalt und christlicher Kirche zwischen dem 1. Konzil von Nicaea (325) und dem 1. Konzil von Konstantinopel (381)*. Stuttgart: Steiner, 2003.

Kafri, Haim. "Mitʿaseḳ." *Gullot* 3 (1994/1995): 3–24.

Kahana, Menahem Izhak. *"Mipenei tiḳḳun ha-ʿolam." Talmud Bavli massekhet Giṭṭin pereḳ reviʿi*. Jerusalem: Magnes, 2020.

Kahlos, Maijastina. *Forbearance and Compulsion: The Rhetoric of Religious Tolerance and Intolerance in Late Antiquity*. London: Duckworth, 2009.

———. *Religious Dissent in Late Antiquity, 350–450*. New York: Oxford University Press, 2020.

Kaizer, Ted. "From Zenobia to Alexander the Sleepless: Paganism, Judaism and Christianity at Late Roman Palmyra." Pages 113–123 in *Zeitreisen: Syrien—Palmyra—Rom: Festschrift für Andreas Schmidt-Colinet zum 65. Geburtstag*. Edited by Beatrix Bastl, Verena Gassner, and Ulrike Muss. Vienna: Phoibos, 2010.

———. "Man and God at Palmyra: Sacrifice, Lectisternia and Banquets." Pages 179–191 in *The Variety of Local Religious Life in the Near East in the Hellenistic and Roman*

Periods. Edited by Ted Kaizer. Religions in the Graeco-Roman World 164. Leiden: Brill, 2008.

———. "Patterns of Worship at Palmyra: Reflections on Methods and Approaches." Pages 7–24 in *Revisiting the Religious Life of Palmyra*. Edited by Rubina Raja. Contextualizing the Sacred 9. Turnhout: Brepols, 2019.

———. *The Religious Life of Palmyra: A Study of the Social Patterns of Worship in the Roman Period*. Oriens et Occidens 4. Stuttgart: Franz Steiner, 2002.

Kalmanson, Binyamin Yosef. "Melakhah she-ʾeinah tserikhah le-gufah." *Gullot* 9 (2000/2001): 195–199. [= *Kotlenu* 16 (2003/2004): 534–539.]

Kalmin, Richard Lee. "The Formation and Character of the Babylonian Talmud." Pages 840–876 in *The Cambridge History of Judaism*. Vol. 4: *The Late Roman-Rabbinic Period*. Edited by Steven T. Katz. Cambridge: Cambridge University Press, 2006.

———. "The Function and Dating of the Stam and the Writing of History." Pages 31*–51* in *Melekhet maḥashevet: Ḳovets maʿamarim be-nośʾe ʿarikhah ṿe-hitpatḥut shel ha-sifrut ha-Talmudit*. Edited by Aharon Amit and Aharon Shemesh. Ramat Gan: Bar Ilan University Press, 2011.

———. *Jewish Babylonia between Persia and Roman Palestine*. New York: Oxford University Press, 2006.

———. "'Manasseh Sawed Isaiah with a Saw of Wood': An Ancient Legend in Jewish, Christian, Muslim, and Persian Sources." Pages 289–318 in *The Archaeology and Material Culture of the Babylonian Talmud*. Edited by Markham J. Geller. IJS Studies in Judaica 16. Leiden: Brill, 2015.

———. "The Post-Rav Ashi Amoraim: Transition or Continuity? A Study of the Role of the Final Generations of Amoraim in the Redaction of the Talmud." *AJS Review* 11 (1986): 157–187.

———. "Quotation Forms in the Babylonian Talmud: Authentically Amoraic, or a Later Editorial Construct?" *Hebrew Union College Annual* 59 (1988): 167–187.

———. *The Redaction of the Babylonian Talmud: Amoraic of Saboraic?* Monographs of the Hebrew Union College 12. Cincinnati: Hebrew Union College Press, 1989.

———. *The Sage in Jewish Society of Late Antiquity*. New York: Routledge, 1999.

———. *Sages, Stories, Authors, and Editors in Rabbinic Babylonia*. Brown Judaic Studies 300. Providence, RI: Brown University Press, 1994.

Kamesar, Adam. *Jerome, Greek Scholarship, and the Hebrew Bible: A Study of the* Quaestiones Hebraicae in Genesim. Oxford: Clarendon, 1993.

Kaplan, Julius. *The Redaction of the Babylonian Talmud*. Ph.D. dissertation. New York: Columbia University, 1933.

Karmann, Thomas R. *Meletius von Antiochien. Studien sur Geschichte des trinitätstheologischen Streits in den Jahren 360–364 n. Chr.* Regensburger Studien sur Theologie 68. Frankfurt am Main: Lang, 2009.

Kats, Steven T. "The Rabbinic Response to Christianity." Pages 259–298 in *The Cambridge History of Judaism*. Vol. 4: *The Late Roman-Rabbinic Period*. Edited by Steven T. Katz. Cambridge: Cambridge University Press, 2006.

Kattenbusch, Ferdinand. "Die Entstehung einer christlichen Theologie. Zur Geschichte der Ausdrücke θεολογία, θεολογεῖν, θεολόγος." *Zeitschrift für Theologie und Kirche* N.F. 11 (1930): 161–205.

Katzoff, Binyamin. "Nine at Once: A Study in the Mutability of Textual Traditions." *Hebrew Union College Annual* 80 (2009): 39–62.

Kaye, Lynne. *Time in the Babylonian Talmud: Natural and Imagined Times in Jewish Law and Narrative*. New York: Cambridge University Press, 2018.

Kelly, John Norman Davidson. *Early Christian Creeds*. London: Longmans, Green, 1950.

———. *Jerome: His Life, Writings, and Controversies*. London: Duckworth, 1975.

Kiel, Yishai. "Cognizance of Sin and Penalty in the Babylonian Talmud and Pahlavi Literature: A Comparative Analysis." *Oqimta* 1 (2013): 1–49.

———. "Penitential Theology in East Late Antiquity: Talmudic, Zoroastrian, and East Christian Reflections." *Journal for the Study of Judaism* 45 (2014): 551–583.

———. "Reimagining Enoch in Sasanian Babylonia in Light of Zoroastrian and Manichaean Traditions." *AJS Review* 39 (2015): 407–432.

———. "Reinventing Yavneh in Sherira's Epistle: From Pluralism to Monism in the Light of Islamicate Legal Culture." Pages 577–598 in *Strength to Strength: Essays in Appreciation of Shaye J.D. Cohen*. Brown Judaic Studies 363. Providence, RI: Brown Judaic Studies, 2018.

———. "Study versus Sustenance: A Rabbinic Dilemma in Its Zoroastrian and Manichaean Context." *AJS Review* 38 (2014): 275–302.

———. "The Systematization of Penitence in Zoroastrianism in Light of Rabbinic and Islamic Literature." *Bulletin of the Asia Institute* 22 (2012): 119–135.

Kim, Sergey. "And They Sealed the Stone with the Seal of the Unit: A Georgian Homily of Meletius of Antioch from the Holy Week Cycle (CPG 3425–7)." *Le Muséon: Revue d'études orientales* 123 (2019): 415–441.

Kim, Young Richard. *Epiphanius of Cyprus: Imagining an Orthodox World*. Ann Arbor: University of Michigan Press, 2015.

King, Benjamin John. *Newman and the Alexandrian Fathers: Shaping Doctrine in Nineteenth-Century England*. Oxford: Oxford University Press, 2009.

King, Daniel. "*Vir Quadrilinguis*? Syriac in Jerome and Jerome in Syriac." Pages 209–223 in *Jerome of Stridon, His Life, Writings and Legacy*. Edited by Andrew Cain and Josef Lössl. Farnham, UK: Ashgate, 2009.

King, J. Christopher. *Origen on the* Song of Songs *as the Spirit of Scripture: The Bridegroom's Perfect Marriage-Song*. Oxford: Oxford University Press, 2005.

King, Karen L. "Social and Theological Effects of Heresiological Discourse." Pages 28–49 in *Heresy and Identity in Late Antiquity*. Edited by Eduard Iricinschi and Holger

M. Zellentin. Texts and Studies in Ancient Judaism 119. Tübingen: Mohr Siebeck, 2008.

Kinzig, Winfram. *Faith in Formulae. A Collection of Early Christian Creeds and Creed-related Texts.* 4 vols. Oxford: Oxford University Press, 2017.

———. *Neue Texte und Studien zu den antiken und frühmittelalterlichen Glaubensbekenntnissen.* Arbeiten zur Kirchengeschichte 132. Berlin: De Gruyter, 2017.

Kiperwasser, Reuven. *Going West: Migrating Personae and Construction of the Self in Rabbinic Culture.* Brown Judaic Studies 369. Providence, RI: Brown Judaic Studies, 2018.

———. Review of Daniel Boyarin, *Socrates and the Fat Rabbis.* Chicago: University of Chicago Press, 2009.

Kissel, Theodor K. "Palmyra: Aufstieg und Fall einer antiken Wirtschaftsmacht." Pages 54–62 in *Pragmata: Beiträge zur Wirtschaftsgeschichte der Antike im Gedenken an Harald Winkel.* Edited by Sven Günther, Kai Ruffing, and Oliver Stoll. Philippika 17. Wiesbaden: Harrassowitz, 2007.

Kister, Menahem. "Allegorical Interpretations of Biblical Narratives in Rabbinic Literature, Philo, and Origen: Some Case Studies." Pages 133–183 in *New Approaches to the Study of Biblical Interpretation in Judaism of the Second Temple Period and in Early Christianity.* Edited by Gary A. Anderson, Ruth A. Clements, and David Safran. Leiden: Brill, 2013.

———. "Meṭaṭron ṿe-ha᾽el u-ve῾ayat shetei ha-reshuyot: Le-virur ha-dinamiḳa shel mesorot, parshanut u-pulmus." *Tarbits. Riv῾on le-mada῾ei ha-Yahadut* 82 (2013/2014): 43–88.

———. "'Panim be-fanim': Tefisot demut ha-᾽El ba-midrashim ṿe-ḳishreihen le-ṭeḳsṭim notsriyim." *Tarbits. Riv῾on le-mada῾ei ha-Yahadut* 81 (2012/2013): 103–142.

———. "Plucking on the Sabbath and Christian-Jewish Polemic." *Immanuel* 24–25 (1990): 35–51.

Klawans, Jonathan. *Heresy, Forgery, Novelty: Condemning, Denying, and Asserting Innovation in Ancient Judaism.* New York: Oxford University Press, 2019.

Klein, Hayman. "Gemara and Sebara." *Jewish Quarterly Review* 38 (1947): 64–88.

———. "Gemara Quotations in Sebara." *Jewish Quarterly Review* 43 (1953): 89–111.

Kopecek, Thomas A. *A History of Neo-Arianism.* 2 vols. Patristic monograph series 8. Cambridge, MA: Philadelphia Patristic Foundation; Winchendon, MA: Greeno, 1979.

Kösters, Oliver. *Die Trinitätslehre des Epiphanius von Salamis: Ein Kommentar zum »Ancoratus«.* Forschungen zur Kirchen- und Dogmengeschichte 86. Göttingen: Vandenhoeck & Ruprecht, 2003.

Kraemer, David Charles. "Concerning the Theological Assumptions of the Yerushalmi." Pages 355–368 in vol. 3 of *The Talmud Yerushalmi in Graeco-Roman Culture.* Edited by Peter Schäfer. 3 vols. Texte und Studien zum antiken Judentum 71, 79, 93. Tübingen: Mohr-Siebeck, 2003.

———. *A History of the Talmud.* Cambridge: Cambridge University Press, 2019.

———. *The Mind of the Talmud: An Intellectual History of the Bavli.* New York: Oxford University Press, 1990.

———. "On the Reliability of Attributions in the Babylonian Talmud." *Hebrew Union College Annual* 60 (1989): 175–190.

———. *Stylistic Characteristics of Amoraic Literature.* Ph.D. dissertation. New York: Jewish Theological Seminary, 1984.

Kreisel, Howard. "Philosophical Interpretations." Pages 88–120 in *The Cambridge History of Jewish Philosophy.* Vol. 3, *From Antiquity through the Seventeenth Century.* Edited by Steven Nadler and Tamar M. Rudavskyin. Cambridge: Cambridge University Press, 2009.

Krüger, Gustav. *Lucifer Bischof von Calaris und das Schisma der Luciferianer.* Leipzig: Breitkopf u. Härtel, 1886.

Kubiak, Aleksandra. "Des 'dieux bons' à Palmyre." *Studia Palmyreńskie* 12 (2013): 227–234.

Kühn, Peter. *Offenbarungsstimmen im Antiken Judentum: Untersuchungen zur Bat Qol und verwandten Phänomenen.* Tübingen: Mohr Siebeck, 1989.

Kuhn, Thomas. *The Structure of Scientific Revolutions.* Chicago: University of Chicago Press, 1962.

Labarriére, Jean-Louis. "*Logos endiathetos* et *Logos prophorikos* dans la polémique entre le Portique et la Nouvelle Académie." Pages 259–279 in *L'animal dans l'antiquité.* Edited by Barbara Cassin, Jean-Louis Labarrière, and Gilbert Romeyer-Dherbey. Paris: Vrin, 1997.

Labourt, Jérôme. *Saint Jérôme: Lettres. Tome I.* Paris: Les Belles lettres, 1949.

Laird, Raymond. "John Chrysostom and the Anomoeans: Shaping an Antiochene Perspective on Christology." Pages 129–149 in *Religious Conflict from Early Christianity to Early Islam.* Edited by Wendy Mayer and Brownen Neil. Berlin: De Gruyter, 2013.

Lakatos, Imre. "Criticism and the Methodology of Scientific Research Programmes." *Proceedings of the Aristotelian Society* 69 (1968): 149–186.

———. "Falsification and the Methodology of Scientific Research Programmes." Pages 91–195 in *Criticism and the Growth of Knowledge.* Edited by Imre Lakatos and Alan Musgrave. Cambridge: Cambridge University Press, 1970.

Lalande, André. *Vocabulaire technique et critique de la philosophie.* 4th ed. 2 vols. Paris: Quadrige/PUF, 1997.

Lançon, Bertrand. "Militia philosophorum. Le rôle des lettrés dans l'entourage des empereurs romains du IVe siècle." Pages 31–47 in *Literature and Society in the Fourth Century AD: Performing* Paideia, *Constructing the Present, Presenting the Self.* Edited by Lieve Van Hoof and Peter Van Nuffelen. Mnemosyne Supplements. Monographs on Greek and Latin Language and Literature 373. Leiden: Brill, 2014.

Lang, Uwe Michael. "The Christological Controversy at the Synod of Antioch in 268/9." *Journal of Theological Studies* 51 (2000): 54–80.

———. "Patristic Argument and the Use of Philosophy in the Tritheist Controversy of the Sixth Century." Pages 79–99 in *The Mystery of the Holy Trinity in the Fathers of the Church: Proceedings of the Fourth International Patristic Conference, Maynooth, 1999*. Edited by Lewis Ayres and D. Vincent Twomey. Dublin: Four Courts, 2007.

Langen, Joseph. *De commentariorum in epistulas Paulinas qui Ambrosii et Quaestionum biblicarum quae Augustini nomine feruntur scriptore dissertatio*. Ph.D. dissertation. Bonn: Rheinische Friedrich-Wilhelms-Universität Bonn, 1880.

Laudan, Larry. *Progress and Its Problems: Toward a Theory of Scientific Growth*. Berkeley: University of California Press, 1977.

Lawler, Thomas Comerford. "Jerome's First Letter to Damasus." Pages 548–552 in vol. 2 of *Kyriakon. Festschrift Johannes Quasten*. Edited by Patrick Granfield and Josef A. Jungmann. 2 vols. Münster: Aschendorff, 1970.

Lawler, Thomas Comerford, and Charles Christopher Mierow. *The Letters of St. Jerome*. Westminster, MD: Newman, 1963.

Lawlor, Hugh Jackson. "The Sayings of Paul of Samosata." *Journal of Theological Studies* (Old Series) 19 (1917): 20–45.

———. "The Sayings of Paul of Samosata: Additional Notes." *Journal of Theological Studies* (Old Series) 19 (1918): 115–120.

Lebon, Joseph. "Le *sermo maior de fide* pseudo-athanasien." *Le Muséon: Revue d'études orientales* 38 (1925): 243–260.

———. Review of Hans-Georg Opitz, *Untersuchungen zur Überlieferung der Schriften des Athanasius*. *Revue d'Histoire Ecclésiastique* 31 (1935): 786–787.

Le Boulluec, Alain. *La notion d'hérésie dans la littérature grecque, IIe–IIIe siècles*. Paris: Études Augustiniennes, 1985.

Lebreton, Jules. "Ἀγέννητος dans la tradition philosophique et dans la littérature chrétienne du IIe siècle." *Recherches de Science Religieuse* 13 (1926): 431–443.

Leemans, Johan. "Logic and the Trinity: Introducing Text and Context of Gregory of Nyssa's *Ad Graecos*." Pages 111–130 in *Gregory of Nyssa: The Minor Treatises on Trinitarian Theology and Apollinarism: Proceedings of the 11th International Colloquium on Gregory of Nyssa (Tübingen, 17–20 September 2008)*. Edited by Margitta Berghaus and Volker Henning Drecoll. Vigiliae Christianae Supplements 106. Leiden: Brill, 2011.

Lefort, Louis-Théophile. *Lettres festales et pastorales en copte*. CSCO 150–151. Scriptores Coptici 19–20. Louvain: L. Durbecq, 1955.

Le Goff, Jacques. *Les intellectuels au Moyen Âge*. Paris: Éditions du Seuil, 1957.

———. *Les intellectuels au Moyen Âge*. Paris: Éditions du Seuil, 1985.

Lenski, Noel Emmanuel. *Constantine and the Cities: Imperial Authority and Civic Politics*. Philadelphia: University of Pennsylvania Press, 2016.

———. *Failure of Empire: Valens and the Roman State in the Fourth Century AD*. Berkeley: University of California Press, 2002.

Leppin, Hartmut. "The Church Historians (I): Socrates, Sozomenus, and Theodoretus." Pages 219–254 in *Greek & Roman Historiography in Late Antiquity: Fourth to Sixth Century AD*. Edited by Gabriele Marasco. Leiden: Brill, 2003.

Leroux, Jean-Marie. "Athanase et la seconde phase de la crise arienne (345–373)." Pages 145–156 in *Politique et théologie chez Athanase d'Alexandrie. Actes du colloque de Chantilly (23–25 septembre 1973)*. Edited by Charles Kannengiesser. Paris: Beauchesne, 1974.

Letteney, Mark. *The Christianization of Knowledge in Late Antiquity: Intellectual and Material Transformations*. Cambridge: Cambridge University Press [forthcoming].

Lettieri, Gaetano. "L'eresia originaria e le sue alterazioni. I. La matrice giudaico-apocalittica dell'eresia di Gesu." *B@belonline* 4 (2018): 26–78.

———. "L'eresia originaria e le sue alterazioni. II. Definizione giovannea e dispositivo dialettico di un'idea cristiana." *B@belonline* 5 (2019): 339–378.

Levinson, Joshua. "Aḥat diber Elohim shetayim zo shamʿati: Ḳeriʾah diʾalogit ba-sipur ha-darshani." Pages 405–432 in *Higayon le-Yona: New Aspects in the Study of Midrash Aggadah and Piyut in Honor of Professor Yona Frankel*. Edited by Jacob Elbaum, Galit Hasan-Roken, and Joshua Levinson. Jerusalem: Magnes, 2006.

Levy, Gabriel. "Rabbinic Philosophy of Language: Not in Heaven." *Journal of Jewish Thought and Philosophy* 18 (2010): 167–202.

Lieberman, Saul. *Hellenism in Jewish Palestine: Studies in the Literary Transmission, Beliefs and Manners of Palestine in the I Century B.C.E.–IV Century C.E.* Texts and Studies of the Jewish Theological Seminary of America 18. 2nd ed. New York: Jewish Theological Seminary of America, 1962.

Liebes, Yehuda. *Ḥeṭʾo shel Elishaʿ: Arbaʿah she-nikhnesu la-pardes ṿe-ṭivʿah shel ha-misṭiḳah ha-Talmudit*. Jerusalem: Magnes, 1990.

Liebeschuetz, J.H. Wolfgang G. *Antioch: City and Imperial Administration in the Later Roman Empire*. Oxford: Oxford University Press, 1972.

Lienhard, Joseph T. "Acacius of Caesarea's *Contra Marcellum*: Its Place in Theology and History." *Cristianesimo nella storia: Ricerche storiche, esegetiche, teologiche* 10 (1989): 1–21.

———. "The 'Arian' Controversy: Some Categories Reconsidered." *Theological Studies* 48 (1987): 415–437.

———. "Basil of Caesarea, Marcellus of Ancyra and 'Sabellius.'" *Church History* 58 (1989): 157–167.

———. "Contra Marcellum: *The Influence of Marcellus of Ancyra on Fourth-Century Greek Theology*." Habilitation thesis. Freiburg im Breisgau: Albert Ludwigs Universität, 1986.

———. Contra Marcellum: *Marcellus of Ancyra and Fourth-Century Theology*. Washington, DC: Catholic University of America Press, 1999.

———. "Did Athanasius Reject Marcellus?" Pages 65–80 in *Arianism after Arius: Essays on the Development of the Fourth Century Trinitarian Conflicts*. Edited by Michel René Barnes and Daniel H. Williams. Edinburgh: T&T Clark, 1993.

———. "Marcellus of Ancyra in Modern Research." *Theological Studies* 43 (1982): 486–503.

———. "*Ousia* and *Hypostasis*: The Cappadocian Settlement and the Theology of 'One Hypostasis.'" Pages 99–122 in *The Trinity: An Interdisciplinary Symposium on the Trinity*. Edited by Stephen T. Davis, Daniel Kendall, and Gerald O'Collins. Oxford: Oxford University Press, 1999.

———. "Two Friends of Athanasius: Marcellus of Ancyra and Apollinaris of Laodicea." *Zeitschrift für Antikes Christentum* 10 (2006): 56–66.

Lieu, Judith. "History and Theology in Christian Views of Judaism." Pages 79–96 in *The Jews among Pagans and Christians in the Roman Empire*. Edited by Judith Lieu, John North, and Tessa Rajak. London: Routledge, 1992.

———. *Image and Reality: The Jews in the World of the Christians in the Second Century*. Edinburgh: T&T Clark, 1996.

Lietzmann, Hans. *Geschichte der Alten Kirche*. 4 vols. Berlin: de Gruyter, 1936–1953.

Lifschitz, Yosef Yitzhak. "Melekhet maḥashevet." *Tekhelet. Ketav-ʿet le-maḥshavah Israʾelit* 10 (2000/2001): 120–147.

Lim, Richard. "Christians, Dialogues and Patterns of Sociability in Late Antiquity." Pages 151–172 in *The End of Dialogue in Antiquity*. Edited by Simon Goldhill. Cambridge: Cambridge University Press, 2008.

———. *Public Disputation, Power, and Social Order in Late Antiquity*. Berkeley: University of California Press, 1995.

Limone, Vito. "Il contributo di Origene alla storia dell'uso di 'ipostasi' nella teologia cristiana." *Cristianesimo nella storia* 2 (2019): 211–256.

———. "I nomi dell'amore: Un'indagine sulla traduzione latina del *Commento al Cantico dei Cantici* di Origene." *Zeitschrift für antikes Christentum* 19 (2015): 407–429.

Lippold, Adolf. "Rolle und Bild der Frauen in der *Historia Augusta*. Bilder—Rollen—Realitäten in den Texten antiker autoren der römischen Kaiserzeit." Pages 355–369 in *Frauen und Geschlechter*. Edited by Robert Rollinger, Kordula Schnegg, and Christoph Ulf. Cologne: Böhlau, 2006.

Logan, Alastair H.B. "Marcellus of Ancyra and the Councils of AD 325: Antioch, Ancyra, and Nicaea." *Journal of Theological Studies* 43 (1992): 428–446.

———. "Marcellus of Ancyra, Defender of the Faith against Heretics—and Pagans." Pages 550–564 in *Studia Patristica XXXVII: Cappadocian Writers; Other Greek Writers; Papers Presented at the Thirteenth International Conference on Patristic Studies Held in Oxford 1999*. Edited by Maurice F. Wiles and Edward J. Yarnold. Louvain: Peeters, 2001.

———. "Marcellus of Ancyra on Origen and Arianism." Pages 159–163 in *Origeniana Septima. Origenes in den Auseinandersetzungen des 4. Jahrhunderts*. Edited by Wolfgang A. Bienert and U. Kuhneweg. Louvain: Peeters, 1999.

Löhr, Winrich Alfried. "Arius Reconsidered (Part 1)." *Zeitschrift für Antikes Christentum* 9 (2006): 524–560.

———. "Arius Reconsidered (Part 2)." *Zeitschrift für Antikes Christentum* 10 (2006): 121–157.

———. *Die Entstehung der homöischen und homöusianischen Kirchenparteien. Studien zur Synodalgeschichte des 4. Jahrhunderts.* Witterschlick: Wehle, 1986.

———. "A Sense of Tradition: The Homoiousian Church Party." Pages 81–100 in *Arianism after Arius: Essays on the Development of the Fourth Century Trinitarian Conflicts.* Edited by Michel René Barnes and Daniel H. Williams. Edinburgh: T&T Clark, 1993.

Lohse, Bernhard. *Das Passafest der Quartadecimaner.* Gütersloh: C. Bertelsmann, 1953.

Longosz, Stanisław. "Argument patrystyczny w okresie sporów ariańskich (318–362)." Pages 196–212 in *Miscellanea patristica in memoriam Joannis Czuj.* Edited by Vincentius Myszor and Aemilius Stanula. Studia Antiquitatis Christianae 2. Warsaw: Akademia Teologii Katolickiej, 1980.

———. *De auctoritate traditionis apud Athanasium alexandrinum.* Th.D. dissertation. Rome: Instititum Patristicum Augustinianum, 1976.

———. "La tradizione nella controversia ariana (a. 318–362). Testimonianze non Atanasiane." *Augustinianum. Periodicum Instituti Patristici «Augustinianum»* 19 (1979): 443–468.

Loofs, Friedrich. "Das Nicänum." Pages 62–82 in *Festgabe von Fachgenossen und Freunden Karl Müller zum siebzigsten Geburtstag dargebracht.* Edited by Otto Scheel. Tübingen: J.C.B. Mohr, 1922.

———. *Leitfaden zum Studium der Dogmengeschichte.* 2nd ed. Halle an der Saale: Max Niemeyer, 1890.

———. *Nestorius and His Place in the History of Christian Doctrine.* Cambridge: University Press, 1914.

———. *Paulus von Samosata. Eine Untersuchung zur altkirchlichen Literatur- und Dogmengeschichte.* TU 44. Leipzig: J.C. Hinrichs, 1924.

———. *Theophilus von Antiochien adversus Marcionem und die anderen theologischen Quellen bei Irenaeus.* TU 46.1. Leipzig: J.C. Hinrichs, 1930.

López, Almudena Alba. "El cisma luciferiano." Pages 177–191 in *Minorías y sectas en el mundo romano. Actas del 3er coloquio de la Asociación Interdisciplinar de Estudios Romanos.* Edited by Gonzalo Bravo and Raúl González Salinero. Monografias y estudios de antigüedad griega y romana 20. Madrid: Signifer Libros, 2006.

López Kindler, Agustín. "Constantino y el arrianismo." *Anuario de historia de la Iglesia* 22 (2013): 37–64.

Lorenz, Rudolf. *Arius judaizans? Untersuchungen zur dogmengeschichtlichen Einordnung des Arius.* Forschungen zur Kirchen- und Dogmengeschichte 31. Göttingen: Vandenhoeck und Ruprecht, 1979.

———. "Die Eustathius von Antiochien zugeschriebene Schrift gegen Photin." *Zeitschrift für die neutestamentliche Wissenschaft und die Kunde der älteren Kirche* 71 (1980): 109–128.

Lowe, Elias Avery, ed. Codices Latini Antiquiores: *A Palaeographic Guide to Latin Manuscripts Prior to the Ninth Century*. 12 vols. Oxford, 1934–1979.

Luibhéid, Colm. "The Arianism of Eusebius of Nicomedia." *Irish Theological Quarterly* 43 (1976): 3–23.

———. *Eusebius of Caesarea and the Arian Crisis*. Dublin: Irish Academic Press, 1978.

Luiselli, Bruno. "Dall'arianesimo dei Visigoti di Costantinopoli all'arianesimo degli Ostrogoti d'Italia." *Rendiconti dell'Accademia Nazionale dei Lincei. Classe di Scienze morali, storiche e filologiche* 16 (2005): 5–30.

Lyman, J. Rebecca. "Arius and Arianism: The Origins of the Alexandrian Controversy." Pages 43–62 in *The Cambridge Companion to the Council of Nicaea*. Edited by Young Richard Kim. Cambridge: Cambridge University Press, 2021.

———. "Arius and Arians." Pages 237–257 in *The Oxford Handbook of Early Christian Studies*. Edited by Susan Ashbrook Harvey and David G. Hunter. Oxford: Oxford University Press, 2008.

———. "Hellenism and Heresy." *Journal of Early Christian Studies* 11 (2003): 209–222.

———. "*Lex Orandi*: Heresy, Orthodoxy, and Popular Religion." Pages 131–141 in *The Making and Remaking of Christian Doctrine: Essays in Honour of Maurice Wiles*. Edited by Sarah Coakley and David A. Pailin. Oxford: Clarendon, 1993.

———. "Natural Resources: Tradition without Orthodoxy." *Anglican Theological Review* 84 (2002): 67–80.

———. "A Topography of Heresy: Mapping the Rhetorical Creation of Arianism." Pages 45–62 in *Arianism after Arius: Essays on the Development of the Fourth Century Trinitarian Conflicts*. Edited by Michel René Barnes and Daniel H. Williams. Edinburgh: T&T Clark, 1993.

MacIntyre, Alasdaire. *After Virtue: A Study in Moral Theory*. 3rd ed. Notre Dame, IN: University of Notre Dame Press, 2007.

MacMullen, Ramsay. *Constantine*. New York: Dial Press, 1969.

———. "The Historical Role of the Masses in Late Antiquity." Pages 250–276 in *Changes in the Roman Empire: Essays in the Ordinary*. Princeton, NJ: Princeton University Press, 1990.

———. "The Search for Orthodoxy A.D. 325–553." *Viator* 38 (2007): 1–17.

———. "Sfiducia nell'intelletto nel quarto secolo." *Rivista storica italiana* 84 (1972): 5–16.

———. *Voting about God in Early Church Councils*. New Haven, CT: Yale University Press, 2006.

Madoz, José. "El Concilio de Éfeso ejemplo de argumentación patrística." *Estudios eclesiásticos* 10 (1931): 305–338.

Maghen, Ze'ev. "The Baffling Coexistence of Legalism and Exuberance in Judaic and Islamic Tradition." Pages 217–237 in *Judaic Sources and Western Thought: Jerusalem's Enduring Presence*. Edited by Jonathan Jacobs. Oxford: Oxford University Press, 2011.

Mai, Angelo. *Nova Patrum Bibliotheca*. 9 vols. in 4. Rome: 1844–1888.

Maier, Johann. *Jesus von Nazareth in der talmudischen Überlieferung*. Darmstadt: Wissenschaftliche Buchgesellschaft, 1978.

Maingueneau, Dominique. "Analyzing Self-Constituting Discourses." *Discourse Studies* 1 (1999): 175–199.

———. "Champ discursif." Page 97 in *Dictionnaire d'analyse du discours*. Edited by Patrique Charaudeau and Dominique Maingueneau. Paris: Éditions du Seuil, 2002.

———. "Constituant (discours —)." Pages 133–134 in *Dictionnaire d'analyse du discours*. Edited by Patrique Charaudeau and Dominique Maingueneau. Paris: Éditions du Seuil, 2002.

———. "Dialectique." Pages 173–174 in *Dictionnaire d'analyse du discours*. Edited by Patrique Charaudeau and Dominique Maingueneau. Paris: Éditions du Seuil, 2002.

———. *Discours et analyse du discours. Introduction*. Paris: Armand Colin, 2014.

———. "Formation discursive." Pages 269–272 in *Dictionnaire d'analyse du discours*. Edited by Patrique Charaudeau and Dominique Maingueneau. Paris: Éditions du Seuil, 2002.

———. "Interdiscours." Pages 324–326 in *Dictionnaire d'analyse du discours*. Edited by Patrique Charaudeau and Dominique Maingueneau. Paris: Éditions du Seuil, 2002.

———. *La philosophie comme institution discursive*. Limoges: Lambert Lucas, 2015.

———. "Positionnement." Pages 453–454 in *Dictionnaire d'analyse du discours*. Edited by Patrique Charaudeau and Dominique Maingueneau. Paris: Éditions du Seuil, 2002.

———. *Sémantique de la polémique: Discours religieux et ruptures idéologiques au XVIIe siècle*. Lausanne, Switzerland: L'Age d'homme, 1983.

Manetti, Giovanni. "«Lógos endiáthetos» e «lógos prophorikós» nel dibattito antico sulla razionalità animale: Traduzione e significato di una coppia emblematica." *I Quaderni del Ramo d'Oro on-line* 5 (2012): 83–95.

Manoir de Juaye, Hubert du. *Dogme et spiritualité chez saint Cyrille d'Alexandrie*. Paris: J. Vrin, 1944.

———. "L'argumentation patristique dans la controverse nestorienne." *Recherches de science religieuse* 25 (1935): 441–461 and 531–560.

Mansi, Giovan Domenico. *Sacrorum conciliorum nova et amplissima collectio*. 31 vols. Florence: Antonius Zatta, 1759–1798.

Marasco, Gabriele. "The Church Historians (II): Philostorgius and Gelasius of Cyzicus." Pages 257–288 in *Greek and Roman Historiography in Late Antiquity*. Edited by Gabriele Marasco. Leiden: Brill, 2003.

Maraval, Pierre, and Pierre Périchon, eds. *Socrate de Constantinople. Histoire ecclésiastique*. 4 vols. SC 477, 493, 505, 506. Paris: Les Éditions du Cerf, 2004–2007.

Marcello, Pietro Maria. *La posizione di Lucifero di Cagliari nelle lotte antiariane del IV secolo*. Nuoro: Tipografia Ortobene, 1940.

Marcheselli, Maurizio. "Daniel Boyarin sur l'origine du Judaïsme et du Christianisme." Pages 507–538 in *Texts, Practices, and Groups: Multidisciplinary Approaches to the History of Jesus' Followers in the First Two Centuries; First Annual Meeting of Bertinoro (2–5 October 2014)*. Edited by Adriana Destro and Mauro Pesce. Judaïsme antique et origines du christianisme 10. Turnhout: Brepols, 2017.

Marcos, Mar. "Current Perspectives on the Notion of Toleration in the Roman World." Pages 325–336 in *Contemporary Views on Comparative Religion: In Celebration of Tim Jensen's 65th Birthday*. Edited by Peter Antes, Armin W. Geertz, and Mikael Rothstein. Sheffield, UK: Equinox, 2016.

———. "De la convivencia a la exclusión. Reflexiones sobre el discurso de la tolerancia religiosa en el Cristianismo antiguo." Pages 631–637 in vol. 1 of *Perfiles de Grecia y Roma: Actas del XII Congreso Español de Estudios Clásicos, Valencia, 22 al 26 de octubre de 2007*. Edited by José Francisco González Castro, Jaime Siles Ruiz, and Jesús de la Villa Polo. 3 vols. Madrid: Sociedad Española de Estudios Clásicos, 2009–2011.

———. "Emperor Jovian's Law of Religious Tolerance (a. 363)." Pages 153–177 in *Política, religión y legislación en el imperio romano (ss. IV y V d.C.)*. Edited by María Victoria Escribano Paño and Rita Lizzi Testa. Munera. Studi storici sulla Tarda Antichità 37. Bari: Edipuglia, 2014.

———. "La idea de la libertad religiosa en el Imperio romano." Pages 61–81 in *Libertad e intolerancia religiosa en el Imperio romano*. Edited by José Fernández Ubiña and Mar Marcos. 'Ilu. Revista de Ciencias de las Religiones. Anejo 18. Madrid: Publicaciones Universidad Complutense de Madrid, 2007.

Marinides, Nicholas, Jonathan Stutz, and Martin Wallraff. *Gelasius of Caesarea. Ecclesiastical History: The Extant Fragments, with an Appendix Containing the Fragments from Dogmatic Writings*. GCS 25. Berlin: De Gruyter, 2018.

Markschies, Christoph. *Christian Theology and Its Institutions in the Early Roman Empire: Prolegomena to a History of Early Christian Theology*. Translated by Wayne Coppins. Waco, TX: Baylor University Press, 2015. [= Translation of Christoph Markschies, *Kaiserzeitliche antike christliche Theologie und ihre Institutionen. Prolegomena zu einer Geschichte der antiken christlichen Theologie*. Tübingen: Mohr Siebeck, 2007.]

———. "Intellectuals and Church Fathers in the Third and Fourth Centuries." Pages 239–256 in *Christians and Christianity in the Holy Land: From the Origins to the Latin Kingdoms*. Edited by Ora Limor and Guy Gedalyah Stroumsa. Cultural Encounters in Late Antiquity and the Middle Ages 5. Leiden: Brill, 2006.

———. "Preface." Pages i–xii in *The Rise of the Early Christian Intellectual*. Edited by Lewis Ayres and H. Clifton Ward. Arbeiten zur Kirchengeschichte 139. Berlin: De Gruyter, 2020.

———."Was ist lateinischer »Neunizänismus«? Ein Vorschlag für eine Antwort." *Zeitschrift für Antikes Christentum* (1997): 73–95.

Marmorstein, Arthur. *Religionsgeschichtliche Studien.* 2 vols. Pressburg: Selbstverlag des Verfasser, 1912.

Martin, Annick. "Antioche aux IVe et Ve siècle. Un exemple de réécriture orthodoxe de l'histoire chrétienne." *Studi e Materiali di Storia delle Religioni* 75 (2009): 279–294.

———. "Antioche ou la difficile unité: Les enjeux d'un schisme." Pages 65–85 in *Les Pères de l'Église et les dissidents: Dissidence, exclusion et réintégration dans les communautés chrétiennes des six premiers siècles. Actes du IVe colloque de La Rochelle, 25, 26 et 27 septembre 2009.* Edited by Pascal-Grégoire Delage. Royan: CaritasPatrum, 2010.

———. *Athanase d'Alexandrie et l'Église d'Égypte au IVe siècle (328–373).* Collection de l'École française de Rome 216. Rome: École française de Rome, 1996.

———. "La réception du concile de Nicée et son impact sur l'évolution des courants théologiques en Orient (325–381)." *Antiquité tardive* 22 (2014): 35–42.

———. "L'Église d'Antioche dans l'*Histoire ecclésiastique* de Théodoret." Pages 481–506 in *Antioche de Syrie. Histoire, images et traces de la ville antique. Colloque organisé par B. Cabouret, P.-L. Gatier et C. Saliou, Lyon, Maison de l'Orient et de la Méditerranée, 4, 5, 6 octobre 2001.* Edited by Bernadette Cabouret, Pierre-Louis Gatier, and Catherine Saliou. Topoi orient-occident. Supplements 5. Lyon: Maison de l'Orient et de la Méditerranée Jean Pouilloux, 2004.

———. Review of Angelo Segneri, *Atanasio. Lettera agli Antiocheni. Introduzione, testo, traduzione e commento. Annuario di Letteratura Cristiana Antica e di Studi Giudeoellenistici* 18 (2012): 589–596.

Maschio, Giorgio. "L'argomentazione patristica di S. Agostino nella prima fase della controversia pelagiana." *Augustinianum. Periodicum Semestre Instituti Patristici* 26 (1986): 459–479.

Matelli, Elisabetta. "ΕΝΔΙΑΘΕΤΟΣ e ΠΡΟΦΟΡΙΚΟΣ ΛΟΓΟΣ. Note sulla origine della formula e della nozione." *Aevum* 66 (1992): 43–70.

May, Gerhard. "Die Chronologie des Lebens und der Werke des Gregor von Nyssa." Pages 51–67 in *Écriture et culture philosophique dans la pensée de Grégoire de Nysse. Actes du colloque de Chevetogne (22–26 septembre 1969).* Edited by Marguerite Harl. Leiden: Brill, 1971.

Mayer, Wendy. "Religious Conflict: Definitions, Problems and Theoretical Approaches." Pages 1–20 in *Religious Conflict from Early Christianity to the Rise of Islam.* Edited by Wendy Mayer and Bronwen Neil. Arbeiten zur Kirchengeschichte 121. Berlin: De Gruyter, 2013.

McCarthy, Daniel P. "The Council of Nicaea and the Celebration of the Christian Pasch." Pages 177–201 in *The Cambridge Companion to the Council of Nicaea.* Edited by Young Richard Kim. Cambridge: Cambridge University Press, 2021.

McGrath, James F. *The Only True God: Early Christian Monotheism in Its Jewish Context.* Urbana: University of Illinois Press, 2009.

McGuckin, John A. "Il lungo cammino verso Calcedonia." Pages 13–41 in *Il Concilio di Calcedonia 1550 anni dopo*. Edited by Antonio Ducay. Rome: Libreria Editrice Vaticana, 2002.

McInnes-Gibbons, Rory. "The Clash for Civilisation: Western Perspectives on Ancient Palmyra through the Image of Zenobia." *Talanta: Proceedings of the Dutch Archaeological and Historical Society* 48–49 (2016): 244–273.

McLynn, Neil B. "Christian Controversy and Violence in the Fourth Century." *Kodai. Journal of Ancient History* 3 (1992): 15–44.

———. "*Curiales* into Churchmen: The Case of Gregory Nazianzen." Pages 277–295 in *Le trasformazioni delle élites in età tardoantica: Atti del convegno internazionale, Perugia, 15–16 marzo 2004*. Edited by Rita Lizzi Testa. Brescia: "L'Erma" di Bretschneider, 2006.

Meijering, Eginhard Peter. "Die Diskussion über den Willen und das Wesen Gottes, theologiegeschichtlich beleuchtet." Pages 35–71 in *L'Église et l'Empire au ive siècle. Sept exposés suivis de discussions. Vandœuvres-Genève, 31 août–3 septembre 1987*. Edited by Dihle Albrecht. Entretiens sur l'antiquité classique 34. Geneva: Fondation Hardt, 1989.

———. "Ἦν ποτε ὅτε οὐκ ἦν ὁ Υἱός: A Discussion on Time and Eternity." *Vigiliae Christianae* 28 (1975): 161–168.

Melamed, Ezra Zion. "Lishana maʿalyah ṿe-kinnuyei soferim be-sifrut ha-Talmud." Pages 112–148 in *Sefer zikaron le-Vinyamin Deh-Fris: Ḳovets meḥḳarim shel ḥaveraṿ ṿe-talmidaṿ*. Jerusalem: Universiṭat Tel-Aviv, Reshut ha-meḥḳar, 1968. [= Pages 263–291 in Ezra Zion Melamed, *ʿIyunim be-sifrut ha-Talmud*. Jerusalem: Magnes, 1986.]

Melamed, Zalman Baruch. "Be-gidrei pesiḳ reisha de-la niḥa leh u-mlakhah she-ʾeinah tserikhah le-gufah." *Me-ʾavnei ha-maḳom* (1992/1993): 29–38.

Meloni, Pietro. "Eusebio di Vercelli 'natione sardus.'" Pages 331–356 in *La Sardegna paleocristiana tra Eusebio e Gregorio Magno: Atti del Convegno nazionale di studi, Cagliari, 10–12 ottobre 1996*. Edited by Attilio Mastino, Giovanna Sotgiu, and Natalino Spaccapelo. Cagliari: Pontificia Facoltà Teologica della Sardegna, 1999.

Ménard, Hélène. "Exil et déploiement d'une théologie, le cas d'Hilaire de Poitiers." Pages 233–240 in *Exil et relégation. Les tribulations du sage et du saint durant l'antiquité romaine et chrétienne (Ier–VIe siècle ap. J.-C.). Actes du colloque organisé par le Centre Jean-Charles Picard, Université de Paris XII-Val-de-Marne, 17–18 juin 2005*. Edited by Philippe Blaudeau. Paris: De Boccard, 2008.

———. "L'exil, enjeu de la sainteté: Réflexions sur la construction de la figure de l'évêque en Italie dans la seconde moitié du IVe s. ap. J.-C." Pages 241–253 in *Exil et relégation. Les tribulations du sage et du saint durant l'antiquité romaine et chrétienne (Ier–VIe siècle ap. J.-C.). Actes du colloque organisé par le Centre Jean-Charles Picard, Université de Paris XII-Val-de-Marne, 17–18 juin 2005*. Edited by Philippe Blaudeau. Paris: De Boccard, 2008.

Meslin, Michel. *Les Ariens d'Occident, 335–430*. Patristica Sorbonensia 8. Paris: Éditions du Seuil, 1967.

Metzler, Karin. "Ein Beitrag zur Rekonstruktion der «Thalia» des Arius (mit einer Neuedition wichtiger Bezeugungen bei Athanasius)." Pages 11–45 in *Ariana et Athanasiana. Studien zur Überlieferung und zu philologischen Problemen der Werke des Athanasius von Alexandrien*. Edited by Karin Metzler and Frank J. Simon. Abhandlungen der Rheinisch-Westfälischen Akademie der Wissenschaft 83. Opladen: Westdeutscher Verlag, 1991.

Meunier, Bernard. "Genèse de la notion de «Pères de l'Église» aux IVe et Ve siècles." *Revue des sciences philosophiques et théologiques* 93 (2009): 315–331.

———. "L'autorité des «Pères» entre Antiquité et Moyen Âge." Pages 565–588 in vol. 2 of *Les réceptions des Pères de l'Église au Moyen Âge. Le devenir de la tradition ecclésiale. Congrès du Centre Sèvres—Facultés jésuites de Paris (11–14 juin 2008). Actes*. Edited by Rainer Berndt and Michel Fédou. 2 vols. Archa verbi. Subsidia 10. Münster: Aschendorff Verlag, 2013.

Milano, Andrea. *Persona in teologia. Alle origini del significato di persona nel cristianesimo antico*. Rome: Edizioni Dehoniane, 1984.

Milburn, Robert Leslie Pollington (*auctor incertus*). "Ο ΤΗΣ ΕΚΚΛΗΣΙΑΣ ΟΙΚΟΣ." *Journal of Theological Studies* 46 (1945): 65–68.

Millar, Fergus. "Paul of Samosata, Zenobia and Aurelian." *Journal of Roman Studies* 61 (1971): 1–17.

Miller, Stuart S. *Sages and Commoners in Late Antique Erez Israel: A Philological Inquiry into Local Traditions in Talmud Yerushalmi*. Texte und Studien zum antiken Judentum 111. Tübingen: Mohr Siebeck, 2005.

Mimouni, Simon Claude. "Il monoteismo: Una forma di totalitarismo attraverso i secoli." *Annali di Storia dell'Esegesi* 35 (2018): 7–22.

Mitchell, Stephen, and Peter Van Nuffelen, eds. *Monotheism between Christians and Pagans in Late Antiquity*. Interdisciplinary Studies in Ancient Culture and Religion 12. Louvain: Peeters, 2010.

———, eds. *One God: Pagan Monotheism in the Roman Empire*. Cambridge: Cambridge University Press, 2010.

Mohrmann, Christine. "Les dénominations de l'église en tant qu'édifice en grec et en latin au cours des premiers siècles chrétiens." *Revue des Sciences religieuses* 36 (1962): 156–174.

Molinier Arbo, Agnès. "Femmes de pouvoir entre Orient et Occident aux derniers siècles de l'Empire: réflexions autour du témoignage de l'«Histoire Auguste»." Pages 47–80 in *Donne, istituzioni e società fra tardo antico e alto medioevo*. Edited by Francesca Cenerini and Ida Gilda Mastrorosa. La Botte di Diogene 8. Lecce: Pensa Multimedia, 2016.

———. "Zénobie reine de Palmyre: Quand une Orientale prend le pouvoir dans l'«Histoire Auguste»." Pages 183–203 in *L'idéalisation de l'autre: Faire un modèle d'un anti-modèle. Actes du 2ᵉ colloque SoPHiA tenu à Besançon les 26–28 novembre 2012.* Edited by Antonio Gonzales and Maria Teresa Schettino. Besançon: Presses Universitaires de Franche-Comté, 2014.

Momigliano, Arnaldo. "The Origins of Ecclesiastical Historiography." Pages 132–152 in Arnaldo Momigliano, *The Classical Foundations of Modern Historiography*. Berkeley: University of California Press, 1990.

———. "Pagan and Christian Historiography in the Fourth Century A.D." Pages 79–99 in Arnaldo Momigliano, *The Conflict between Paganism and Christianity in the Fourth Century*. Oxford: Clarendon, 1963.

Mommsen, Theodor, Eduard Schwartz, and Friedhelm Winklemann, eds. *Die Kirchengeschichte*. 2nd ed. GCS 9. Eusebius Werke 2. Berlin: Akademie-Verlag, 1999.

Monnickendam, Yifat. *Jewish Law and Early Christian Identity: Betrothal, Marriage, and Infidelity in the Writings of Ephrem the Syrian*. New York: Cambridge University Press, 2019.

Montaigne, Michel de. *Les Essais*. Edited by Pierre Villey. Paris: Presses Universitaires de France, 1992.

Montana, Fausto. "The Making of Greek Scholiastic «Corpora»." Pages 105–161 in *From Scholars to Scholia: Chapters in the History of Ancient Greek Scholarship*. Edited by Franco Montanari and Laura Pagani. Trends in Classics. Supplementary Volumes 9. Berlin: De Gruyter, 2011.

Montinari, Franco. "Hypomnema." Translated by Theodor Heinze. Columns 813–815 in vol. 5 of *Der neue Pauly: Enzyklopädie der Antike*. Edited by Hubert Cancik and Helmuth Schneider. Stuttgart: Metzler, 2001.

Moore, Michael Edward. *A Sacred Kingdom: Bishops and the Rise of Frankish Kingship, 300–850*. Washington, DC: Catholic University of America Press, 2011.

———. "The Spirit of the Gallican Councils, A.D. 314–506." *Annuarium Historiae Conciliorum: Internationale Zeitschrift für Konziliengeschichtsforschung* 39 (2007): 1–52.

Mopsik, Charles. *Le Livre hébreu d'Hénoch ou Livre des palais*. Paris: Verdlier, 1989.

Morales, Xavier. *La théologie trinitaire d'Athanase d'Alexandrie*. Collection des Études Augustiniennes. Série antiquité 180. Paris: Institut d'études augustiniennes, 2006.

Morawski, Stefan. "The Basic Functions of Quotation." Pages 690–705 in *Sign, Language, Culture = Signe, langage, culture = Znak, język, kultura = Znak, i͡azyk, kul'tura*. Edited by Algirdas Julien Greimas. Janua linguarum. Series maior 1. The Hague: Mouton, 1970.

Morison, Stanley. "An Unacknowledged Hero of the Fourth Century, Damasus I, 366–384." Pages 241–264 in vols. 2 of *Classical, Mediaeval, and Renaissance Studies in Honor of Berthold Louis Ullman*. Edited by Charles Henderson. 2 vols. Rome: Edizioni di Storia e Letteratura, 1964.

Morlet, Sébastian. "Aux origines de l'argument patristique? Citation et autorité dans le *Contre Marcel* d'Eusèbe de Césarée." Pages 69–94 in *On Good Authority: Tradition, Compilation and the Construction of Authority in Literature from Antiquity to the*

Renaissance. Edited by Reinhart Ceulemans and Pieter De Leemans. Lectio: Studies in the Transmission of Texts and Ideas 3. Turnhout: Brepols, 2015.

———. "L'Antiquité tardive fut-elle une période d'obscurantisme? À propos d'un ouvrage récent." *Annuario di Letteratura Cristiana Antica e di Studi Giudeoellenistici* 16 (2010): 413–421.

Morray-Jones, Christopher R.A. "Hekhalot Literature and Talmud Tradition: Alexander's Three Test Cases." *Journal for the Study of Judaism in the Persian, Hellenistic, and Roman Periods* 22 (1991): 1–39.

Morson, Gary Saul. *The Words of Others: From Quotations to Cultures*. New Haven, CT: Yale University Press, 2011.

Mortley, Raoul. "The Alien God in Arius." Pages 205–215 in *Platonism in Late Antiquity*. Edited by Stephen Gersh and Charles Kannengiesser. Notre Dame, IN: University of Notre Dame Press, 1992.

Moscovitz, Leib. "The Formation and Character of the Jerusalem Talmud." Pages 663–670 in *The Cambridge History of Judaism*. Vol. 4, *The Late Roman-Rabbinic Period*. Edited by Steven T. Katz. Cambridge: Cambridge University Press, 2006.

———. *Ha-ṭerminologyah shel ha-Yerushalmi: Ha-munaḥim ha-ʿiḳariyim*. Jerusalem: Magnes, 2009.

———. "Sugyot maḳbilot u-masoret nosaḥ ha-Yerushalmi." *Tarbits* 60 (1991): 523–549.

———. "Sugyot muḥlafot ba-Yerushalmi." *Tarbits* 60 (1990): 19–66.

———. *Talmudic Reasoning: From Casuistics to Conceptualization*. Texte und Studien zum antiken Judentum 89. Tübingen: Mohr Siebeck, 2002.

Moss, Yonatan. "Fish Eats Lion Eats Man. Saadia Gaon, Syriac Christianity, and the Resurrection of the Dead." *Jewish Quarterly Review* 106 (2016): 494–520.

Mosshammer, Alden A. *The Easter Computus and the Origins of the Christian Era*. Oxford: Clarendon, 2008.

Mottolese, Maurizio. *Dio nel giudaismo rabbinico. Immagine e mito*. Scienze e storia delle religioni 15. Brescia: Morcelliana, 2010.

Mueller, Joseph Gerard. *L'ancien testament dans l'ecclésiologie des pères. Une lecture des Constitutions apostoliques*. Instrumenta Patristica et Mediaevalia 41. Turnhout: Brepols, 2004.

———. "The Ancient Church Order Literature: Genre or Tradition?" *Journal of Early Christian Studies* 15 (2007): 337–380.

Mühl, Max. "Der λόγος ἐνδιάθετος und προφορικός von der älteren Stoa bis zur Synode von Sirmium 351." *Archiv für Begriffsgeschichte* 7 (1962): 7–56.

Mühlenberg, Ekkehard. "Griechische Florilegien." Columns 215–219 in vol. 11 of *Theologische Realenzyklopädie*. 36 vols. Berlin: De Gruyter, 1977–2005.

Müller, Christian. "Die Synode von Mailand 355, Eusebius von Vercelli und die Folgen." Pages 95–190 in *Die Synoden im trinitarischen Streit: Über die Etablierung eines synodalen Verfahrens und die Probleme seiner Anwendung im 4. und 5. Jahrhundert*.

Edited by Uta Heil and Annette von Stockhausen. TU 177. Berlin: De Gruyter, 2017.

Nacke, Ewald. *Das Zeugnis der Väter in der theologischen Beweisführung Cyrills von Alexandrien nach seinen Briefen und anti-nestorianischen Schriften*. Ph.D. dissertation. Münster: Westfälische Wilhelms-Universität Münster, 1964.

Naeh, Shlomo. "ʿAśeh libekha ḥadrei ḥadarim: ʿYiun nosaf bedivrei Ḥazal ʿal hamaḥloḳot." Pages 851–875 in vol. 2 of *Meḥuyavut yehudit mitḥadeshet: ʿAl ʿolamo vehaguto shel David Hartman*. Edited by Abraham Sagi and Tsevi Zohar. 2 vols. Jerusalem: Shalom Hartman Institute and Hakkibutz Hameuchad, 2001.

Naiweld, Ron. "Au commencement était la pratique. Les commandements comme exercices spirituels—la subjectivation pratique rabbinique." *Yod. Revue des études hébraïques et juives* 15 (2010): 13–41.

———. "The Discursive Machine of Tannaitic Literature: The Rabbinic Resurrection of the Logos." Pages 405–434 in *Les judaïsmes dans tous leurs états aux Ier–IIIe siècles. Les judéens des synagogues, les chrétiens et les rabbins. Actes du colloque de Lausanne 12–14 décembre 2012*. Edited by Claire Clivaz, Simon Claude Mimouni, and Bernard Pouderon. Turnhout: Brepols, 2015.

———. "La littérature rabbinique classique: La création d'une machine discursive." *Annuaire de l'École pratique des hautes études (EPHE). Section des sciences religieuses* 121 (2014): 209–210.

———. *Les antiphilosophes: Pratiques de soi et rapport à la loi dans la littérature rabbinique classique*. Paris: A. Colin, 2011.

———. "The Not So Significant Other: On the Ideological Roots of Rabbinic-Christian Polemics." Pages 191–207 in *Jews and Christians in Antiquity: A Religious Perspective*. Interdisciplinary Studies in Ancient Culture and Religion 18. Edited by Pierluigi Lanfranchi and Joseph Verheyden. Louvain: Peeters, 2018.

———. "The Organization of Religious Signs and the Imperial Mind of Some Early Rabbis." *Images re-vues. Histoire, anthropologie et théorie de l'art. Hors-série* 6 (2018). Retrieved March 29, 2020, at http://journals.openedition.org/imagesrevues/4378.

———. "Qu'est-ce qu'une culture sans foi?" *La cause du désir* 90 (2015): 26–32.

———. "Some Considerations on the History of the Talmud and Christianity and a Proposition of a New Method." Paper presented at the conference Talmud and Christianity: Rabbinic Judaism after Constantine, Cambridge University, Cambridge, June 27–28, 2016.

Nau, François. "Littérature canonique syriaque inédite. Concile d'Antioche. Lettre d'Italie. Canons 'des saints pères' de Philoxène, de Théodose, d'Anthime, d'Athanase, etc." *Revue de l'Orient Chrétien* 14 (1909): 1–31.

Nautin, Pierre. "Le premier échange épistolaire entre Jérôme et Damase: Lettres réelles ou fictives?" *Freiburger Zeitschrift für Philosophie und Theologie* 30 (1983): 331–334.

Navascués Benlloch, Patricio de. “El fr. 37 de Pablo de Samosata: Una hipóstasis particular del Logos.” *Augustinianum. Periodicum Semestre Instituti Patristici* 39 (1999): 275–293.

———. “La *communio*: Unidad y diversidad en torno a Nicea.” *Scripta Theologica* 41 (2009): 843–860.

———. “Osio en Sárdica (343): Método, doctrina y gobierno.” Pages 381–407 in *El siglo de Osio de Córdoba: Actas del Congreso Internacional*. Edited by Antonio Javier Reyes Guerrero. Madrid: Biblioteca de Autores Cristianos, 2015.

———. *Pablo de Samosata y sus adversarios. Estudio histórico-teológico del cristianismo antioqueno en el s. III*. Rome: Institutum Patristicum Augustinianum, 2004.

Nebenzahl, Avigdor. “Melekhet maḥashevet.” *Kotlenu* 16 (2003/2004): 436–439.

Nemeshegyi, Peter. *La paternité de Dieu chez Origène*. Paris: Desclée, 1960.

Neria, Moshe Tzvi. “Melekhet maḥashevet u-fṭor meḳalḳel.” *Orot ʿEtsion* 30 (1998/1999): 112–113.

Neumark, David. *Geschichte der jüdischen Philosophie des Mittelalters*. 2 vols. Berlin: Reimer, 1907.

Neusner, Jacob. *The Documentary Foundation of Rabbinic Culture: Mopping Up after Debates with Gerald L. Bruns, S.J.D. Cohen, Arnold Maria Goldberg, Susan Handelman, Christine Hayes, James Kugel, Peter Schaefer, Eliezer Segal, E.P. Sanders and Lawrence Schiffman*. South Florida Studies in the History of Judaism. Atlanta: Scholars Press, 1995.

———. *The Formation of the Babylonian Talmud: Studies in the Achievements of Late Nineteenth and Twentieth Century Historical and Literary-Critical Research*. Leiden: Brill, 1970.

———. *A History of the Jews in Babylonia*. Vol. 3, *From Shapur I to Shapur II*. Leiden: E.J. Brill, 1968.

———. *Judaism and Christianity in the Age of Constantine: History, Messiah, Israel, and the Initial Confrontation*. Chicago: University of Chicago Press, 1987.

———. *Narrative and Document in the Rabbinic Canon*. 2 vols. Lanham, MD: University Press of America, 2010.

———. *Rabbinic Political Theory: Religion and Politics in the Mishnah*. Chicago: University of Chicago Press, 1991.

———. Review of Richard Lee Kalmin, *Sages, Stories, Authors, and Editors in Rabbinic Babylonia*. *Hebrew Studies* 31 (1990): 182–188.

———. *The Three Stages in the Formation of Judaism*. Chico, CA: Scholars Press, 1985.

Neusner, Jacob, and William S. Green. *Writing with Scripture: The Authority and Uses of the Hebrew Bible in the Torah of Formative Judaism*. Minneapolis: Fortress, 1989.

Newman, John Henry. *The Arians of the Fourth Century*. London: E. Lumley, 1871.

Nirenberg, David. *Anti-Judaism: The Western Tradition*. New York: W.W. Norton, 2013.

Nongbri, Brent. *Before Religion: A History of a Modern Concept*. New Haven, CT: Yale University Press, 2013.

Norris, Frederick W. "Paul of Samosata: *Procurator Ducenarius*." *Journal of Theological Studies* 35 (1984): 50–70.

Novick, Tzvi. "Etiquette and Exemplarity in Judaism." Pages 522–537 in *New Directions from Philosophy, Psychology, and Theology*. Edited by William Fleeson, Angela Knobel, Michael Furr, and Christian B. Miller. New York: Oxford University Press, 2015.

Nyman, J.R. "The Synod at Antioch (324–325) and the Council of Nicaea." Pages 483–489 in *Studia Patristica IV: Papers Presented to the Third International Conference on Patristic Studies, Held at Christ Church, Oxford, 1959*. Edited by Kurt Aland and Frank Leslie Cross. Berlin: Akademie-Verlag, 1957.

O'Connell, Patrick J. "The «Patristic Argument» in the Writings of Patriarch St Nicephorus I of Constantinople († 828)." Pages 210–214 in *Studia Patristica XI: Papers Presented to the Fifth International Conference on Patristic Studies Held in Oxford 1967. Vol. 2, Classica, Philosophica et Ethica, Theologica, Augustiniana; With a Cumulative Index of Contributors to Studia Patristica, vol. I–XI*. Edited by Frank Leslie Cross. TU 108. Berlin: Akademie-Verlag, 1972.

Ó Cróinín, Dáibhí, and Immo Warntjes. *The Easter Controversy of Late Antiquity and the Early Middle Ages*. Turnhout: Brepols, 2011.

Olmi, Amiram. "Mitʿaseḳ be-shabat u-vi-shʾar mitsṿot." *Gullot* 9 (2000/2001): 201–209.

O'Meara, Dominic J. *Platonopolis: Platonic Political Philosophy in Late Antiquity*. Oxford: Oxford University Press, 2005.

———. "The Transformation of Metaphysics in Late Antiquity." Page 36–52 in *The Science of Being as Being: Metaphysical Investigations*. Edited by Gregory T. Doolan. Washington, DC: Catholic University of America Press, 2012.

Opelt, Ilona. "Formen der Polemik bei Lucifer von Calaris." *Vigiliae Christianae* 26 (1972): 200–226.

Opitz, Hans-Georg, *Athanasius Werke. Dritter Band. Erster Teil. 1. Lieferung*. Berlin: De Gruyter, 1934.

———. *Athanasius Werke. Zweiter Band. 5. Lieferung*. Berlin: De Gruyter, 1940.

———. "Das syrische Corpus Athanasianum." *Zeitschrift für die neutestamentliche Wissenschaft und die Kunde der älteren Kirche* 33 (1934): 18–31.

———. *Untersuchungen zur Überlieferung des Schriften des Athanasius*. Arbeiten zur Kirchengeschichte 23. Berlin: De Gruyter, 1935.

Oppenheimer, Aharon. *The ʿAm Ha-arets: A Study in the Social History of the Jewish People in the Hellenistic-Roman Period*. Translated by I.H. Levine. Leiden: E.J. Brill, 1977.

Orbe, Antonio. "Orígenes y los monarquianos." *Gregorianum* 72 (1991): 39–72.

Orbe, Antonio, and Manlio Simonetti. *Il Cristo*. Vol. 2, *Testi teologici e spirituali in lingua greca dal IV al VI secolo*. Milan: Fondazione Lorenzo Valla/A. Mondadori, 1986.

Orlandi, Tito. "Papiro di Torino 63, 1. Damiano di Alessandria, *Sul Natale*." Pages 593–613 in *Papyri in Honorem Johannis Bingen Octogenarii (P. Bingen)*. Edited by Rudolf

De Smet, Henri Melaerts, and Cecilia Saerens. Studia varia Bruxellensia ad orbem Graeco-Latinum pertinentia 5. Louvain: Peeters, 2000.

Ortiz de Urbina, Ignacio. "L'*homoousios* preniceno." *Orientalia Christiana Periodica* 8 (1942): 194–209.

Ortuño Córcoles, Eduardo. "Jerónimo en Antioquía: La vocación monástica y el sueño condenatorio." *Vichiana* 3 (2001): 227–228.

Paget, James Nicholas Carleton. "Anti-Judaism and Early Christian Identity." *Zeitschrift für Antikes Christentum* 1 (1997): 195–225.

———. "The Definition of the Terms Jewish Christian and Jewish Christianity in the History of Research." Pages 22–52 in *Jewish Believers in Jesus: The Early Centuries*. Edited by Reidar Hvalvik and Oskar Skarsaune. Peabody, MA: Hendrickson, 2007.

———. "Jewish Christianity." Pages 731–775 in *The Cambridge History of Judaism*. Vol. 3, *The Early Roman Period*. Edited by William Horbury, W.D. Davies, and John Sturdy. Cambridge: Cambridge University Press, 1999.

Panaccio, Claudio. *Le discours intérieur de Platon à Guillaume d'Ockham*. Paris: Éditions du Seuil, 1999.

Panken, Aaron D. *The Rhetoric of Innovation: Self-Conscious Legal Change in Rabbinical Literature*. Lanham, MD: University Press of America, 2005.

Pardini, Alessandro. "Citazioni letterali dalla «ΘΑΛΕΙΑ» in Atanasio." *Orpheus* N.S. 12 (1911): 411–428.

Paredi, Angelo. "L'esilio in Oriente del vescovo Milanese Dionisio e il problematico ritorno del suo corpo a Milano." Pages 229–244 in *Atti del Convegno di Studi sulla Lombardia e l'Oriente, Milano, 11–15 giugno 1962*. Milan, 1963.

Parkes, James. *The Conflict of the Church and the Synagogue: A Study in the Origins of Antisemitism*. London: Soncino, 1934.

Parmentier, Léon. *Theodoret Kirchengeschichte*. GCS 19. Leipzig: J.C. Hinrichs, 1911.

Parmentier, Martin F.G. "Rules of Interpretation Issued against the Heretics (CPL 560)." *Journal of Eastern Christian Studies* 60 (2008): 231–273.

Parvis, Paul. "Constantine's *Letter to Arius and Alexander*?" Pages 89–95 in *Studia Patristica XXXIX: Historica, Biblica, Ascetica et Hagiographica; Papers Presented at the Fourteenth International Conference on Patristic Studies Held in Oxford*. Edited by Francis Young, Mark Edwards, and Paul Parvis. Studia Patristica 39. Louvain: Peeters, 2006.

Parvis, Sara. "Joseph Lienhard, Marcellus of Ancyra and Marcellus' Rule of Faith." Pages 89–108 in *Tradition and the Rule of Faith in the Early Church: Essays in Honor of Joseph T. Lienhard*. Edited by Alexander Y. Hwang and Ronnie J. Rombs. Washington, DC: Catholic University of America Press, 2010.

———. *Marcellus of Ancyra and the Lost Years of the Arian Controversy, 325–345*. Oxford: Oxford University Press, 2006.

———. "The Reception of Nicaea and *Homoousios* to 360. Pages 225–255 in *The Cambridge Companion to the Council of Nicaea.* Edited by Young Richard Kim. Cambridge: Cambridge University Press, 2021.

Pascal, Blaise. *The Provincial Letters.* Translated by Thomas M'Crie. Boston: Houghton Mifflin, 1887.

Pasté, C.R. "Del simbolo «Quicumque»." *La Scuola cattolica* 60 (1932): 142–147.

Pastor Muñoz, Mauricio, and Héctor F. Pastor Andrés. "Zenobia." Pages 323–347 in *En Grecia y Roma.* Vol. 3, *Mujeres reales y ficticias.* Edited by Jesús María García González and Andrés Pociña Pérez. Granada: Universidad de Granada, 2009.

Pelttari, Aaron. *The Space That Remains: Reading Latin Poetry in Late Antiquity.* Ithaca, NY: Cornell University Press, 2014.

Pépin, Jean. "Attitudes d'Augustin devant le vocabulaire philosophique grec. Citation, translitération, traduction." Pages 277–307 in *La langue latine, langue de la philosophie. Actes du colloque de Rome (17–19 mai 1990).* Collection de l'École Française de Rome 161. Paris: De Boccard and École française de Rome, 1992.

Pérès, Jacques-Noël. "The 'Episcopos' in Ancient Syriac Christianity: A Matrix of 'Monarchical' Episcopate?" *The Jurist: Studies in Church Law and Ministry* 66 (2006): 129–143.

Pérez Mas, Javier. *La crisis luciferiana: Un intento de reconstrucción histórica.* Studia Ephemeridis Augustinianum 110. Rome: Institutum Patristicum Augustinianum, 2008.

Perrin, Michel-Yves. "À propos de la participation des fidèles aux controverses doctrinales dans l'antiquité tardive: Considérations introductives." *Antiquité tardive* 9 (2001): 179–199.

———. Civitas confusionis: *De la participation des fidèles aux controverses doctrinales dans l'Antiquité tardive (début III*e *s.–c. 430).* Paris: Nuvis, 2017.

———. "The Limits of the Heresiological Ethos in Late Antiquity." Pages 201–227 in *Religious Diversity in Late Antiquity.* Edited by Susanne Bangert, Luke Lavan, Carlos Machado, and Michael Mulryan. Late Antique Archaeology 6. Leiden: Brill, 2010.

Perrone, Lorenzo. "'The Bride at the Crossroads': Origen's Dramatic Interpretation of the Song of Songs." *Ephemerides Theologicae Lovanienses* 82 (2006): 69–102.

———. "Der formale Aspekt der origeneischen Argumentation in den Auseinandersetzungen des 4. Jahrhunderts." Pages 119–134 in *Origeniana Septima. Origenes in den Auseinandersetzungen des 4. Jahrhunderts.* Edited by Wolfgang A. Bienert and Uwe Kuhneweg. Louvain: Peeters, 1999.

———. "L'enigma di Paolo di Samosata. Dogma, chiesa e società nella Siria del III secolo. Prospettive di un ventennio di studi." *Cristianesimo nella Storia* 13 (1992): 253–326.

Person, Ralph E. *The Mode of Theological Decision Making at the Early Ecumenical Councils: An Inquiry into the Function of Scripture and Tradition at the Councils of Nicaea and Ephesus*. Theologischen Dissertationen 14. Basel: Friedrich Reinhardt Kommissionsverlag, 1978.

Petersen, William L. "Eusebius and the Paschal Controversy." Pages 311–325 in *Eusebius, Christianity, and Judaism*. Edited by Harold W. Attridge and Gohei Hata. Detroit: Wayne State University Press, 1992.

Peterson, Erik. *Heis theos. Epigraphische, formgeschichtliche und religionsgeschichtliche Untersuchungen zur antiken "Ein-Gott"-Akklamation*. Göttingen: Vandenhoeck & Ruprecht, 1926. [= Vol. 8 of Erik Peterson, *Ausgewählte Schriften*. Edited by Christoph Markschies, Henrik Hildebrandt, and Barbara Nichtweiss. 12 vols. Würzburg: Echter, 2012.]

Petuchowski, Jakob J. "The Concept of 'Teshuvah' in the Bible and the Talmud." *Judaism* 17 (1968): 175–185.

Pflaum, Hans-Georg. *Les carrières procuratoriennes équestres sous le haut-empire romain*. 4 vols. Paris: P. Geuthner, 1960–1961.

———. *Les procurateurs équestres sous le haut-empire romain*. Paris: A. Maisonneuve, 1950.

Pieper, Max. "Zwei Blätter aus dem Osterbrief des Athanasius vom Jahre 364 (Pap. Berol. 11948)." *Zeitschrift für die neutestamentliche Wissenschaft und die Kunde der älteren Kirche* 37 (1938): 73–76.

Pietras, Henryk. *Concilio di Nicea (325) nel suo contesto*. Rome: Pontificia Università Gregoriana, 2021.

Pietri, Charles. "Appendice prosopographique à la Roma christiana (311–440)." *Mélanges de l'École française de Rome. Antiquité* 89 (1977): 371–415.

———. "Damase évêque de Rome." Pages 29–58 in *Saecularia damasiana. Atti del convegno internazionale per il XVI centenario della morte di Papa Damaso I (11–12–384—10/12–12–1984) promosso dal Pontificio Istituto di Archeologia Cristiana*. Studi di antichità cristiana 39. Vatican City: Pontificio Istituto di Archeologia Cristiana, 1986.

Pietri, Charles, and Luce Pietri. *Prosopographie chrétienne du Bas-Empire*. Vol. 2, *Prosopographie de l'Italie chrétienne* (313–604). 2 vols. Rome: École française de Rome, 2000.

Pinggéra, Karl. "Syrische Tradition." Pages 397–407 in *Athanasius-Handbuch*. Edited by Peter Gemeinhardt. Tübingen: Mohr Siebeck, 2011.

Piras, Antonio. "Kritische Bemerkungen zur Schrift 'De Athanasio' des Lucifer von Calaris." *Vigiliae Christianae* 46 (1992): 57–74.

Pitra, Jean Baptiste. *Analecta sacra spicilegio solesmensi parata*. Paris: Ex publico Galliarum typographeo, 1883.

Pohlenz, Max. "Die Begründung der abendländischen Sprachlehre durch die Stoa." *Nachrichten von der Königlichen Gesellschaft der Wissenschaften zu Göttingen, Philologisch-Historische Klasse. Fachgruppe 1* N.F. 3 (1939): 151–198.

———. *Die Stoa. Geschichte einer geistigen Bewegung*. 2 vols. 4th ed. Göttingen: Vandenhoeck & Ruprecht, 1970.

Pollard, Thomas Evan. "The Exegesis of Scripture and the Arian Controversy." *Bulletin of the John Rylands Library Manchester* 41 (1959): 414–429.

———. "Logos and Son in Origen, Arius and Athanasius." Pages 282–287 in *Studia Patristica*. Vol. 2, *Liturgica, Iuridica, Theologica, Philosophica, Monastica, Ascetica; Papers Presented to the Second International Conference on Patristic Studies Held at Christ Church, Oxford 1955*. Edited by Kurt Aland, and Frank Leslie Cross. Berlin: Akademie-Verlag, 1957.

———. "Marcellus of Ancyra, a Neglected Father." Pages 187–196 in *Epektasis: Mélanges patristiques offerts à Jean Daniélou*. Edited by Jacques Fontaine and Charles Kannengeisser. Paris: Beauchesne, 1972.

———. "The Origins of Arianism." *Journal of Theological Studies* 9 (1958): 103–111.

Pouderon, Bernard. "L'évêque chef du peuple dans le roman pseudo-clémentin." Pages 237–250 in *Anthropos laïkos. Mélanges Alexandre Faivre à l'occasion de ses 30 ans d'enseignement*. Edited by Marie-Anne Vannier, Otto Wermelinger, and Gregor Wurst. Paradosis. Études de Littérature et de Théologie Ancienne 44. Freiburg: Éditions universitaires, 2000.

Pourkier, Aline. *L'hérésiologie chez Épiphane de Salamine*. Paris: Beauchesne, 1992.

Prestige, George Leonard. "Ἀγέν[ν]ητος and Cognate Words in Athanasius." *Journal of Theological Studies* 34 (1933): 258–265.

———. "Ἀγέν[ν]ητος and γεν[ν]ητός, and Kindred Words, in Eusebius and the Early Arians." *Journal of Theological Studies* 24 (1923): 486–496.

———. *God in Patristic Thought*. 2nd ed. London: SPCK, 1952.

Price, Richard. "Conciliar Theology: Resources and Limitations." Pages 1–18 in *Die Synoden im trinitarischen Streit: Über die Etablierung eines synodalen Verfahrens und die Probleme seiner Anwendung im 4. und 5. Jahrhundert*. Edited by Uta Heil and Annette von Stockhausen. TU 177. Berlin: De Gruyter, 2017.

Prinzivalli, Emanuela. "Callisto I, santo." Pages 237–246 in vol. 1 of *Enciclopedia dei Papi*. 3 vols. Rome: Istituto della Enciclopedia italiana 2.

———. "A Fresh Look at Rufinus as a Translator." Pages 274–275 in *Origeniana undecima: Origen and Origenism in the History of Western Thought; Papers of the 11th International Origen Congress, Aarhus University, 26–31 August 2013*. Edited by Anders-Christian Jacobsen. Bibliotheca Ephemeridum Theologicarum Lovaniensium 279. Louvain: Peeters, 2016.

Rabinovitch, Nachum Eliezer. "Be-ʿinyan pesiḳ reisha." *Maʿaliyot* 8 (1986/1987): 2–4.

Ramelli, Ilaria L.E. "Cristo-Logos in Origene: Ascendenze medioplatoniche e filoniane, passaggi in Clemente e Bardesane, e anti-subordinazionismo." Pages 295–317 in *Dal logos dei greci e dei romani al Logos di Dio. Ricordando Marta Sordi*. Edited by Roberto Radice, and Alfredo Valvo. Pubblicazioni del Centro di Ricerche di Metafisica. Temi metafisici e problemi del pensiero antico. Studi e testi 122. Milan: Vita e Pensiero, 2011.

———. "*Hebrews* and Philo on Ὑπόστασις: Intersecting Trajectories?" Pages 27–49 in *Pascha nostrum Christus: Essays in Honour of Raniero Cantalamessa*. Edited by Pier Franco Beatrice and Bernard Pouderon. Théologie historique 123. Paris: Beauchesne, 2016.

———. "Origen, Eusebius, the Doctrine of *Apokatastasis*, and Its Relation to Christology." Pages 307–323 in *Eusebius of Caesarea: Tradition and Innovations*. Edited by Aaron P. Johnson and Jeremy M. Schott. Hellenic Studies 60. Washington, DC: Center for Hellenic Studies, 2013.

———. "Origen's Anti-Subordinationism and Its Heritage in the Nicene and Cappadocian Line." *Vigiliae Christianae* 65 (2011): 21–49.

Rankin, David Ivan. "Tertullian's Vocabulary of the Divine 'Individuals' in *adversus Praxean*." *Sacris Erudiri: A Journal of Late Antique and Medieval Christianity* 40 (2001): 5–46.

Ratti, Stéphane. "Malalas, Aurélien et l'«Histoire Auguste»." *Historia: Zeitschrift für alte Geschichte/Revue d'histoire ancienne* 55 (2006): 482–492.

Rauschen, Gerhard. *Jahrbücher der christlichen Kirche unter dem Kaiser Theodosius*. Freiburg: Herder, 1897.

Rebenich, Stefan. *Hieronymus und sein Kreis: Prosopographische und sozialgeschichtliche Untersuchungen*. Stuttgart: F. Steiner, 1992.

———. *Jerome*. London: Routledge, 2002.

———. "Jerome: The *Vir Trilinguis* and the *Hebraica veritas*." *Vigiliae Christianae* 37 (1993): 50–77.

Rebillard, Éric. "Augustin et ses autorités. L'élaboration de l'argument patristique au cours de la controverse pélagienne." Pages 245–263 in *Studia Patristica XXXVIII: Papers Presented at the Thirteenth International Conference on Patristic Studies Held in Oxford 1999; St. Augustine and His Opponents; Other Latin Writers*. Edited by Paul M. Parvis, Maurice F. Wiles, and Edward J. Yarnold. Louvain: Peeters, 2001.

———. "A New Style of Argument in Christian Polemic: Augustine and the Use of Patristic Citations." *Journal of Early Christian Studies* 8 (2000): 559–578.

Redfield, James Adam. "Redacting Culture: Ethnographic Authority in the Talmudic Arrival Scene." *Jewish Social Studies* 22 (2016): 29–80.

———. "Traveling Rabbis and the Talmud as History." Paper presented at Teaching and Transmitting the Past: Sixth Annual Symposium on Medieval and Renaissance Studies. Center for Medieval and Renaissance Studies. Saint Louis University. St. Louis, MO, June 20, 2018.

———. "'When X Arrived, He Said': The Historical Career of a Talmudic Formula (Appendix to 'Redacting Culture')." Published open-access on November 5, 2016, at https://www.academia.edu/29627483/_When_X_Arrived_he_said_The_Historical_Career_of_a_Talmudic_Formula_appendix_to_Redacting_Culture. Retrieved on January 6, 2022.

Reed, Annette Yoshiko. "'Jewish Christianity' after the 'Parting of the Ways': Approaches to Historiography and Self-Definition in the Pseudo-Clementine Literature." Pages 188–231 in *The Ways That Never Parted: Jews and Christians in Late Antiquity and the Early Middle Ages*. Edited by Adam H. Becker and Annette Yoshiko Reed. Tübingen: Mohr Siebeck, 2003.

———. *Jewish-Christianity and the History of Judaism: Collected Essays*. Texte und Studien zum antiken Judentum 171. Tübingen: Mohr Siebeck, 2018.

Regier, Willis Goth. *Quotology*. Lincoln: University of Nebraska Press, 2010.

Reiser, William E. "Dogma and Heresy Revisited: A Heideggerian Approach." *Thomist* 46 (1982): 509–538.

———. "An Essay on the Development of Dogma in a Heideggerian Context: A Non-Theological Explanation of Theological Heresy." *Thomist* 39 (1975): 471–495.

Reutter, Ursula. *Damasus, Bischof von Rom (366–384): Leben und Werk*. Studien und Texte zu Antike und Christentum 55. Tübingen: Mohr Siebeck, 2009.

Réville, Albert. "La christologie de Paul de Samosate." Pages 189–208 in *Études de critique et d'histoire*. 2ème série. Bibliotheque de l'École des Hautes-Études, Sciences Religieuses 7. Paris: École Pratique des Hautes Études, 1896.

Reyes Guerrero, Antonio Javier, ed. *El siglo de Osio de Córdoba: Actas del Congreso Internacional*. Madrid: Biblioteca de Autores Cristianos, 2015.

Ribas Alba, José María. *Persona: Desde el derecho romano a la teología cristiana*. Granada: Comares, 2012.

Richard, Marcel. "Léonce et Pamphile." *Revue des sciences philosophiques et théologiques* 27 (1938): 27–52. [= Pages 1197–1222 in vol. 3 of Marcel Richard, *Opera minora*. 3 vols. Turnhout: Brepols, 1976–1977.]

———. "Les florilèges diphysites du Ve et du VIe siècle." Pages 721–748 in vol. 1 of *Das Konzil von Chalkedon. Geschichte und Gegenwart*. Edited by Heinrich Bacht and Aloys Grillmeier. 3 vols. Würzburg: Echter-Verlag, 1951. [= Pages 79–106 in vol. 1 of Marcel Richard, *Opera minora*. 3 vols. Turnhout: Brepols, 1976–1977.]

———. "Malchion et Paul de Samosate. Le témoignage d'Eusèbe de Césarée." *Ephemerides Theologicae Lovanienses* 35 (1959): 325–338. [= Pages 615–628 in vol. 2 of Marcel Richard, *Opera minora*. 3 vols. Turnhout: Brepols, 1976–1977.]

———. "Pamphile de Jérusalem." Pages 277–280 in *Le Muséon: Revue d'études orientales* 90 (1977).

Ricken, Friedo. "Das Homousios von Nikaia als Krise des altchristlichen Platonismus." Pages 74–99 in *Zur Frühgeschichte der Christologie. Ihre bibl. Anfänge u. d. Lehrformel von Nikaia*. Edited by Heinrich Schlier and Bernhard Welte. Quaestiones Disputatae 51. Freiburg im Breisgau: Herder, 1970.

———. "Die Logoslehre des Eusebios von Caesarea und der Mittelplatonismus." *Theologie und Philosophie* 42 (1967): 341–358.

———. "Emanation und Schöpfung." *Theologie und Philosophie* 49 (1974): 483–486.

———. "Nikaia als Krise des altchristlichen Platonismus." *Theologie und Philosophie* 44 (1969): 321–341.

———. "Zur Rezeption der platonischen Ontologie bei Eusebios von Kaisareia, Areios und Athanasios." *Theologie und Philosophie* 53 (1978): 321–352. [= Pages 92–127 in *Metaphysik und Theologie*. Edited by Klaus Kremer. Leiden: Brill, 1980.]

Riedmatten, Henri de. *Les actes du procès de Paul de Samosate: Étude sur la christologie* du 3e au 4e *siècle*. Paradosis. Études de Littérature et de Théologie Ancienne 6. Freiburg: Éditions St-Paul, 1952.

Rigolio, Alberto. *Christians in Conversation.* New York: Oxford University Press, 2019.

Rist, John M. "Paul von Samosata und Zenobia von Palmyra: Anmerkungen zu Aufstieg und Fall eines frühchristlichen Bischofs." *Römischen Quartalschrift* 92 (1997): 145–161.

Rist, Josef. "Cyprian von Karthago und Paul von Samosata. Überlegungen zum Verständnis des Bischofsamtes im 3. Jahrhundert." Pages 257–286 in *Rom und das himmlische Jerusalem. Die frühen Christen zwischen Anpassung und Ablehnung.* Edited by Raban von Haehling. Darmstadt: Wissenschaftliche Buchgesellschaft, 2000.

Ritter, Adolf Martin. *Das Konzil von Konstantinopel und sein Symbol. Studien zur Geschichte und Theologie des II. ökumenischen Konzils.* Forschungen zur Kirchen- und Dogmengeschichte 15. Göttingen: Vandenhoeck & Ruprecht, 1965.

———. "Zum homoousios von Nizäa und Konstantinopel. Kritische Nachlese zu einigen neueren Diskussionen." Pages 298–310 in *Kerygma und Logos. Beiträge zu den geistesgeschichtlichen Beziehungen zwischen Antike und Christentum. Festschrift für Carl Andresen zum 70. Geburstag.* Edited by Adolf Martin Ritter. Göttingen: Vandenhoeck & Ruprecht, 1979.

Rius-Camps, Josep. *El dinamismo trinitario en la divinización de los seres racionales según Orígenes.* Rome: Pontificium Institutum Orientalium Studiorum, 1970.

———. "¿Subordinacionismo en Orígenes?" Pages 154–186 in *Origeniana Quarta. Die Referate des 4. Internationales Origeneskongresses (Innsbruck, 2.–6. September 1985).* Edited by Lothar Lies. Innsbruck: Tyrolia-Verlag, 1987.

Robertson, Jon M. *Christ as Mediator: A Study of the Theologies of Eusebius of Caesarea, Marcellus of Ancyra, and Athanasius of Alexandria.* Oxford: Oxford University Press, 2007.

Rosenberg, Michael. "Penetrating Words: A Babylonian Rabbinic Response to Syriac Mariology." *Journal of Jewish Studies* 67 (2016): 121–134.

Rosenberg, Shimʿon Gershon. "Be-gidrei meḳalḳel." *Kotlenu* 8 (1975/1976): 36–43.

Rosenthal, Avraham. "Le-masoret girsat ha-Mishnah." Pages 29–47 in *Sefer ha-zikaron le-Rabi Shaʾul Liberman.* Edited by Shamma Friedman. New York: Bet ha-midrash le-rabanim be-Ameriḳah, 1993.

Rosenthal, David. "Torah she-be-ʿal peh ṿe-Torah mi-Sinai." Pages 448–487 in vol. 2 of *Meḥḳerei Talmud. Kovets meḥḳarim ba-Talmud u-v-tḥumim govlim muḳdash le-zikhro shel Prof. Efraim E. Urbakh.* Edited by David Rosenthal and Yaakov Sussmann. 3 vols. in 4. Jerusalem: Magnes, 1993.

Rosenthal, Eliezer Shimshon. "Toldot ha-nosaḥ u-veʿayot ʿarikhah be-ḥeḳer ha-Talmud ha-Bavli." *Tarbits* 57 (1988): 1–36.

Rosen-Zvi, Ishay. *Demonic Desires: Yetzer Hara and the Problem of Evil in Late Antiquity.* Philadelphia: University of Pennsylvania Press, 2011.

Rosilio, Yaron. "Bi-gdar din mitʿaseḳ." *Nitsanei erets* 13 (1998/1999): 111–131.

Roth, Joel. "*Gufei Torah*: The Limit to Halakhic Pluralism." Pages 207–220 in *Tifʾeret le-Yiśraʾel. Jubilee Volume in Honor of Israel Francus.* Edited by Yaacov Francus, Joel Roth, and Menahem Schmelzer. New York: Jewish Theological Seminary, 2010.

Rothschild, Jean-Pierre. "Au fondement de la notion de «Pères»: Paternités réelles et paternités symboliques dans le judaïsme." Pages 493–514 in vol. 1 of *Les réceptions des Pères de l'Église au Moyen Âge. Le devenir de la tradition ecclésiale. Congrès du Centre Sèvres—Facultés jésuites de Paris (11–14 juin 2008). Actes.* Edited by Rainer Berndt and Michel Fédou. 2 vols. Archa verbi. Subsidia 10. Münster: Aschendorff Verlag, 2013.

Rousseau, Philip. "Jerome as Priest, Exegete, and 'Man of the Church.'" Pages 186–207 in *Christians Shaping Identity from the Roman Empire to Byzantium: Studies Inspired by Pauline Allen.* Edited by Geoffrey Dunn and Wendy Mayer. Supplements to Vigiliae Christianae 132. Leiden: Brill, 2015.

Rovner, Jay. "Pseudepigraphic Invention and Diachronic Stratification in the Stammaitic Components of the Bavli: The Case of Sukka 28." *Hebrew Union College Annual* 68 (1997): 11–62.

———. "Structure and Ideology in the Aher Narrative (bHag 15a and b)." *Jewish Studies: An Internet Journal* 10 (2012): 1–73.

Rubenstein, Jeffrey L. "Criteria of Stammaitic Intervention in Aggada." Pages 417–439 in *Creation and Composition: The Contribution of the Bavli Redactors (Stammaim) to the Aggada.* Edited by Jeffrey L. Rubenstein. Texte und Studien zum antiken Judentum 114. Tübingen: Mohr Siebeck, 2005.

———. *The Culture of the Babylonian Talmud.* Baltimore: Johns Hopkins University Press, 2003.

———. "Elisha ben Abuya: Torah and the Sinful Sage." *Journal of Jewish Thought and Philosophy* 7 (1998): 139–225.

———. *Rabbinic Stories.* New York: Paulist, 2002.

———. "Some Structural Patterns of Yerushalmi Sugyot." Pages 303–314 in vol. 3 of *The Talmud Yerushalmi in Graeco-Roman Culture.* Edited by Peter Schäfer. 3 vols. Texte und Studien zum antiken Judentum 71, 79, 93. Tübingen: Mohr-Siebeck, 2003.

———. *Talmudic Stories: Narrative Art, Composition, and Culture.* Baltimore: Johns Hopkins University Press, 1999.

———. "The Thematization of Dialectics in Bavli Aggadah." *Journal of Jewish Studies* 53 (2003): 71–84.

———. "Translator's Introduction." Pages xvii–xxx in David Weiss Halivni, *The Formation of the Babylonian Talmud.* Introduced, translated, and annotated by Jeffrey L. Rubenstein. Oxford: Oxford University Press, 2013. [= Translation of *Meḳorot u-msorot: Be'urim ba-Talmud: Massekhet Bava batra.* Jerusalem: Magnes, 2007.]

Ruether, Rosemary Radford. "Judaism and Christianity: Two Fourth-Century Religions." *Sciences Religieuses/Studies in Religion* 2 (1972): 1–10.

Rüpke, Jörg. *Fasti sacerdotum: A Prosopography of Pagan, Jewish, and Christian Religious Officials in the City of Rome, 300 BC to AD 499.* Translated by David Richardson. Oxford: Oxford University Press, 2008.

Rustow, Marina. *Heresy and the Politics of Community: The Jews of the Fatimid Caliphate*. Ithaca, NY: Cornell University Press, 2008.

Sabato, Mordechai. *Talmud Bavli massekhet Sanhedrin perek̦ shelishi. Mahadurah, perush ṿe-ʿiyun mashṿeh ba-mak̦bilot*. Jerusalem: Mosad Byalik̦, 2018.

Safrai, Shmuel. "Oral Torah." Pages 39–45 in vol. 1 of Shmuel Safrai, *The Literature of the Sages*. 2 vols. Assen, Netherlands: Van Gorcum and Fortress Press, 1987.

Salaverri, Joaquín. "El argumento de tradición patrística en la antigua Iglesia." *Revista española de teología* 5 (1945): 107–119.

Salmon, Haim. "Melakhah she-ʾeinah tserikhhah le-gufah u-fsik̦ reisheh." *Mi-beit midrashenu—Shabat* (2010–2011): 280–290.

Saltet, Louis. "Fraudes littéraires des schismatiques Lucifériens aux IVe et Ve siècles." *Bulletin de littérature ecclésiastique* 7 (1906): 300–326.

———. "La formation de la légende des Papes Libère et Félix." *Bulletin de littérature ecclésiastique* 6 (1905): 223–236.

Samely, Alexander. *Forms of Rabbinic Literature and Thought: An Introduction*. Oxford: Oxford University Press, 2007.

———. "Text and Time: Ten Propositions on Early Rabbinic Hermeneutics." *International Journal for the Semiotics of Law* 14 (2001): 143–159.

Sample, Robert L. "The Christology of the Council of Antioch (268 C.E.) Reconsidered." *Church History* 48 (1979): 18–26.

———. *The Messiah as Prophet: The Christology of Paul of Samosata*. Evanston, IL: Northwestern University, 1977.

Satlow, Michael. "'And on the Earth You Shall Sleep': 'Talmud Torah' and Rabbinic Asceticism." *Journal of Religion* 83 (2003): 204–225.

Saxer, Victor. "Fonti storiche per la biografia di Eusebio." Pages 122–152 in *Eusebio di Vercelli e il suo tempo*. Edited by Enrico Dal Covolo, Renato Uglione, and Giovanni Maria Vian. Biblioteca di scienze religiose 133. Rome: Libreria Ateneo Salesiano, 1997.

Schäfer, Peter. *Jesus in the Talmud*. Princeton, NJ: Princeton University Press, 2007.

———. *The Jewish Jesus: How Judaism and Christianity Shaped Each Other*. Princeton, NJ: Princeton University Press, 2012.

———. "Metatron in Babylonia." Pages 29–39 in *Hekhalot Literature in Context: Between Byzantium and Babylonia*. Edited by Ra'anan S. Boustan, Martha Himmelfarb, and Peter Schäfer. Tübingen: Mohr Siebeck, 2013.

———. "New Testament and Hekhalot Literature: The Journey into Heaven in Paul and in Merkavah Mysticism." *Journal of Jewish Studies* 35 (1984): 19–35.

———. *The Origins of Jewish Mysticism*. Princeton, NJ: Princeton University Press, 2009.

———. *Synopse zur Hekhalot-Literatur*. Texte und Studien zum Antiken Judentum 2. Tübingen: J.C.B. Mohr, 1981.

———. *Two Gods in Heaven: Jewish Concepts of God in Antiquity*. Translated by Allison Brown. Princeton, NJ: Princeton University Press, 2020. [= Translation of *Zwei Götter in Himmel: Gottesvorstellungen in der jüdischen Antike*. Munich: C.H. Beck, 2017.]

Schaff, Philip, and Henry Wace, ed. *A Select Library of Nicene and Post-Nicene Fathers of the Christian Church. Second Series*. 14 vols. New York: Christian Literature, 1890–1900.

Schaffer, Simon, and Steven Shapin. *Leviathan and the Air-Pump: Hobbes, Boyle, and the Experimental Life*. Princeton, NJ: Princeton University Press, 2011.

Schamp, Jacques. "Gélase ou Rufin: Un fait nouveau. Sur des fragments oubliés de Gélase de Césarée (CPG, N° 3521)." *Byzantion. Revue internationale des études byzantines* 57 (1987): 360–390.

Schechter, Solomon. *Some Aspects of Rabbinic Theology*. New York: Macmillan, 1909.

Scheidweiler, Felix. "Paul von Samosata." *Zeitschrift für die neutestamentliche Wissenschaft und die Kunde der älteren Kirche* 46 (1955): 116–129.

———. *Theodoret Kirchengeschichte*. GCS 44. Berlin: Akademie-Verlag, 1954.

———. "Wer ist der Verfasser des sog. *Sermo Maior de Fide*." *Byzantinische Zeitschrift* 47 (1954): 333–357.

Schermann, Theodor. *Die Geschichte der dogmatischen Florilegien vom V–VIII Jahrhundert*. TU 28.1 N.F. 13.1. Leipzig: J.C. Heinrichs, 1904.

Scholem, Gerschom Gerhard. *Jewish Gnosticism, Merkabah Mysticism, and Talmudic Tradition*. 2nd ed. New York: Jewish Theological Seminary of America, 1965.

Schoo, George. *Die Quellen des Kirchenhistorikers Sozomenos*. Neue Studien zur Geschichte der Theologie und der Kirche 11. Berlin: Trowitsch, 1911.

Schremer, Adiel. "Beyond Naming: Laws of *Minim* in Tannaitic Literature and the Early Rabbinic Discourse of *Minut*." Pages 383–397 in *Jews and Christians in the First and Second Centuries: How to Write Their History*. Edited by Joshua Schwartz and Peter J. Tomson. Compendia rerum Iudaicarum ad Novum Testamentum 13. Leiden: Brill, 2012.

———. *Brothers Estranged: Heresy, Christianity, and Jewish Identity in Late Antiquity*. Oxford: Oxford University Press, 2010.

———. "Midrash, Theology, and History: Two Powers in Heaven Revisited." *Journal for the Study of Judaism in the Persian, Hellenistic and Roman Period* 39 (2007): 1–25.

———. "The Religious Orientation of Non-Rabbis in Second-Century Palestine: A Rabbinic Perspective." Pages 319–341 in *Follow the Wise: Studies in Jewish History and Culture in Honor of Lee I. Levine*. Edited by Zeev Weiss, Oded Irshai, Jodi Magness, and Seth Schwartz. Winona Lake, IN: Eisenbrauns, 2010.

———. "Stammaitic Historiography." Pages 219–235 in *Creation and Composition: The Contribution of the Bavli Redactors (Stammaim) to the Aggada*. Edited by Jeffrey L. Rubenstein. Texte und Studien zum antiken Judentum 114. Tübingen: Mohr Siebeck, 2005.

———. *Zakhar u-nḳevah bera'am. Ha-niśu'im be-shilhei yemei ha-bayit ha-sheni u-vi-tḳufat ha-Mishnah ṿe-ha-Talmud.* Jerusalem: Merkaz Zalman Shazar le-Toldot Yiśra'el, 2003.

Schubert, Christoph. "Ein wiedergewonnenes Schreiben des Eusebius von Vercelli." *Zeitschrift für antikes Christentum* 10 (2006): 15–18.

Schulthess, Friedrich. *Die syrischen Kanones der Synoden von Nicaea bis Chalcedon, nebst einigen zugehörigen Dokumenten.* Berlin: Weidmann, 1908.

Shustri, Rabin. "Me-'agadah le-halakhah: Le-gilguleiha shel sugyiat mitsṿah ha-ba'ah be-'aveirah (Bavli Sukah k"ṭ '[amud]"b–l '[amud]"'[alef])." *Hebrew Union College Annual* 81 (2010): י-מד.

Schwab, Moïse. Le Talmud de Jérusalem. Vol. 3, *Traités Troumoth, Maasseroth, Maasser schéni, Ḥalla, Orla, Biccurim.* Paris: Maisonneuve, 1879.

Schwartz, Eduard. "Der s. g. Sermo maior de fide des Athanasius." Pages 1–63 in *Sitzungsberichte der Bayerischen Akademie der Wissenschaften.* Philosophisch-philologische und historische Klasse 1924.6. Munich: Verlag der Bayerischen Akademie der Wissenschaften, 1925.

———. "Eine fingierte Korrespondenz mit Paulus dem Samosatener." Pages 1–58 in *Sitzungsberichte der Bayerischen Akademie der Wissenschaften.* Philosophisch-philologische und historische Klasse 1927.3. Munich: Verlag der Bayerischen Akademie der Wissenschaften, 1927.

———. "Über die Sammlung des *Cod. Veronensis LX.*" *Zeitschrift für die neutestamentliche Wissenschaft und die Kunde der älteren Kirche* 35 (1936): 1–23. [= Pages 30–72 in vol. 3 of Eduard Schwartz, *Gesammelte Schriften.* 5 vols. Berlin: De Gruyter, 1938–1963.]

———. "Zur Geschichte des Athanasius, VI: Die Dokumente des arianischen Streites bis 325." *Nachrichten von der Königlichen Gesellschaft der Wissenschaften zu Göttingen. Philologisch-historische Klasse* (1905): 257–299. [= Pages 117–168 in vol. 4 of Eduard Schwartz, *Gesammelte Schriften.* 5 vols. Berlin: De Gruyter, 1938–1963.]

———. "Zur Geschichte des Athanasius, VII: Das antiochenische Syndodalschreiben von 325." *Nachrichten von der Königlichen Gesellschaft der Wissenschaften zu Göttingen. Philologisch-historische Klasse* (1908): 305–374. [= Pages 169–187 in vol. 4 of Eduard Schwartz, *Gesammelte Schriften.* 5 vols. Berlin: De Gruyter, 1938–1963.]

———. "Zur Kirchengeschichte des vierten Jahrhunderts." *Zeitschrift für die neutestamentliche Wissenschaft und die Kunde der älteren Kirche* 34 (1935): 129–213. [= Pages 1–110 in vol. 4 of Eduard Schwartz, *Gesammelte Schriften.* 5 vols. Berlin: De Gruyter, 1938–1963.]

Schwartz, Marcus Mordecai. "As They Journeyed from the East: The Nahotei of the Fourth Century and the Construction of the Rabbinic Diaspora." *Hebrew Union College Annual* 86 (2015): 63–99.

Schwyzer, Eduard. *Griechische Grammatik auf der Grundlage von Karl Brugmanns Griechischer Grammatik. Band II.* Handbuch der Altertumswissenschaft 2.1. Munich: C.H. Beck, 1950.

Scott, Alan B. *Origen and the Life of the Stars: A History of an Idea.* Oxford: Clarendon and Oxford University Press, 1991.

Scourfield, John Howell David. "Jerome, Antioch, and the Desert: A Note on Chronology." *Journal of Theological Studies* 37 (1986): 117–121.

Secord, Jared. *Christian Intellectuals and the Roman Empire: From Justin Martyr to Origen.* University Park: Pennsylvania State University Press, 2020.

———. "Julius Africanus, Origen, and the Politics of Intellectual Life under the Severans." *Classical World* 110 (2017): 211–235.

Seeberg, Erich. *Die Synode von Antiochien im Jahre 324/325: Ein Beitrag zur Geschichte des Konzils von Nicäa.* Neue Studien zur Geschichte der Theologie und der Kirche 16. Berlin: Trowitzsch, 1913.

Segal, Alan F. *Rebecca's Children: Judaism and Christianity in the Roman World.* Cambridge, MA: Harvard University Press, 1986.

———. "'Two Powers in Heaven' and Early Christian Trinitarian Thinking." Pages 73–96 in *The Trinity: An Interdisciplinary Symposium on the Trinity.* Edited by Stephen T. Davis, Daniel Kendall, and Gerald O'Collins. New York: Oxford University Press, 1999.

———. *Two Powers in Heaven: Early Rabbinic Reports about Christianity and Gnosticism.* Leiden: Brill, 1977.

Segal, Eliezer. "Anthological Dimensions of the Babylonian Talmud." Pages 81–107 in *The Anthology in Jewish Literature.* Edited by David Stern. New York: Oxford University Press, 2004.

Segelman, Aviv. "Ḥissorei meḥassera ṿe-hachi ḳatanei." *Ḥayeinu* 3 (2014/2015): [without page numbers].

———. "Melakhah she-ʾeinah tserikhah le-gufah." *Ḥayeinu* 3 (2014/2015): [without page numbers].

Segneri, Angelo. *Atanasio. Lettera agli Antiocheni. Introduzione, testo, traduzione e commento.* Bologna: Edizioni Dehoniane, 2010.

Seibt, Klaus. *Die Theologie des Markell von Ankyra.* Arbeiten zur Kirchengeschichte 59. Berlin: De Gruyter, 1994.

———. "Ein *argumentum ad Constantium* in der Logos- und Gotteslehre Markells von Ankyra." Pages 415–420 in *Studia Patristica XXVI: Liturgica, Second Century, Alexandria before Nicaea, Athanasius and the Arian Controversy; Papers Presented at the Eleventh International Conference in Patristic Studies Held in Oxford 1991.* Edited by Elizabeth Anne Livingstone. Louvain: Peeters, 1993.

Sellers, Robert Victor. *Eustathius of Antioch and His Place in the Early History of Christian Doctrine.* Cambridge: Cambridge University Press, 1928.

———. *Two Ancient Christologies: A Study in the Christological Thought of the Schools of Alexandria and Antioch in the Early History of Christian Doctrine.* London: Society for Promoting Christian Knowledge, 1940.

Septimus, Bernard. "Iterated Quotation Formulae in Talmudic Narrative and Exegesis." Pages 371–398 in *The Idea of Biblical Interpretation: Essays in Honor of James L. Kugel*. Edited by Hindy Najman and Judith H. Newman. Leiden: Brill, 2004.

Septimus, Dov. "Ḥeṭ᾽o shel Meṭaṭron bi-svakh leshonot ṿe-nusḥa᾽ot." *Leshonenu* 69 (2007): 291–300.

Septimus, Zvi. "Revisiting the Fat Rabbis." Pages 421–456 in *Talmudic Transgressions: Engaging the Work of Daniel Boyarin*. Edited by Charlotte Elisheva Fonrobert, James Adam Redfield, Ishay Rosen-Zvi, Aharon Shemesh, and Moulie Vidas. Supplements to the Journal for the Study of Judaism 181. Leiden: Brill, 2017.

Sesboüé, Bernard. *Saint Basile et la Trinité: Un acte théologique au IV*[e] *siècle. Le rôle de Basile de Césarée dans l'élaboration de la doctrine et du langage trinitaires*. Paris: Desclée, 1998.

Sfameni Gasparro, Giulia. "Monoteismo pagano nella Antichità tardiva? Una questione di tipologia storico-religiosa." *Annali di scienze religiose* 8 (2003): 97–127.

———. "Religious Tolerance and Intolerace in the Ancient World: A Religious-Historical Problem." Pages 11–37 in *Tolerancia e intolerancia religiosa en el Mediterráneo antiguo. Temas y problemas*. Edited by Mar Marcos and Ramón Teja. [= *Bandue. Revista de la Sociedad Española de Ciencias de las Religiones* 2. Madrid: Trotta, 2008.]

Shapere, Dudley. Review of Thomas Kuhn, *The Structure of Scientific Revolutions*. *Philosophical Review* 73 (1964): 383–394.

Shepardson, Christine C. *Anti-Judaism and Christian Orthodoxy: Ephrem's Hymns in Fourth-Century Syria*. Patristic monograph series 20. Washington, DC: Catholic University of America Press, 2008.

———. "Christian Division in Ancient Edessa: Ephrem the Syrian's *Carmina Nisibena* XXVII–XXVIII." *Journal of the Assyrian Academic Society* 12 (1999): 29–41.

———. *Controlling Contested Places: Late Antique Antioch and the Spatial Politics of Religious Controversy*. Berkeley: University of California Press, 2014.

———. "Defining the Boundaries of Orthodoxy: Eunomius in the Anti-Jewish Polemic of His Cappadocian Opponents." *Church History* 76 (2007): 699–723.

———. "'Exchanging Reed for Reed': Mapping Contemporary Heretics onto Biblical Jews in Ephrem's *Hymns on Faith*." *Hugoye* 5 (2002): 15–33.

Shinan, Avigdor. *Aggadatam shel meturgemanim: Te᾽ur ṿe-nittuaḥ sifruti shel ha-ḥomer ha-᾽aggadi ha-meshuḳa῾ be-khol ha-targumim ha-᾽aramiyim ha-᾽erets iśre᾽eliyim le-ḥamishah ḥumshei Torah*. 2 vols. Jerusalem: Maḳor, 1979.

Sieben, Hermann Josef. *Die Konzilsidee der Alten Kirche*. Paderborn: F. Schöningh, 1979.

Siegal, Michal Bar-Asher. *Early Christian Monastic Literature and the Babylonian Talmud*. Cambridge: Cambridge University Press, 2013.

———. "Ethics and Identity Formation: Resh Lakish and the Monastic Repentant Robber." Pages 53–72 in *L'identité à travers l'éthique: Nouvelles perspectives sur la formation des identités collectives dans le monde greco-romain*. Edited by Katell Berthelot, Ron Naiweld, and Daniel Stökl Ben Ezra. Bibliothèque de l'École des hautes études. Section des sciences religieuses 128. Turnhout: Brepols, 2015.

———. *Jewish-Christian Dialogues on Scripture in Late Antiquity: Heretic Narratives of the Babylonian Talmud*. Cambridge: Cambridge University Press, 2019.

———. "Mountains Hanging by a Strand? Re-Reading Mishnah Ḥagigah 1:8." *Journal of Ancient Judaism* 4 (2013): 235–256.

Simon, Marcel. "From Greek Hairesis to Christian Heresy." Pages 101–116 in *Early Christian Literature and the Classical Intellectual Tradition: In Honorem Robert M. Grant*. Edited by William R. Schoedel and Robert L. Wilken. Théologie historique 53. Paris: Éditions Beauchesne, 1979.

Simonetti, Manlio. "All'origine della formula teologica una essenza/tre ipostasi." *Augustinianum. Periodicum semestre Instituti Patristici* 14 (1974): 173–175.

———. "Ancora su *Homoousios* a proposito di due recenti studi." *Vetera Christianorum* 17 (1980): 85–98.

———. "Ancora sul concilio di Alessandria del 362, e dintorni." *Augustinianum. Periodicum semestre Instituti Patristici* 50 (2010): 5–25.

———. "Ancora sulla datazione della *Thalia* di Ario." *Studi Storico-Religiosi* 4 (1980): 349–354.

———. "Ancora sulla paternità dello ps. atanasiano «Sermo maior de fide»." *Vetera Christianorum* 11 (1974): 333–343.

———. "Appunti per una storia dello scisma luciferiano." Pages 67–81 in *Atti del Convegno di studi religiosi sardi, Cagliari 24–26 maggio 1962*. Padua: CEDAM, 1963.

———. "Arianesimo latino." *Studi medievali* 8 (1967): 663–744.

———. "Ariomaniti." Page 512 in vol. 1 of *Nuovo Dizionario Patristico e di Antichità Cristiane*. Edited by Angelo Di Berardino. 3 vols. Genoa: Marietti, 2006–2008.

———. "Dal nicenismo al neonicenismo. Rassegna di alcune publicazioni recenti." *Augustinianum. Periodicum semestre Instituti Patristici* 38 (1998): 5–25.

———. "Dal subordinazionismo all'egalitarismo: Rivisitazione dell'esito della controversia ariana." *Rassegna di Teologia* 24 (1983): 175–177.

———. "Dibattito trinitario e tensioni ecclesiali in Cappadocia e Ponto dal 360 al 380." Pages 7–23 in *L'*Epistula fidei *di Evagrio Pontico. Temi, contesti, sviluppi. Atti del III Convegno del Gruppo italiano di ricerca su Origene e la tradizione alessandrina*. Edited by Paolo Bettiolo. Studia Ephemeridis Augustinianum 72. Rome: Institutum Patristicum Augustinianum, 2000.

———. "Eresia e ortodossia ad Antiochia nei primi tre secoli." *Salesianum* 58 (1996): 656–659.

———. "Eusebio di Vercelli nella controversia ariana." Pages 155–179 in *Eusebio di Vercelli e il suo tempo*. Edited by Enrico Dal Covolo, Renato Uglione, and Giovanni Maria Vian. Biblioteca di scienze religiose 133. Rome: Libreria Ateneo Salesiano, 1997.

———. "Faustini opera." Pages 359–392 in Vinzenz Bulhart, *Gregorii Iliberritani episcopi quae supersunt*. CCSL 69. Turnhout: Brepols, 1967.

———. "Genesi e sviluppo della dottrina trinitaria di Basilio di Cesarea." Pages 169–197 in vol. 1 of *Basilio di Cesarea. La sua età, la sua opera e il basilianesimo in Sicilia. Atti del congresso internazionale (Messina, 3–6 XII 1979)*. 2 vols. Messina: Centro di Studi umanistici, 1983.

———. "Il concilio di Alessandria del 362 e l'origine della formula trinitaria." *Augustinianum. Periodicum semestre Instituti Patristici* 30 (1990): 353–360.

———. *Ippolito. Contro Noeto*. Biblioteca Patristica 35. Bologna: Edizione Dehoniane Bologna 2.

———. *La crisi ariana nel IV secolo*. Studia Ephemeridis Augustinianum 11. Rome: Institutum Patristicum Augustinianum, 1975.

———. "La tradizione nella controversia ariana." *Augustinianum. Periodicum semestre Instituti Patristici* 12 (1972): 37–50.

———. "Le origini dell'arianesimo." *Rivista di storia e letteratura religiosa* 7 (1971): 317–330.

———. "L'imperatore arbitro nelle controversie ideologiche." *Mediterraneo Antico. Economie, Società e Culture* 5 (2002): 449–459.

———. "Lucifero di Cagliari nella controversia ariana." *Vetera Christianorum* 35 (1998): 279–299. [= Pages 9–28 in *La figura e l'opera di Lucifero di Cagliari: Una rivisitazione. Atti del 1° Convegno Internazionale, Cagliari, 5–7 dicembre 1996*. Edited by Sonia Laconi. SEA 75. Rome: Institutum Patristicum Augustinianum, 2001.]

———. "Melezio di Antiochia." Pages 3190–3191 in vol. 2 of *Nuovo Dizionario Patristico e di Antichità Cristiane*. Edited by Angelo Di Berardino. 3 vols. Genoa: Marietti, 2006–2008.

———. *Origene. Commento al Cantico dei Cantici*. Rome: Città Nuova Editrice, 1976.

———. "Paolo di Samosata e Malchione. Riesame di alcune testimonianze." Pages 7–25 in *Hestíasis. Studi di tarda antichità offerti a Salvatore Calderone*. Studi tardoantichi 1. Messina: Sicania, 1986.

———. "Per la rivalutazione di alcune testimonianze su Paolo di Samosata." *Rivista di storia e letteratura religiosa* 24 (1988): 155–210.

———. "«Persona» nel dibattito cristologico dal III al VI secolo." *Studium* 91 (1995): 529–548.

———. Review of Klaus Seibt, *Die Theologie des Markell von Ankyra*. *Rivista di Storia e Letteratura Religiosa* 31 (1995): 259–269.

———. "Sabellio e il sabellianismo." *Studi Storico-Religiosi* 4 (1980): 7–28.

———. "Scritti di e attribuiti a Eusebio di Vercelli." Pages 449–461 in *La Sardegna paleocristiana tra Eusebio e Gregorio Magno: Atti del Convegno nazionale di studi, Cagliari, 10–12 ottobre 1996*. Edited by Attilio Mastino, Giovanna Sotgiu, and Natalino Spaccapelo. Cagliari: Pontificia Facoltà Teologica della Sardegna, 1999. [= *Cassiodorus* 3 (1997): 37–48.]

———. *Studi sulla cristologia del II e III secolo.* Rome: Institutum Patristicum Augustinianum, 1993.

———. *Studi sull'arianesimo.* Verba Seniorum 5. Rome: Editrice Studium, 1965.

———. "Su alcune opere attribuite di recente a Marcello d'Ancira." *Rivista di storia e letteratura religiosa* 9 (1973): 313–329.

———. "Sulla corrispondenza tra Dionigi di Alessandria e Paolo di Samosata." *Augustinianum. Periodicum Semestre Instituti Patristici* 47 (2007): 321–334.

———. "Un libro recente su Marcello di Ancira." *Augustinianum. Periodicum Semestre Instituti Patristici* 48 (2008): 103–121.

Sirinelli, Jean. *Les vues historiques d'Eusèbe de Césarée durant la période prénicéenne.* Dakar: Université de Dakar. Faculté des lettres et sciences humaines, 1961.

Slootjes, Daniëlle. "Bishops and Their Position of Power in the Late Third Century CE: The Cases of Gregory Thaumaturgus and Paul of Samosata." *Journal of Late Antiquity* 4 (2011): 100–115.

Smallwood, E. Mary. *The Jews under Roman Rule from Pompey to Diocletian.* Leiden: Brill, 1976.

Smulders, Pieter. *Hilary of Poitiers' Preface to His* Opus Historicum. Vigiliae Christianae Supplements 29. Leiden: Brill, 1995.

———. "Two Passages of Hilary's *Apologetica Responsa* Rediscovered." *Bijdragen: Tijdschrift voor Philosophie en Theologie* 39 (1978): 234–243. [= *Texte und Textkritik. Eine Aufsatzsammlung.* Edited by Jürgen Dummer, Johannes Irmscher, Franz Paschke, and Kurt Treu. TU 133. Berlin: Akademie-Verlag, 1987: 539–547.]

Soden, Hans Freiherr von. "Neue Forschungen zu Paul von Samosata." *Zeitschrift für Kirchengeschichte* 44 (1925): 161–170.

Sofer, Itiel. "Ḥissorei—mi ḥaserah? Be-ʿinyian ḥissorei meḥassera she-ba-Sha"s." *Asif* 2 (2014/2015): 417–434.

Sokoloff, Michael. *A Dictionary of Jewish Babylonian Aramaic of the Talmudic and Geonic Periods.* Ramat Gan: Bar Ilan University Press; Baltimore: Johns Hopkins University Press, 2002.

Sotinel, Claire."Les éveques italiens dans la société de l'Antiquité tardive: L'émergence d'une nouvelle élite?" Pages 377–404 in *Le trasformazioni delle élites in età tardoantica: Atti del convegno internazionale, Perugia, 15–16 Marzo, 2004.* Edited by Rita Lizzi Testa. Rome: "L'Erma" di Bretschneider, 2006.

Souter, Alexander. *A Study of Ambrosiaster.* Texts and Studies. Contributions to Biblical and Patristic Literature 7.4. Cambridge: Cambridge University Press, 1905.

Spanneut, Michel. "La position théologique d'Éustathe d'Antioche." *Journal of Theological Studies* N.S. 5 (1954): 220–224.

———. *Recherches sur les écrits d'Eustathe d'Antioche.* Lille: Faculté catholique, 1948.

Spiegel, Yaakov L. "Leshonot perush ṿe-hosafot meʾuḥarot ba-Talmud ha-Bavli." *Teʿudah: Ḳovets meḥḳarim shel Beit ha-sefer le-madaʿei ha-Yahadut ʿal shem Ḥayyim Rosenberg* 3 (1982/1983): 93–112.

Spoerl, Kelley McCarthy. "The Schism at Antioch since Cavallera." Pages 101–126 in *Arianism after Arius: Essays on the Development of the Fourth Century Trinitarian Conflicts.* Edited by Michel René Barnes and Daniel H. Williams. Edinburgh: T&T Clark, 1993.

Staats, Reinhart. *Gregor von Nyssa und die Messalianer: Die Frage der Priorität zweier altkirchlicher Schriften.* Berlin: De Gruyter, 1968.

———. *Makarios-Symeon, Epistola Magna: Eine messalianische Monchsregel und ihre Umschrift in Gregors von Nyssa "De instituto christiano."* Abhandlungen der Akademie der Wissenschaften in Göttingen. Philologisch-Historische Klasse. Dritte Folge 134. Göttingen: Vandenhoeck & Ruprecht, 1984.

Stav, Moshe. "Pesiḳ reisha." *Be-lekhtekha ba-derekh* 20 (2002/2003): 30–32.

———. "Pesiḳ reisha de-la niḥa leh." *Be-lekhtekha ba-derekh* 8 (1995/1996): 17–20.

Stead, George Christopher. "Athanasius' Earliest Written Work." *Journal of Theological Studies* 39 (1988): 76–91.

———. *Divine Substance.* Oxford: Clarendon, 1977.

———. "«Eusebius» and the Council of Nicea." *Journal of Theological Studies* 24 (1973): 85–100.

———. "Homoousios." Pages 364–433 in vol. 16 of *Reallexikon für Antike und Christentum. Sachwörterbuch zur Auseinandersetzung des Christentums mit der antiken Welt.* Edited by Ernst Dassman, Theodor Klauser, and Georg Schöllgen. 29 vols. and 1 suppl. Stuttgart: A. Hiersemann, 1994.

———. "«Homoousios» dans la pensée de saint Athanase." Pages 231–253 in *Politique et théologie chez Athanase d'Alexandrie. Actes du colloque de Chantilly (23–25 septembre 1973).* Edited by Charles Kannengiesser. Théologie Historique 27. Paris: Beauchesne, 1974.

———. "Marcel Richard on Malchion and Paul of Samosata." Pages 140–150 in *Logos. Festschrift für Luise Abramowski zum 8. Juli 1993.* Edited by Hanns Christof Brennecke, Ernst Ludwig Garsmück, and Christoph Markschies. Beihefte zur Zeitschrift für die neutestamentliche Wissenschaft und die Kunde der älteren Kirche 67. Berlin: De Gruyter, 1993.

———. "Philosophy in Origen and Arius." Pages 101–108 in *Origeniana septima. Origenes in den Auseinandersetzungen des 4. Jahrhunderts. International Colloquium for Origen Studies (7th: 1997. Hofgeismar, Germany, and Marburg, Germany).* Edited by Wolfgang A. Bienert and Uwe Kühneweg. Bibliotheca Ephemeridum theologicarum Lovaniensium 137. Leuven: Leuven University Press and Peeters, 1999.

———. "The Platonism of Arius." *Journal of Theological Studies* 15 (1964): 16–31.

———. "The Significance of the Homoousios." *Studia Patristica* 3 (1961): 397–412.

———. "The *Thalia* of Arius and the Testimony of Athanasius." *Journal of Theological Studies* 29 (1978): 20–52.

———. "The Word 'from Nothing.'" *Journal of Theological Studies* 49 (1998): 671–684.

Stein, Siegfried. "The Concept of the 'Fence': Observations on Its Origin and Development." Pages 301–329 in *Jewish Religious and Intellectual History: Presented to Alexander Altmann on the Occasion of His Seventieth Birthday.* Tuscaloosa: University of Alabama Press, 1979.

Stern, David. "Midrash and Indeterminacy." *Critical Inquiry* 5 (1988): 132–161.

———. *Midrash and Theory: Ancient Jewish Exegesis and Contemporary Literary Studies.* Evanston, IL: Northwestern University Press, 1996.

Stern, Sacha. "Attribution and Authorship in the Babylonian Talmud." *Journal of Jewish Studies* 45 (1994): 28–51.

———. "The Concept of Authorship in the Babylonian Talmud." *Journal of Jewish Studies* 46 (1995): 183–195.

———. *Jewish Identity in Early Rabbinic Writings.* Arbeiten zur Geschichte des antiken Judentums und des Urchristentums 23. Leiden: Brill, 1994.

Sternberg, Mordechai. "Davar she-ʾeino mitkaɣɣein—Maḥloḳet Rabi Yehudah ɣe-Rabi Shimʿon." *Orot ʿEtsion* 25 (1994/1995): 17–31.

Stewart, Alastair C. *The Original Bishops: Office and Order in the First Christian Communities.* Grand Rapids, MI: Baker Academic, 2014.

Stiglmayr, Joseph. "Mannigfache Bedeutung von 'Theologie' und 'Theologen.'" *Theologie und Glaube* 11 (1919): 296–309.

Stockhausen, Annette von. "Athanasius in Antiochien." *Zeitschrift für Antikes Christentum* 10 (2006): 86–102.

———. "Der Brief der Synode von Ankyra 358 (Dok. 55)." Pages 191–205 in *Die Synoden im trinitarischen Streit: Über die Etablierung eines synodalen Verfahrens und die Probleme seiner Anwendung im 4. und 5. Jahrhundert.* Edited by Uta Heil and Annette von Stockhausen. TU 177. Berlin: De Gruyter, 2017.

———. "Die pseud-athanasianische *Disputatio contra Arium.*" Pages 138–155 in *Von Arius zum Athanasianum. Studien zur Edition der Athanasius Werke.* Edited by Hanns Christof Brennecke and Annette von Stockhausen. TU 164. Berlin: De Gruyter, 2010.

———. "Epistula ad Rufinianum." In *Athanasius Handbuch.* Edited by Peter Gemeinhardt. Tübingen: Mohr Siebeck. 2011.

———. "Praefatio." Pages xi–cxii in *Athanasius Werke. Zweiter Band. Erster Teil. 8. Lieferung.* Edited by Hanns Christof Brennecke, Uta Heil, Hans-Georg Opitz, and Annette von Stockhausen. Berlin: De Gruyter, 2006.

———. "Textüberlieferung: Handschriften und frühe Drucke." Pages 2–8 in *Athanasius-Handbuch.* Edited by Peter Gemeinhardt. Tübingen: Mohr Siebeck, 2011.

Stommel, Eduard. "Bischofsstuhl und hoher Thron." Pages 52–78 in *Jahrbuch für Antike und Christentum* 1. Münster: Aschendorff, 1958.

Stoneman, Richard. *Palmyra and Its Empire: Zenobia's Revolt against Rome.* Ann Arbor: University of Michigan Press, 1992.

Stroumsa, Guy Gedalyah. "Aḥer: a Gnostic." Pages 228–238 in vol. 2 of *The Rediscovery of Gnosticism: Proceedings of the International Conference on Gnosticism at Yale, New Haven, Connecticut, March 28–31, 1978*. Edited by Bentley Layton. 2 vols. Studies in the history of religions. Supplements to Numen 41. Leiden: Brill, 1980.

Strutwolf, Holger. *Die Trinitätstheologie und Christologie des Euseb von Caesarea. Eine dogmengeschichtliche Untersuchung seiner Platonismusrezeption und Wirkungsgeschichte*. Forschungen zur Kirchen- und Dogmengeschichte 72. Göttingen: Vandenhoeck & Ruprecht, 1999.

Studer, Basil. "Argomentazione patristica." Columns 497–503 in vol. 1 of *Nuovo Dizionario Patristico e di Antichità Cristiane*. Edited by Angelo Di Berardino. 3 vols. Genoa: Marietti, 2006–2008.

———. "Eusebio e i rapporti con la Chiesa di Roma." Pages 181–189 in *Eusebio di Vercelli e il suo tempo*. Edited by Enrico Dal Covolo, Renato Uglione, and Giovanni Maria Vian. Biblioteca di scienze religiose 133. Rome: Libreria Ateneo Salesiano, 1997.

Sussman, Yaakov. "'Torah she-be-ʿal peh': Peshuṭah ke-mashmaʿah. Koḥo shel ḳotso shel yod." Pages 209–384 in vol. 3.1 of *Meḥḳerei Talmud. Kovets meḥḳarim ba-Talmud u-v-tḥumim govlim muḳdash le-zikhro shel Prof. Efraim E. Urbakh*. Edited by David Rosenthal and Yaakov Sussmann. 3 vols. in 4. Jerusalem: Magnes, 2005. [Reprinted with additions in *"Torah she-be-ʿal peh": Peshuṭah ke-mashmaʿah. Koḥo shel ḳotso shel yod*. Jerusalem: Magnes and Hebrew University Press, 2019.]

Swartz, Michael D. "Jewish Visionary Tradition in Rabbinic Literature." Pages 198–221 in *The Cambridge Companion to the Talmud and Rabbinic Literature*. Edited by Charlotte Elisheva Fonrobert and Martin S. Jaffee. Cambridge: Cambridge University Press, 2007.

Tabacco, Giovanni. "Gli intellettuali del medioevo nel gioco delle istituzioni e delle preponderanze sociali." Pages 7–46 *Storia d'Italia. Annali 4: Intellettuali e potere*. Edited by Corrado Vivanti. Turin: Einaudi, 1981.

Tal, Shemuel. "Davar she-ʾeino mitkayyein." *Ṭal ḥayim—Shabat* 1 (2009/2010): 29–143.

———. "Melakhah she-ʾeinah tserikhah le-gufah." *Ṭal ḥayim—Shabat* N.S. 1 (2009/2010): 197–232.

———. "Melakhah she-hi ḳerovah li-fsiḳ reisha." *Ṭal ḥayim—Shabat* N.S. 1 (2009/2010): 144–163.

———. "Pesiḳ reisha bi-de-rabanan." *Ṭal ḥayim—Shabat* N.S. 1 (2009/2010): 164–196.

Tannous, Jack. *The Making of the Medieval Middle East: Religion, Society, and Simple Believers*. Princeton, NJ: Princeton University Press, 2018.

Taylor, Justin. "St Basil the Great and Pope St Damasus I." *Downside Review* 91 (1973): 186–203 and 262–274.

Taylor, Miriam S. *Anti-Judaism and Early Christian Identity: A Critique of the Scholarly Consensus*. Studia Post-Biblica 46. Leiden: Brill, 1995.

Teixidor, Javier. "Antiquités sémitiques." *Annuaire du Collège de France* 98 (1997): 713–731.

Teja, Ramón. "Pablo de Samosata: Obispo de Antioquía y procurador imperial." *Semanas de Estudios Romanos* 7–8 (1986): 305–320.

Telfer, William. "The Codex Verona LX(58)." *Harvard Theological Review* 36 (1943): 169–246.

Tenenblatt, Mordechai. *Ha-Talmud ha-bavli be-hithavvuto ha-hisṭorit: Yetsirah, ʿarikhah ve-siddur*. Tel Aviv: Devir, 1972.

ter Haar Romeny, Robert Bas. "Les Pères grecs dans les florilèges exégétiques syriaques." Pages 63–76 in *Les Pères grecs en syriaque*. Edited by Andrea B. Schmidt and Dominique Gonnet. Études syriaques 4. Paris: Paul Geuthner, 2007.

Tetz, Martin. "'Ante omnia de sancta fide et de integritate veritatis.' Glaubensfragen auf der Synode von Serdika (342)." *Zeitschrift für die neutestamentliche Wissenschaft und die Kunde der älteren Kirche* 76 (1985): 243–269.

———. "Die Kirchweihsynode von Antiochien (341) und Marcellus von Ancyra. Zu der Glaubenserklärung des Theophronius von Tyana und ihren Folgen." Pages 199–217 in Oecumenica et patristica. *Festschrift für Wilhelm Schneemelcher zum 75. Geburtstag*. Edited by Wolfgang A. Bienert, Damaskinos Papandreou, and Knut Schäferdiek. Stuttgart: Kohlhammer, 1989.

———. "Ein enzyklisches Schreiben der Synode von Alexandrien (362)." *Zeitschrift für die neutestamentliche Wissenschaft und die Kunde der älteren Kirche* 79 (1988): 262–281. [= Pages 207–225 in Martin Tetz, *Athanasiana. Zu Leben und Lehre des Athanasius*. Edited by Wilhelm Geerlings and Dietmar Wyrwa. Beihefte zur Zeitschrift für die neutestamentliche Wissenschaft und die Kunde der älteren Kirche 78. Berlin: De Gruyter, 1995.]

———. "Les écrits «dogmatiques» d'Athanase. Rapport sur les travaux relatifs à l'édition des oeuvres d'Athanase, tome I." Pages 181–188 in *Politique et théologie chez Athanase d'Alexandrie. Actes du colloque de Chantilly (23–25 septembre 1973)*. Edited by Charles Kannengiesser. Théologie Historique 27. Paris: Beauchesne, 1974.

———. "Markellianer und Athanasios von Alexandrien. Die markellianische *Expositio fidei ad Athanasium* des Diakons Eugenios von Ankyra." *Zeitschrift für die neutestamentliche Wissenschaft und die Kunde der älteren Kirche* 64 (1973): 75–121.

———. "Über nikäische Orthodoxie. Der sog. *Tomus ad Antiochenos* des Athanasios von Alexandrien." *Zeitschrift für die neutestamentliche Wissenschaft und die Kunde der älteren Kirche* 66 (1975): 194–222 [= Pages 107–134 in *Athanasiana: Zu Leben und Lehre des Athanasius*. Edited by Wilhelm Geerlings and Dietmar Wyrwa. Beihefte zur Zeitschrift für die neutestamentliche Wissenschaft und die Kunde der älteren Kirche 78. Berlin: de Gruyter, 1995].

———. "Zur Theologie des Markell von Ankyra I. Eine Markellische Schrift 'De Incarnatione et contra Arianos.'" *Zeitschrift für Kirchengeschichte* 75 (1964): 217–270.

———. "Zur Theologie des Markell von Ankyra II. Markells Lehre von der Adamssohnschaft Christi und eine pseudoklementinische Tradition über die wahren Lehrer und Propheten." *Zeitschrift für Kirchengeschichte* 74 (1963): 3–42.

———. "Zur Theologie des Markell von Ankyra III. Die pseudathanasianische *Epistula ad Liberium*, ein Markellisches Bekenntnis." *Zeitschrift für Kirchengeschichte* 83 (1972): 145–194.

Teuber, Binyamin. "Melakhah ke-darkah u-v-shinnui be-shabat u-va-Torah kullah." *She'arim la-gmara—Shabat* (2015/2016): 167–180.

Thomassen, Einar. "What Is Heresy, and Why Did It Matter?" Pages 191–201 in *Invention, Rewriting, Usurpation: Discursive Fights over Religious Traditions in Antiquity*. Edited by David Brakke, Anders-Christian Jacobsen, and Jörg Ulrich. Early Christianity in the Context of Antiquity 11. Frankfurt am Main: Peter Lang, 2011.

Thompson, Glen L. *The Correspondence of Pope Julius I*. Washington, DC: Catholic University of America Press, 2015.

———. *The Earliest Papal Correspondence*. Ph.D. dissertation. New York: Columbia University, 1990.

Thümmel, Hans Georg. "Logos und Hypostasis." Pages 347–398 in *Die Weltlichkeit des Glaubens in der Alten Kirche. Festschrift für Ulrich Wickert zum siebzigsten Geburtstag*. Edited by Dietmar Wrywa. Beihefte zur Zeitschrift für die neutestamentliche Wissenschaft und die Kunde der älteren Kirche 85. Berlin: De Gruyter, 1997.

Tietze, Walter. *Lucifer von Calaris und die Kirchenpolitik des Constantius II. Zum Konflikt zwischen Kaiser Constantius II. und der nikäisch-orthodoxen Opposition (Lucifer von Calaris, Athanasius von Alexandria, Hilarius von Poitiers, Ossius von Córdoba, Liberius von Rom und Eusebius von Vercelli)*. Stuttgart: Sprint, 1976.

Todde, Mauro. *Peccato e prassi penitenziale secondo Lucifero di Cagliari*. Saggi e ricerche 1. Dissertationes ad lauream in Pontificia Facultate Theologica Marianum 9. Vicenza: Edizioni Patristiche, 1965.

Tuilier, André. "Le sens du terme ὁμοούσιος dans le vocabulaire théologique d'Arius et de l'école d'Antioche." Pages 421–430 in *Studia Patristica III: Papers Presented to the 3rd International Conference on Patristic Studies at Christ Church, Oxford, 21–26 September 1959*. Edited by Frank Leslie Cross. TU 78. Berlin: Akademie-Verlag, 1961.

Turcescu, Lucian. "Prosōpon and Hypostasis in Basil of Caesarea's *Against Eunomius* and the *Epistles*." *Vigiliae Christianae* 51 (1997): 374–395.

Turner, Cuthbert Hamilton. *Ecclesiae Occidentalis monumenta iuris antiquissima. Canonum et conciliorum Graecorum interpretationes latinae*. 2 vols. in 9. Oxford: Clarendon, 1899–1939.

Twersky, Yitzchak. "Make a Fence around the Torah." *Torah U-Madda Journal* 8 (1998/1999): 25–40.

Twik, Eliezer. "Pesiḳ reisheh bi-f'ulah mitsṭaberet." *Emunat 'itteikha* 124 (2018/2019): 79–82.

Ullucci, Daniel. "What Did He Say? The Ideas of Religious Experts and the 99%." Pages 21–31 in *Religious Competition in the Third Century C.E.: Jews, Christians, and the Greco-Roman Worlds*. Edited by Nathaniel P. DesRosiers, Jordan D. Rosenblum, and Lily C. Vuong. Journal of Ancient Judaism Supplements 15. Göttingen: Vandenhoeck & Ruprecht, 2014.

Ulrich, Jörg. *Die Anfänge der abendländischen Rezeption des Nizänums*. PTS 39. Berlin: De Gruyter, 1994.

Urbach, Ephraim Elimelech. "Ha-mesorot ʿal torat ha-sod bi-tḳufat ha-tannaʾim." Pages 1–28 in *Studies in Mysticism and Religion, Presented to Gershom G. Scholem on His Seventieth Birthday by Pupils, Colleagues and Friends*. Edited by Ephraim Elimelech Urbach, Raphael Jehuda Zwi Werblowsky, and Chaim Wirszubski. Jerusalem: Magnes and Hebrew University Press, 1967.

———. "Masoret ṿe-halakhah." *Tarbits. Rivʿon le-madaʿei ha-Yahadut* 50 (1981/1982): 136–163.

———. "Redemption and Repentance in Talmudic Judaism." Pages 190–206 in *Types of Redemption: Contributions to the Theme of the Study-Conference Held at Jerusalem, 14th to 19th July 1968*. Edited by C. Jouco Bleeker and Raphael Jehuda Zwi Werblowsky. Leiden: Brill, 1970.

———. *The Sages: Their Concepts and Beliefs*. Jerusalem: Magnes, 1975.

Urciuoli, Emiliano Rubens. *Servire due padroni. Una genealogia dell'uomo politico cristiano (50–313 e.v.)*. Saggi 101. Brescia: Morcelliana, 2018.

Uríbarri Bilbao, Gabino. "Trasfondo escriturístico del nacimiento de Cristo en los fragmentos de Pablo de Samosata." Pages 259–264 in *Studia Patristica XLII: Other Greek Writers, John of Damascus and Beyond, The West to Hilary; Papers Presented at the Fourteenth International Conference on Patristic Studies Held in Oxford 2003*. Edited by Mark Julian Edwards, Paul M. Parvis, and Frances Margaret Young. Louvain: Peeters, 2006.

Vaggione, Richard Paul. *Eunomius of Cyzicus and the Nicene Revolution*. Oxford: Oxford University Press, 2000.

Van Dam, Raymond. "Imperial Fathers and Their Sons: Licinius, Constantine, and the Council of Nicaea." Pages 19–42 in *The Cambridge Companion to the Council of Nicaea*. Edited by Young Richard Kim. Cambridge: Cambridge University Press, 2021.

van der Heide, Albert. "Midrash and Exegesis." Pages 43–56 in *The Book of Genesis in Jewish and Oriental Christian Interpretation: A Collection of Essays*. Edited by Judith Frishman and Lucas Van Rompay. Traditio Exegetica Graeca 5. Louvain: Peeters, 1997.

Van Deun, Peter. "The Church Historians after Eusebius." Pages 151–176 in *Greek and Roman Historiography in Late Antiquity*. Edited by Gabriele Marasco. Leiden: Brill, 2003.

Van Hoof, Lieve, and Peter Van Nuffelen. "The Social Role and Place of Literature in the Fourth Century AD." Pages 1–15 in *Literature and Society in the Fourth Cen-*

tury AD: Performing Paideia, *Constructing the Present, Presenting the Self.* Edited by Lieve Van Hoof and Peter Van Nuffelen. Mnemosyne supplements. Monographs on Greek and Latin Language and Literature 373. Leiden: Brill, 2014.

Van Nuffelen, Peter. "Arius, Athanase, et les autres: Enjeux juridiques et politiques du retour d'exil au IVe siècle." Pages 147–175 in *Exil et relégation. Les tribulations du sage et du saint durant l'antiquité romaine et chrétienne (Ier–VIe siècle ap. J.-C.). Actes du colloque organisé par le Centre Jean-Charles Picard, Université de Paris XII-Val-de-Marne, 17–18 juin 2005.* Edited by Philippe Blaudeau. Paris: De Boccard, 2008.

———. "Beyond Categorisation: 'Pagan Monotheism' and the Study of Ancient Religion." *Common Knowledge* 18 (2012): 451–463.

———. "The End of Open Competition? Religious Disputation in Late Antiquity." Pages 149–172 in *Religion and Competition in Antiquity.* Edited by David Engels and Peter Van Nuffelen. Collection Latomus 343. Brussels: Éditions Latomus, 2014.

———. *Penser la tolérance durant l'Antiquité tardive.* Conférences de l'École pratique des hautes études 10. Paris: Les Éditions du Cerf, 2018.

Van Roey, Albert. "Le traité contre les Trithéites (CPG 7245) de Damien d'Alexandrie." Pages 229–250 in *Philohistôr. Miscellanea in honorem Caroli Laga septuagenarii.* Edited by Antoon Schoors and Peter Van Deun. Orientalia Lovaniensia Analecta 60. Louvain: Peeters, 1994.

Van Rompay, Lucas. "A Letter of the Jews to the Emperor Marcian concerning the Council of Chalcedon." *Orientalia Lovaniensa Periodica* 12 (1981): 215–224.

Verheyden, Joseph. "Eustathius of Antioch on 'The Witch of Endor' (1 Sam 28): A Critique of Origen and Exegetical Method." *Ephemerides Theologicae Lovanienses* 93 (2017): 107–132.

———. "Origen on the 'Witch of Endor' (1 Sam 28): Some Comments on an Intriguing Piece of Reception History." Pages 589–598 in *The Book of Samuel: Stories—History—Reception History.* Edited by Walter Dietrich, Cynthia Edenburg, and Philippe Hugo. Bibliotheca Ephemeridum Theologicarum Lovaniensum 284. Leuven: Peeters, 2016.

Vessey, Mark. "The Forging of Orthodoxy in Latin Christian Literature: A Case Study." *Journal of Early Christian Studies* 4 (1996): 495–513.

———. "Jerome's Origen: The Making of a Christian Literary *Persona.*" Pages 135–145 in *Studia Patristica XXVIII: Papers Presented at the Eleventh International Conference on Patristic Studies Held in Oxford 1991; Other Latin Authors, Nachleben of the Fathers, Index Patrum.* Edited by Elizabeth Anne Livingstone. Louvain: Peeters, 1993. [= no. 4 in Mark Vessey, *Latin Christian Writers in Late Antiquity and Their Texts.* Collected Studies 837. Aldershot, UK: Ashgate, 2005.]

———. "'La patristique, c'est autre chose': André Mandouze, Peter Brown, and the Avocations of Patristics as a Philological Science." Pages 443–472 in *Patristic Studies in the Twenty-First Century: Proceedings of an International Conference to Mark the 50th Anniversary of the International Association of Patristic Studies.* Edited by Brouria

Bitton-Ashkelony, Theodore de Bruyn, Carol Harrison, and Oscar Velásquez. Turnhout: Brepols, 2015.

———. "Literary History: A Fourth-Century Roman Invention?" Pages 16–30 in *Literature and Society in the Fourth Century AD: Performing* Paideia, *Constructing the Present, Presenting the Self.* Edited by Lieve Van Hoof and Peter Van Nuffelen. Mnemosyne Supplements. Monographs on Greek and Latin Language and Literature 373. Leiden: Brill, 2014.

Vianès, Laurence. "Des ossements dispersés au corps de l'Église. Ézéchiel 37, 1–14 dans un groupement de citations chez Origène." Pages 191–207 in Hôs ephat', dixerit quispiam, *comme disait l'autre. Mécanisme de la citation et de la mention dans les langues de l'Antiquité.* Edited by Christian Nicolas. Recherches & Travaux. Hors-série 15. Grenoble: Ellug—Université Stendhal, 2006.

Vidas, Moulie. *Tradition and the Formation of the Talmud.* Princeton, NJ: Princeton University Press, 2014.

———. *The Rise of Talmud and the Limits of* Midrash. Unpublished manuscript shared by the author (version of November 2016), PDF.

Vilella Masana, Josep. "Constantino y Osio: La última etapa del conflicto arriano preniceno." *Antiquité Tardive* 22 (2014): 27–33.

Vinzent, Markus. *Athanasius und Markell von Ankyra.* Pages 129–131 in *Athanasius Handbuch.* Edited by Peter Gemeinhardt. Tübingen: Mohr Siebeck, 2011.

———. *Markell von Ankyra: Die Fragmente und der Brief an Julius von Rom.* Leiden: Brill, 1997.

———. Review of Wonfram Kinzig, *Neue Texte und Studien zu den antiken und frühmittelalterlichen Glaubensbekenntnissen. Theologische Literaturzeitung* 143 (2018): 1287–1290.

Visonà, Giuseppe. "Ostern / Osterfest / Osterpredigt I." Columns 517–530 in vol. 25 of *Theologische Realenzyklopädie.* 36 vols. Berlin: De Gruyter, 1977–2005.

Visotzky, Burton L. *Golden Bells and Pomegranates: Studies in Midrash Leviticus Rabbah.* Texte und Studien zum antiken Judentum 94. Tübingen: Mohr Siebeck, 2003.

Voelker, John T. "An Anomalous Trinitarian Formula in Marius Victorinus' «Against Arius»." Pages 517–522 in *Studia Patristica XLIII: Augustine, Other Latin Writers; Papers Presented at the Fourteenth International Conference on Patristic Studies Held in Oxford 2003.* Edited by Mark Julian Edwards, Paul M. Parvis, and Frances Margaret Young. Louvain: Peeters, 2006.

———. *The Trinitarian Theology of Marius Victorinus: Polemic and Exegesis.* Ph.D. dissertation. Milwaukee: Marquette University, 2006.

Vogt, Hermann Josef. "Die Trinitätslehre des Papstes Kalixt I." *Theologische Quartalschrift* 179 (1999): 195–209.

Voss, Bernd Reiner. "Vernachlässigte Zeugnisse klassischer Literatur bei Augustin und Hieronymus." *Rheinisches Museum für Philologie* N.F. 112 (1969): 154–166. [= Pages

300–311 in *Lemmata. Donum natalicium W. Ehlers sexagenario a sodalibus Thesauri linguae Latinae oblatum*. Munich, 1968.]

Wald, Stephen G. *Pereḳ Ellu ʿovrin. Bavli Pesaḥim, pereḳ shelishi. Mahadurah biḳortit ʿim beʾur maḳif.* New York: Beit ha-midrash le-rabanim ba-Ameriḳah, 2000.

Walraff, Martin. *Der Kirchenhistoriker Sokrates. Untersuchungen zu Geschichtsdarstellung, Methode und Person*. Forschungen *zur Kirchen- und Dogmengeschichte* 68. Göttingen: Vandenhoeck & Ruprecht, 1997.

———. "Il «sinodo di tutte le eresie» a Constantinopoli (383)." Pages 271–279 in vol. 2 of *Vescovi e pastori in epoca teodosiana. In occasione del XVI centenario della consacrazione episcopale di S. Agostino. XXV incontro di studiosi dell'antichità cristiana. Roma, 8–11 maggio 1996*. 2 vols. Studia Ephemeridis Augustinianum 58. Rome: Institutum Patristicum Augustinianum, 1997.

Ward, Robin. *The Schism at Antioch in the Fourth Century*. Ph.D. dissertation. London: King's College London, 2003.

Wasserman, Mira. *Jews, Gentiles, and Other Animals: The Talmud after the Humanities*. Philadelphia: University of Pennsylvania Press, 2001.

Weber, Anton. *Arché. Ein Beitrag zur Christologie des Eusebius von Caesarea*. Munich: Neue-Stadt-Verlag, 1965.

Weidner, Daniel. "Reading Gerschom Scholem." *Jewish Quarterly Review* 96 (2006): 203–231.

Weijenborg, Reginald. "Apollinaristic Interpolations in the *Tomus ad Antiochenos* of 362." Pages 324–330 in *Studia Patristica III: Papers Presented to the 3rd International Conference on Patristic Studies at Christ Church, Oxford, 21–26 September 1959*. Edited by Frank Leslie Cross. TU 78. Berlin: Akademie-Verlag, 1961.

———. "De authenticitate et sensu quarundam epistularum S. Basilio Magno et Apollinario Laodiceno." *Antonianum* 33 (1958): 197–240, 371–414; *Antonianum* 34 (1959): 245–298.

Weiss, Abraham. *ʿAl ha-yetsirah ha-sifrutit shel ha-ʾamoraʾim*. New York: Horeb Yeshiva University and the Lucius N. Littauer Foundation, 1961/1962.

———. *Ha-Talmud ha-bavli be-hithavvuto ha-sifrutit*. Warsaw: Ha-maḥon le-hafatsat maddaʿei ha-Yahadut be-Folin—Ḳeren be-shem Y. Spielvogel, 1937.

———. *Ha-yetsirah shel ha-savoraʾim*. Jerusalem: Magnes, 1953.

———. *Le-ḥeḳer ha-Talmud*. Sefarim le-zikhrono shel ha-Doḳṭor Michael Higger 1. New York: Feldheim, 1954.

———. *Meḥḳarim ba-Talmud*. Jerusalem: Mosad ha-Rav Ḳuḳ and Bar Ilan University Press, 1975.

Wells, Colin. "Spotting an Elephant." *Arion* 19 (2011): 159–172.

Welte, Bernhard. "Die Lehrformel von Nikaia und die abendländische Metaphysik." Pages 100–117 in *Zur Frühgeschichte der Christologie. Ihre bibl. Anfänge u. d. Lehrformel von Nikaia*. Edited by Heinrich Schlier and Bernhard Welte. Quaestiones Disputatae 51. Freiburg im Breisgau: Herder, 1970.

Whaling, Frank. "The Development of the Word 'Theology.'" *Scottish Journal of Theology* 34 (1981): 289–312.

Whiting, Colin M. *Christian Communities in Late Antiquity: Luciferians and the Construction of Heresy*. Ph.D. dissertation. Riverside: University of California Riverside, 2015.

Wickham, Lionel R. *Hilary of Poitiers: Conflicts of Conscience and Law in the Fourth-Century Church*. Translated Texts for Historians 25. Liverpool: Liverpool University Press, 1997.

Wickman, Eric. "Shaping Church-State Relations after Constantine: The Political Theology of Hilary of Poitiers." *Church History* 86 (2017): 287–310.

Widdicombe, Peter. *The Fatherhood of God from Origen to Athanasius*. Oxford: Clarendon and Oxford University Press, 1994.

Wieber, Anja. "Die Augusta aus der Wüste: Die palmyrenische Herrscherin Zenobia." Pages 281–310 in *Frauenwelten in der Antike: Geschlechterordnung und weibliche Lebenspraxis*. Edited by Thomas Späth and Beate Wagner-Hasel. Stuttgart: Metzler, 2000.

Wiles, Maurice F. *Archetypal Heresy: Arianism through the Centuries*. Oxford: Clarendon, 1996.

———. "Attitudes to Arius in the Arian Controversy." Pages 31–44 in *Arianism after Arius: Essays on the Development of the Fourth Century Trinitarian Conflicts*. Edited by Michel René Barnes and Daniel H. Williams. Edinburgh: T&T Clark, 1993.

———. "In Defence of Arius." *Journal of Theological Studies* 13 (1962): 339–347.

Williams, Daniel H. *Ambrose of Milan and the End of the Arian-Nicene Conflicts*. Oxford: Clarendon, 1995.

———. "The Anti-Arian Campaigns of Hilary of Poitiers and the 'Liber Contra Auxentium.'" *Church History* 61 (1992): 7–22.

———. "The Council of Ariminum (359) and the Rise of the Neo-Nicene." Pages 305–324 in *The Cambridge Companion to the Council of Nicaea*. Edited by Young Richard Kim. Cambridge: Cambridge University Press, 2021.

———. "A Reassessment of the Early Career and Exile of Hilary of Poitiers." *The Journal of Ecclesiastical History* 42 (1991): 202–217.

Williams, Megan Hale. *The Monk and the Book: Jerome and the Making of Christian Scholarship*. Chicago: University of Chicago Press, 2006.

Williams, Rowan D. *Arius: Heresy and Tradition*. Grand Rapids, MI: Eerdmans, 2002.

———. "Does It Make Sense to Speak of Pre-Nicene Orthodoxy?" Pages 1–23 in *The Making of Orthodoxy: Essays in Honour of Henry Chadwick*. Edited by Rowan D. Williams. Cambridge: Cambridge University Press, 1989.

———. "The Logic of Arianism." *Journal of Theological Studies* 34 (1983): 56–81.

———. "The Son's Knowledge of the Father in Origen." Pages 146–153 in *Origeniana Quarta: Die Referate des 4. Internationalen Origeneskongresses (Innsbruck, 2.–6. Sep-*

tember 1985). Edited by Lothar Lies. Innsbrucker theologische Studien. Innsbruck: Tyrolia-Verlag, 1987.

Wilmart, André. "L'*Ad Constantium liber primus* de Saint Hilaire de Poitiers et les fragments historiques." *Revue Bénédictine* 24 (1907): 149–179 and 291–317.

———. "Les 'Fragments Historiques' et le synode de Béziers de 356." *Revue bénédictine* 25 (1908): 225–229.

Wilson, Stephen G. *Related Strangers: Jews and Christians, 70–170 C.E.* Minneapolis: Fortress Press, 1995.

Wimpfheimer, Barry Scott. "The Dialogical Talmud: Daniel Boyarin and the Rabbinics." *Jewish Quarterly Review* 101 (2011): 245–254.

———. *Narrating the Law: A Poetics of Talmudic Legal Stories*. Philadelphia: University of Pennsylvania Press, 2011.

Winsbury, Rex. *Zenobia of Palmyra: History, Myth and the Neo-classical Imagination*. London: Duckworth, 2010.

Wirth, Gerhard. "Jovian: Kaiser und Karikatur." Pages 353–384 in *Vivarium: Festschrift Theodor Klauser zum 90. Geburtstag*. Edited by Theodor Klauser. Jahrbuch für Antike und Christentum. Ergänzungsband 11. Münster: Aschendorff, 1984.

Wolf, Sarah. "'Haven't I Told You Not to Take Yourself outside of the Law?': Rabbi Yirmiyah and the Characterization of a Scholastic." *AJS Review* 44 (2020): 384–410.

———. "Suffering and Sacrifice: The Hermeneutics of *Yisurin* in the Babylonian Talmud." *Studies in Late Antiquity* 3 (2019): 56–76.

Wolfson, Harry Austryn. *Philo: Foundations of Religious Philosophy in Judaism, Christianity, and Islam 1*. Cambridge, MA: Harvard University Press, 1948.

———. "Philosophical Implications of Arianism and Apollinarianism." *Dumbarton Oaks Papers* 12 (1958): 3–28.

———. *The Philosophy of the Church Fathers*. Vol. 1, *Faith, Trinity, Incarnation*. Structure and Growth of Philosophic Systems from Plato to Spinoza 3. Cambridge, MA: Harvard University Press, 1956.

Yadin-Israel, Azzan. "Christian, Jewish, and Pagan Authority and the Rise of the Christian Intellectual." Pages 165–191 in *The Rise of the Early Christian Intellectual*. Edited by Lewis Ayres and H. Clifton Ward. Arbeiten zur Kirchengeschichte 139. Berlin: De Gruyter, 2020.

———. "The Hammer on the Rock: Polysemy and the School of Rabbi Ishmael." *Jewish Studies Quarterly* 10 (2003): 1–17.

Yanir, Tzvi. "Melakhah she-ʾeinah tserikhah le-gufah." *Orot ʿEtsion* 11 (1985/1986): 23–59.

Yeum, Changseon. *Die Synode von Alexandrien (362). Die dogmengeschichtliche und kirchenpolitische Bedeutung für die Kirche im 4. Jahrhundert*. Münster: LIT, 2005.

Yon, Jean-Baptiste. "Zénobie et les femmes de Palmyre." *Annales archéologiques arabes syriennes* 45–46 (2002): 215–220.

Yuval, Israel Jacob. "The Orality of Jewish Law: From Pedagogy to Ideology." Pages 237–260 in *Judaism, Christianity, and Islam in the Course of History: Exchange and Conflicts*. Edited by Lothar Gall and Dietmar Willoweit. Schriften des Historischen Kollegs 82. Munich: R. Oldenbourg Verlag, 2011.

———. *Two Nations in Your Womb: Perceptions of Jews and Christians in Late Antiquity and the Middle Ages*. Translated by Barbara Harshav and Jonathan Chipman. Berkeley: University of California Press, 2006. [= Translation of *Shenei goyim be-viṭnekh: Yehudim ṿe-notsrim: Dimuyim hadadiyim*. Tel Aviv: Am Oved, 2000].

Zachhuber, Johannes. "The Antiochene Synod of AD 363 and the Beginnings of Neo-Nicenism." *Zeitschrift für Antikes Christentum* 4 (2000): 83–101.

———. "Basil and the Three-Hypostases Tradition. Reconsidering the Origins of Cappadocian Theology." *Zeitschrift für antikes Christentum* 5 (2001): 65–85.

———. "Gregor von Nyssa und das Schisma von Antiochien: Zur Interpretation der Schrift *Ad Graecos. Ex communibus notionibus*." *Theologie und Philosophie* 72 (1997): 481–496.

———. "Individuality and the Theological Debate about 'Hypostasis.'" Pages 91–110 in *Individuality in Late Antiquity*. Edited by Alexis Torrance and Johannes Zachhuber. Farnham, UK: Ashgate, 2014.

———. *The Rise of Christian Theology and the End of Ancient Metaphysics: Patristic Philosophy from the Cappadocian Fathers to John of Damascus*. Oxford: Oxford University Press, 2020.

Zahn, Theodor. *Marcellus von Ancyra. Ein Beitrag zur Geschichte der Theologie*. Gotha: F.A. Perthes, 1867.

Zahran, Yasmine. *Zenobia between Reality and Legend*. Oxford: Archaeopress, 2003.

Zecchini, Giuseppe. "Latin Historiography: Jerome, Orosius and the Western Chronicles." Pages 317–345 in *Greek and Roman Historiography in Late Antiquity*. Edited by Gabriele Marasco. Leiden: Brill, 2003.

———. "Religione pubblica e libertà religiosa nell'impero romano." Pages 187–198 in *Politiche religiose nel mondo antico e tardoantico. Poteri e indirizzi, forme del controllo, idee e prassi di tolleranza. Atti del Convegno Internazionale di Studi, Firenze, 24–26 settembre 2009*. Edited by Giovanni A. Cecconi and Chantal Gabrielli. Bari: Edipuglia, 2011.

Zedda, Claudio. "La dottrina trinitaria di Lucifero di Cagliari." *Divus Thomas* 52 (1949): 276–329.

Zellentin, Holger M. *Rabbinic Parodies of Jewish and Christian Literature*. Texte und Studien zum antiken Judentum 139. Tübingen: Mohr Siebeck, 2011.

Ziegler, Thierry. *Les petits traités trinitaires de Grégoire de Nysse: Témoins d'un itinéraire théologique (379–383)*. Ph.D. dissertation. Strasbourg: Université de Strasbourg, 1987.

Zoepfl, Friedrich. "Die trinitarischen und christologischen Anschauungen des Bischofs Eustathius von Antiochien." *Theologische Quartalschrift* 104 (1923): 170–201.

Zurutuza, Hugo Andrés. "La intolerancia religiosa de Constancio II: Algunas puntualizaciones sobre el exilio de los adversarios." Pages 115–126 in *Libertad e intolerancia religiosa en el Imperio romano*. Edited by José Fernández Ubiña and Mar Marcos. 'Ilu. Revista de Ciencias de las Religiones. Anejo 18. Madrid: Publicaciones Universidad Complutense de Madrid, 2007.

Index of Subjects

Additional references to ancient authors and works may be found in the Index of Ancient Sources.

Aba, Rabbi, 33–34
Abuyah, Elisha ben: curiosity of, 37; cutting the shoots by, 28–30, 203n29; deliverance and, 37; excommunication of, 19; discernment attempt by, 48; inquiry of, 49, 50; memorialization of, 38; Metatron encounter of, 20, 21–28, 48; misprision of, 21–28; overview of, 178; prostitute and, 28, 34–35, 48; radish and, 34–35; rejection of, 50; Sabbath transgression of, 20, 30–36, 48; story of, 36–37
Acacius of Caesarea, 73–74, 99, 101, 134
Acher. *See* Abuyah, Elisha ben
a collection (Athanasius's corpus), 108–9
Adam, 35
adoptionism, 39
Aëtius, 73
Agapetos, 97, 109
Agelius, 174
Alexander of Alexandria, 53–54, 56, 57, 112, 146–47
Alexandria, Council of. *See* Council of Alexandria
Ambrose of Milan, 287
Ammi, Rabbi, 46
amoraic dicta, 153–54
amora'im, 162–63, 166, 172, 173, 282n159
anathematisms, 14, 64, 115
Ancyra, Council of. *See* Council of Ancyra
anhypostatos, 133
Antioch, 40, 81–83, 136
Antioch, Council of. *See* Council of Antioch
Antiochene Church, 42
Antiochene corpus. *See b* tradition (Athanasius's corpus)
Antiochene events of 363, 99–103
Antiochene New Nicene, 108
Antiochia of Caria, Council of. *See* Council of Antiochia of Caria

Arabianos of Antros, 99
argumentation, 173
Ariminum, Council of. *See* Council of Ariminum
Arius: allies of, 56; criticism of, 60; influence of, 187–88n5; interpretations by, 2; letter to, 146–47; overview of, 54; rejection of, 57–58; support for, 55; Trinitarian controversies and, 53–55; viewpoint of, 211n9, 212n11, 213n21; writings of, 62
Arles, Council of. See Council of Arles
ascent apocalypse, 24–25
Ashi, Rav, 160, 161
Athanasius of Alexandria: banishment of, 76; contributions of, 52–53; convincing by, 58–59; Coptic text "A" and, 99–100, 101–2, 103; Coptic text "B" and, 112; exile of, 100; Jovian and, 100–101; leadership of, 75, 79, 80, 107; Meletius and, 99; biblical metaphors of, 112; ousting of, 73; Paulinus and, 97–98, 102; treatment of Paul and Samosata and Zenobia by, 43, 44; readmission policy of, 92; reinstatement of, 59, 75; theology of, 112; viewpoint of, 68, 69–70; rendition of the Trinitarian controversies of, 14; see of Antioch and, 95–99.
Athenodorus, 39
Atticus, 212n11
Augustine of Hippo, 16, 155–56, 289
Aurelian, 41
authority, 4, 26–27

Babylonian Talmud: 151, 152, 162–64, 170, 172; characteristics of, 170–71; citations within, 154, 157, 160–70; dialectic within, 171; editorial efforts regarding, 169–70; Jewish allegiance to, 152. *See also specific topics*
Barhebraeus. *See* Grigorios Bar ʿEbroyo
Basil of Ancyra, 74, 256n92
Basil of Caesarea: 98, 102–3, 143, 155, 289–90; viewpoint of, 13, 132–33; writings of, 89
Bavli. *See* Babylonian Talmud
betrothal, 165–69
Bézier, Council of. *See* Council of Bézier
Binitarianism, 6
b tradition (Athanasius's corpus), 109

Callixtus of Rome, 132
Cappadocians, 13, 16
Carthage, 1
Chalcedon, Council of. *See* Council of Chalcedon
Chalcedonian formula, 196n59
Christendom, 2, 150
Christian dialectic, 170–77
Christian intellectuals: authoritarian proclivities of, 179; dogmatization and, 148; heretical denial of truth by, 160; preclusion of, 180; scholarly activities of, 7–8; theology of, 158
Christianity: asymmetric parting of ways and, 47–50; "doings" of, 8; first century of, 4–5; intellectual tradition of, 9–13, 18, 47; Judaism's line of demarcation with, 150; parting of the ways and, 177–80, 181–82; as a self-standing tradition of inquiry, 10; theological codes within, 5
Christian-Jewish continuum, fracture of, 18
Christian literary activity, 8
Christian literate elites, 151–60, 153, 179
Christians, 10, 19
Christian theologians, 180, 182

Christian theological literature, 152, 154, 156–57, 158
Christian theology, 12. *See also* theology
Christian thought, 54–55, 192n35, 196n59
Christological controversies, 13
Chrysostom, 82
Church, 147, 159
Church of Euzoius, 83
Church of Syria, 41
citation: in the Babylonian Talmud, 160–70; by Christians, 158; formulas of, 162–63; functions of, 153–54, 160; history regarding, 154; patristic argument and, 151–60, 177
citeme *(Citem)*, 272n89
Clement of Alexandria, 132, 192n35, 290
Codex Veronensis LX, 103
conformism, 149–50
Constans (Emperor), 58, 63–64, 72
Constantine (Emperor), 1, 5, 55–56, 58
Constantinian theology, 113
Constantinople, Council of. *See* Council of Constantinople
Constantius Gallus, 73, 74–75
Constantius II, 58, 72–73, 80
constituting discourse, 12
Coptic text "A" (Athanasius of Alexandria), 99–100, 101–2, 103
Coptic text "B" (Athanasius of Alexandria), 112
Cornelius, 40
Council of Alexandria: disciplinary action of, 92–95; doctrinal positions of Meletians within, 106; hypostaseis at, 115; importance of, 79–80; influence of, 79; Jerome of Stridon and, 140; Meletians and, 106, 108, 110; significance of, 120; *Tome to the Antiochenes* (Athanasius of Alexandria) at, 68–70
Council of Ancyra, 74
Council of Antioch (*in encaeniis*), accusations against, 102; Alexander of Alexandria within, 112; effects of, 145; formulas of, 59-64; homoousios and, 99, 106; overview of, 102, 110–11; tri-hypostatic view within, 113
Council of Antiochia of Caria, 60
Council of Ariminum, 74, 83, 115, 116, 118
Council of Arles, 73, 75–76, 86
Council of Bézier, 73, 86
Council of Chalcedon, 148
Council of Constantinople: bishops within, 87, 99; creed of, 117; effects of, 5; focus of, 14–15; hypostasis banning at, 118; overview of, 14, 74
Council of Ephesus, 156, 176
Council of Lampsacus, 60
Council of Milan, 73, 75, 76
Council of Nicaea: agenda of, 1–2; doctrine of, 17; Eustathius of Antioch at, 126; homoousios and, 14–15; legacy of, 13–18; overview of, 2; support for, 197n67. *See also* Nicene Creed
Council of Nike, 74, 118
Council of Paris, 89, 92–93, 94
Council of Sardica, 64–65, 68, 69, 78, 82, 130
Council of Seleucia, 60, 74, 99, 134
Council of Sirmium, 99, 115
Council of the Thebaid, 83–92
Council of Tyre, 86
Creed of Antioch, 117
Creed of Ariminum, 116–17
Creed of Constantinople, 117
Creed of Nike, 116, 117, 118
creeds/credal declarations, 52. *See also specific creeds*

cutting the shoots, 28–30, 35–36, 203n29
Cyril of Alexandria, 156, 290

Damasus (Pope), 136–42, 177
Damian of Alexandria, 128, 129
Dated Creed (Fourth Creed of Sirmium), 116
Dedication council. *See* Council of Antioch (*in encaeniis*)
Demetrianus, 39, 46
dialectic, Jewish and Christian chronologies of, 170–77
dialogue, 148, 149
Didymus the Blind, 192n35, 291
Dionysius of Alexandria, 39, 40, 155, 291
Dionysius of Milan, 76
Dionysius of Rome, 57
discourse, as primary objective of investigation, 194n47
discourse analysis, 194n47
discursive tradition, 9–10
disputation, 148
dogmatization, 148, 263n7
Domnus, 38–39

Easter, 1–2
ecclesiastical institutionalization, 194n43
Edict of Milan, 2, 150
Edict of Thessalonica, 150
Egyptian Church leaders, 108
Eliezer, Rabbi, 171–72, 178
enhypostatos, 133–34, 143–44
en prefix, 134–35
enhydros, 135
Ephesus, Council of. *See* Council of Ephesus
Epictetus, 291
Epiphanius of Salamis, 102, 142–45, 291
episcopal ententes, 11
Esau, 4
Eudoxius of Germanicia, 73, 74, 82
Eugenius of Ancyra, 292
Eunomius, 73
Eusebian alliance, 59, 61, 65
Eusebians, 92, 188n5
Eusebius of Caesarea: conflict of, 129; death of, 73; Jerome of Stridon and, 136; leadership of, 56; Nicene Creed and, 57; support for Arius from, 55; theology and, 192n35; three ousiai formulation of, 116; treatment of Paul and Samosata and Zenobia by, 41, 42; viewpoint of, 39, 45–46, 61, 113; writings of, 132, 155
Eusebius of Nicodemia: accusations against, 59; Eustathius of Antioch and, 125; letter from, 56; letter to, 53; Nicene Creed and, 57; reinstatement of, 58; support for Arius from, 55;
Eusebius of Samosata, 99
Eusebius of Vercellae, 84, 86, 87–88, 91–92, 98, 110
Eusebius of Vercellae (Pseudo-), 72, 76, 81, 292
Eustathians/Eustathianism, 96, 107, 108, 110, 118
Eustathius of Antioch: exile of, 81–82; leadership of, 56; overview of, 248–49n31; Fragment 142 attributed to, 128–36; theology of, 125–28; viewpoint of, 113, 253n57; writings of, 125, 250n38
Eutychios of Eleutheropolis, 99
Euzoius, 81–82
Evagrius, 136, 137, 138
Eve, 35
explicit theology, 10

Fabius of Antioch, 40
Facundus of Hermaine, 292

Fathers of the Church, 155, 156, 175
Faustinus and Marcellinus, 90–91, 293
Faustus of Riez, 156
Firmilian of Caesarea of Cappadocia, 39, 40
flesh, mouth's connection with, 23
formulas of faith, 59–66, 124
Fourth Creed of Sirmium (Dated Creed), 116

Galen, 293
Gallican bishops, 93–94, 231–32n86
Gelasius of Cyzicus, 72, 293
Gelasius of Cyzicus (Pseudo-), 293
gemara, 22, 33–34
gemire/gemiri, 25, 26
George of Alexandria, 73, 134
George of Laodicea, 74
Germinius of Sirmium, 73
Giwargis, 293
God: adoption by, 39; anger of, 28; anti-Marcellan clause regarding, 59–60; as creator, 46; creeds regarding, 60–64, 66, 117; within *Against Damian*, 129–30; dignity of, 54; early viewpoints regarding, 10; existence of, 56; generation by, 15, 54, 256n92; grace of, 122; Christ's equality with, 15, 54; Christ's similarity to, 114, 116; Jewish scrutiny of, 7; Logos of, 132; as marker of nature, 129; Metatron and, 24; monarchy of, 113; relationship to the Word by, 113; revelation of, 12; within Trinity, 129
Golden Church, 82
grace, 122
Great Commission, 61–62
Gregory of Nazianzus, 13, 132, 293
Gregory of Nyssa: Old Nicene and, 249n35; viewpoint of, 13; writings of, 250n38
Gregory the Wonder-Worker, 39
Grigorios Bar ʿEbroyo, 45, 294

halakhah le-Mosheh mi-Sinai (a law given to Moses at Sinai), 25
Helenus of Tarsus, 39, 40
Hellenic philosophical tradition, 189n17
Herennios, 97, 109
heresies, 19–21, 159–60
heteroousian movement, 73
Hilary of Jerusalem, 86
Hilary of Poitiers: banishment of, 86; leadership of, 93; promotion of synods by, 75
Hilary of Rome, 86, 88, 90
Hillel, 284–85n175
Hippolytus, 132, 295
Holy Spirit: creeds regarding, 60–62, 64; distinction of, 65, 104, 105, 111, 129, 143; expressions regarding, 126; generation of, 256n92; Jesus Christ as conceived from, 117, 127; nature of, 130; presence of, 39; as *prosōpon* of God, 116, 117, 132; reduction to a creature of, 102; wisdom from, 134
homoousios: affirmation of, 99; Athanasius and, 77; defined, 14–15; overview of, 56–57; viewpoint of the tri-hypostatic party on, 106–7
homophony, 148
Hormisdas (Pope), 156
hyparxis, 56
hypostasis: at Council of Alexandria, 115, 124; difference of, 128–29; overview of, 112; subsistent person *(prosōpon enhypostaton)* and, 142; unicity of, 126; usage of, 133; within the godhead, 14–15; within *Tome to the Antiochenes* (Athanasius of Alexandria), 95, 120-121, 124
hypostatos, 135

implicit syllogism, 24
implicit theology, 10
in encaeniis, council. *See* Council of Antioch (*in encaeniis*)
intellectual culture, parting ways under, 3
intellectuals, 189n14
intellectual tradition, Christianity as, 9–13
inter-discourse, discursive fields within, 195n51
intolerance, 153, 177–80
intra-communal pluralism, 178
Irenaeus of Lyons, 134, 295

Jacob, 4
Jansenists, 122–23
Jerome of Stridon: 89–90, 136–42, 259n119; overview of, 136–37; quote about the Council of Alexandria by, 79; travels of, 136–37; writings of, 74, 116–17
Jesus Christ: begetting of, 2, 53–54, 59, 174, 175; cosmogonic role of, 127; creeds regarding, 61–64, 126; within *Against Damian,* 129–30; disputes regarding, 2; divine and human elements within, 13, 39; equality with God of, 6, 14, 15, 54; expressions regarding, 126; generation of, 15, 16, 53, 211n9, 212n11, 213n21, 256n92; God's similarity to, 114, 116; as homoousios to the Father, 14, 56, 65, 74–77; hypostasis of, 15, 59, 65; individuated character of, 66; Jewish viewpoint regarding, 4, 6, 7; as "out of non-existence," 211n9; Paul of Samosata's viewpoint of, 38–39; resurrection of, 2; saving action of, 127; debate regarding the self-standing of, 120; as subsistent person (*prosōpon enhypostaton*), 104, 111, 117, 133, 135, 143; as Wisdom, 134
Jewish Christianity, 4
Jewish commoners, 179
Jewish dialectic, 170–77
Jewish literate elites, 151–60, 152, 153, 179
Jews, 19, 149–50
John Chrysostom, 43–44, 132, 296
John of Damascus, 132
Jovian (Emperor), 100–101, 296
Judah, Rabbi, 33–34
Judaism: asymmetric parting of ways and, 47–50; binitarianism within, 6; Christian intellectual tradition and, 18; Christianity's line of demarcation with, 150; conflicts within, 7; disassociation from, 2–3; "doings" of, 8; first century of, 4–5; focus of, 7; interests within, 6; disinterest in Jesus within, 6; parting of the ways within, 177–80, 181–82
Julian (Emperor), 75, 80, 100
Julian solar calendar, 1
Julius I (Pope), 58–59, 66–72, 296
Justin Martyr, 148, 192n35

Kalemeros, 96–97, 109
Karterios, 110

Lampsacus, Council of. *See* Council of Lampsacus
Leontius, 74, 82
Liberius (Pope), 76, 89, 296–97
Life of Constantine (Eusebius of Caesarea), 146–47
literary dialogues, production of, 148
living tradition, 9
Logos Christology, 39
Lucian of Antioch, 55, 61
Luciferians, 92

Lucifer of Calaris: influence of, 81, 145; leadership of, 87–88, 92; Paulinus and, 97, 111; request to, 76; subscriptions of the *Tome to the Antiochenes* by, 109; travels of, 86; viewpoint of, 84, 89–90
Lucius, Bernicianus, et. al., 297

Magnentius, 75
Malchion, 38
Marcellans, 143, 144
Marcellus of Ancyra, 56, 59, 65, 113, 144, 243n195
Marius Victorinus, 158, 297
Mark of Arethusa, 63–64, 73
Maximos, 109
Maximus of Bosra, 39, 96–97
melakhah (work), 31–36
Meletians/Meletian group: attitude toward, 103; Council of Alexandria and, 106, 108, 110; criticism of, 139; dispute involving, 137; doctrinal positions of, 106; Jerome of Stridon's criticism of, 140; overview of, 83; readmission of, 96; signatories of, 107–11; tradition of thought by, 118
Meletius of Antioch: conflict involving, 92, 102–3; Council of Antioch and, 110–11; leadership of, 81–82, 98; letter to, 98; overview of, 134; writings of, 134
merits, 26–27
Merkabah mysticism, 24–25
metaphors, 112
Metatron, 20, 21–28, 48
mia-hypostatism, 112–13, 115, 116, 118, 140
Michael the Great, 45
Michael the Syrian, 297–98
Milan, Council of. *See* Council of Milan
mitsyot, 27
Monarchianism, 56, 69, 113
monodoxy, 148
monology, 178
monotheism, 190–91n24, 190n23
Montalte, Louis de, 122–24
mouth, flesh's connection with, 23

Narcissus of Neronias, 63–64, 116
Nectarius, 174
New Nicenism, 120, 144, 197n67
Nicaea and Its Legacy (Ayres), 15–17
Nicaenum, 56, 67, 75–78
Nicaea, Council of. *See* Council of Nicaea
Nicene Creed: acceptance of, 110; anachronistic identification of adherence to, 15; declaration within, 56; usage of homoousios within, 56–57; letter of, 67; signing of, 57; writing of, 68
Nicenism, 197n67
Nicomas of Iconium, 39
Nike, Council of. *See* Council of Nike
Nikephoros Kallistos Xanthopoulos, 298
Novatianism, 40, 176

Old Nicenism 83, 141-142, 145, 197g67, 249n35
"one *persona*" heresy, 115
Optatus of Milevis, 298
Origenist theology of the Logos, 15
Origen of Alexandria: admiration for, 175; Firmilian and, 40; use of hypostasis by, 133; influence of, 156; theology and, 192n35; viewpoint of, 54; writings of, 133–34
orthodoxy, 29
ortholalia, 122–25
orthopraxy, 29
Ossius of Cordoba, 55, 66–72, 77, 299

ousia, 56–57, 64–65, 106, 116, 120–21, 128–29
"out of non-existence," 211n9

Palestinian Talmud, 152, 163
Pamphilus the Theologian, 299
Pancratius, 86
Paris, Council of. *See* Council of Paris
Parmenides, 211n9
parting of the ways metaphor, 4–9, 188n8
Passover, 1–2
patristic ways of citing, 151–60, 177
Patrophilus of Scythopolis, 101
Paulinus: Athanasius of Alexandria and, 97–98, 102; consecration of, 111; death of, 137; elevation of, 92; leadership of, 81–82; ordination of, 97; political weakness of, 143; representatives of, 96–97; subscriptions of, 110, 111–12; within *Tome to the Antiochenes* (Athanasius of Alexandria), 108; viewpoint of, 102–3
Paul of Samosata: within Christian tradition, 49–50; condemnation of, 19, 57; excommunication of, 37–39; geo-ecclesiological context of affair of, 39–42; the Jew, 42–47; as Monarchian, 39; overview of, 21; Syrian bishops' clash with, 41–42; writings of, 134; Zenobia of Palmyra (queen) and, 42–47
Paul of Samosata (Pseudo-), 299
Pelagius of Laodicea, 99
"perhaps, God forbid" expression, 30
Peter of Alexandria, 103
Peter of Callinicus, 128, 129–30, 299
Peter of Hippo of Palestine, 99
Philastrius of Brescia, 43, 299
Philoponus, John, 129
Philostorgius, 299
Photinus of Sirimum, 72, 128
Photius, 44–45, 300
pittakion, 71–72
plants, cutting the shoots of, 29
Plato, 213n21, 300
Platonic doctrine, 54–55, 242n195
Plutarch, 300
positioning, 12, 194n45
Possessor, 300
pro-Nicene culture, 16–17, 142–45, 197n67
prostitute/prostitution, 28, 34–35, 48
Protogenes of Sardica, 66–72, 77, 299
Protopaschism, 1
Provincial Letters (Pascal), 122–25, 140
psilanthropism, 39
Ptolemy the Gnostic, 300

Quartodeciman movement, 1
quotations, preceeded by citation formulas, 162

rabbinic Judaism, 151–60, 171, 269–70n67
rabbinic literature, 200n13
rabbis: characteristics of, 9; dialectics and, 171; processual truth of, 177; research life of, 20–21; Sabbath practices of, 31; self-identification of, 157–58; as social group, 171; socialized forms of learning of, 177–78; Torah and, 157–58; totalitarian urges of, 179; viewpoints of, 180
Rava, 166–69, 173
readmission, 92–93
Refinus of Aquileia, 301
religious expression, 147
religious knowledge, 36–37
religious phenomena, 9

representation, psychological sense of, 193–94n43
research tradition, 193n38
Res Gestae (Aristotle), 287
Roman Empire, 7–8, 159
Roman society, 147–48
Rufinus, 84, 94–95, 97, 132, 172
Rufinus of Aquileia, 176

Sabbath, 20, 30–36, 48
Sabellius, 132, 242–43n195
Safra, Rav, 166
Sardica, Council of, 64–65, 68, 69, 78, 82, 130
Sardican creed, 67
savora 'im, 161
scholium, 70–71
science, 192n38
scientific paradigms, 192–93n38
Second Creed of Antioch, 74
Second Creed of Sirmium, 115–16
sectarianism, 5
Seleucia, Council of. *See* Council of Seleucia
self-generation, 211n9
self-production, 211n9
Senatus consultum de bacchanalibus 147
Sepphoris, 144
seyag la-Torah (a safeguard around the Torah), 206n66
Shammai, 284–85n175
Shemuel, Rabbi, 46
Sherira bar Hanina, 301
Shimon, Rabbi, 33
sin offering, 31
Siricius (Pope), 301
Sirmium, Council of. *See* Council of Sirmium
Sisinnius, 174, 175–76
Sixtus II, 40
Socrates of Constantinople, 84, 97, 134, 173–74, 175–76, 301
Sozomen, 61, 66, 67–68, 84, 97, 301
speech, straying, 28
spolium, 71
stam, 151, 161, 162
straying speech, 28
subsistent person *(prosōpon enhypostaton)*: history of the reception of, 139; hypostasis and, 135, 142; Jerome of Stridon's comments regarding, 140–41; Old Nicene standpoint regarding, 141–42; overview of, 124–25, 131–36; usage of, 143–44; viewpoints regarding, 130–31, 144–45
substantia, 115–16
sugyah, 20, 151. *See also specific cases*
Sulpicius Severus, 88–89, 301–2
synods, 11

Tertullian, 132, 156, 302
Thebaid, Council of the. *See* Council of the Thebaid
Theodore of Heraklea, 63–64
Theodoret of Cyrrhus: formula of Nike and, 117; treatment of Paul and Samosata and Zenobia by, 44; writings of, 85–87, 100, 116, 126
Theodosius (Emperor), 51, 173–74
Theognis of Nicaea, 57, 58
theologians, characteristics of, 9
theology, 3, 10, 11–12, 159, 192n35. *See also* Christian theology
Theophronius of Tyana, 63–64
Thesaurus de sancta et consubstantiali Trinitate (Cyril of Alexandria), 290
3 Enoch, 291
three hypostaseis formula, 79, 95, 111–18, 124, 135–36, 140

Thritheists, 128–29
time, creation of, 212n11
Tome to the Antiochenes (Athanasius of Alexandria): alterations within, 110; battle of formulas regarding, 111–18; doctrinal contents of, 108; effects of, 95; hypostaseis within, 124; manuscripts within, 109; novelty of, 118–21; overview of, 68–70, 80–81, 95, 103–7; recensions within, 109–10; reconciliation and, 95–96; rehabilitation practices within, 94; viewpoints regarding, 72; viewpoint within, 140
Torah, 157–58
totalitarianism, 285n179
tradition, Christian reverence for, 154–55
triadicity, 130
tri-hypostatism, 112–13, 115, 118, 140
Trinitarian controversies: barren contentiousness and, 13; characteristics of, 3; Council of Nicaea and, 13–18; creeds within, 52; dates of, 15; disputes regarding, 2, 11; division during, 5; effects of, 182; fading of, 5–6; first two decades of, 55–58; origins of, 53–55; overview of, 17, 187–88n5; positioning within, 12; research regarding, 11; significance of, 18; terminologies within, 52; as unitary whole, 18
Trinitarian relations, 16
Trinitarian theology, 15–16
Trinity, 51, 256n92. *See also* God; Holy Spirit; Jesus Christ
tri-prosopic hypostasis, 132
tritheism, 130
truth, integrity of, 159
two sovereignties *(shetei reshuyot)*, 23, 26, 29, 30, 37, 201
Tyre, Council of. *See* Council of Tyre

unity, 130
Ursacius of Singidunum, 73

Valens of Mursia, 73, 86
Vincent of Lérins, 156, 159, 303
violence, within social and intellectual fields, 5
Vitalis, 259n119

wisdom, 134
women, relationships of, 276n116
Word of God, preexistence of, 39, 132

Xanthopoulos, Nikephoros Kallistos, 46
x collection (Athanasius's corpus), 109

y collection (Athanasius's corpus), 109
Yehudah ha-Nasi, 151
Yehudah, Rav, 167
Yosef, Rav, 166–69

Zakkai, Raban Yoḥanan ben, 170
Zenobia of Palmyra (Queen), 42–47, 49
Zier bar Ḥinena, 46
Zoilos of Larissa, 99

Index of Ancient Sources

Hebrew Bible

Gen
1:28 168
2:17 206n63
3:3 206n63
25:24 188n8

Exod
35:2 205n58
35:32 204n44
35:33 204n44, 205n58
35:34 204n44

Lev
19:18 166, 168, 276n116
23:3 31

Nah
1:9 26

Job
14:7–9 203n21

Ps
116:15 22

Prov
8:22 134, 245n10
25:16 22

Qoh 23, 29
5:04 28
5:5 22, 25(203n24), 28(203n26)
5:5b 28(203n28)

Jer
3:22 22

Dan
4:11–12:23 203n21
7 6
7:13 30

Apocrypha, Pseudepigrapha, and Para-biblical Writings

2 Enoch
23:4–6 201n16

3 Enoch 6, 23(199n8), 29, 30, 199n11, 201n16, 204n35

Jubilees
4:23 201n16

Merkavah Rabah
202n19

New Testament

Matt
12:30 139
28:16–19 61

Mark
3:29 203n22

Luke
10:22 112
14:23 264n19

John 10
1:1–2 127
1:3 127

Rom
11 203n29

Gal
1:3 133
4:4 127

Early Christian Writings

Acta concilii nicaeni secundi
6 126(246n14)

Contra Artemonem
267n42

Aphrahat

Demonstratio XIV
207n71

Alexander of Alexandria

Epistula ad Alexandrum Constantinopolitanum
9 213n17

Alexander of Jerusalem

Epistula ad Origenem 267n48

Altercatio Heracliani laici cum Germinio episcopo sirmiensi
Initium 226n39

Ambrose of Milan

Expositio Evangelii secundum Lucam
1.5.61 255n83

Ammianus Marcellinus

Res Gestae
22.9.4 216n49
25.10.4 234n115

Apophthegmata patrum 267n43

Ascensio Esaïae 10

Arius

Epistula ad Alexandrum Alexandrinum 60(217n63), 62, 245n10
45 60(217n64)
66 60(217n64)

Thaleia 214n24

Athanasius of Alexandria

Apologia de fuga sua
3.3 248n31

Apologia secunda contra arianos

20–36 216n53
21–35 216n57
51–57 233n103

De decretis Nicaenae synodi 233n109
19–20 56, 214n32
23.2 239n153

De sententia Dionysii
24.3 239n153

De synodis Arimini in Italia et Seleucia in Isauria 233n109
16.2 217n603
22.2–7 59(216n56)
22.3 60(216n58)
23.2 60(216n60)
23.2–10 217n65
23.5 61(217n68)
23.7–10 62(217n70)
24.2–5 217n71
25.2–4 64(217n74)
25.5 64(217n75)
26.4.1 66(218n78)
30 228n52
30.9 244n209
41 234n117
41.8 239n153
53.2 238n151

Epistula ad Iovianum de fide 234n117
1.6 101(236n124)

Epistula ad Rufinianum 89(228n60, 229n63), 94, 221n112, 229n61

Epistula festalis XXXVI (?) 236n129

Historia Arianorum ad monachos
4.1 245n6, 248n31
5.6 216n49
21–23 233n103
31–34 226n45
36 239n158
41.1–2 86(227n47)
71.1 43(209n92)
76 226n45

Oratio I contra arianos
13.1 212n11
14.7 212n11

Oratio II contra arianos
2.5 238n153

Oratio III contra arianos
22.1 238n151

Tomus ad Antiochenos 80(222n4), 81, 91, 94, 95, 102, 103, 105, 106, 107, 108, 109, 110, 111, 124, 125,135, 139, 140, 143, 145, 241n175
1.1 96(232n91)
3.1 96, 110
3.3 110
4 96, 97
4.1 94
5.1–2 105
5.3 105

Athanasius (*continued*)
5.3–4 67(219n890), 71, 96, 105
5–6 103, 104, 105(237n137), 107, 112
5.3–6.4 95
6 105, 106
6.1 94
6.1–2 95, 105
6.2 105, 106
6.3 111
6.3–4 105
9.1 80(222n6), 81
9.3γ 96, 97(232n100), 240n172
10.1–2 240n173
10.3 72(221n106), 77
11.2 112(241n178)

Vita Antonii 237n131
14 258n108

Athanasius of Alexandria (*dubia*)

De virginitate 112

Epistula ad cunctos episcopos (= *Epistula Alexandri Alexandrini*) 191n28

In illud: Omnia mihi tradita sunt a patre meo (Lc 10:22) 112

Athanasius of Alexandria (*falsa*)

De sancta Trinitate dialogus III
1.2.15 217n66

Epistula ad Liberium (= *Contra Theopaschitas*) 110, 241n176

Epistula catholica 102, 110, 222n3, 241n176

Fragmentum (= *Fragmentum Magni Athanasii*) 44(209n97)

Sermo maior de fide 10, 241n176

Augustine of Hippo

Epistulae
ep. XCIII (= *ad Vincentium*)
2.5 264n19

Basil of Caesarea

Adversus Eunomium
1.2 228n52

De spiritu sancto 155
72–74 268n55

Epistulae
ep. LVII 233n105
ep. LXVI 102
ep. LXVII 102
ep. LXVIII 233n105
ep. LXXXIX 98(233n105)
ep. C 250n35
ep. CXX 233n105
ep. CXXV 106
ep. CXXIX 233n105
ep. CXXXIX 233n105
ep. CLVI
3 137(258n105)
ep. CCIV

6 89(228n61), 221n112
ep. CCVIII 233n105
ep. CCX
3 238n152
5 133(254n72)
ep. CCXIV 233n104
ep. CCLI
4 221n112
ep. CCLVIII 143, 233n105, 233n107
ep. CCLXVI
2 103(237n135)

Chronicon Paschale
I, 542 (ed. Dindorf) 228n52
I, 547–548 (ed. Dindorf) 223n11

Clement of Alexandria

Hypotyposeis 221n103

Paedagogus
1.7.57.2 254n64

Stromateis
1.1.3 267n43
5.6.3 243n196

Continuatio Eusebii Antiochiensis 225n35

Clement of Rome (*falsa*)

Homiliae et *Recognitiones* 207n71

Cyril of Alexandria

Thesaurus de sancta et consubstantiali Trinitate 254n65

Damian of Alexandria

Epistula prolixa (= *Πολύστιχος ἐπιστολή*) 251n39

Tractatus adversus tritheistas 129
5 251n39

Damnatio blasphemiae Arrii 115(243n202)

Dialogus Timothei et Aquilae 148

Didymus the Blind

Commentarii in Zachariam 192n35

Dionysius of Alexandria

Epistula ad Philemonem presbyterum Romanum 267n48

Epistula ad Stephanum Romanum 208n76

Doctrina Addaï 208n79

Doctrina apostolorum 207n71

Epictetus

Dissertationes ab Arriano digestae
3.21.6 221n103

Epiphanius of Salamis

Adversus haereses 142
25.6.4 261n142
33.7.8 215n40
63–64 255n85
65.2.5 209n94
68.11.3 234n117, 235n119
68.11.4 235n122
69.8.5 217n603
69.80.3 261n142
72.1.3 143(261n143), 261n142
73.12–22 256n92
73.16.1–4 256n91
73.23.4 228n52
73.29–33 243n199
73.31.6–7 256n91
73.34.2 261n142
73.36.4 261n142
77.20.5–8 236n131
78.24.5 261n142

Ancoratus 142, 143
6.5 143(261n140)
6.8 143(261n141)
25.2 262n145
31.3 262n145
34.8 262n145
35.1 262n145
36.4 262n145
38.2 262n145
39.3 262n145
39.4 262n145
39.5 262n145
39.6 262n145
54–55 255n85
54.5 262n145
55.8 262n145
62–63 255n85
67.4 143(262n144)
67.7 143(262n145)
68.2 262n145
83.4 262n145
87 255n85

Epistula episcoporum Italiae ad episcopos Inlyrici 91(230n72), 232n87

Epistula Hymenaei 39(207n74), 134

Epistula legatorum 226n43

Epistula synodi Parisiensis (ca. 360) 93(231n79, 231n80, 231n83)

Eugene of Ancyra

Expositio fidei 249n35

Eusebius of Caesarea

De ecclesiastica theologia 132(254n70)
1.14 268n52

De Pascha 187n3

Historia ecclesiastica 267n48
6.14.9 267n48
7.4.1 208n76
7.7.5 267n48
7.13.2 208n82
7.27.2 38(207n72)

7.27–30 39(207n73), 46(209n104)
7.30.18–19 41(208n80)
7.30.20 42(208n87)

Vita Constantini 146, 187n3
2.64–65.1 147(262n1)
2.68.1–2 147(262n1)
2.71.2 147(262n1)

Eusebius of Vercellae (*falsa*)

Epistula ad Gregorium Illiberitanum 230n73

Eustathius of Antioch

Commentarius in Ps. 92 125(245n10), 126(246n22)

Contra Arianos 125(245n10)

Contra Ariomanitas et de anima 125(245n10)

De Engastrimytho contra Origenem 125(245n10)
24 127(247n24)

De fide contra arianos 125(245n10)

De temptationibus 125(245n10)

In illud: Dominus creavit me initium viarum suarum (Prov 8:22) 125(245n10)

In inscriptiones Psalmorum graduum 125(245n10)

In inscriptiones titulorum 125(245n10)

In Ioseph 125(245n10)

In Samaritanam 125(245n10)

Oratio coram tota Ecclesia in: Verbum caro factum est (Ioh 1:14) 125(245n10)

Secunda oratio coram tota Ecclesia 125(245n10)

Eustathius of Antioch (*dubia*)

Contra Photinum (Fragmentum 142) 125, 128, 131, 248n31, 249n32, 250n38, 251n39, 251n40

Expositio prolixa (= *Ἔκθεσις Μακρόστιχος*) 65, 66, 68, 72, 134, 248n31

Facundus of Hermiane

Pro defensione trium capitulorum
11.2.1 80(222n4)
11.2.4 80(222n4)

Faustinus and Marcellinus

Libellus precum 91
50–51 90(230n70)
63 229n665

Galen

Commentarius in Hippocratis De medici officina librum
3.1.18 221n103

Gelasius of Cyzicus

Historia ecclesiastica 225n35

Syntagma
26.3 72(221n105)

Gelasius of Cyzicus (*falsa*)
De libris recipiendis et non recipiendis 156, 269n62

Giwargis I, Catholicos

Epistula ad Minam 253n56

Gregory of Nazianzus

Orationes
21.33 234n117

Gregory of Nyssa

Ad Graecos ex communibus notionibus 128(249n33), 249n34, 250n38
1.1–23.3 250n38
23.4–28.8 250n38
28.9–29.3 250n38

De instituto christiano 250n38

Epistulae
ep. V
2 249n35

Grigorios Bar ʿEbroyo

Chronicon 45(209n102)

Historia compendiosa Dynastiarum
7 45(209n103)

Hilary of Poitiers

Apologetica responsa 89
5 226n41

De synodis, seu De fide Orientalium 89
29–30 60(216n60), 217n65
91 75(221n115)

Fragmenta historica 262n152
Series A, I, 1 231n79, 231n80
Series A, I, 4 93(231n83)

Series A, VII 226n43
Series A, VII, 6 222n116
Series A, IX, 1, 3 115(243n204)
Series B, IV, 1 89(229n62)
Series B, IV, 2 91(230n72), 232n87

Liber I ad Constantium
2 227n46
8 226n45

Hippolytus

Contra Noëtum
14 132(254n66)

Refutatio omnium haeresium (= *Philosophoumena*)
10.27.4 254n68

Historia acephala Athanasii
2.7 237n136
4.4 234n115, 235n119
4.7 235n122
8.10 221n111

Historia ecclesiae alexandrinae
5.75 235n122

Hormisdas, Pope

Epistulae
ep. LXX (= *ad Possessorem Episcopum*) 269n63

Ignatius of Antioch

Epistulae 10

Irenaeus of Lyons

Adversus haereses
1.5.1 215n40
1.5.5 215n40

Fragmenta
134(255n86)

Jerome of Stridon

Altercatio Luciferiani et orthodoxi
18 117(243n206)
19 74(221n107)
20 79(222n2), 89, 229n64, 229n66
21 226n41, 227n49
25 226n41
26 90(229n67), 226n41
26–27 90(230n68)
27 226n40, 226n41

Chronicon
a.a.R. XVIII 227n46
a.a.R. XXII 227n50
a.a.R. XXIII 227n50
a.a.R. XXXVI 223n10
a.a.R. XXXVII 234n111

De viris illustribus
Prologus 269n60
85 245n6

Epistulae
ep. III
3.1 257n97
ep. VII
2 136(257n102)
ep. XV 136(257n95), 138, 141, 257n95, 258n107, 258n109,

Jerome of Stridon (*continued*)
258n112, 259n115, 259n116, 259n119
2.2–3.2 139(260n125)
4–5 260n131
5.1 139(259n121), 140(260n130)
ep. XVI 257n95, 258n112, 259n116
2 138(258n113)
ep. XVII 257n100, 261n133
2.2 141(260n133)
3 137(258n108)
ep. XVIII 257n95
ep. XX 257n95
ep. XXI 257n95
ep. XXXVI 257n95
ep. CXII
3 269n60

Epistula praefatoria ad Homilias Origenis in Ezechielem 221n103

John Chrysostom

In Ioannem Homiliae
4.1 209n95
8.1 43(209n95)

Laudatio S. patris nostri Eustathii Antiochaeni
4 82(224n16), 248n31

Jovian, Emperor

Epistula ad Athanasium 235n119

Julius I, Pope

Epistulae
ep. II 59(216n54)

Justin Martyr

Dialogus cum Tryphone 148

Liberius, Pope

Epistula ad catolicos episcopos Italiae 89 (229n62), 232n87

Liberius, Pope (*falsa*)

Olim et ab initio 229n62

Lucifer of Calaris

De regibus apostaticis
5 226n41

Moriundum esse pro Dei Filio
1 226n45

Lucius, Bernicianus, et al.

Petitio ad Iovianum imperatorem 235n122

Marius Victorinus

Adversus Arium
2.4 238n143
2.7 158(270n76)
3.4 238n143

Meletius of Antioch

In illud: Dominus creavit me initium viarum suarum (Prov 8:22) 113, 134(256n91)

De sigillatione sepulcri 114(243n199)

Michael the Syrian

Chronicon

6.8 45(209n101)

Nikephoros Kallistos Xanthopoulos

Historia ecclesiastica

6.27 46(209n105)

Odes Salomonis 10

Optatus of Milevis

De schismate Donatistarum

Appendix 4 187n2

Origen of Alexandria

Adnotationes in Deuteronomium

In Deut 16:20 255n81

Commentarius in Canticum

3.43 132(254n59)

Commentarius in Epistulam ad Romanos

1.7.4 54(212n11)

Commentarium in Epistulam ad Titum 132

Commentarius in Evangelium Ioannis

1.24.151 243n196

2.10.75 255n78

13.151 54(213n16)

Contra Celsum

8.12 255n78

8.14 255n78

8.67 255n78

Conversatio cum Heraclide

2 211n4

De principiis

1.2.2 134(255n84)

1.2.9 54(212n11)

1.7.1 255n83

4.4.1 54(212n10, 212n11)

Epistula ad Photium et Andream 255n81

Expositio in Proverbia

88 134(255n82)

Ossius of Cordoba and Protogenes of Sardica

Epistula ad Iulium papam 67(218n86), 68, 70, 77

Pamphilus the Theologian

Capitulorum diversorum seu dubitationum solutio de recta erga Christum religione 209n98

Passio Sancti Artemii

70 17n66

Pastor Hermae 10

Paul of Samosata (*falsa*)

Ad Zenobiam 44(209n98), 47

Peter of Alexandria

Epistula ad episcopos Aegyptios fidei causa exules 222n4

Peter of Callinicus

Tractatus contra Damianum 129

3.40.62–67 251n39
3.40.119–124 251n39
3.40.130–160 251n39
3.40.171–178 251n39
3.40.179–184 251n39
3.40–42 250n39
3.42.26–31 251n39
3.43.33–38 251n39

Philastrius of Brescia

Diversarum haereseon liber

36(64).2 43(209n93)

Philostorgius

Historia ecclesiastica 217n66

2.12 216n49
5.1 87(228n53)
8.2 235n120
8.6 235n121
8.8 217n66

Photius

Bibliotheca

265 44(209n100)

Possessor, Bishop

Epistula ad Hormisdam 156(269n63)

Ptolemy the Gnostic

Epistula ad Floram 57(215n40)

Refutatio hypocriseos Meletii et Eusebii 102

1–6 114(243n201)

Regulae definitionum contra haereticos prolatae 51(211n1)

Rufinus of Aquileia

De adulteratione librorum Origenis

13 176(284n174)

Historia ecclesiastica

1.9 216n49
1.12 216n49
1.20 233n104

1.27 223n10
2.1 235n119
10.3 172(282n153)
10.21 227n46
10.20 226n45
10.27 223n9
10.28.3 84(224n28)
10.29 94(232n90)
10.29–30 222n1
10.30 241n173
11.1 234n117

Sabinus of Heraklea

Collectio (= *Συναγωγή*) 61

Severus of Antioch

Epistulae
ep. III 126

Siricius, Pope

Epistula ad Himerium Tarraconensem
2 229n62

Socrates of Constantinople

Historia ecclesiastica 175
1.7 262n1
1.9 187n3
1.23 251n40, 253n57
1.25 216n49
2.1 225n33
2.10.4–8 59(216n56)
2.10.10–18 60(216n60), 217n65
2.18.3–6 217n74
2.19.3–28 218n78
2.20.9 217n73
2.23 233n104
2.36 226n45
2.36.3–5 227n46
2.37.1 227n46
2.42 228n52
2.44.5–7 224n20
3.4.2 235n122
3.5–6 84(224n25)
3.7 222n1
3.9 223n9, 223n10, 224n21
3.9.3 223n11
3.10 221n112
3.21.17 234n115
3.24 235n119
3.24.2 234n117
3.25.2–4 235n123
3.25.6–19 234n111
3.25.10–18 233n110, 234n112
4.14.3–4 248n31
5.1.3 224n22
5.5 237n134
5.10.6–15 173(283n166)

Sozomen

Historia ecclesiastica
1.16 187n2
2.18 251n40
2.27 216n49
3.11.4–9 217n73
3.12.5–6 66(218n80)
3.12.5 220n95
3.20 233n104
3.20.4 233n102
3.5.8–9 61(217n65)
4.9 226n45
4.9.3 227n46
4.13 221n108
4.13.2 248n31

Sozomen (*continued*)
4.22.9–10 216n59
4.24–25 228n52
4.28.9–10 224n20
5.12 223n9, 223n10
5.12.1 84(224n26, 224n27)
5.12.3–5 222n1
5.13.3 223n11
6.4.3–5 235n123
6.4.6–11 234n111
6.4.7–10 234n110
6.5.1 234n115, 234n116
6.5.2 235n122
6.7.5 216n59
6.12.4 216n59
7.3 237n134

Sulpicius Severus

Chronica
2.42.1–2 226n39
2.45 88(228n56), 89(228n59), 221n112, 226n39
2.45.2–4 226n39

Vita sancti Martini Turonensis
6.7 229n62
7.1 226n39

Tertullian

Adversus Praxean
132

Theodoret of Cyrrhus

Commentarii in Esaïam
17.14 85(225n31)

Haereticarum fabularum compendium
2.8.1 44(209n96)

Historia ecclesiastica
225n37, 246n13
1.3 245n7
1.9 187n3
2.3 216n49
2.8.39–40 64(217n76)
2.15 226n45
2.15.4 227n46
2.21.7 116(243n205), 117(244n208)
2.27–28 228n52
2.32.11 224n20
2.33.2 85(225n32)
3.2 222n10
3.4.2 223n11
3.4.2–3 85(224n30)
3.4.3 224n20
3.4.5 248n31
3.4.6–3.5.2 88(228n55)
3.5 223n9
4.2.4–5 234n117
4.3 234n117
5.3.9–20 237n134

Vincent of Lérins

Commonitorium
2.5(6) 268n59
3.4(8) 156(268n59)
17–18 269n61

GREEK AND LATIN WRITERS

Aristotle

Categoriae

5 196n58

Cicero

Ad Atticum
16.7.3 70(220n100)

Plato

Cratylus
390C 264n16

De republica
509B 215n38

Timaeus
28C 213n21
38B–39 212n11
41B 211n9

Plutarch

Quaestiones platonicae
2 213n21

Porphyry

Commentarius in Aristotelis Categorias 253n52

Isagoge 253n52

Theognis of Megara

Theognidea 268n57

Rabbinic literature

Mishnah

Ḥagigah 32(205n51)
1:8

ʿEduyot
1:4–6 266n37

Avot
1:1 203n29

Tosefta

Shabat
1:16–17 206n64

Ḥagigah
2:3 22(198n3)

Sotah
7:11–12 279n138

Kipurim
4:6–8 202n22

Palestinian Talmud

Terumot
8:10 (46b) 46(209n106)

Shabat
1:4 (3c) 206n64

Sheḳalim
2:5 (47a) 266n37

Yoma
8:8 (45b–c) 202n22

Ḥagigah
2:1 (77b) 25, 199n9

Yevamot
1:6 (3b) 279n138

Sanhedrin
10:1 (27c) 202n22

Shevuʿot
1:9 (33b) 202n22

Babylonian Talmud

Berakhot
18a 276n117
59a 26(202n19)

Shabat

Babylonian Talmud (*continued*)
29b 204n47
41b 204n47
49b 204n44
73a 204n43
73b 33(205n54)
93b 33(205n55)
94a 205n57
103a 205n47
119a 168, 278n128
141a 206n60
146b 276n118
150b 276n119

ʿEruvin
13b 279n138, 284n175

Pesaḥim
25b 204n47
49b 284n180

Yoma
34b 204n47
77a 211n117
85a 277n123
86a 202n22

Sukah
33b 277n124
35b 277n123

Beitsah
13b 204n44, 277n122

Ḥagigah 20, 21, 24, 202n19
3a–3b 284n175
3b 279n138
10a 33, 36
10b 22, 23, 32, 35, 48, 205n56, 206n59
15a 21, 23, 25, 26, 29, 30, 35, 36, 37, 38, 48, 199n10, 199n11, 201n16, 201n17, 204n42, 206n61
15b 206n61

Yevamot
104b 277n123
118b 274n112

Ketubot
12a 276n120
15b 277n123
18b 277n123
72b 276n121
75a 274n112

Nazir
42a 204n47

Sotah
9a 277n124

Giṭṭin
6b 284n175
86a 276n122

Ḳiddushin 165(274n111)
7a 274n112
41a 164
46a 276n123
65a 276n124

Bava ḳamma
26b 205n48
44b 204n47
56a 277n123
75b 276n125
111a 274n112
114a 277n123

Bava metsiʿa
30a 276n126
59b 203n23
59b 284n177

Bava batra
24b 277n122
87b 276n127
88b 277n122

Sanhedrin
88b 284n175

ʿAvodah zarah
3b 191n26
10b 211n116

Zevaḥim
11b 276n128

Menaḥot
62b 201n18
70b 277n122

Ḥullin
44a 203n23, 284n177

Bekhorot
13b 276n129

Meʿilah
13b 277n123

Niddah
11b 277n123
55a 277n122
68a 276n130

Midrash

***Avot de-Rabi Natan* (version A)**
1 206n64
29 202n22

Bereshit Rabah
19:3 35(206n64)

Mekhilta de-Rabi Yishmaʿel
Yitro 7 202n22

Other ancient rabbinic texts

Sherira bar Hanina

Epistula 278n132

Index of Modern Authors

Abramowski, Luise, 105–6
Alexander, Elizabeth Shanks, 157
Armstrong, C. B., 96, 97
Arnauld, Antoine, 122
Asad, Talal, 9–10
Ayres, Lewis, 15–17, 77, 197n67, 197n70

Balberg, Mira, 28
Bauer, Walter, 160
Beeley, Christopher, 197n70
Behr, John, 197n70
Berzon, Todd, 160
Bion, Wilfred, 146
Boltanski, Luc, 9, 11
Bourdieu, Pierre, 16
Boyarin, Daniel, 8–9, 30, 170, 171–172

Camplani, Alberto, 105, 106–7
Cohen, Shaye, 170
Compagnon, Antoine, 158

Declerck, José H., 128
Dolgopolski, Sergey, 171

Elliott, Thomas, 96
Elon, Menachem, 157
Epstein, Yaakov Nahum, 273n106

Friedman, Shamma, 161, 164

Goshen-Gottstein, Alon, 30
Graumann, Thomas, 155, 174–75
Grillmeier, Aloys, 196n59
Grossberg, David, 29–30

Halivni, David Weiss, 32–33, 161
Halleux, André de, 15
Hanson, Richard, 18, 96
Harnack, Adolf von, 14, 17
Hayes, Christine, 34
Hübner, Reinhard, 128

Jaffee, Martin, 33
Kalmin, Richard, 162–63
Kaplan, Julius, 160
Kim, Richard, 143–44
Kister, Menachem, 200n13
Kösters, Oliver, 142
Kraemer, David, 172–73
Kuhn, Thomas, 192n38

Lakatos, Imre, 192–93n38
Laudan, Larry, 9, 11, 192–93n38
Le Goff, Jacques, 189n14
Loofs, Friedrich, 14, 17, 127

Lorenz, Rudolf, 128

MacIntyre, Alasdaire, 9
Maingueneau, Dominique, 9, 11–12, 149
Markschies, Christoph, 10
Morales, Xavier, 112
Morawski, Stefan, 153, 158
Morlet, Sébastien, 148

Opitz, Hans-Georg, 17

Pascal, Blaise, 122–25, 140
Pêcheux, Michel, 195n51
Prestige, George Leonard, 15

Régnon, Théodore de, 15–16

Schäfer, Peter, 30
Schwartz, Eduard, 17
Simonetti, Manlio, 18, 106, 113, 130
Spanneut, Michel, 127–28
Stead, Christopher, 15
Stern, Sacha, 163–64

Vaggione, Richard, 120
Van Nuffelen, Peter, 148
Vidas, Moulie, 161

Weidner, Daniel, 169
Weiss, Abraham, 160

Zachhuber, Johannes, 250n38
Zahn, Theodor, 14, 17